AF339219

SUZANNE
LACY

SUZANNE LACY

WE ARE HERE

EDITED BY

RUDOLF FRIELING, LUCÍA SANROMÁN, AND DOMINIC WILLSDON

WITH CONTRIBUTIONS FROM

Jessica D. Brier, Christa Cesario, Lucia Fabio, Taylor Shoolery, and Tanya Zimbardo

SAN FRANCISCO MUSEUM OF MODERN ART

IN ASSOCIATION WITH

DelMonico Books • Prestel Munich, London, New York

6   **FOREWORD**
Neal Benezra and Deborah Cullinan

8   **WHERE ARE WE? A CURATORIAL INTRODUCTION**
Rudolf Frieling, Lucía Sanromán, and Dominic Willsdon

14   **TO REENACT, TO RETHINK, TO REDISTRIBUTE SUZANNE LACY**
Lucía Sanromán

24   **THE TEXT IS ACTIVE**
Rudolf Frieling

34   **GEOMETRY IN MOTION**
Dominic Willsdon

42   **ILLUSTRATED SURVEY**
WITH TEXTS BY Jessica D. Brier, Christa Cesario, Lucia Fabio, Taylor Shoolery, and Tanya Zimbardo

42   BODIES
68   PERSONAS
88   VIOLENCE AGAINST WOMEN
124 NETWORKS
150 IMAGE AND DIALOGUE
182 YOUTH
216 WORK AND CLASS

246 ACKNOWLEDGMENTS
250 CHRONOLOGY OF SELECTED WORKS
258 SELECTED BIBLIOGRAPHY
263 FEATURED WORKS
264 COLLABORATORS, PARTICIPANTS, AND ASSOCIATES
266 CREDITS

FOREWORD

Over more than four decades, artist, writer, and educator Suzanne Lacy has established a creative practice that blurs the lines between art and political activism. Her performances and installations are typically created in collaboration with other artists and members of the communities in which she works, often evolving from intensive participatory dialogue and collaborative choreography. One of the foremost thinkers involved in initiating the discourse and scholarship around social practice art, Lacy has used her work to promote gender and racial equality, address ageism and poverty, and confront violence against women. This may sound like activism, and it is. But, as Lacy has explained: "I am totally identified as an artist. I would act differently if I were only a political activist. The creative identification is important strategically, in the same way that people used to say 'I'm a feminist' as a political statement. 'I'm an artist' means that I'm intent on addressing the language of that field, that I'm interested in form."

Lacy's work is undeniably political, but it is also deeply visual, finding its form in "the 'shape' of ideas, relationships, and social processes." The San Francisco Museum of Modern Art (SFMOMA) and Yerba Buena Center for the Arts (YBCA) are proud to present this work in *Suzanne Lacy: We Are Here*, a partnership of impressive scope honoring an artist whose efforts to engage multiple voices, explore collaborative authorship, and promote public pedagogy in the San Francisco Bay Area and beyond have been foundational to the public dialogue initiatives championed today by many cultural institutions—including our own.

Conceived of as one exhibition at two venues, this retrospective encompasses the wide range of art forms Lacy has explored throughout her career, including photography, film, sculpture, video installations, drawings, books, and related ephemera. The presentation at SFMOMA spans from her earliest projects, completed in the 1970s, to recent video installations. At YBCA the exhibition updates two of Lacy's key collaborative works from the 1990s. Notably, the presentation of *The Oakland Projects* (1991–2001, pp. 184–211) has taken shape in dialogue with former participants as well as with local youth arts and activist organizations. In partnership with contemporary Bay Area artists and arts organizations—including Caleb Duarte; the Center for Media Justice; YBCA teaching artists and Dr. Martin Luther King Jr. Academic Middle School; Youth Speaks; and YR Media (formerly Youth Radio)—new works have been created for the exhibition that reflect on the urgent issues affecting young people today.

Lacy's roots in the Bay Area are deep, and we could not be more pleased to premiere her retrospective in San Francisco. The timing of this endeavor is particularly fitting: SFMOMA recently completed a strategic plan that bolsters its commitment to making art a meaningful part of civic life, and YBCA has reinvented the role of arts institutions by becoming a public square and a home for creativity and action that prioritizes diverse perspectives, gender equity, and inclusion. This project would not have moved forward, however, without the ambition and passion of the exhibition's curators: Rudolf Frieling, SFMOMA curator of media arts; Lucía Sanromán, YBCA curator at large; and Dominic Willsdon, who began this venture as Leanne and George Roberts Curator of Education and Public Practice at SFMOMA and assumed the role of director of the Institute for Contemporary Art at Virginia Commonwealth University, Richmond, in December 2018. Each of them came to this undertaking with a strong track record in supporting performative, participatory work and public dialogue, and we are extremely proud of their collaboration on *Suzanne Lacy: We Are Here*.

Suzanne Lacy: We Are Here has been years in the making and has benefited from the support and dedication of numerous organizations and individuals, as well as of the wider museum community. During its development, the project was awarded a curatorial research fellowship grant from The Andy Warhol Foundation for the Visual Arts that supported a convening at Independent Curators International, New York, on exhibiting social practice in museums. Similar questions were explored in the four-day symposium *Does Art Have Users?*, which was presented as part of both SFMOMA's Phyllis Wattis Distinguished Lecture Series and its Public Knowledge initiative, and was organized in partnership with the Asociación de Arte Útil and YBCA in conjunction with the exhibition *Tania Bruguera: Talking to Power / Hablándole al Poder*. At SFMOMA, major support for the exhibition is provided by The Andy Warhol Foundation for the Visual Arts. Generous support is provided by Lionel F. Conacher and Joan T. Dea. The YBCA presentation is made possible in part by the Circle of Advisors for Changing the Ratio: Female Artists at YBCA: Abundance Foundation, Berit Ashla, Diana Cohn, EMIKA Fund, Jennifer C. Haas Fund, La Mar Cebichería Peruana, Rekha Patel, Catalina Ruiz-Healy and Jonathan Kevles, Vicki Shipkowitz, and Meg Spriggs, with thanks to the Facebook Artist in Residence Program. Additional support is provided by Amanda Weil. YBCA also extends thanks to its exhibition supporters: The Andy Warhol Foundation for the Visual Arts, Panta Rhea Foundation, Mellon/American Council of Learned Societies Public Fellows Program, and Kevin King and Meridee Moore. YBCA

Programs are made possible in part by Bloomberg Philanthropies and The James Irvine Foundation, with additional funding by the National Endowment for the Arts, Grosvenor, and YBCA Members. YBCA is also grateful to the City of San Francisco for its ongoing support.

Finally, we join the curators in acknowledging the many SFMOMA and YBCA staff members, listed on pages 247–48, whose efforts, commitment, and expertise made this complex project possible. We extend our deepest thanks to Suzanne Lacy for modeling a form of engaged citizenship to which we can all aspire and for reminding us that we are all here, and in this together.

—NEAL BENEZRA HELEN AND CHARLES SCHWAB DIRECTOR, SFMOMA

—DEBORAH CULLINAN CHIEF EXECUTIVE OFFICER, YBCA

The quotes by Suzanne Lacy above are from Paul David Young, "The Suzanne Lacy Network," *Art in America*, May 31, 2012, https://www.artinamericamagazine.com/news-features/magazines/the-suzanne-lacy-network/, and Thom Donovan, "Five Questions for Contemporary Practice with Suzanne Lacy," *Art21*, November 13, 2012, http://magazine.art21.org/2012/11/13/5-questions-for-contemporary-practice-with-suzanne-lacy/.

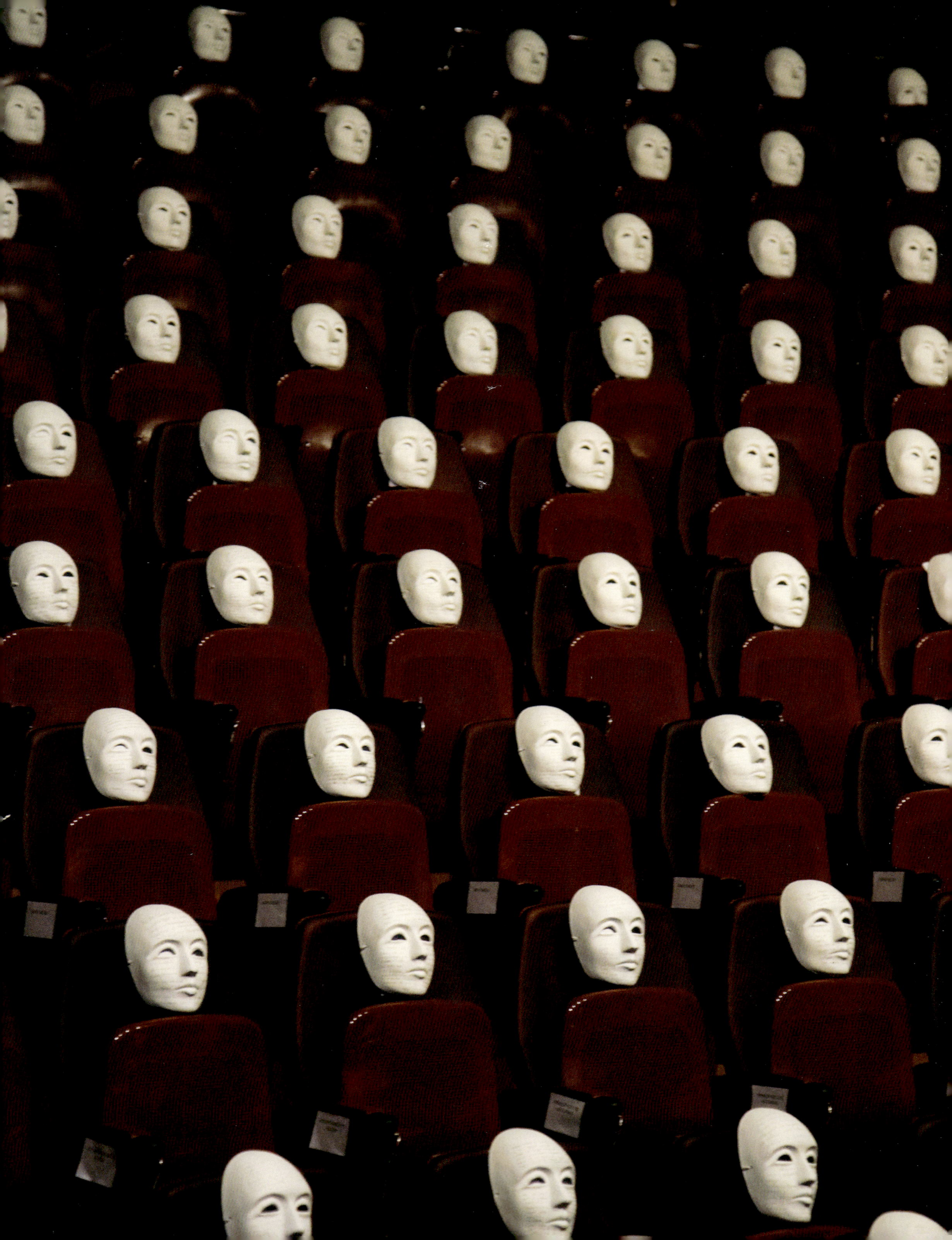

WHERE ARE WE?
A CURATORIAL INTRODUCTION

Within the realm of major arts institutions, the history of social practice struggles to be seen. This is not surprising given that it is the privilege of this work to be situated in contexts far removed from the flattening, straitened spaces of traditional white cube galleries. Museums—the San Francisco Museum of Modern Art (SFMOMA) being no exception—tend to do well with monographic exhibitions and catalogues that present painting, photography, or sculpture in an orderly march of carefully sequenced single images. Today, the curatorial field recognizes that the histories of contemporary art are more varied and complex than this model typically allows. Yet while performance and media-based works have come to be incorporated at least to some degree in these narratives, social practice (also called, among other names, socially engaged art), which has rarely (or only secondarily) produced artifacts to be exhibited or collected, has remained on the margins. This retrospective of California artist Suzanne Lacy, who over more than four decades has created an incredibly rich and nuanced body of collaborative, socially engaged, ephemeral, and context-specific work, aims to address this glaring oversight.[1] It is also an attempt to collaborate across institutional structures—those of SFMOMA and Yerba Buena Center for the Arts (YBCA)—and to consider the question of how to present such a practice within the frameworks of twenty-first-century arts organizations.

SFMOMA and YBCA are neighbors, yet they have very different mandates and capacities. These differences have strengthened our partnership on this project. Surveying Lacy's complex works required "making art history"—a process best achieved under the auspices of an established collecting museum designed to ratify art practices, as exemplified by this catalogue and the retrospective presentation in SFMOMA's galleries. But one might well ask how the field of social practice relates to the postminimal aesthetics of core SFMOMA artists such as Ellsworth Kelly, Sol LeWitt, and Richard Serra. We argue that works by such artists share with Lacy's an aesthetic complementarity, but with an essential difference, found chiefly in the contingency, mobility, and agency of forms—as, of course, Lacy's forms are composed of people, not inanimate materials.[2] This opened the related question of what "activating" Lacy's past work might look like. *Suzanne Lacy: We Are Here* takes up this challenge in three pieces, two of which—*Alterations* (1994–95, p. 218) and *Cleaning Conditions* (2013, pp. 236–37)—Lacy has performed on more than one occasion, and one—*The Oakland Projects* (1991–2001, pp. 184–211)—that the artist has never attempted to revisit as a process, but that she has partially re-created as installations for past exhibitions. Presenting such work requires an institutional commitment to the present, to current constituents. This aspect of the project made it a natural fit for YBCA, where a pronounced focus on civic engagement guides the exhibition programming. As a center for live and visual art forms whose mission is to connect with the various communities that make up the Bay Area, YBCA is well positioned to highlight the participatory processes of institutional inclusion and to expand Lacy's collaborative approach toward these forms of co-creation and others that often lie beyond a traditional retrospective format.

Although our partnership made us well situated in many respects to achieve the standard goals of a solo retrospective—to collate and historicize the artist's works, provide an optimal experience of them, assess their abiding value, and make them public in new ways—Lacy's work required both institutions to apply some nonstandard methods. When projects evolve with many participants over considerable periods of time, as hers do, and are recorded and reflected on in an array of variable media, one question emerges almost from the start: what set of acts, objects, and agents constitutes a work? Moreover, in such a practice the notion of sole authorship is quickly jeopardized: what does it mean to apply the single name "Suzanne Lacy" to an exhibition of projects created by so many participants and collaborators—including many other artists—and how should those stakeholders be involved and recognized now? It was also unclear how we might best look back at these projects, which were impelled by the politics of particular times and places. Thankfully, we didn't have to start from scratch. In recent years, a number of artists working in socially engaged, process-driven ways have received solo museum shows that could be looked to for insight. We were particularly keen on learning from the Getty Research Institute's 2008 retrospective of Allan Kaprow, who was hugely influential for Lacy.[3] The partial survey focused on Lacy herself, organized by the Centro per l'Arte Contemporanea Luigi Pecci at Museo Pecci, Milan, in 2014, was also informative.[4] In addition, we each had experience with presenting socially engaged work in earlier projects at SFMOMA and YBCA, respectively.[5] *Suzanne Lacy: We Are Here*, then, is less a departure than a continuation of a nascent collective effort to make time and space for art like Lacy's in museums—which is to say, in the public history of art.

Another fundamental curatorial question posed by Lacy's work centered on what it would mean to produce a retrospective that is not only guided by the task of remembrance but also seeks to engage the here and now of 2019. This led us to consider the specificity of our "now"—politically, culturally—and the specificities of our institutional settings. We initially explored this question through organizing a 2017 convening at Independent Curators International in which curators, researchers, and artists jointly reflected on the framing of such projects and ways of engaging with social practice in museum settings.[6] For Lacy, one of the core elements of revisiting earlier works for a museum context has been the use of the installation space to structure the reconsideration of past issues and questions for the present, while also "re-investigating" the evolution of the social and political issues at the center of the original performance. Indeed, this aspect of "rethinking," as Lacy has sometimes termed it, is not only an integral part of her own praxis and writing but has also become an essential and much-needed tool in contemporary art history and museology.[7] Implicit but similarly important is Lacy's stance that process—typically invisible to an exhibition audience—is part of the durational performance and therefore is also part of the artwork. Looking beyond existing curatorial models, we asked how participants might be involved with and represented in both the process of remaking these works and their presentation. *The Oakland Projects*, which were created in the San Francisco Bay Area and embody an evolving set of concerns related to youth, race, and public policy, seemed like a particularly fitting lens through which to examine this question. Reassembling any of Lacy's works of collective action means drawing again on the experiences and perspectives of those who participated originally, yet we also wanted to treat these historic projects in a more expansive way and carefully consider how we might rethink their relevance for the present.[8] To that end, YBCA invited a group of youth organizations from Oakland and the wider Bay Area, as well as a number of socially engaged contemporary artists who work with local youths, to use its presentation of the retrospective as a platform for surfacing their current concerns, activities, and responses. Our aim here is not to reframe these projects as "process artworks" but rather to consider *The Oakland Projects* as yet another set of transferable tools, or perhaps even a loose "script," for the engagement of youth today—on their own terms.

Keeping such questions in mind, this publication does not represent each project through one or two key images but instead presents a broad range of materials that evoke Lacy's process and actions, contextualizing her work with other visuals, texts, and firsthand commentary by many of her original collaborators. We hope that these stories and histories will generate more in-depth explorations of the strategies and concerns central to Lacy's practice and will help forge a more complex account of how art of recent decades agitates, politically and artistically, at times and in places beyond our personal experiences. After all, most of the time, most of us weren't there.

Indeed, it is easy for any exhibition or study of past actions to underscore the sense that "we weren't there"—perhaps this is the risk of all exhibitions of performance. The challenge, which we also faced in the exhibition, is to present two contexts at once, to enable visitors and readers to hold in their minds the reality that the work was of its time and yet persists. Lacy's projects and the issues that prompted them—violence against women; race, youth, and the state; immigration; the culture of the working class—are as present today as ever. We need to historicize and de-historicize the work simultaneously. We can't be there, but *we are here*. In recognition of this duality, *Suzanne Lacy: We Are Here* is a movement toward the live, the present, and the political. Despite the natural desire to identify a "definitive" form of presentation for each work within the retrospective and catalogue, we ultimately had to acknowledge that no single way of representing social practice art, which is invariably iterative and open ended, could capture its complexity and processual quality.[9] These projects are not over—"the text is active."[10] Nothing is fully present, and nothing can be fully absent. What persists is the agitation, and this is why, even and especially today, *we are all here* to take on this work.

—RUDOLF FRIELING, LUCÍA SANROMÁN, AND DOMINIC WILLSDON

NOTES

Significant portions of this introduction are adapted from Dominic Willsdon, "Where Are We and What Time Is It? On Beginning to Curate Suzanne Lacy," A Blade of Grass, September 2018, http://www.abladeofgrass.org/fertile-ground/time-beginning-curate-suzanne-lacy/.

1. Lacy was active in the San Francisco Bay Area as an artist and educator for more than twenty-five years. In addition to the many projects she produced in the region, presented in the Illustrated Survey in this volume, other local highlights include her participation in 1977 in The Floating Museum, a San Francisco–based "museum without walls" organized by artist Lynn Hershman Leeson that aimed to critique gender inequality in the arts. Two years later, her twenty-four-hour performance *International Dinner Party* (pp. 130–35) was featured among the opening events for SFMOMA's presentation of *The Dinner Party* (1979), an iconic installation by her mentor Judy Chicago. In 1982 SFMOMA supported the staging of Lacy's performance *Freeze Frame: Room for Living Room* (pp. 140–46) as part of the International Theater Festival conference and the International Sculpture Conference in San Francisco. Lacy has since pioneered feminist and performance art education and public practice programs at institutions throughout the region and beyond. As dean of fine arts at the California College of Arts and Crafts (CCAC, now California College of the Arts [CCA]) in Oakland from 1987 to 1997, she fostered critical discourse on contemporary art and the idea of the artist as an engaged citizen. In 1989 she directed City Sites: Artists and Urban Strategies, a series of site-specific artist lectures in Oakland, and in 1991 she convened artists, curators, and educators working in the public sphere for *Mapping the Terrain: New Genre Public Art*, a symposium co-hosted by SFMOMA. More recently, in 2008, Lacy and her collaborator Leslie Labowitz presented *The Performing Archive: Restricted Access* (2007, pp. 108–9) at YBCA.

2. For further discussion of the forms of Lacy's art, see the essay by Dominic Willsdon in this volume.

3. That presentation is documented in the catalogue *Allan Kaprow—Art as Life*, ed. Eva Meyer-Hermann, Andrew Perchuk, and Stephanie Rosenthal (Los Angeles: Getty Research Institute, 2008). Lacy herself frequently situates her practice in relation to both contemporary art and activism. Her references include peers such as Ant Farm, Judy Chicago, Yvonne Rainer, Kaprow, Lynn Hershman Leeson, and others who have championed actions or events that are not framed by specific issues or agendas. She has also aligned herself with activists within the traditions of education and theater, such as Paulo Freire, Augusto Boal, and Bertolt Brecht. The impact of such traditions of media art, performance, sculpture, and theater in an expanded field of social practice is evident in her methodology.

4. See *Suzanne Lacy: Gender Agendas*, curated by Fabio Cavallucci in collaboration with Megan Steinman for the Centro per l'Arte Contemporanea Luigi Pecci, Museo Pecci, Milan, November 14, 2014–January 6, 2015.

5. Lucía Sanromán recently organized surveys of the work of Tania Bruguera and Futurefarmers at YBCA. During his tenure at SFMOMA, Dominic Willsdon spearheaded the framing of "public practice" and "public knowledge." Rudolf Frieling organized an expansive early survey at SFMOMA called *The Art of Participation: 1950 to Now* (2008–9).

6. Some twenty-plus colleagues gathered from February 27 to March 1, 2017. The convening was supported by a generous grant from The Andy Warhol Foundation for the Visual Arts. A full participant list is available on the Independent Curators International website: http://curatorsintl.org/events/curatorial-research-convening.

7. For further discussion of this aspect of Lacy's practice, see the essay by Lucía Sanromán in this volume.

8. Two of Lacy's former collaborators on *The Oakland Projects*, Unique Holland and Moriah Ulinskas, embarked on a different, complementary research path that reflected on the works' histories and legacies of collaboration. Similar themes were explored on September 30, 2017, in the roundtable discussion "What Role Should Art Have in Civic Life?" as part of the symposium *Does Art Have Users?*, organized by SFMOMA in collaboration with YBCA. This event convened original participants and collaborators in *The Oakland Projects*, socially engaged Bay Area artists, students, and others, and took place in the YBCA galleries. The University of Southern California (USC) provided generous support for Lacy's rethinking of *The Oakland Projects* for this exhibition through the James H. Zumberge Faculty Research and Innovation Fund and RAP (Race, Arts & Placemaking), an initiative supported by the USC Provost Research Collaboration Fund. Lacy's work on the video installation of *De tu puño y letra* (By Your Own Hand, 2014–15/2019, pp. 118–23) created for this presentation was supported by Lauren Bon and Metabolic Studio.

9. In our curatorial decision-making process, we considered both the artist's previous modes of translating large-scale offsite projects into installation formats for museums and our own interest in reimagining and re-viewing select works through a contemporary lens. This guided our focus on particular aspects of projects and led us to emphasize the surfacing of previously unseen materials.

10. See the essay by Rudolf Frieling in this volume.

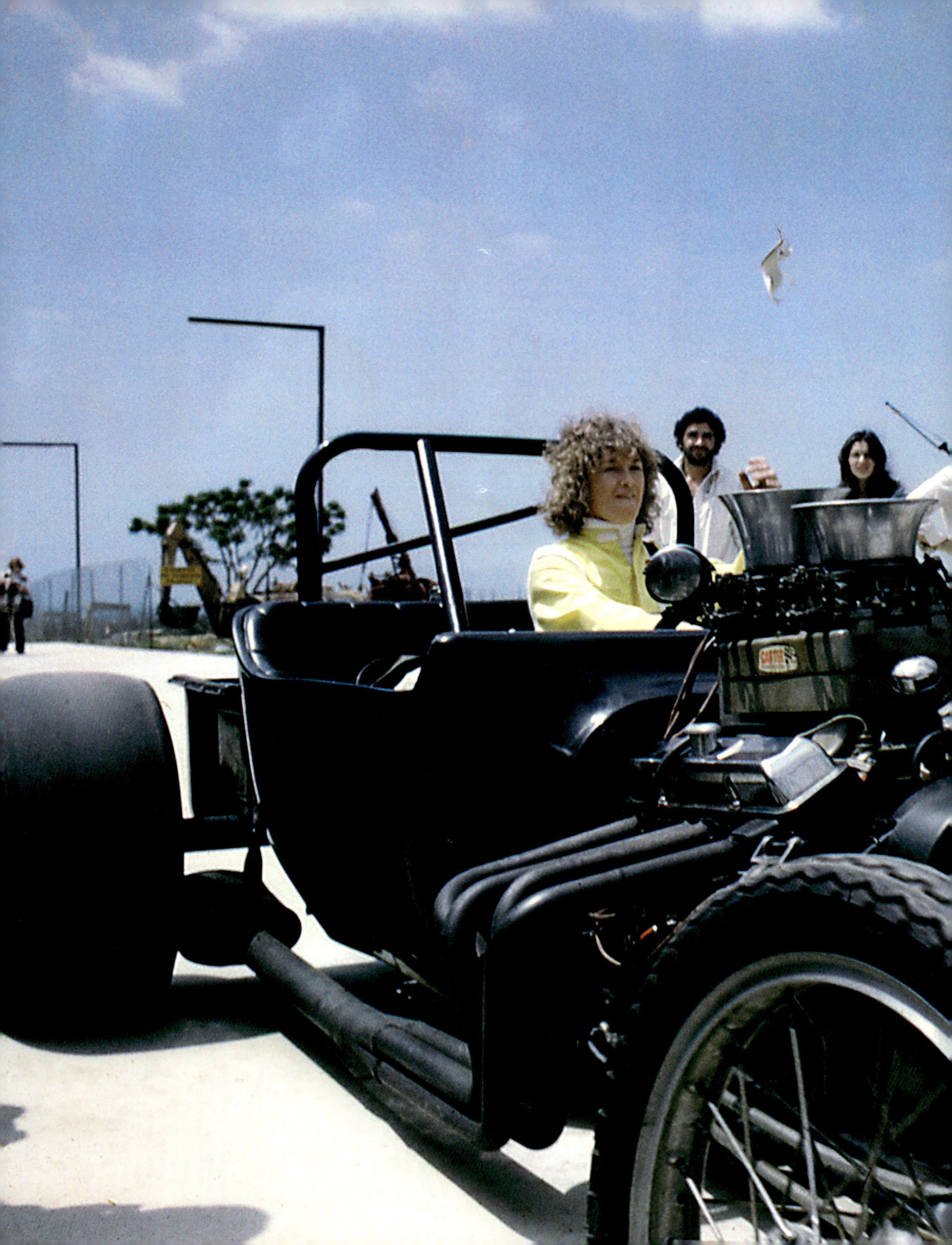

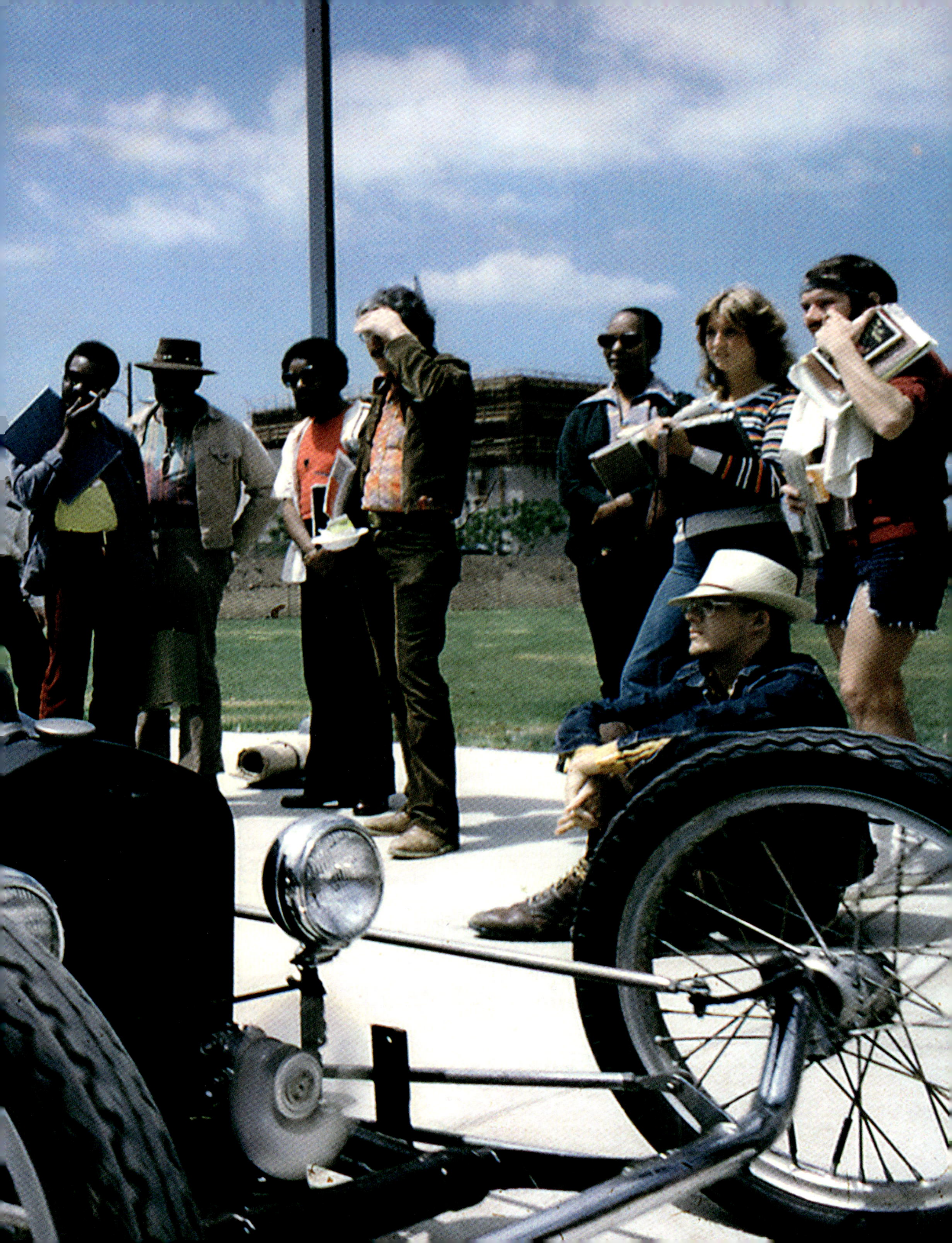

TO REENACT, TO RETHINK, TO REDISTRIBUTE SUZANNE LACY

Lucía Sanromán

What is performance art? Much of what I do I label performance because there's nothing better to call it. One definition of performance at this moment could be "that which cannot be encompassed by other forms."
—SUZANNE LACY[1]

The above statement was made in 1985, when Suzanne Lacy was deeply involved with creating some of her most iconic participatory performance works. Despite—or perhaps because of— her intensive exploration of the genre, she questioned the use of the term "performance" to describe these projects. This was no rhetorical gesture. She, along with other feminist artists working in the 1970s and early 1980s, had redefined the ways in which "political performance art" (as she later described it) might radically blur the line between life and art. Creating ethically committed, engaged public works involved linking, as she noted, "avant-garde art and the feminist goal to diversify audiences."[2] This question of what performance—and, indeed, art—*is* in Lacy's manifestation of the genre is central to any consideration of her practice, which insistently spills over boundaries between categories and genres, tests the limits of authorship, and addresses social and political issues of broad public concern.

A key aspect of Lacy's practice has been to synergize dialogue toward collective consciousness raising and to make this process an art genre. In a sense, her life's work has been to expand her mentor and professor Allan Kaprow's ideas of making "life itself" a formal element in visual art, such that "political art need not be simply an art of symbolic action, but might include actual action."[3] She extends performance art into the social sphere, where it can encompass ideas and disciplines outside of art, always working in deep collaboration with individuals and communities. Lacy creates conditions for pluralistic and democratic processes by making the subject of performance the intimate concerns of the structurally underrepresented—such as women victims of violence, elderly women, or youth of color. Hers is sometimes regarded as a "useful" practice whose social efficacy can be measured—in terms of media representations of women, for instance, or youth policy.[4]

At various times Lacy's practice has included mapping, sociological research, community organizing, workshops in a variety of media, and choreographed and/or directed dialogue-performances, which in turn may become the subjects of video productions and mass-media interventions, whether in newspaper or television coverage. But for any given work, it is not necessarily clear how we might pull apart the constituent elements— research, engagement with collaborators and participants, choreographed public dialogue, media intervention—because although there is a form to every stage, the stages are not necessarily conceived of as discrete, nor does Lacy see them as part of a linear progression (an assertion supported by her mind maps and process diagrams).

Over the years Lacy has been continually called upon to circle back to earlier works, either for exhibitions or out of her own desire to follow up with old friends and collaborators. And given the nature of the work, a persistent question has necessarily followed: What does it mean to "re-perform" a work whose making involved social research and collective creation, and that was staged in public spaces with a loose script informed by questions rather than answers? To answer that question, it seems, we need to ask another one first: Where do the performances begin and end? Do they take shape when Lacy initiates private discussions with potential collaborators and participants, or through the social research that informs the questions that guide public and private conversations? Is the performance *only* the moment of public dialogue staged for an audience? Lacy argues that it is all of the above, which leads to the proposition—which I will argue for here—that her works, especially those that are months or years in duration, cannot be endlessly, exactly re-created or re-performed. Lacy herself questions whether they should be re-performed at all, pointing to the politics of "re-presentation" that such processes imply.

Within certain parameters, however, and depending on the work, could *aspects* of Lacy's engaged performances become scripts, scores, or sets of guidelines to be (re)interpreted by the artist herself or others into the future? Could her methodologies be reproduced and transferred, learned and applied, in different contexts than she originally intended—or even entirely in her absence? Seeking answers, we might begin by looking at Lacy's own approaches, applied to a handful of projects over the past eleven years, and considering what we in the field tend to call "re-performance" or "restaging"—although these are terms that she rarely, if ever, uses. We might also ask, what words *does* she use?

Consider *Stories of Work and Survival* (2007, p. 147, fig. 1), which was created for the exhibition *WACK! Art and the Feminist Revolution*, organized by the Museum of Contemporary Art, Los Angeles. In it Lacy, together with collaborators, "revisited," as she describes it, two prior performances: *Freeze Frame: Room for Living Room* (1982, pp. 140–46) and *Immigrants and Survivors* (1983). Notably, the term "revisited" implies a return to a familiar place, project, or process. While a re-performance might be tied to the rigors of a script or score, a revisitation is liberated from the need to closely follow the original performance. This revisiting may lead to new tactics, alternative routes, and, certainly, new outcomes.

Freeze Frame took place in a Roche Bobois furniture showroom in San Francisco. There, 120 women gathered in small groups (of sex workers, Jews, people with disabilities, et cetera) based on shared circumstances for structured conversations on crucial

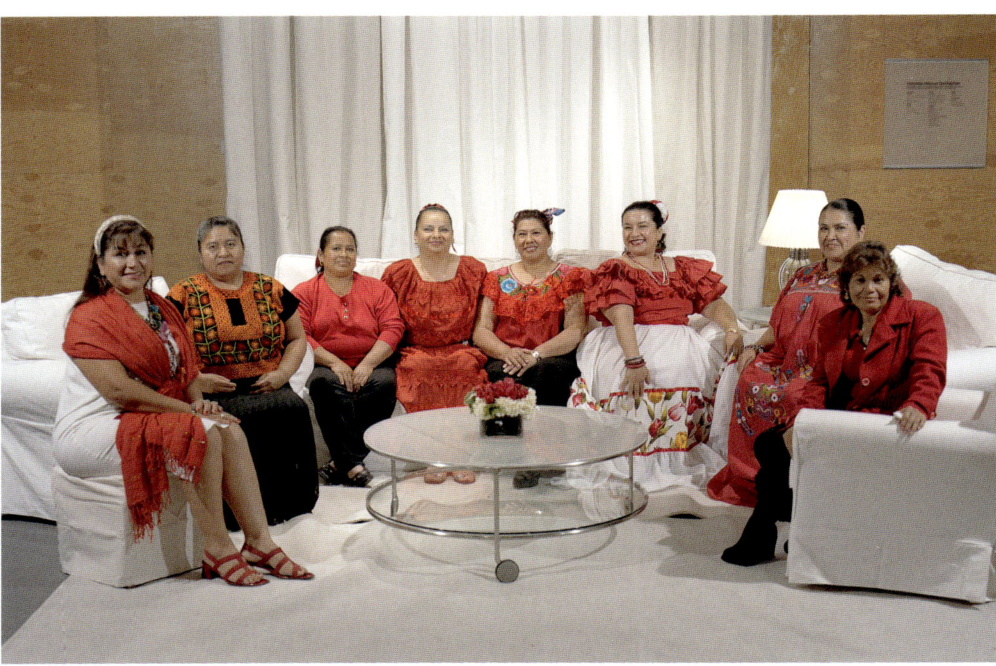

Fig. 1. Suzanne Lacy with Kelly Akashi and Susan Barnet, *Stories of Work and Survival*, 2007. Performance for *WACK! Art and the Feminist Revolution*, Museum of Contemporary Art, Los Angeles

topics—namely survival and constituency building—while an audience of about six hundred people listened in. It was one of the earliest instances in which Lacy staged dialogue as performance. The following year, *Immigrants and Survivors* also brought women's networks to the fore—this time around questions of immigration, race, and age—in an experimental exercise that prefigured "intersectional" feminist encounters before that term was coined. Co-created with a large planning committee of women of many backgrounds, this conversation featured food as a starting point and took place in Los Angeles. Both works resonated with the methods and processes of Augusto Boal's Theater of the Oppressed and consciousness-raising feminist gatherings, using the contingency of dialogue in non-art contexts to create powerful, multivocal performances—in the form of a potluck dinner—that literally brought public attention to the participants' voices.

Lacy describes *Stories of Work and Survival* as an exploration of how representations of feminism, race, and class in visual and performance art had changed in the twenty-five years since *Freeze Frame*. Besides "revisiting" the two earlier works, it addressed the exhibition itself as an integral context for the project. In considering how to represent her earlier dialogue-based projects in a museum show, Lacy foregrounded something she had been thinking about since the 1970s: the idea that her "art performance" is durational and inclusive of all parts of the organizing process—meetings and workshops, gatherings and private conversations. She wanted to explore representations of activism and women "in four parts, inside and outside the museum: 1) conversations not witnessed, taking place in women's homes and workplaces; 2) group conversations seen [through a window], but not heard, by visitors to the *WACK!* exhibition; 3) these same conversations heard, via recordings, in a subsequent installation; and 4) conversations [between women] over dinner outside the doors of the museum, representing public voice."[5]

Conceiving of the exhibition as a frame, tracking the evolution of a given topic or network of people, and extending the notion of a performance to encompass the production steps that preceded it remained key aspects of Lacy's next revisitation. *La piel de la memoria revivida/Skin of Memory Revisited* (pp. 219–23) was a dialogue-performance and installation produced in 2011 for Encuentro Internacional de Medellín 2011 (MDE11). As Lacy writes, "The new work took advantage of the reflective space of the museum to review the past decade in Medellín in terms of progress and setbacks on the incidence of violence; to imagine possible futures for the city; and to bring those who produced [the earlier performance] together again, to celebrate the fabric of relations formed earlier that continues today."[6]

The original project, *La piel de la memoria/Skin of Memory* (1999–2000, pp. 219–23), had its roots in 1998, when Lacy was invited by noted anthropologist Pilar Riaño-Alcalá to create an art project in Medellín, Colombia, in collaboration with local social workers, academics, and activists. Aimed at addressing collective trauma in barrio Antioquia, then one of the city's most violent neighborhoods, this public art project was a part of a broader program put together by a consortium of government and nongovernment organizations.[7] Workshops centered on remembering as a means of community building and healing in a place torn asunder by drug trafficking, youth gangs, paramilitary violence, and territorial divisions. For several months, twenty local leaders trained by Riaño-Alcalá gathered meaningful objects from residents (such as photos or mementos of family members felled by violence) to place in an itinerant "museum of memory." Each lender also wrote or dictated an anonymous letter expressing positive desires for the neighborhood, to be delivered in the future to a neighbor. About five hundred objects were gathered and placed in a borrowed bus that was transformed into a beautiful mobile reliquary. Over ten days in July 1999 the bus-museum traversed internal territorial borders and parked at five different locations. More than four thousand people visited and then participated in a culminating parade, during which time the letters were delivered. Today the project is widely considered one of the most important social-impact performance artworks in Colombia.[8]

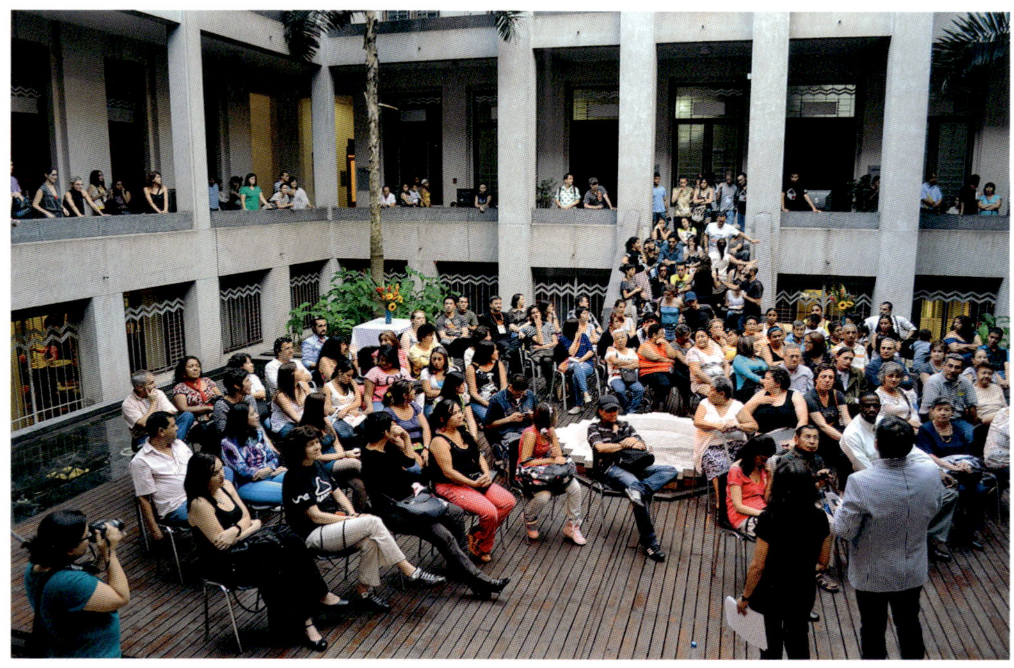

By 2011 Medellín had come to be recognized across the globe for the rapid and positive transformation of its urban, social, and civic infrastructures. In *La piel de la memoria revivida*, Lacy and Riaño-Alcalá decided to foreground reconnection with their past collaborators and contributors in an afternoon dialogue-performance in which some seventy previous participants reflected on the project and the great changes the city had witnessed in the intervening eleven years (fig. 2). Lacy and Riaño-Alcalá also created an art installation that remade the original bus interior in a new format featuring a single shelf of artifacts from the original lenders. There were two new videos as well, one featuring the participants' current reflections, and a second containing earlier documentary footage.

La piel de la memoria revivida makes one thing evident: as a performance becomes more engaged with civic processes and a wide variety of actors, and as its impact spreads well beyond the agency of a single author, the idea of "re-performance" as it is usually understood within contemporary art seems inapplicable, or even irrelevant. To ask the lenders of the original artifacts to remake the bus-museum, or to drive it along its previous route with the original goals in mind, would make no sense given the social changes that had occurred in Medellín, which were dramatic enough to have ameliorated or erased the violent social divides that the original performance had sought to heal. What *did* make sense in 2011 was to transform the bus into a sculptural piece—the single shelf—presented as a "relational" object. Most visitors to MDE11, steeped as they were in Colombia's civic renewal process, understood this as an exercise in public memory (fig. 3). It was not a re-performance but a new installation. While the public dialogue organized by Lacy and Riaño-Alcalá was described as a "performance" that brought together previous participants, it was also a reunion among old friends.

In 2017 Lacy and Riaño-Alcalá gathered a subset of the original artifacts, along with elements from the 2011 exhibition, for installations in Santa Barbara and New York. A key

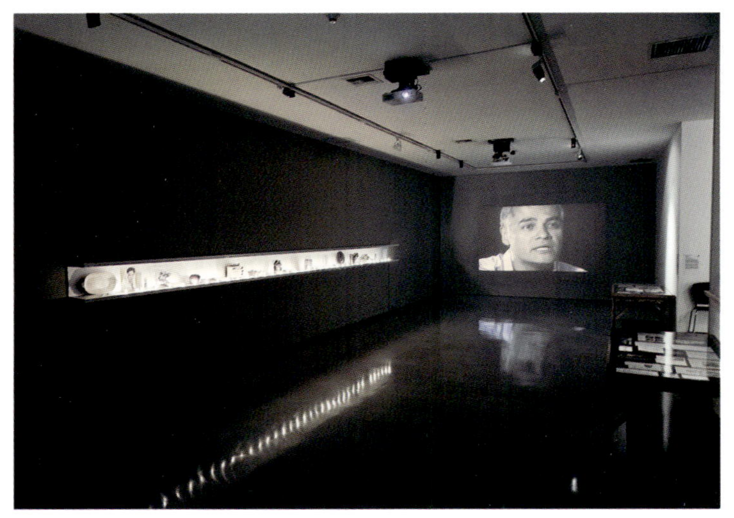

TOP: Fig. 2. Public gathering for Suzanne Lacy and Pilar Riaño-Alcalá, *La piel de la memoria revivida/Skin of Memory Revisited*, 2011. Part of Encuentro Internacional de Medellín 2011 (MDE11), Museo de Antioquia, Medellín, Colombia
BOTTOM: Fig. 3. Lacy and Riaño-Alcalá, *La piel de la memoria revivida/Skin of Memory Revisited*, 2011. Installation view, MDE11

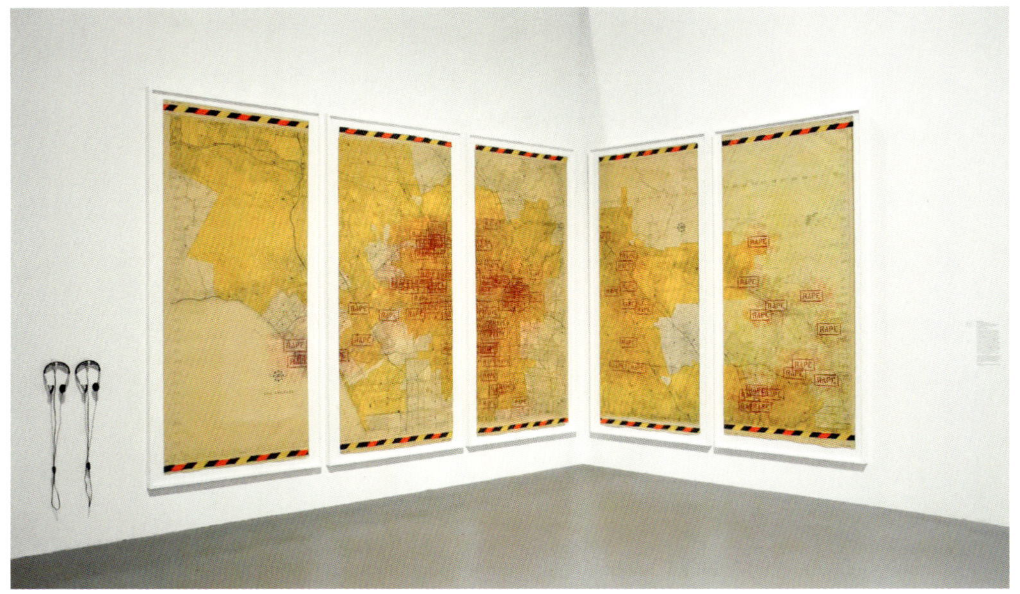

addition was a research time line of United States–Colombia relations since 1999. Featuring quotes, newspaper clippings, and infographics, it contextualized the original presentation for American audiences unfamiliar with the negative impact of their government's intervention in Colombia. Each of these "revisitings" of *La piel de la memoria* has required the material re-creation of specific elements as well as the inclusion of contextual information that allows for new understandings of global politics.

In contrast to revisiting, to "re-create," or create again, connotes a more object-based form of fabrication or making. In 2014 Lacy used the title *Three Weeks in May Re-creation* for a new version of her iconic public performance *Three Weeks in May* (pp. 95–99), a project executed in 1977 with Leslie Labowitz that she considers foundational to her subsequent efforts to develop works that address and include a broader, non-art public. A culminating moment in her long-term investment in combating violence against

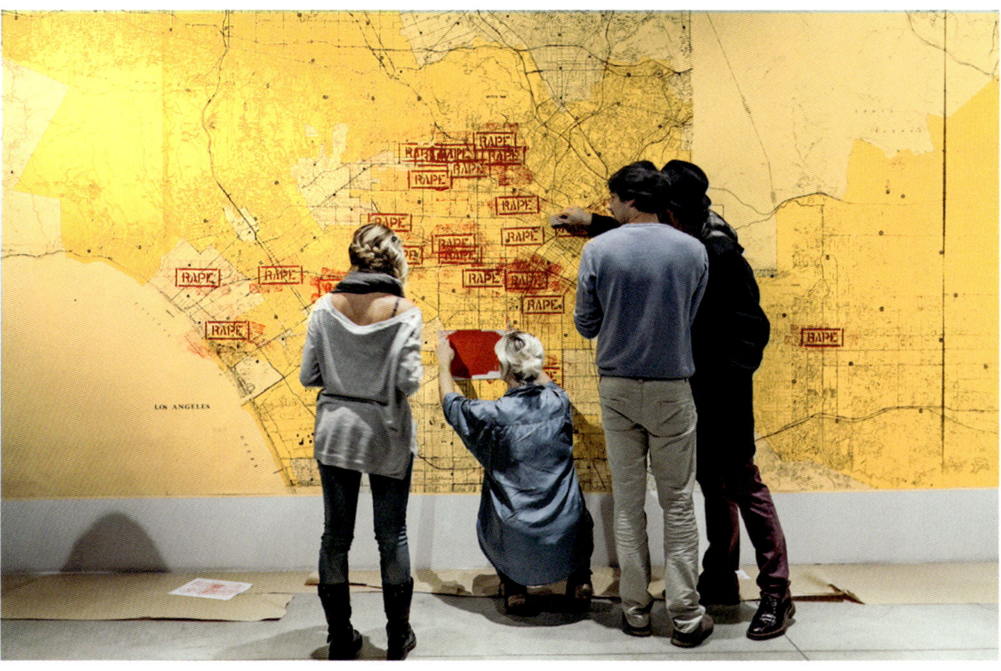

TOP: Fig. 4. Suzanne Lacy, *Three Weeks in May*, 1977. Ink on printed maps, with sound, dimensions variable. Hammer Museum, Los Angeles, purchased through the Board of Overseers Acquisitions Fund with additional support from Dori Peterman Mostov, Susan Bay Nimoy, and Ruth Bloom BOTTOM: Fig. 5. Suzanne Lacy and Megan Steinman with Franziska Rauh, *Three Weeks in May Re-creation*, 2014. Installation in progress for *Suzanne Lacy: Gender Agendas*, Museo Pecci, Milan

women, it represented a major commitment to using performance to communicate with civic leaders, with the aim of influencing policy and intervening in the mass media. The project included approximately thirty public and private performances, conversations, meals, self-defense classes, and other gatherings involving a broad group of feminists, public health professionals, and elected officials. Central to the work was a twenty-five-foot-wide map of Los Angeles that was posted in a commercial area close to City Hall. Each day for three weeks, Lacy stamped it with the locations of the previous day's rapes (obtained by the artist from the police department). A rare instance of an object functioning as a central component in one of Lacy's works, the map operated as a "social sculpture" (fig. 4). A second map presented the sites of organizations and programs for victims of rape and other violence. The cartographic format made the ubiquity and proximity of rape inescapable.

The 2014 *Re-creation* version, made for a survey of Lacy's work organized by the Centro per l'Arte Contemporanea Luigi Pecci at Museo Pecci, Milan, featured a facsimile of the twenty-five-foot-wide map, over which the locations of rapes recorded in the 1977 police reports were stamped by visitors over three days (fig. 5). This re-creation thus involved what Lacy called a "partial reenactment" of the earlier work and was likewise rare in her oeuvre in that it translated a longer-term, socially engaged, process-based performance into a synthesized "manual," where elements of the earlier participatory piece were "played" based on instructions given to an exhibition's visitors. While Lacy herself does not consider this a significant project, it is important to my argument as it exemplifies the potential pitfalls of "re-performing" her artworks. Notably, in 2012, Lacy had already carried out a deeper revisiting of *Three Weeks in May* under the title *Three Weeks in January* (pp. 116–17). Lacy has noted that this reenactment involved focusing "on where Los Angeles is now."[9] A new map of the city was installed for three weeks in front of the Los Angeles Police Department and stamped daily with locations of rapes based on police reports. Once again the project included a series of public and private events, but this time a special social media campaign, *I Know Someone, Do You?*, allowed for a new social networking element to be performed.

Three Weeks in January represents one of Lacy's closest re-creations of an earlier performance. While some elements were adapted, the new iteration remained visually related to the original—for example, the map was essentially the same, but now with stamps indicating the locations of current rapes. The methods of engaging with and organizing feminist and activist organizations and communities were likewise updated. A push toward the present could be seen in the restaging of heightened moments of public ritual around violence, which gave voice to stakeholder communities, as well as in the behind-the-scenes organizing this implied. More importantly, in step with what we have seen with the recent #MeToo movement—albeit at a smaller scale—*Three Weeks in January* underscored the ways social media is transforming organizing, allowing for the sharing of live, intimate, direct accounts of personal experiences and laying the foundations for the public to empathize with the victims of rape and condemn perpetrators. The term "reenactment" is thus appropriate, since it describes the acting out of a past event and suggests the idea of "acting again"—not simply to repeat what once was but to execute the processes anew and make the work relevant to Los Angeles in 2012. Unlike *Three Weeks in May Re-creation*, this reenactment brought the work into the present through engagement with new communities, new organizers, and new politicians. In this sense, Lacy highlighted a significant shift in the perception of and openness to dialogue around rape and sex-violence in public life and emphasized a deepening awareness of the conditions that perpetuate it.

A perhaps more succinct but equally appropriate approach to rethinking occurred in 2013, when Lacy was invited by Tate Modern, London, to make a project exploring the themes, populations, and dialogues central to what is possibly her most famous performance tableau: *The Crystal Quilt* (1987, pp. 166–73). The culmination of two years of organizing and community engagement, that project focused on combating the social invisibility of elderly women and highlighting their experiences of aging. As part of a mass-media campaign, 430 participants were assembled around square tables placed over a carpet made to resemble a quilt in a large interior plaza at the IDS Center shopping mall in Minneapolis. The result was an artful montage of colors, experiences, and people that was viewed by a live audience and was broadcast live on PBS.

Titled *Silver Action* (2013, pp. 178–79), Lacy's rethinking of the project took the form of a six-hour choreographed dialogue-performance. Structured in four acts, it focused on the legacy of British women activists from the 1960s to 1985, allowing them to "write themselves into history" by projecting live transcriptions of a selection of personal narratives. Other new elements included a social media campaign aimed at bringing visibility to the leading role women activists have played in establishing progressive policy in Britain since the 1960s. Lacy considered *Silver Action* a "rethinking" because while the performance was centered on the image of a group of women around square tables with yellow tablecloths, and some of the participants were of advanced age, in other ways it differed pointedly from *The Crystal Quilt*. As she noted: "This is actually not a project about aging, and not a sentimental project about older women. . . . This is a project about discrimination and inequality."[10] Lacy attributes this shift in focus to her desire to respond to the government's characterization of older women as a burden on Britain's social welfare system.

There were formal *and* methodological elements uniting the two projects: both were informed by workshops and other gatherings of women who determined the topics of discussion. Nevertheless, Lacy's description of *Silver Action* as a "rethinking" is telling, and it highlights her decision to allow for aspects of the earlier project to function differently. For example, with *The Crystal Quilt* Lacy played a more involved and constant role, even moving from Southern California to Minnesota for two years to work on the project. She actively devised a work that would utilize community organizing methodologies in real time and allow for a later TV broadcast. In London, she described her role as "facilitator," and she delegated the pedagogical work to the Tate's education team. The workshops they organized, she reports, were essential in helping "frame the discourse that would take place during the piece."[11]

This looser relationship to the original performance points to the potential of thinking of the earlier works as scripts or scores that can be interpreted anew, not only by the artist but also by a growing and/or changing group of facilitators dedicated to engagement as a core component of an arts institution's civic role. For a work by Lacy to serve as a script or score, however, requires full institutional commitment. Arts professionals cannot simply regard themselves as "interpreters" of an object-based piece on view for a temporary visitor. They must be empowered co-creators. The score or script for "replaying" a Lacy work, therefore, must include annotations or instructions for both the performers and the producer, whether this is an individual or an institution. The instructions have to allow for some rethinking of the original to make it appropriate to the new institution and its geography and social milieu.

For *Suzanne Lacy: We Are Here*, the artist, along with the San Francisco Museum of Modern Art (SFMOMA) and Yerba Buena Center for the Arts (YBCA), will "activate" several past works. Like Kaprow's score-based happenings and performances, *Alterations* (1994–95, p. 218) is readily synthesized as a set of instructions: Create three large piles of used clothes in red, white, and blue. Hire seamstresses, preferably local garment-industry workers. Seat them among the piles and ask them to hand-stitch the garments one to the other into long red, white, and blue strips, for long periods at a stretch, over the duration of the exhibition (fig. 6). The repetitive actions enact labor in the context of the exhibition space and also recall Kaprow's love of absurd, mundane gestures that "infect" art with everyday life and vice versa. This is a case in which the term "activation" points to a freeing of the project from Lacy's direct management and authorship.

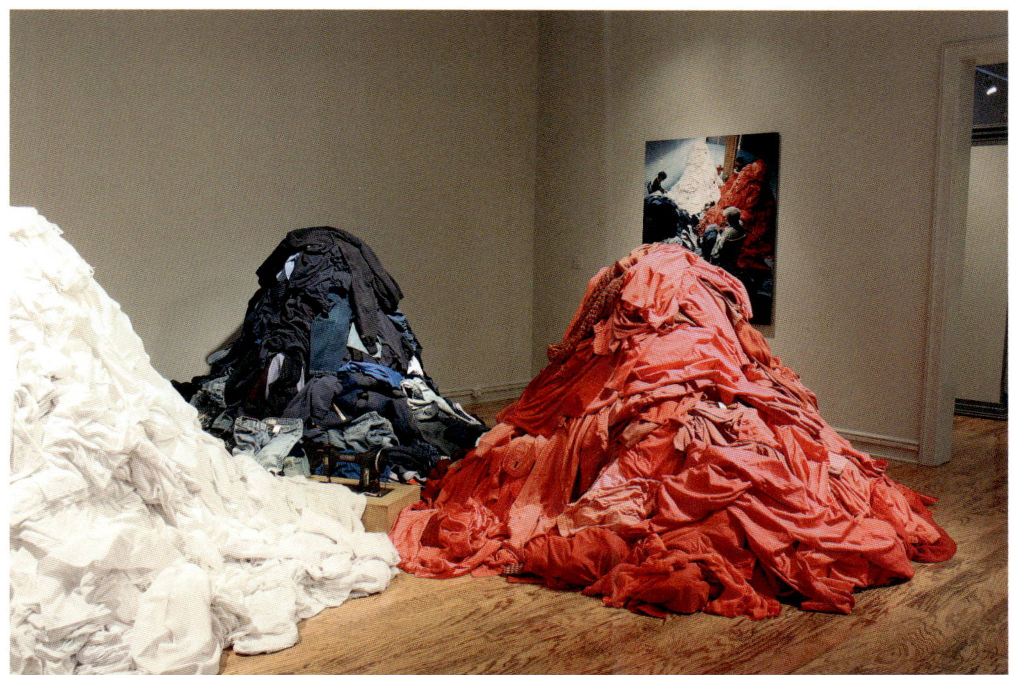

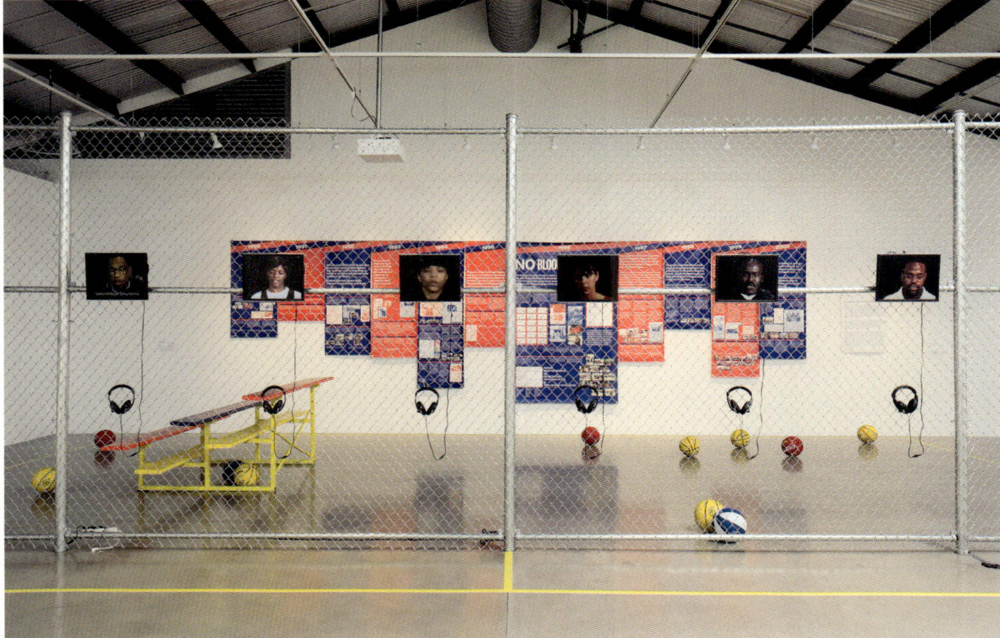

This idea of "activating" a score is even more explicit in *Cleaning Conditions* (2013, pp. 236–37), another gallery-sited performance, in which Lacy pays homage to Kaprow by interpreting his instructions "Chores" (1995). Lacy's piece addresses the history of labor organizing as well as the labor conditions of facilities departments in art institutions. It was first produced for the Manchester Art Gallery, England, where groups of sweepers redistributed political labor-organizing flyers (as opposed to the dust called for in Kaprow's version) from one gallery to the next for two weeks. At the end of each day's sweep, entities and individuals associated with labor organizing conducted public discussions in the galleries. At SFMOMA this action will be performed again but rethought in relation to the museum's unique architecture, and with attentiveness to current labor conditions in San Francisco.

While these examples demonstrate how straightforward "reactivating" a Lacy work can be, in the absence of specific instructions created with the exhibition space in mind it can be far more complicated. Indeed, re-creating or reenacting civically engaged works such as *The Oakland Projects* (1991–2001, pp. 184–211)—as YBCA is doing for this retrospective—is exceptionally challenging. As Lacy has explained, the original works were collaborations "with scores of Oakland artists and youth to produce performances and installations on public schooling, health care, criminal justice, and public policy issues. Our strategies included reflection on core issues (community policing, schooling, neighborhood safety, youth leadership, and civic participation), skill building (public speaking, computer literacy, writing, media analysis, video and photography), and workshops on team building, mentoring, and antiracism."[12] YBCA's presentation will take the form of video documentation and artist-directed installations. As of this writing, Lacy is in the process of revisiting some of her past relationships with individuals who contributed to *The Oakland Projects*, in a way reminiscent of her "revisitation" of *La piel de la memoria*. Her video and photographic representations of the encounters, focused on the changes that nearly twenty to thirty years have brought—to the individuals and more broadly to Oakland's urban, social, and political fabric—will be central to the exhibition.

Lacy's work has consistently defied the idea of a single author and proposed instead a participatory, distributive model of artistic creation. Thus, for this retrospective it seemed important to carry forward the concept of distributed authorship. The YBCA presentation will include a platform for activists, organizations, and youths who have been working in Oakland and the Bay Area from the 1990s to today, including Youth Speaks, YR Media (formerly Youth Radio), and the Center for Media Justice. Visitors will encounter their active, participatory group investigations of youth culture, policy, and media representation in a variety of exhibition formats, including sound pieces and time lines. The aim of this strategy is to begin a more explicit process of redistributing Lacy's legacy and authorship, one in which her work is *mined* for methodologies but not re-performed, per se.

Lacy herself is clear that this process—which is perhaps more in line with how musicians and actors interpret scripts or scores—does not and cannot lead to new "Suzanne Lacy performances." She realizes that giving continued life to works like *The Oakland Projects* requires widening the lens to other cultural actors and institutions who are responding to evolving contexts. In this way, a Lacy retrospective can serve as a useful tool for understanding the present. Ultimately, while the artist might reject the concept of re-performance, redistribution of her participatory, multidisciplinary, activist, and civically engaged work extends her tools and methods to new generations of collaborators and organizers. And it is through this process that Lacy's legacy will continue to contribute to a more heterogeneous and equitable future.

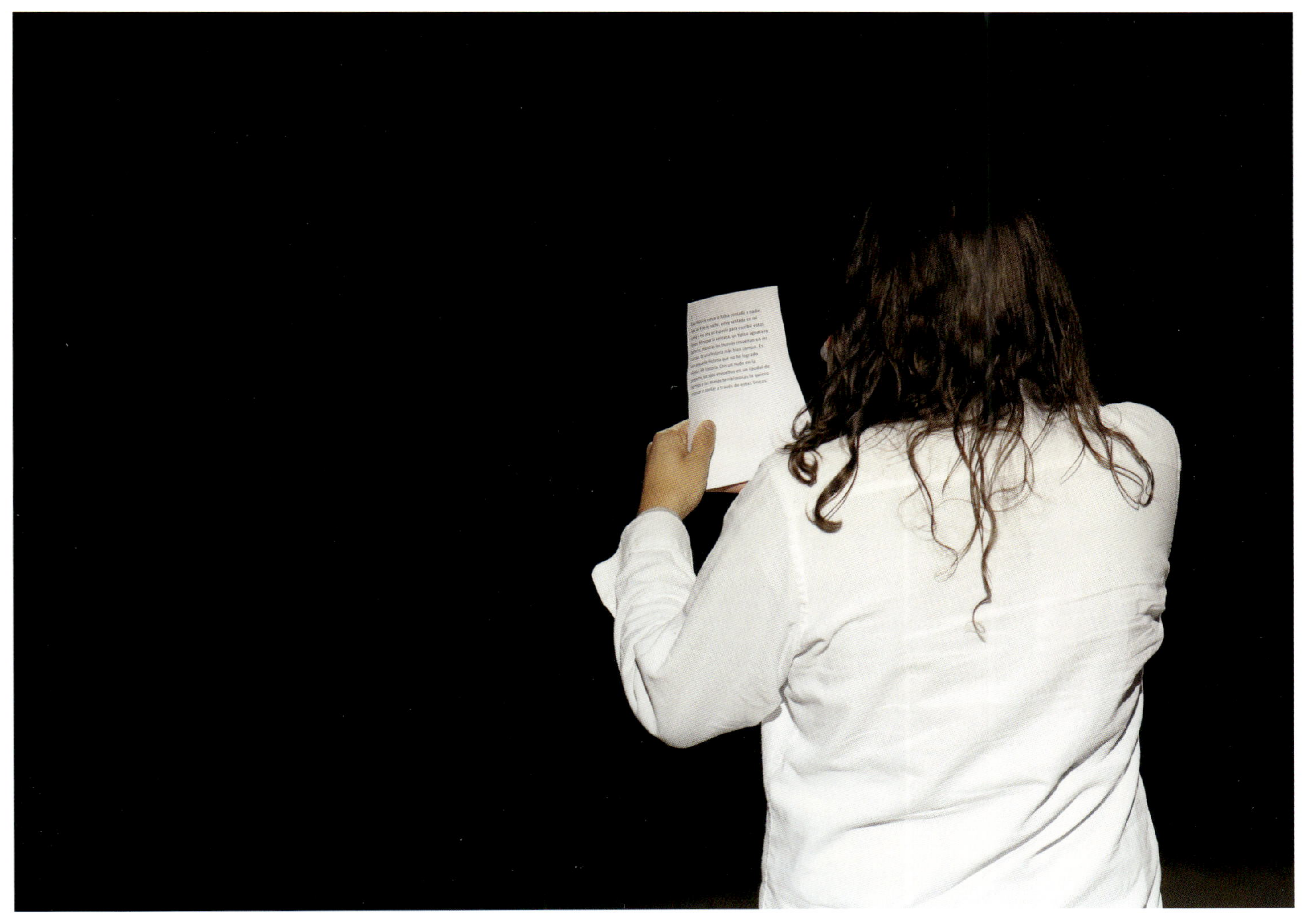

take center stage, compelling me to listen more closely and read more attentively. Such works span the arc of Lacy's career, from voices reading the artist's writing in *Prostitution Notes* (1974–75, pp. 90–93) to the letters about abuse and violence written by women and read by men in *De tu puño y letra* (By Your Own Hand, 2014–15/2019, pp. 118–23, fig. 1).[3] In Lacy's art, words carry a particular weight that asserts their centrality. And the text is often both a response to previous conversations and an active agent in the continuum of her oeuvre and social practice more broadly. What is said counts as much as when and where it is said. We may not isolate a single flash of epiphany, but sudden memories of physical experiences of power or abuse may be sparked in our minds and bodies as readers or listeners.

Lacy regards process as inseparable from the final result or event: for her, to reflect on process and actions through post-factum statements, whether as text, verbal reflection, or installation, keeps a work open and active over time. As opposed to "re-performance," a term that some artists in the field use, Lacy's term "rethinking" allows for a more radical shift and for the articulation of temporal specificity. I would call these continuous shifts "acts of translation," as if each iteration of the original "text" calls for a new actualization in a different register, be it the language of visual art, theater, or activism. This essay's title, "The Text Is Active," is not only the result of my process of reflection but also a way of articulating the artist's ongoing exploration of voices and agency in dialogue with exhibitions as another form of rethinking.[4]

Fig. 1. Suzanne Lacy, *De tu puño y letra*
(By Your Own Hand), 2014–15/2019.
Production photo, 2014

ACT I: FALLING APART

Lacy's *Three Love Stories* (1975–76, p. 54, figs. 2–3), an early series of photo-text montages, pairs narrative sequences of photographs with commentary. Despite their clearly dialectical structure, the collages embody an ambiguity in which text acts as annotation, juxtaposition, critique, and interpretation for images whose sequencing nods toward genres such as comic strips and popular photo novels.

"She gave her heart away./He treated it carelessly." The personal and even comic lament about love's unequal power dynamic is an old story, but here it accompanies an unusual, even blunt pictorial element: raw intestines. Lacy's practice has been an ongoing quest to explore ways of speaking publicly about topics others deem too intimate, too political, or too artistic.[5]

Similarly, a multipart essay related to the eponymous photo-text collage *Falling Apart* (1976, see p. 64) addresses in a pronounced yet elusive way the key role of language in Lacy's practice, where there is never one text or message but rather a multiplicity of voices, sources, and registers, as well as a continuous feedback loop of production and reflection. This "tale of four bodies" points to real blood, real stories, and "questionable monsters" via narrative jumps from a personal diary and dreams to an authorial voice. The fourth story, "To Hang without Falling," recounts a dream of being inside another body, "that of a man, a monk from a time long ago."[6] Here violence comes from the inside, from an unspoken memory of a traumatic event previously suffered. This is difficult to bear, and Lacy's text struggles with its own weight, leaving open the extent to which it is an account from her own biography.

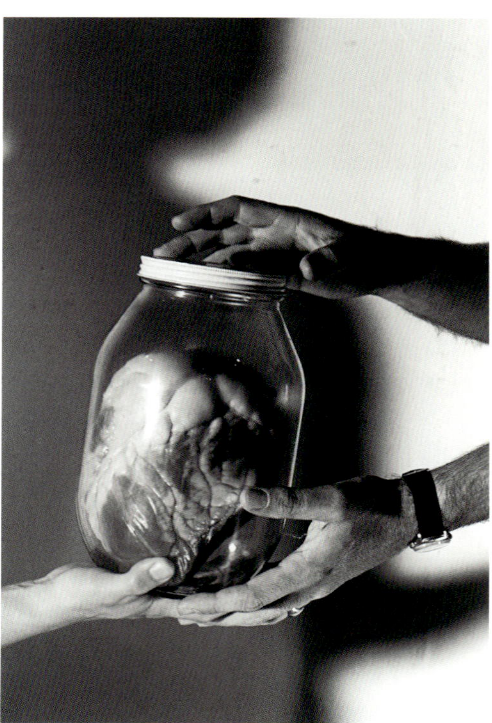

She gave her heart away.

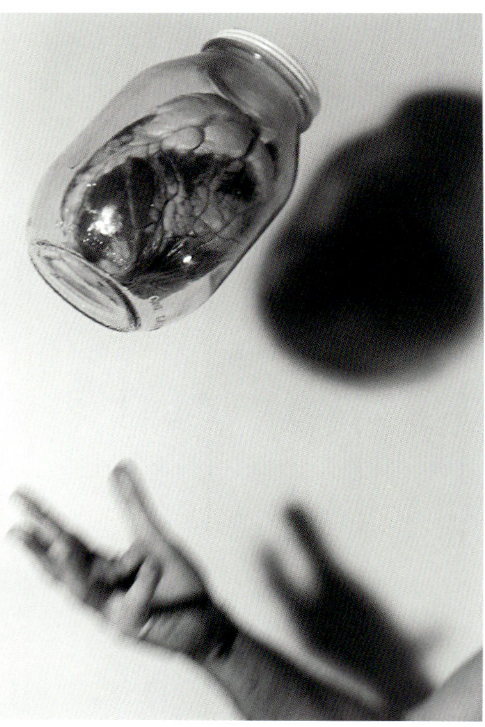

He treated it carelessly.

ACT II: PROSTITUTION NOTES

Prostitution Notes, in which the artist serves as ethnographer and scribe to the intimidating world of prostitutes and pimps, introduces mappings of narratives and operates with the informality of writings on a wall, a practice Lacy situates in relation to, among others, Allan Kaprow's happenings (see, for example, *Words*, 1962, fig. 4), Joan Jonas's performances, or Joseph Beuys's performance lecture notations on blackboards.[7] For her "field notes" Lacy adopted whatever strategy seemed most appropriate for the given context. The notes—informal, handwritten, casual, performative, processual, and often personal—along with questions asked, marks made with added color, visual explications, and commentary, all contribute to what we experience in the gallery as a temporary form, a sketch or didactic tool, not something to be scrutinized for acceptance or rejection as a "successful" artistic expression. The notes tend toward the diagram, as also seen in *Three Weeks in May* (1977, pp. 95–99) and *Cancer Notes: Seven-Day Genesis* (1991). They record events over time, giving a concept a first embodiment by tracing activities and dialogues. They don't serve as visual condensations of something larger and more durational; they are single layers of narratives we know to be multilayered. It seems especially appropriate here that the artist re-created the stories in a different format at a later point. When rethinking the forms in which she makes things public, Lacy tests her narratives in multiple ways, mirroring them in different registers and tonalities. It all starts, however, with the hand following discursive events. "If Movement Is the Form of 'The Life,' Place Is Its Language."[8]

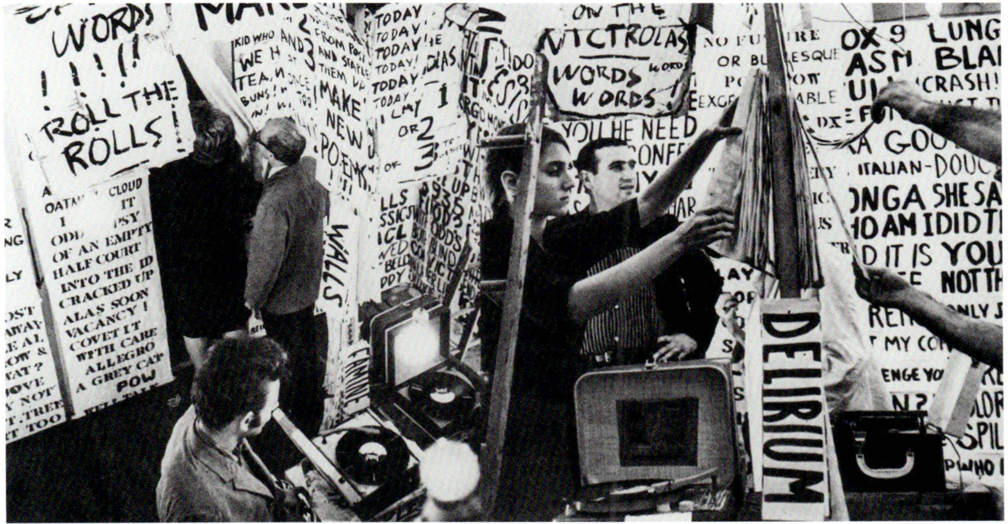

Prostitution Notes was Lacy's first use of notes to keep track of fleeting, half-understood personal narratives. She translated these "echoes" into a series of drawings on cheap brown sheets of paper, all equally sized, forming a sequence of ten diagrams or narrative maps. The research began in San Francisco but soon moved to Los Angeles:

MAY 14 Cappucino [*sic*] with Margo (San Francisco)
A centrally placed black-and-white photograph captures the artist running toward the San Francisco Art Institute.[9] The itinerary of that day is recorded as an abstracted hand-drawn street map that includes two cafés in the city's North Beach neighborhood and arrows indicating the direction of movement and progression. This first calendar entry acts as a prologue introducing Lacy's intention as well as her anxieties and feelings: "[I] realized my fear of being rejected by the 'Outsiders' with whom I identified." The text is organized as a body around the central map, with three main paragraphs and marginal notes in smaller handwriting. There is a beginning and an end to that day, the conclusion written in red ink at the bottom right.

OPPOSITE: Figs. 2–3. Suzanne Lacy, *Three Love Stories: A Gothic Love Story*, 1975 (details)
RIGHT: Fig. 4. Allan Kaprow, *Words*, 1962. Performance at Smolin Gallery, New York. The Getty Research Institute, 2014.M.7

The map for this entry, with Los Angeles's Sunset and Wilshire Boulevards as coordinates, traces Lacy's movements but lacks a narrative conclusion. At the end of the day she is "chalking the whole eve up to a big 0." She uses black and red ink, exclamation points, underscoring, and circles for annotation and commentary, but it remains unclear how to differentiate the types of writing. July 23 is atmospheric, indebted more to John Cage's acceptance of noise than to some Hollywood idea of narrative progression.

Comparing these handwritten and drawn "notes" to the printed version in her 2010 book *Leaving Art: Writings on Performance, Politics, and Publics, 1974–2007*, two changes stand out: the consistent present tense, lending the text a sense of urgency, and the insertion of questions as interruptions.[10] "Have you ever been to a whore?" While the maps express narrative shifts through letter size and modes of writing, these direct addresses to the reader serve as Brechtian devices of alienation, breaking up whatever linearity there had been before.

Stories resonate and echo, producing a certain vagueness and unease about this diary that eschews direct quotes from the prostitutes and pimps, instead filtering their utterances through the artist's perception. The ten maps are probes into a coded territory and its protagonists: actors, divas, and supporting cast. Scratching the surface to reveal not "roles" but human beings—a supporting cast of a different order—is for Lacy a way of dissecting that mystical place called Hollywood. The dreams pursued in her encounters are neither directly addressed nor ultimately revealed. What emerges is a system of exploitation not unlike the movie industry, centered on exchanges of money, illusion, and power. Violence never surfaces explicitly, but it is systematically embodied in every transaction.

As mentioned, *Prostitution Notes* is a compilation of notes, not a finished text. Within Lacy's work it opened a new chapter of research and a practice of subjective anthropology, helping her break the frame of making drawings for galleries and museums. She would again take her concerns to the street in works such as *Three Weeks in May*.

Prostitution Notes also has a postscript from 1996 that reminds me of the final credits of a movie based on real events, in which one learns what eventually happened to the people depicted. Margo, Lois, Brian, and Paul reappeared at various moments in the artist's career, and their stories continued—some became activists, while others took a break from "the life" only to return to it later. In book format, the work becomes a document, a set of testimonies, a factual account beyond Lacy's interior reminiscences and recollections.

This storyboard of traces, memories, and ephemera collected from fleeting encounters assumed a final form when the artist respoke the narrative, alongside a slide show of drawings and additional documentation that never made it into the original ten maps, for the 2010 "Map Marathon" at Serpentine Galleries in London. The call and response of two voices, the artist's and that of another performer on a balcony, and the hand of a third performer who retraced the maps (projected onto a blackboard) all contributed to the process of echoing and resonance. The performance was carried along by an urgency—the voices seemed to have no time to dwell on details or nuances. The narrative, it seems, keeps slipping away, eluding the artist's control.

No one story can be gleaned from these notes, but they offer a glimpse of complexities, failures, monetary transactions, and illusions in the City of Angels. They (re)connect stories of pimps, prostitutes, and the artist's processes at work in mythic Hollywood, jazzed up with a dose of cinema verité not unlike a John Cassavetes film—a hard and focused look, but with rhythm and some wrong notes. Street corners and cafés are sites of brief interludes, missed connections, mistaken identities. Our view into the life beneath the veneer uses the urgency of a voice—a resonant body, if you will—to pierce through stereotypes. *Prostitution Notes* was a score for Lacy's work to come: listening to people, being mindful of her own condition, and hanging in there through the twists and turns of a given social dynamic.

"What do you exchange for sex?"
—Suzanne Lacy, *Prostitution Notes*

ACT III: CONVERSATION PIECES—SPEAKING AS THEATER

The voice—the artist's or other women's and men's—carries through the processes of production, exhibition, and reflection. It is one of the defining features of Lacy's work that the sound of women talking is heard without falling into the trap of narrative closure. In fact, Lacy's stagings and choreographies create a particular relationship between speaker and listener, as first tested in *Freeze Frame: Room for Living Room* (1982, pp. 140–46). On the surface, it was a project about coalition and survival. But as the artist puts it, "The real undercurrent of the evening was the experience of compassion evoked when people come into communion with each other—particularly when they are an oppressed group whose experience is in the public shadows."[11] Later she clarified that an appropriate language for this communion must come out of everyday rituals, an expanded field of ethnography and field notes where speaking, writing, and commenting are theorized as a process of being in the "active voice."[12]

But *Freeze Frame* achieved more than a communal experience. Keen on sculpting an image, a "tableau performance," as she called it, Lacy organized the work in the context of a conference on sculpture in San Francisco. She set up parallel stages featuring different groups representing diverse communities and using the aesthetics of a luxury furniture store—a place where consumers stroll, following their whims and desires. The theatricality of the spoken word around a table or in a tableau as an unscripted performance, operating with the illusion of a "fourth wall" by apparently ignoring the surrounding audience, was embedded in a multisensory experience. Words were not only spoken but tested, whispered, shouted, and otherwise embodied in a continuum that also allowed the audience its own space for quiet reflection. The closing was staged as a formal juxtaposition of audience versus performers (fig. 5). Yet the confrontation looked more like people versus people, a theatrical *shattering* of the fourth wall in keeping with Bertolt Brecht's revolutionary theater method of direct address. The moment equally alluded to the tradition of a family reunion expressed in the ritual of a group picture, but it also expanded the notion of communion into the political realm of calls to action.

But why give the performance the title *Freeze Frame*—a term borrowed from video technology to mean literally stalling on a captured moment in time? To freeze means to suspend the relentless course of events and allow for a medium-specific Brechtian break from the usual illusion of time-based media in which the spectator identifies with the camera's perspective.[13] Individual faces and groupings were assembled as a sequence of "frames" that were then overcome in the final juxtaposition, where participants stood up to deliver personal reflections, as if the play had already ended. In this moment of Brechtian alienation, the public was directly addressed and literally situated within the larger social "frame" by being included in an affective experience of making the personal political.

Dismantling the usual distinction between speakers and listeners, individual voices carried the urgency that each one of them had experienced. The words freely spoken in this safe space advocated for action and change beyond the comfort of communal expression. From this point on, the new language Lacy was looking for was one of public and political address, yet without betraying the intimacy of a whisper.[14]

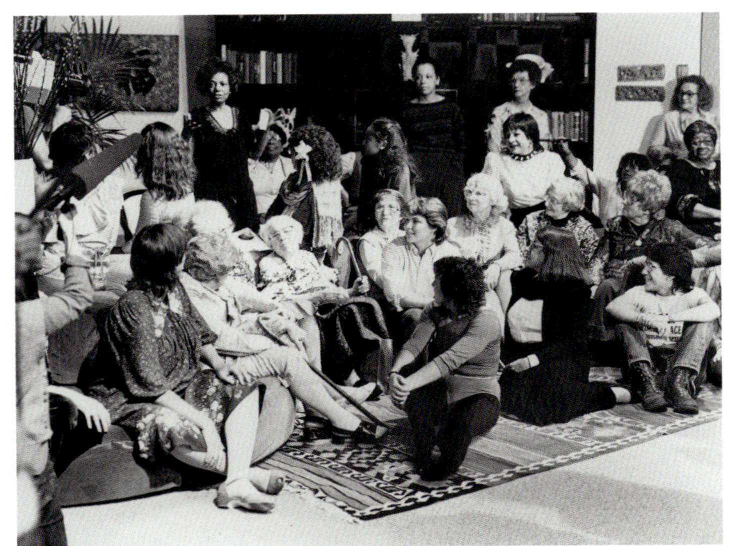

Fig. 5. Suzanne Lacy and Julia London with Jan Chattler, Joya Cory, Natalia Rivas, Ngoh Spencer, and Carol Szego, *Freeze Frame: Room for Living Room*, 1982

ACT IV: FRAMING VS. REHEARSING—*DE TU PUÑO Y LETRA*

Drawing on her deep roots in the traditions of both theater and the visual arts, Lacy's most recent approach transforms the framing of a conversation or participation into a more complex "rehearsal." Notably, *De tu puño y letra* has undergone significant transformations since it premiered in 2015, with Lacy not only rethinking but literally reproducing its components. In this regard, it is a key work for my larger arguments here, involving as it does the public reading of very intimate letters and the representation of these readings in strikingly different formats.

De tu puño y letra first took the form of a large-scale performance in a historic bullring in Quito, Ecuador; it was the outcome of a yearlong period in which Lacy discussed the theme of domestic violence with men, women, and local social agencies. The theatrical event in four acts was based on letters written by real women about domestic abuse they had suffered.[15] Lacy sourced men of all ages to each "adopt" a letter and publicly read it as a performed act of solidarity. While the anonymous letters weren't addressed to these men personally, they implicated each one as part of the male population at large in its tolerance of hierarchical and abusive relationships.

The seeming dissonance between the highly personal letters and the massive public performance was a key element. The brief stories, rooted in the familiarity of the everyday, touched on rape, abuse of children, and antagonism, but here they were embedded in a collective enactment, a chorus intoned by a community of mostly men and some women, embodying a dialogue between genders and voices. There were moments of noise and silence, music and mass spectacle, individual voices and face-to-face encounters.

Three years later, concerned about the effect on museum audiences, Lacy decided to re-produce the reading as a video installation translating the bullring into a circle of five vertical projections approximating human scale, each representing a male performer dressed in a white shirt and dark trousers. The time is evening, the lights are out, and a spotlight shifts toward each in turn. One by one, they approach the camera to read their letters in Spanish or English. In an appropriate reversal, the museum audience is now gathered in the center, surrounded by the performers. This new format closely resonates with the final act of the original performance, where the reading contracted to small groups of people, transitioning from mass spectacle to intimate dialogue—not unlike *Freeze Frame*, where the audience could also choose between various "stages" while listening to the voices.

I call this act of translation "appropriate" because it makes the letters of women the core of the work. One voice in particular arrested me in its poetic translation of a violent act into the image of a white paper crumpled, flattened, reused, but never the same as before. To stay with this analogy for a moment, the white paper may have contained some writing or traces of another kind, like marks of history, but the act remains a violent gesture of refusal and disposal. It is a striking image of a life lived after dehumanizing violence.

Lacy often wonders about ways to narrativize what otherwise is left to languages coded by the police, the law, and the media.[16] The Brazilian dramatist Augusto Boal would call this "dressing the word."[17] The Ecuadorian women, protected by their anonymity, leave the listener longing for more information—and yet it is precisely the lack of resolution that makes their stories powerful beyond their historical and geographical context. The more they evoke specific absent faces and bodies, the more they operate poetically, affectively, transculturally.

Lacy's artistic use of literary, cinematic, and theatrical tools complements the political messaging strategies also associated with every project. She finds responsive forms for complex stories and evolves them over time, embracing periods of reflection and distancing. In *De tu puño y letra* her process of rethinking led to a clarification of form involving a different letter read by a new person, in sequence. Listening to the totality of the letters over half an hour effectively blends them into one another, piling statement on statement on statement on memory on injustice, the lamenting ritual always foregrounding the gesture of speaking to the camera.

In art, an additive process that gradually erases the particulars of a narrative—a single, forceful gesture applied with a durational approach that fundamentally changes the tenor of what is conveyed—recalls Glenn Ligon's continuous rewriting on the same piece of paper in *White #13* (1994, fig. 6) or Hiroshi Sugimoto's photographic series *Theaters*, in which the artist leaves the camera shutter open in a darkened movie theater, so that the screen blanches to a blank rectangle on the exposed film. Between these two artistic poles that counter the siren song of narrative, Lacy makes room for the individual and

Fig. 6. Glenn Ligon, *White #13*, 1994. Paintstick on linen, 84 1/2 x 60 1/4 in. (214.6 x 153 cm). San Francisco Museum of Modern Art, gift of Vicki and Kent Logan

embodied voice, the noise and murmur of community conversations, as much as for the single sentence uttered or performed affectively onstage. She carefully balances the spectacle of a mass performance with individual detail to locate the connective interpersonal tissue. And when gendered stories of abuse intersect with stories of refugees exploited by systemic violence, all of a sudden, here we are in the present tense.

In one of Lacy's earliest collaborative works, *Ablutions* (1972, pp. 44–45), the voice of a woman who was held captive in a car driving across the Golden Gate Bridge struggles to narrate the moment she realized the danger she was in. She focused on one thought: as long as she could keep a conversation going, she wouldn't die.[18] As long as there is language and a story to tell, death is averted—which is precisely the upshot of one of the oldest stories about storytelling, *One Thousand and One Nights*, a mythic work of collective authorship. But in Lacy's texts, stories don't become myths; they get taken apart and reassembled differently, for it is important to "not get stuck in the myth."[19] Again and again throughout her career, she has staged polyphonies of voices and demonstrated the impossibility of a final closing: her hand connects dots, establishes lines of relations, and implicates her own body and biography in the process of taking notes while letting the voice, her own and that of others, embody the text, which in the process continues to be an active agent.

Looking at Lacy's scribbles on a manila folder she used while planning the 1995–96 work *No Blood/No Foul* (fig. 7), I realize that she was filing notes under the category of "Active." With that in mind, I find myself thinking of the exhibition as a re-performance—but an open-ended one—of notes in time and space. Whether knowledge will manifest as an epiphany or via a close listening and reading, the experience of voices in the exhibition will depend on our active use of our senses and our deployment of language toward a communal experience.

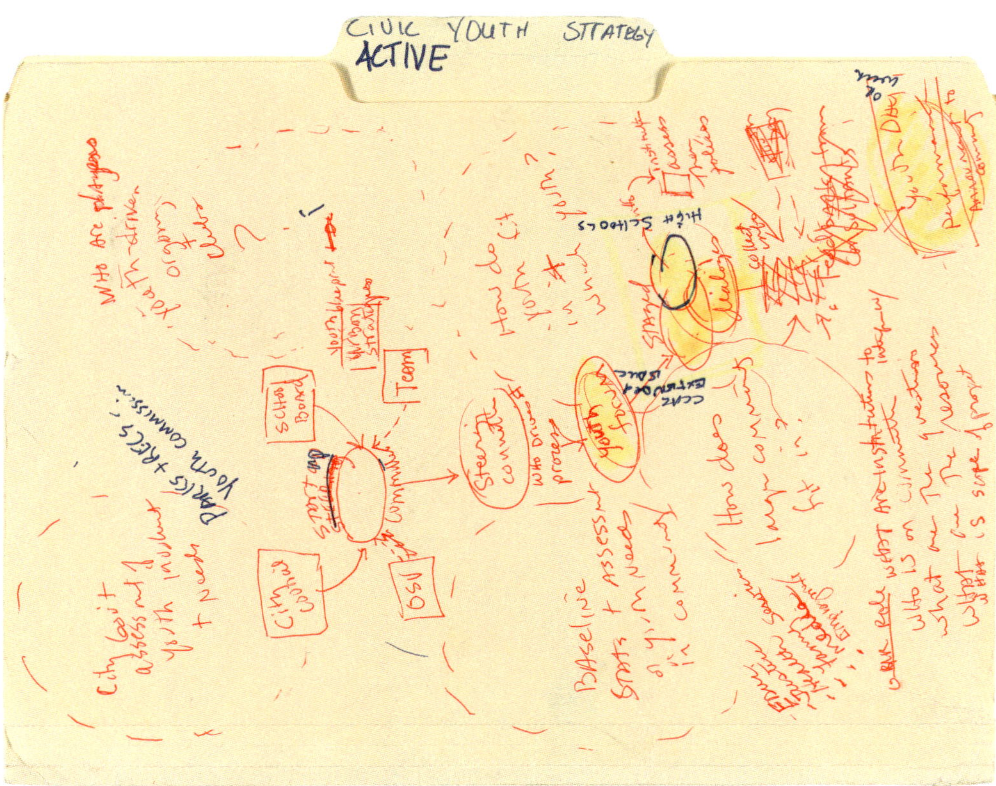

Fig. 7. Undated preparatory notes for Suzanne Lacy, Annice Jacoby, and Chris Johnson, *No Blood/No Foul* (1995–96)

LACY: I tend to see my work as [having] two components. One is the way it deals with an issue and interfaces in a strategic way with society (or doesn't, when I do really personal things). I found that the fewer images my work has in it, the stronger I rely on the geometric shape that underlies the piece, and I think it would be different for different pieces. *Three Weeks in May* feels like a grid; [inaudible] feels like parallel lines, historical lines, and a current line of interaction. *Tree: [A Performance for] Women of Ithaca* felt like a rectangle. . . .

ROTH: Allan, what's your formal deal with your art? What forms do you use?

KAPROW: It's very hard to find a root metaphor, or even a geometric metaphor, that would make sense the way Suzanne spoke of a square or rectangle or some kind of figure like that, but a prevailing one occurs to me at this moment, and that is the mirror. The mirror implies a kind of symmetry, but of course everybody knows that a mirror is backward.[2]

■

LACY: I want to say something about shape. Stepping back, rather than looking at individual pieces, I would say that a grid or a network—not even a grid, but a sort of net—would be the thing that would best describe most of my work. I don't know whether this is a content issue or a formal issue, but I've been trying with that notion of a network to make clear in some form what exists in the space between people and the relationships between people. It's almost literally a physical object. Like, what is the line you could draw from one person to another on which you could hang the interaction of the words of their exchanges. . . .

KAPROW: A net stretched taut or loose?

LACY: I would say stretched.

KAPROW: So that's a little bit closer to a grid.

LACY: Except not necessarily square, but yes. Do grids have to be square?

KAPROW: Yes.[3]

■

LACY: A good piece will have . . . a very strong image, although there are several that don't have a strong individual image that I'm still very satisfied with. As the image becomes less important, then what becomes more important is the sense of internal coherence, and that probably is some internal sense of form I'm following. I don't know if I can say what constitutes that form except for me it has a great deal to do with geometry and with motion. When I have a real sense of motion in a piece, that doesn't mean I'm moving it. You know when I saw Yvonne Rainer, at Pasadena . . . I was riveted by it because somehow she had tapped into an internal formal language, which had an awful lot to do with her content. I could see in the way she was moving and the way objects were moving that her internal sense of form was playing itself out. When I tap into that, for me, it's a rolling movement, and it has a clear sense of an internal thing that holds it together. It can be geometric form; it can also be a kind of thought process that to me is very complex. I like it when they sort of revolve in spirals. I don't like them to be closed. . . . I like line drawings. I love open-ended space. But for that complexity not to be confusing it has to rest on something. I can say, yes, there's a grid, and on top of that is interaction. And part of that is observing the subtleties, complexities, and oddities of relationships between people.[4]

Listen to how certain formal terms are used. First, "image" is differentiated from "shape." The two are said to be somehow complementary, each compensating for the withdrawal of the other. Shape is underlying; image seems auxiliary. Shape is a term for internal coherence, where "internal" means not so much internal to the artist (a sensibility, a volition) but rather internal to the work. The work has an internal geometry, and that geometry is in movement, in a manner akin to dance.

The Rainer performance to which Lacy refers is *This Is the Story of a Woman Who* . . . (1973), an autobiographical piece about a deteriorating sexual relationship between a man and a woman who is a dancer.[5] As the emotion drains, the devolving connection is rendered in objectified, abstracted ways—including as stylized physical violence. Doubtless the content mattered for Lacy, but what she notes is how abstract shape can move, unroll, out of an internal language. Language, like geometry, is relational. Let us not think of "geometry" too mathematically but just as a language of points, lines, and surfaces, and of abstract relations. We hear that an individual work has its shape but that there is also a shape, a geometry, characteristic of her work more generally. This general geometry is described in two ways: as the grid (or the net) and as the spiral.

Listening to the language, let us imagine how these forms might move. The grid is an open-ended, extensive plane, spreading in two dimensions through the addition of nodes and lines. The spiral is open-ended, too, but turning around a center. We may see it both expanding and at the same time returning to its source. The spiral moves simultaneously in different directions. It is extensive and intensive. The grid and the spiral are two ways of seeing relationships that are in motion and growing, yet maintaining a certain structure.

Contrast those forms with the mirror, as described by Kaprow. He no doubt has in mind the mirror as metaphor (art as a mirror of life), but in his remarks the mirror is also a geometry. It has symmetry, like the recto and verso leaves of a book. We can see what he means when he cites a recent piece, *Company* (1981–82), an instructional performance that, so to speak, turns full circle.[6] Like the mirror, the circle begins and ends at the same point. They are closed forms. The open forms of the circle and the mirror, respectively, are the spiral and the grid.

We are trying to think about all these forms in abstract terms, but sociopolitical meaning is always close by. Kaprow's remarks on the circle, and Lacy's response, show how geometry and politics might connect:

> KAPROW: One of the forms I adopted from feminist consciousness raising was the form of a group of people sitting around in a circle and sharing their personal experience, without being interrupted or challenged. Up until that moment, in the earlier happenings and activities, I had never provided a way for people to share their experience once they had finished a piece. . . . It tied in with the kinds of forms I had been using for a long time in my work without understanding the implications—that is, the symmetrical or mirror form, the circular form.

> LACY: I think that's probably the core of what I'd think of as political art. That form of people processing experience information and creating a group reality. That's a form that art can contribute to politics.[7]

> •

> KAPROW: What feminism and especially feminist performance made possible for a lot of men's performance, including mine, is intimacy. That is, the actual experience of intimacy, not necessarily in private, but between individuals and groups, and that shareable aspect of experience which had been pretty much erased from high culture because of alienation, which artists had experienced for over three hundred years as the increasing isolation of the artist and symbolic celebration of the isolated self, which the artist could best communicate. That isolation now seemed to be at an end with the feminist movement.[8]

For Kaprow, the politics of the circle is that the individual (artist) is opened to others, in an intimate group, but also that the group is closed to itself. Kaprow's circle is a protective formation (a circle of wagons) against a wider image culture. The circle is a contribution of art to politics, Lacy says. But that circle needs to be opened, expanded, and set in motion. We are put in mind of the diagram of audiences as concentric circles (fig. 1) that Lacy included in her book *Mapping the Terrain: New Genre Public Art* (1995). This is

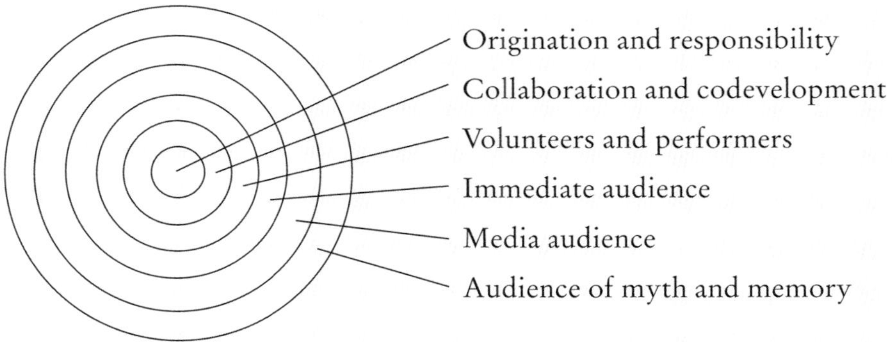

how her work—or "new genre public art"—is said to circulate and become public: "One possible evaluative construct might be to see the audience as a series of concentric circles with permeable membranes that allow continual movement back and forth."[9] She continues: "Fundamental to the above construction of the audience is its flexible and fluid nature. At no point is the level of participation fixed, and depending on the criteria established through the work, participants move back and forth between levels."[10]

We can see that these are not circles after all. What is a set of concentric circles moving back and forth between levels but a spiral? If for Lacy the circle (of feminist consciousness raising) is the core of political art, then the formal movement of political art, for her, may be the spiraling out of and around that core. If the circle is a geometry of shared, intimate, personal space, then the spiral is the space of intimacy opening, expanding, and becoming public.

At the time of the conversations with Kaprow and Roth, Lacy's most notable work on intimacy and otherness was no doubt *Evalina and I: Crimes, Quilts, and Art* (1975–80, pp. 126–29), a series of actions shared over several years with Evalina Newman, an older African American woman. That work, which has a straightforward linear shape (a time line with spurs to related actions), gave way to *Freeze Frame: Room for Living Room* (1982, pp. 140–46), in which the distinctive visual and spatial character of Lacy's social practice (the tableau image) came together, performatively, for the first time. With *Freeze Frame*, a constellation of irregular, broken circles of women of various identities was staged in a San Francisco furniture showroom—a domestic space made public. If the closed circle of consciousness raising is the core of political art, *Freeze Frame* opened that circle to a more expansive, spiraling public intimacy. *Freeze Frame* projected an image. It was made to be seen.

In Lacy's remarks quoted above, we heard that if shape is an internal coherence, image is something else. The stronger the shape, she says, the less the work needs a strong image, and perhaps vice versa. When Kaprow says he finds it hard to see any geometric *shape* in his work, he means, in our terms, geometric *image*. A work such as *Company* has a structural geometry (the mirror, the circle), but we do not see that. There is no image because there is no viewer; all the relevant participants are in the circle. We have only a textual description of a form that is out of sight. As Lacy's work is designed to circulate more broadly, to become public and be seen by others, viewer and image matter more. We can talk about the geometric shapes of Lacy's works and the sociopolitical meanings of those shapes, and we can also talk about her geometric images. It is the difference between the body and the face.

Many of Lacy's geometric images are also variations on the circle and the square. *Whisper, the Waves, the Wind* (1983–84, pp. 152–57) features an approximate oval (a stretch of beach in La Jolla, California) that contains square tables. Miriam Schapiro's

Fig. 1. Suzanne Lacy, diagram of degrees of engagement, with each circle representing a form of interaction between making and witnessing, 1995

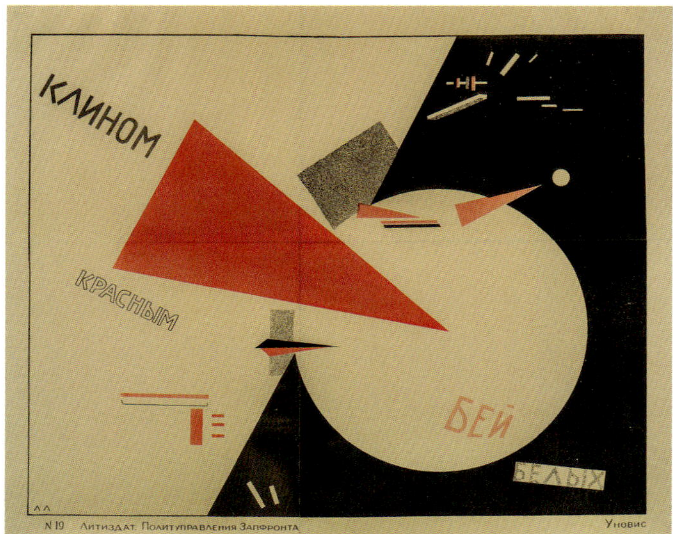

Fig. 2. El Lissitzky, *Klinom krasnym bei belykh* (Beat the Whites with the Red Wedge), 1920. Lithograph, 20 1/16 × 24 7/16 in. (51 × 62 cm). Museum of Fine Arts, Boston, gift of Azita Bina and Elmar W. Seibel in memory of Charlotte Vershbow

quilt template for *The Crystal Quilt* and the staging of the performance take the form of a grid of diamonds. *Meeting in the Water*, the fourth part of *The Road of Poems and Borders* (1989–90, pp. 174–75, a collaboration with Kaprow), is a circle (of red-shirted teenagers) within a circle (an island lagoon). *Between the Door and the Street* (2013, pp. 180–81) is a long rectangle (the width of the street) edged by squares (the stoops) accommodating circles (of women). In *The Circle and the Square* (2015–17, pp. 238–45), these two shapes are juxtaposed within the larger rectangle of the Brierfield Mill in Pendle, England. The meaning of a geometric image is not quite the same as that of shape. It is less structural and more optical and associative. With *The Circle and the Square*, the meanings are quite specific: the forms of the circle and the square refer to the musical traditions of the two local communities assembled. But more general cultural or sociopolitical associations of the two shapes come freely: the circle is associated with equity and fairness, and with nature; the square is associated with public space, the polis, the city. Think of the round kitchen table and the public square.

In terms of image making, Lacy's art is in a tradition of geometric abstraction. She uses a few recurring shapes and primary colors—occasionally blue, but mainly yellow and red—plus white and black. We see affinities with geometric abstractions that picture or diagram social relations—for example, constructivist images such as El Lissitzky's *Klinom krasnym bei belykh* (Beat the Whites with the Red Wedge, 1920, fig. 2)—and geometric abstractions that are produced through the actions of others—such as the mural art of Sol LeWitt.[11] The big difference, of course, is that Lacy's abstractions are composed of people, not paint, which means they are, by design, open to contingency. John Baldessari's *Throwing four balls in the air to get a square (best of 36 tries)* (1974) is open to the contingency of physics, as is Lacy's takeoff of Baldessari, *Anatomy Lesson #3: Falling Apart* (1976, p. 63), in which irregular, imperfect flesh substitutes for the perfect geometries of the balls. In both cases, the artists' human attempts to realize a pure geometry necessarily, humanly, fail.

In her social practice works, however, Lacy is collaborating not with physics but with disparate, willful human beings. Her geometries contain an ungovernable element, an element of disobedience. She is the author of the aesthetic, but it admits the lived experiences and interpretations of others. She may direct participants to form a circle or a straight line, but if they do not quite do this, so be it. (LeWitt imposed a stricter control over those who executed his geometries, and that was the point.) In her recent work *Across and In-Between* (2018), children in kayaks, negotiating with one another, attempt to make a straight line in a river in Ireland (fig. 3). It is the difference between a negotiated line and a geometric line that energizes Lacy's aesthetics. Hers is a geometric abstraction that vibrates with the contingency of the social.

Images are always to be seen from a certain viewpoint. The angle of view adds another vector to the geometry of the work. If Kaprow's geometry denies a viewpoint outside (the circle has no outside) and so denies us any image, Lacy's work offers, at different times, three viewpoints, each at a different angle to the image. Each angle has sociopolitical meaning. There is the face-to-face view at 0 degrees to the image. Most common and distinctive is the view from above at an oblique angle (typically 30 to 45 degrees). And most rare, there is the 90-degree view from directly overhead. We are talking about the angles from which actions are viewed in the representations of the work selected by the artist (that is, in photographs and video footage). As such, they are integral to the work.

For example, certain photographs of the women seated at tables in *Whisper, the Waves, the Wind* and *The Crystal Quilt* are 0-degree views: the viewer is positioned as if

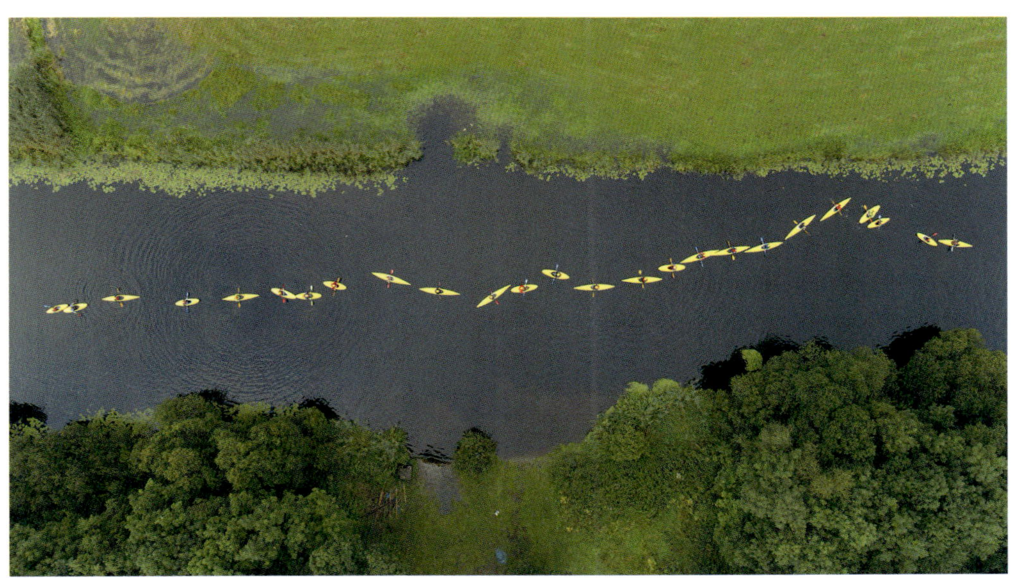

Fig. 3. Suzanne Lacy with Cian Smyth, Garrett Carr, Eva Grosman, Helen Sharp, Helen Sloan, Pedro Rebelo, and Mark Thomas, *Across and In-Between*, 2018 (still)

seated there, too, and as if able, imminently, to join their conversations.[12] The 0-degree view includes us, or implicates us, in the standing video portraits that comprise part of the installation forms of *De tu puño y letra* (By Your Own Hand, 2014–15/2019, pp. 118–23) and *The Circle and the Square*. If there is an aesthetic tradition in play here, it may be the "face of our time" tradition of ethnographic photography that runs from August Sander to Zanele Muholi.

The view from an oblique angle is the most common. We see this in other representations of *The Crystal Quilt* and *Whisper, the Waves, the Wind*—representations that approximate the viewpoint of the audiences for the performances. The audience, in each case, is offered a 30-degree angle down onto the participants from the second floor of the IDS Center Crystal Court shopping mall in Minneapolis and from the sea cliffs at La Jolla. This is the angle of view not only when the audience is at an upper level but also when, during the performance, they descend to the level of the women. Since they are standing, they still look down at an oblique angle on the seated participants.[13] The oblique angle both includes and excludes us as viewers. We are present for the story, but it is not ours. We acknowledge our elevated status, but we are to listen. At this angle, and at this distance, the geometric image comes into view. But it is as if Lacy has taken the vertical images of Lissitzky or LeWitt, asked us to step back, and then flipped them onto a horizontal plane and invited us to view them from above and to the side.

The oblique view also has geographic connotations. If the grid is composed of squares and has associations with city blocks, we may be reminded of a city familiar to us. This most distinctive geometry of Lacy's art—this net rolling across open space, layered with human interactions and viewed at an angle from above, an angle that is both/neither observation and/nor participation—resembles nothing so much as the city of Los Angeles as seen from the Hollywood Hills. Our everyday environments are themselves composed of relationships, movements, and vectors that are both spatial and ethical. Lacy's art has affinities with street space and other vernacular forms.

Then there is the 90-degree view from above. This is the viewpoint of objectivity and of the didactic. The yellow *Three Weeks in May* map, viewed at 90 degrees, as maps tend to be, is stamped with the facts that matter for its sociopolitical meaning: rape is not a matter of perspective. Representations at 90 degrees typically take the form not of photography or video (scenes in *Across and In-Between* are exceptions) but rather of maps and diagrams. The diagram is where the movement of geometry may be most vivid in Lacy's art. Her diagrams are often formative. They fall approximately into two types, which we might

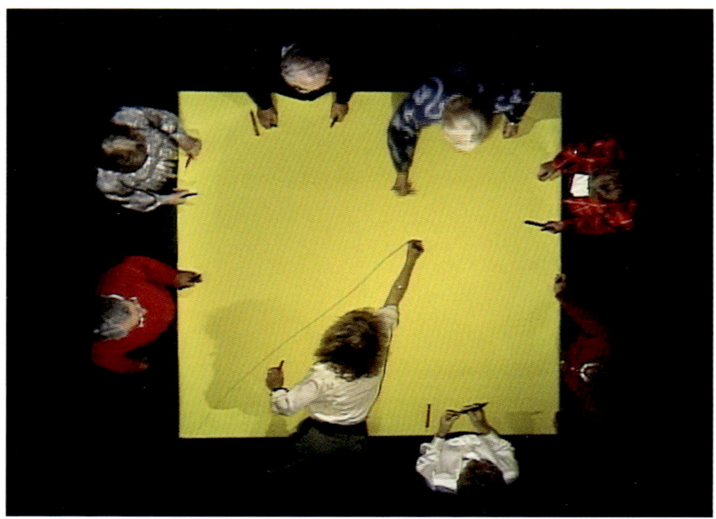

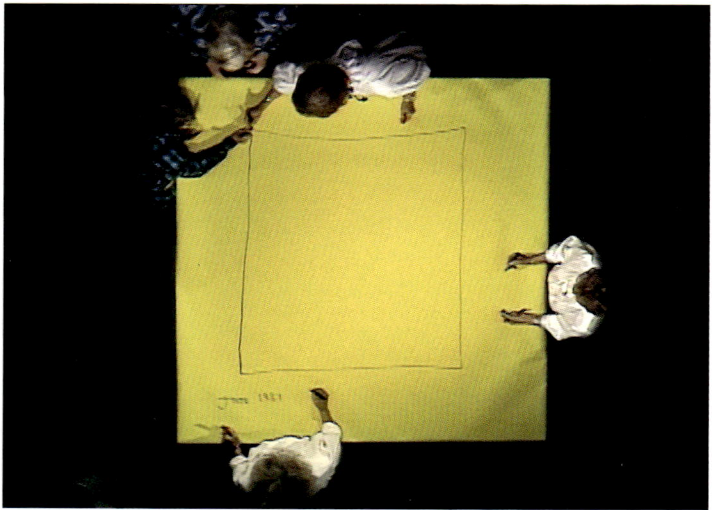

call process diagrams and production diagrams (the latter for the production of a performance). Examples of each type, in this case related to *The Dark Madonna* (1985–86, pp. 158–65), appear on pages 160–61. The vernacular of the process diagram is that of organizational project management. Unlike with institutional diagrams, the nodes are not limited to individuals (they can be groups, organizations, or agents of other kinds), and the lines tend to represent actions rather than static hierarchies. The process diagrams are not linear, but they do tend to express a chronology from one side of the page to the other. The production diagrams describe not a chronology, but a space within which time unfolds—in the case of *The Dark Madonna*, the space of the Franklin D. Murphy Sculpture Garden at the University of California, Los Angeles. The nodes are locations within the planned production; the lines are the movements of performers. Most of Lacy's diagrams are meant to be explanatory (diagrams are pedagogical), not for us but for herself or her collaborators in the creation of a project. Once the work is made, it takes the place of any preparatory diagrams.

There are instances, though, where diagrams became works in themselves.[14] Groups of collaborators on *The Crystal Quilt* came together to recollect, five years later, aspects of how that project was created and made two drawings and videos. One group comprised producers, the other production coordinators. In the resulting video works, as nowhere else in Lacy's practice, we see geometry and movement unfolding. Our viewpoint is the 90-degree angle from above, meaning we are purely observers and not in any way participants. The collaborators' viewpoint on the arena is oblique (they stand over a table); this is their story, but it is past. Their view of one another is at 0 degrees. The first drawing, made by the producers, is a process diagram: partner relations, funding, the evolution of the concept. With the first gesture, Lacy draws a diagonal time line between the bottom left and top right corners of the square (fig. 4). Partly, this determines that this will be a process diagram. Partly, it gives the participants permission to use the whole space and, in so doing, establishes the artist as the first among equals. The task of creating a time line quickly gives way to other things: the proximity of ideas and people, relationship lines, expressions of movement or energy, maps, pictures of elements of the project.

The second drawing is a production diagram: the logistics and implementation of the performance at the IDS Center (fig. 5). With her opening gesture, Lacy draws a square within the square—it is the quilt, it is the Crystal Court. This establishes the drawing as a spatial diagram that will be overlaid by events. The production coordinators describe the preparations for the performance as outside the square, at the margins. As it happens, the time of production is expressed spatially as being from the outside in—from staging areas into the arena. The process drawing recollects the geometry of the structural shape of *The Crystal Quilt*. The production drawing recollects its geometric image. They are the most complete and discerning expressions—in shape, image, and dialogue—of the movement of geometry in Lacy's art.

When we pay attention to Lacy's geometries and to those rare occasions when she has remarked on forms, a language of form becomes available. This is not the only way to elaborate such a language.[15] Yet thinking through geometry reveals something essential about her work: that one of its central functions is to enable us to *see relationships*, and that those relationships can be as much sociopolitical as they are aesthetic. The sociopolitical aspect of Lacy's art need not be a matter only of bringing voice and visibility to less heard and seen constituencies, nor of raising awareness of certain social issues or contributing to policy change. It can be a matter of bringing sociopolitical relations into view. This art enables us to discern the various modalities of those relations—their dimensions, scale, angles, perspectives, vectors, convergence, and divergence—and also their contingencies, negotiated imperfections, and irregularities. These are the traits of the social geometry we inhabit every day. Lacy's work does not just apply itself to social matters; the social is the medium of this art.

NOTES

1. A transcript of three conversations Suzanne Lacy and Allan Kaprow recorded in this period may be found in the Suzanne Lacy papers. The first two were conducted with Moira Roth. The third and longest conversation was conducted on four different occasions during the spring and summer of 1981. The following citations indicate the pages on which the quoted passages appear in the transcript. All excerpts have been lightly edited for readability.

2. Suzanne Lacy, Allan Kaprow, and Moira Roth in conversation, unpublished transcript in the Suzanne Lacy papers, 4–5.

3. Ibid., 7–8.

4. Ibid., 10–11.

5. Yvonne Rainer with John Erdman and Shirley Soffer, *This Is the Story of a Woman Who . . .* (1973), Pasadena Museum of Art (now the Norton Simon Museum) and California Institute of the Arts, Valencia. I am indebted to Ana Janevski and Yvonne Rainer for this reference.

6. *Company* takes the form of the following text: "A person locates a bare room and sits in it for a long time. Then she or he brings into the room a cement block and sits with it for a long time. A second block is brought in, a third, a fourth, a fifth and so on, up to the number corresponding to the person's age. At each addition, the person sits with the blocks for a long time. Then, one by one the blocks are removed. The person sits, as before, at each stage, for a long time, until the room is empty. Then, she or he sits in the empty room. Allan Kaprow 1981–82."

7. Lacy, Kaprow, and Roth in conversation, 4–6.

8. Ibid., 8.

9. Suzanne Lacy, "Debated Territory: Toward a Critical Language for Public Art," in *Mapping the Terrain: New Genre Public Art*, ed. Lacy (Seattle: Bay Press, 1995), 178.

10. Ibid., 180.

11. Much more could be said about the influence of the Russian avant-garde on Lacy, in relation not only to geometric abstraction but also to performance spectacles such as Nikolai Evreinov, *The Storming of the Winter Palace* (1920).

12. A viewpoint can be suggested without an image. We know from their tweets (see p. 179) that the social media staff in *Silver Action* (2013, pp. 178–79) had this 0-degree viewpoint. It placed them both inside and outside the conversation.

13. This oblique view from above is there too in, for instance, the performance of *De tu puño y letra* and many of the camera angles in *The Circle and the Square*. We can note the oblique view from below in, for example, the view of the stoop from the sidewalk in *Between the Door and the Street*.

14. Besides the drawings described here, *Cancer Notes: Seven-Day Genesis* (1991) is another example of a work that takes the form of diagramming.

15. If we were to consider how the aesthetics of early twentieth-century American pageants have informed Lacy's socially engaged tableaux since the early 1980s, then a different yet complementary language of form would follow.

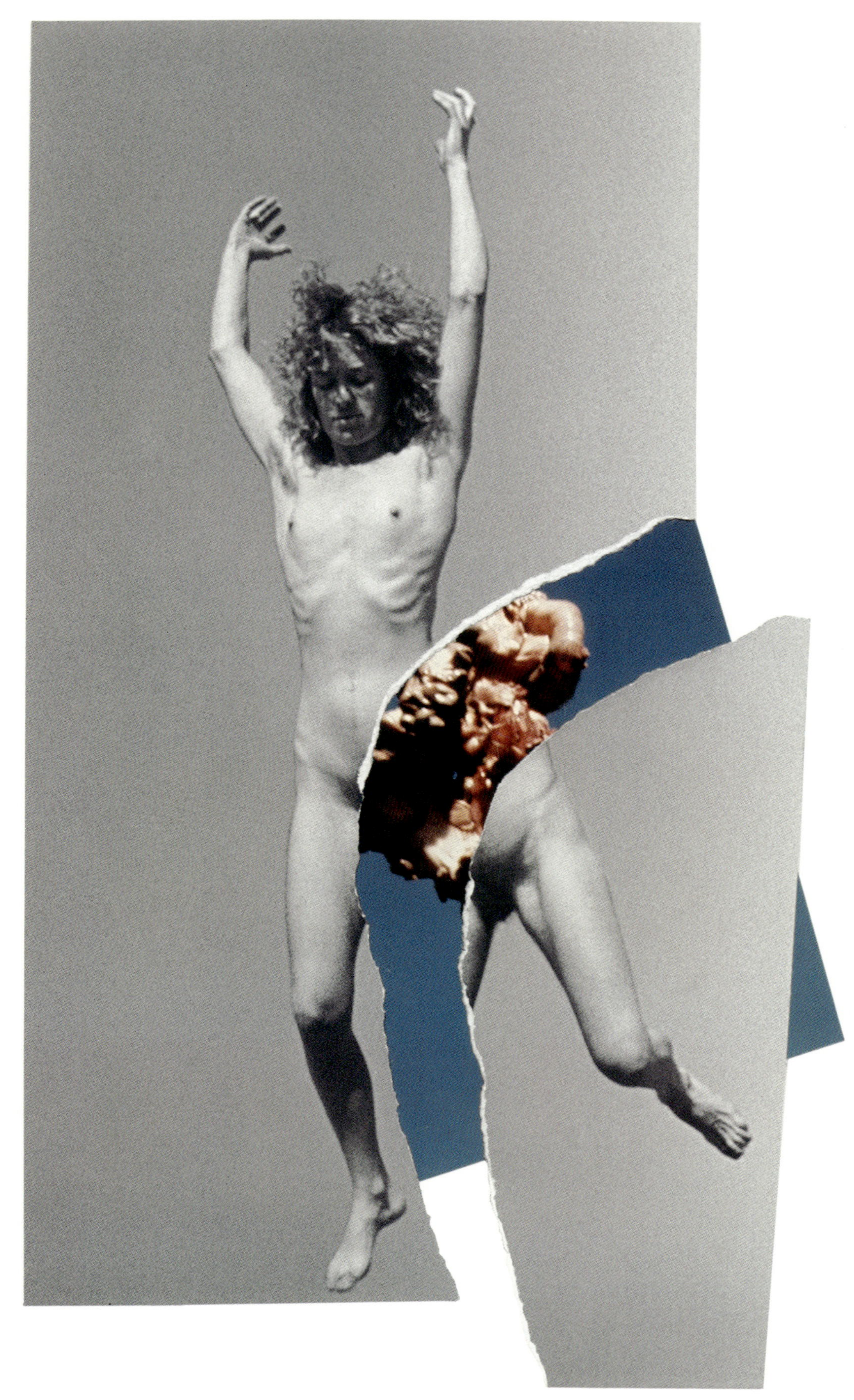

BODIES

As a student inspired by the feminist movement, Lacy shifted the trajectory of her graduate studies in psychology to join the inaugural cohort of Judy Chicago's Feminist Art Program at Fresno State College (now California State University, Fresno) and followed its relocation to California Institute of the Arts, Valencia. In these classes and in feminist consciousness-raising groups, participants questioned many aspects of their identities and relationships. Challenging the divide between the personal and the political, feminism created a space for engagement with how the lived experiences of women could provide meaningful content for their art.

Presenting a female perspective to counter mediated images of women became a major thrust of the 1970s. In this era activists drew attention to the issue of rape and reframed the definition of sexual assault as an act of power. Lacy's first artist's book, *Rape Is* (1972, p. 46), reflects these concerns by outlining a progression of forms of violence in women's lives. One of the first artworks on the subject of rape from the perspective of women, the group performance *Ablutions* (1972, pp. 44–45) was premised on the belief "that by revealing the extent of the crime and personalizing the reality of the victims one could raise public awareness and mobilize action."[1] These pieces would anticipate Lacy's collaborative efforts in the second half of the decade, which theorized connections between violence against women and its representation in the media.

Performance offers artists a way to deal with the physicality and intimacies of their own bodies. Lacy's interest in revealing women's hidden stories of violence corresponded with her broader explorations of what lies beneath the surface. Her early live pieces and performances for the camera confronted the interiority of the body and the psyche. She developed her signature aesthetics of drawing into comparison human and animal anatomy, informed by her prior zoology studies and medical training: Having gained access to slaughterhouses through her zoology degree, Lacy quickly began incorporating animal organs and lamb carcasses as sculptural elements, stand-ins for the human body, and charged symbols. She moved from temporary sculptural installations of strings and organs to live performances, foregrounding the process of assembling or disassembling parts. Sewn together, ripped apart, peeled off, bound up—recurrent physical actions in her performance imagery such as these were fundamental to her thinking around what it meant to be a body with a consciousness. *Three Love Stories* (1975–76, p. 54) parodies how certain romantic clichés use the language of affect in relation to vital organs—*she gave her heart away.*

In this vein Lacy also developed feminist reworkings of the tales of Frankenstein and Dracula, which have long occupied the popular imagination. She drew from the gothic literature genre and its monster metaphors to consider "the process of birth, the fear and awe associated with physical existence, and a visualization of and identification with the monstrous."[2] The moral story of Frankenstein resonated with her research into contemporary news accounts about medical advancements in altering the body, from organ transplants to plastic surgery.

—TANYA ZIMBARDO

NOTES
1. Suzanne Lacy, "Time, Bones, and Art: Anatomy of a Decade," an essay written prior to its first presentation at a symposium in 1995 and reprinted in *Leaving Art: Writings on Performance, Politics, and Publics, 1974–2007* (Durham, NC: Duke University Press, 2010), 97.
2. Suzanne Lacy, unpublished artist statement, 1974. Suzanne Lacy papers.

OPPOSITE: Collage from *Anatomy Lesson #3: Falling Apart* (1976, p. 63)

Ablutions (1972)

SUZANNE LACY, JUDY CHICAGO, SANDRA ORGEL, AND AVIVA RAHMANI

Ablutions made a provocative statement about rape to the art community. In the studio of Guy Dill, in Venice, California, one woman was slowly bound with bandages while two others bathed in each of three galvanized metal tubs filled with eggs, blood, and clay. As each woman emerged from the final tub, she was wrapped in a sheet. Throughout the ritualistic performance Lacy nailed beef kidneys to the wall and created a web of rope. Lacy and Chicago had recorded graphic testimonies of rape by seven women for the soundtrack, which played continuously. The tape repeated at the end: "I felt so helpless, all I could do was just lie there."

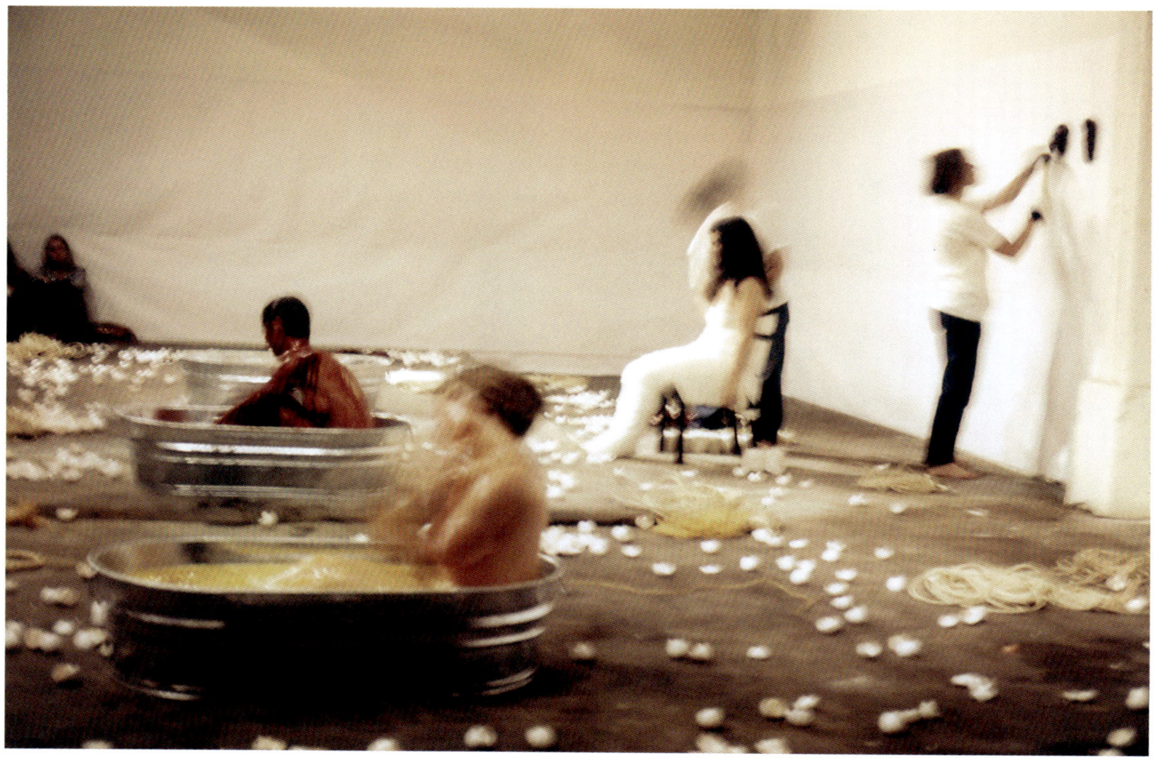

When I encountered the women's liberation movement I had already confronted plenty of sexism, harassment, abuse, and hostility and had produced and exhibited work on those topics. At California Institute of the Arts I approached Judy, Suzanne, and Sandy with exactly that idea of coeval collaboration in mind that had evolved in my earlier work: how might we externalize our experiences as equals to express a new analysis?

—Aviva Rahmani, 2018

Audience watches as Shawnee Wollenman (background) and Jan Oxenberg (foreground) bathe in metal tubs, Jan Lester Martin wraps Orgel (seated) in bandages, and Lacy nails kidneys to the wall
OPPOSITE: Wollenman and Oxenberg

From the beginning of my 1970–71 Feminist Art Program . . . I discovered that performance was an effective tool in helping my young female students transform their (often traumatic) sexual experiences into visual form. . . . *Ablutions* was probably the first public work of art about rape, and it was met with total silence.

—Judy Chicago, 2018

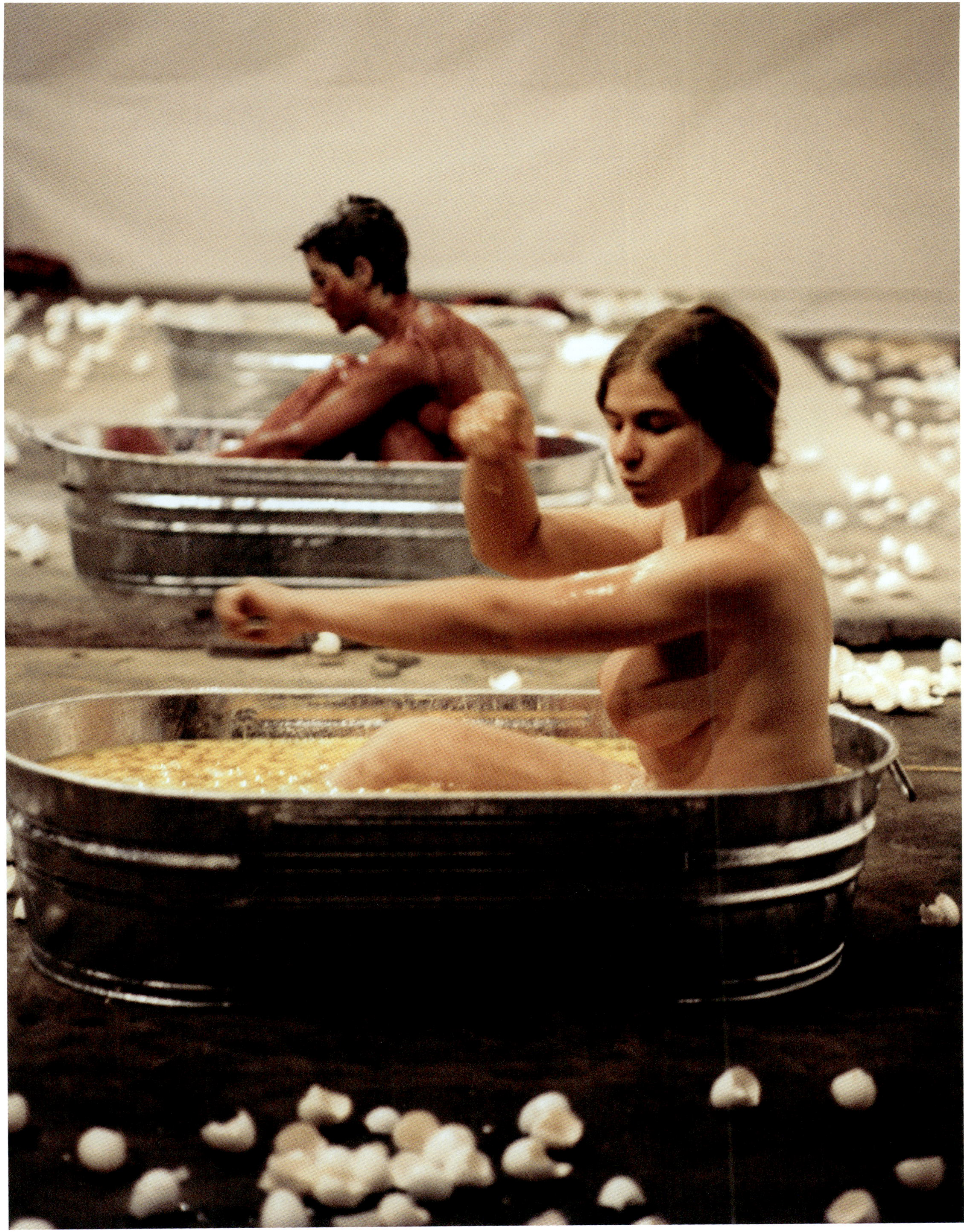

Rape Is (1972)

Lacy tackled the subject of rape and the cultural attitudes that promote it in her first artist's book, produced in the Women's Design Program at California Institute of the Arts, Valencia. The title riffs on the *Happiness Is* book genre. Her mentor Sheila Levrant de Bretteville suggested that it open down the middle, the flaps joined with a sticker seal, to make the reader consciously aware of invading a private experience. Another of her teachers, the writer Deena Metzger, supported the development of the text.

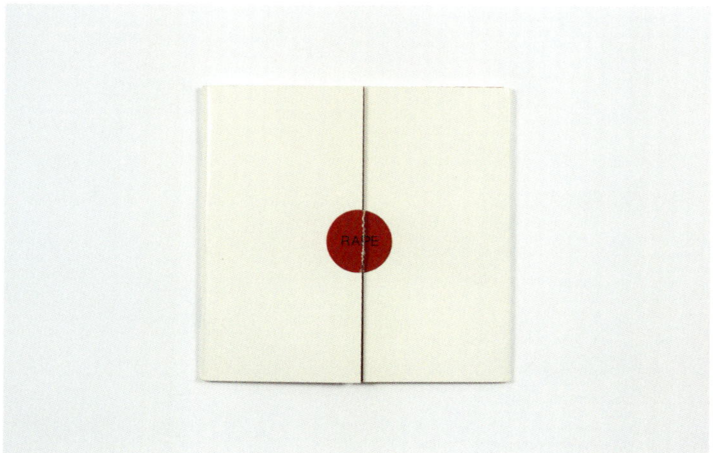

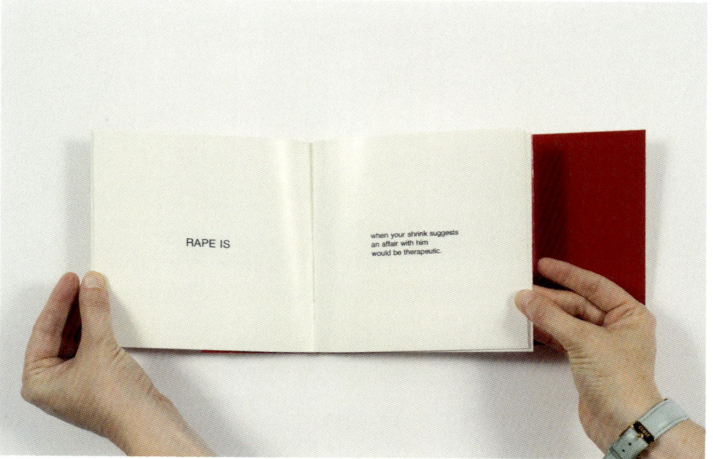

SUSAN GRIFFIN, "RAPE: THE ALL-AMERICAN CRIME," *RAMPARTS*, 1971 (EXCERPT)

Rape is an act of aggression in which the victim is denied her self-determination. It is an act of violence which, if not actually followed by beatings or murder, nevertheless always carries with it the threat of death. And finally, rape is a form of mass terrorism, for the victims of rape are chosen indiscriminately, but the propagandists for male supremacy broadcast that it is women who cause rape by being unchaste or in the wrong place at the wrong time—in essence, by behaving as though they were free.

The threat of rape is used to deny women employment. . . . The fear of rape keeps women off the streets at night. Keeps women at home. Keeps women passive and modest for fear that they be thought provocative.

It is part of human dignity to be able to defend oneself, and women are learning. . . . And yet we will not be free until the threat of rape and the atmosphere of violence is ended, and to end that the nature of male behavior must change.

But rape is not an isolated act that can be rooted out from patriarchy without ending patriarchy itself. The same men and power structure who victimize women are engaged in the act of raping Vietnam, raping Black people and the very earth we live upon.

I Tried Everything (1972)

SUZANNE LACY, DORI ATLANTIS, JAN LESTER MARTIN, AND NANCY YOUDELMAN

This collaboration parodies breast enhancement products and their false advertising using the format of a pseudoscientific study. The artists pooled money to send away for various creams and devices that Youdelman methodically tried out. She jotted notes about her findings on index cards, and Atlantis photographed her in a sequence that playfully recalls the trend in Conceptual art of information gathering and body measurement. The artists presented advertisements, products, their notes, and documentation of their correspondence with various companies.

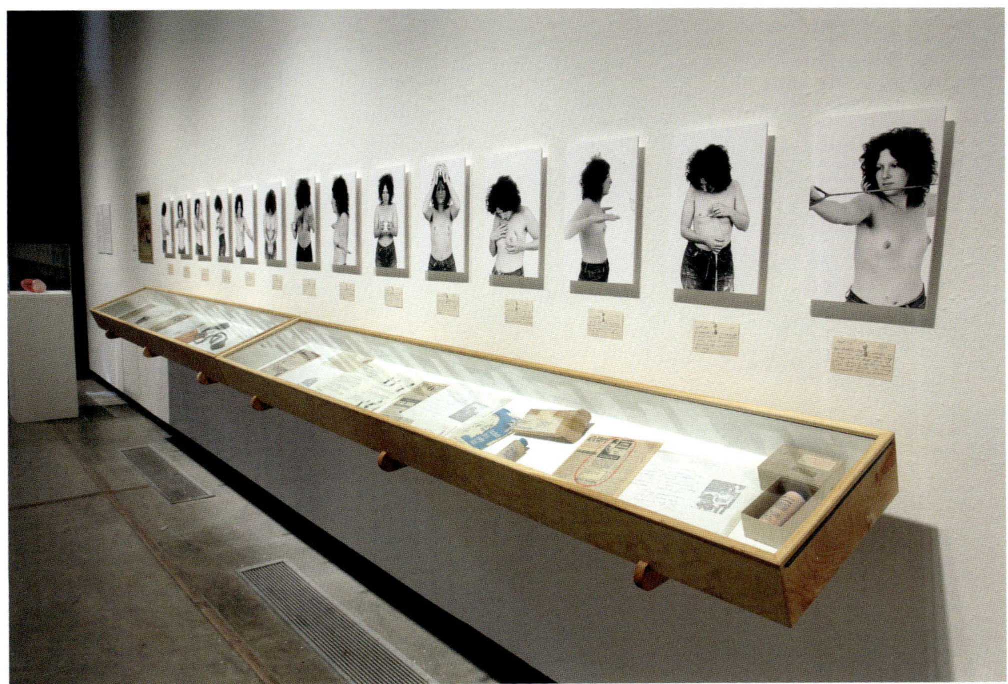

LEFT: Installation view, *A Studio of Their Own: The Legacy of the Fresno Feminist Experiment*, Phebe Conley Art Gallery, California State University, Fresno, August 26–October 9, 2009
BOTTOM, LEFT TO RIGHT: Poster for *I Tried Everything—A Documentary Exhibition*, California Institute of the Arts Library, Valencia, June 4–July 1, 1972; promotional materials from the installation

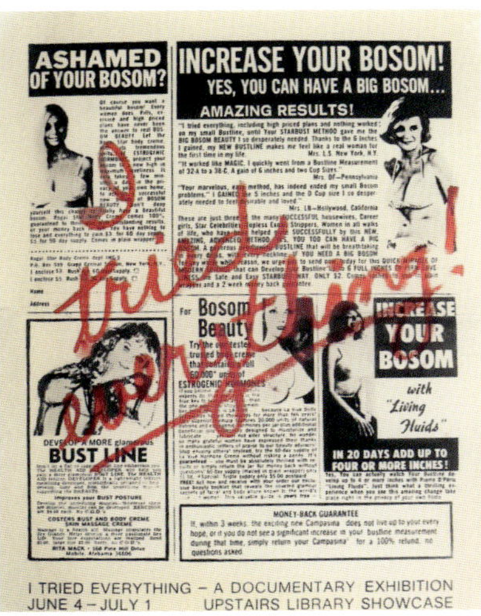

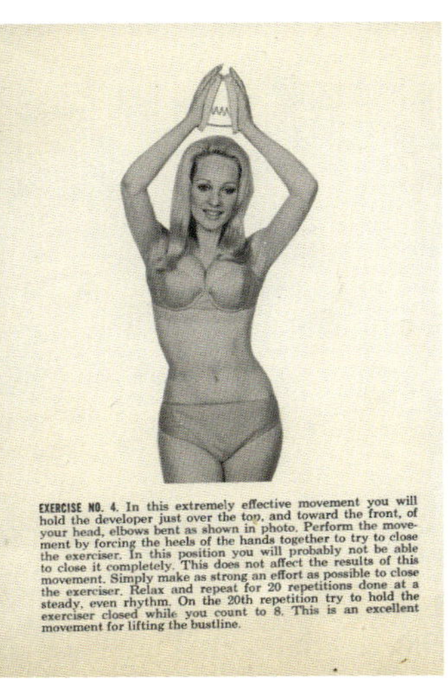

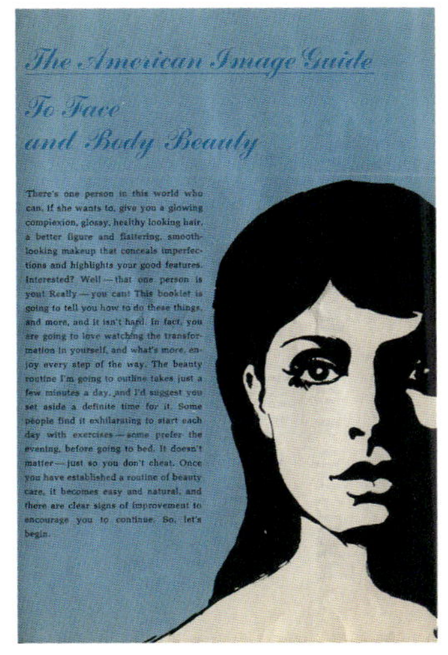

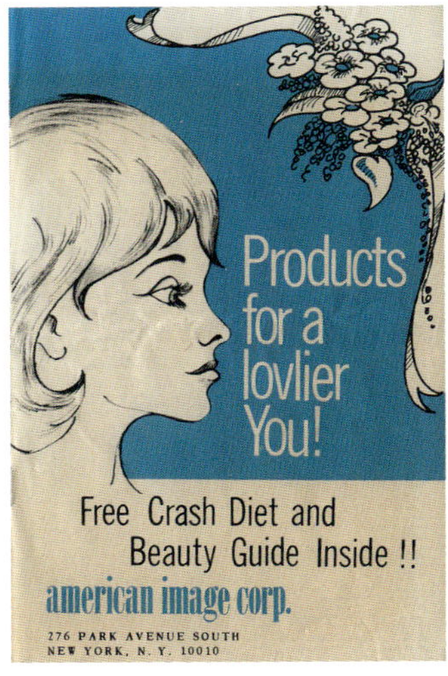

Net Construction (1973)

Lacy's early performances often had a participatory aspect, connecting her with other performers or the audience. In *Net Construction*, staged at the University of California, Santa Barbara, she explored the notion of mutual visceral entrapment and what links us as biological creatures. She tied beef kidneys along a handmade net and, using a giant needle, threaded the kidneys to audience members with strands of twine. She then removed her clothes, tied the ends of the strings to various parts of her own body, and began a slow series of movements. Bound to the audience through this configuration of strings and net, Lacy both influenced and was manipulated by their movements.

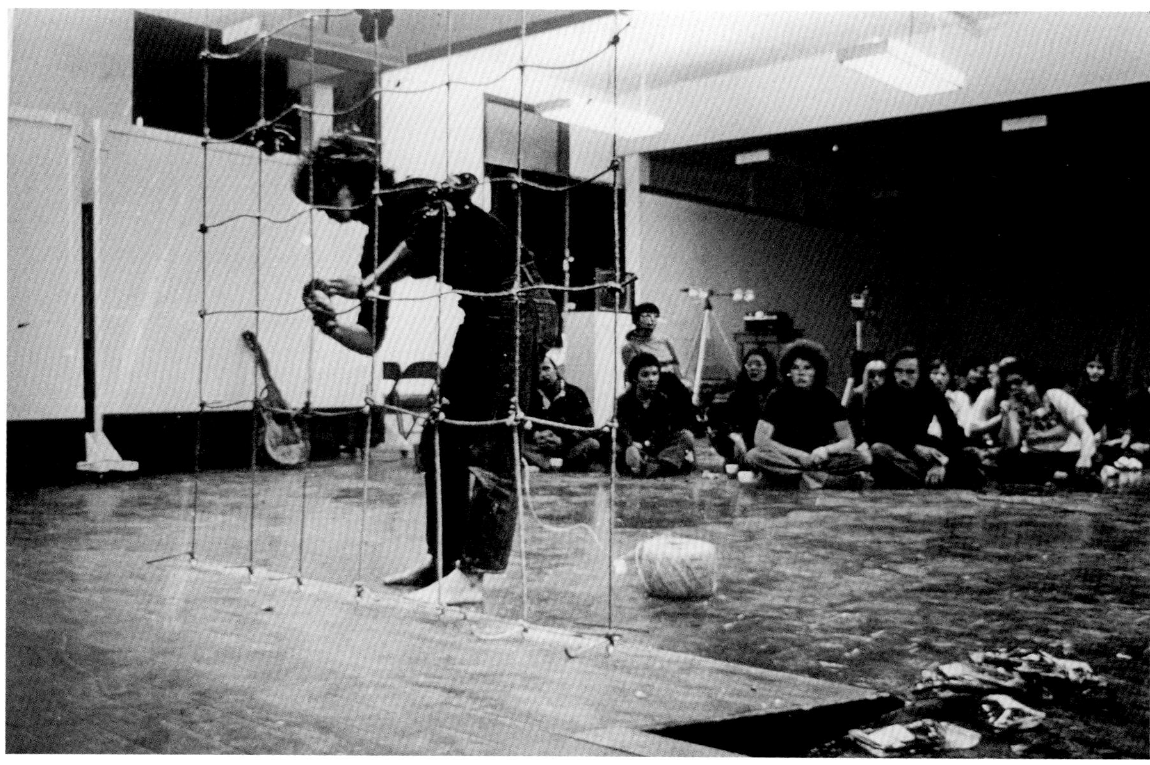

Lamb Construction (1973)

In this surreal exploration of gender and mortality Lacy reconstructed a lamb carcass, nailing internal organs to a saw-horse and adding a head and tail. Black and white mice ran up and down strings suspended from the ceiling with beef kidneys, while a man dressed as a woman made sausage links from ground meat and hung them from a meat hook on the wall. Dishes were set on a long white runner, and two young girls dressed in white brought pieces of birthday cake out for the audience. *Lamb Construction* was performed twice, once at Womanspace Gallery, Los Angeles, and once at the opening of the Woman's Building, Los Angeles.

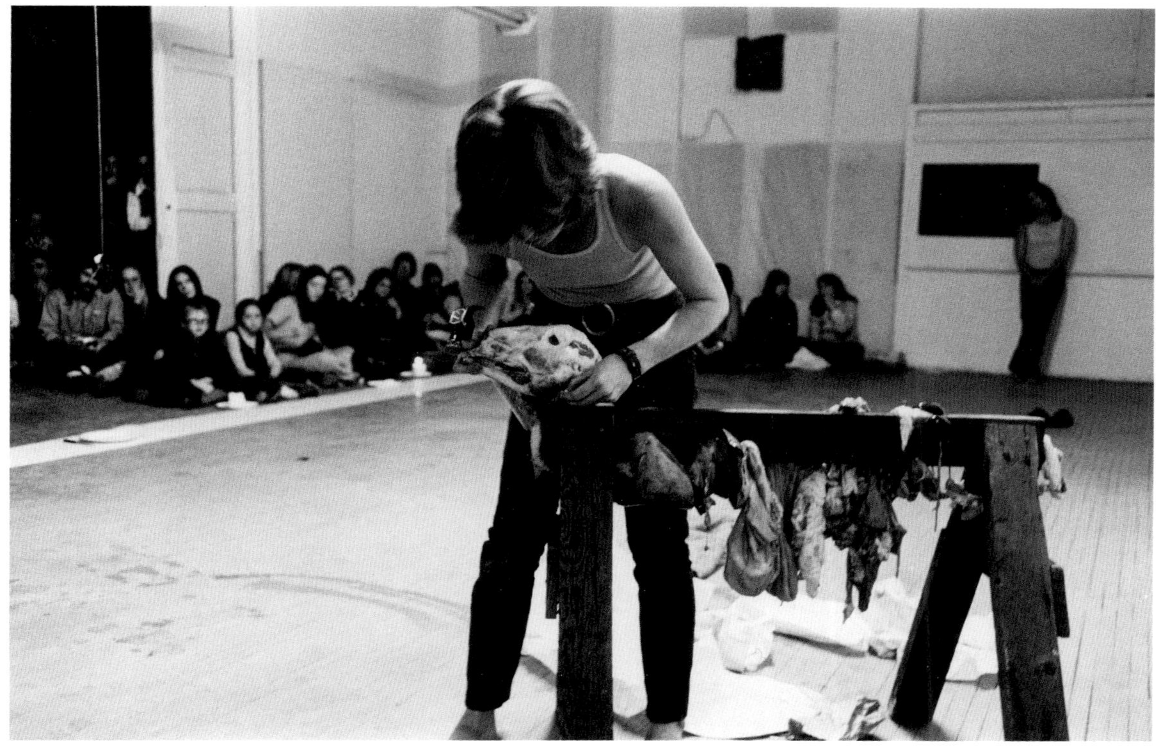

Maps (1973)

Maps involved a journey through Los Angeles based on a set of instructions. At California Institute of the Arts, Valencia, for Allan Kaprow's class, Lacy gave sheep parts to ten participants to nail to a wall according to their anatomical locations. The participants then carried these organs in paper bags through a hospital for people with developmental and learning disabilities, alternately moving separately, converging, and splitting up again. Later, at a meatpacking shed in Vernon, Lacy gave everyone pressed but bloodstained lab coats. They carried their respective organs separately through this abandoned space, later reassembling them on a fence in the back.

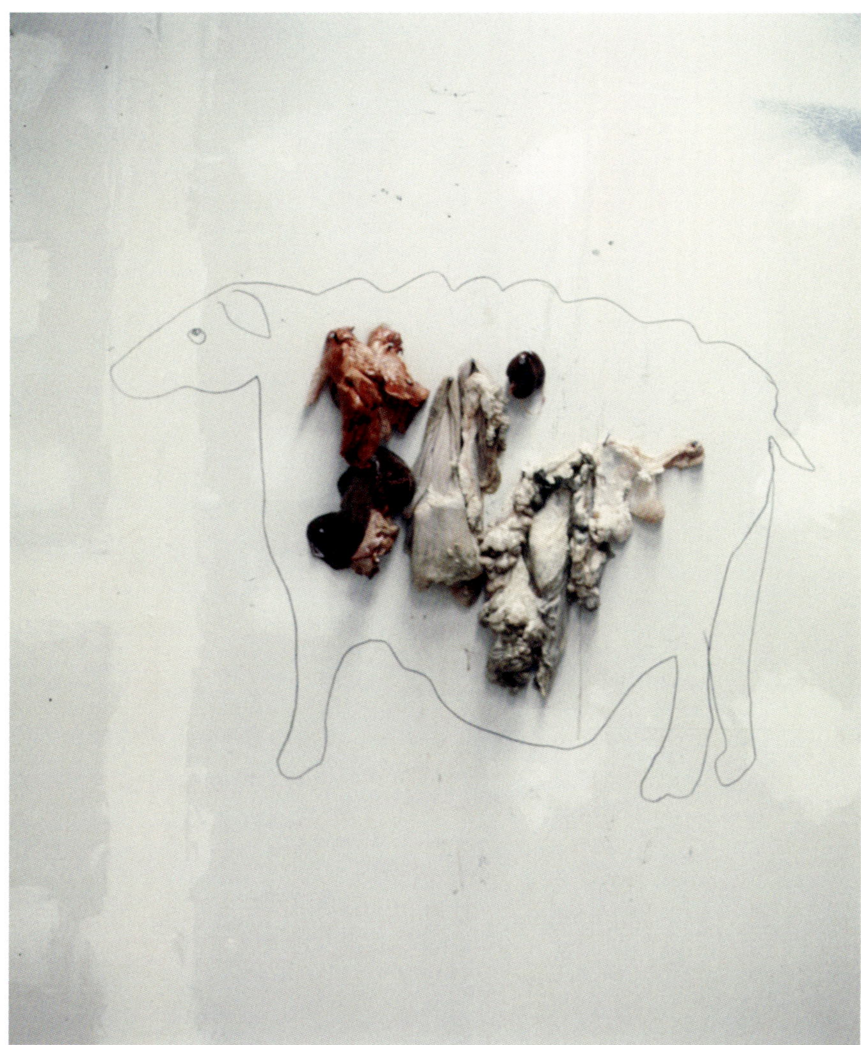

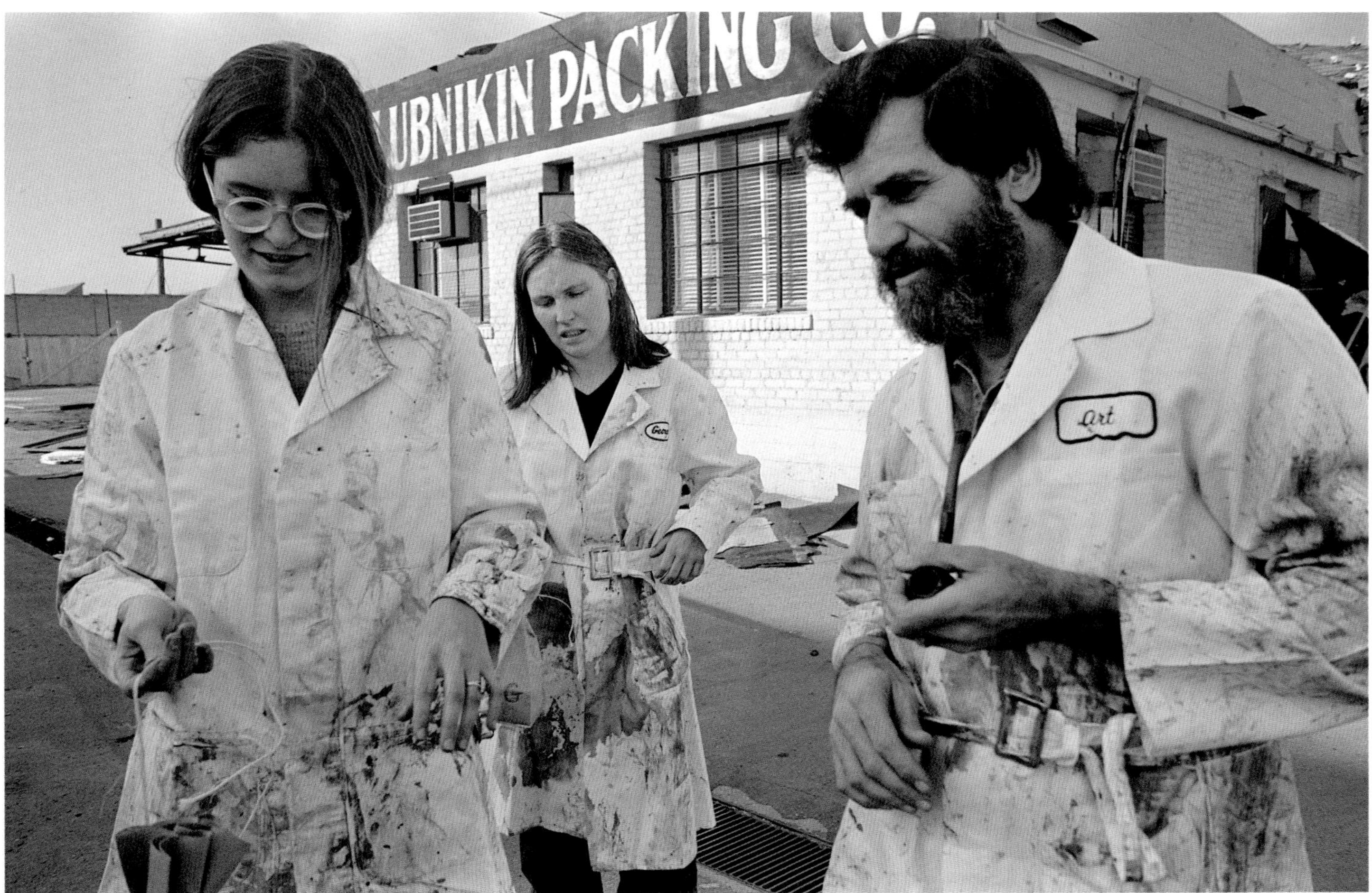

Left to right: participants Gail [?], Bia Lowe, and Kaprow

MOIRA ROTH: Why were you both interested in talking together and producing a taped conversation?
. . .

ALLAN KAPROW: Well, I went to the—whatever year that was, 1978 or something like that—

SUZANNE LACY: 1979.

KAPROW: —College Art Association meeting back East somewhere, I can't remember where—

LACY: Washington, D.C.

KAPROW: —and Suzanne was dynamically holding forth on the issues of feminism and how it has affected the art world. I was very impressed by her, as usual. . . . I thought Suzanne was among the most comprehensive speakers, as she usually is.

LACY: Too bad the tape recorder can't see my blush.

KAPROW: She had the clear sense of both the history of the subject and its ramifications. So, filled with a kind of eagerness of response, at the time I said . . . "Listen, let's do an article together." Because the issue of politics interested me very much, and it seemed to me that we'd gotten to the point where we understood that there were a number of applications of that word, a number of nuances to it, from what some people would call personal politics—the ways in which people transact and negotiate their relationships—to [the] large-scale arena or realpolitik, which is the street version, or the global version of negotiations.

ROTH: Do you see your work as concerned with personal politics?

KAPROW: Well, I saw it then as being more associated with that, but what I was interested in was really the model-making nature of both of our work, even though by comparison Suzanne's scale at that time was much larger.

ROTH: Why were you interested in talking to Allan?

LACY: I think there were a couple of things. . . . I'm always fascinated with the quality of people's relationships and what goes on in relationships and the sort of intellectual/emotional exchange that happens. I felt both I'd learned a great deal personally [about] how an artist lives through time . . . as well as aesthetically. You were really my only contact with the formal art world. I mean, Judy [Chicago] and you are sort of like my two major contacts. . . . I've always liked the dynamics that show up interpersonally. That was sort of part of the intrigue of an article. At this point in history you're involved in the art world in a different way than I am—you've been involved longer, you're a man, I'm a female, you've been my teacher. That interests me a lot too. That sort of teaching pattern passes down. Like one very personal thing I learned from you was watching how you showed up at students' performances and thinking to myself how I don't show up at my students' performances that much. It's that kind of observation that was interesting. Also, on an aesthetic level, I liked the notion that you sort of represent for me one way of thinking about art, and Judy represents another way of thinking about art. Obviously I don't want to hold you in that place . . . and make that real kind of rigid definition . . . but I'm intrigued with the quality of that relationship. That's one thing. And the other is . . . you're probably the only person except for Leslie [Labowitz] that's an artist that I know of that really will engage [with the] straight, formalist kind of shape and structure of things, and that can understand that content exists in work, and political intent exists in work, but underneath the work there's this real clear, formal way of playing with it.

—Excerpt from recorded conversation, 1981

Monster Series: Construction of a Novel
Frankenstein (1974/1975)

SUZANNE LACY WITH SARAH MACY

Building on Mary Shelley's gothic novel *Frankenstein* (1831) and its themes of creation and responsibility, this performance deconstructed aspects of both the book and the author's life. Mary Wollstonecraft, one of the earliest feminist theorists, died soon after giving birth to Shelley, who herself experienced miscarriages. In this work, first staged at the Woman's Building, Los Angeles, two simultaneous soliloquies were delivered, one by Dr. Frankenstein and one by the monster. Projected imagery included medical literature and news articles on organ transplantation, Shelley's introduction to the book, and a silent black-and-white film in which two women (Lacy and Macy) sew their clothes together and then rip them apart. In a lab coat, Lacy drew blood from her arm and left paint imprints of her body on the wall. In a second version of the work, staged at Western Washington State College (now Western Washington University), Bellingham, Lacy, a new mother, and thirteen students discussed creation and the experience of childbirth for an audience while stitching together their clothing.

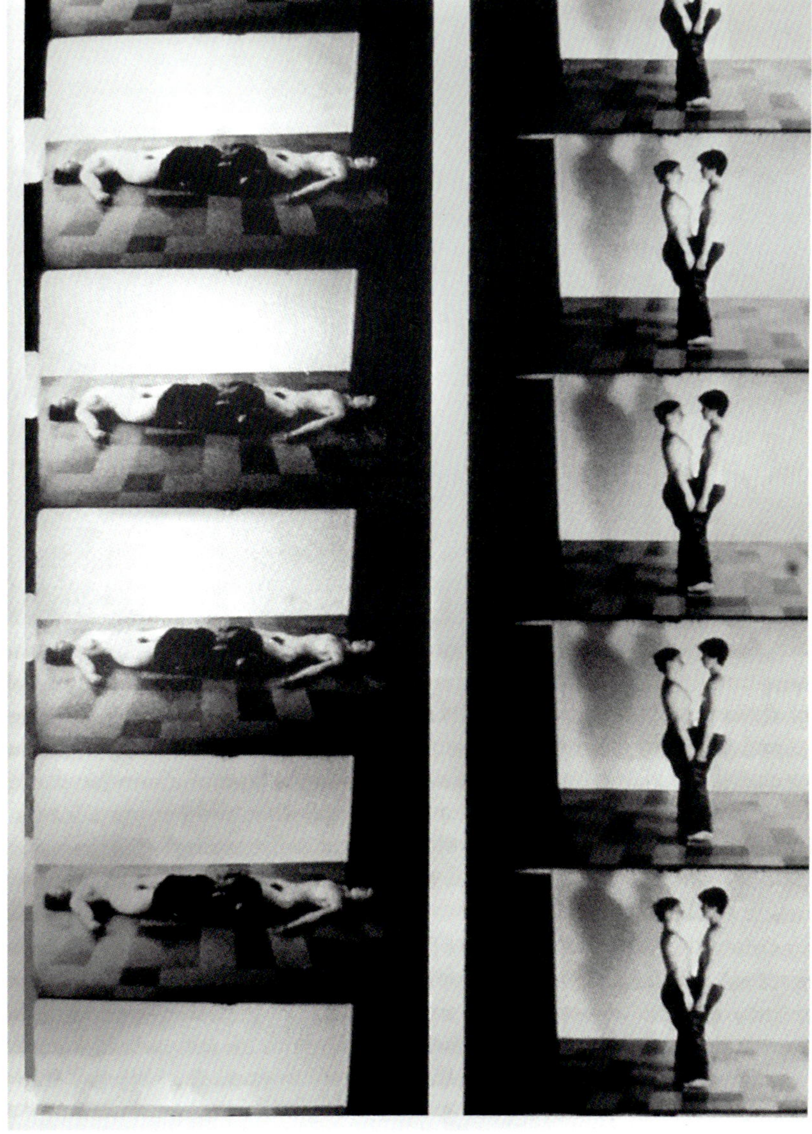

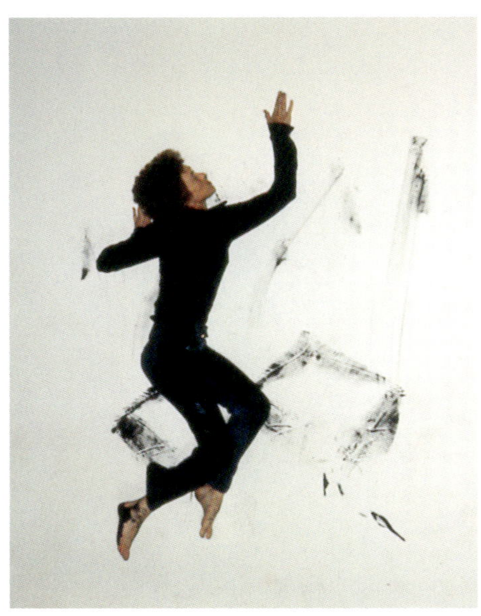

LEFT: Film sequence of Lacy and Macy moving with their clothes sewn together
RIGHT: Lacy slamming against the wall in paint-soaked clothes to leave imprints of her body, Western Washington State College
OPPOSITE: Source materials used in a slide projection during the performance

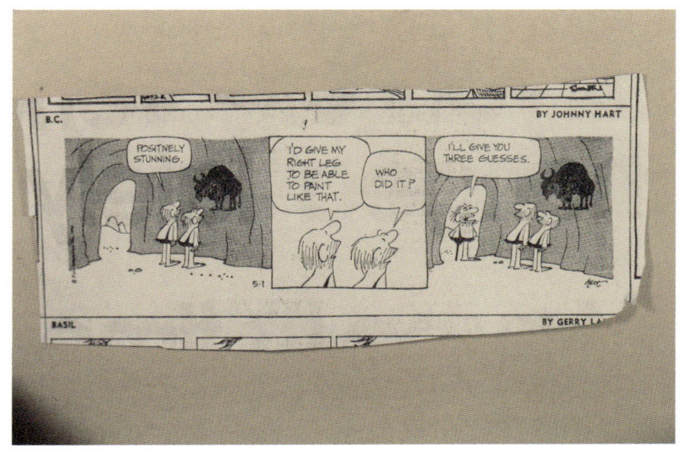

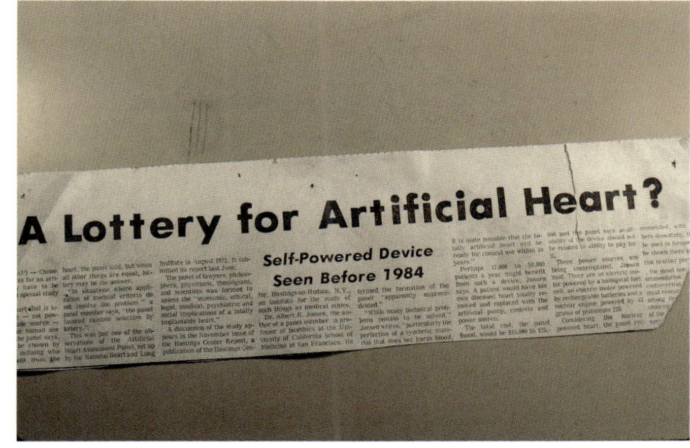

A Lottery for Artificial Heart?

Self-Powered Device Seen Before 1984

Eye for Sale at $35,000

GRASS VALLEY (UPI)—Herbert Gibboney, 58, wants to sell one of his eyes for $35,000 to pay for a costly operation for his wife.

"I'm desperate," said Gibboney, who placed an advertisement in a local newspaper offering to sell an eye for $35,000 in cash, with the buyer paying the cost of transferring the eye.

Gibboney said his wife Jean requires surgery to replace a portion of

He sold his small business in Los Angeles and came to Grass Valley to live on Social Security after doctors advised him to retire following a heart attack. He said his hospitalization insurance was canceled after his heart attack.

"You just try to get your wife in a hospital with no insurance and no money—it's impossible," said Gibboney, who is unwilling to accept wel-

Planting Teeth

The ancient Egyptians replaced missing teeth with carved ivory, making tooth implantation possibly the oldest form of major oral surgery. But most implant techniques—ancient or modern—have proved disappointing, forcing dentists to rely for the most part on costly and troublesome bridges and dentures. Now, however, dental researchers are testing a new way of replacing a missing tooth with a crown anchored to an artificial root made of vitreous carbon, a tough and inert material developed in the 1930s and used more recently for the heat shields of space capsules.

Several types of dental implants have been developed since World War II, but all have had serious drawbacks. In one type, the patient's gum is opened and a metal frame placed directly on the jawbone. Crowns are then attached to vertical posts protruding from the frame through the gum. The procedure involves complicated surgery requiring hospitalization and costs as much as $3,000. Often, the bone shrinks away from the metal frame, the teeth become loose and the frame must be removed. Other types of implants, in which a metal device is inserted directly into the tooth socket, have also failed because of bone tissue loss, inflammatory reactions and infection. The vitreous-carbon implant, first tested by Dr. Dale Grenoble of the University of Southern California School of Dentistry, has been done on some 800 persons in the U.S. in the last three years without causing such problems.

Plug: Vitreous carbon is made of a plastic-like material subjected to very high temperatures in much the same way that synthetic diamonds are produced. The result is a hard, black, glassy substance that won't corrode like metal or

or for securing a loose full denture. The implants, notes Dr. Richard Stallard of BU, can only be used when an adequate amount of bone is present. They are ideal for children, he adds, because they permit normal growth and development of the mouth in cases where missing teeth could lead to speech impairment or facial deformity with attendant emotional problems.

But largely because of the failures encountered with other types of dental implants, many dentists will regard the vitreous-carbon devices with extreme caution until more trials have established their usefulness. For the present, in fact, the American Dental Association will not permit the implants to be advertised in its publications. But those who have

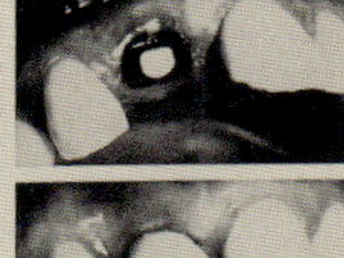

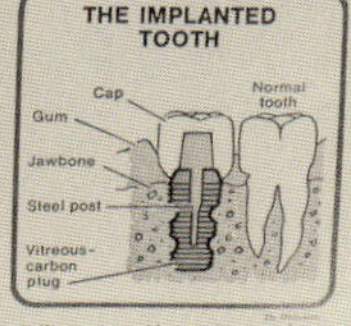

Filling a gap: Above, vitreous plug; below, finished implant with crown

lymphoblastic leukemia of children, which can often be brought under control by intensive drug therapy, AML responds poorly to conventional treatment and few of its victims survive more than a year.

Therapy: In a study begun four years ago, Powles and his group chose patients who had gone into remission after receiving standard drug therapy for two months. Immunotherapy was then begun to destroy leukemic cells remaining in the body. The patients received weekly injections of BCG, a TB vaccine widely used in Europe, followed by inoculation of leukemic cells that had been removed and then killed by irradiation. The BCG, which is being tested in a number of centers for anti-cancer effects, theoretically provides a general stimulus to the pa-

used the vitreous-carbon implants believe them to be the most promising such devices yet to come along. "The other

tient's immune system. The killed leukemic cells, which presumably contain special antigens that the body should

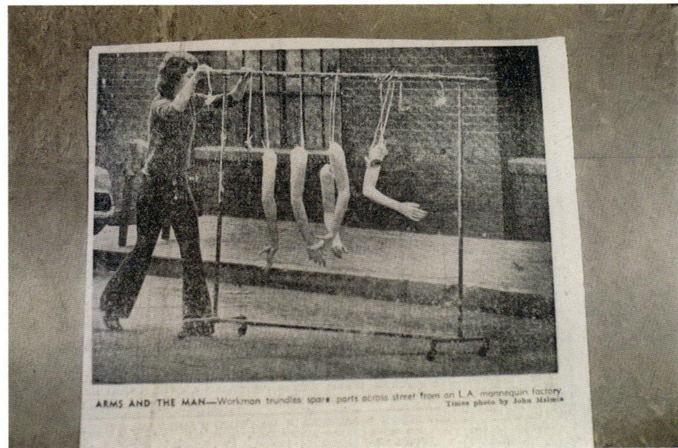

ARMS AND THE MAN—Workmen trundles spare parts across street from an L.A. mannequin factory.
Tissue photo by John Malmin

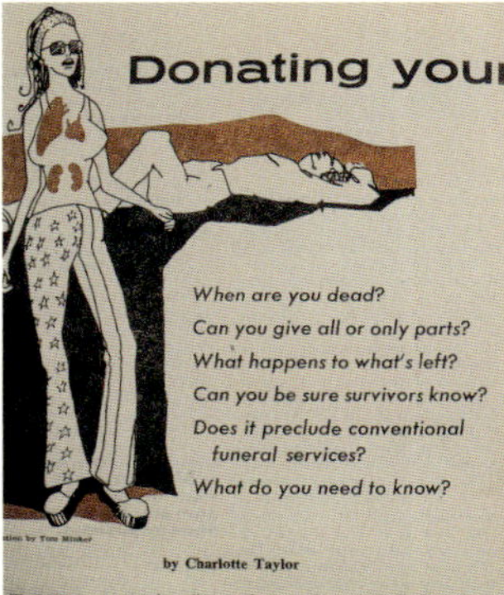

Donating your body to science

When are you dead?

Can you give all or only parts?

What happens to what's left?

Can you be sure survivors know?

Does it preclude conventional funeral services?

What do you need to know?

by Charlotte Taylor

Dr. Samuel L. Kountz, presently with the State University Hospital in Brooklyn, N.Y., and formerly co-chief of one of the world's largest kidney transplant centers at the University of California's San Francisco Medical Center, estimates that there are currently less than one-tenth of the needed kidney donors registered.

The Eye-Bank for Sight Restoration in New York, the U.S.'s largest and first eye bank, estimates that five times the current number of corneas are needed in the N.Y. area alone, even though that institution received over 2400 last year.

Fifty-four percent of the medical schools surveyed by the Living Bank, a non-profit organization which promotes the donation of bodies to science, have indicated that they need more bodies for instruction purposes. St. Louis University medical school now gets 50 bodies annually but could double that amount.

Today people needing kidney transplants must wait years for the needed organ, and those for corneal transplants, months. Yet a Gallup Poll conducted in January, 1968—shortly after the first human heart transplant made world-wide headlines—indicated that seven out of ten Americans would willingly donate their vital organs to medical science after death.

Why the shortage? Is the process of donating one's body that difficult?

tomical gifts so complex and cumbersome that it was almost impractical. Today every state has enacted legislation based on the uniform model, and bequeathing your body to science is a fairly simple process.

The problem, simply stated, is that people die with their bequests unknown. This is particularly true in the donation of kidneys and eyes, where speed is vital in bridging the gap between a donor's death and his gift of viable tissue to a recipient.

Corneas must be removed within two hours of death and transplanted within 24 hours. Kidneys can only be kept viable for 70 hours, but must be removed within 30 minutes after the heart stops beating. For those people whose wills and papers are locked in a safety deposit box, buried in a file, or even made verbally to a relative who may be unreachable at the time of death, it is too late.

Roger Harris, who is organizing the American International Funeral Registry in Washington, D.C., so that burial and donation wishes can be known quickly, points to the framed copy of Franklin D. Roosevelt's funeral wishes over his desk as the perfect example. Four pages long, the papers were opened and read three days after his burial.

One of the major breakthroughs in body donation was the stipulation in the 1968 Uniform Act that the legal document of consent can be a card-

ST. LOUIS, a young boy lives with the kidney of a housewife died of a brain hemorrhage. In ston, a laborer can count on a more years of life because of the of a Texas businessman. Although firm figures are difficult establish, it is estimated that 200,-

plants could cut this fatality rate in half.

Eye tissues could restore the sight of some 35,000 Americans, or aid research into this affliction of a half million people. Bodies given to medical schools are instrumental in providing adequate instruction of our

Three Love Stories (1975–76)

With deadpan humor, this work illustrates popular figures of speech that dramatically link romantic emotional states with vital organs, such as, "You are the air I breathe!" Each sequence of six black-and-white photographs involves a different organ and is paired with short captions that describe a cycle or arc of longing and loss. *A Gothic Love Story* narrates the drama of a broken heart. *Under My Skin: A Pornographic Novel* depicts guts spilled on a bed and then wrapped and tied up. Lacy breathes into a set of animal lungs in *A True Romance Story, or She's Got Quite a Set of Lungs.* She self-published the three stories together as an artist's book in 1978.

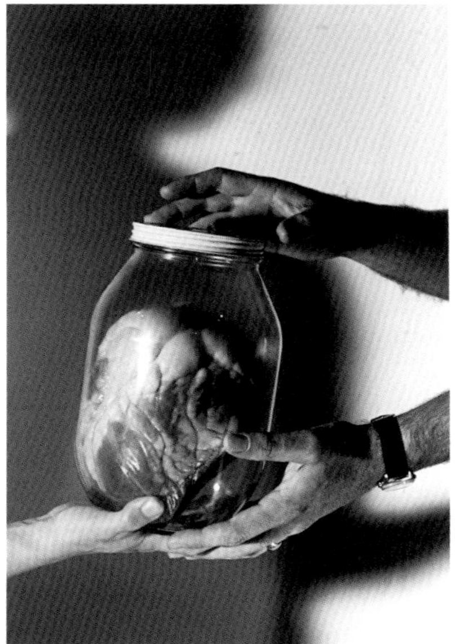

She gave her heart away.

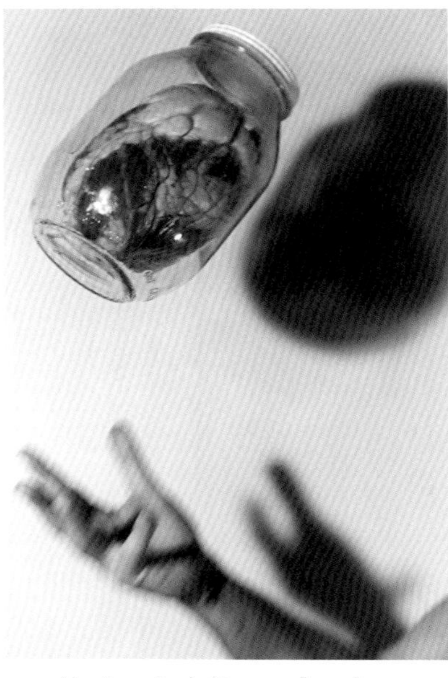

He treated it carelessly.

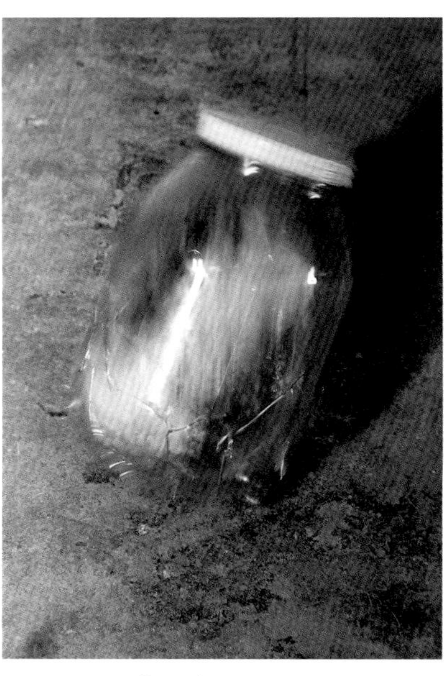

One day . . .

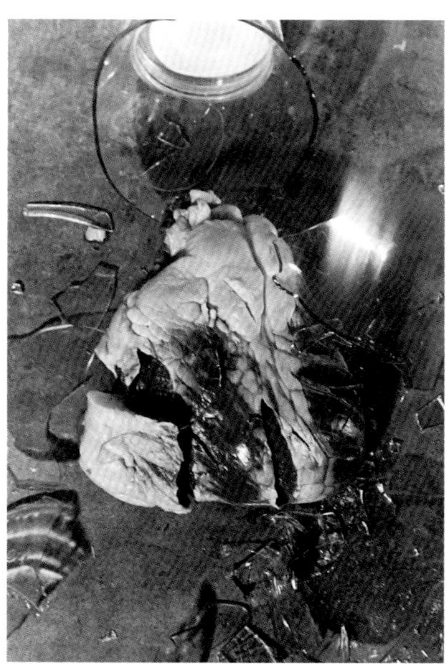

he broke it.

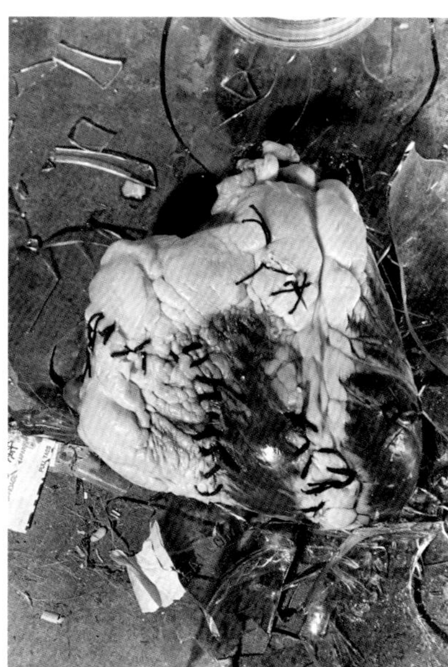

She pulled herself together,

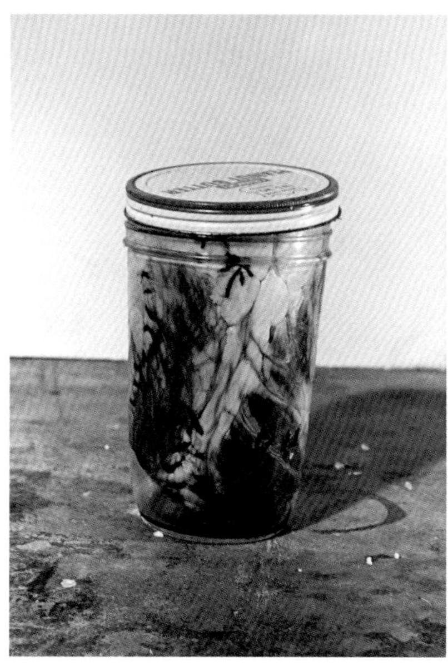

but she was never quite the same.

Three Love Stories: A Gothic Love Story, 1975

Under My Skin: A True-Life Story (1975/1977)

Exploring the idea of embedded memories of violence and the nature of evil, in this work Lacy combined imagery from three sources—her own childhood injuries, a vampire prostitute character, and Dracula mythology. The performance was divided into seven sections, respectively titled "Book of the Body," "Book of the Tooth," "Book of the Eye," "Book of the Hand," "Book of the Head," "Book of the Heart," and "Book of the Bones." It began with a film of two actions: Lacy peeling the "skin" (dried paste) off her face and then baring vampire fangs.

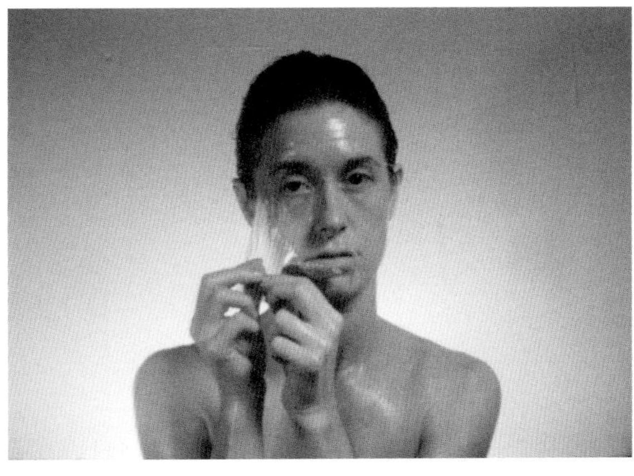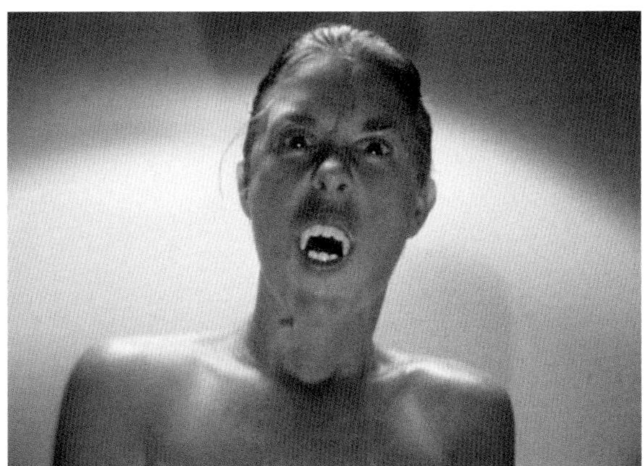

```
MOVIE: UNDER MY SKIN: A TRUE-LIFE STORY

SLIDES:                          READINGS:

1.   This is a tale of four bodies, or parts of bodies, or even a single body in
     pieces. Some may see it as fragmentation. Others will recognize dismemberment.
     It could also be understood as memory, the memory which resides in each cell,
     each vessel and bone of my body.

2.   It is a story gothic in nature, filled with shadows and horrors and pathos,
     monsters real and imagined, and blood. The blood is real. The stories are real.
     Only the monsters are questionable.

3.   body 1: the beginnings of memory

(Hold)  4.   I remember falling . . .

                         I REMEMBER DREAMING AND I REMEMBER IT WELL, HOW OFTEN I WOULD AWAKEN,
                         ALTHOUGH MAYBE NOT ENTIRELY, AND FEEL SOMETHING EVIL IN MY ROOM.
                         I COULD FEEL SHADOW, BLACK CLOTH OR A CAPE, AND TERROR TOO GREAT TO
                         SEE CLEARLY. I REMEMBER SCREAMING AND THIS WITHOUT SOUND, AND RUNNING
                         AS IF THROUGH THICK CLAY, BUT NEVER QUITE FAR ENOUGH, AND I REMEMBER
                         HOW I WOULD BE PULLED BACK, SUCKED BACK, AT LAST AND WITHOUT HELP,
                         I WOULD FEEL MYSELF FALLING BACK INTO THE ROOM.
```

Film stills of Lacy from the black-and-white version
of the 8mm film shown during the performance at the
San Francisco Art Institute Annual, December 1975

Body Contract (1974)

Lacy researched the new science of organ transplants and organ donations that were possible at the time under California law. Prepared by a lawyer, this multipage document outlines different designations for the distribution of Lacy's body parts and a bill of sale. The conceptually driven work reflects a larger discussion in contemporary art around the relationship of the artist to commerce and the production of non-salable art.

AGREEMENT OF PURCHASE AND SALE OF THE RIGHT

TO DESIGNATE THE DISPOSITION OF ORGANS

THIS AGREEMENT OF PURCHASE AND SALE OF THE RIGHT TO DESIGNATE THE DISPOSITION OF ORGANS ("Agreement") is made and entered into by and between SUZANNE LACY (hereinafter referred to as "Seller") and (hereinafter referred to as "Buyer").

This Agreement is made pursuant to the following facts and circumstances:

A. Seller, under the provisions of California law, has the right to control the disposition of her remains at her death.

B. Seller desires to sell, transfer, and assign the right to designate at her death the disposition of certain of her organs.

C. Buyer desires to acquire the right to designate, at Seller's death, the recipient of certain of Seller's organs.

NOW, THEREFORE, in consideration of the mutual covenants and agreements herein contained, the parties agree as follows:

1. Purchase and Sale:

a. Buyer hereby purchases from Seller, and Seller hereby sells to Buyer, subject to the restrictions set forth in

<u>PRICE LIST</u>

Currently Transplantable Body Parts:

Adrenal Gland	$100
Artery (five inches at doctor's discretion)	$ 50
Articular Cartilage of Hip (two)	$ 50 ea.
Articular Cartilage of Knee (two)	$ 50 ea.
Blood (approximately 4000 ml)	$ 80
Bone (includes marrow, femur or comprable)	$ 75
Bowel	$ 50
Cerebral Dura Mater	$100
Cornea (two)	$100 ea.
Fascia (two x two inch of fibro-areolar)	$ 50
Hair (surface of head)	NFS
Heart (includes valves)	$400
Kidney (two)	$300 ea.
Liver	$300
Lung (two)	$250 ea.
Ovary (two)	$200 ea.
Pancreas	$150
Parathyroid Gland	$100
Peripheral Nerves (five inches at doctors discretion)	$ 50
Pituitary Gland	$100
Skin (six x six inches at doctor's discretion	NFS
Teeth (complete set as available at death)	$ 75
Tendon (Achilles t. or comprable)	$ 50
Thymus Gland	$100
Thyroid Gland	$100
Ureter	$ 50
Vein (five inches at doctor's discretion)	$ 50

Exhibit A shall be made up of organs drawn from this
price list.

ANATOMY LESSONS

(1976–1977)

Anatomy Lesson #1: Chickens Coming Home to Roost (for Rose Mountain and Pauline) /
Anatomy Lesson #2: Learn Where the Meat Comes From / Anatomy Lesson #3: Falling Apart /
Falling Apart / Anatomy Lesson #4

Lacy's early work brings a medical sensibility to the study of personal identity and the gendered, biological body. As a medical student she had been exposed to autopsies and was inspired by their depiction in Stan Brakhage's film *The Act of Seeing with One's Own Eyes* (1971). Lacy has described the insides of bodies as "very beautiful, awesome and awful at the same time. I use sheep organs as a metaphor for the inside revealed, for a deeper, physical awareness of our connection to our bodies." The series *Anatomy Lessons* comprises some of Lacy's most iconic solo performances for the camera, as well as several photographic sequences that were rarely or only later exhibited. In one photo session Lacy tossed sacks of organs up into the blue sky in a riff on John Baldessari's conceptually driven *Throwing Three Balls in the Air to Get a Straight Line (Best of Thirty-Six Attempts)* (1973).

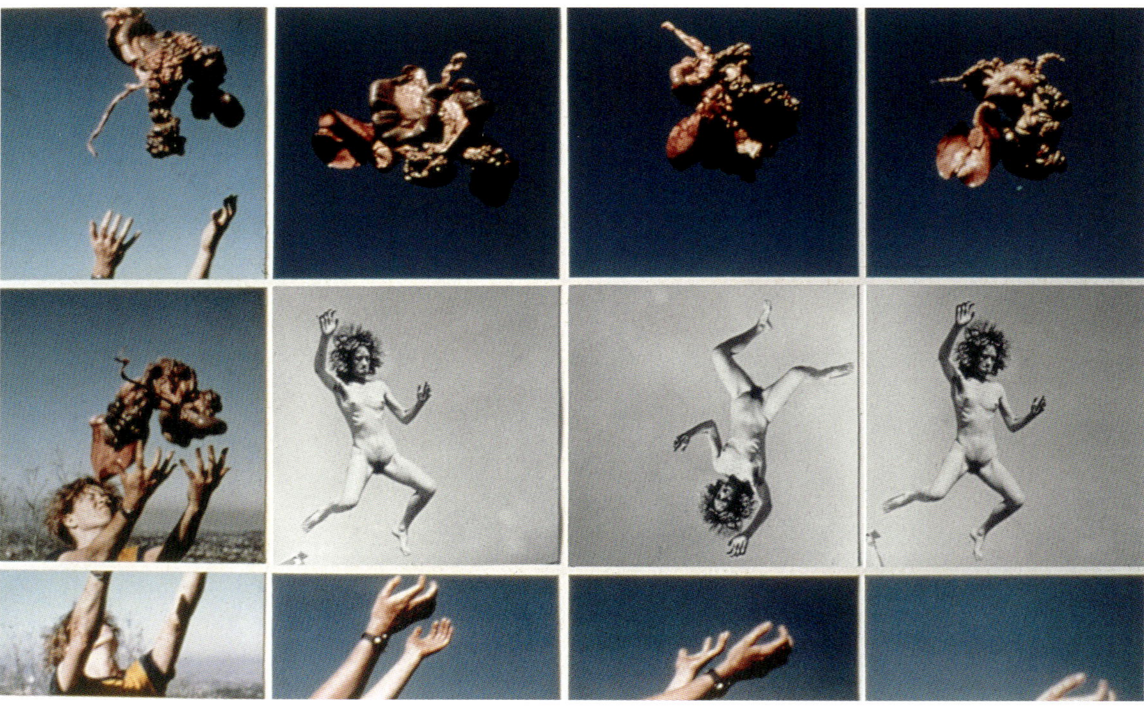

Anatomy Lesson #3: Falling Apart,
1976. Chromogenic prints on board.
Hammer Museum, Los Angeles,
gift of Lynn Hershman Leeson

Anatomy Lesson #1: Chickens Coming Home to Roost (for Rose Mountain and Pauline) (1976)

This work makes a deadpan comparison between Lacy's own body and corresponding parts of a chicken: breast, wings, and drumsticks. Sitting in a kitchen, she was photographed by Susan Mogul eating the various cuts of meat and then circulated the pictures as a set of four postcards. The dedication on the back of each, "For Rose Mountain and Pauline," refers to the artist Linda Montano, whose early performance personas included Rose Mountain and Chicken Woman, and the composer Pauline Oliveros.

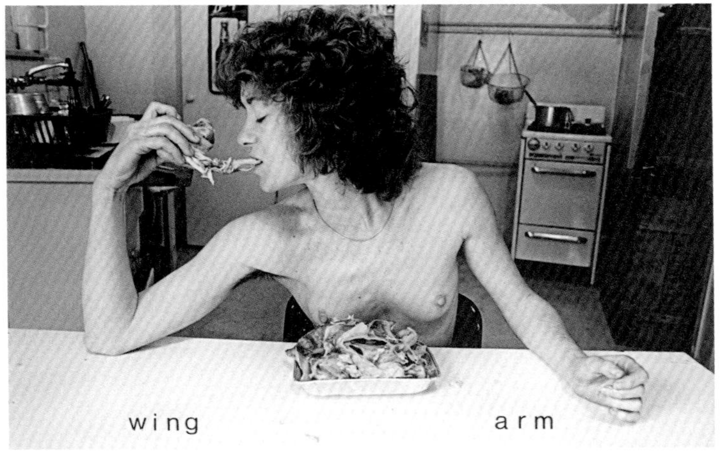

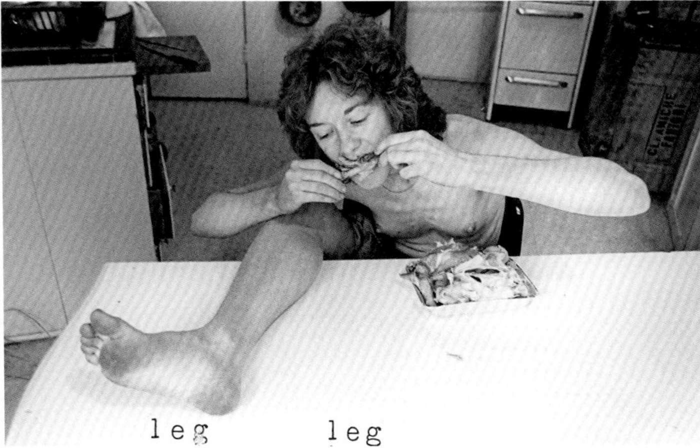

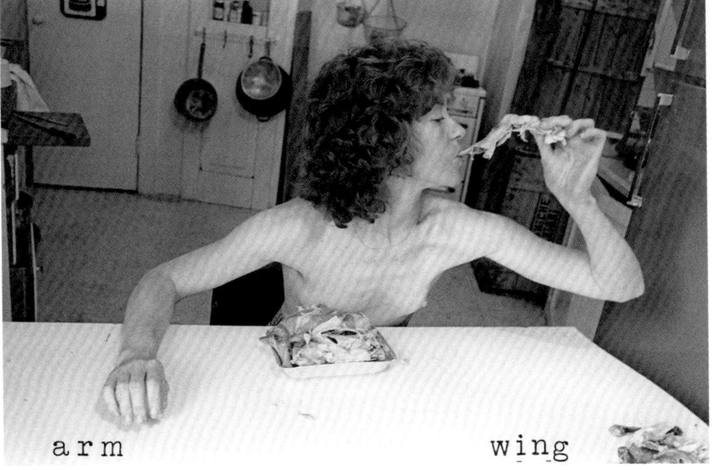

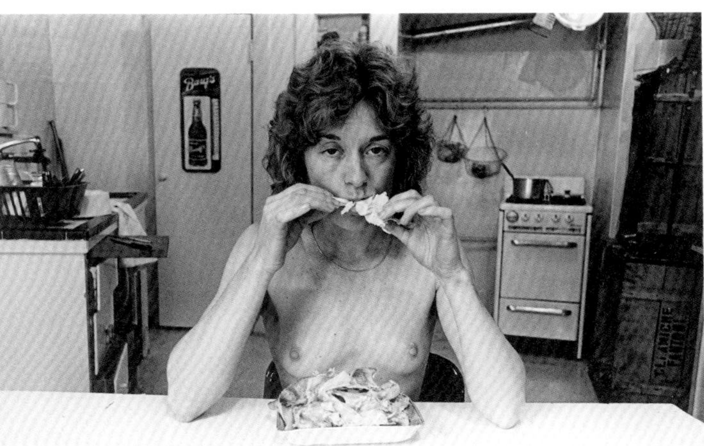

Anatomy Lesson #2: Learn Where the Meat Comes From (1976)

Through photography and a video, Lacy delivers an anatomy lesson in the format of a cooking show. With a lamb carcass splayed on a chopping block, she undergoes a series of physical transformations—baring protruding, animalistic false teeth, then vampire teeth—as her monologue progresses. She based this comparison of human and animal bodies on the work of the chef Julia Child and that of the nutrition experts Adelle Davis and Jack LaLanne. Her first significant work on video, it was directed by Hildegarde Duane and produced by David A. Ross for his pioneering video art program at the Long Beach Museum of Art, California. The photographs were taken by Raúl Vega.

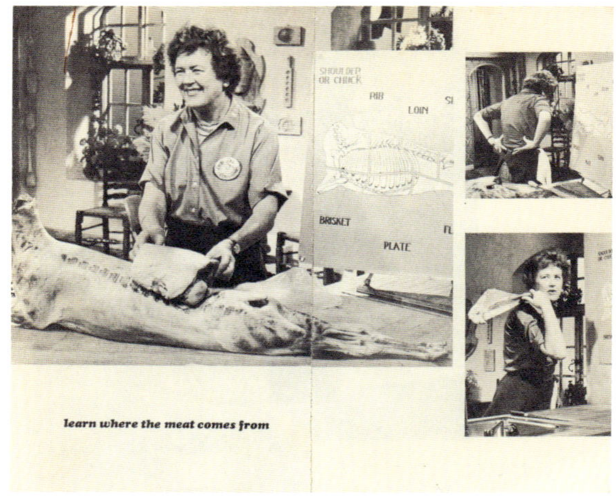

Preparatory concept study with images of Child

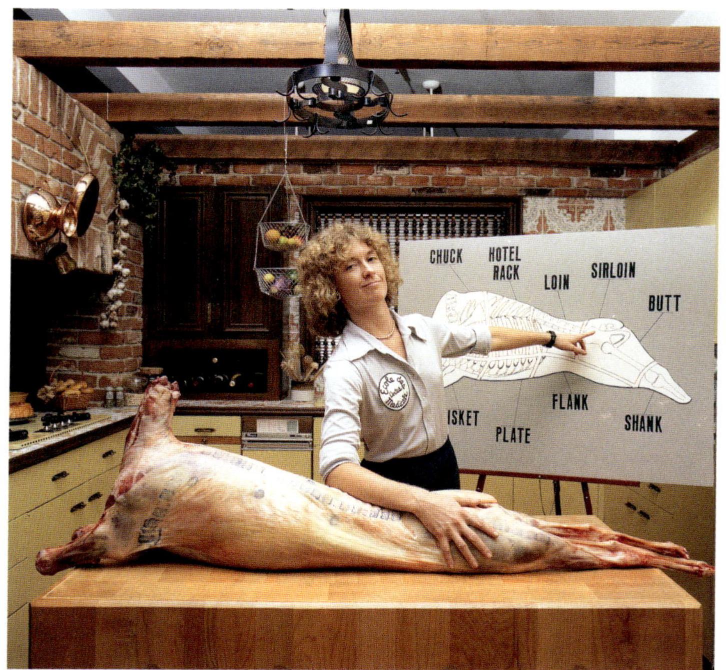

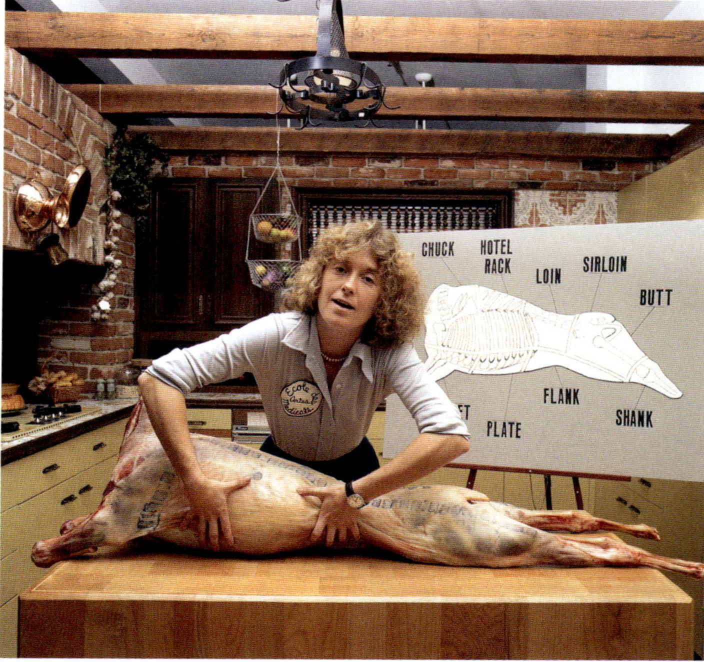

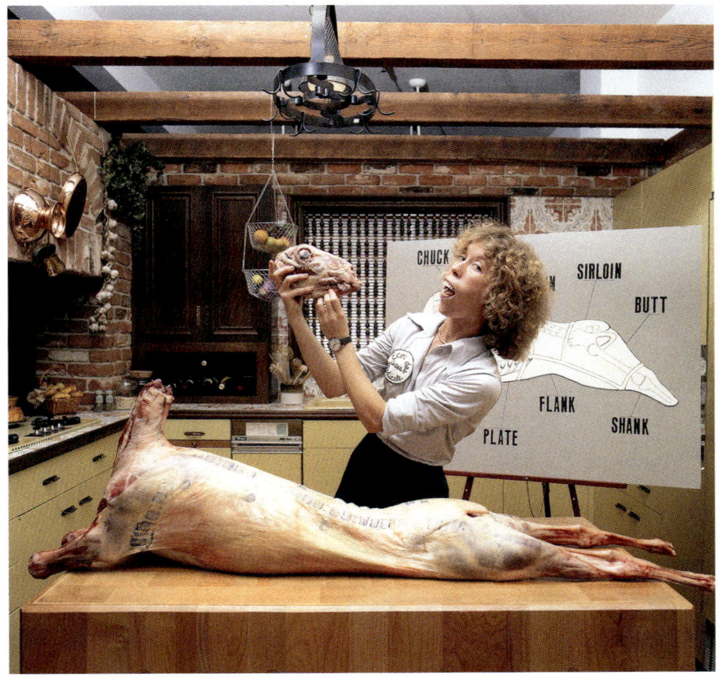

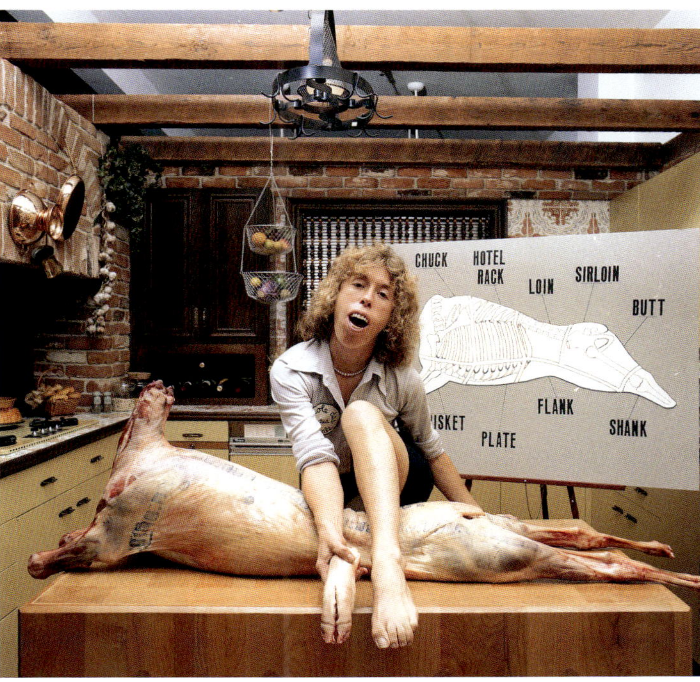

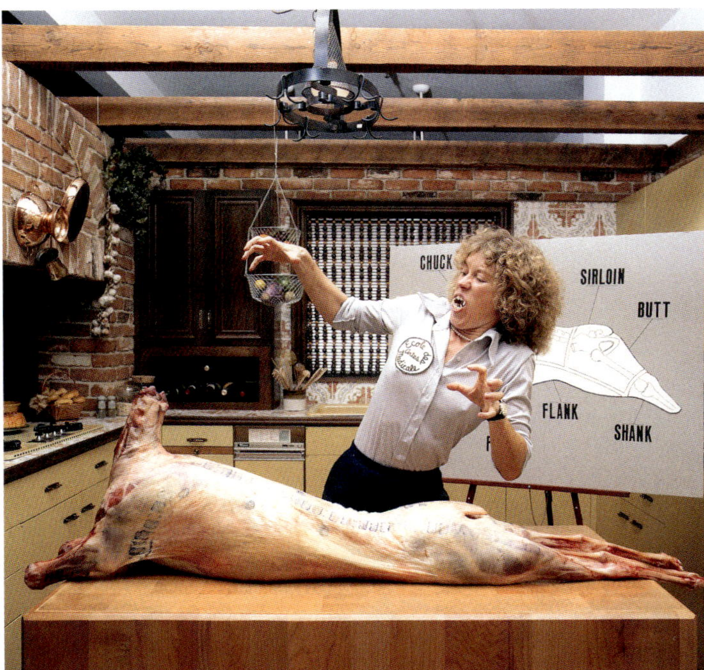

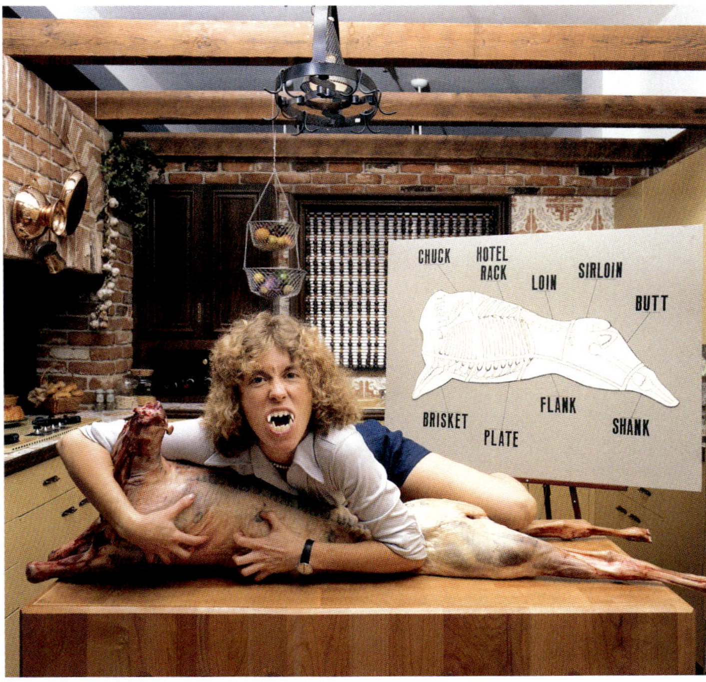

The video was shown at the time when women artists were coming to the fore, asserting equality creatively and in terms of being exhibited. Naturally there was resistance. One of the male directors who saw the piece said to me, "How can you call yourself the director when there is a stationary camera and she barely moves around?" and I said, "I told her when to slap the meat."

—Hildegarde Duane, 2018

SCRIPT (EXCERPT)

Now you want to locate the hole at the large end of the meat from which the leg bone was removed; push the stuffing down into it. (Notice the location of the thickest part of the meat, for this is where we'll put the thermometer later.) If the outside skin has been pierced through at the knee, close it with a skewer. Now we'll skewer the meat at the large end to hold in our stuffing, and just lace it up. (Just like a surgeon!) Baste the roast with our mustard and herb coating, and put in the pan vegetables we prepared earlier, and voila! The roast is ready for the oven.

Sign: Learn where the meat comes from.

Today's lamb means zesty flavors and serving possibilities that challenge the imagination. Shish [kebabs] impaled over the barbeque, sizzling lamb chops, roasted leg of lamb, bubbling lamb stew. Lamb is today's word for good eating. Sounds good? Yes, when it's done right! Innumerable housewives buy meat year after year, often spending hundreds of dollars, without any conception of why one roast or chop is delicious and another is a failure.

Today we'll learn the cuts of meat on a young spring lamb, and get you acquainted with what you need to know to ensure success after success in the kitchen. The first thing you want to do is establish a good relationship with your butcher. Learn to speak his language. You and I know the leg, the rump, the ribs, the neck, but the butcher calls them: chuck, rack, loin, sirloin, brisket, shank and so on. Sounds confusing? Let's see it in the flesh.

. . .

Tell your butcher you want the double or kidney loin and point it out on yourself. It is the small of your back on both sides from the top of your hip up to and including your thirteenth or floating ribs and following around to your front, or flank in butcher language. The best or choicest quality saddles come from so-called spring lambs, everything up to forty-five pounds, which is what we have here. Moving upward is the rack, or hotel rack, also called the standing rib roast.

You can fashion the rack into a French roast by removing about 1½ inches of meat from the ends of the ribs. Then after roasting cover the rib ends with paper frills for a decorative touch.

<u>VOICE-OVER:</u> If this sounds too complicated, there's a simple method. If you're willing to make yourself utterly ridiculous, you can learn the cuts of meat in a few minutes. Here's what you do: Get down on all fours and imagine you are a lamb. Try to imitate the movements a lamb would make, and notice which muscles you use. Imagine you are a curious animal, often turning, lowering, and raising your head: the muscles of your neck will be rich in flavor. Wiggle the muscles on either side of your backbone to frighten away a fly: these will certainly be tender. Breathe deeply and pull your head grassward. The front of your chest, from your neck to just above your waist and from a cut along your breastbone to your shoulders is the brisket. Walk around on your hands and knees. The sections from your hands to elbows and from feet to knees are sold as soup bones. Begin peacefully chewing grass. The large muscles in your cheeks will be used for soup meat, hamburgers or may be fried. Move your tongue: this can be baked, boiled or pickled, and in lambs is a real delicacy!

I was working as curator and deputy director at the Long Beach Museum of Art. With support from the Rockefeller Foundation, we had opened the region's first video-editing facility designed to help . . . artists produce finished video artworks and performance video documentaries. . . . Suzanne Lacy was among the first generation of L.A. artists who quickly found video an appropriate way of recording her actions, and like several other Southern California feminists . . . she was interested in the way that video mocked the oppressive role of television in contemporary American society. . . . *Learn Where the Meat Comes From* [was] a parody of domesticity and the ways traditional television was complicit in the construction and maintenance of stereotypical roles for women.

—David A. Ross, 2018

Anatomy Lesson #3: Falling Apart (1976)

Lacy created five collages of pictures of herself seemingly falling through the air and ripped apart to reveal organs. Susan Mogul, a fellow feminist artist who collaborated with Lacy on a few performances and photographed others, shot her jumping from a ladder in the early morning light. The resulting set of photocollages with excerpts from the artist's book *Falling Apart* (1976, p. 64) were reproduced in *Dreamworks: An Interdisciplinary Quarterly* in 1980.

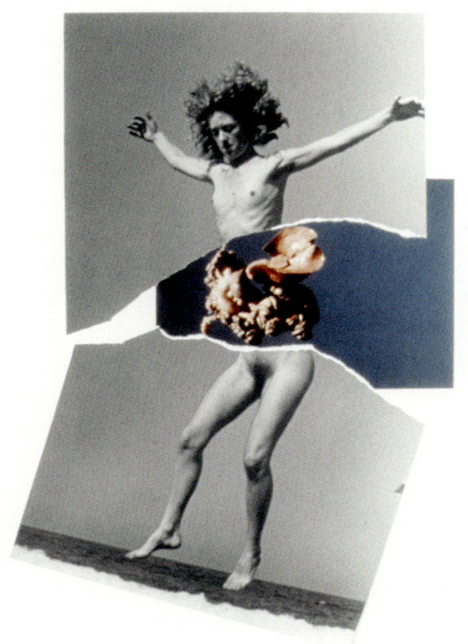

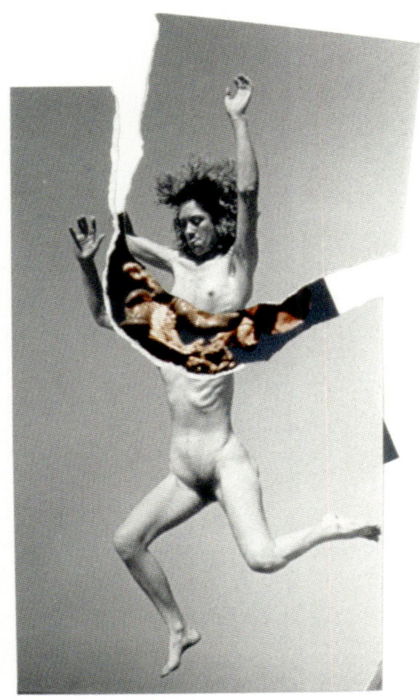

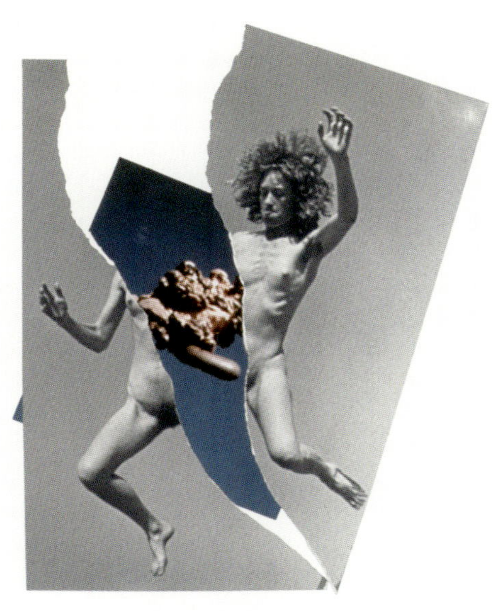

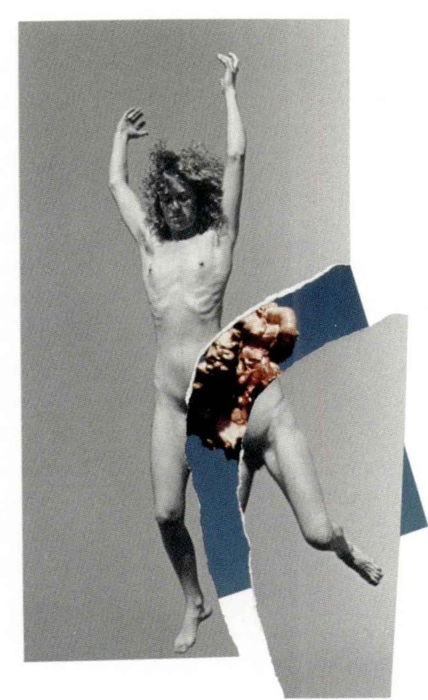

Falling Apart (1976)

Wrapped in a protective elastic bandage, this handmade artist's book traces the impact of various forms of violence, from accidents to deliberate cruelty, on the body. Lacy included newspaper clippings on political and sexual violence. The first version was titled *Falling Woman*.

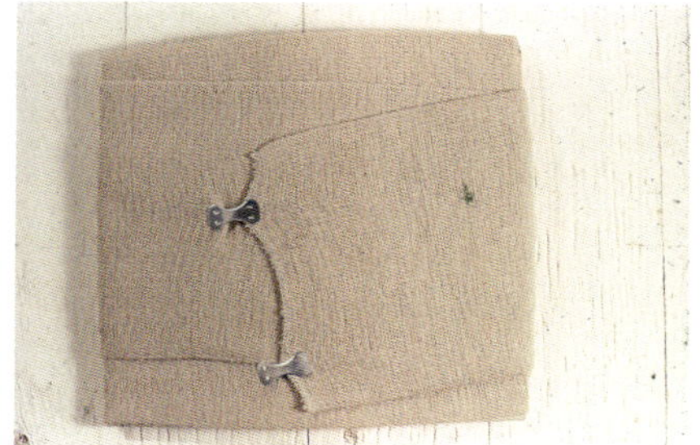

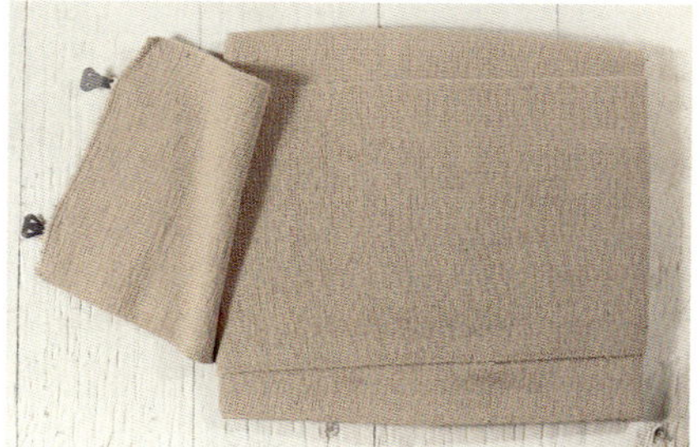

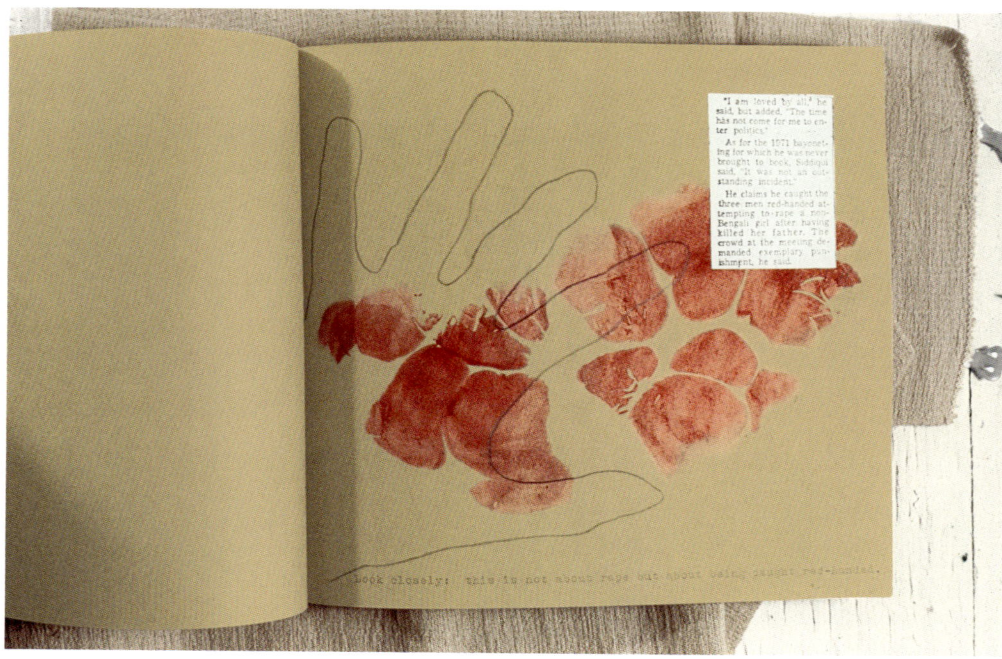

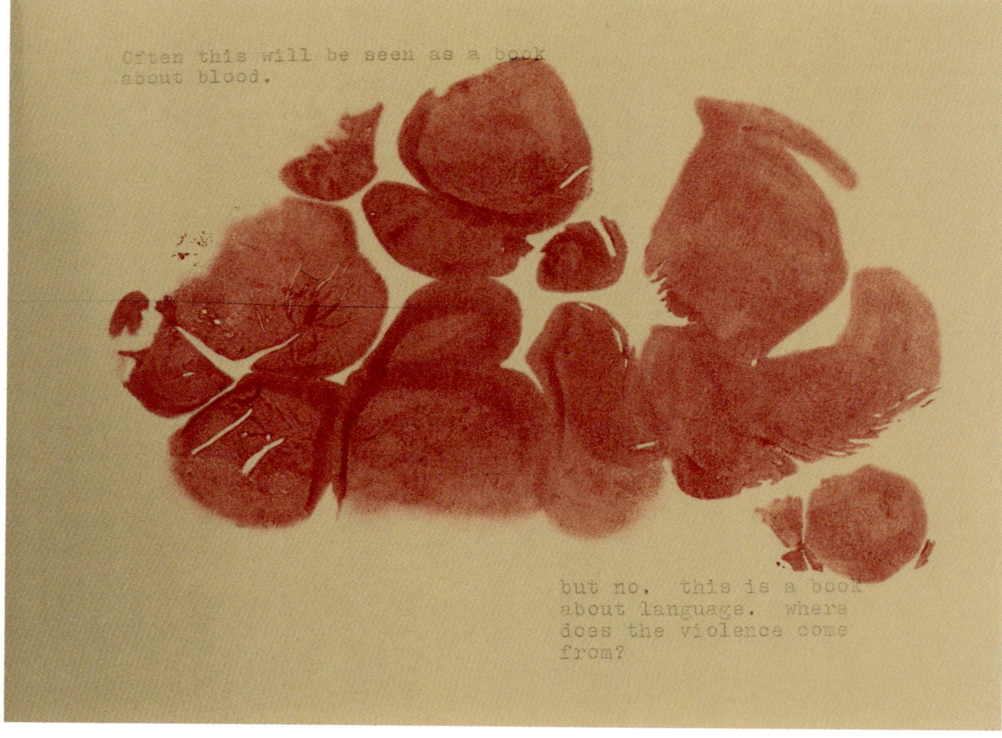

Anatomy Lesson #4 (1977)

These uncanny, dreamlike pictures show the artist serenely floating in or lying beside a pool with sheep organs positioned on or near her torso as if she has been eviscerated. Lacy explored different compositions and sequences of the images. Several of her earlier body-based works used imagery of organs and peeling skin to suggest psychological states such as the humiliation of exposure or the experience of confinement.

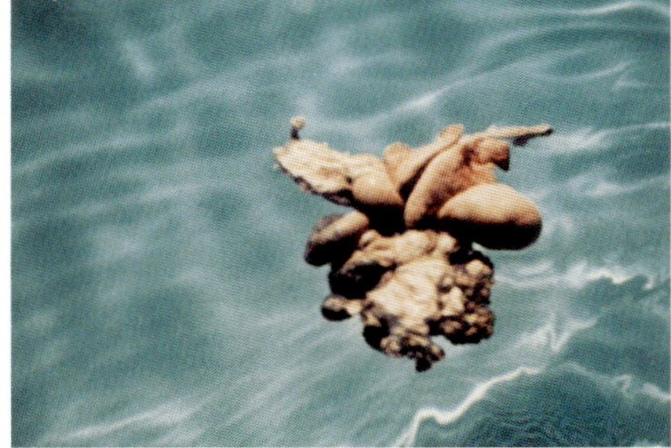

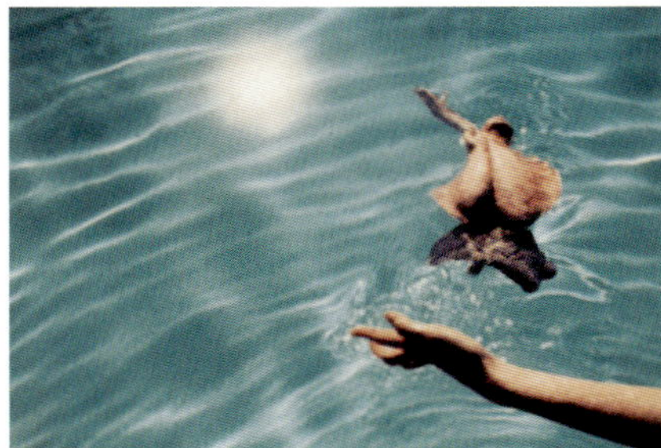

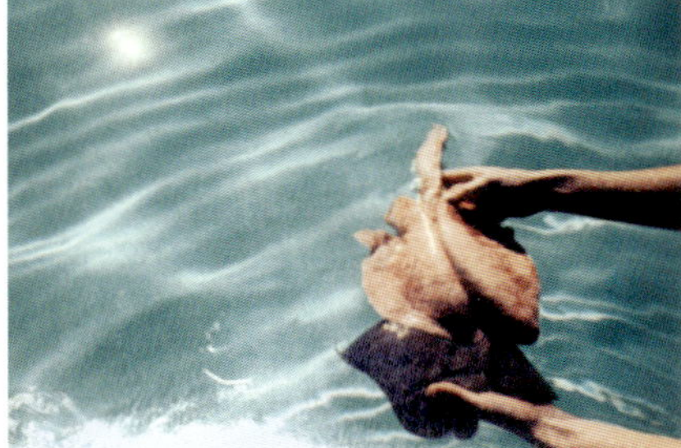

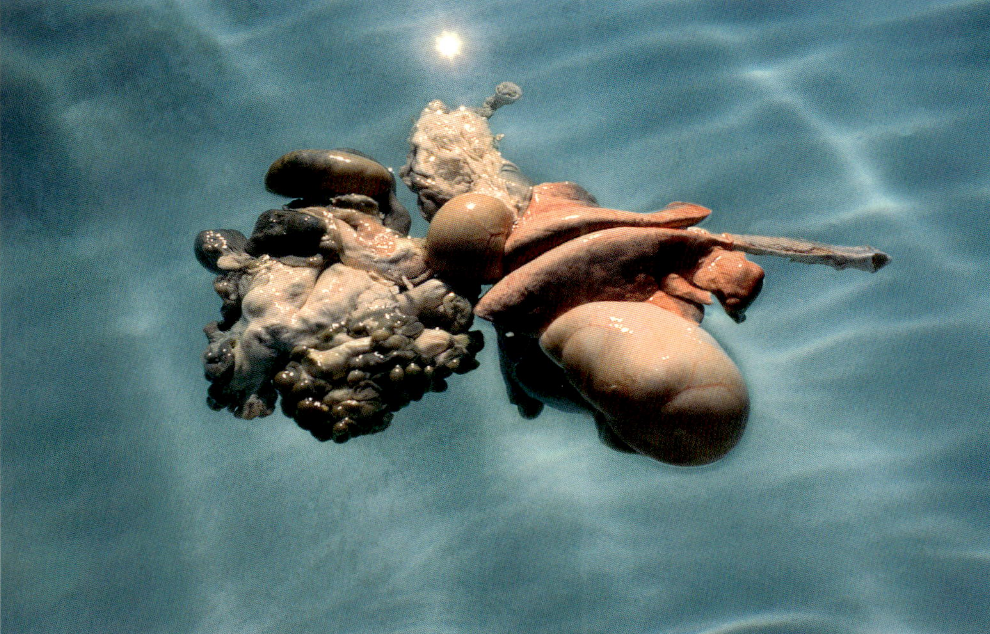

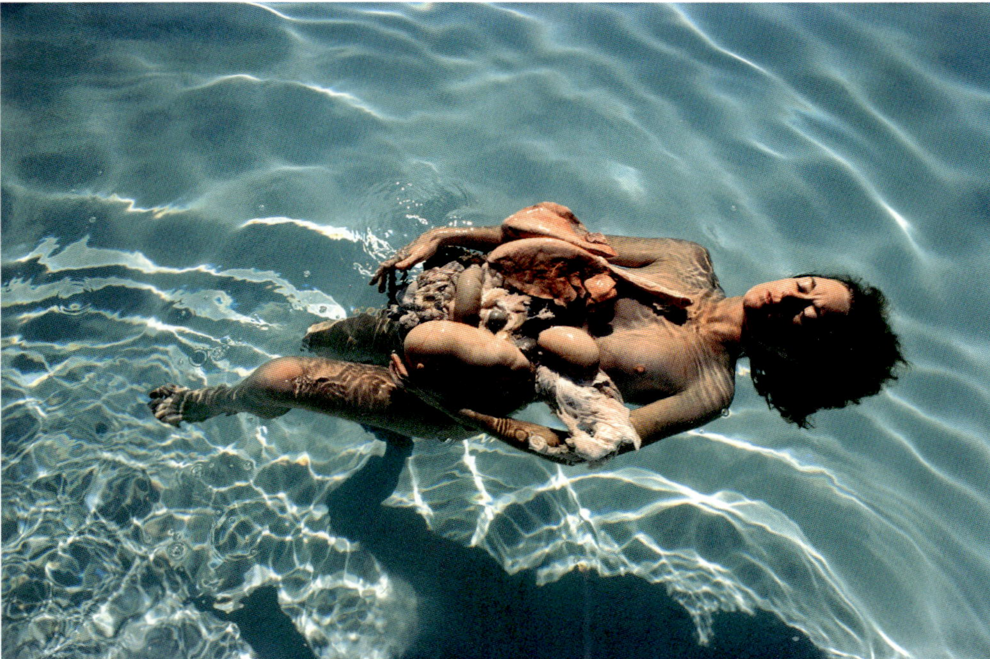

ABOVE: *Anatomy Lesson #4: Flying*
TOP RIGHT: *Anatomy Lesson #4: Still Life*
BOTTOM RIGHT: *Anatomy Lesson #4: Dreaming*
FOLLOWING PAGES: *Anatomy Lesson #4: Untitled*

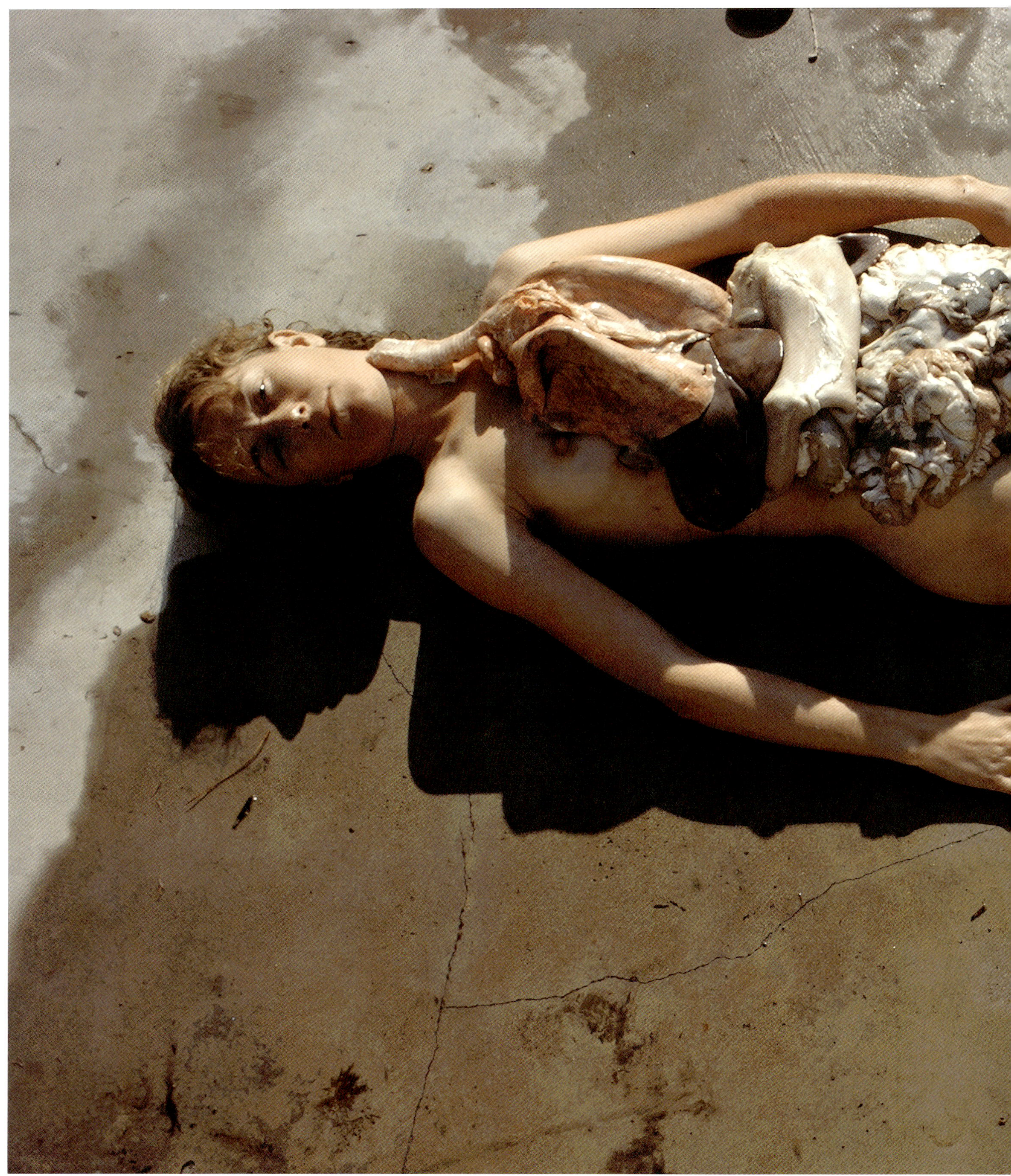

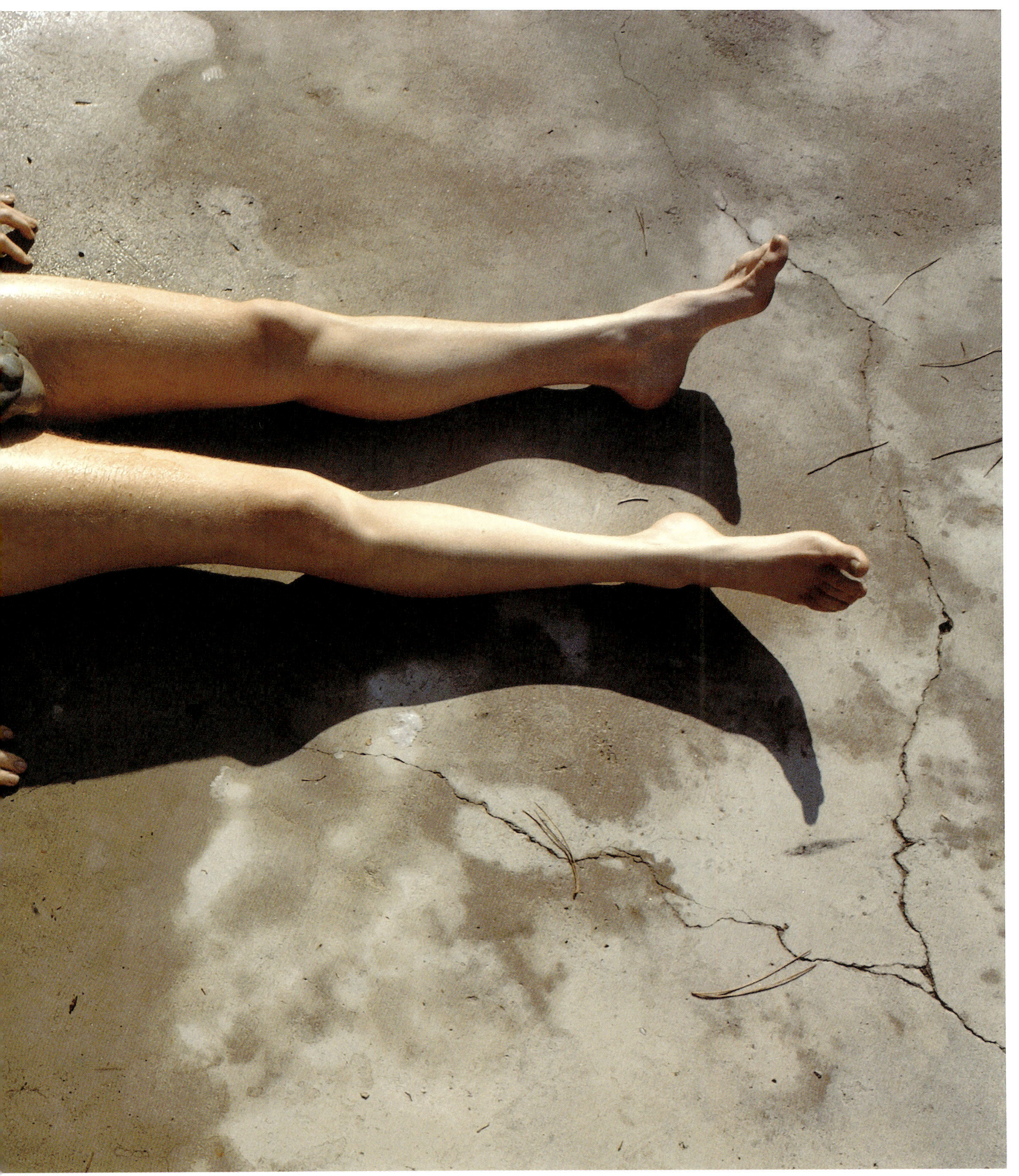

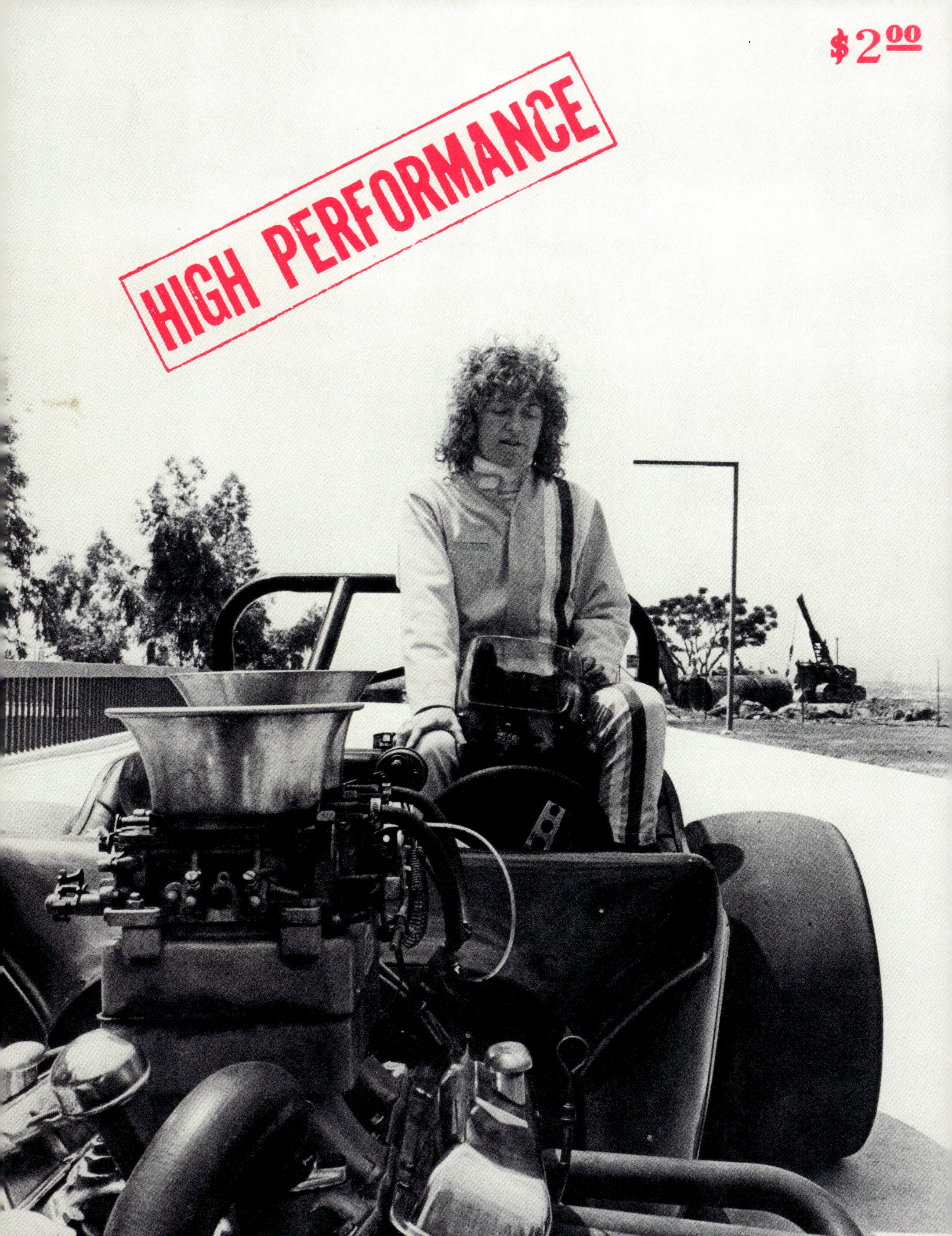

$2.00
HIGH PERFORMANCE

PERSONAS

Lacy participated in the burgeoning performance scene in Southern California during the 1970s as an artist and an educator at multiple schools. She belonged to the pioneering faculty of the Feminist Studio Workshop at the Woman's Building in Los Angeles, which fostered a community that integrated art and activism. Her curatorial projects there—including the exhibition *Performance!* (1974) at Womanspace Gallery and a conference in 1975—were among the first to highlight performance art by women. As a member of the cooperative Grandview Galleries in the Woman's Building complex, she developed a performance structure in *One Woman Shows* (1975) that created a chain of invitations designed to also include women who were not artists. The performance *Cinderella in a Dragster* (1976, p. 72) framed her role as a visiting lecturer and the mobile lifestyle of commuting to teach in Los Angeles, San Francisco, and San Diego.

During this period Lacy also began to contribute to the international discourse on performance, Conceptual art, and the rise of artist-run galleries through writings and interviews in various periodicals, as well as through artist-produced publications, which offered another form of alternative space.[1] Her forays into mail art included *Travels with Mona* (1977–78, p. 84), which adopted the format of fold-out tourist postcards. There and in *In the Last Throes of Artistic Vision* (1980, pp. 86–87), Lacy employed paint-by-number replicas of great masterpieces to parody "high art" and the romantic idea of the monolithic artist. These works comment on the role of performance artists in attempting to formulate a new discipline.

Many of Lacy's contemporaries examined the intersections of private and public experience through character explorations. At issue for feminists was how the construction of identity affected the lives of women, and their alternate personas were often encountered by passersby in the streets. Lacy was interested in the possibility of identifying with others, in moving inside a character to represent a social status or condition. Her character-based works often incorporated aspects of her own autobiography and voice. In several performances, starting with *Inevitable Associations* (1976, pp. 74–77), Lacy transformed her physical appearance from that of a thirty-year-old to that of an elderly woman using prosthetic makeup applied by a Hollywood makeup artist. She would continue in the next decade to critically respond to the relative invisibility of older women in American society on a much larger scale, through events that brought numerous participants into the dialogue.

One strategy of Lacy's performances was to include a moment of transparency about the development of a given piece. In the third part of *The Life and Times of Donaldina Cameron* (1977, pp. 82–83), Lacy and Kathleen Chang stepped out of character to share how they addressed problems that arose in creating the performance together. It was among the first works to confront racial and cultural divisions within the women's movement. The context for that site-specific performance was the historic feminist action *(H)errata*, led by Lynn Hershman Leeson's The Floating Museum in response to a San Francisco Museum of Modern Art (SFMOMA) program series that featured only men. For this public critique of gender inequality, pieces by women artists were presented simultaneously and at the same outdoor sites as the artworks sponsored by SFMOMA.[2]

—TANYA ZIMBARDO

NOTES

1. The artist Howardena Pindell first characterized artists' publications as an alternative space in her article "Alternative Space: Artists' Periodicals," *The Print Collector's Newsletter* 8, no. 4 (September/October 1977): 96–109, 120–21.

2. *Installation and Performance Pieces: Golden Gate National Recreation Area* (1977) was organized in conjunction with the touring exhibition *America 1976*. A "museum without walls," The Floating Museum produced temporary and site-specific works in public and nontraditional spaces from 1975 to 1978. Lacy was included in two of its exhibitions in 1977 and 1978.

OPPOSITE: *Cinderella in a Dragster* (1976, p. 72) illustrated on the cover of the first issue of *High Performance* (1978)

Autobiography of a Young Vampire (ca. 1974–75)

"Once upon a time a little Dracula was born in the small town of Wasco." Lacy developed an "autobiographical" tale about her childhood as a vampire that appeared in published writings and that she integrated as material into a performance. She made a series of collage, ink, and gouache interventions into her family snapshots, using consecutive close-ups of one photo altered to reveal baby vampire teeth as imagery in *Under My Skin: A True-Life Story* (1975/1977, p. 55).

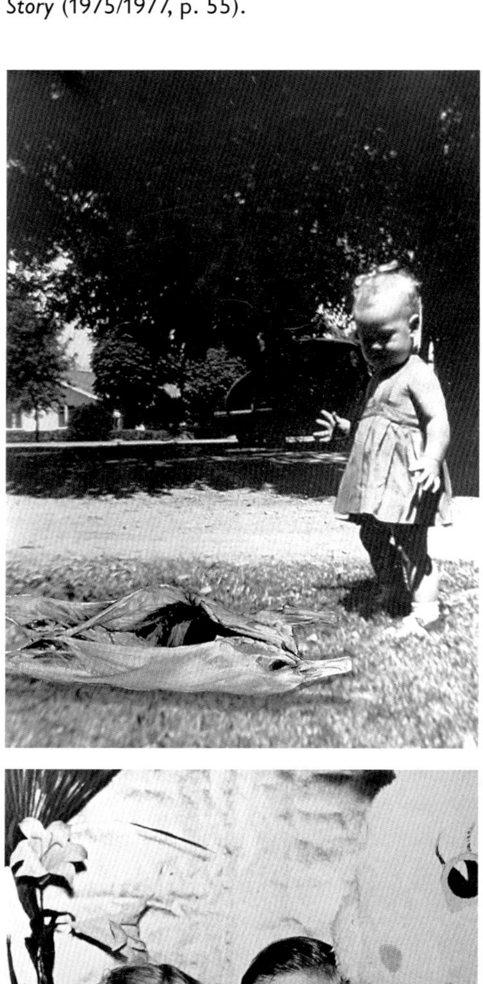

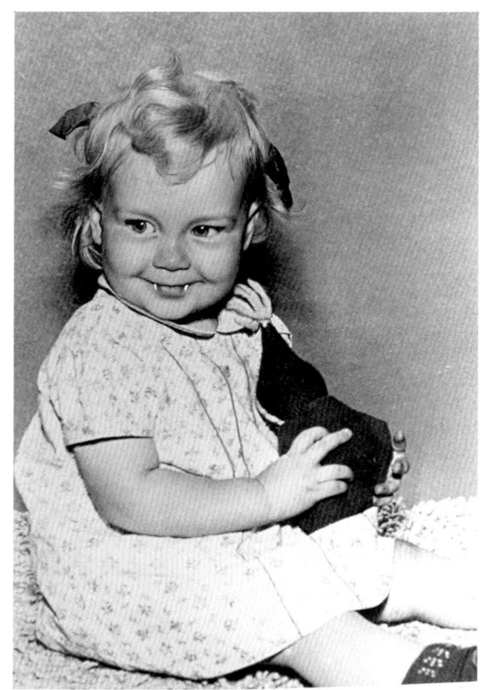

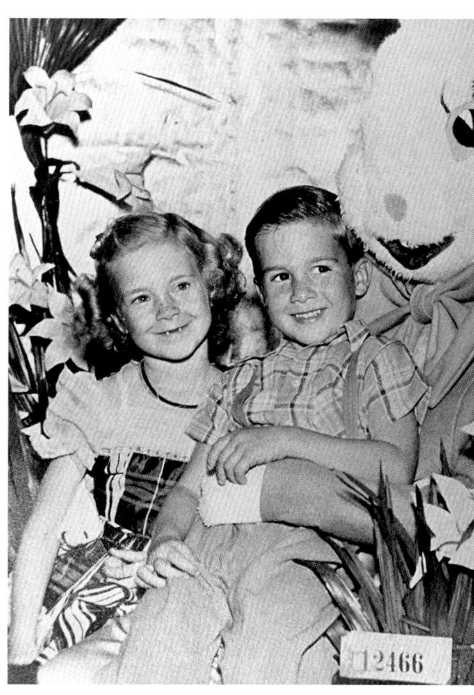

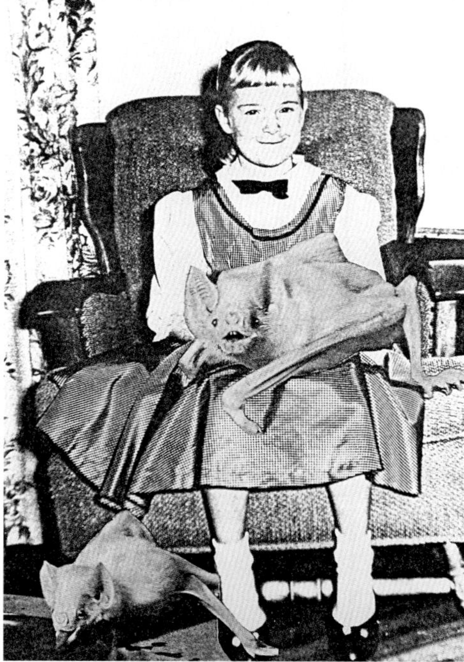

Running to San Francisco (1975)

Lacy made her weekly trip from her home in Los Angeles to the San Francisco Art Institute, where she taught a class, in a track uniform for this performance. She timed herself and posed for the camera like an athlete for a news profile. One photograph would appear alongside a diaristic entry in *Prostitution Notes* (1974–75, pp. 90–93), where Lacy describes "the act of performing in total awareness of each moment. I ran, I was always running in the piece, and what I didn't say was I was experiencing the usual fear that propels me through action."

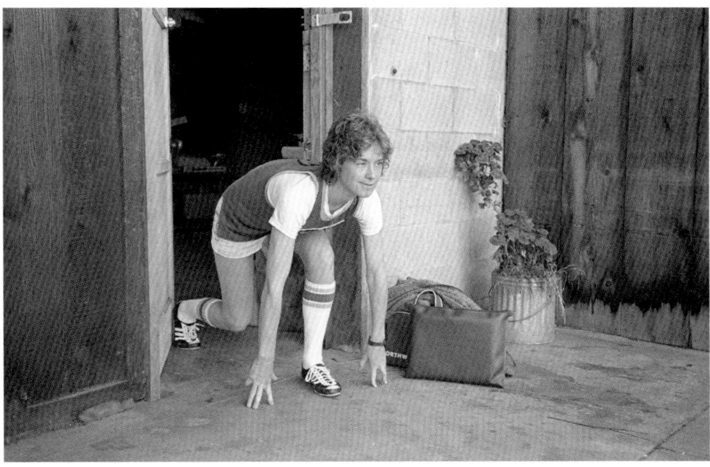

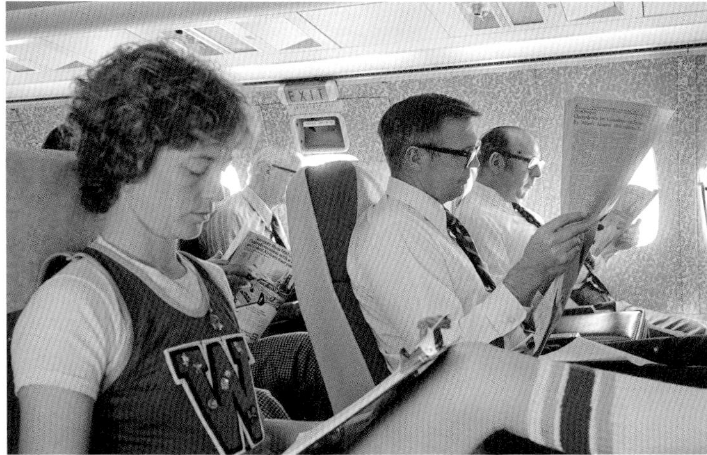

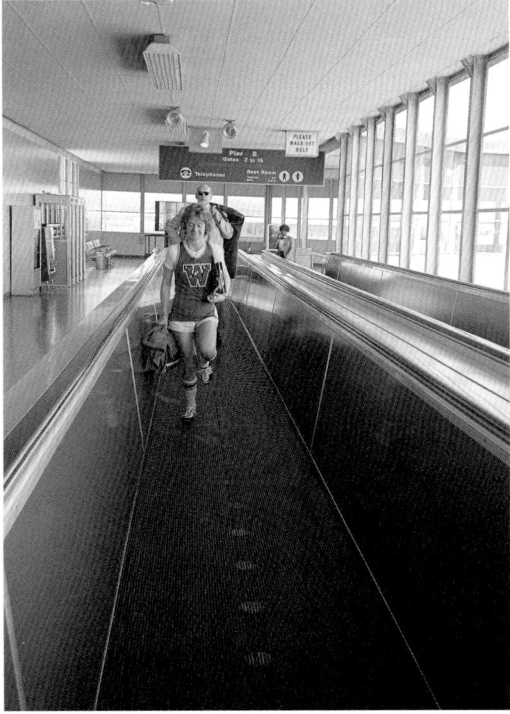

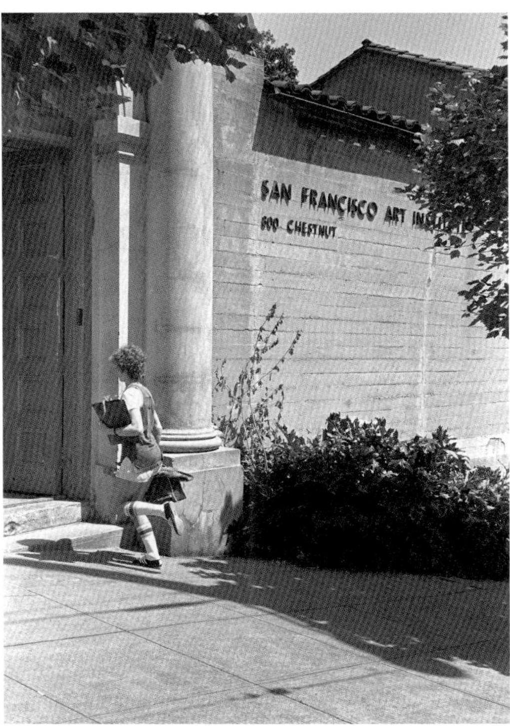

Cinderella in a Dragster (1976)

Lacy drove onto the campus of California State College, Dominguez Hills (now California State University, Dominguez Hills), Carson, in a yellow jumpsuit and a borrowed dragster. Near the library, she delivered a rapid-fire monologue about time and movement across space. Beginning with her childhood in Wasco, California, she calculated the exponential growth of her daily travels up to that week, in which she crossed the state to teach in San Francisco, Los Angeles, and San Diego. She likened artists to Cinderella: "The sign of visibility for an artist, and that might include anybody, is the ability to survive the collapse of one fairy tale and the creation of the next, that is, to not get stuck in the myth. It's a time-honored quotation in performance art which goes, 'Don't ever forget: what is a carriage today might be a pumpkin tomorrow.' " At the end, she tossed a glass slipper out of the dragster and drove off.

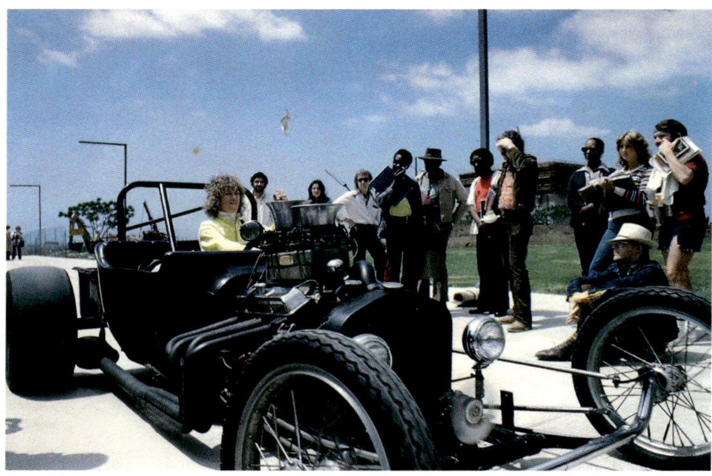 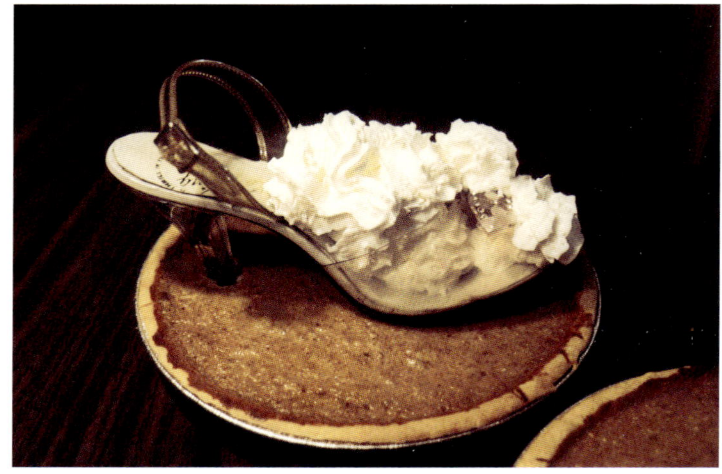

I went to the Grand Prix Racetracks to drive one of their formula cars around the track. You pay a dollar a lap, which mounts up quickly since a satisfactory time is under three minutes a lap. You pay your dollar then you drive for all you're worth, trying to make each lap in a shorter time. Or you can collapse time by doing two things at once, like putting on nylons as you drive down the Santa Monica Freeway, listening to music on your way from working as a carpenter to attending an art opening.

Sometimes the rate of acceleration gets too intense and my body protests, like it did a few nights ago, by getting sick. One thing they never tell you about Cinderella: she changed three times in three days (if you read the French version she went to the ball twice) and then she lived happily ever after. But did she get sick before the happy part?

Now you may be wondering what all of this has to do with art, or at least performance art, and that brings us to Cinderella. Because Cinderella is a fairy tale and that's a lot like performance art, creating elaborate structures so that everything in your life seems to relate to the story at hand. When I was young, in Wasco, I never noticed cars, or at least made a point of not noticing them (I had decided it was superficial to be interested in cars). But since I've been doing this piece I've looked at cars, met drag racing drivers (a couple of them are here now), and read car magazines; I've learned the difference between formula cars and dragsters and funny cars, and I've seen that there are some people—and probably quite a few—who embrace acceleration.

So, whatever it is that I experience in this lifestyle as it intersects with mine I synthesize into an image and that's this one which hangs in the air between us now, that's this fairy tale about how Cinderella became a metaphor for my life as a metaphoric drag racer. Then this image and this information becomes a point of contact between you and me, and my life becomes, in this limited sense, your own material, out of which you will make your images, and that may be art and it may be something else, if only anecdote.

LEFT: *Cinderella in a Dragster*, April 28, 1976
RIGHT: *Cinderella Cooks a Pumpkin Pie*, the second part of the performance, in which Lacy met her class at the University of California, San Diego, wearing one glass slipper and carrying a pumpkin, April 28, 1976

Edna, May Victor, Mary, and Me:
An All-Night Benediction (1977)

For a College Art Association conference at the Hilton Hotel in Los Angeles, Lacy created an all-night performance filmed by Nancy Angelo and Linda Montano and broadcast live to televisions in the hotel rooms. Made-up as an elderly woman, she sorted through various items belonging to Edna, May Victor, and Mary—three older female friends whom Lacy had worked with on the performance *Inevitable Associations* (1976, pp. 74–77)—while tape-recorded monologues by the women offered ruminations on aging. Occasionally the program was interrupted by an audio or textual command to stay tuned, and Lacy periodically tended to a concealed form in the bed. In the early hours of the morning she finally lifted the form, a lamb carcass, out of the bed, placed it on a chair, and climbed into the bed in its place to sleep.

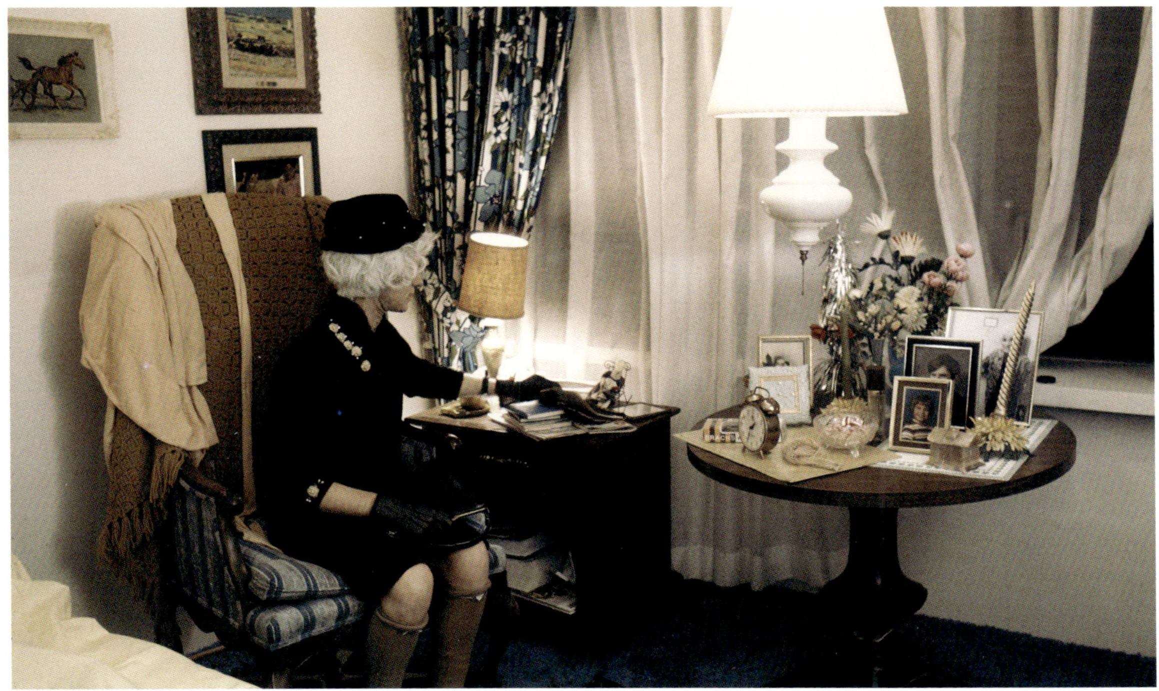

Inevitable Associations (1976)

This two-day performance, the first in a series exploring aging women, was staged for the American Theater Association at the Biltmore Hotel, Los Angeles, at the invitation of David Antin, Frantisek Deak, and Allan Kaprow. On day one, Lacy placed three demonstration booths in the lobby. The first provided information on the hotel's renovation and the attendant media coverage. At the second, a surgeon's assistant provided "before and after" information on plastic surgery. At the final booth, a Hollywood makeup artist aged Lacy with prosthetics while ten old women dressed in black slowly filled a long line of red chairs. When Lacy's makeup was finished, the women surrounded her and pulled black clothes from their purses to dress her. With the transformation complete, they all posed together in the red chairs as a tableau. The next day an audience was seated in three circles, each with a red chair for a woman from the previous day's performance. Lacy discussed her interpretation of aging through text-based slides, after which the older women talked about their lives after sixty.

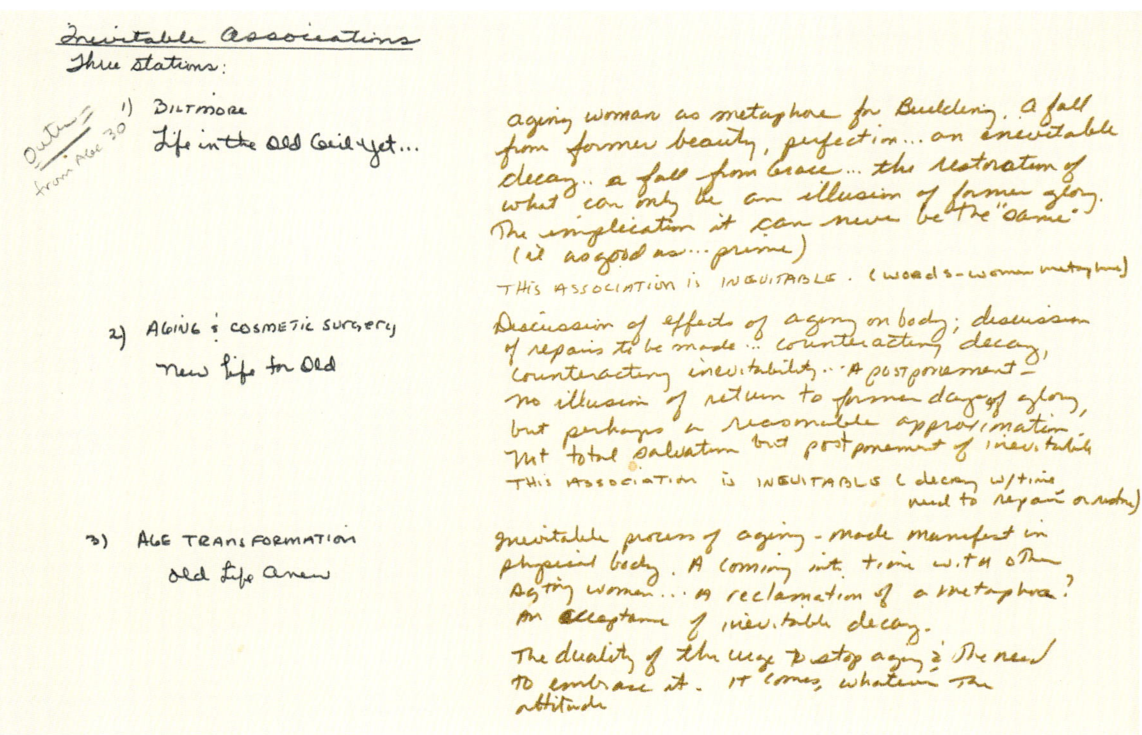

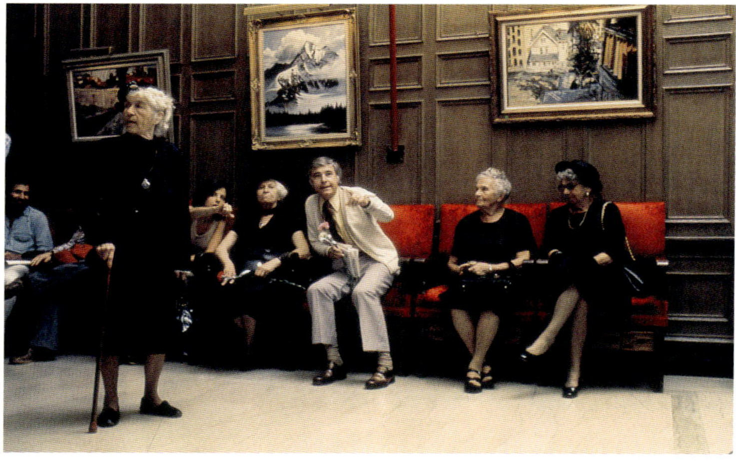

TOP: Notes on the concepts of the three stations
BOTTOM: Norma Jean Deak (foreground) and other performers "invade" the space of the audience in the hotel lobby, August 8, 1976
OPPOSITE, BOTTOM: Photo and preparatory sketch of the first booth featuring an attendant, Cheri Gaulke, with news clippings comparing the building to an aging widow

he Biltmore: Life in the Old Girl Yet

Renovation Under Way on Olive St. Dowager

BY LYNN SIMROSS
Times Staff Writer

"In spite of all that has been said of California and its sunshine and oranges and the blueness of the ocean off its shores, there is still some uncertainty in the East as to the accommodations for travelers out here. The wild and woolly idea dies hard . . . I see great changes in the city since I was here last (1913), but of all the improvements the Biltmore ranks first. Without doubt it's the finest hotel in the world."

—Albert S. Crockett of New York City, editor of World Traveler magazine, the day after he saw the Los Angeles Biltmore open on Oct. 1, 1923.

Oh, Mr. Crockett. We aren't wild and woolly anymore, but it's been a while since the old Biltmore was first in anything. She has spent her recent years as a somewhat dowdy dowager, plaster peeling from some of her ceilings, carpets faded and torn.

The Biltmore went the way of Pershing Square, that once-lovely park in front of her on Olive St., between 5th and 6th. They grew old ungracefully together: the park became a haven for downtown vagrants, panhandlers; the Biltmore a transient home for foreign tour groups that had not got the word that she had slipped from her pedestal.

The Biltmore still hosts conventions—film groups, Shriners, various trade organizations, a recent White House consumer conference. But things are not as they were in her prime when kings and queens and presidents, athletes and aviators were her guests. Academy Awards ceremonies, held at the Biltmore in 1931, 1935-39, 1941-42, have moved elsewhere. The last large gathering of political luminaries under her roof was in 1960 when the Biltmore was headquarters hotel for the Democrats, holding their national convention at the Sports Arena to nominate John F. Kennedy.

Although the downstairs ballrooms, lobby and meeting rooms have been kept in better repair than the guest

BILTMORE GIRL—Peggy Hamilton, official hostess for Biltmore's opening, recalls hotel as "mecca for royalty, stars."
Times photo by Larry Bessel

BILTMORE DRESS—Miss Hamilton in special 1923 gown.

Suzanne was an excellent mentor—part nurturing mother, part drill sergeant. . . . In *Inevitable Associations*, I played the "smartly clad woman" handing out news articles that compared the Biltmore Hotel to an aging dowager. In a culture that devalues older women, her performance affirmed their wisdom and beauty. Now, at sixty-four, I appreciate that even more than I did then.

—Cheri Gaulke, participant, 2018

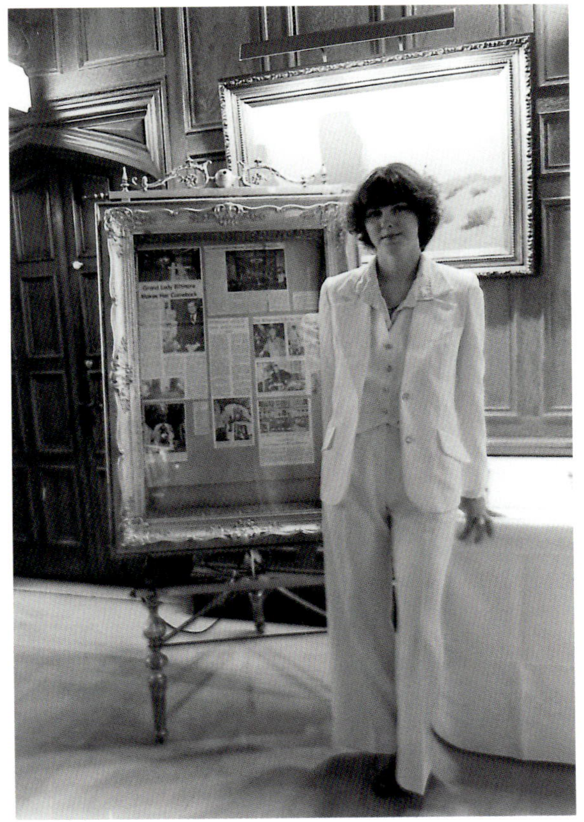

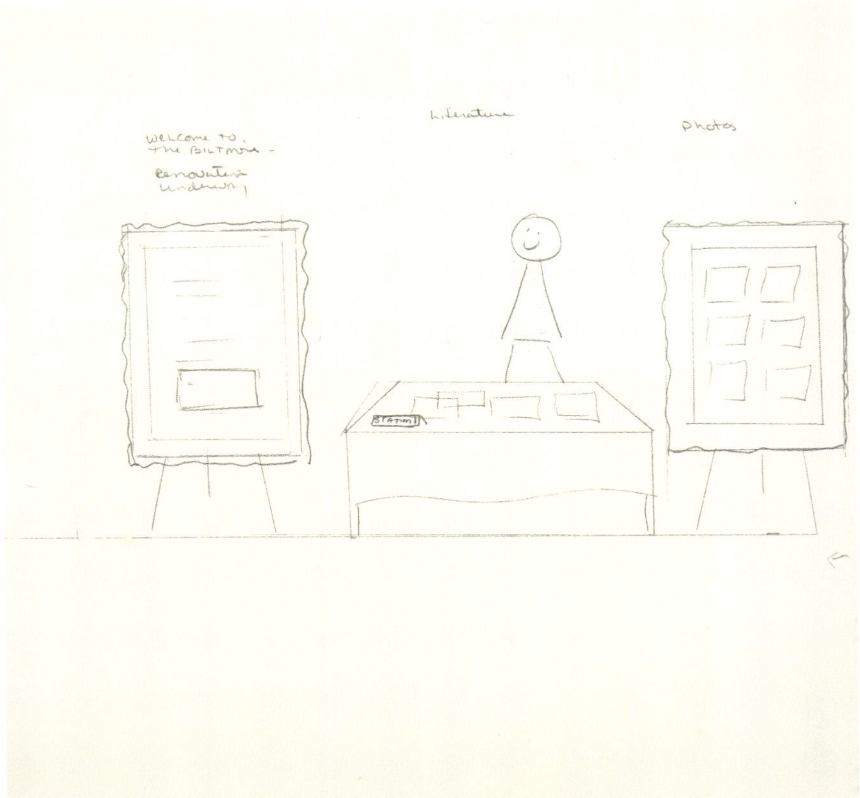

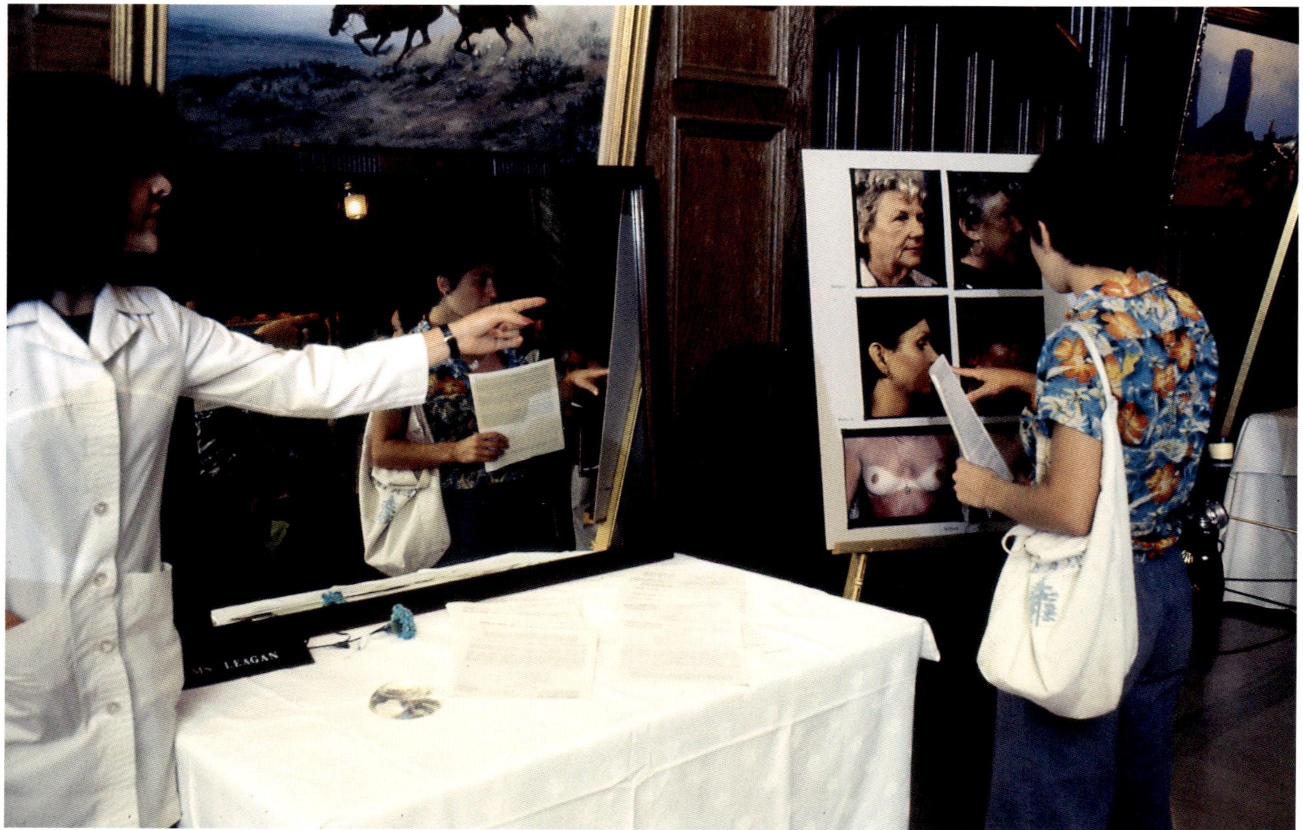

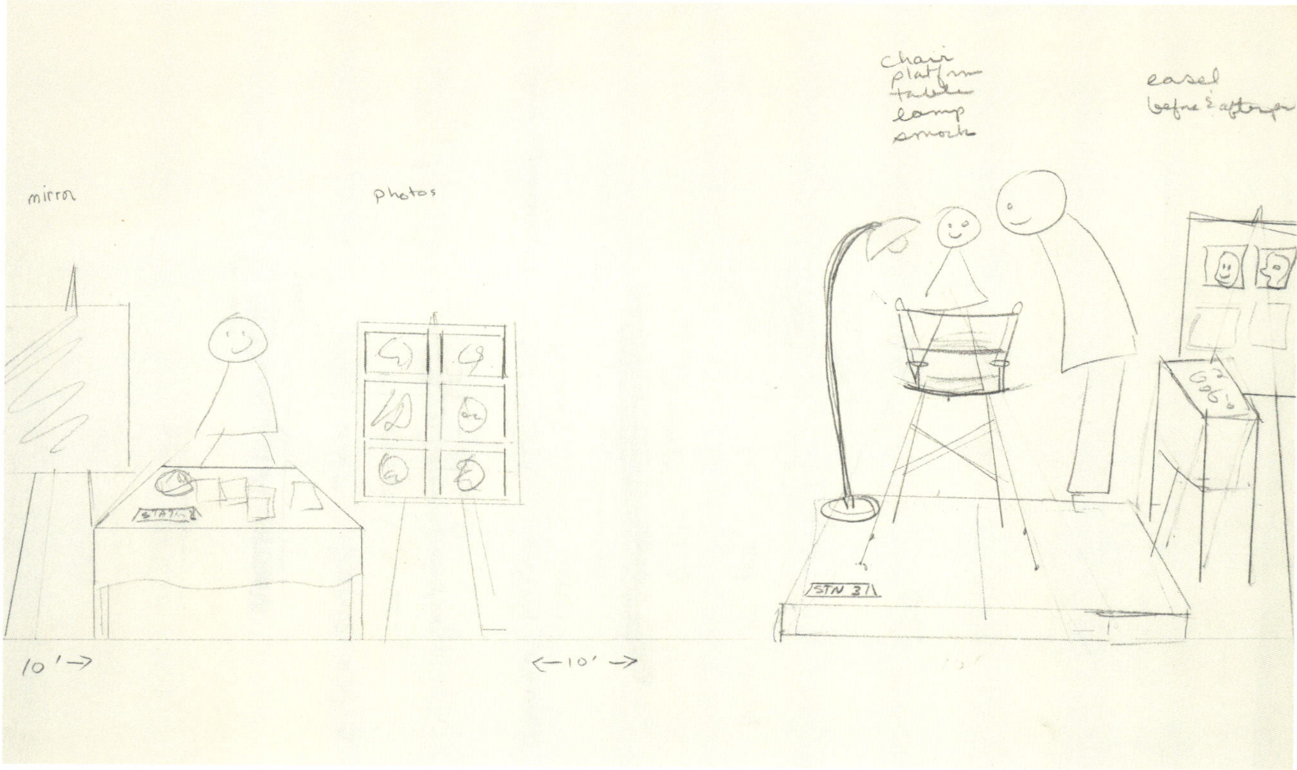

Photo and preparatory sketch of the second booth
OPPOSITE, TOP: Lacy having prosthetic makeup applied at the third booth

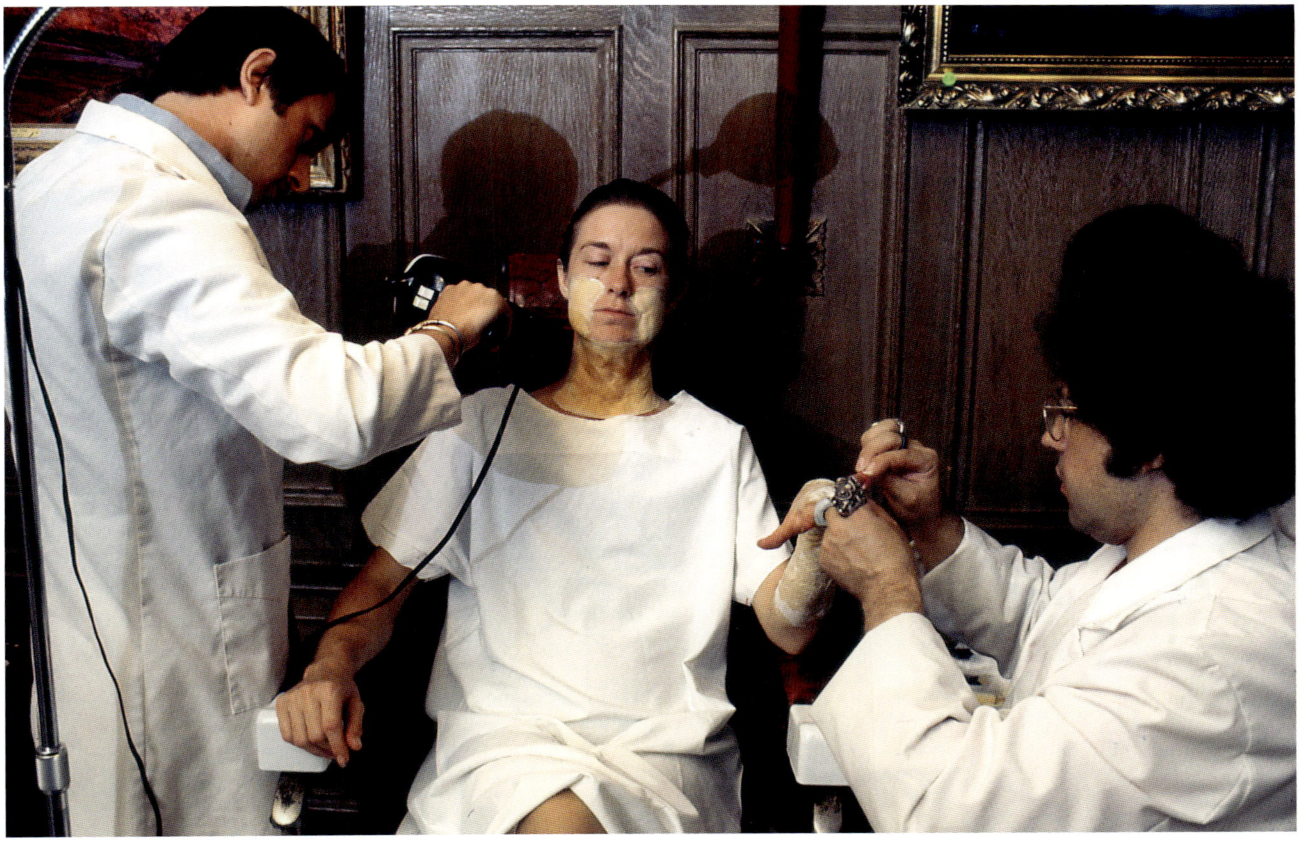

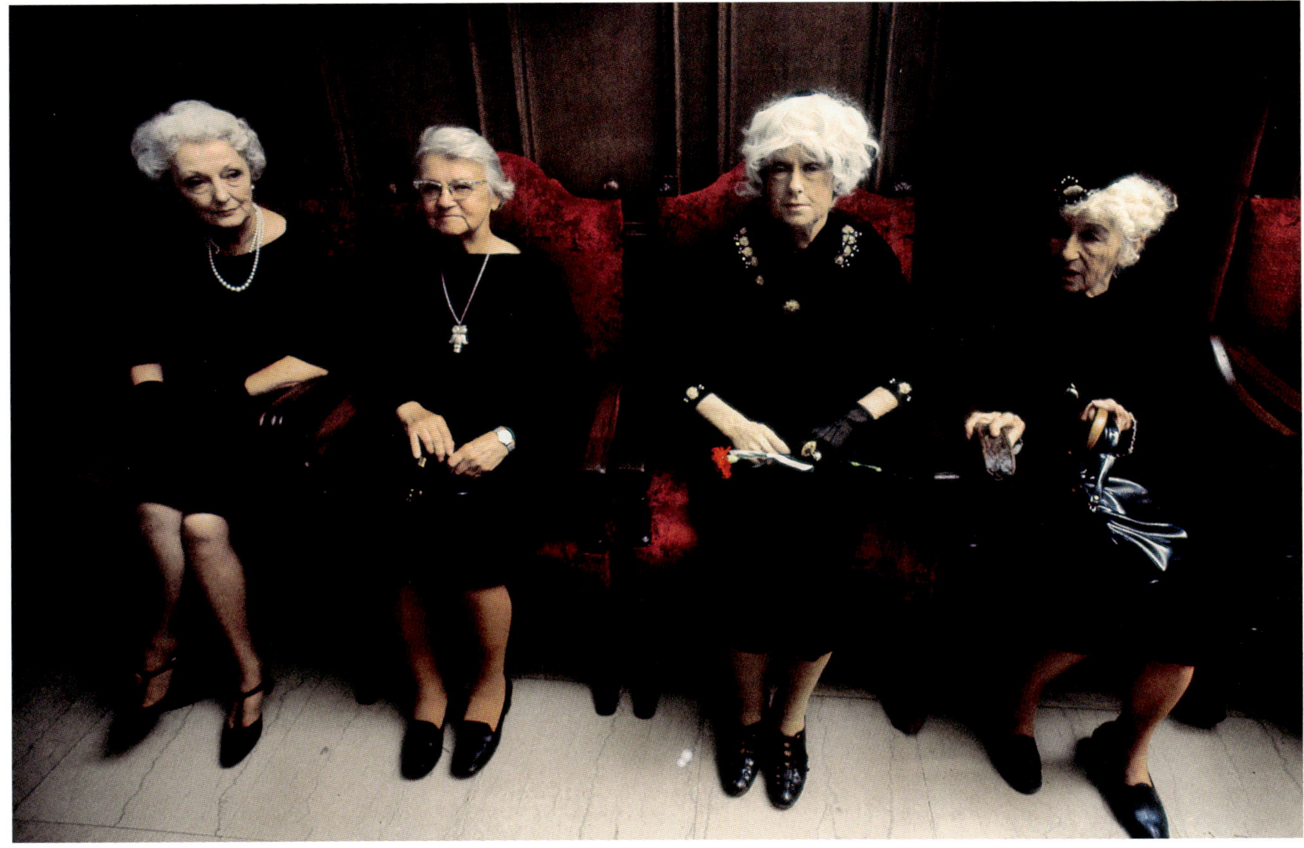

The Bag Lady (1977)

Dressed as a "bag lady" clutching several shopping bags, Lacy slept in the doorway of the Fine Arts Museums of San Francisco Downtown Center as visitors stepped over her. She then entered the gallery with a shopping cart and meandered through the exhibition *Cityscapes: San Francisco and Los Angeles*, stopping repeatedly to rearrange her possessions. Overhead speakers featured anecdotes narrated by an elderly friend about digging through trash, collecting tinsel, and packaging leftovers, all drawn from the artist's childhood. The soundtrack then deconstructed the making of the performance: Lacy explained how she had transported trash from Los Angeles to San Francisco and tried unsuccessfully to engage a homeless woman. When Lacy encountered her again in the Civic Center area, the woman began yelling about being left alone to no one in particular. Only Lacy knew it was a direct communication to her.

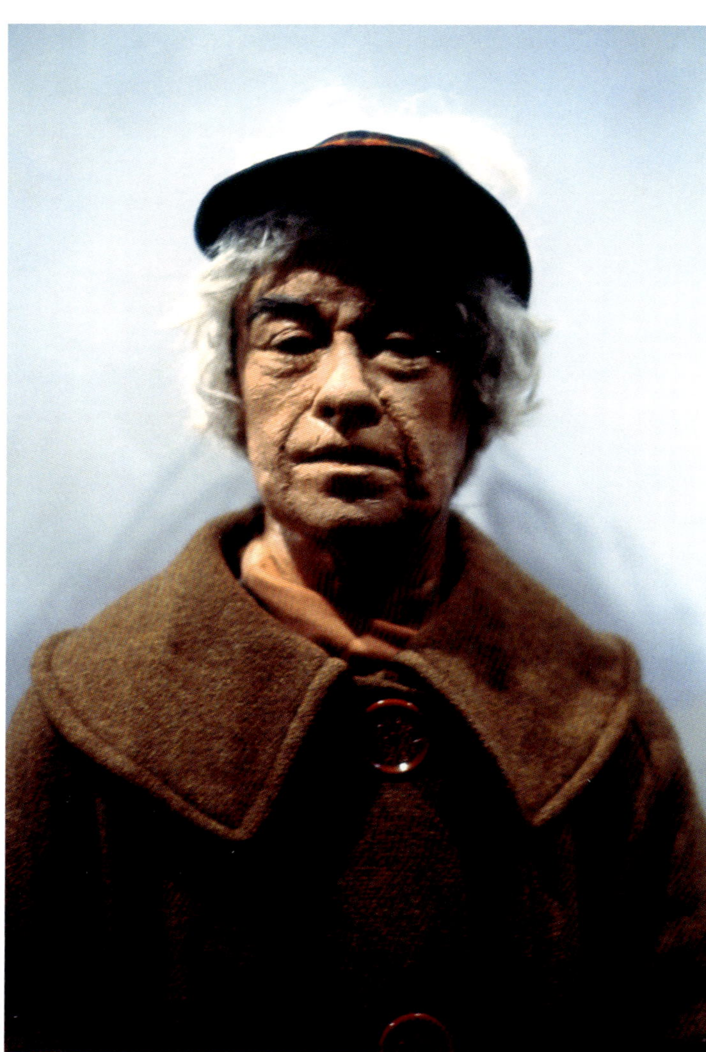

Forgetting

grandmother's discarded purse
orange juice's plastic container
platform tennis shoes from a sale
Leonard Cohen's second album
ceramic saucer as cat dish
what I looked like at 20
yellow dish draining rack
six inches purple flowered fabric
recyclable aluminum cans
photoplay magazines from 1975
faded orange acrylic blanket
life-sized Davy Crockett doll
three used nylon support hose
dried gardenia prom corsage
bottle wishbone french dressing
teflon coated sauce pan
almost every letter ever received
turquoise melmac plate
two mismatched orlon socks
leather bag that no longer zips
set of toy horses
a hardback copy of "Arrowsmith"
assorted knives and forks
old women on Los Angeles street corners

—Suzanne Lacy, excerpt from article
"The Bag Lady," 1982

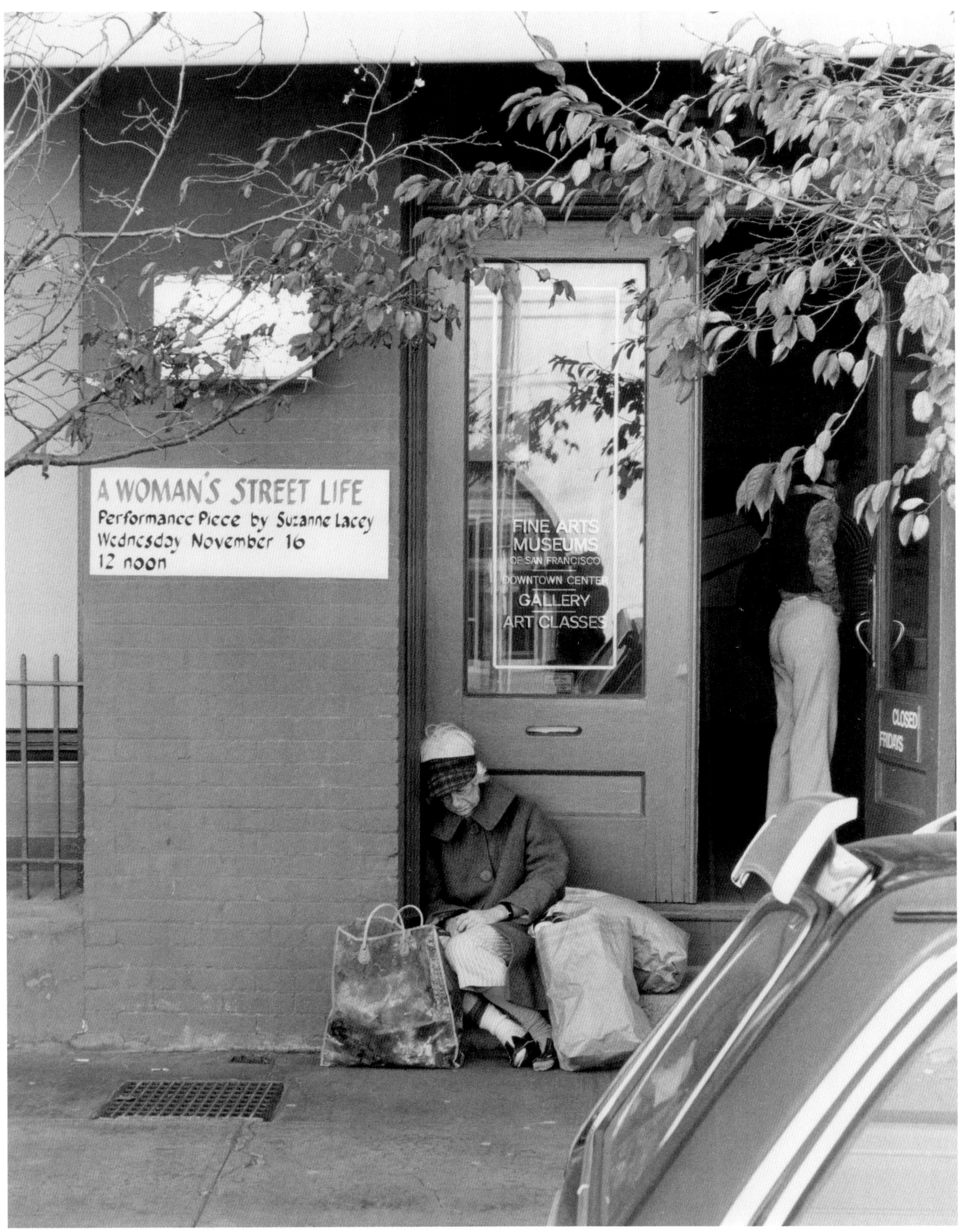

A WOMAN'S STREET LIFE
Performance Piece by Suzanne Lacey
Wednesday November 16
12 noon
FINE ARTS
MUSEUMS
OF SAN FRANCISCO
DOWNTOWN CENTER
GALLERY
ART CLASSES
CLOSED
FRIDAYS

The Vigil/Incorporate (1978)

SUZANNE LACY AND BARBARA T. SMITH

The all-night performance of *The Vigil* took place at the University Art Gallery, University of California, Irvine. Lacy, as an elderly woman, and Smith, as a young girl spirit, occupied two bedroom environments and wrote stream-of-consciousness texts on the gallery walls throughout the evening. The audience was asleep when the artists unwrapped the body—a lamb carcass—in Lacy's bed and suspended it from the ceiling. *Incorporate* took place later, during an opening at Los Angeles Contemporary Exhibitions. Dressed in white, Lacy and Smith consumed a cooked shank of lamb with their hands and ritually arranged condiments while a series of artists and scholars— Linda Burnham, Beatrice Manley, Nancy Angelo, Phranc, and Lynn Phillips—performed individual interpretations in response.

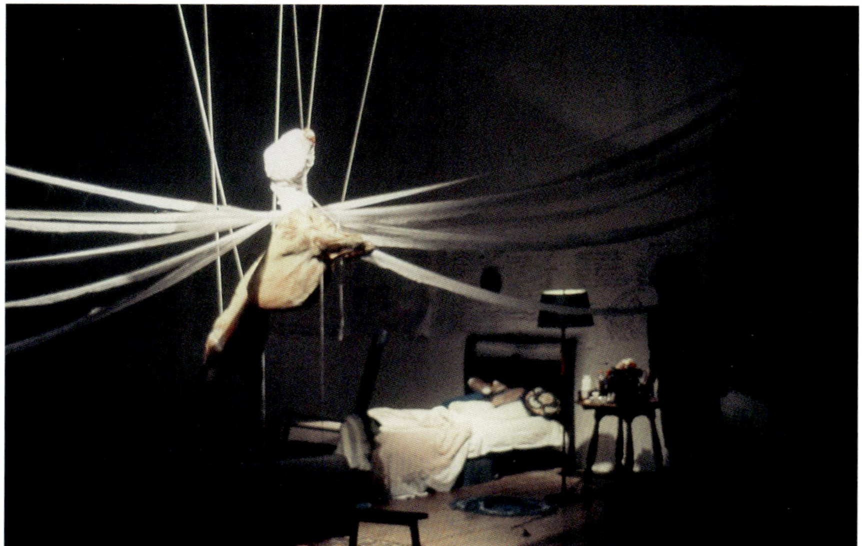

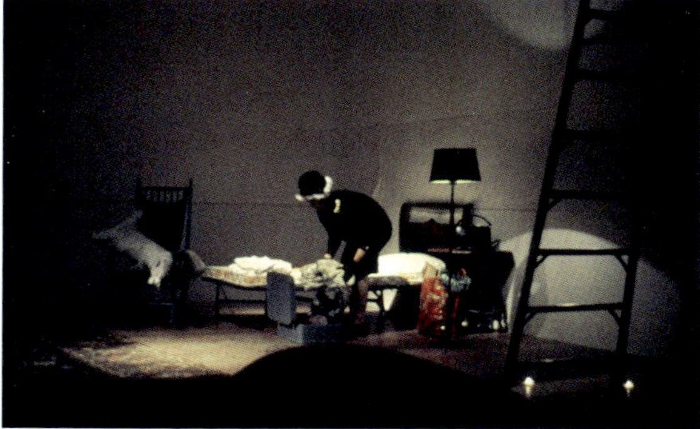

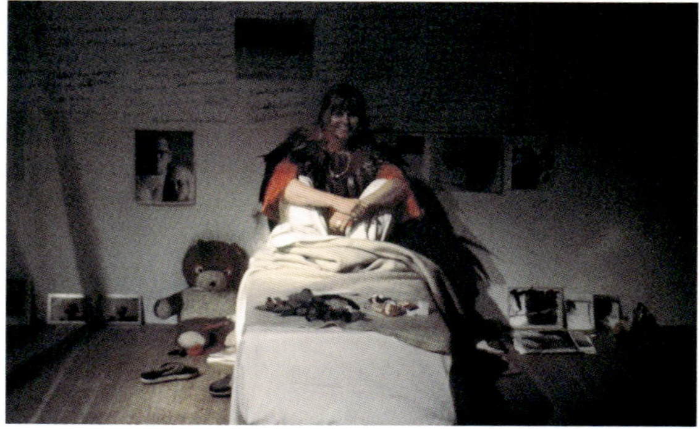

TRANSCRIPT: *The Vigil* (EXCERPT)

I'm beginning to feel a more insistent pressure in my ear . . . pushing against my eardrum. My left ear. What don't I want to hear from my past?

Is that all garbage, about transcending through a total immersion in the body? A woman's form of flight? Is flight in this body or out of it? Last night when I woke up with an earache at 2:00 a.m., I had been dreaming of slaughtered animals. I still smelled the meat. I think the lamb last week was connected to the earache.

Barbara told me this morning that she had mastitis when she was a little girl and she had to have some of her mastoid bone carved away. I decided I'd better at least see a doctor.

It's like admitting defeat to admit my body can't always heal it-self. Like admitting mortality. It's also stubborn, like my grandmother.

I'm so tired of trying to hold my head up.

—SUZANNE LACY

The Vigil, March 14–15, 1978.
The bandages formed soaring wings over the space as the performers sat waiting for the audience to awaken

TRANSCRIPT: *The Vigil* (EXCERPT)

I am a mother and feel like a child. My skin was always dry and ages very rapidly.

Suzanne is in pain and has a dead lamb in bed with her. I wonder what that means. I see her as any age. She thinks she is already old and I though older and all—am childlike—that's so but not all together. I feel old and enjoy it. I would enjoy slowing down a bit—there's plenty for all to do and plenty of others to do it. I enjoy for example sharing this performance together. I'm wondering where we'll get. We have her EAR and my fatigue, my disengaged feeling. It's cold in here, can we realize anything at all about our bodies? I feel so often not *in* mine and then needy. Very. To love . . . etc. Then wings are odd. I have struggled for wings for a long long time. They are my power and freedom. I have had images of me with wings for a long long time. I must rest and dream of the problems. I can't seem to see it clearly.

It's awful to see oneself aging—it's utterly unbelievable.

Suzanne, have you forgotten something?

—BARBARA T. SMITH

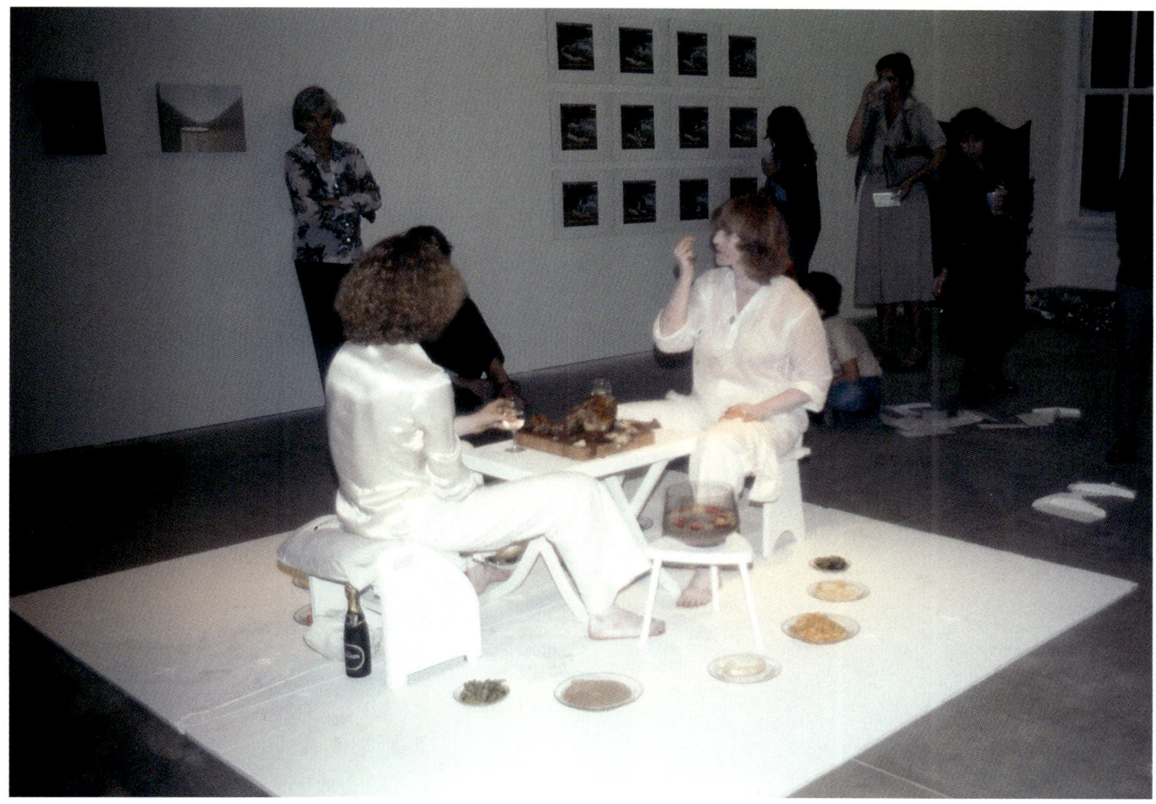

TRANSCRIPT: *The Vigil* (EXCERPT)

SIGNS of the BODY AGING— 1) My appendicitis last year? NO it was told to me that usually only twenty-five-year-olds or younger have their appendices out. 2) An arthritic spur in my knee. YU[C]K. 3) Facial lines. 4) My period is irregular. 5) Not such an urgent desire—irrational passion, *drive* to get the work out. 6) Sense that there are only so many more years and I have *so much* to do. 7) Desire to unite my children. 8) Sense also that there is a whole new beginning now.

But I cannot tell *what* reality *is*!

—BARBARA T. SMITH

The Life and Times of Donaldina Cameron (1977)

SUZANNE LACY AND KATHLEEN CHANG

As a ferry approached Angel Island, the historical point of entry for Asian immigrants in the San Francisco Bay, on October 29, 1977, a schooner sailed past with two women in period clothes. Landing on the island near the ferry port, the women walked up a hill with an audience behind them. At the top they presented two perspectives: Lacy, as the real-life missionary and social reformer Donaldina Cameron, spoke of rescuing Chinese girls smuggled into the country for prostitution and slavery, and Chang, as the fictional immigrant Leung Ken-Sun, spoke of her escape from China to the New World. Their narratives indicted, challenged, and enhanced historical understanding of the role of missionaries. Later, breaking character over a picnic, Lacy and Chang discussed the conflicts they negotiated during their development of the work and their own aesthetic differences regarding performance.

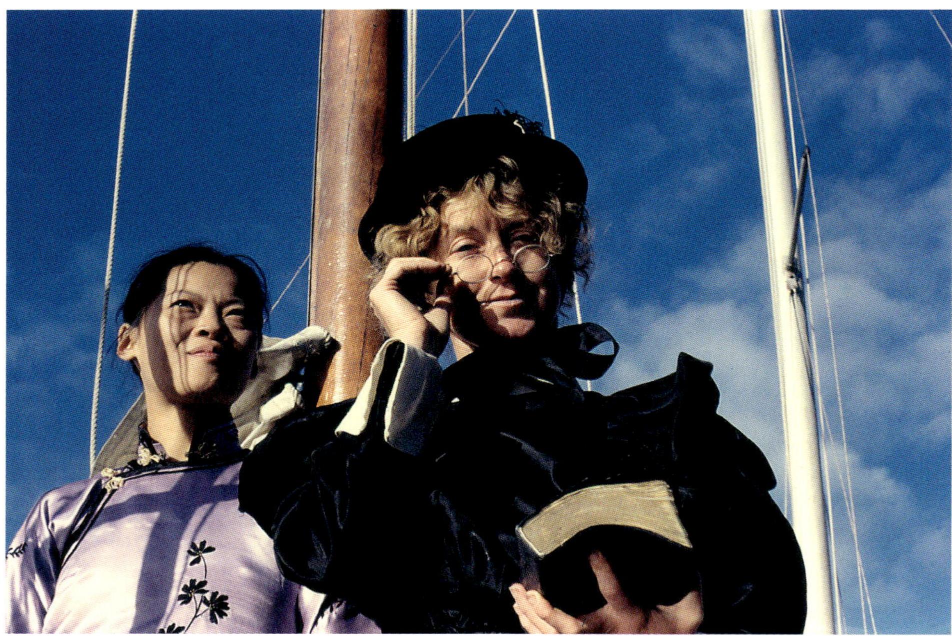

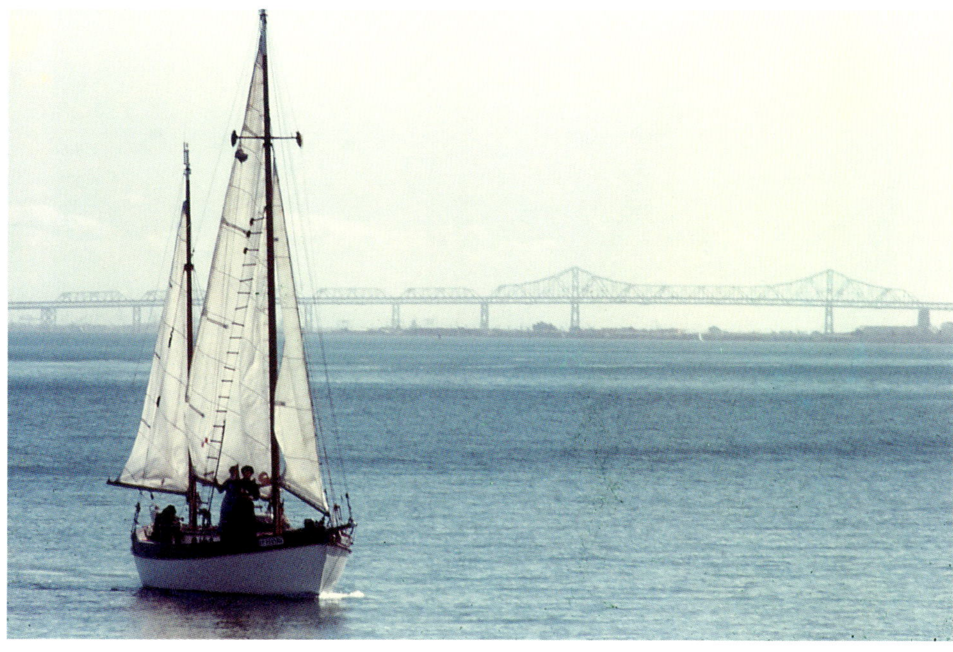

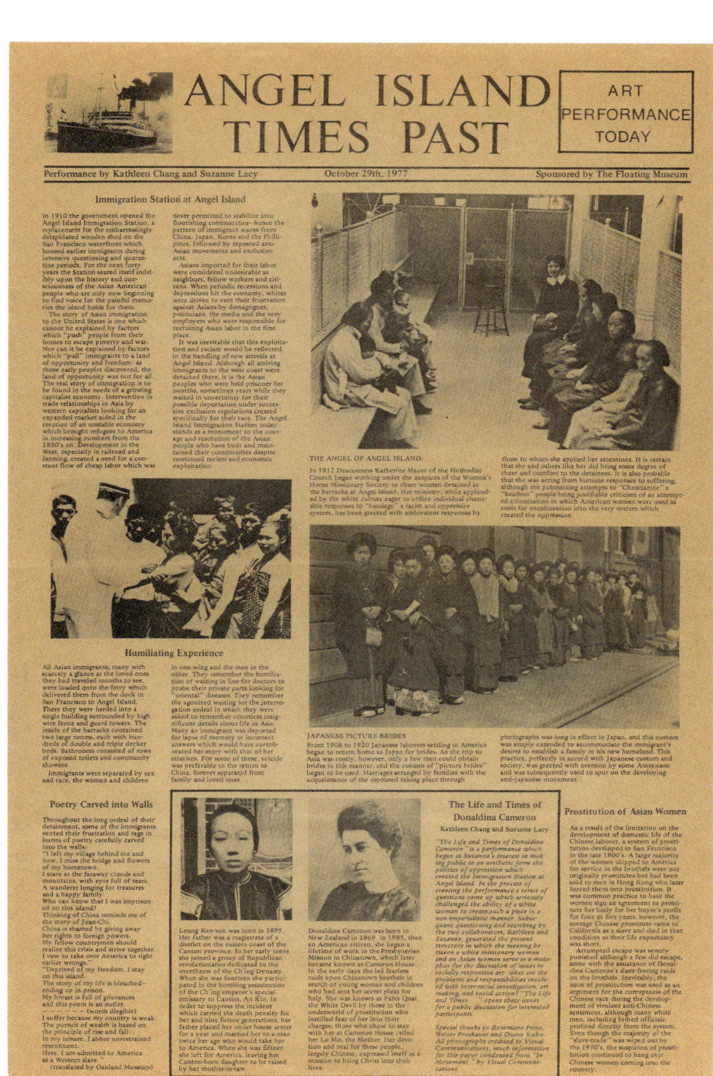

ANGEL ISLAND TIMES PAST

ART PERFORMANCE TODAY

Performance by Kathleen Chang and Suzanne Lacy | October 29th, 1977 | Sponsored by The Floating Museum

Immigration Station at Angel Island

In 1910 the government opened the Angel Island Immigration Station, a replacement for the embarrassingly delapidated wooden shed on the San Francisco waterfront which housed earlier immigrants during intensive questioning and quarantine periods. For the next forty years the Station seared itself indelibly upon the history and consciousness of the Asian American people who are only now beginning to find voice for the painful memories the island holds for them.

The story of Asian immigration to the United States is one which cannot be explained by factors which "push" people from their homes to escape poverty and war. Nor can it be explained by factors which "pull" immigrants to a land of opportunity and freedom; as those early peoples discovered, the land of opportunity was not for all. The real story of immigration is to be found in the needs of a growing capitalist economy. Intervention in trade relationships in Asia by western capitalists looking for an expanded market aided in the creation of an unstable economy which brought refugees to America in increasing numbers from the 1850's on. Development in the West, especially in railroad and farming, created a need for a constant flow of cheap labor which was never permitted to stabilize into flourishing communities—hence the pattern of immigrant waves from China, Japan, Korea and the Phillipines, followed by repeated anti-Asian movements and exclusion acts.

Asians imported for their labor were considered undesirable as neighbors, fellow workers and citizens. When periodic recessions and depressions hit the economy, whites were driven to vent their frustration against Asians by demagogues, politicians, the media and the very employers who were responsible for recruiting Asian labor in the first place.

It was inevitable that this exploitation and racism would be reflected in the handling of new arrivals at Angel Island. Although all arriving immigrants to the west coast were detained there, it is the Asian peoples who were held prisoner for months, sometimes years while they waited in uncertainty for their possible deportation under successive exclusion regulations created specifically for their race. The Angel Island Immigration Station today stands as a monument to the courage and resolution of the Asian people who have built and maintained their communities despite continued racism and economic exploitation.

THE ANGEL OF ANGEL ISLAND

In 1912 Deaconness Katherine Mauer of the Methodist Church began working under the auspices of the Women's Home Missionary Society to cheer women detained in the barracks at Angel Island. Her ministry, while applauded by the white culture eager to utilize individual charitable responses to "bandage" a racist and oppressive system, has been greeted with ambivalent responses by those to whom she applied her attentions. It is certain that she and others like her did bring some degree of cheer and comfort to the detainees. It is also probable that she was acting from humane responses to suffering, although the patronizing attempts to "Christianize" a "heathen" people bring justifiable criticism of an attempted colonization in which American women were used as tools for enculturation into the very system which created the oppression.

Humiliating Experience

All Asian immigrants, many with scarcely a glance at the loved ones they had traveled months to see, were loaded onto the ferry which delivered them from the dock in San Francisco to Angel Island. There they were herded into a single building surrounded by high wire fence and guard towers. The inside of the barracks contained two large rooms, each with hundreds of double and triple decker beds. Bathrooms consisted of rows of exposed toilets and community showers.

Immigrants were separated by sex and race, the women and children in one wing and the men in the other. They remember the humiliation of waiting in line for doctors to probe their private parts looking for "oriental" diseases. They remember the agonized waiting for the interrogation ordeal in which they were asked to remember countless insignificant details about life in Asia. Many an immigrant was deported for lapse of memory or incorrect answers which would have corroborated her story with that of her relatives. For some of these, suicide was preferable to the return to China, forever separated from family and loved ones.

Poetry Carved into Walls

Throughout the long ordeal of their detainment, some of the immigrants vented their frustration and rage in bursts of poetry carefully carved into the walls:

"I left my village behind me and now, I miss the bridge and flowers of my hometown.
I stare at the faraway clouds and mountains, with eyes full of tears.
A wanderer longing for treasures and a happy family.
Who can know that I was imprisoned on this island?
Thinking of China reminds me of the story of Juan-Chi..."

JAPANESE PICTURE BRIDES

From 1908 to 1920 Japanese laborers settling in America began to return home to Japan for brides. As the trip to Asia was costly, however, only a few men could obtain brides in this manner, and the custom of "picture brides" began to be used. Marriages arranged by families with the acquaintance of the concerned taking place through photographs was long in effect in Japan, and this custom was simply extended to accommodate the immigrant's desire to establish a family in his new homeland. This practice, perfectly in accord with Japanese custom and society, was greeted with aversion by some Americans and was subsequently used to spur on the developing anti-Japanese movement.

The Life and Times of Donaldina Cameron

Kathleen Chang and Suzanne Lacy

"The Life and Times of Donaldina Cameron" is a performance which begins as Suzanne's interest in making public an aesthetic form the politics of oppression which created the Immigration Station at Angel Island. In the process of creating the performance a series of questions came up which seriously challenged the ability of a white woman to create such a piece in a non-imperialistic manner. Subsequent questioning and searching by the two collaborators, Kathleen and Suzanne, generated the present structure in which the meeting between a white missionary woman and an Asian woman serve as a metaphor for the discussion of issues in racially responsive art—ideas on the prominent and responsibilities involved in cross-racial investigation, art-making, and social action. "The Life and Times..." is open these issues for a public discussion for interested participants.

Special thanks to Rosemaire Pena, Walter Proebster and Diana Yudko. All photographs credited to Visual Communications, much information for this paper condensed from "In Movement" by Visual Communications.

Prostitution of Asian Women

As a result of the limitation on the development of domestic life of the Chinese laborer, a system of prostitution developed in San Francisco in the late 1800's. A large majority of the women shipped to America for service in the brothels were not originally prostitutes but had been sold to men in Hong Kong who later forced them into prostitution. It was common practice to have the women sign an agreement to prostitute her body for her buyer's profit for four or five years, however, the average Chinese prostitute came to California as a slave and died in that condition as their life expectancy was short.

Attempted escape was severely punished although a few did escape, some with the assistance of Donaldina Cameron's slave-freeing raids on the brothels. Inevitably, the issue of prostitution was used as an argument for the corruption of the Chinese race during the development of virulent anti-Chinese sentiments, although many white men, including bribed officials, profited directly from the system. Even though the majority of the "slave-trade" was wiped out by the 1930's, the suspicion of prostitution continued to hang over Chinese women coming into the country.

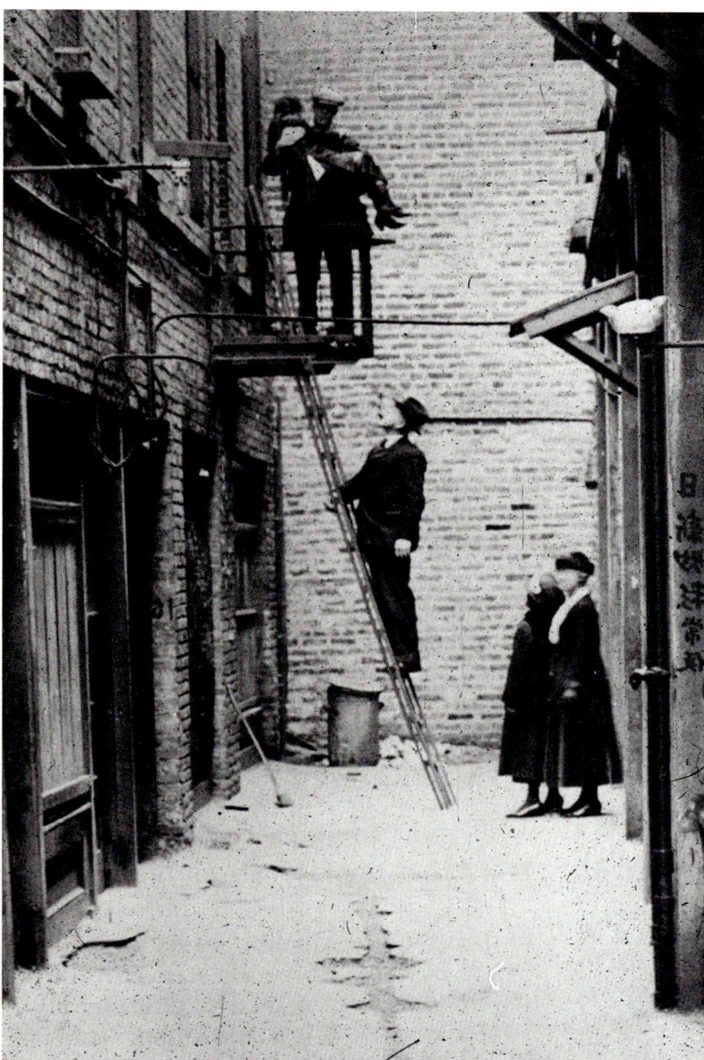

I was intrigued when I heard from Suzanne about participating in this piece, but at first I questioned her motives. I was fearful of using Chinese prostitution as a source; too often it has been exploited as a gimmick to sensationalize, rather than investigate, racism. Although I did not believe audience titillation was Suzanne's aim, I did suspect her of having a white missionary complex. My fears and her drives—it was the Chinese community reacting to Donaldina Cameron all over again; I certainly didn't have to look too hard for ambivalence. But I did like Suzanne, and I was intrigued at working with another artist, so I committed myself to our collaboration. . . .

One of our major sources of distrust was aesthetics. My acting background made me feel as if the piece required that form. I was unfamiliar with performance art. Suzanne, on the other hand, was averse to acting—was afraid of it, mostly. In addition, there was Suzanne's desire to render an idealized woman-to-woman relationship, to avoid the stereotype of women hating women that, to me, violated the truth. The piece moved uneasily in the direction of conflict and drama that I felt it required. We hit upon a combination of dramatic reading and acted monologue, again making this layer of the piece a compromise corresponding to the differences inherent in our aesthetics.

—Kathleen Chang, 1978

LEFT: Broadsheet distributed to audience members on the ferry providing context for the performance, including information on the Angel Island Immigration Center and historical accounts of Asian Pacific women
RIGHT: Historical photo reproduced in an article about the project in *Chrysalis: A Magazine of Women's Culture* in 1979 with the caption, "A daring rescue or a police bust?"

Travels with Mona (1977–78)

SUZANNE LACY WITH ARLENE RAVEN

In the summer of 1977 Lacy traveled to great monuments of Europe and Latin America with a paint-by-number reproduction of Leonardo da Vinci's *Mona Lisa* (ca. 1503–19). At every location an artist or critic photographed her filling it in. Twelve photographs were reproduced with narrative captions as a fold-out postcard travelogue, to which the feminist art historian Raven contributed ironic commentary: "Painting by numbers is like touring; the uninitiated traveler/artist can be assured of the route and the outcome—Education and Culture. But this Mona is an imitation made in the image of Leonardo. She smiles and does not speak. A performance artist speaks but does not generally paint canvases. In this journey, a performance about tourism, imitation, art, artists, art objects, women and culture, she seeks the promises of art long ago whispered to Mona (is that why she's smiling?)—visibility, acknowledgment, fortune, even immortality. Under these circumstances, it is best to have a Famous Painting by a Great Artist along."

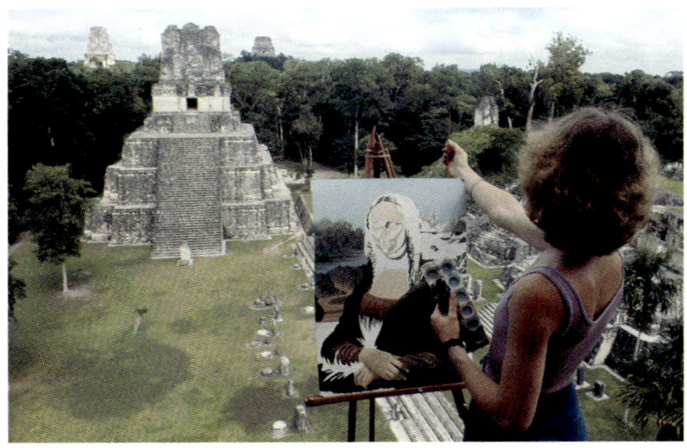
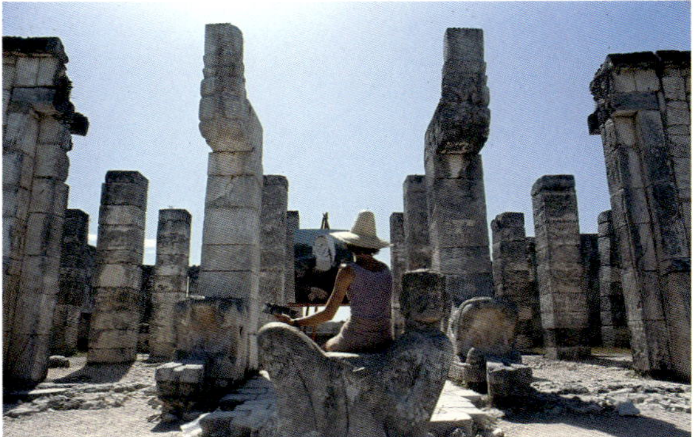

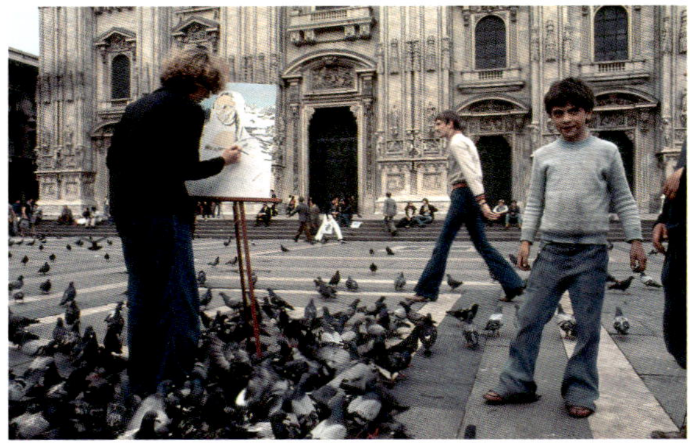
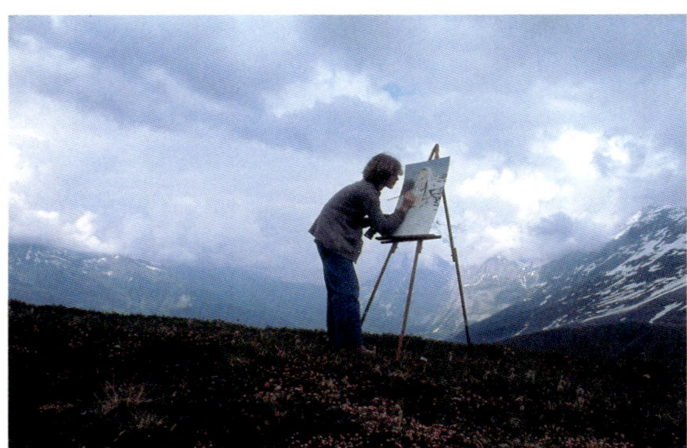

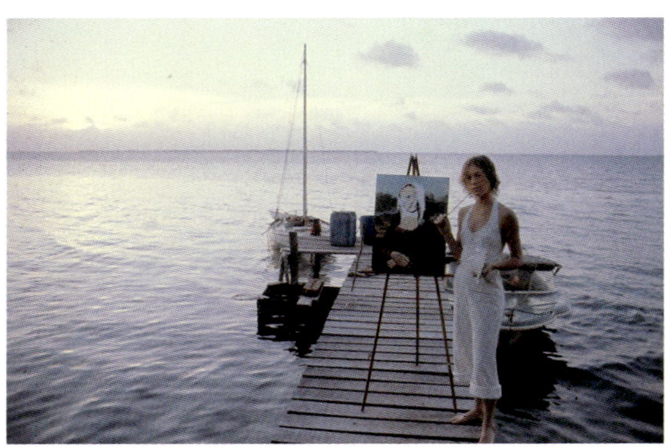
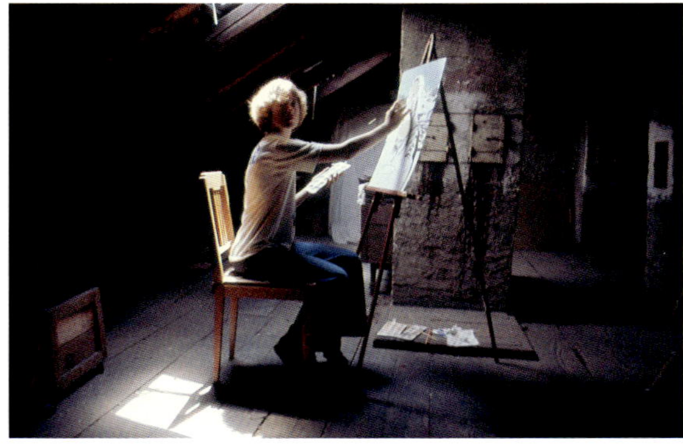

CLOCKWISE FROM TOP LEFT: Postcards showing Lacy in Tikal, Guatemala; Chichén-Itzá, Mexico; the Swiss Alps; Basel; British Honduras (now Belize); and Milan

Mona by Number (1978)

In this installation at the San Francisco Museum of Modern Art (SFMOMA), Lacy sat in a booth with a glass window reminiscent of the presentation of Leonardo da Vinci's *Mona Lisa* (ca. 1503–19) at the Musée du Louvre, Paris, which she had visited as part of *Travels with Mona* (1977–78, p. 84). She colored in a *Mona Lisa* paint-by-number replica over a period of two weeks. Lacy had participated in *Global Space Invasion Phase I* (1977), sponsored by Lynn Hershman Leeson's The Floating Museum at the Bologna Art Fair. The performance at SFMOMA was featured in one of six guest-organized exhibitions that comprised *The Floating Museum: Global Space Invasion Phase II*.

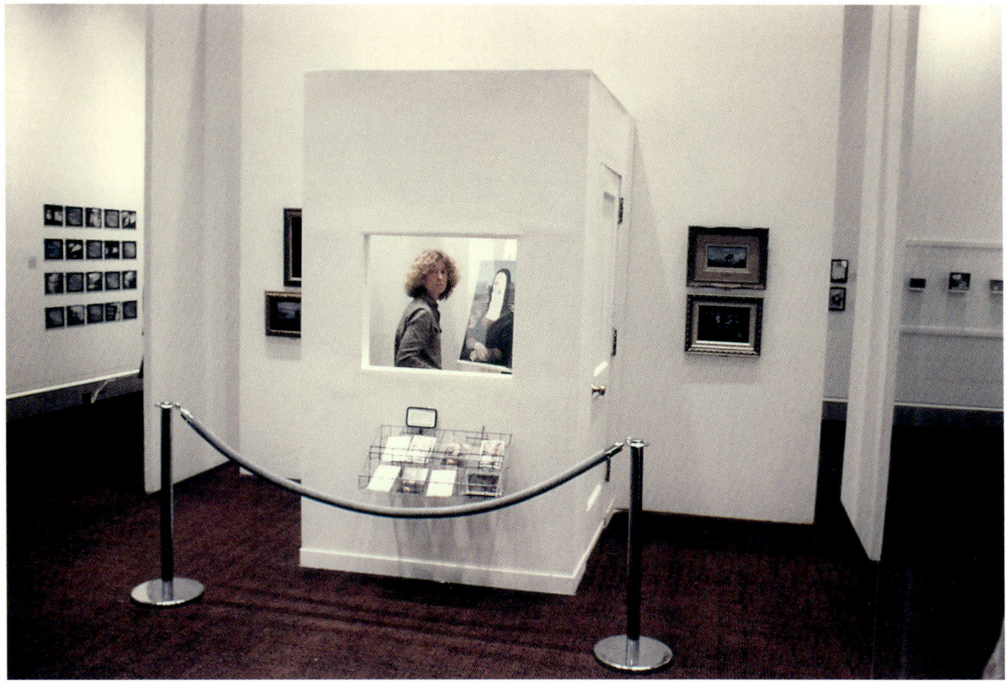

LEFT: Installation view, July 20, 1978
BOTTOM, LEFT TO RIGHT: *Mona by Number* postcard, 1978; Lacy's unfinished reproduction of the *Mona Lisa*

The Floating Museum . . . was dedicated to work that was not exhibited in formal institutions like museums or galleries. I was interested in a more egalitarian situation that brought art to the streets, to places people did not expect to find it. This was intended to also incorporate into exhibition[s] politics of representation and institutional critique. . . . Suzanne Lacy was doing provocations about issues of identity, aging, history, and repression. She was doing mainly performances and seemed a key artist to include in these ventures that took place in several cities and non-art locations, bringing a new sense of history and relevance through the works she made during this time.

—Lynn Hershman Leeson, 2018

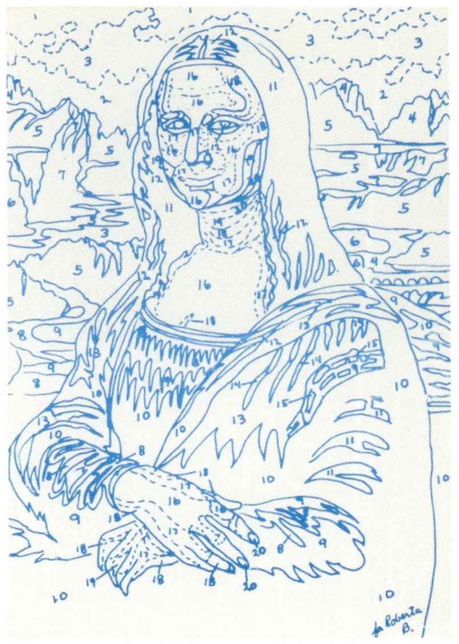

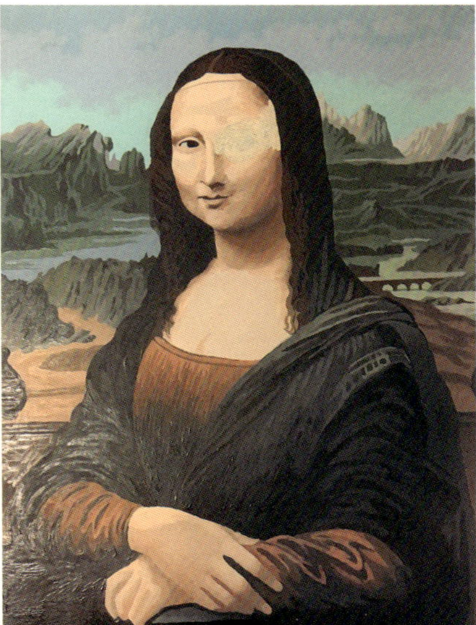

In the Last Throes of Artistic Vision (1980)

This forty-eight-hour performance installation was staged in an abandoned warehouse and open to the public. Led by wraiths carrying candles, visitors walked up five flights of stairs, passing writings from Bram Stoker's journal on the walls. On the top floor they encountered a dramatically lit tableau. In Lacy's final enactment of a vampire character, she slept by day in a coffin filled with earth. By night she worked on a paint-by-number reproduction of Rembrandt van Rijn's *The Slaughtered Ox* (1655), a masterpiece from the Musée du Louvre, Paris. An accompanying soundtrack featured swelling music and a monologue that ruminated on artistic genius and the nature of evil. The performance spanned Halloween and was sponsored by the Public Spirit: Live Art LA festival.

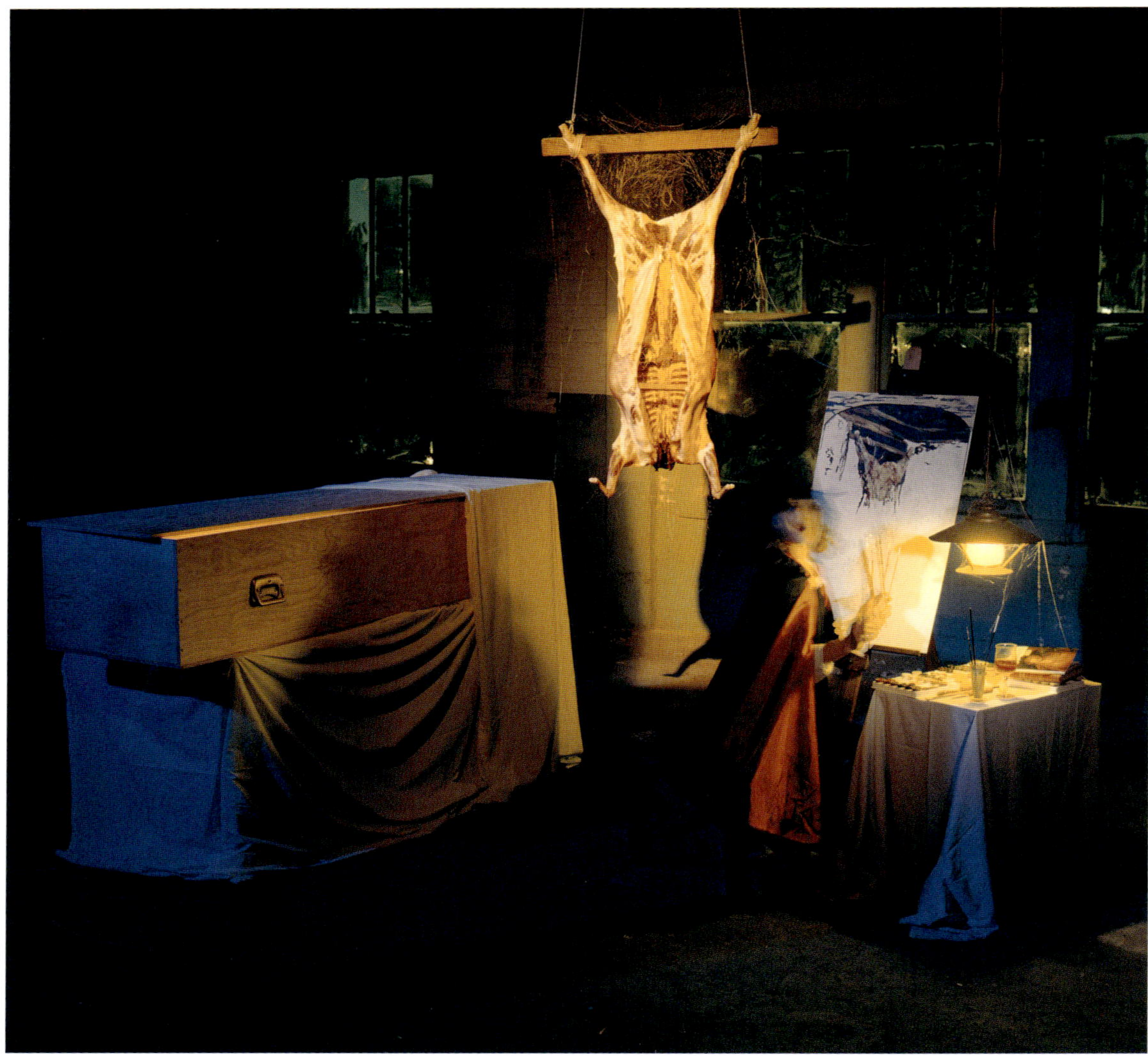

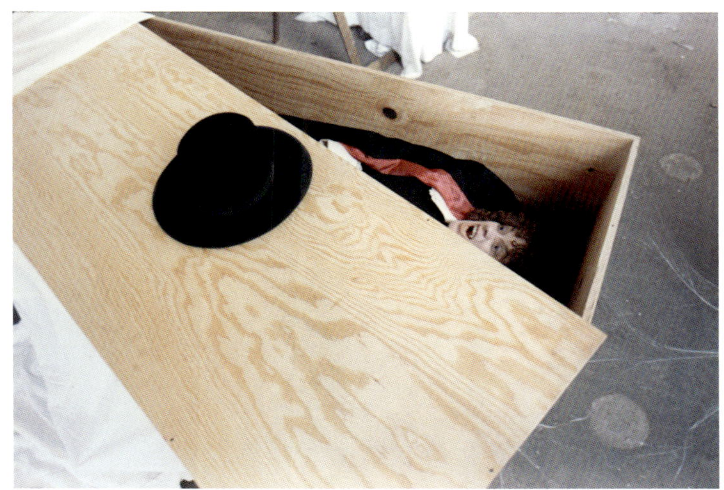

Here they come; these aimless images parade into the early hours before dawn, mocking me with their senselessness. They come in threes: enter this particular unholy trio. Two are locked in mortal embrace, the third watches with fascinated wonder. It is always thus: of the two who dance grimly, one is marked evil and has no body, but a black and terrible presence. The other, oh how vulnerable, how carnate! The other is he to whom evil is done. And what of the third, the observer, he who completes this strange menage? This time he appears as an artist from long ago, one who was called the "son of darkness." Scorned, even ruined, yet he is immortal! He lives forever, for, oh strange paradox, how can there be shadows without light?

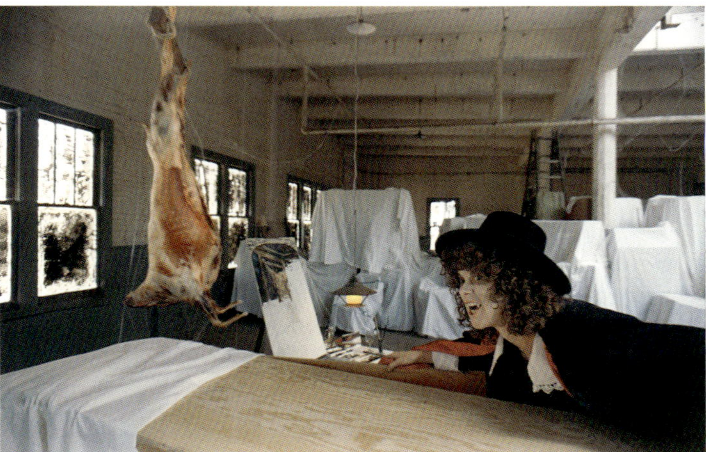

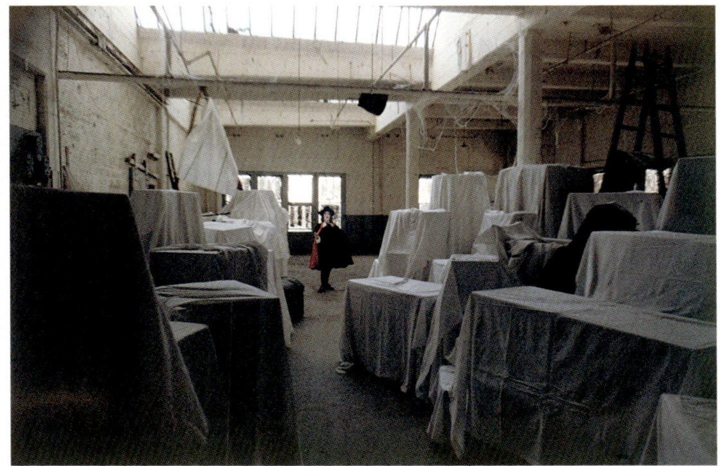

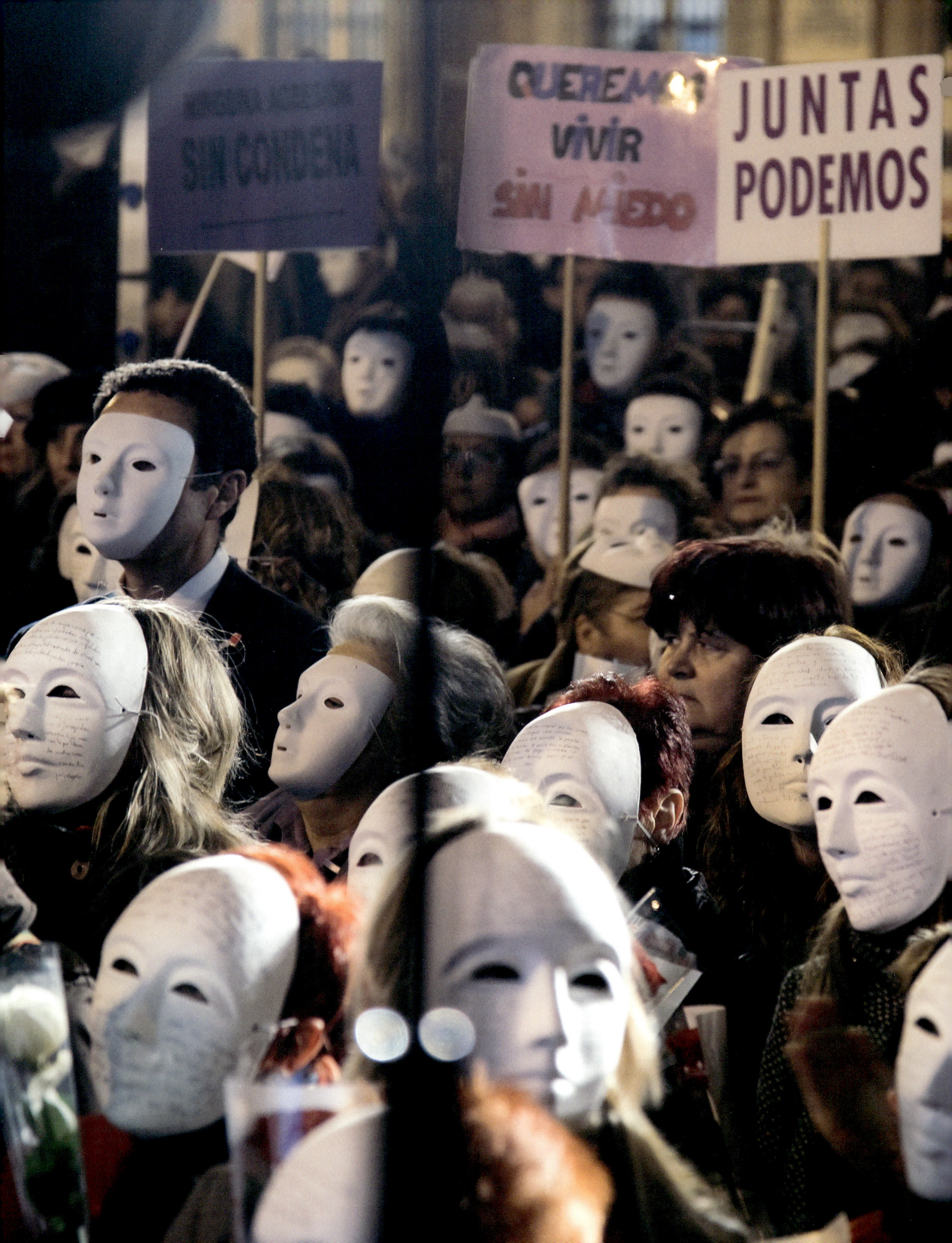
SIN CONDENA
QUEREMOS
VIVIR
SIN MIEDO
JUNTAS
PODEMOS

VIOLENCE AGAINST WOMEN

Stamping the locations of rapes in Los Angeles taken from daily police reports onto a map in an art gallery was Lacy's first conceptualization of the work that would become *Three Weeks in May* (1977, pp. 95–99). This initial vision soon led her to question restricting the discussion of rape to a gallery, when one could be raped on the way home from such a space. Lacy wanted to speak to and influence more than just artists when it came to the topic of violence against women—she wanted to intervene in the culture at large. *Three Weeks in May* would be a major turning point in her work, an intentional move out of the gallery that would launch a progression of increasingly large-scale, issue-based, durational public performances.

Lacy's early work addressing violence against women interrogated representations of women in and by the news media and popular culture, particularly the "sex-violent" imagery. She applied her keen eye as a visual artist to advance societal critique, teaming up with Leslie Labowitz on much of this work in the 1970s under the auspices of the coalition Ariadne: A Social Art Network. To reach broader audiences, the pair developed and honed a media strategy whose interventions fell into two categories: public information campaigns and media performances. The public information campaigns included long-term media coverage with the goal of educating and organizing communities, while the media performances were one-time events designed specifically for newscasts, allowing Lacy and Labowitz to maintain tight control over their message. They published a fourteen-point strategy for successful media events in the magazine *Heresies: A Feminist Publication on Art and Politics*, providing a tool for the feminist community at large. Lacy's media strategy has evolved over time to adapt to the changing media landscape; a prior focus on the television newscast has given way to a use of social media as an organizing and promotional strategy, as seen in *Three Weeks in January* (2012, pp. 116–17).

It was through her work on violence against women and due to a desire to spur policy change that Lacy began to build strong civic partnerships, a shift that would become significant in shaping her unique form of social practice. Her collaborations extended beyond working with other artists to engaging feminist political organizations, social service nonprofits, government departments, city officials, and even the police. Not only were such collaborations the backbone of key works on violence against women in the Ariadne series and in projects such as *Auto on the Edge of Time* (1993–94, pp. 110–11), *Esqueleto tatuado* (Tattooed Skeleton, 2010, pp. 112–15), and *De tu puño y letra* (By Your Own Hand, 2014–15/2019, pp. 118–23), but this commitment to relationship building came to characterize her practice more broadly, especially in long-term works such as *The Oakland Projects* (1991–2001, pp. 184–211). While Lacy's approach to the theme of violence against women has evolved from guerrilla-style activist interruption, as in the Ariadne series, to a more operatic style, as in *De tu puño y letra*, the role of civic partnerships has remained a fundamental element.

—CHRISTA CESARIO

OPPOSITE: Protesters in masks from *Esqueleto tatuado* (Tattooed Skeleton, 2010, pp. 112–15) on the International Day for the Elimination of Violence against Women, Madrid, November 25, 2010

Prostitution Notes (1974–75)

Rather than positioning herself in performance as if she were a prostitute—something other women artists had experimented with—Lacy explored the connections between actual and imagined experiences of prostitution through a work combining performance and research. She began by tracing links among her friends, acquaintances, and contacts that might help surface the sites and dynamics of prostitution in Los Angeles. Moving from one lead to another, Lacy met with people in their local bars or coffee shops, itemizing what she ate and collecting matchbook covers to affix to hand-drawn maps charting her physical and psychological routes through the city. The maps also include photographs and annotations of her personal revelations as she "tracked" prostitutes around California and considered the relationship between her life and the lives of sex workers.

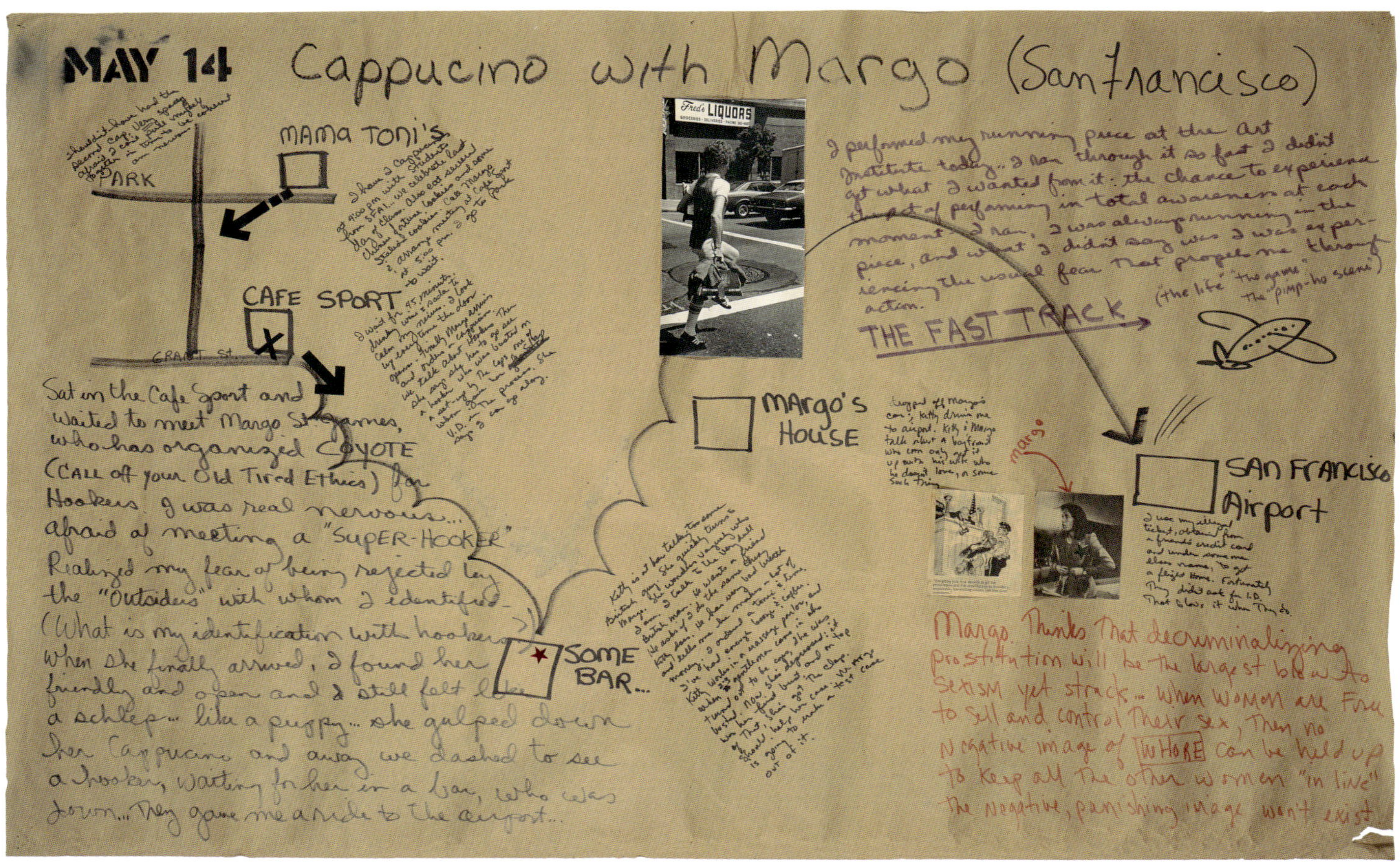

I decided to do a project on prostitution. I wondered who they were, these women whose lives were such powerful icons for my gender. How did I carry their condition inside my own experience?

I didn't want to put myself inside their shoes, walk the streets as an art performance, or dress up like a prostitute in order to flirt with their reality. I also didn't want to relate their individual stories, except as their stories appeared along my journey. Rather, I thought to locate the work in my own experience, to record the process of my entry into an understanding of "The Life," as I looked for the echo of their situation inside my own.

The media portrayals of sex workers in reality shows or movies, they're still keeping women in a net. Usually women die in the movie, or they get arrested, or they're brutalized by their pimps. They show sex workers being punished. Why don't they ever show the cops hassling them instead? . . . You can't divide economic injustice from sex-worker injustice. The two go together. The men and women on the streets are the ones who are going to be hassled by the police. I think we need to look at that, and we've got to leave the policy answers up to the sex workers. The criminalization of marginalized people is the problem we need to fix.

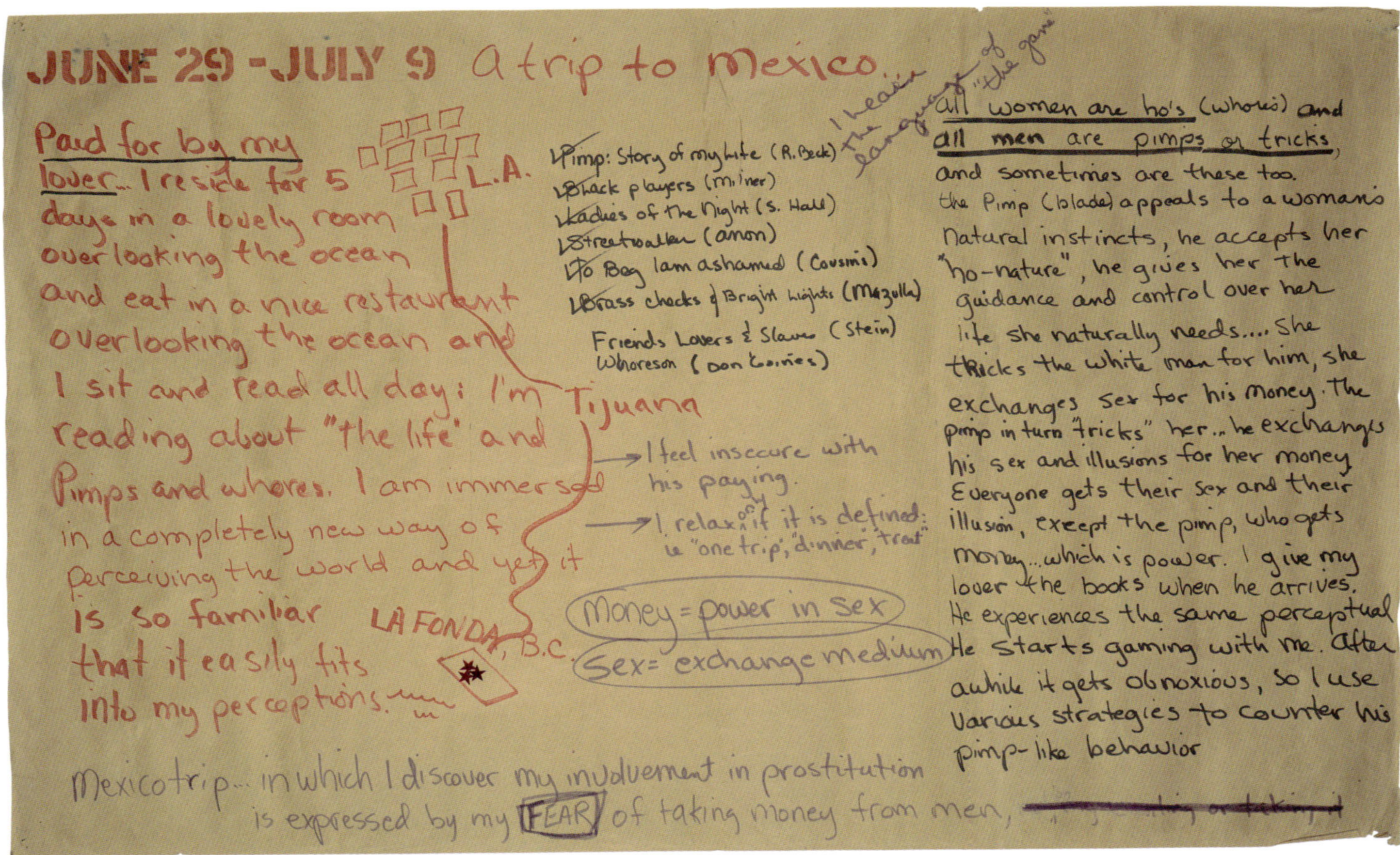

I had no idea where to find prostitutes. I began simply by asking friends and acquaintances. I found that within the "field" of my intimate friends, there were those who had "tricked," or knew firsthand someone who had. "The Life" wasn't far from mine. I followed friends' leads and entered another world—one that lies just below the surface, if you know where to look. The street corners, restaurants, and bars of Los Angeles took on a new appearance.

—Suzanne Lacy, 1974

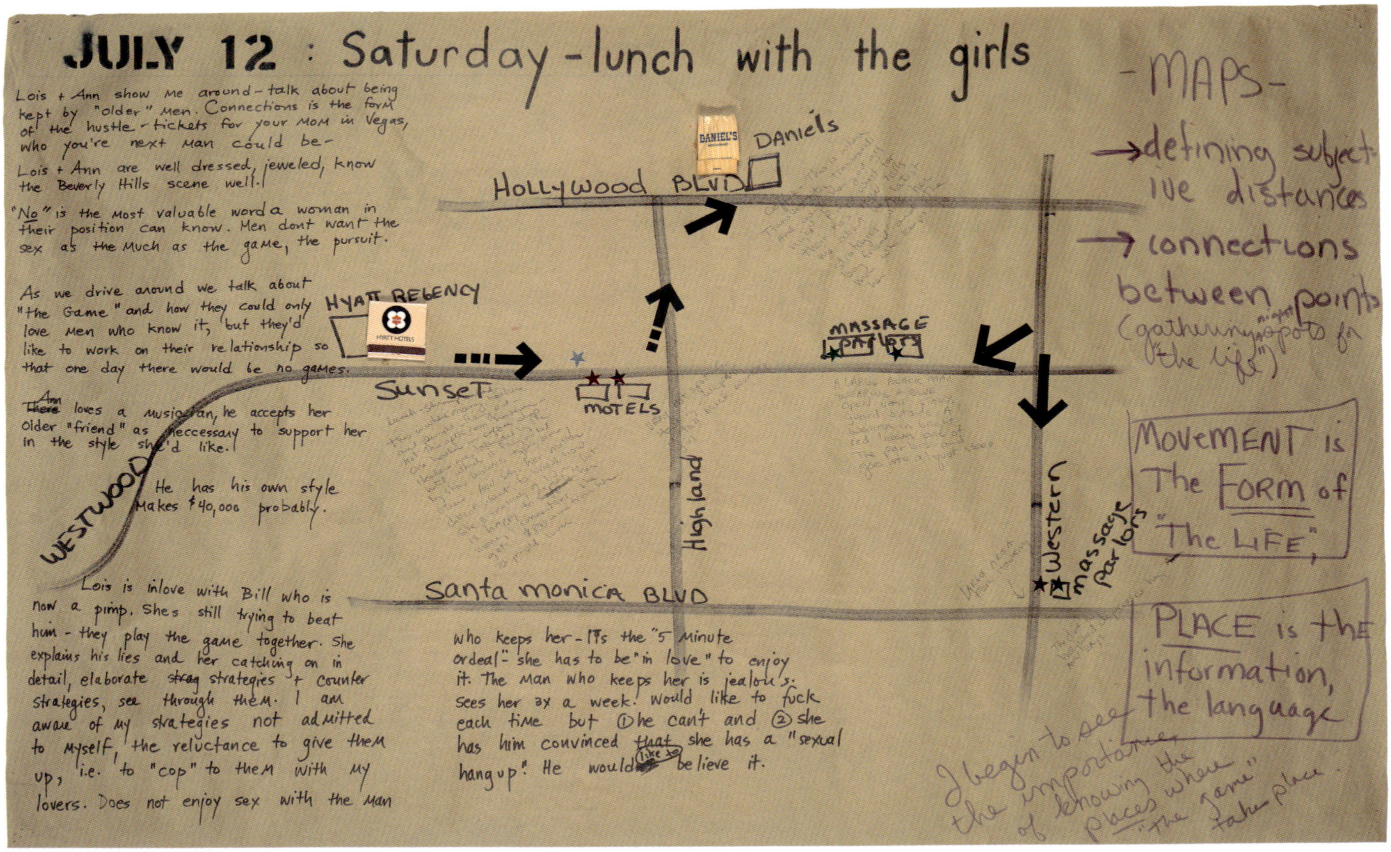

JULY 12 : Saturday - lunch with the girls

Lois + Ann show me around - talk about being kept by "older" men. Connections is the form of the hustle - tickets for your mom in Vegas, who you're next man could be -

Lois + Ann are well dressed, jeweled, know the Beverly Hills scene well.

"No" is the most valuable word a woman in their position can know. Men don't want the sex as the much as the game, the pursuit.

As we drive around we talk about "the Game" and how they could only love men who know it, but they'd like to work on their relationship so that one day there would be no games.

Ann loves a musician, he accepts her older "friend" as neccessary to support her in the style she'd like.

He has his own style. Makes $40,000 probably.

Lois is inlove with Bill who is now a pimp. She's still trying to beat him - they play the game together. She explains his lies and her catching on in detail, elaborate strag strategies + counter strategies, see through them. I am aware of my strategies not admitted to myself, the reluctance to give them up, i.e. to "cop" to them with my lovers. Does not enjoy sex with the man who keeps her - It's the "5 minute ordeal" she has to be "in love" to enjoy it. The man who keeps her is jealous: sees her 3x a week. Would like to fuck each time but ① he can't and ② she has him convinced that she has a "sexual hangup". He would (like to) believe it.

- MAPS -

→ defining subjective distances

→ connections between points (gathering spots for "the life")

MOVEMENT is The FORM of "The LIFE"

PLACE is the information, the language

I begin to see the importance of knowing the places where "the game" takes place.

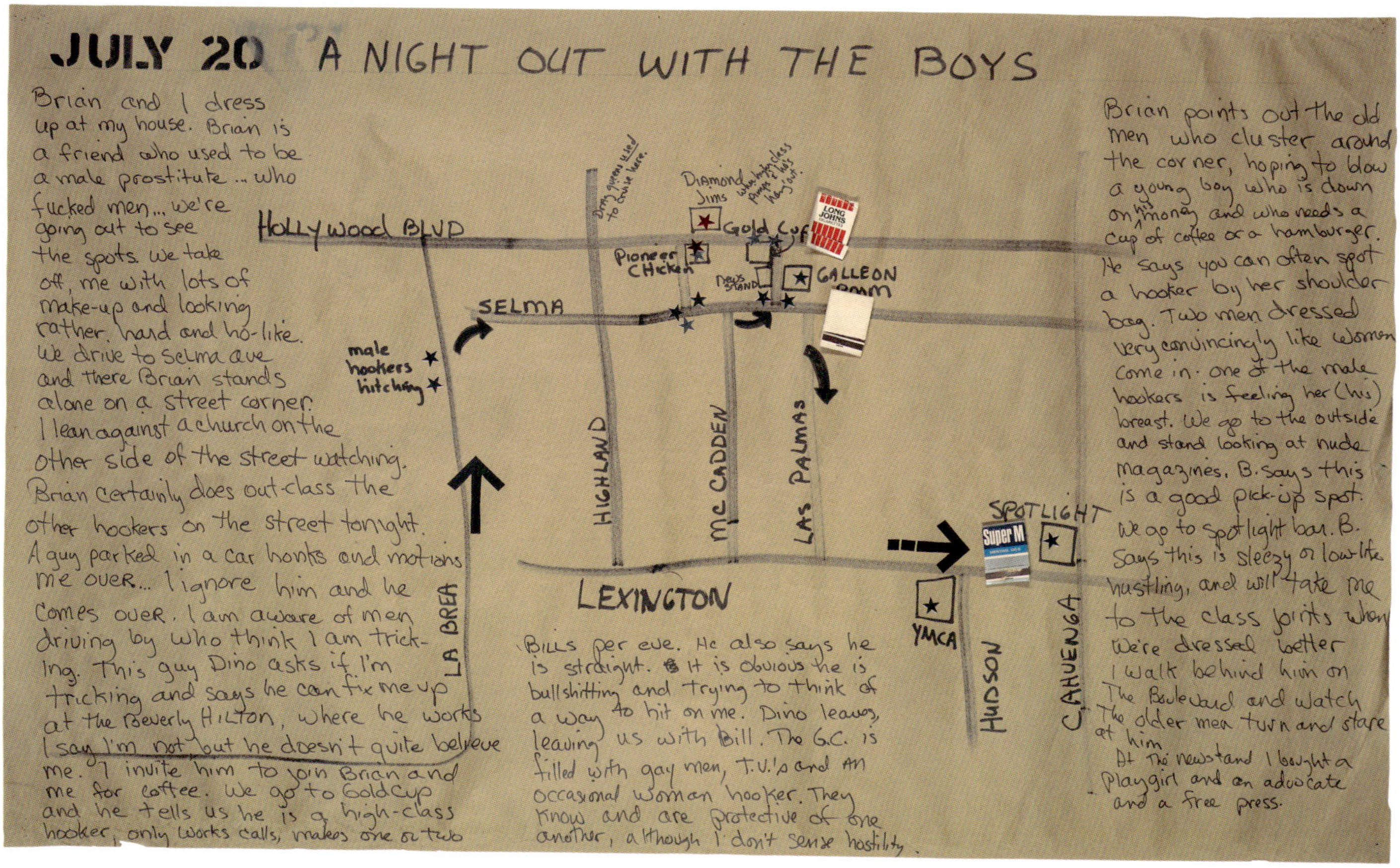

JULY 20 : A NIGHT OUT WITH THE BOYS

Brian and I dress up at my house. Brian is a friend who used to be a male prostitute ... who fucked men... we're going out to see the spots. We take off, me with lots of make-up and looking rather hard and ho-like. We drive to Selma ave and there Brian stands alone on a street corner. I lean against a church on the other side of the street watching. Brian certainly does out-class the other hookers on the street tonight. A guy parked in a car honks and motions me over... I ignore him and he comes over. I am aware of men driving by who think I am tricking. This guy Dino asks if I'm tricking and says he can fix me up at the Beverly Hilton, where he works. I say I'm not but he doesn't quite believe me. I invite him to join Brian and me for coffee. We go to GoldCup and he tells us he is a high-class hooker, only works calls, makes one or two bills per eve. He also says he is straight. ✗ It is obvious he is bullshitting and trying to think of a way to hit on me. Dino leaves, leaving us with Bill. The G.C. is filled with gay men, T.V.'s and an occasional woman hooker. They know and are protective of one another, although I don't sense hostility.

Brian points out the old men who cluster around the corner, hoping to blow a young boy who is down on his money and who needs a cup of coffee or a hamburger. He says you can often spot a hooker by her shoulder bag. Two men dressed very convincingly like women come in. One of the male hookers is feeling her (his) breast. We go to the outside and stand looking at nude magazines. B. says this is a good pick-up spot. We go to spotlight bar. B. says this is sleezy or low-life hustling, and will take me to the class joints when we're dressed better I walk behind him on the Boulevard and watch the older men turn and stare at him At the newstand I bought a Playgirl and an advocate and a free press.

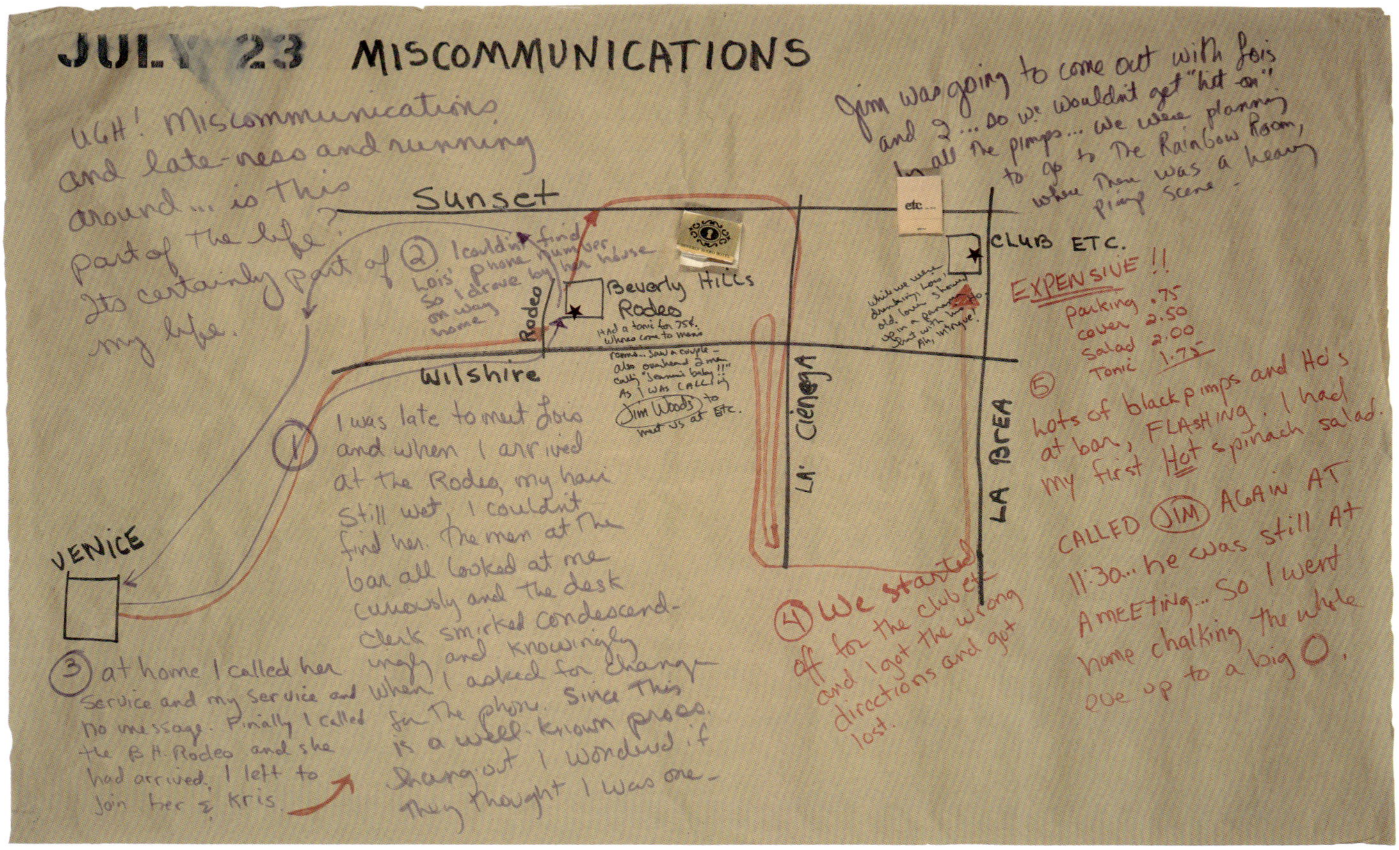

JULY 23 MISCOMMUNICATIONS

UGH! Miscommunications
and late-ness and running
around... is this
part of The life?
Its certainly part of
my life.

Sunset

Wilshire

VENICE

Rodeo

Beverly Hills Rodeo

La Cienega

La Brea

② I couldn't find Lois' phone number so I drove by her house on way home.

Had a tonic for .75¢. Whores come to mind... Saw a couple - also overheard a man call "Jemima baby!!!" As I was calling Jim Woods to meet us at Etc.

① I was late to meet Lois and when I arrived at the Rodeo, my hair still wet, I couldn't find her. The men at The bar all looked at me curiously and the desk clerk smirked condescend- ingly and knowingly and when I asked for change for The phone. Since This is a well-known pross. hangout I wondered if They thought I was one-

③ at home I called her service and my service. No message. Finally I called the B.H. Rodeo and she had arrived, I left to join her & Kris.

Jim was going to come out with Lois and I... so we wouldn't get "hit on" by all the pimps... We were planning to go to The Rainbow Room, where there was a heavy pimp scene.

etc...

while we were drinking Lois' old. lover showed up in a Camaro. Sent with her to (?) Ah, intrigue!

CLUB ETC.

EXPENSIVE!!
parking .75
cover 2.50
salad 2.00
Tonic 1.75

⑤ lots of black pimps and Ho's at bar, FLASHING. I had my first Hot spinach salad.

CALLED (JIM) AGAIN AT 11:30... he was still at a meeting... So I went home chalking The whole eve up to a big O.

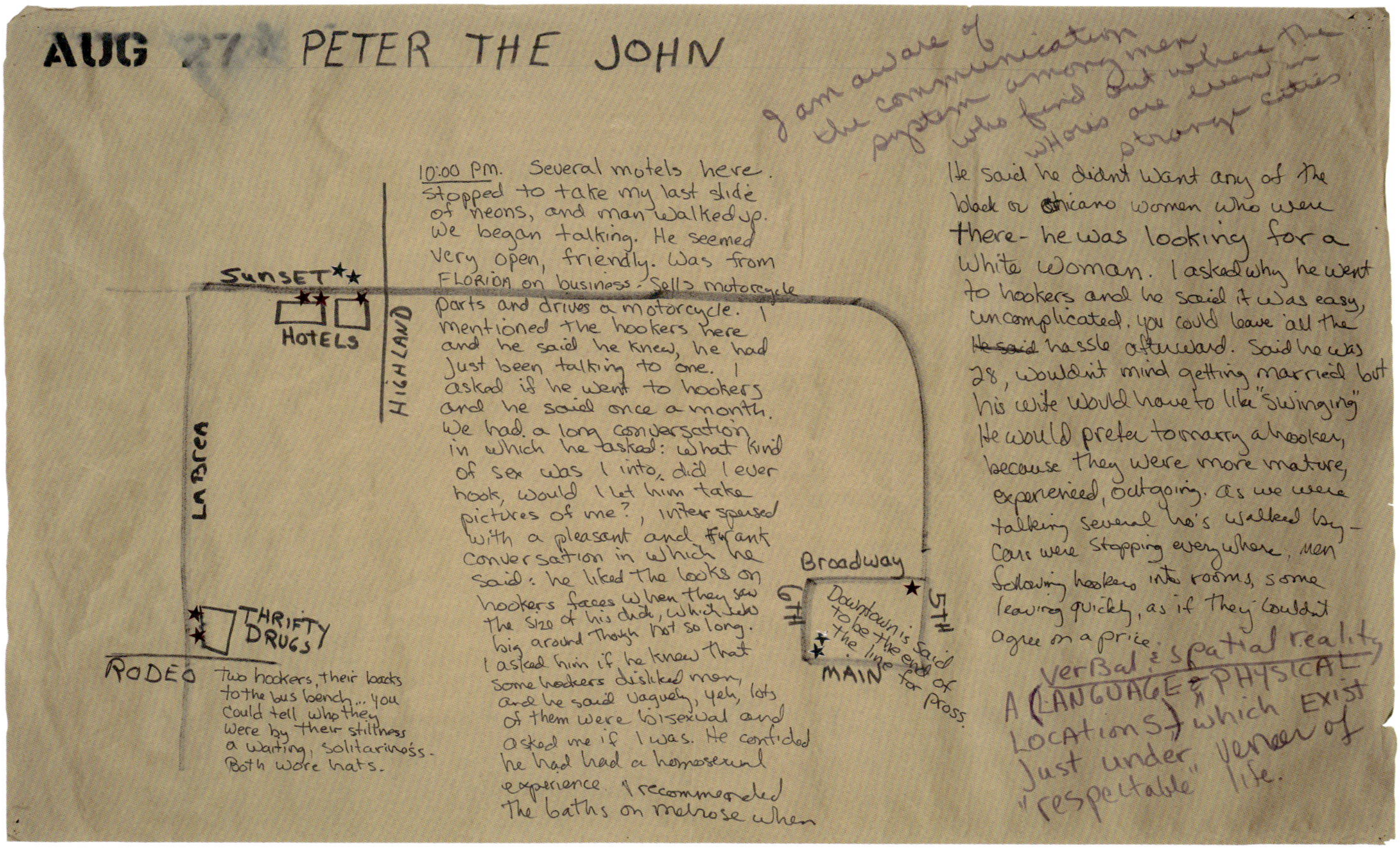

④ we started off for the club et and got The wrong directions and got lost.

AUG 27 PETER THE JOHN

I am aware of the communication system among men who find out where the whores are even in strange cities

SUNSET

HOTELS

HIGHLAND

LA BREA

THRIFTY DRUGS

RODEO

Two hookers, their backs to the bus bench... you could tell who they were by their stillness a waiting, solitariness. Both wore hats.

10:00 PM. Several motels here. Stopped to take my last slide of neons, and man walked up. We began talking. He seemed very open, friendly. Was from FLORIDA on business. Sells motorcycle parts and drives a motorcycle. I mentioned the hookers here and he said he knew, he had just been talking to one. I asked if he went to hookers and he said once a month. We had a long conversation in which he asked: what kind of sex was I into, did I ever hook, would I let him take pictures of me?, interspersed with a pleasant and frank conversation in which he said: he liked the looks on hookers faces when they saw the size of his dick, which was big around Though not so long. I asked him if he knew that some hookers disliked men, and he said vaguely, yeh, lots of them were bisexual and asked me if I was. He confided he had had a homosexual experience. I recommended the baths on melrose when

He said he didn't want any of the black or chicano women who were there- he was looking for a white woman. I asked why he went to hookers and he said it was easy, uncomplicated. you could leave all the hassle afterward. Said he was 28, wouldn't mind getting married but his wife would have to like "swinging" He would prefer to marry a hooker, because they were more mature, experienced, outgoing. As we were talking several ho's walked by- Cars were stopping everywhere, men following hookers into rooms, some leaving quickly, as if they couldn't agree on a price.

Broadway

6TH

MAIN

5TH

Downtown is said to be the end of the line for Pross.

A (LANGUAGE & PHYSICAL LOCATIONS) which EXIST Just under "respectable" life.

verBal & spatial reality

ARIADNE

(1977–1982)

Three Weeks in May / In Mourning and in Rage / Record Companies Drag Their Feet /
A Woman's Image of Mass Media / From Reverence to Rape to Respect /
Take Back the Night / Making It Safe / Hardcore Screening / Incest Awareness Project /
The Performing Archive: Restricted Access

After collaborating on multiple works addressing violence against women, Lacy and Leslie Labowitz established Ariadne: A Social Art Network to formalize and provide structure to the fluid network of artists, activists, reporters, and politicians with whom they had built relationships. As Lacy and Labowitz had done in earlier works, Ariadne focused on critiquing the trend of sex-violent images of women in media and pornography.

Ariadne developed during a period that saw a proliferation of coalition-based feminist organizations, such as Women against Violence against Women (WAVAW) in Los Angeles and the Combahee River Collective in Boston, and politically active artist coalitions, such as Political Art Documentation and Distribution (PAD/D) and Group Material in New York. Lacy and Labowitz's commitment to coalition building can been seen in Ariadne's numerous collaborations with organizations including COYOTE (Call Off Your Old Tired Ethics), the Los Angeles Commission on Assaults against Women (now Peace over Violence), and the Lesbian and Gay Community Services Center (now the Lesbian, Gay, Bisexual, and Transgender Community Center). Its activities centered around education (media workshops, political performance classes, and organizing), vision and theory (sponsored events, funding development, and writings on the subjects of critical theory, performance, and violence), communication networks, and art itself. By cultivating an environment that would generate theory and practice related to feminist art and activism, Ariadne supported the inclusion of women artists in political organizing and public critique.

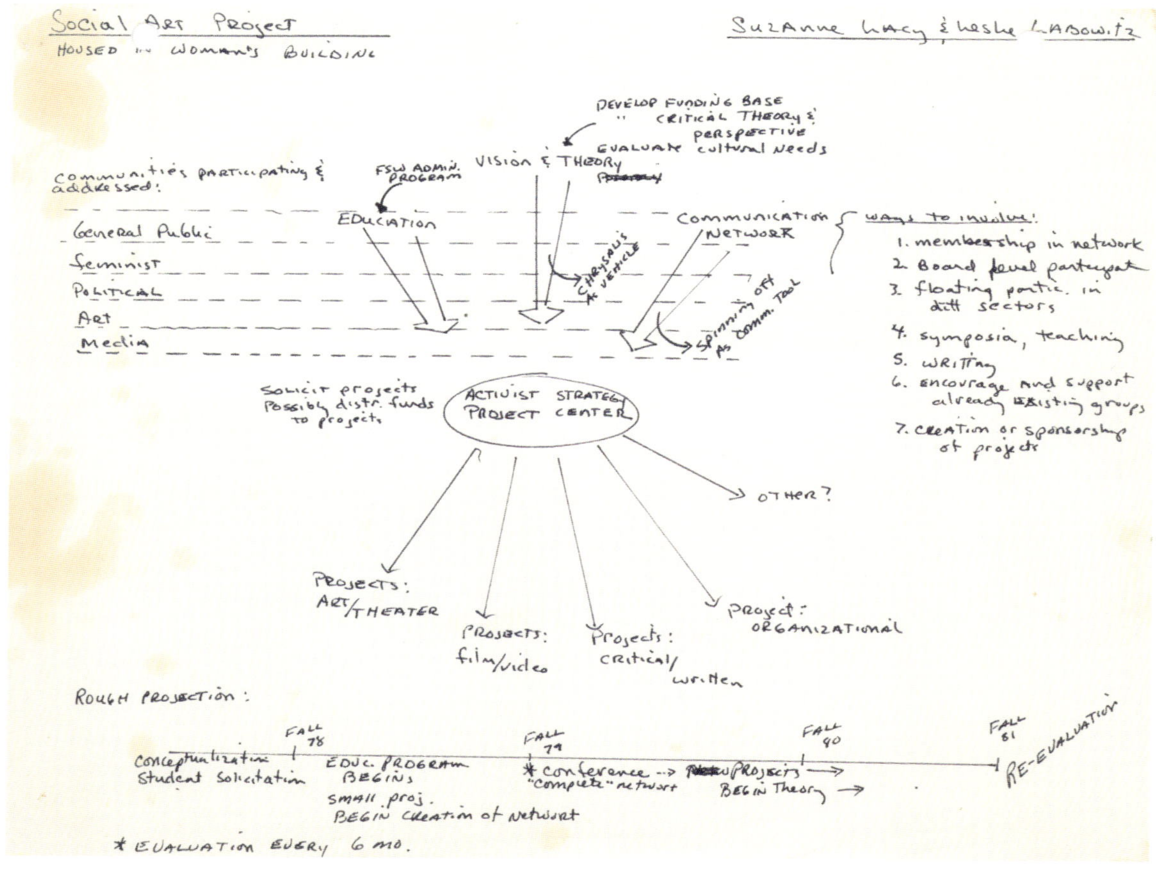

Three Weeks in May (1977)

Every day over the course of *Three Weeks in May* Lacy stamped the locations of rapes reported the day before on a large map of Los Angeles in the mall below City Hall. Fainter stamps symbolized the estimated nine additional rapes for every one reported. A second map showed sites of organizations and self-help activities for injured women, revealing a schedule of three weeks of events—many covered by the media—on violence prevention including performances, rituals, a dinner facilitating coordination and conversation between women activists and law enforcement, and a self-defense demonstration. Lacy also created the installation *She Who Would Fly*, in which a lamb carcass with white-feathered wings was suspended in a small gallery with women's descriptions of sexual violation pinned to maps of the United States on the walls. Four women sat perched above the door, nude, their bodies stained bright red. Staring down intently, they reminded visitors that they were voyeurs to the pain of real experiences.

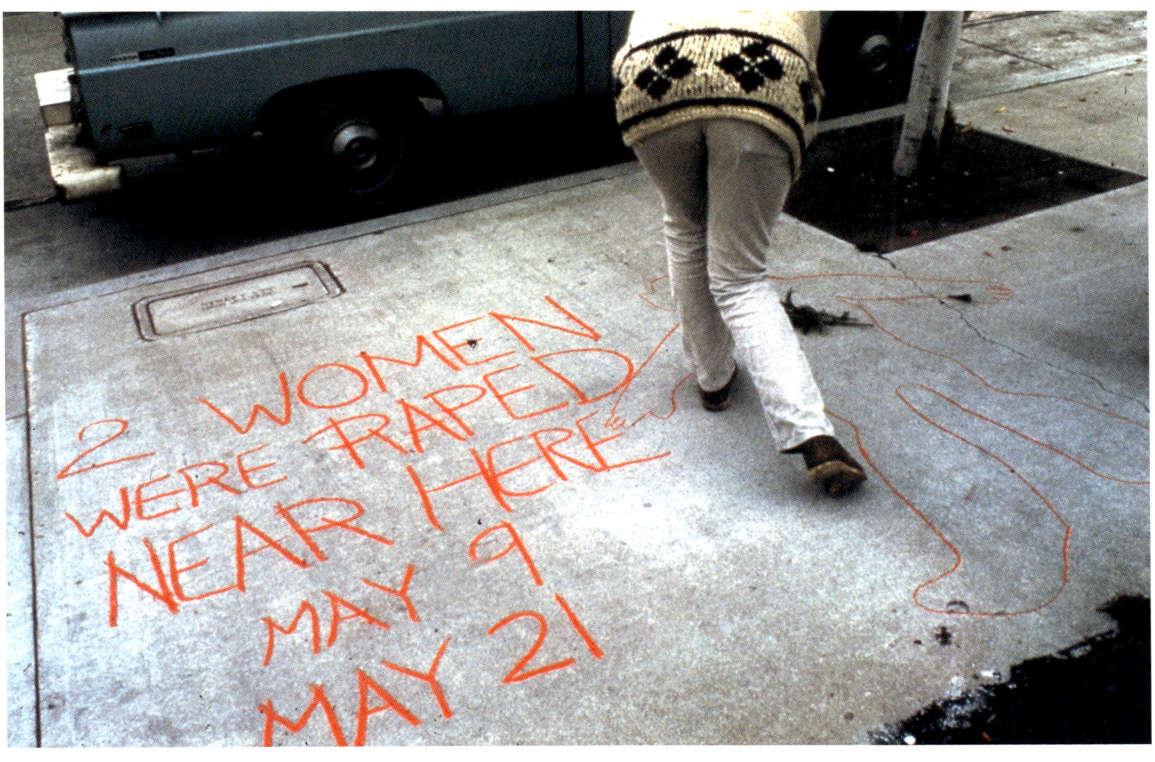

OPPOSITE: Diagram of Ariadne's planned approach to activist networking
TOP: View of a guerilla performance in which sidewalks near rape sites were marked throughout Los Angeles, 1977
BOTTOM AND FOLLOWING PAGES: Lacy's notations on police rape reports, read on *Close Radio*, a weekly radio program that aired on the Los Angeles station KPFK

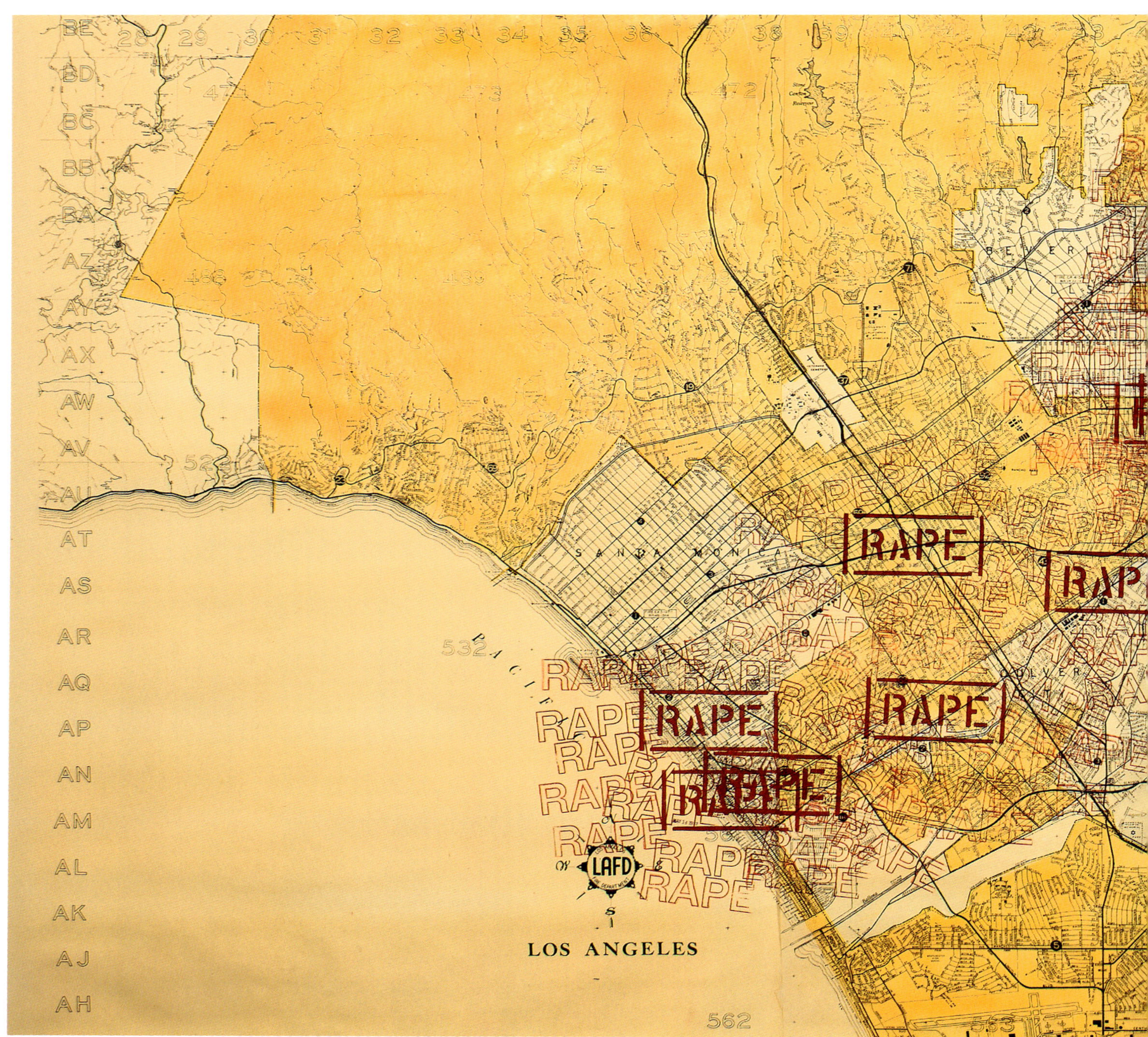

Mon May 9 1977
~~Sat, April 5, 1975~~
11:00 am this mornig

This incident occurred at the victims
residente in the southwest area of LA

V-~~F-C-60~~
S-~~M-N-34~~

Victim talked to S. earler in liquor store.
S. knocked on V's door and V. let him in.
S. stated he wanted some "Hanky panky"
V. refused. S. hit V. about face and head
with fists. V. possibly lost consciousness.

Mon May 9 1977
~~Saturday, Apr 5, 1975~~
2:50 am this morning

This incident occurred in the ~~Venice area~~. Inglewood area

V-~~F-C-19~~
S-M-O-26

Victim parked with date in car. Susp
approached with shotgun. ~~S. forced vict
to orally copulate him then forced vict
to engage in act of sexual intercourse.
V. again forced to orally cop. susp. Susp
then sodomized vict~~) S. threatened to
kill vict with knife and shotgun.

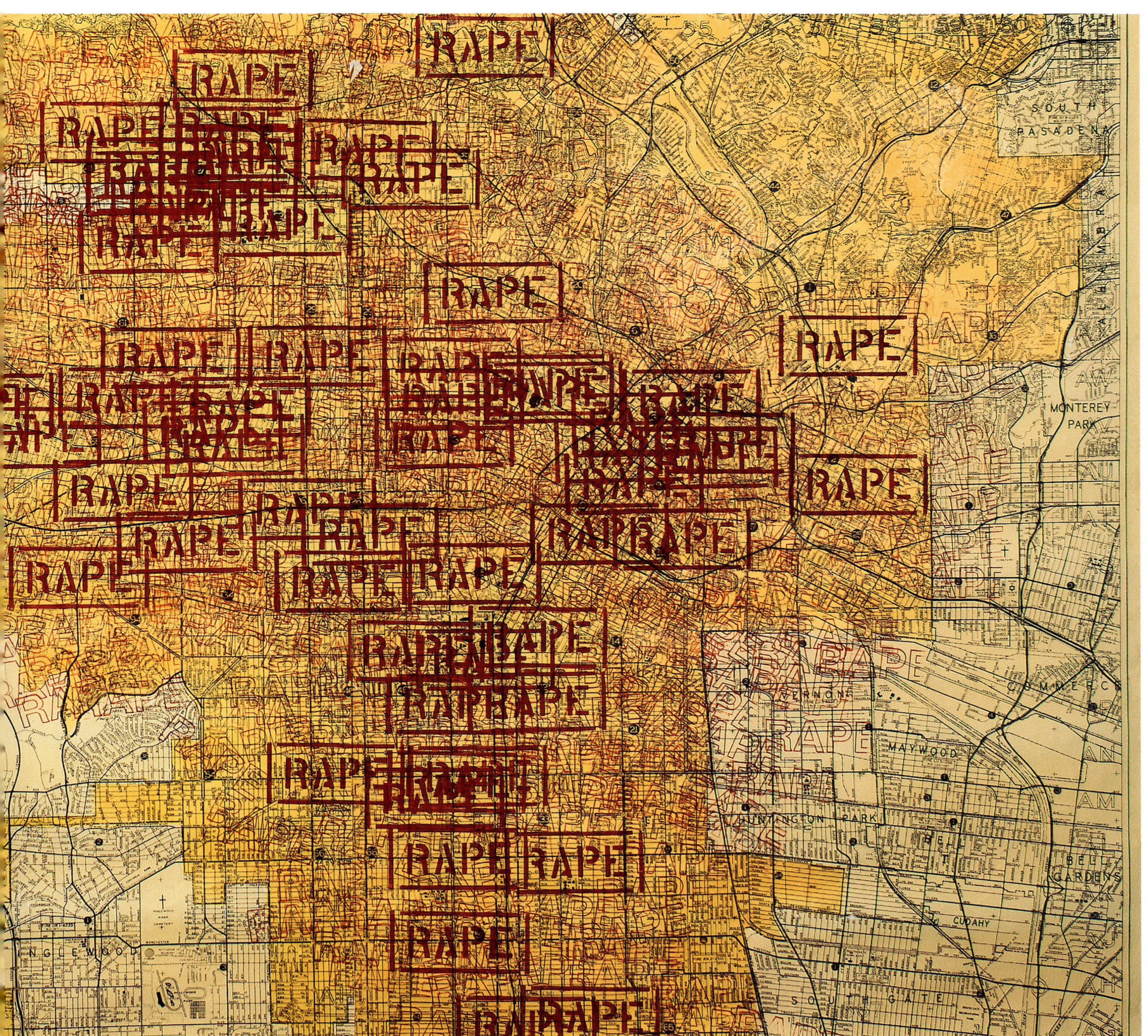

Tues May 11 1977
~~Saturday, April 5, 1975~~
2:30 am this morning.

Set 8 M + J

This incident occurred in a church parking lot in ~~Devonshire, Grnada Hills~~.
Van Nuys

~~Victim-Female-Caucasian-age 19~~
~~Suspect-male-Caucasian-age approx 24~~

Suspect jumped over a wall, grabbed ~~vict~~ *victim* by neck and stated "don't scream" ~~Suspect removed victs tampon and began spitting on her vagina. Suspect made slight penetration for approx 5 min.~~

Mon May 9
~~Sat, April 5, 1975~~
7:30 pm this evening

This incident occurred in the ~~downtown~~ *Hollywood* ~~los Angeles area~~.

~~V-F-Latin 24~~
~~S- 2M- L- 25/27~~

S. approached V, as V was proceeding to Bus stop. S. grabbed V's arm and twisted it behind her...

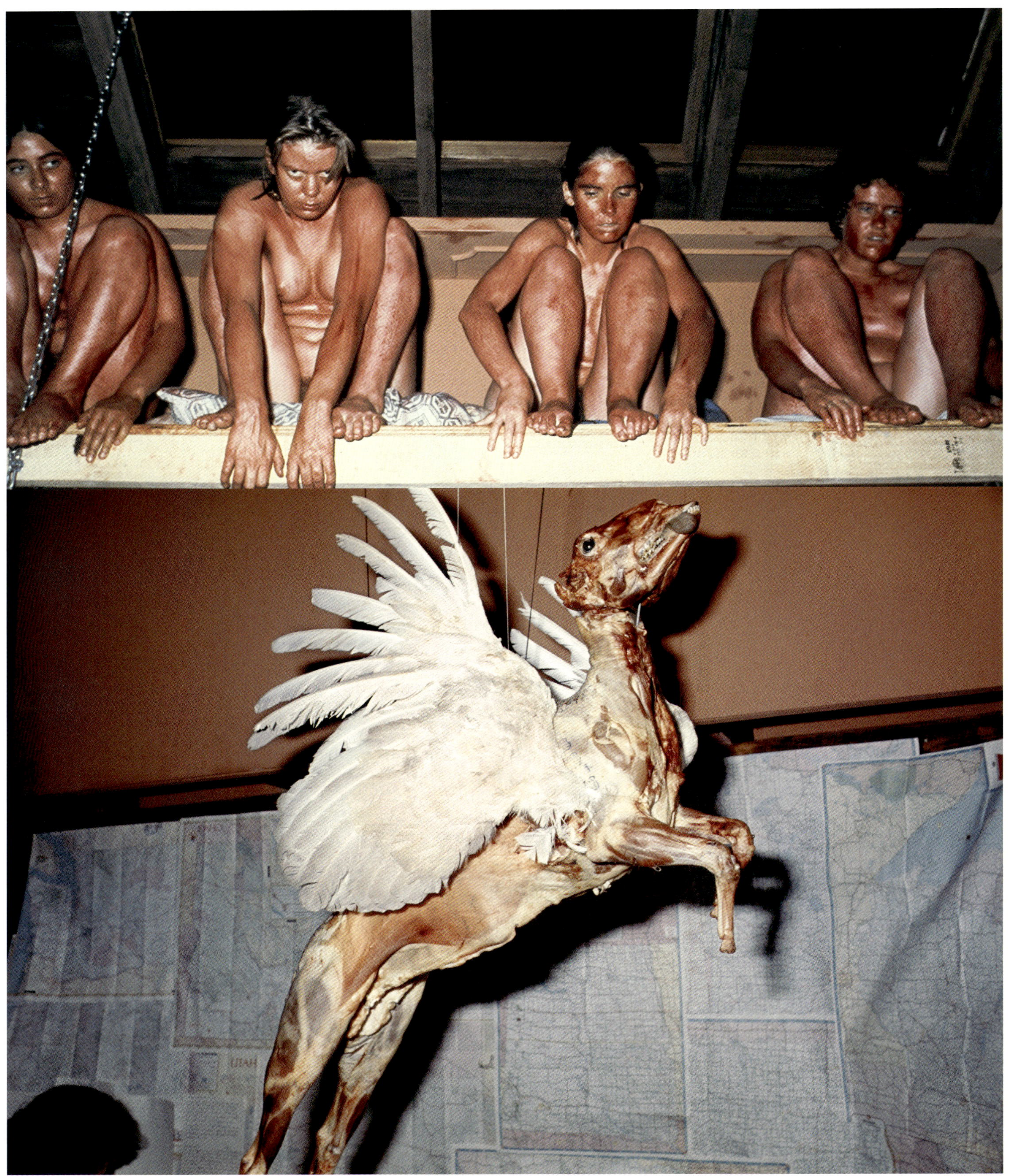

Installation view, *She Who Would Fly*, Garage Gallery, Los Angeles, May 20–21, 1977

"TAKE your clothes off," he says.
My body is shaking. The dress peels
from me like skin, a heap of feathers
disordered, plucked live from the skin,
a mound of fresh leather in a corner.
The animal is still alive! And the
animal is still alive!
I want to reach for a knife to carve
myself into morsels, to divide into portions
to carve a slit downwards from my
navel to my spine. Pain is a relief. I
cherish a distraction from knowing.
But there is no distraction. There is
a gun resting on my shoulder. I do not
forget death is a voyeur at this encounter.

> —Deena Metzger, untitled poem from *Skin: Shadows/
> Silence* for the installation *She Who Would Fly*, 1976

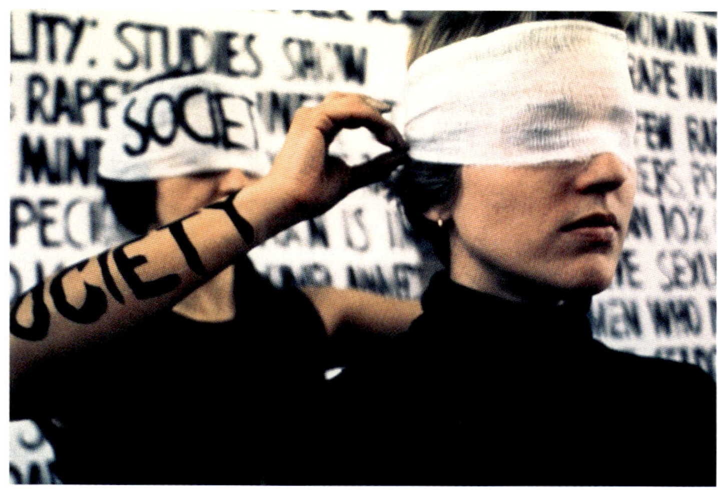

Leslie Labowitz tightening a bandage over the eyes of Signe Dowse for one of Labowitz's four street performances titled *Myths of Rape*, May 19, 1977

Schedule of Events (Excerpt)

<table>
<tr><td>

Opening Press Conference
May 4
Office of City Attorney

</td><td>

Breaking Silence — Anne Gauldin and Melissa Hoffman
May 15
Private studio in Pasadena

</td></tr>
<tr><td>

Business and Professional Women's Meeting
May 5
Restaurant in Santa Monica

</td><td>

Reading from the Maps — Suzanne Lacy
May 16
CLOSE Radio, KPFK-FM

</td></tr>
<tr><td>

Women's Coalition Luncheon
May 5
Bunker Hill, Downtown Los Angeles

</td><td>

Women's Pursepower Jobs
May 18 and 19
Los Angeles Trade Technical School

</td></tr>
<tr><td>

Moment of Concern
May 8
Churches throughout the city
Sponsored by COMMIT, Ecumenical Women Committed to Women

</td><td>

Myths of Rape — Leslie Labowitz
May 19
Los Angeles Mall

</td></tr>
<tr><td>

Installation Ceremonies for the Maps
May 9
Los Angeles City Mall

</td><td>

The Rape — Leslie Labowitz
May 20
Los Angeles Mall

</td></tr>
<tr><td>

Performance and Banquet for Heads of Organizations
May 9
Prepared and Performed by Barbara Smith and Cheri Gaulke in their studio, Pasadena

</td><td>

All Men Are Potential Rapists — Leslie Labowitz
May 21
Los Angeles Mall

</td></tr>
<tr><td>

Slide Presentation, Los Angeles Commission on Assaults against Women
May 11
Southern California Edison Building

</td><td>

Women Fight Back — Leslie Labowitz
May 22
Los Angeles Mall

</td></tr>
<tr><td>

Discussion with Artists from Three Weeks in May Project
May 11
City Mall, site of the maps

</td><td>

She Who Would Fly — Suzanne Lacy
May 20 and 21
Garage Gallery, Studio Watts Workshop

</td></tr>
<tr><td>

Battered Women: A Time for Action
May 14
University of Southern California

</td><td>

Self-Defense Demonstrations
May 20 and 26
Employee Lounge, ARCO Plaza

</td></tr>
<tr><td>

Notes on the Process of Three Weeks
May 15
Garage Gallery, Studio Watts Workshop

</td><td>

Rape Prevention Workshop, Women in County Government
May 20
County Offices

</td></tr>
</table>

In Mourning and in Rage (1977)

SUZANNE LACY AND LESLIE LABOWITZ

In Mourning and in Rage offered a feminist analysis of the violence captivating Los Angeles at the time. Sensational media coverage of the "Hillside Strangler" focused on the life circumstances of the women victims, the randomness and inevitability of the violence, and the personality of the unknown murderer. Lacy and Labowitz's public ritual of rage and grief began with a motorcade of sixty women following a hearse to City Hall, where reporters waited. Nine tall women robed in black like nineteenth-century mourners, followed by one woman in red, climbed out of the hearse, representing the Strangler's victims. On the steps of City Hall each "victim" announced a different form of violence against women, connecting them as part of a fabric of social consent. After every performer spoke, the women from the motorcade, now surrounding the steps like a Greek chorus, yelled, "In memory of our sisters, we fight back!" The woman in red represented the capacity for self-defense. City council members voiced support to the press, the Rape Hotline Alliance pledged to start self-defense classes, and the singer-songwriter Holly Near sang "Fight Back," which she had written the night before. The performance, produced with significant contributions from Bia Lowe, received extensive coverage in local and statewide news.

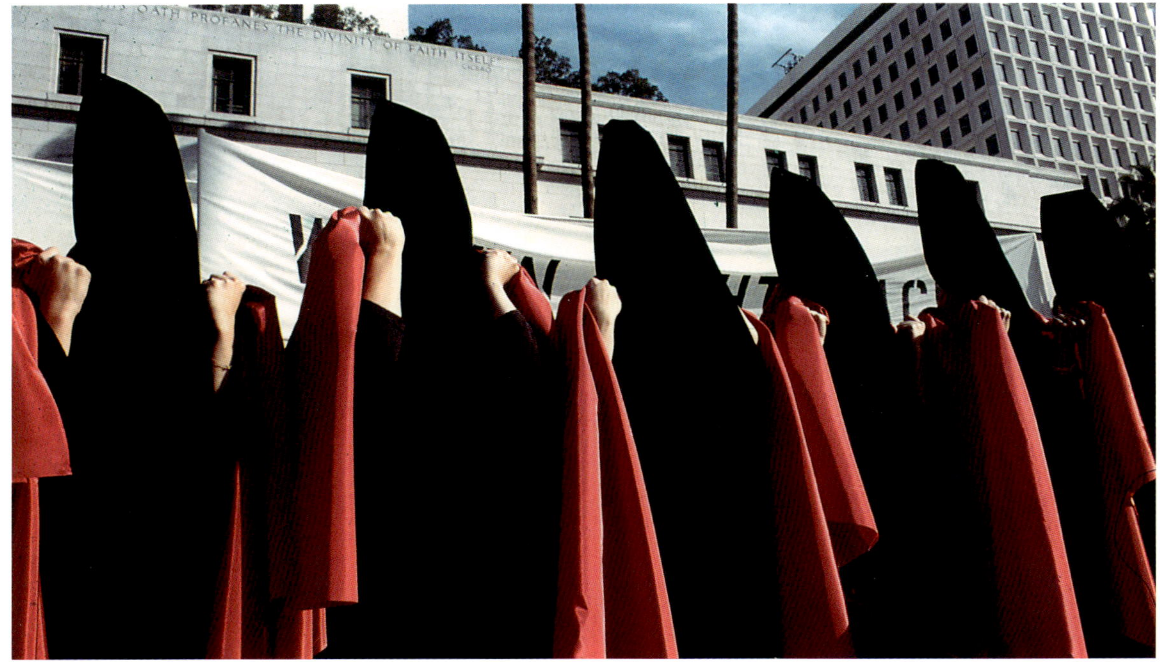

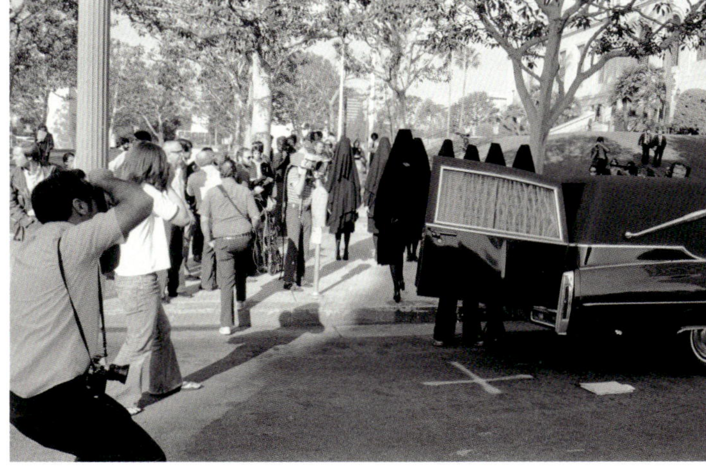

OPPOSITE, RIGHT: Left to right: councilwoman Pat Russell, deputy mayor Grace Montañez Davis, Holly Near, councilman Dave Cunningham, councilwoman Joy Picus, Rape Hotline Alliance member Midori Tabata, and Los Angeles Commission on Assaults against Women organizer Joan Robins

I AM HERE . . .

for the ten women who were raped and strangled between
    October 13th and November 29th

for the 388 women who have been raped in Los Angeles
    between October 18th and November 29th

for the 4,033 women who have been raped in L.A. last year

for the half-million women who are being beaten in
    their own homes

for the one out of four of us who is sexually abused
    before the age of eighteen

for the hundreds of women who are portrayed as victims
    of assault in film, television, and magazines

to speak for the thousands of women who have been raped
    and beaten and who have not yet found their voices

for the women whose lives are limited daily by the
    threat of violence

for the reality of violence against women

for the rage of all women

for women fighting back

. . . IN MEMORY OF OUR SISTERS, WE FIGHT BACK!

FIGHT BACK (EXCERPT)
A song by Holly Near

By day I live in terror
By night I live in fright
For as long as I can remember
A lady don't go out alone at night, no no
A lady don't go out alone at night
But I don't accept the verdict
It's a wrong one anyway
'Cause nowadays a woman
Can't even go out in the middle of the day, safely
Can't go out in the middle of the day
And so we've got to fight back
In large numbers
Fight back, I can't make it alone
Fight back, in large numbers
Together we can make a safe home
Together we can make a safe home
Women all around the world
Every color, religion, and age
One thing we've got in common
We can all be battered and raped
We can all be battered and raped
Some have an easy answer
They buy a lock, and they live in a cage
But my fear is turning to anger
And my anger's turning to rage
And I won't live my life in a cage, no!
By day I live in terror
By night I live in fright
For as long as I can remember
A lady don't go out alone at night
Fight back!

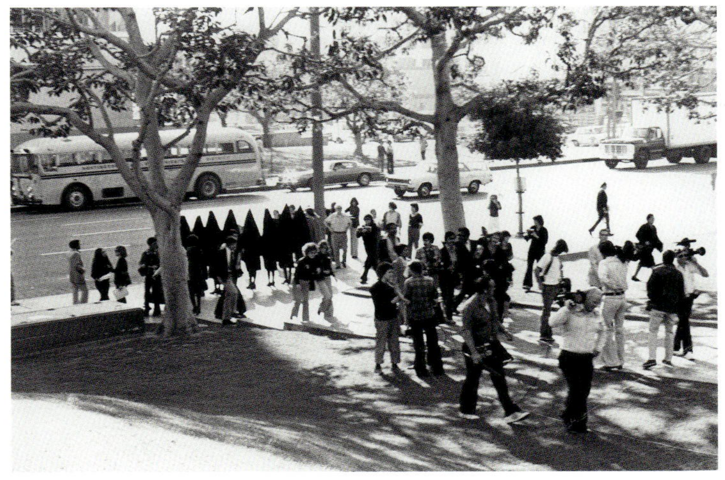

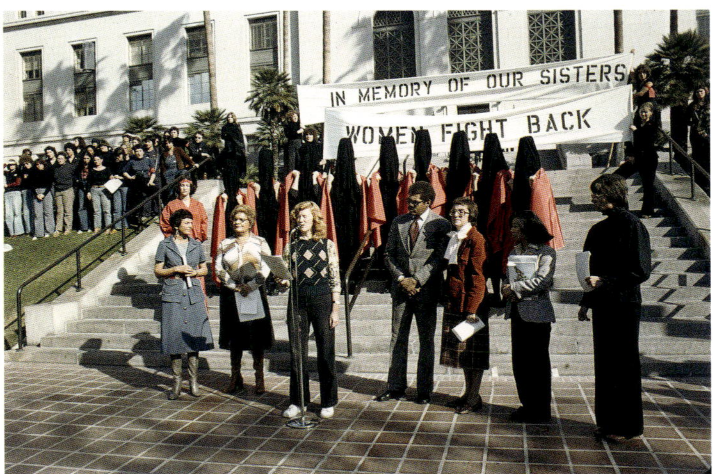

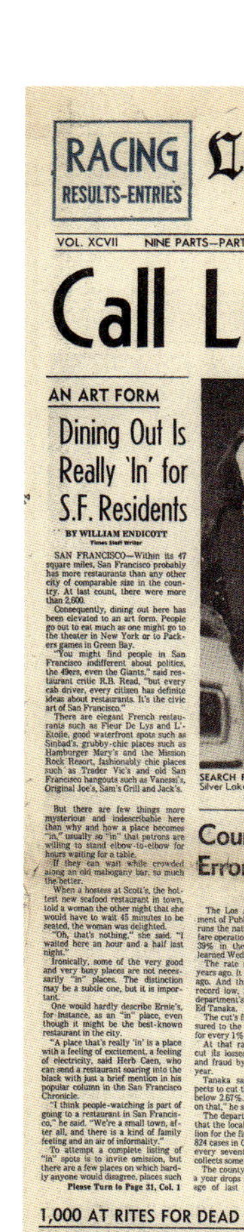
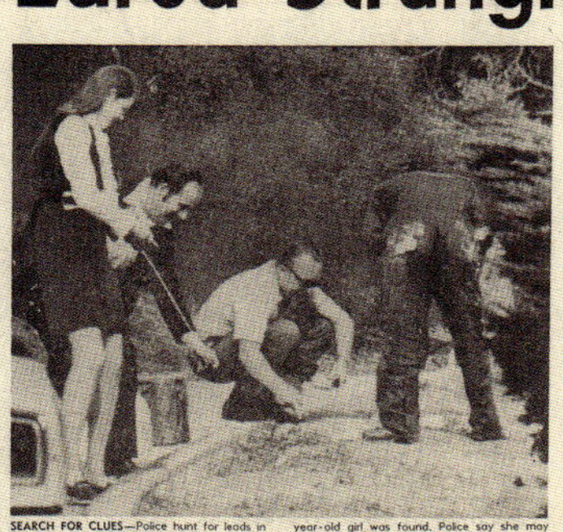

Call Lured Strangler Victim

Slain Girl, 17, Linked to Hollywood Prostitution

(Los Angeles Times, Thursday, December 15, 1977 — Morning Final)

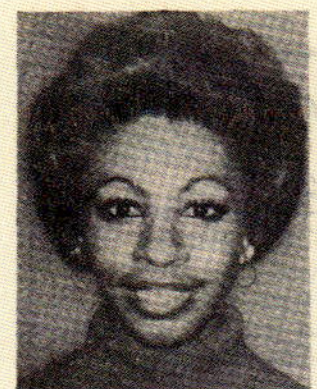
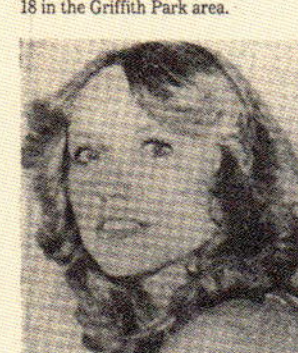
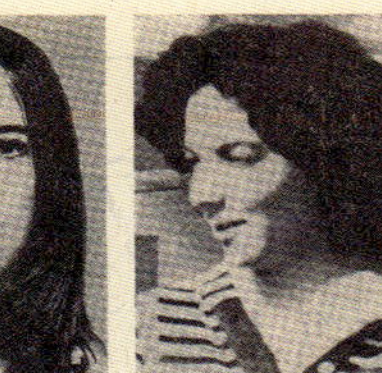
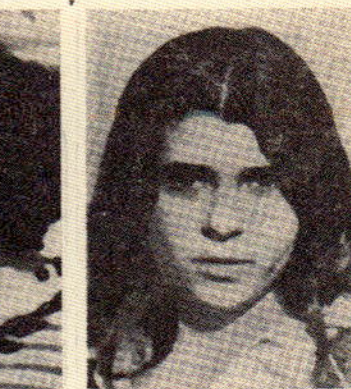
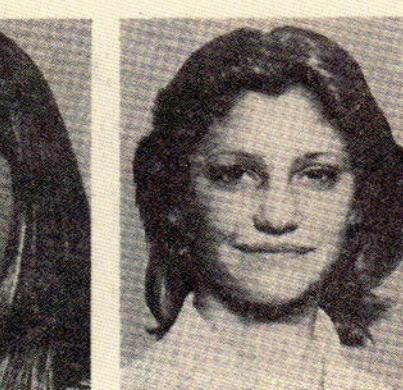
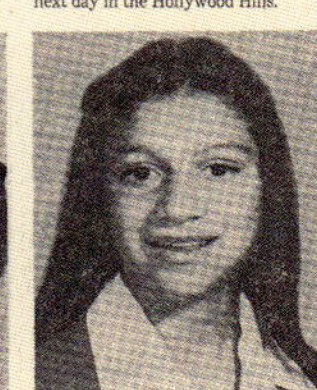
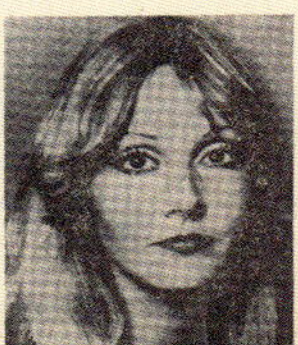
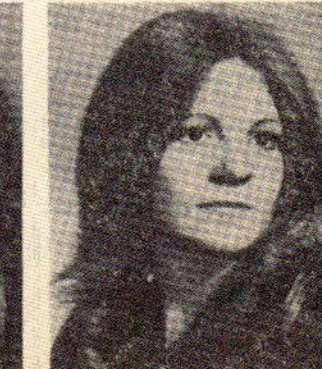

Yolanda Washington, 20, believed to be the strangler's first victim and only black victim, was a former student at Sawyer Business College and the mother of a 2-year-old daughter. She was found at about 1:45 p.m. Oct. 18 in the Griffith Park area.

Judith Ann Miller, 15, a former student at Hollywood High School, had been reported as a runaway by her mother. Last seen at 1:30 a.m. Oct. 31 in the Hollywood area, her nude and strangled body was found hours later in La Crescenta.

Lissa Teresa Kastin, 21, was a former waitress at a health food restaurant in the Hollywood area. She was last seen Nov. 5 in the 1600 block of Vine St. in Hollywood and she was found, nude and strangled, at 10:15 the next morning in Glendale.

Jill Barcomb, 18, was a newcomer to the West Coast from upstate New York and was living at a motel in Hollywood. She was last seen at 7 p.m. Nov. 9 in the Hollywood area and was found nude and strangled the next day in the Hollywood Hills.

Kathleen Robinson, 17, a high school student, was last seen at 9:30 p.m. Nov. 17 at Pico and Ocean Blvd. in Santa Monica. Her remains were found the next day at 8:30 a.m. in the Wilshire District. She had been strangled, but was fully clothed.

Kristina Weckler, 20, was a second-year student at the Art Center College of Design in Pasadena. Last seen at 6 p.m. Nov. 19 in Glendale, her body was discovered at 10:15 a.m. the next day in Highland Park. She had been strangled and was nude.

Sonja Johnson, 14, was a student at St. Ignatius School in Highland Park. She was last seen alive at 6:30 p.m. Nov. 13 at York Blvd. and Ave. 46. Her remains were found Nov. 20 at 4 p.m. near Elysian Park. She had been strangled and was nude.

Dolores Cepeda, 12, was also a St. Ignatius student. Police theorized she was kidnaped at the same time as Sonja Johnson. She, too, was last seen Nov. 13, and her remains were found Nov. 20 near those of the older girl in the Elysian Park area.

REWARDS OFFERED IN 10 L.A. STRANGLINGS

Jane King, 28, eldest of the victims, was a student at the Church of Scientology Celebrity Center. Friends said she was an occasional hitchiker. Last seen at 11:20 p.m. Nov. 9 in Hollywood, she was found, nude and strangled, Nov. 23 near Griffith Park.

Lauren Rae Wagner, 18, was a student at the Sawyer Business College and had hoped to become a legal secretary. Last seen a little after 10 p.m. Nov. 28 in Sepulveda, she was found nude and strangled at 7:30 a.m. the following day near Mt. Washington.

Defense to Escape Strangler Outlined

Fighting Knowledge Might Have Saved Women, Expert Says

Labowitz and Betty Brooks

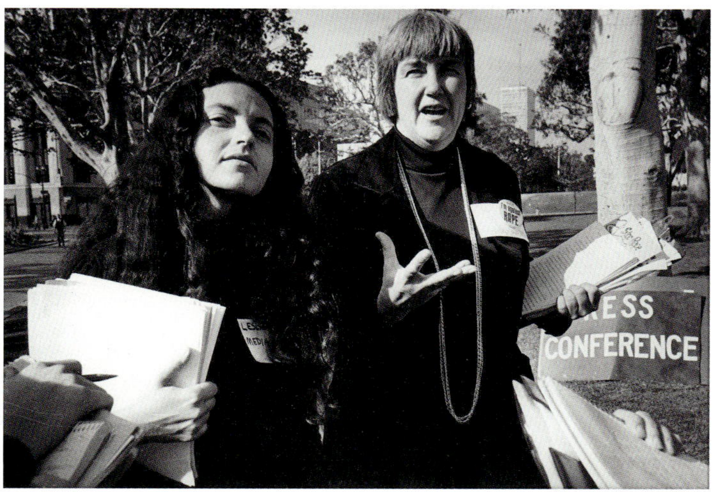

I did a lot of going on television news. . . . They're going, "Well, you're criticizing the media and the way we're sensationalizing this, and don't you want us to report it?" or "Don't you want people to know?". . . I wouldn't say it was the most supportive environment. . . . [But] they really couldn't fight back on what I was saying. You know, there's no way that they could say, "Well, yeah, showing a picture of a woman spread-eagle on a hill, naked, is not a sensationalized image.". . . They just didn't analyze images in the way that they do today, sometimes, some places. Again, I don't really think much has changed.

—Leslie Labowitz, 2011

Record Companies Drag Their Feet (1977)

LESLIE LABOWITZ

After *Three Weeks in May* (1977, pp. 95–99) put news media in the service of art, Labowitz designed another type of intervention, in which the media itself became the performance venue. Staged on Sunset Boulevard under a billboard for the band Kiss, *Record Companies Drag Their Feet* was a protest performance produced specifically for the news media. The press event announced the California National Organization for Women and Women against Violence against Women's national boycott of major record labels such as Warner, Elektra, and Atlantic due to their commodification of sex-violent images of women on album covers.

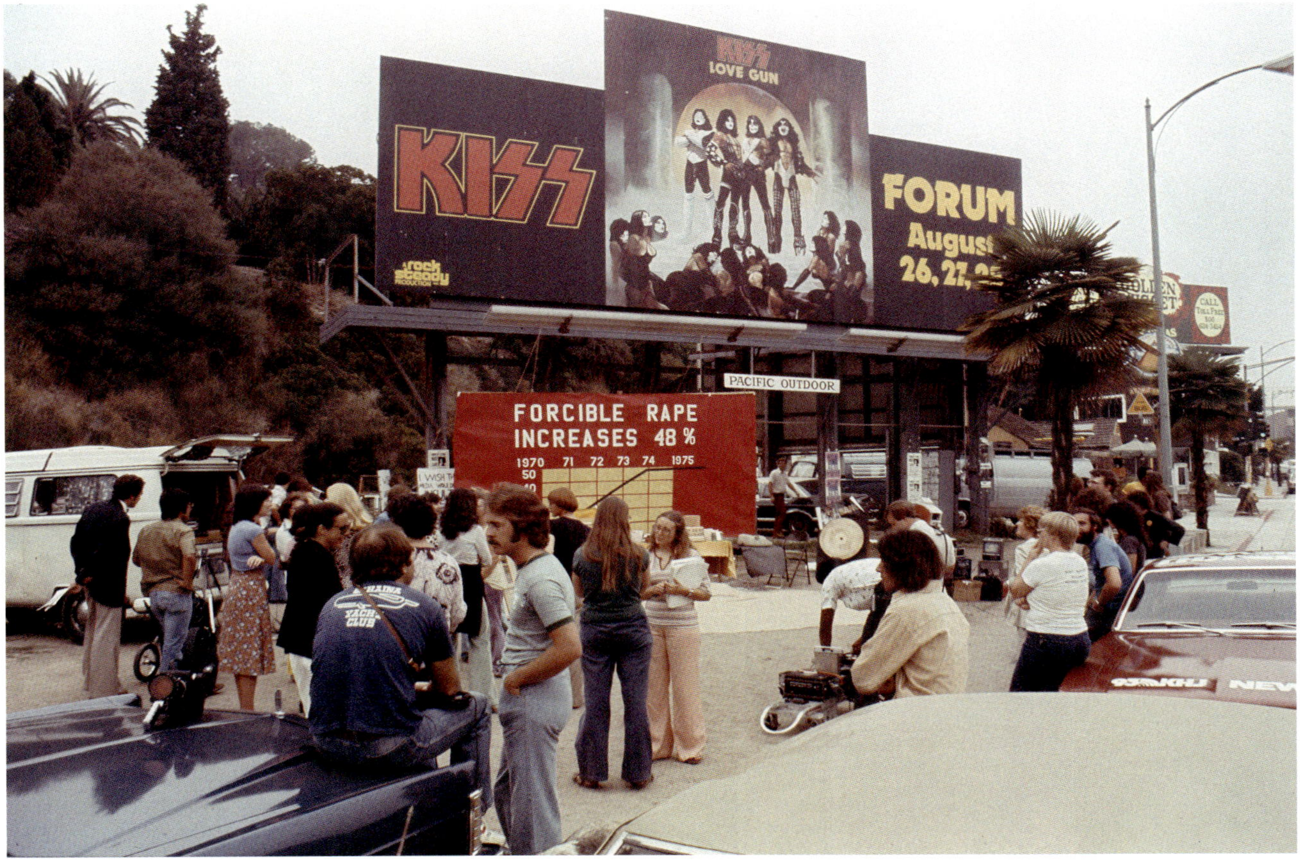

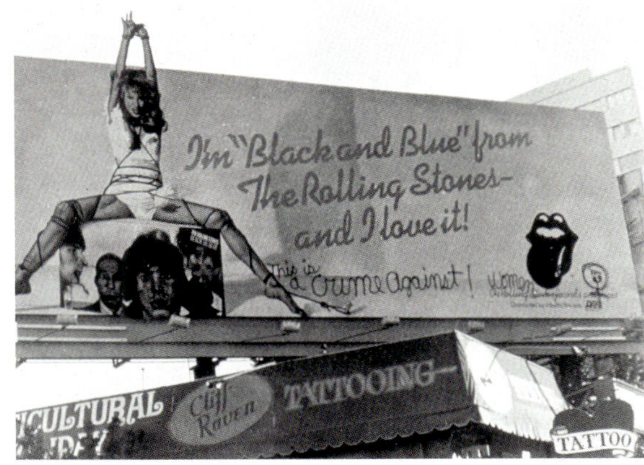

RIGHT: Billboard advertising the 1976
Rolling Stones album *Black and Blue*

A Woman's Image of Mass Media (1979)

LESLIE LABOWITZ

This photomontage brings into stark relief the news and entertainment industries' parallel uses of sex-violent images of women: one to sell newspapers, the other to sell records. It presents a collage of pictures from two Ariadne media performances: on the far right, *In Mourning and in Rage* (1977, pp. 100–102), a response to the news media's sensationalized coverage of the "Hillside Strangler," and on the far left, *Record Companies Drag Their Feet* (1977, p. 103), a protest against major record labels that put demeaning images of women on album covers.

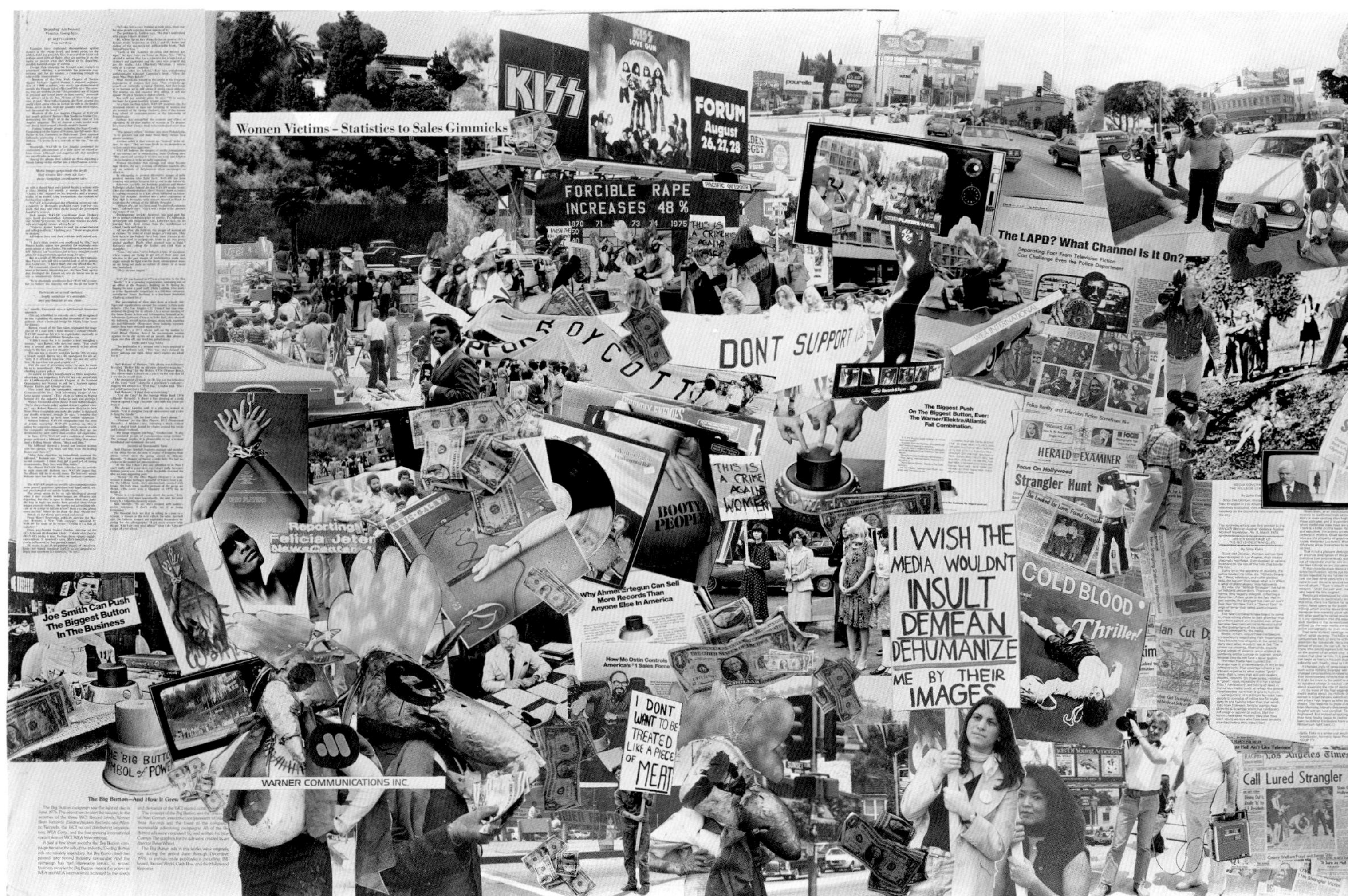

Looking at the mural today, I realize how well it visualized our intent for Ariadne to exist as a framework to build support and community participation among women in the media, artists, activists, and government. Our concern with educating the public about violence against women brought us together. We wanted to put a stop to the use of images of victimized women as entertainment to sell records and newspapers. In the mural I attempted to create a visual representation of the actual performances from the perspective of a woman engaged in these media interventions. I wanted the mural to

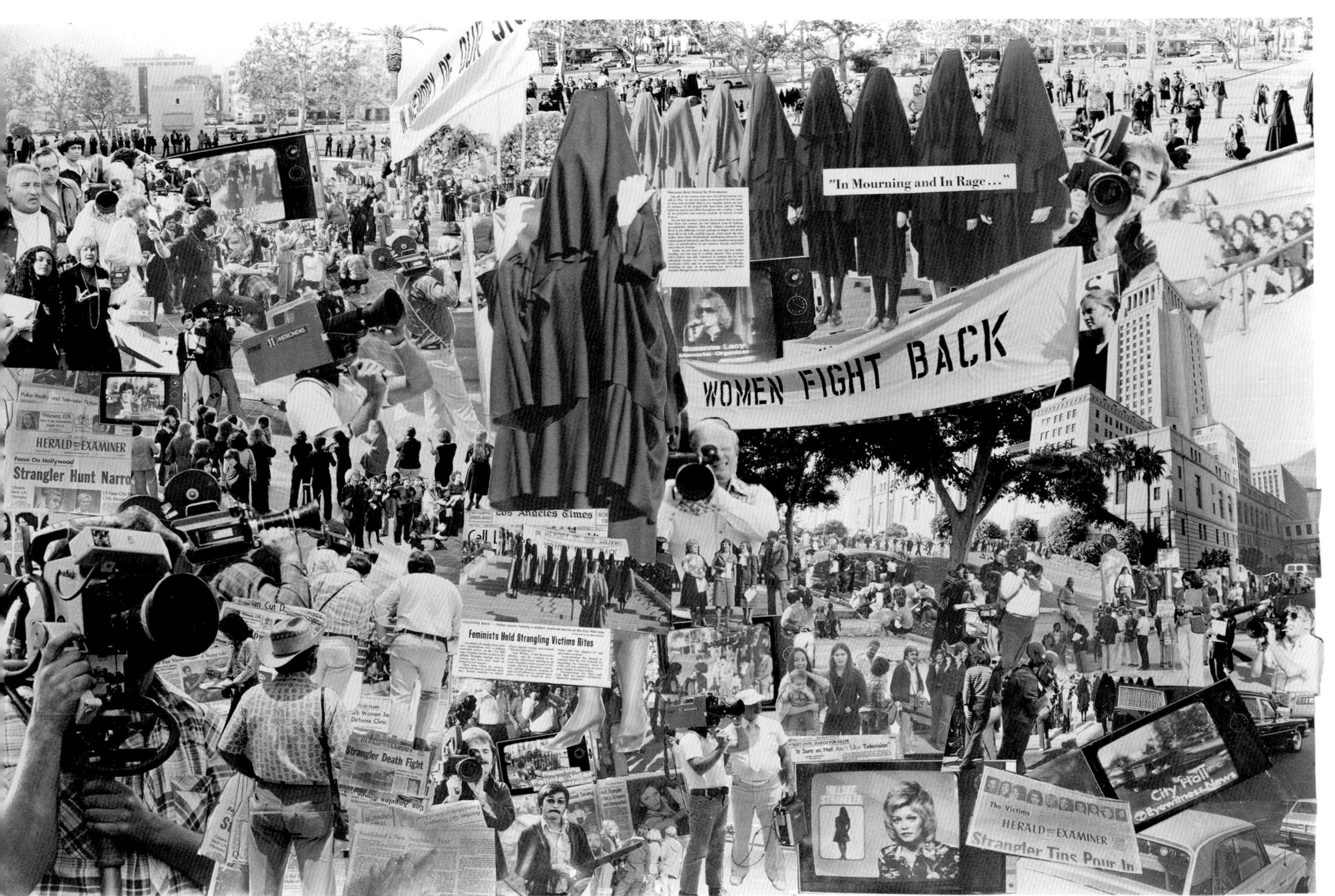

hit hard and have an effect on the viewer that characterized our activist art. Each photo image was cut out and assembled by hand. The images that make up the mural are the real women, reporters, and cameramen who participated in the performances. It is important to be aware that the movement to stop violence against women is grounded in a long history that is more relevant than ever today.

—Leslie Labowitz, 2018

From Reverence to Rape to Respect (1978)

SUZANNE LACY, LESLIE LABOWITZ, AND CLAUDIA KING

This durational performance sought to expose the objectification and exploitation of women in Las Vegas through a media campaign that included two billboards, local press coverage, and a PBS documentary. It incorporated a media event by Labowitz in front of a billboard by Deborah Feldman, a bus tour/performance by Feminist Art Workers, a conference, a talk by Margo St. James, a performance by Kathy Kauffman, and an exhibition featuring Lacy's installation *There Are Voices in the Desert*, which women could enter in solitude to write their experiences of violence on the wall.

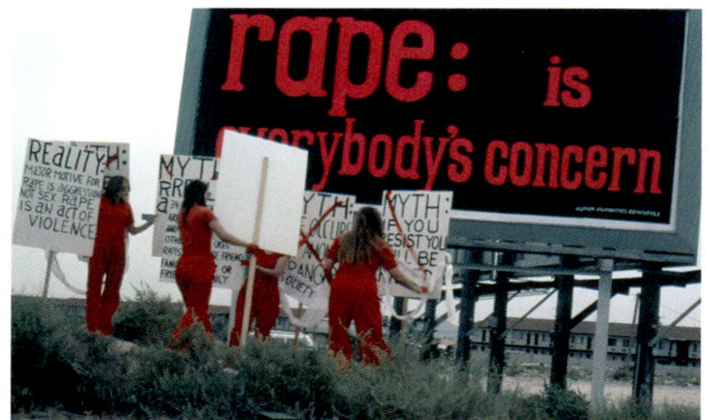

Take Back the Night (1978)

SUZANNE LACY AND LESLIE LABOWITZ

Three thousand women marched from the Feminist Perspectives on Pornography conference in San Francisco to the city's pornography district in this public performance. As Holly Near sang "Fight Back," a brightly lit Janus-faced float moved slowly through the crowd. Labowitz created the front, a madonna bedecked with flowers and electric candles, as in Spanish and Latin American Semana Santa (Holy Week) celebrations. Lacy created the back, a lamb carcass with three heads, like the goddess Hecate, that leaked black-and-white pornography from its open gut. Rose Marie Prins, Mónica Mayer, Betsy Irons, and Ann Klix also contributed to the float. Ariadne organized the participation of over a dozen artists from across the state in the conference.

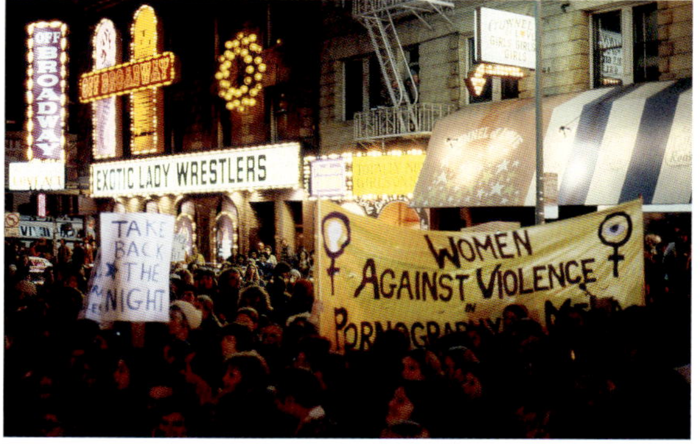

Making It Safe (1979)

Communitas, a community organizing group in Santa Monica, commissioned Lacy to create a work that would raise awareness of violence against women. She and her collaborators distributed leaflets, curated an exhibition spanning thirty windows in the commercial district, and staged events including speak-outs, small dialogues, and self-defense classes. A guerilla group papered a porn shop with images of women protesting, and a series of meals in residents' homes culminated in a candlelit dinner performance at a park featuring 250 women who had participated in the project.

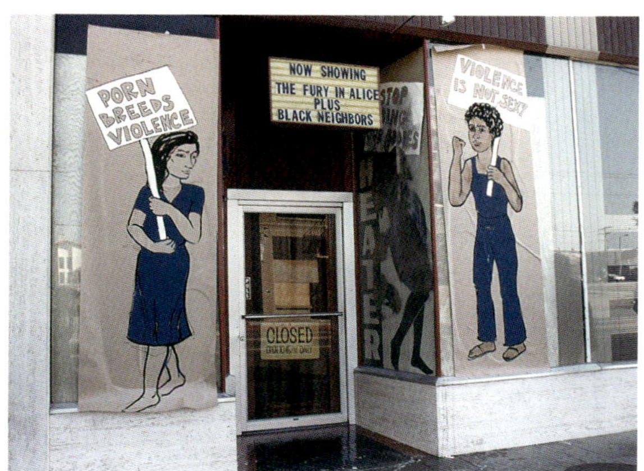

Hardcore Screening (1978)

SUZANNE LACY AND LESLIE LABOWITZ

Ariadne and the California Advocates for Trollops cosponsored a Columbia Pictures screening of *Hardcore*, a film about a father's search for his missing teenage daughter, who reemerges in a pornographic film. Lacy and Lois Lee, founder of Children of the Night and a leading expert on rescuing child sex trafficking victims, moderated a post-screening critique that centered on the film's portrayal of women. Around 150 women attended the event, which received local news coverage.

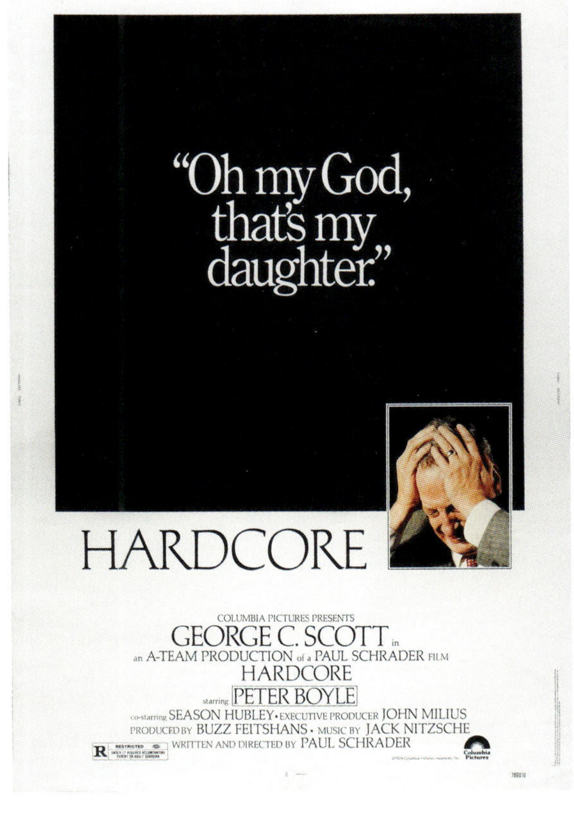

Incest Awareness Project (1979–80)

LESLIE LABOWITZ, NANCY ANGELO, LESLIE BELT, BIA LOWE, PAULA LUMBARD, AND TERRY WOLVERTON

Incest Awareness Project sought to bring an invisible topic into mainstream discourse. The first public dialogue on incest in Los Angeles, it coined the term "incest survivor," taught survivors how to use media to educate the public about incest, and presented the first national art exhibition by incest survivors. Mayor Tom Bradley signed a proclamation making November 1979 Children's Defense Month and formally recognizing the efforts of Ariadne to raise awareness of this issue.

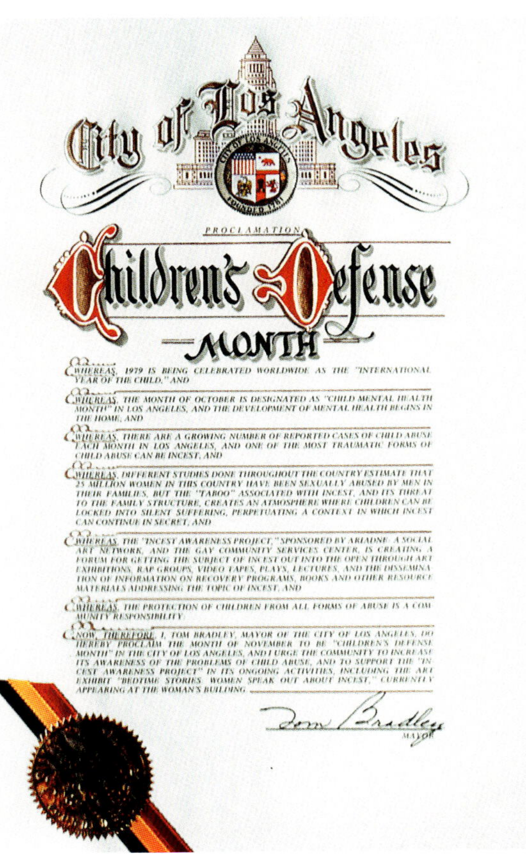

The Performing Archive: Restricted Access (2007)

SUZANNE LACY AND LESLIE LABOWITZ

This installation featured fifty white bankers boxes of archival photographs and ephemera from Lacy and Labowitz's art of the 1970s. Twelve monitors displayed women born that decade interpreting the materials from their own perspectives, representing the transmission of feminist art history. The installation also included a re-creation of Labowitz's *A Woman's Image of Mass Media* (1979, pp. 104–5), vitrines of archival materials selected by the women in the videos, and a projection of the women searching through the archives. At Yerba Buena Center for the Arts, San Francisco, the installation also featured planned visits by scholars and their students.

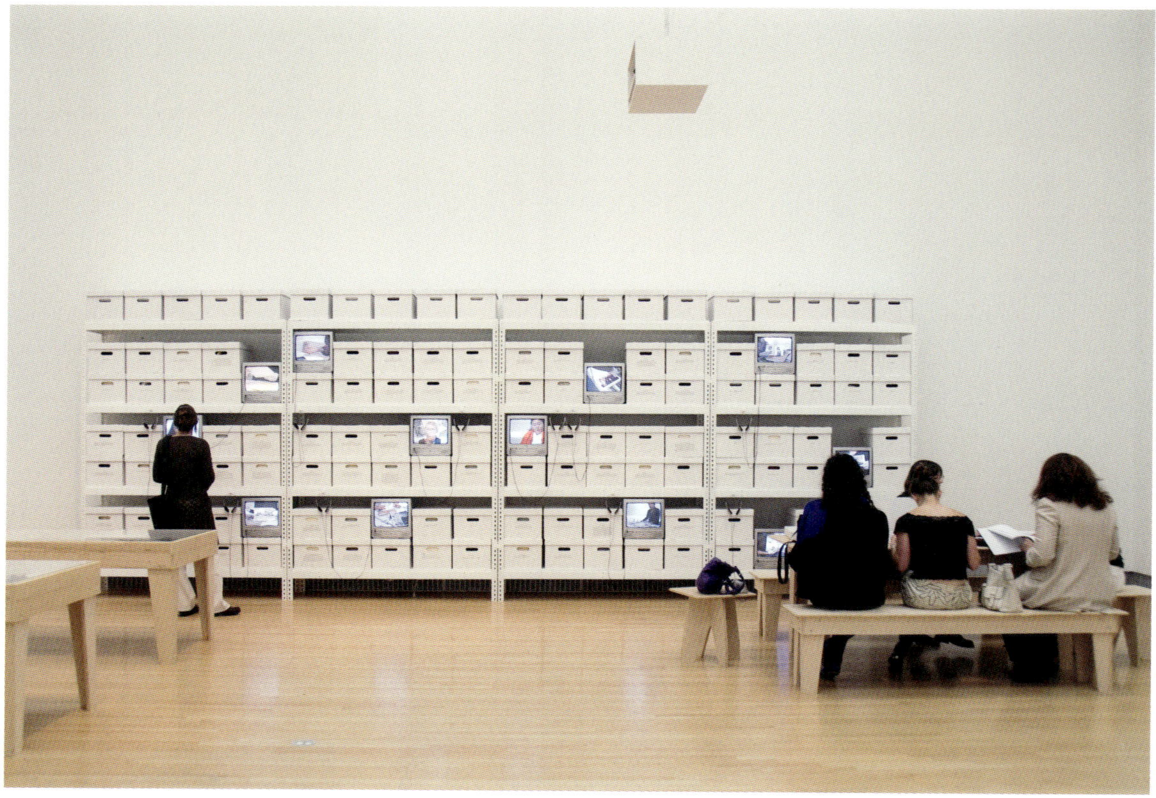

Installation view, *The Way That We Rhyme: Women, Art, and Politics*, Yerba Buena Center for the Arts, March 29–June 29, 2008

DOMINIC WILLSDON: What was the impulse for doing *The Performing Archive*?

LESLIE LABOWITZ: The archives of most women artists of that time were hidden in their garages or apartments. They were not out in the public sphere. So we decided to bring all our archives together. In fact, we brought them to the 18th Street Arts Center, Santa Monica—we started here—and Suzanne brought in her analysis of 1970s performance art and brought in other artists to talk about archives. And we made a time line of feminist performance art from 1970 to 1980.

SUZANNE LACY: We got together—I don't think Martha Wilson was there, but Faith Wilding was, and Cheri Gaulke, Susan Mogul. . . . We had all these women laughing hysterically and talking about who slept with who and sticking notes up on the time line and fighting about where things occurred in their résumés. Subsequently, I also interviewed a lot of people about archives, like Martha and Alastair MacLennan and whoever came through L.A. We were looking at how individual memory differs from institutional memory. L.A. performance had been reduced in institutional memory to Paul McCarthy, Mike Kelley, and Chris Burden, and then it expanded to include Asco and feminism, but that still is a very small band. Actually, there were tons of people doing performance at that moment. So I think it was an essentially democratic impulse to say, wait a minute, we lived in that era, and we knew that work and how it impacted men and women at the same time. We were also interested in how the idea of feminism had been translated—through college art classes, mostly—into kind of a white, middle-class movement in the 1970s, which wasn't exactly the way we remembered it. So, against the institutional reduction of feminist history, performance history, and different political movements, we were doing our own reclaiming.

LABOWITZ: The artists who had participated in these works, they were represented in all of our archives. Media reporters were also in our archives, activists were in our archives—within our archives we were valuing the work that was done throughout that whole period.

WILLSDON: When the younger women artists who were part of the work engaged with this history, and with the Ariadne history, particularly—what do you think had the most impact on them?

LACY: I think a lot of it was that they were shocked that they didn't get this in feminist history courses in college, that they got a very different point of view.

LABOWITZ: To just add a little context about what we asked them to do: Suzanne came up with the idea of integrating these younger women artists into the piece, and when we brought them in, we didn't tell them about our work. They were told to go through the archive and pick ten things that interested them and then talk about them. We didn't tell them what this was. We were trying to see how they would, in their time, look at this work, and what they would see in the work.

LACY: That's a very important point.

LABOWITZ: What I got from it, which was very moving, really, was the recognition that we were a generation that had stepped away from our mothers. Our mothers were not our role models. But we were these women's role models. And they were so happy and thrilled and honored to look at our work and to think that we invited them in and that there was this whole other kind of matriarchal history.

WILLSDON: What about the ways in which the political moment of 1977 differs from that of 2007 or today?

LABOWITZ: So much now, in a good way, is about diversity, antiracism, and immigration rights, and so many women are working in all these areas—plus there's the #MeToo movement. *The Performing Archive* really did relate to mostly women in the arts, in terms of the way it was shown, and that was on purpose. The thought was: How can we do something within the broad cultural community that brings the history of feminist art into that community? Something that deals with violence against women and shows what strategies of media intervention were used in the past to make social change, as some of those models might also work today? Because social media is not enough. That's the message. Social media is not enough. Firing men—that's helpful, I guess. What we're talking about here, and what I was trying to talk about with the Ariadne website I recently created, is that we need to engage the media, the government, and other people—artists, in this case, and activists. To achieve real social change, you can't just do it by putting it on the internet. I wanted the website to be an educational tool, originally. One that would be available, free, and accessible on all devices, and then I would invite educators to recommend it as part of their curricula. My plan was also to do salons, inviting people to have the same kind of discussion we're having right now.

—Excerpt from recorded conversation, 2018

Auto on the Edge of Time (1993–94)

This series by Lacy and various collaborators explores domestic violence. Evoking the flight from abuse in the family car as today's "underground railroad," *Underground* comprised three sculptural cars representing interior and exterior monologues, escape plans, and memory. They were placed in Pittsburgh's Three Rivers Park along a railroad track inscribed with a poem that led to a phone booth, where you could talk to a live person, listen to recordings of survivors, or record your own story. For *Doing Time*, Lacy worked for a year with a domestic violence shelter in White Plains, New York, and fifteen women at Bedford Hills Correctional Facility, New York. Together they developed a two-week workshop, during which participants created three more sculptural cars: the Abuse Car, the Wall of Silence, and the Healing Car. For *The Children's Car* and *Children Speak*, Lacy interviewed kids, mothers, and counselors at Cleveland's Center for the Prevention of Domestic Violence. In workshops the children drew their homes, neighborhoods, and families on car doors that were exhibited at the Museum of Contemporary Art Cleveland. Public service announcements with children and their mothers were also produced. In 1994 cars from *Underground* and *Doing Time* were reinstalled in an abandoned Niagara Falls gas station, where they served as a backdrop for rallies, presentations, and meetings about domestic violence. Susanne Cockrell, Virginia Cotts, David Katzive, Carol Kumata, Sharon Smolick, and Charlotte Watson each collaborated with Lacy on one or more projects in the series.

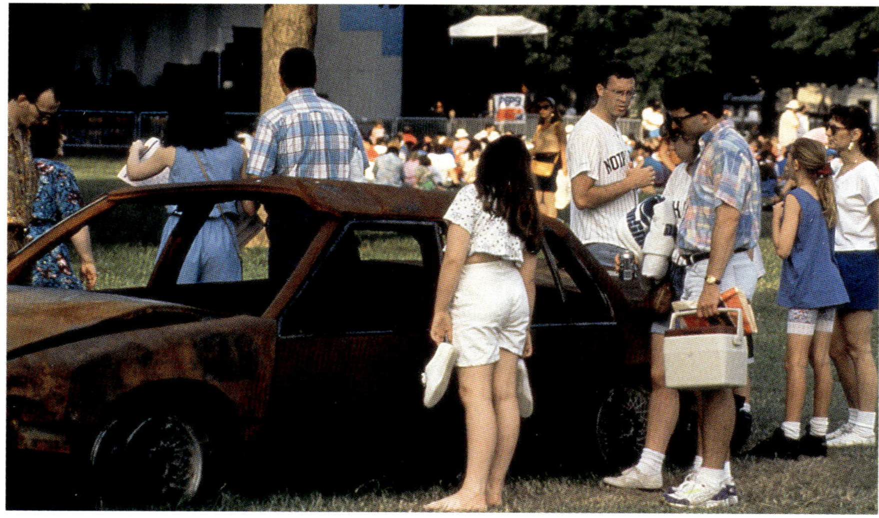

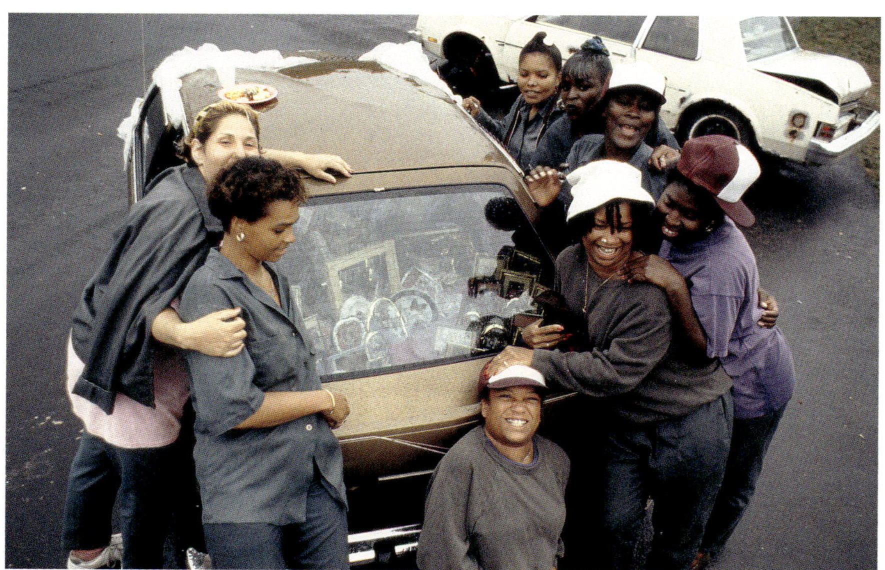

TOP: Audience members with the Car of Memory, from *Underground*
BOTTOM: Women from the Family Violence Program at the Bedford Hills Correctional Facility posing with the Healing Car, from *Doing Time*
OPPOSITE, TOP: The Abuse Car, from *Doing Time*
OPPOSITE, MIDDLE (LEFT TO RIGHT): The Car of Interior and Exterior Monologues, from *Underground*; the Healing Car, from *Doing Time*
OPPOSITE, BOTTOM (LEFT TO RIGHT): The Car of Memory, from *Underground*; the Car of Escape Plans, from *Underground*

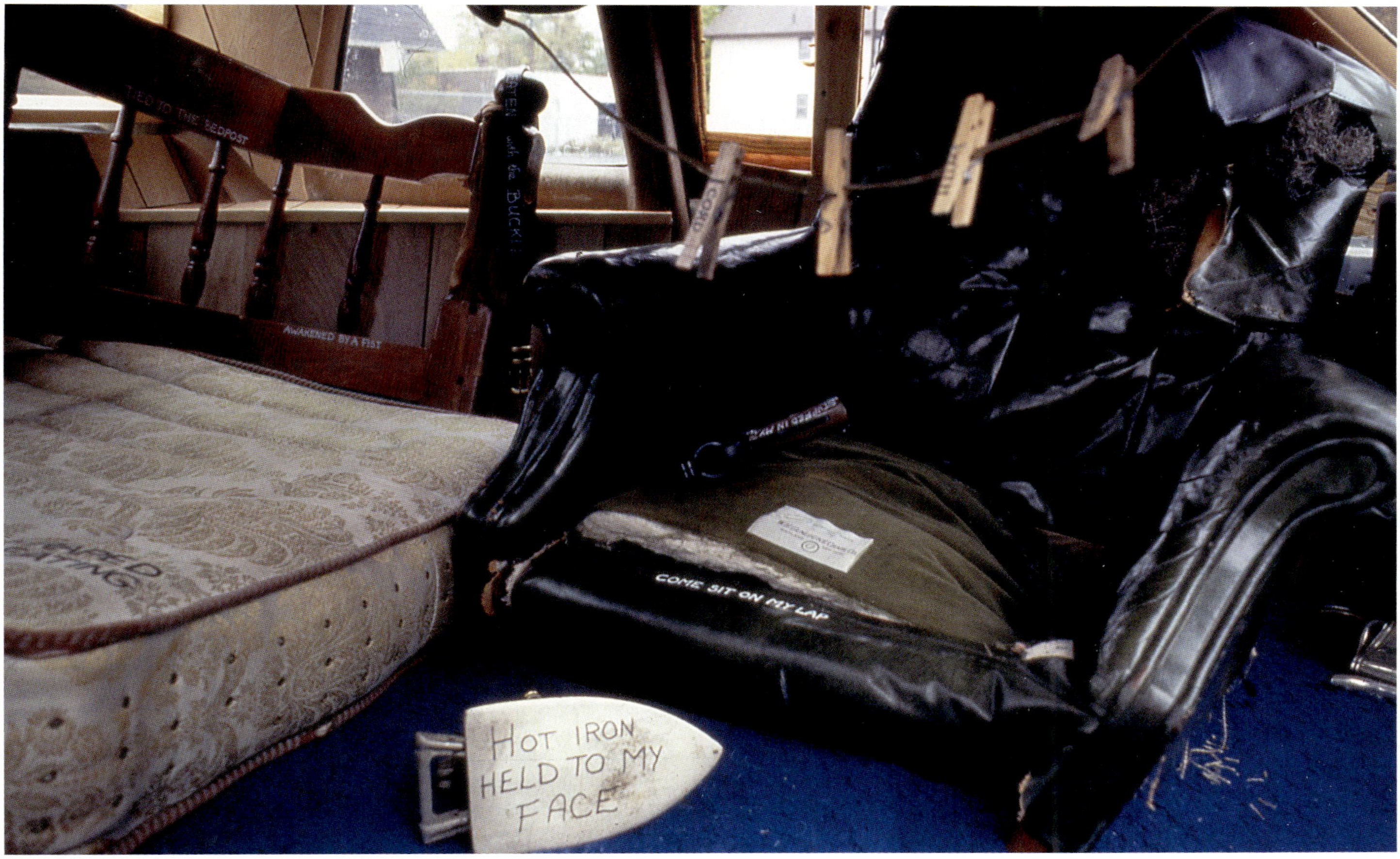

TIED TO THE BEDPOST
AWAKENED BY A FIST
HOT IRON HELD TO MY FACE
COME SIT ON MY LAP

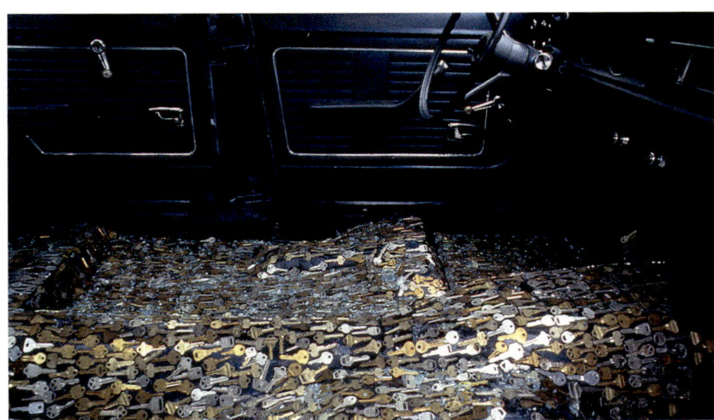

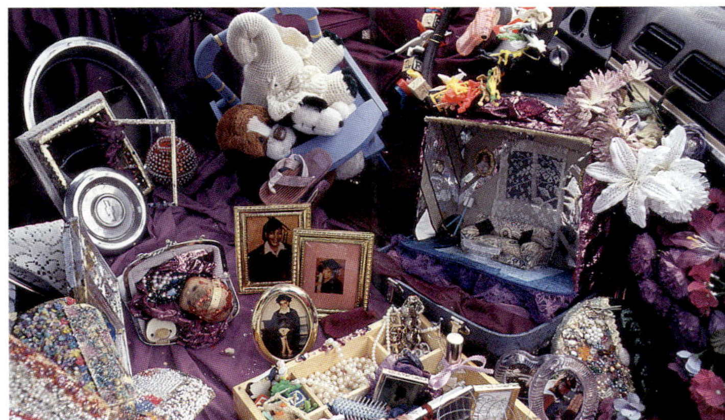

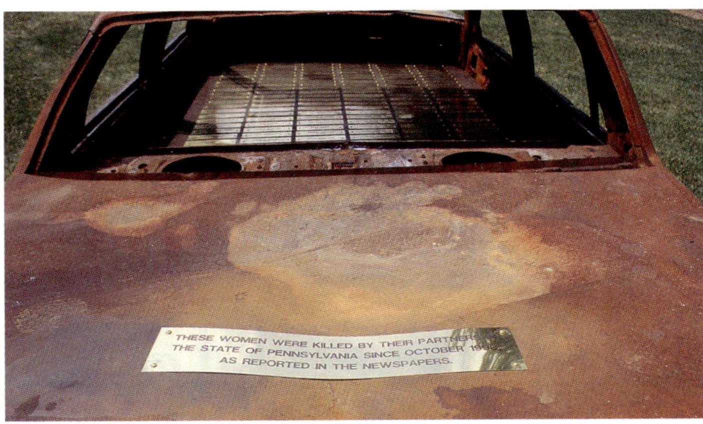
THESE WOMEN WERE KILLED BY THEIR PARTNERS IN
THE STATE OF PENNSYLVANIA SINCE OCTOBER 19
AS REPORTED IN THE NEWSPAPERS.

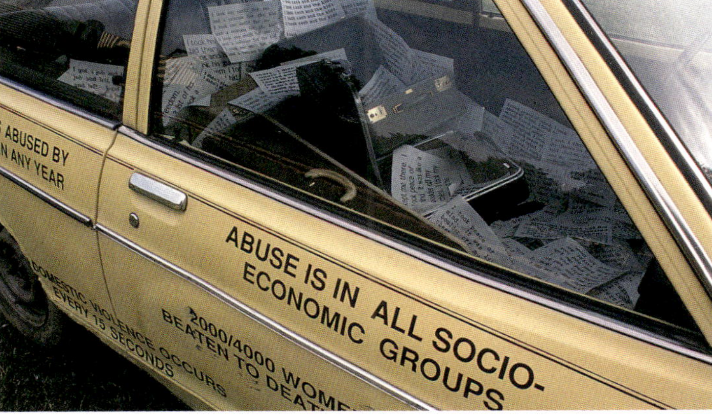
ABUSE IS IN ALL SOCIO-
ECONOMIC GROUPS
2000/4000 WOMEN
BEATEN TO DEATH
DOMESTIC VIOLENCE OCCURS
EVERY 15 SECONDS

Esqueleto tatuado (Tattooed Skeleton) (2010)

Esqueleto tatuado was a yearlong project in Madrid that examined how media and political discourse construct narratives of domestic violence, the impact of those narratives in the public sphere, and new ways of confronting the issue. Lacy and her collaborators explored the gaps between the experiences of survivors and society's laws and practices, taking as a starting point the white masks Spanish protesters used to symbolize how victims of domestic violence remain hidden, fearing retribution. Four hundred personal narratives of abuse from women across the country were handwritten onto masks employed throughout the project, which included four months of performances and civic interventions: videotaped interviews with women living in a shelter; a film by Cecilia Barriga; a film screening during an awards ceremony for social service providers; a conversation among activists, journalists, and government officials; an exhibition at the Museo Nacional Centro de Arte Reina Sofía; a live-streamed performance with school-age youth; and a massive protest on November 25, the International Day for the Elimination of Violence against Women.

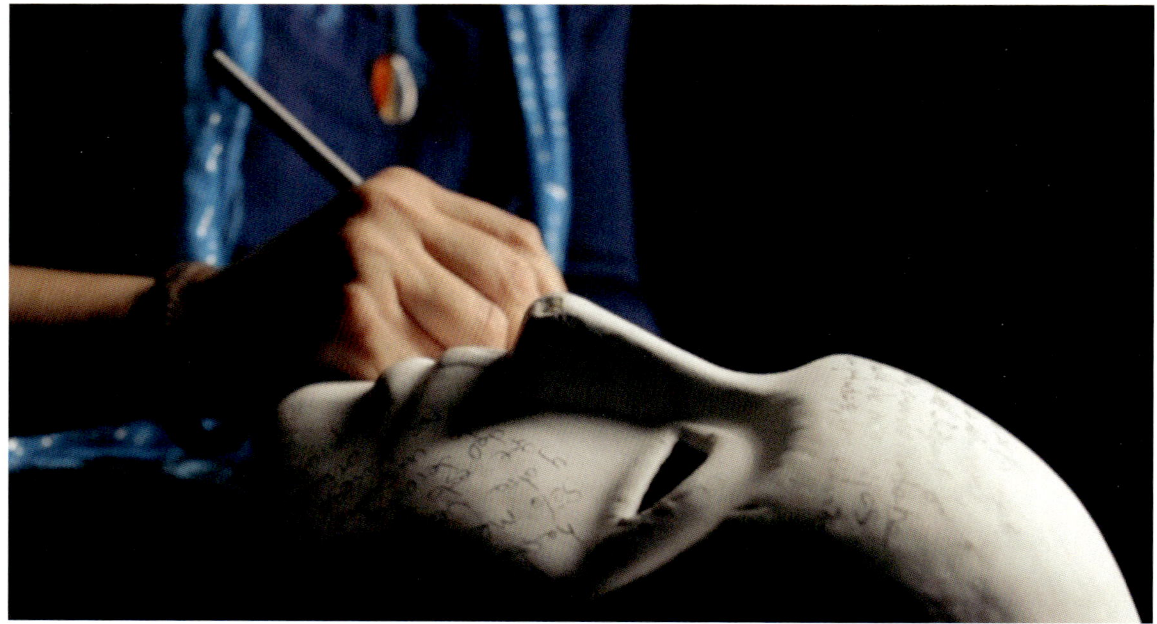

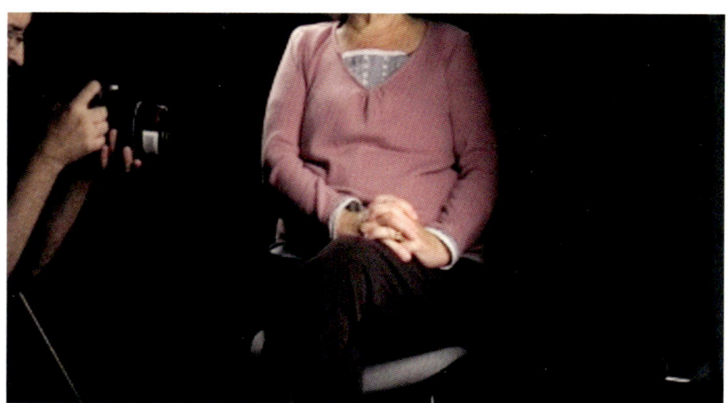

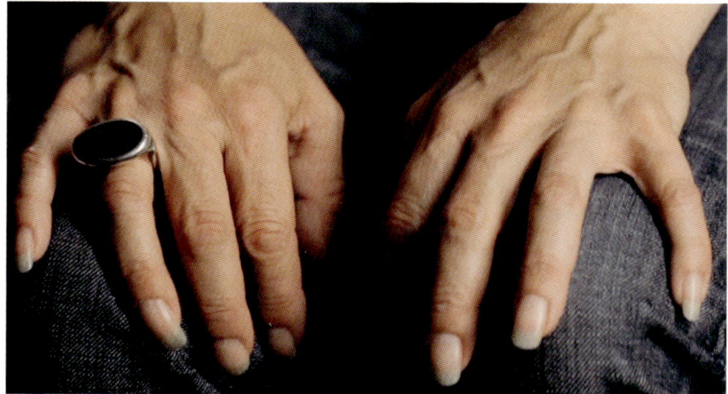

Just as literary critics have recognized that powerful stories come not necessarily from following traditional genres but from combining them, so those working to prevent sexual assault might combine story genres to produce the kind of stories that are capable of shattering pernicious myths about what constitutes a real rape.

—Francesca Polletta, Monica Trigoso, Britni Adams, and Amanda Ebner, "The Limits of Plot: Accounting for How Women Interpret Stories of Sexual Assault," 2013

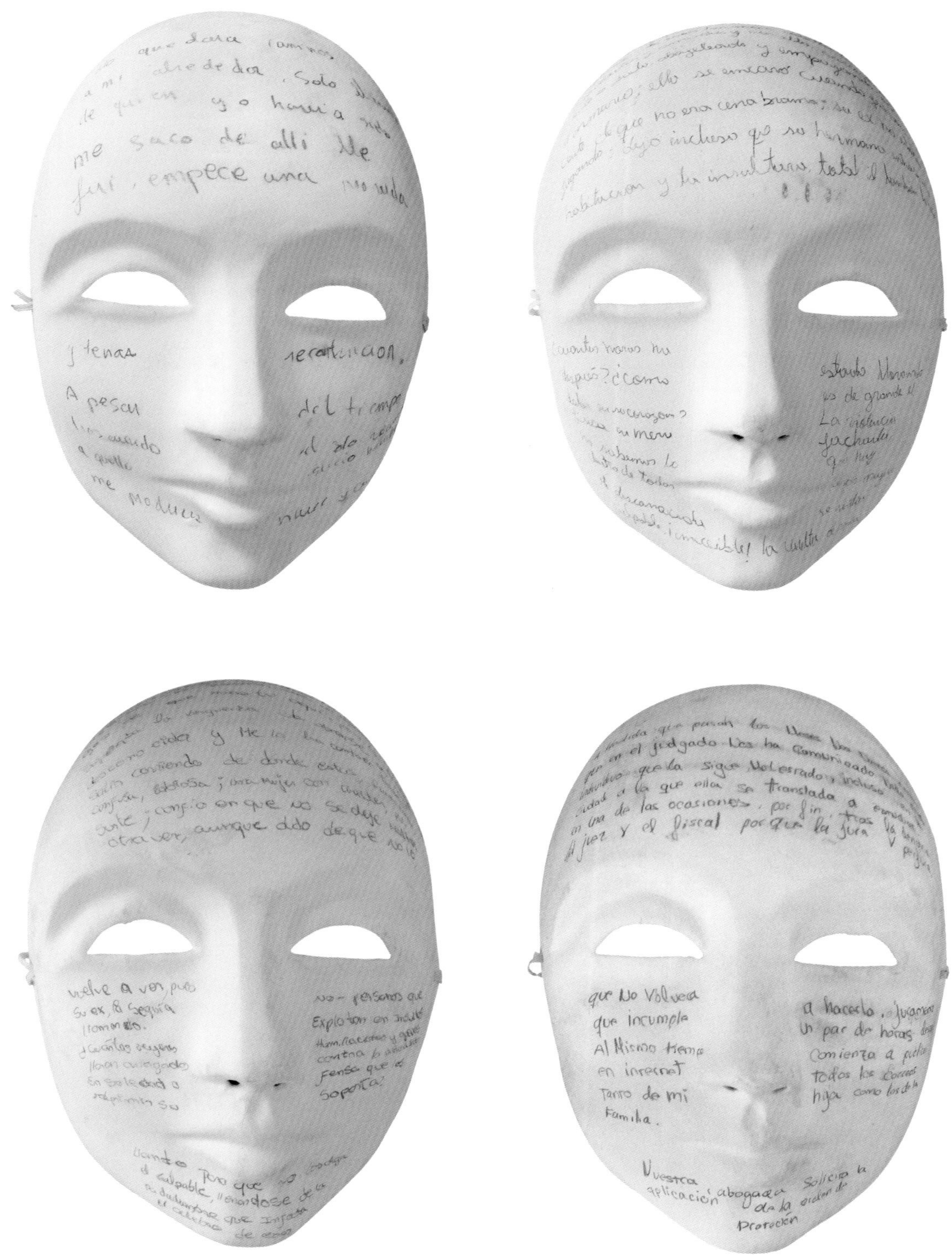

OPPOSITE: Production stills from the film *Esqueleto tatuado* (Tattooed Skeleton, 2010) by Barriga

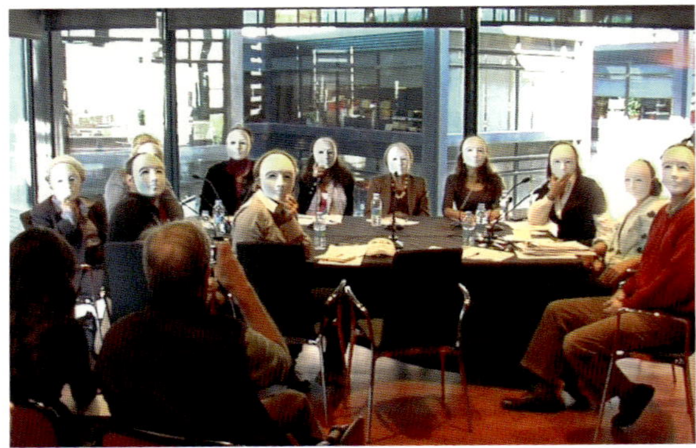
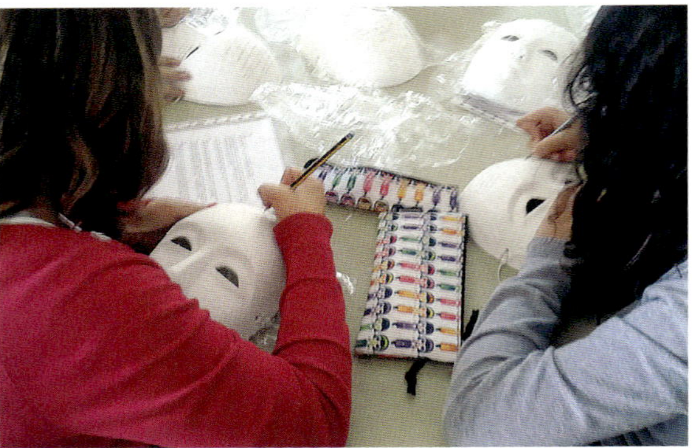

TOP LEFT: A conversation among activists, journalists, and government officials exploring new narratives to counter domestic violence, Madrid, 2010
TOP RIGHT: Students writing women's personal narratives of abuse on masks, Madrid, 2010
BOTTOM: Spanish protesters wearing masks similar to those Lacy employed in *Esqueleto tatuado*, 2016
OPPOSITE, TOP: Audience members wearing masks from *Esqueleto tatuado* during an awards ceremony organized by the Spanish government for providers of social services, November 23, 2010
OPPOSITE, BOTTOM: International Day for the Elimination of Violence against Women, Madrid, November 25, 2010

When Suzanne Lacy made contact, Toxic Lesbian was working on a gender perspective project with highly invisible groups, the very groups feminists usually approach least. Specifically, Toxic Lesbian was working with gender violence victims from communities affected by mental health problems, as well as with Roma women, lesbians, and transgender women.

—Toxic Lesbian, collaborator, 2018

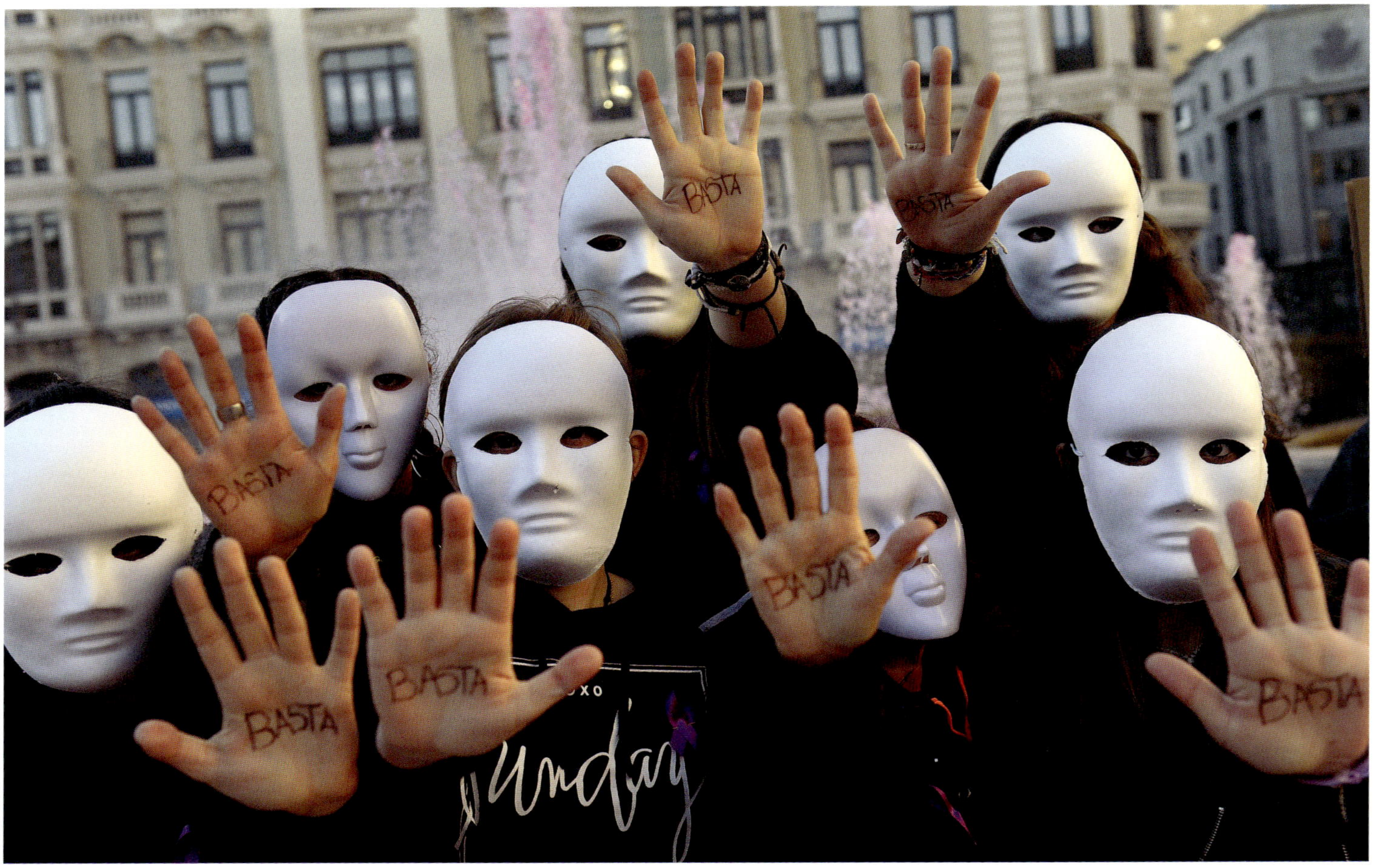

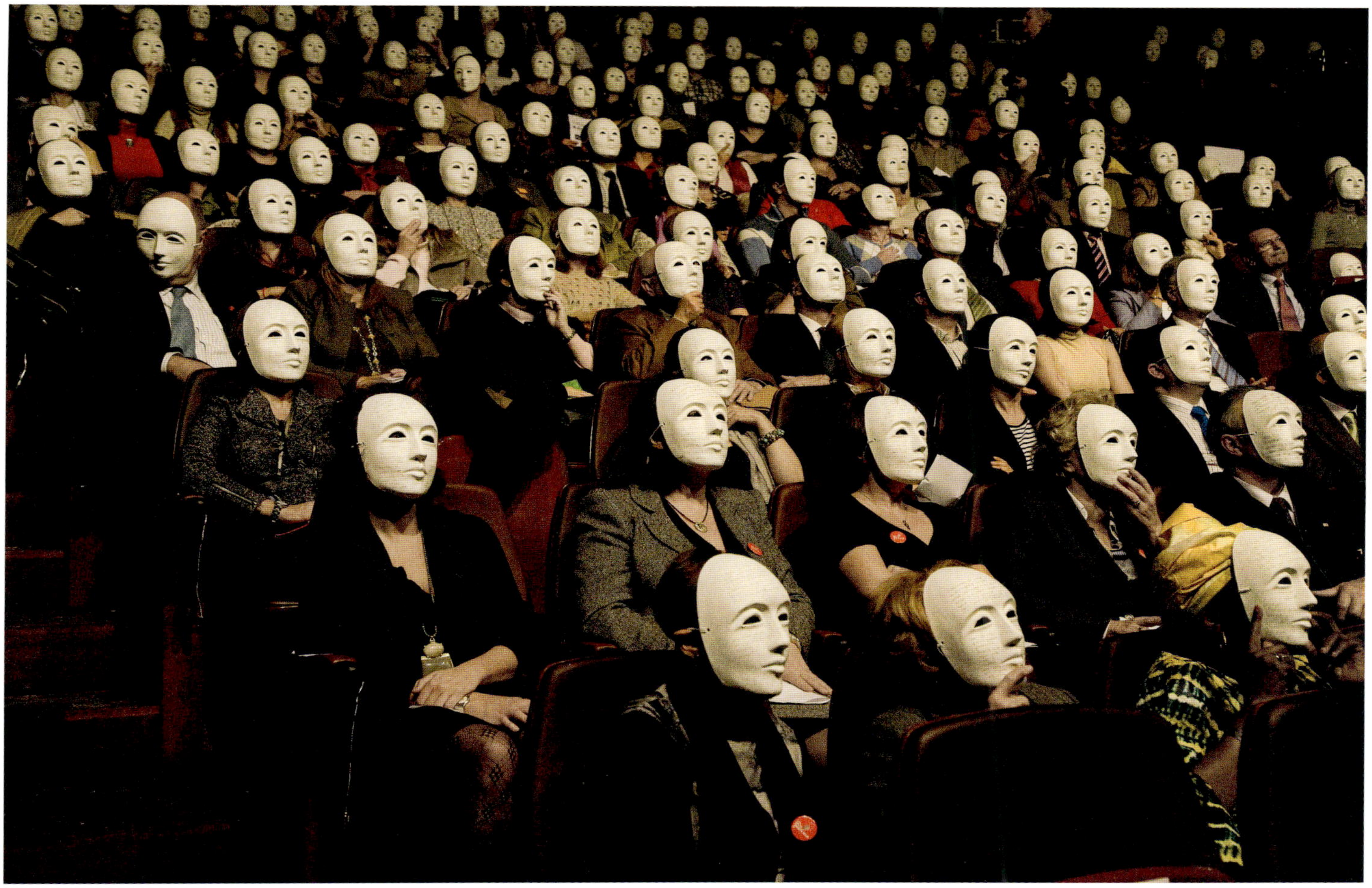

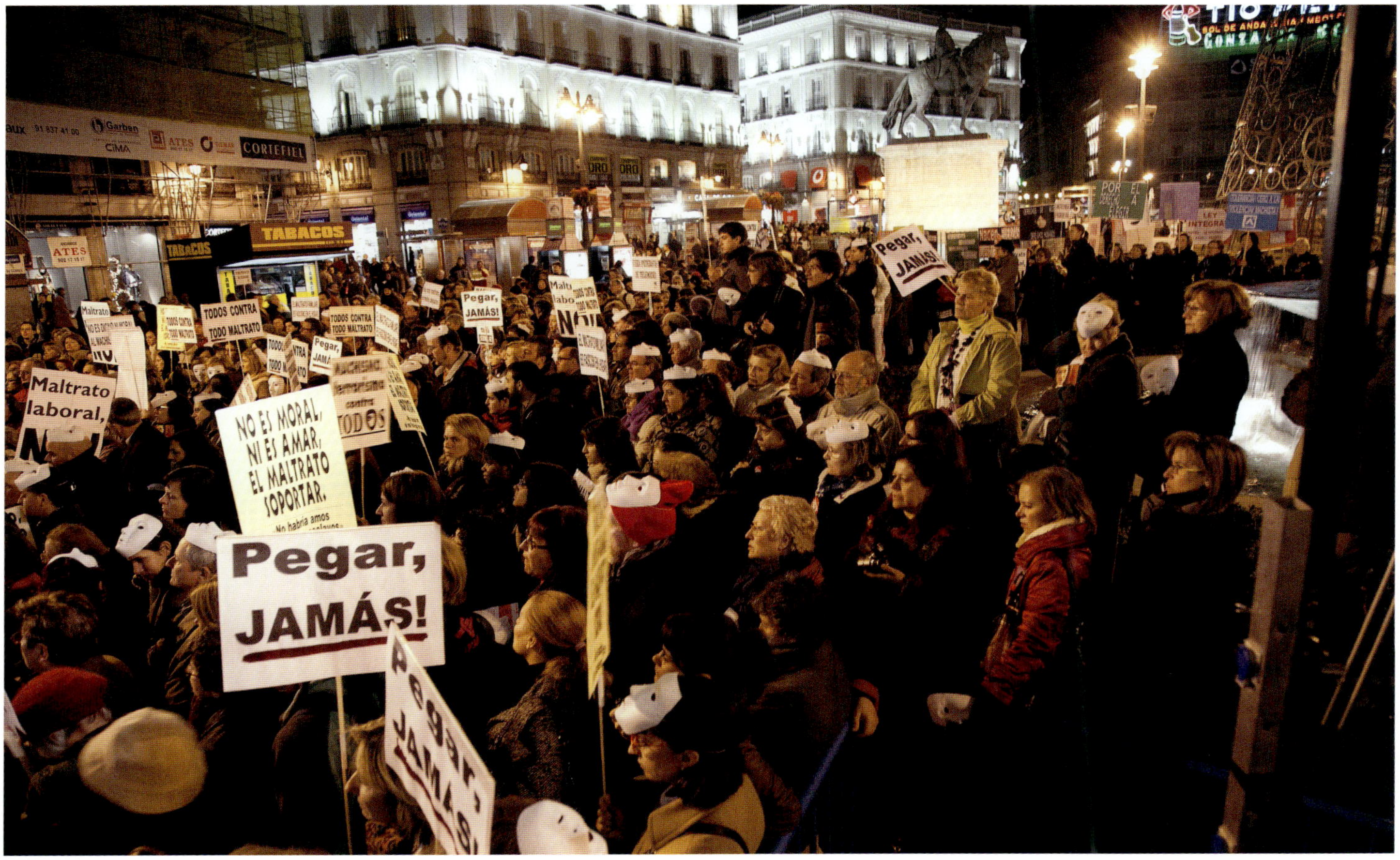

Maltrato laboral,
TODOS CONTRA TODO MALTRATO
NO ES MORAL, NI ES AMAR, EL MALTRATO SOPORTAR.
No habría amos
Pegar, JAMÁS!
CORTEFIEL
TABACOS
ATES
POR EL
LEY INTEGRA

Three Weeks in January (2012)

To reimagine *Three Weeks in May* (1977, pp. 95–99) forty years into the anti-rape movement, Lacy reenacted some of its key performances but also focused on new issues and organizing strategies. The project included fifty public and private events with activists, educators, media makers, politicians, and artists, many of which were covered extensively by the news media; a map of Los Angeles in front of the police department with daily markings of the sites of the prior day's reported rapes; a bench projecting a soundtrack of survivor narratives, created by Bruno Louchouarn; and a social media campaign, *I Know Someone, Do You?* It concluded with two performances: *Storying Rape*, at the top of City Hall, and *Call to Action/Candlelight Vigil*, which paired audience participation with filmed and animated instructions, exploring the range of communication techniques used in contemporary organizing.

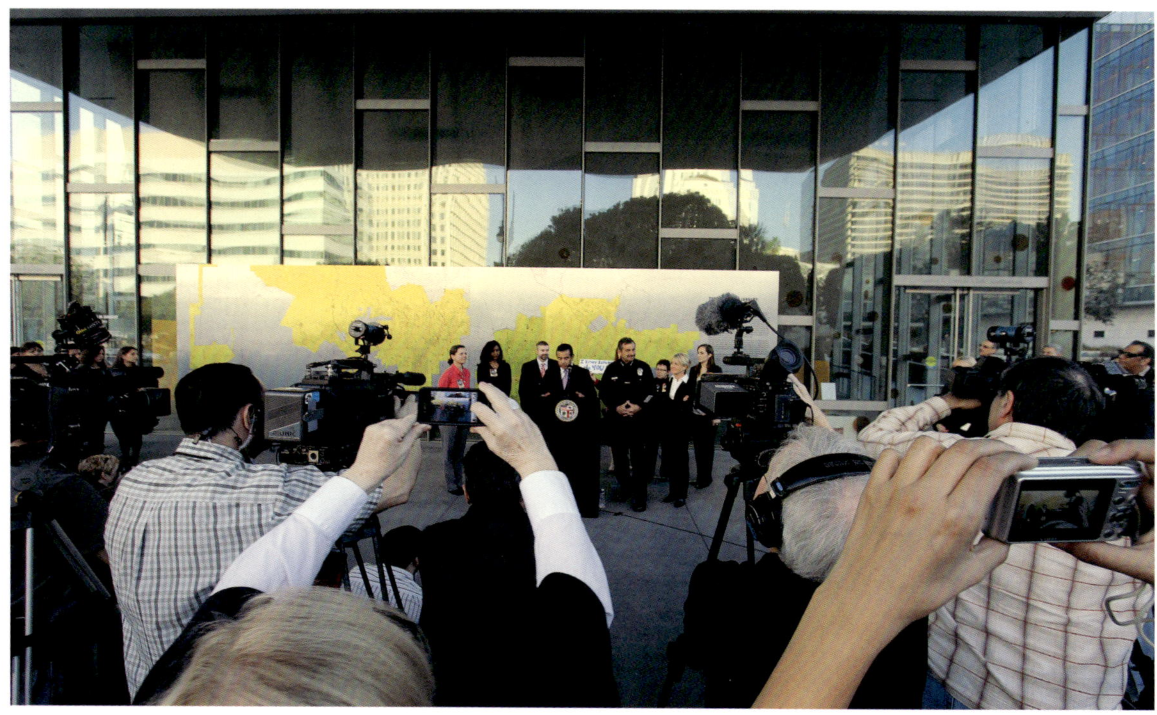

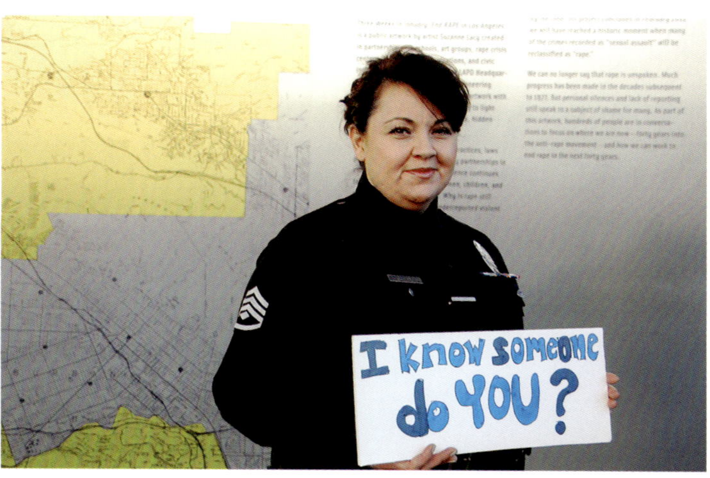

Six hundred eighty-three rapes is 20 percent less than we had the year before. It's one quarter of what we had in 1977. It's much less than the city has ever had in its recent history. But let's not forget: one rape is one too many. One of the ways that we can keep women safe against sexual violence is to increase awareness, and to me, that is the core, that is the result that I wish from this project.

—Charlie Beck, Los Angeles Police Department chief, 2012

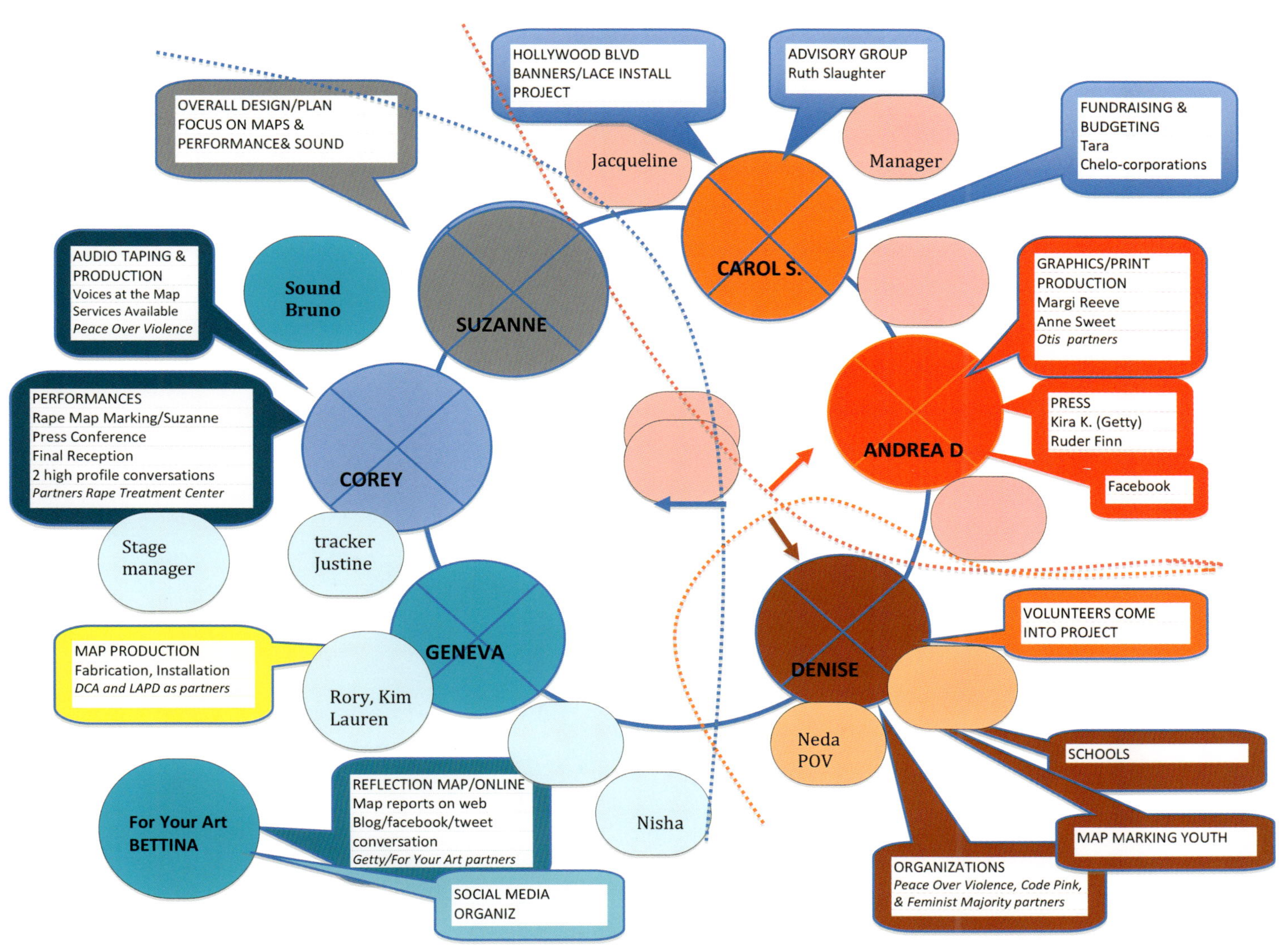

OPPOSITE, TOP: Los Angeles mayor
Antonio Villaraigosa, with Lacy and police
chief Charlie Beck, speaking in front of
the map of rapes in Los Angeles
OPPOSITE, BOTTOM: Photograph from
I Know Someone, Do You?
ABOVE: Diagram of project organizers

De tu puño y letra (By Your Own Hand) (2014–15/2019)

When Lacy arrived in Quito, Ecuador, in 2014, she encountered the Cartas de Mujeres project, for which ten thousand Ecuadorian women wrote letters about their experiences of violence. *De tu puño y letra* invited men to address the issue of domestic abuse by representing these letter writers. On the night of the final performance more than fifteen hundred people entered Plaza Belmonte with the city band. The first three "acts" inside the bullring featured a relentless narrative drawn from the letters of the Ecuadorian women discussing childhood, the body, and intimate partner violence. The ring slowly filled with hundreds of men from all walks of life reading the letters, their crescendo eventually broken by an abrupt silence. The voice of an elderly woman then asked, "Why do you call this love?" The last act took place amid the audience, where 350 men huddled over candles to read letters to groups of two or three. Mediators fostered conversations between the readers and audience members that collaborators hoped would continue long after the project concluded. Contributors to the work included Bruno Louchouarn, Oderay Game, Gabriela Ponce, Timm Kroeger, Paulina León, María Fernanda Cartagena, and Mónica Moreira.

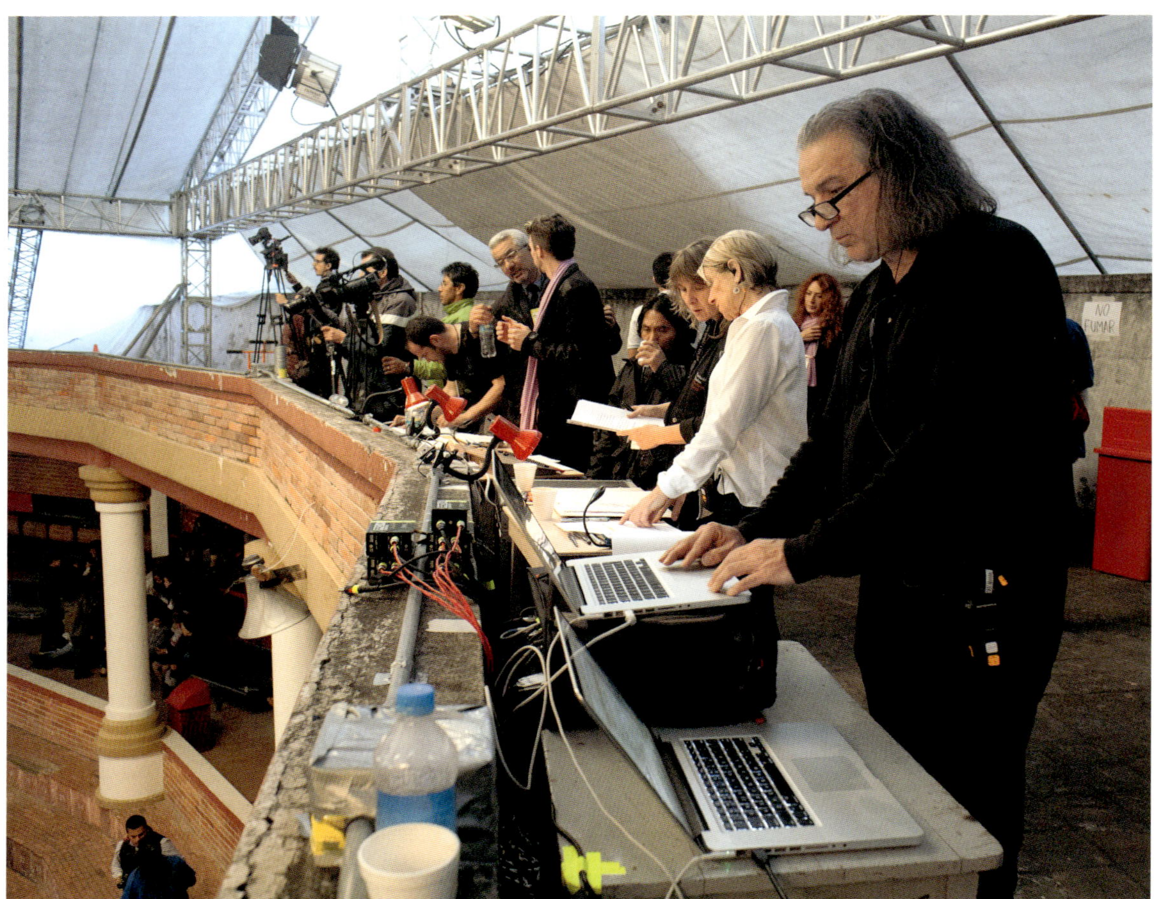

Lacy with composer Louchouarn
(foreground) in a production booth
during the performance, 2015

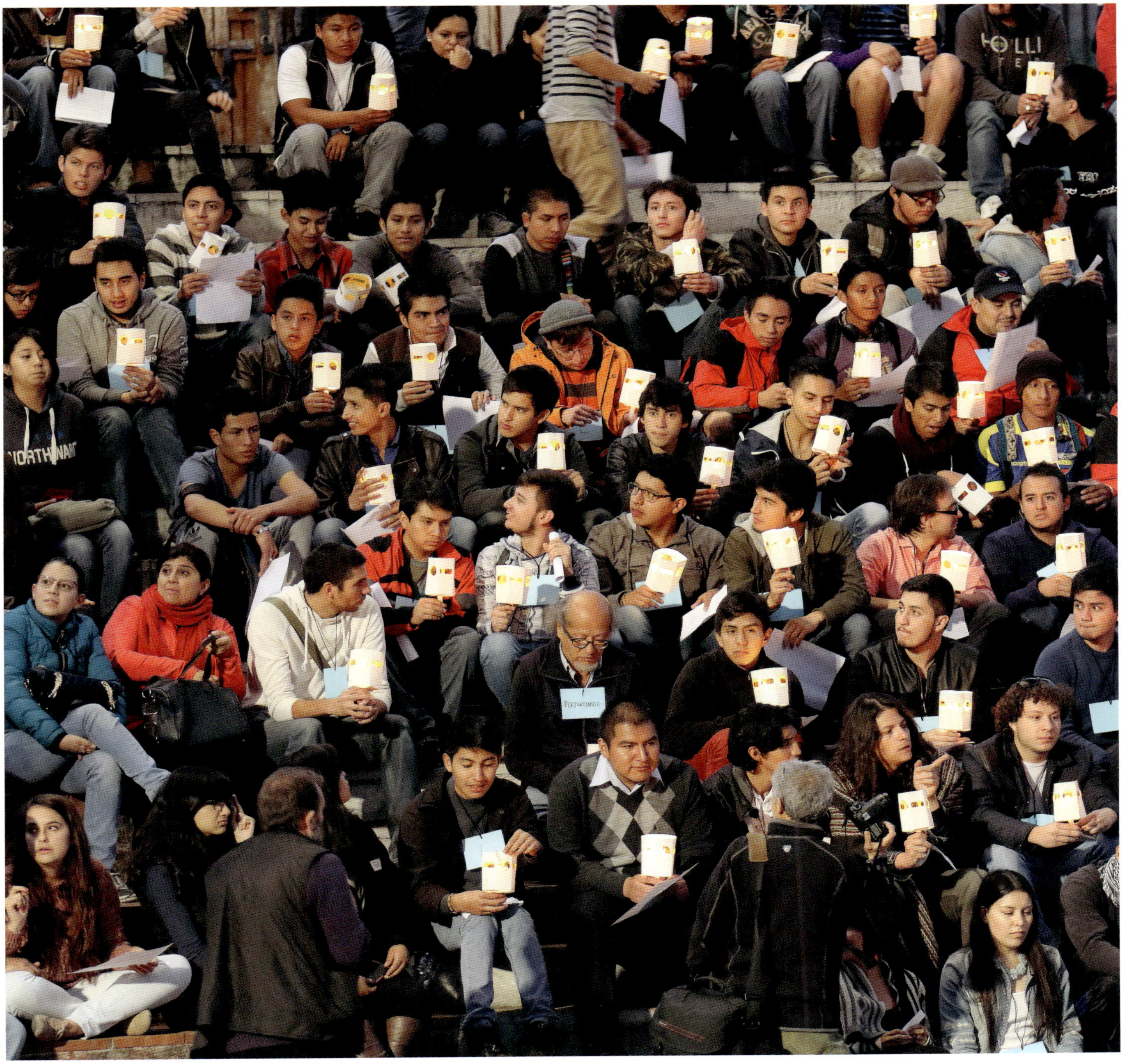

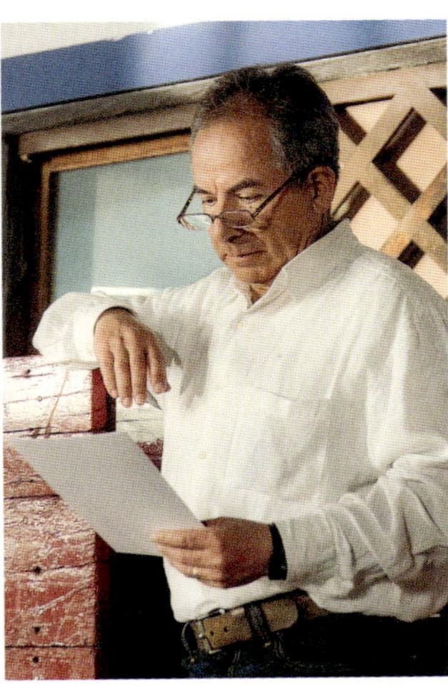

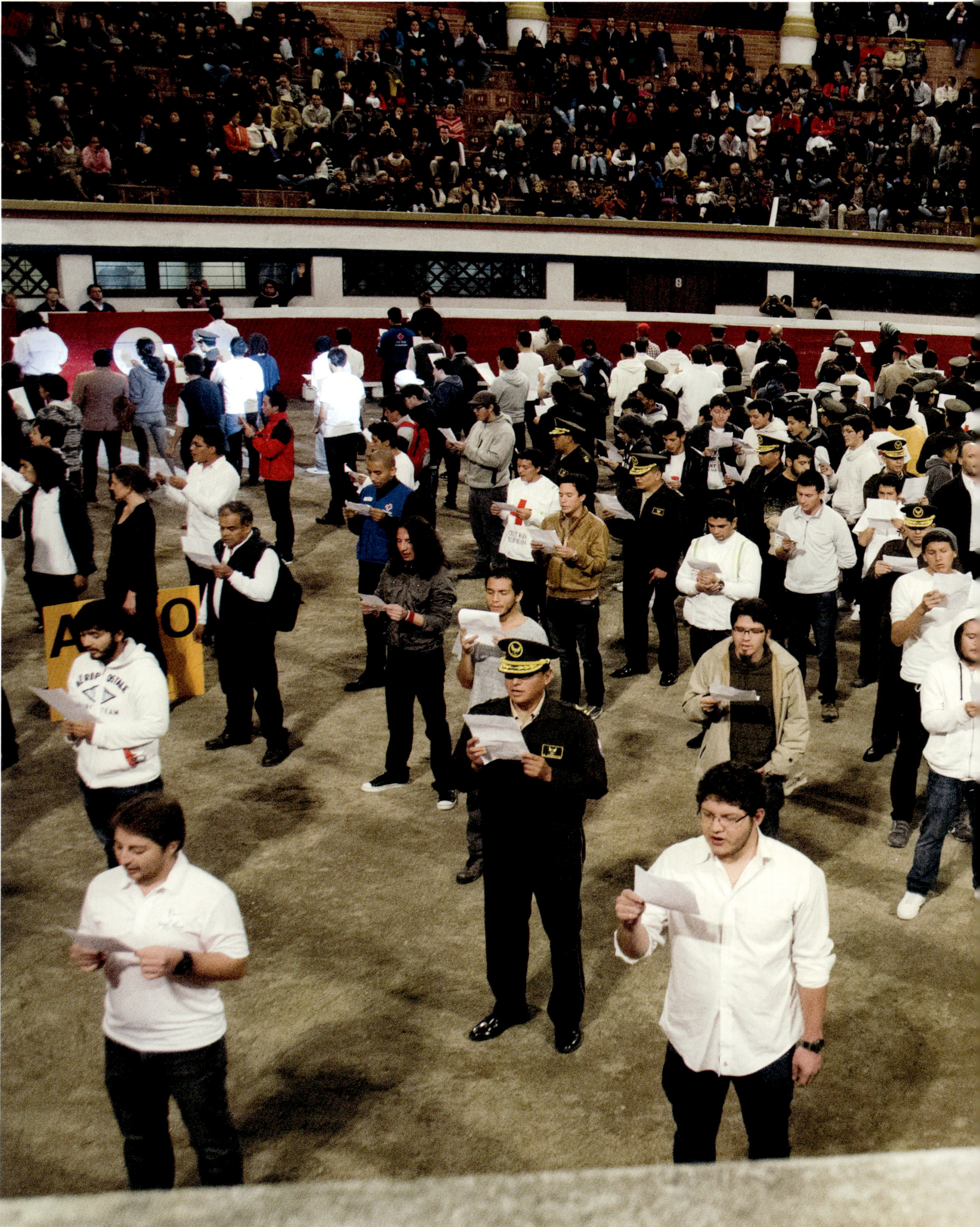

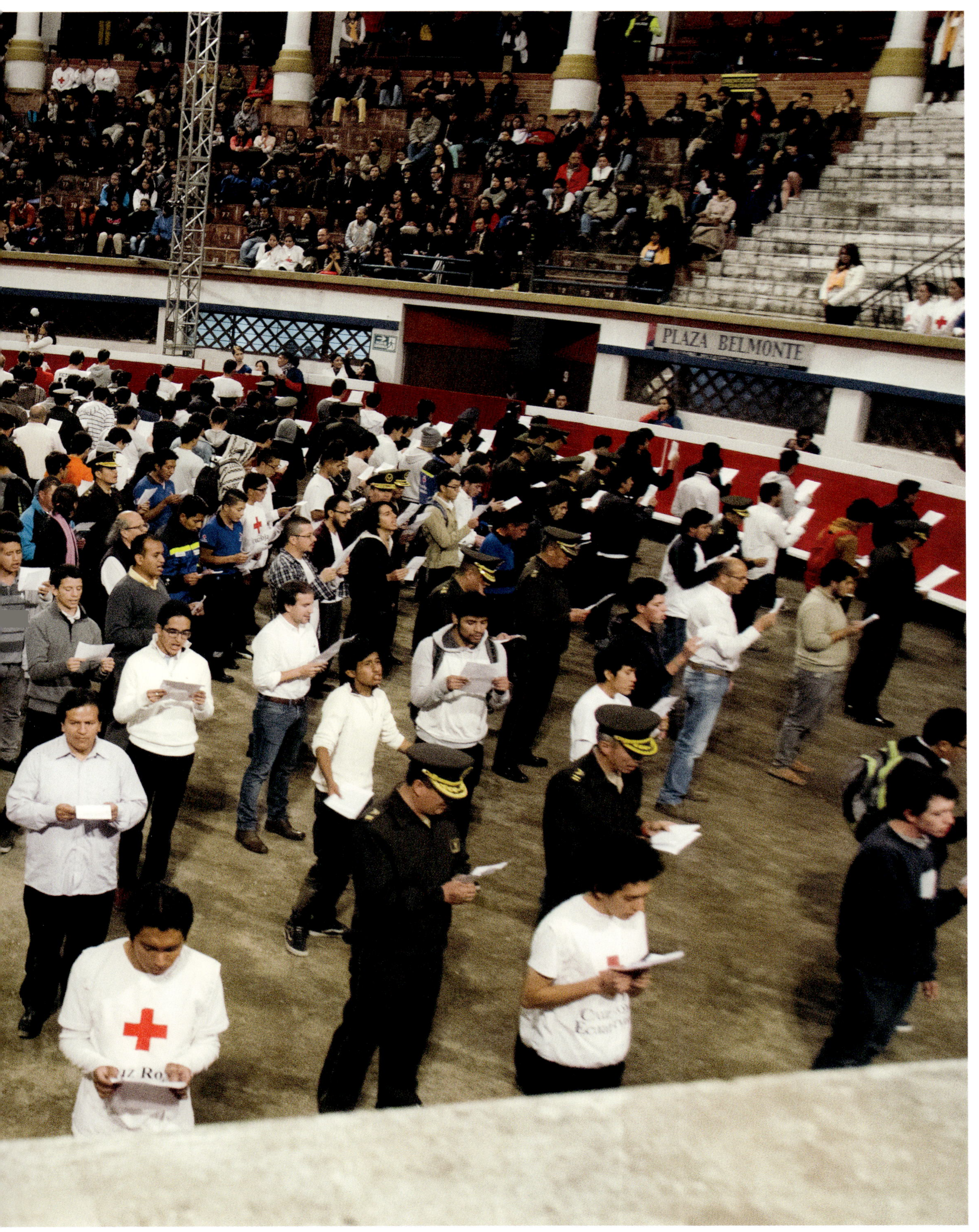
PLAZA BELMONTE

SCRIPT (EXCERPTS)

Maybe you won't understand why is this happening now, because it has been a long time and you have forgotten the past that has to do with me. The episodes that happened so long ago have marked my life, and today I want to let you know. This is the right moment to deal with the pain that is inside of me. Maybe the passing of time and the experiences of your life have opened [in] your heart a space for my story.

Act I: The Idea of the Past

What do I remember from when I was six? A man who appeared to be a good person told me he would take me to have ice cream. Instead he pulled up my uniform skirt and introduced his fingers into me. He started doing it often. Don't ask me for details, but I remember being at the edge of the terrace of the building waiting to fall, and listening to him say that he would kill me.

One day the mother arrived early and saw her husband raping her daughter. She didn't say a thing because she was afraid of losing him. The girl grew up being abused by her father who was to all a good and hardworking man. The girl—tired of the abuse—decided to take her own life. That girl was my cousin.

I am Mariela. Since I was a girl I was bullied in school. They asked me if I was a man or a woman. They told me that I looked like a boy, asked me if I was homosexual. Once a group of men beat me until I was unconscious, calling me butch and dyke. That night is still alive in my memory.

Act II: These Bodies

The first week after the marriage my brand new husband broke my front teeth with his fist, and gave me swollen eyes that I couldn't open for a week. Since then he raped me regularly. When I was pregnant he kicked me in the belly, that's how I lost my baby.

What I am looking for with this letter is to open those intimate spaces where violence is practiced. The dark room where so many women have died from loss of blood in an abortion, because of the lesions, lesions with spoons, with knifes, with pliers, the hidden faces, the phantoms of fear, the solitude of death all around with the smells, the sensations. We are not stati[sti]cs. We have some rights over our body, or don't we?

She opened her eyes and didn't know where she was. She tried to stand up but the pain in her hips was tremendous. Her skirt was missing buttons and she was dirty with blood. She cried, screamed, cursed her luck. He didn't want to go to jail or die in the hands of her father. She didn't want to be judged by society. The fear of recriminations had more power, because without knowing each other, without loving each other, with only a history of terror between them, they married.

Act III: Living Together

This was not the first time he beat me. He threw me as if I was a stone. My two [clavicles] were broken. He kicked me, as he insulted me: "You can't survive without me. Nobody will take you with three children and no money. You are a whore!"

At the age of 55, I am sharing my great pain with you. My husband used threats with me, while the church and the community said that my marriage was for my whole life. One day the priest said, "Don't fear if your husband kills you, you will die for the glory of god as a good Christian. Endure him and forgive him."

I learned to die. Each time I received a kick, a punch, I closed my eyes and learned to die little by little. After the beating he would ask for my forgiveness and I always gave it. "Things are going to change. At heart he is good. I can help him," I told myself, knowing deep inside this was not true.

The children are still asleep. I hope they didn't hear the dry hits you gave me last night, in order to quell that rage that was rising up in you. Just in case, I smothered my cries, the pain of the punches, and my crying in the sheets, in the covers, by your side. You always say, without you I am nothing. But I ask myself, what am I at your side?

The story that I am going to tell you changed our lives forever. On September 2 my cousin arrived home to prepare lunch for her family. Her husband arrived an hour later and a discussion started that ended up in a tragedy. Her husband stabbed her twenty times in the chest. Her death took her away from her dreams and her two children. Two years have gone by and he is still in the streets as a normal citizen.

That night I finished washing the dishes and started washing my husband's clothes, as I did since I married him. I waited for him, like every Friday, with my nose pressed to the window. Suddenly I heard the door opening and I asked him why he was so late. He was drunk with his friends and he started beating me, and all of them started beating and raping me. They abandoned my naked body on the floor, almost dead.

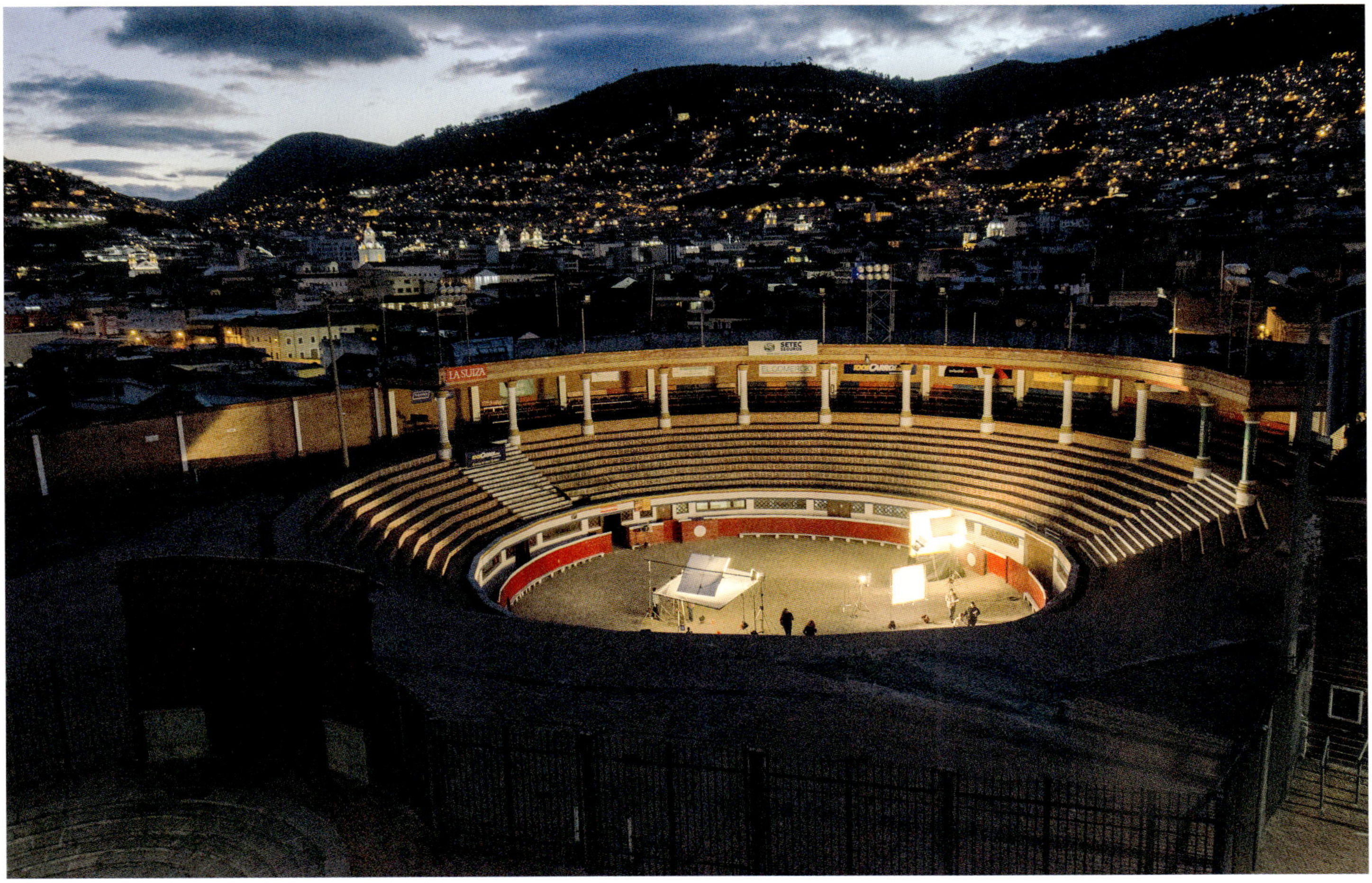

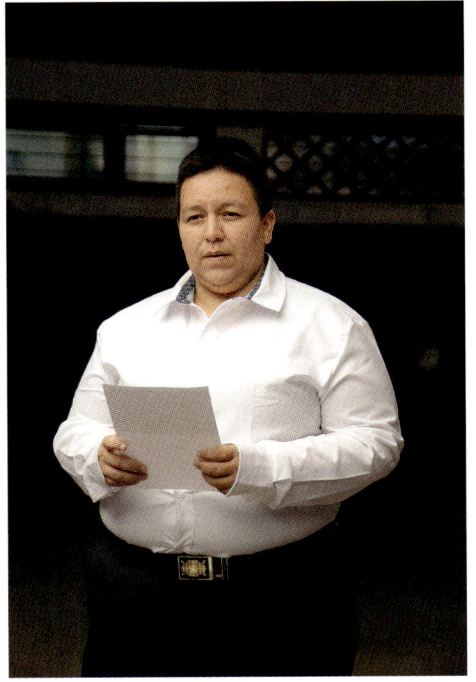
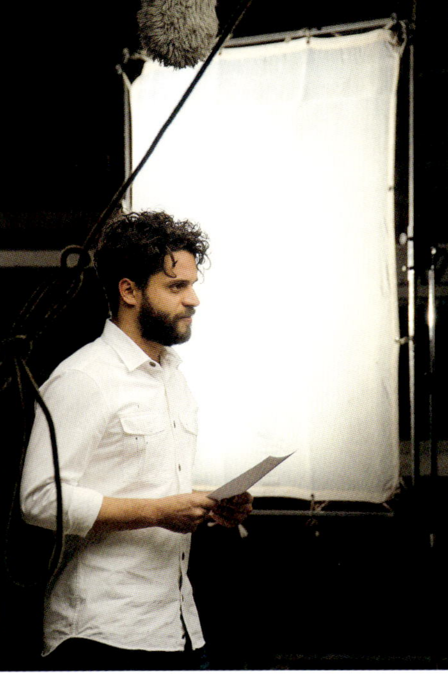
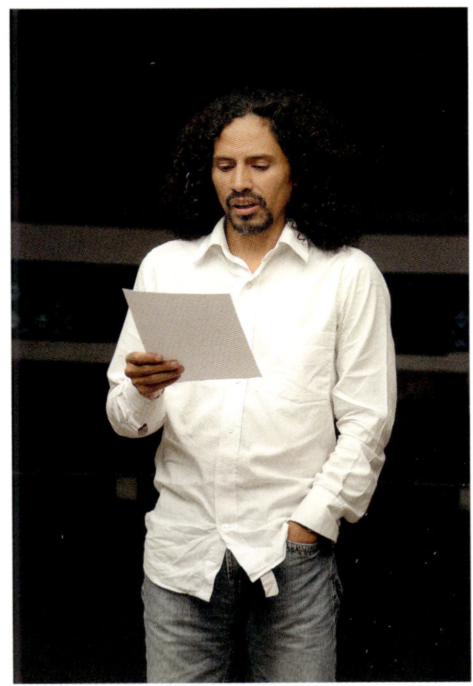

TOP: Plaza Belmonte
BOTTOM: Performers reading lines before the performance, July 20–23, 2017

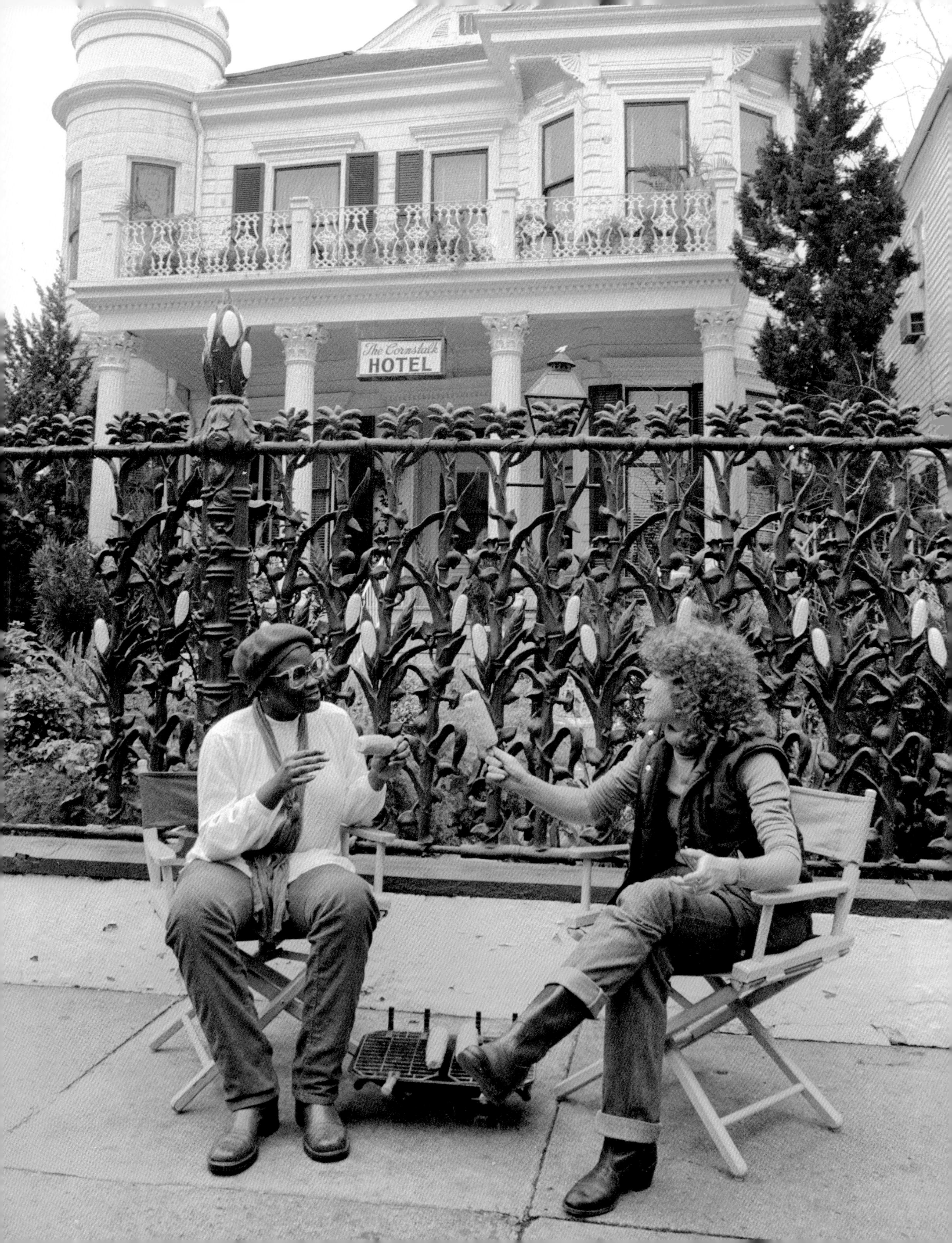

The Cornstalk
HOTEL

NETWORKS

Following her activist work around violence against women in the 1970s, Lacy shifted her focus to amplifying women's individual stories and lived experiences in increasingly complex performances. By using mass media to engage an extended audience and aligning herself with international feminist groups and local community members, Lacy was able to incorporate the voices of women of various races, ages, and socioeconomic groups into sophisticated dialogues that celebrated and empowered them.

Lacy cultivated authentic connections through everyday environments and routines—in addition to adopting the tactics of the early abolitionist and women's labor movements, which used dinners, birthday parties, and gift giving as rituals to entice participation. The meal became a cornerstone of Lacy's practice, as the sharing of both physical and emotional nourishment, through food and conversation, proved an effective means of community organizing.[1] *International Dinner Party* (1979, pp. 130–35) used dinners to connect diverse groups of women around the globe in a synchronized celebration. In *River Meetings: Lives of Women in the Delta* (1980, pp. 136–39) Lacy employed eating as the foundation of images that brought attention to Louisiana's failure to sign the Equal Rights Amendment. She also used it to organize local women, facilitating small "chain-letter" dinners that led to a final, five-hundred-woman dinner performance.

Intimate spaces and relationships are important both conceptually and visually to Lacy's practice. *Dinner at Jane's* (1993, p. 149) was a private meal that served as a symbolic gesture of feminist advancement, while *Evalina and I: Crimes, Quilts, and Art* (1975–80, pp. 126–29) was rooted in a personal friendship, the mutual trust between Lacy and Evalina Newman enabling a durational performance about crime and fear.[2] Lacy places emphasis on creating genuine relationships with the members of the communities she works with, encouraging them to contribute content and engage in collective image making. In *Freeze Frame: Room for Living Room* (1982, pp. 140–46) she organized the performers in small tableaux, grouping the participating women by race, religion, age, or occupation to create striking scenes for the audience to encounter. This framework became crucial in later large-scale productions such as *Whisper, the Waves, the Wind* (1983–84, pp. 152–57) and *The Crystal Quilt* (1987, pp. 166–73), where visual presentations of collective groups complemented individual stories.

Lacy thus experimented with different ways of organizing, using both common, comfortable settings and grander gestures—sometimes within a single work. *Stories of Work and Survival* (2007, p. 147) was her first piece to revisit prior projects, a method that she has employed several times since, as it allows her to layer experiences and draw connections between past inequalities and present attitudes. Though she has continued to focus on conversation, enhancing the theatrical dimension of her work has helped Lacy promote personal narratives within larger, shared experiences and create more possibilities for changes of perspective.

—LUCIA FABIO

International Dinner Party (1979)

SUZANNE LACY AND LINDA PREUSS

As a gift performance for her mentor Judy Chicago, Lacy organized more than two hundred women to host dinners on the opening of Chicago's *The Dinner Party* at the San Francisco Museum of Modern Art (SFMOMA). Every dinner honored a woman from its region in this twenty-four-hour happening. As each meal took place—all on March 14, 1979, but in different time zones—participants sent telegrams to the museum. Lacy put them in a binder and marked their points of origin on a large map with inverted red triangles. A trove of letters, photographs, and images arrived documenting more than two thousand participants, a testament to Lacy's feminist networking capabilities in a pre-internet world.

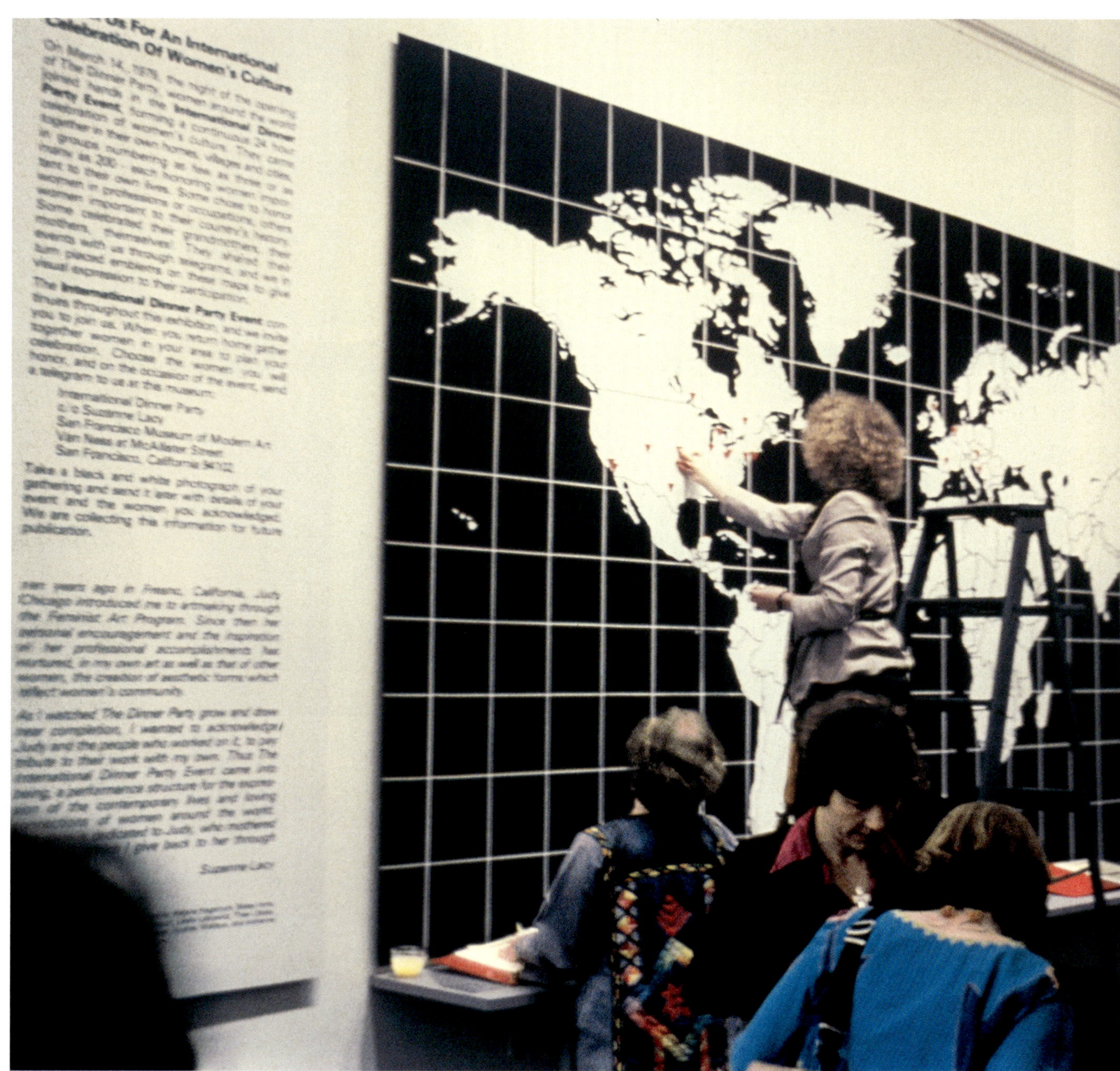

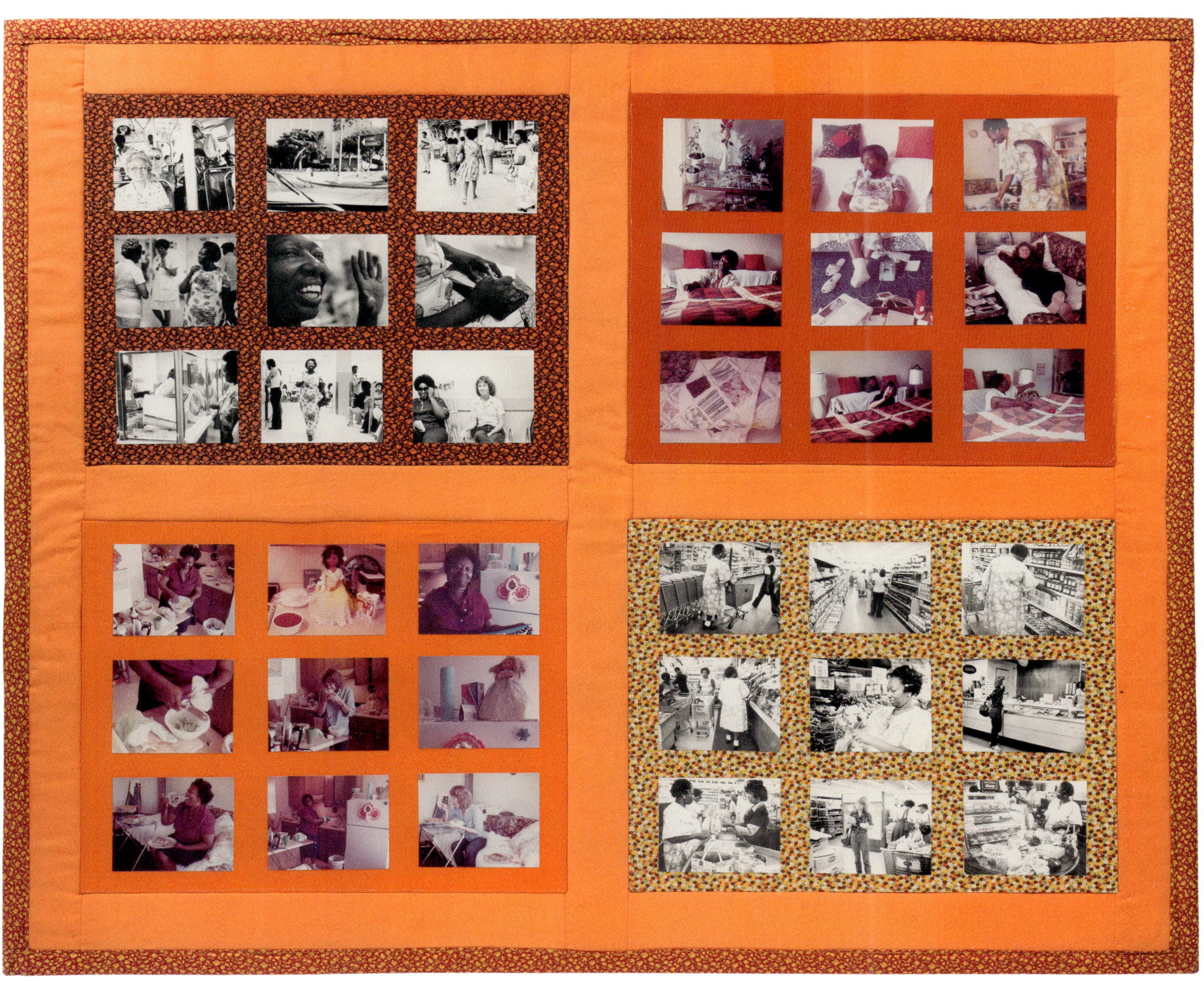

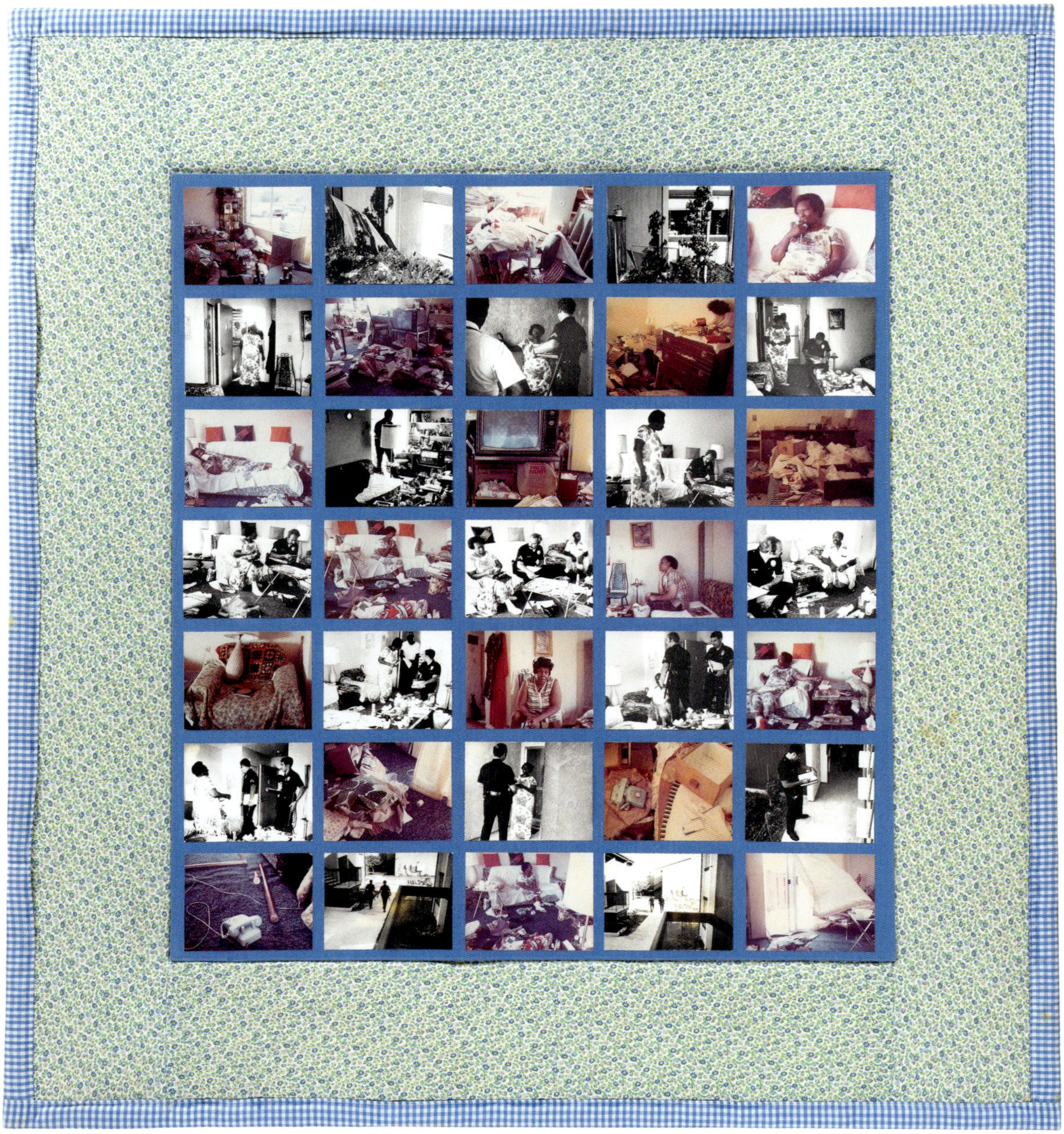

BOTTOM: Newman's apartment after a break-in; *Evalina and I* examined the violence within and around the Watts neighborhood
OPPOSITE: Images from the slide show for *Bus Ride from Watts*, a durational performance in which Lacy traveled from the Guy Miller Homes to a gallery in downtown Los Angeles, 1978

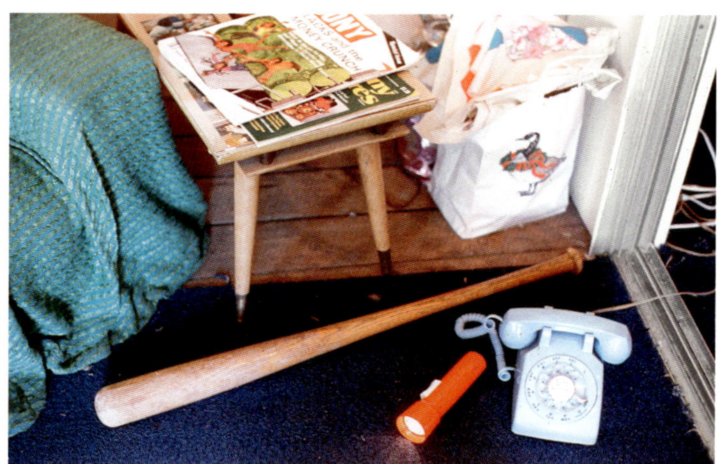

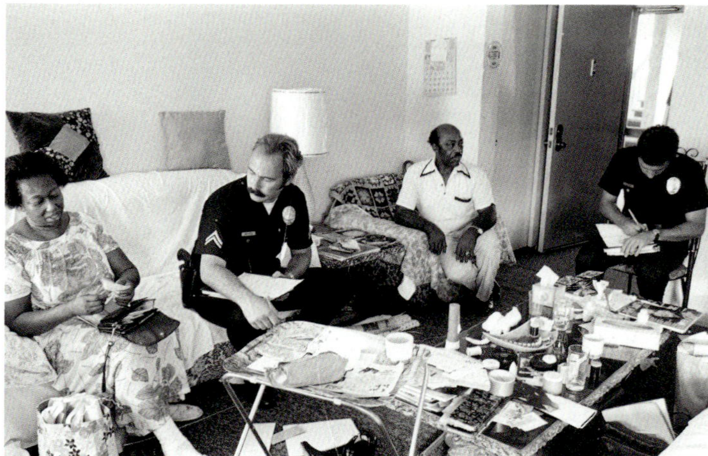

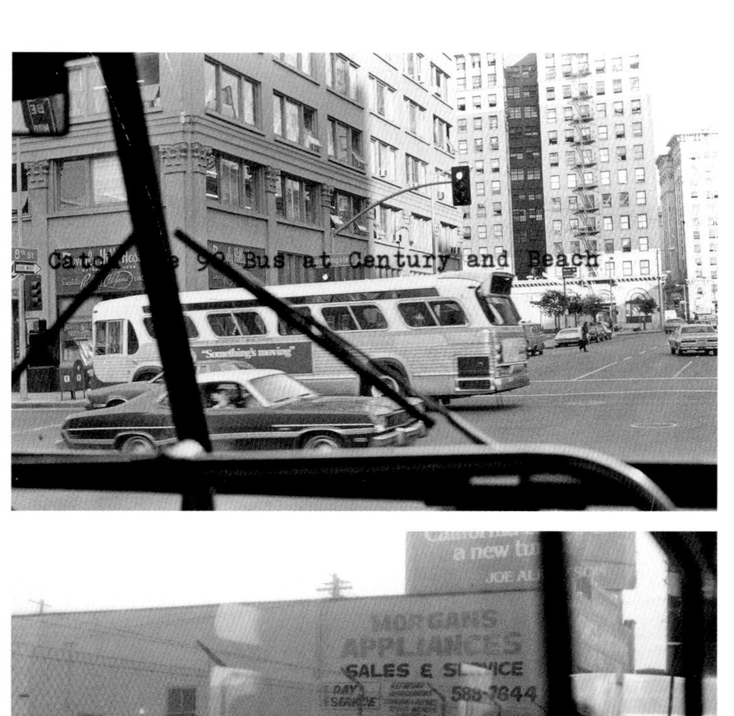

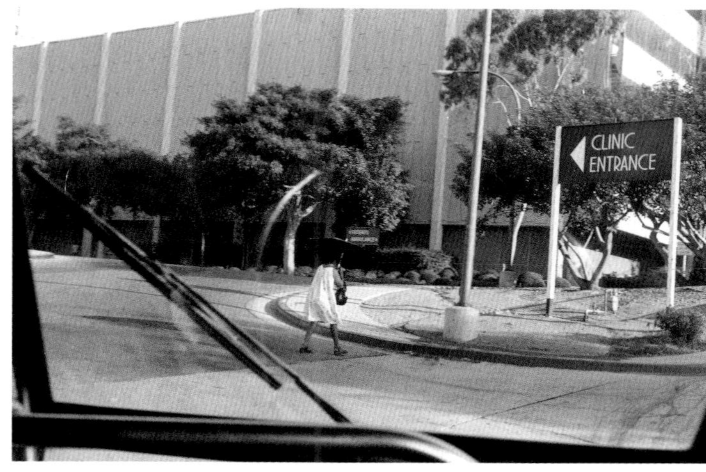

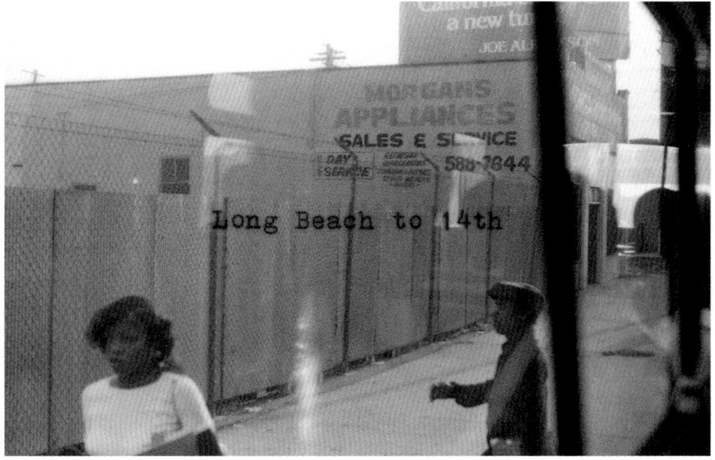

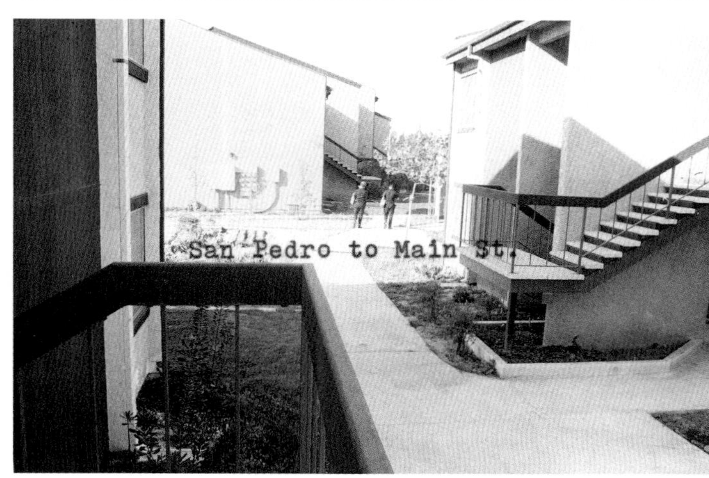

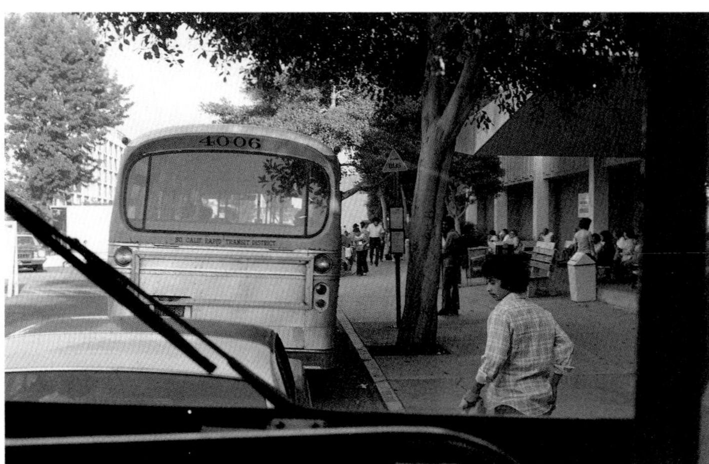

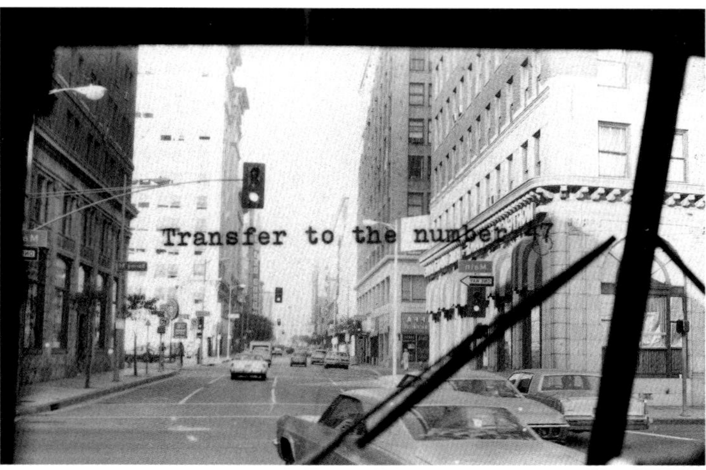

Evalina walked me to the bus stop early one Saturday evening, a gun in her apron pocket, to see me off. I had invited her to do a performance with me, to travel via bus from her house in Watts, with three transfers and a few blocks' walk, to a performance venue in downtown Los Angeles. I tape-recorded our phone conversation in which I'd proposed the piece and Evalina had replied that her heart condition would make a Saturday night trip on a public bus (during those more unsettled days) dangerous. As I set off from Watts, Nancy Buchanan announced [that] the journey was beginning to an audience gathered at the gallery, played the recording, showed slides of the journey, and announced when I arrived.

—Suzanne Lacy, 2018

International Dinner Party (1979)

SUZANNE LACY AND LINDA PREUSS

As a gift performance for her mentor Judy Chicago, Lacy organized more than two hundred women to host dinners on the opening of Chicago's *The Dinner Party* at the San Francisco Museum of Modern Art (SFMOMA). Every dinner honored a woman from its region in this twenty-four-hour happening. As each meal took place—all on March 14, 1979, but in different time zones—participants sent telegrams to the museum. Lacy put them in a binder and marked their points of origin on a large map with inverted red triangles. A trove of letters, photographs, and images arrived documenting more than two thousand participants, a testament to Lacy's feminist networking capabilities in a pre-internet world.

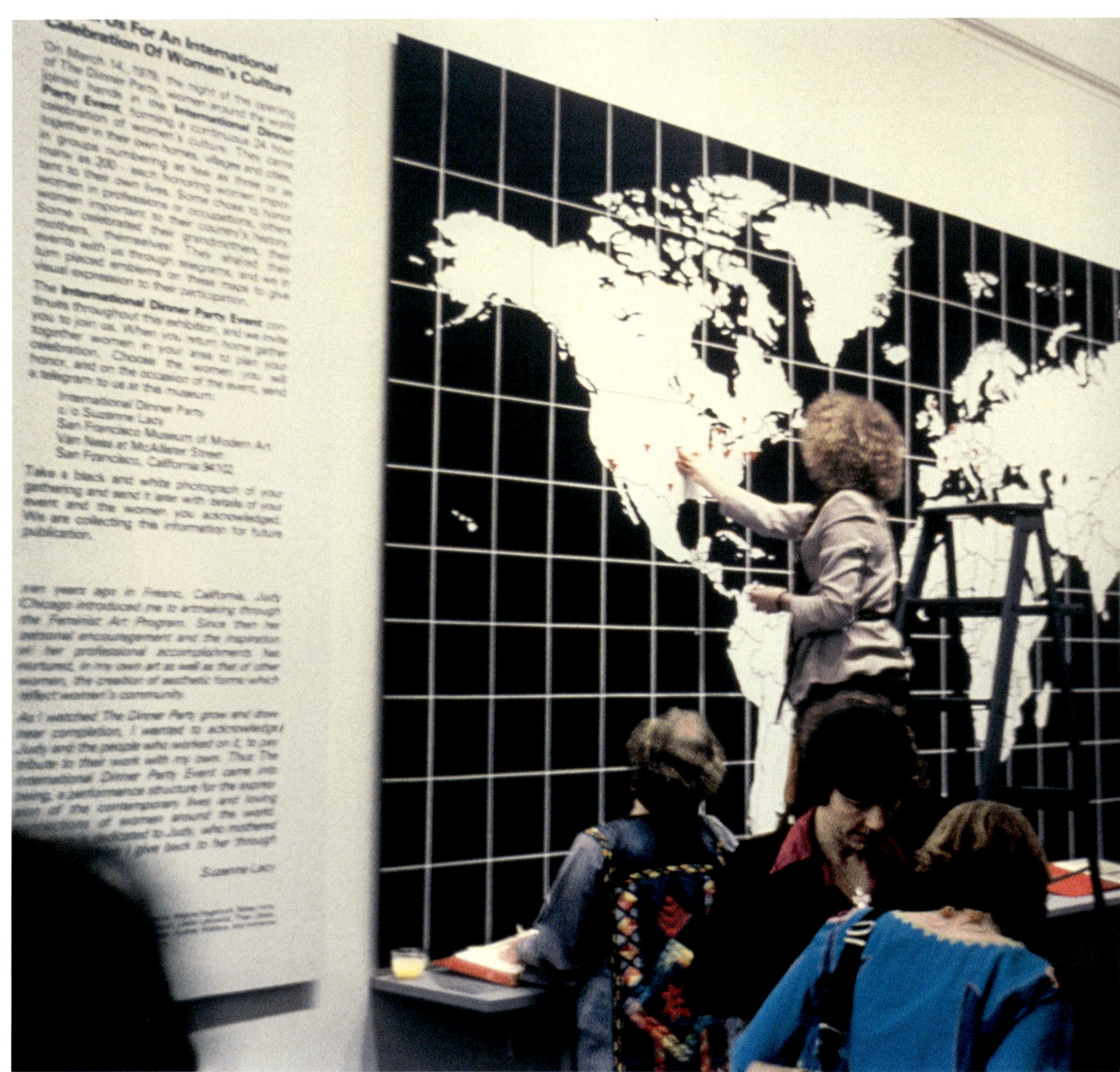

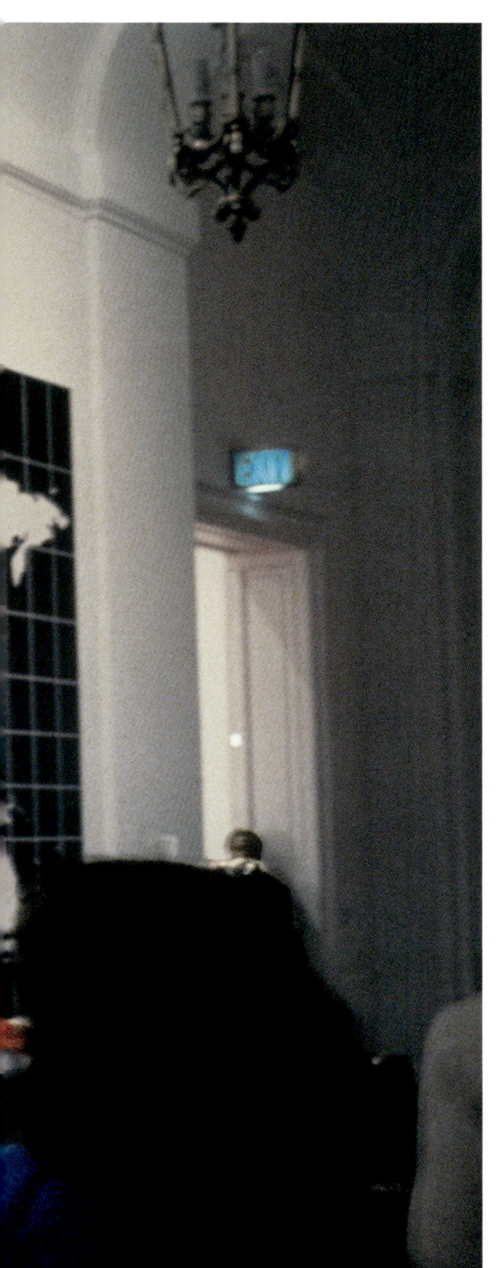

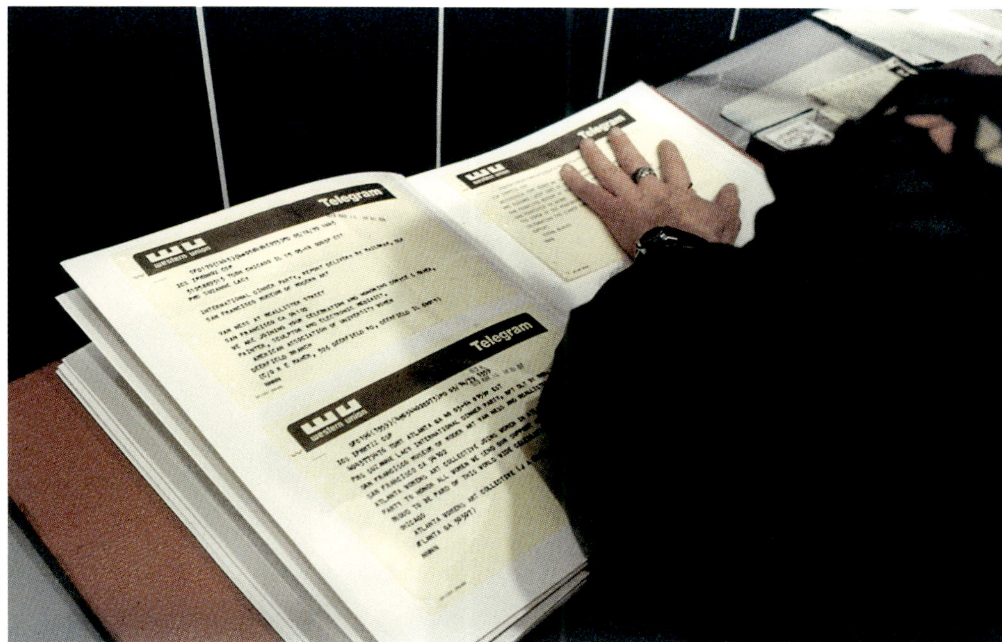

INSTRUCTIONS: International Dinner Party Event

1. Plan your celebration for the evening of **MARCH 14, 1979.** With women in your area, decide who you will invite and who you will honor.

2. Send us a telegram or mailgram so that it reaches the Museum in San Francisco during the day of March 14. In your message you should include who you (or your group) are, who you will be honoring, and any other message you'd like to be posted for women to read. These messages will remain up during the "Dinner Party" exhibition, and women who see it will be invited to continue the dinner parties in their own homes. Thus our first posted messages will be added to throughout several weeks.

   Address messages to: Suzanne Lacy
   International Dinner Party
   San Francisco Museum of Modern Art
   Van Ness at McAllister Street
   San Francisco, California 94102

3. Take a black and white photograph of your celebration and send it to us with a letter telling us about your event. We will collect the documentation for printing at a later date.

From the U.S., telegrams will reach us in 2-5 hours; mailgrams in one day. From Outside the U.S., telegrams will take 1-2 days, depending upon your local service. If cost is prohibitive to telegraph from your area, please mail postcard and allow time to arrive on March 14.

PLEASE PASS THIS ON!

On March 14, 1979, *The Dinner Party* premiered at . . . SFMOMA, which was headed up by the visionary director Henry Hopkins. He was probably the first museum professional to open the doors to feminist art because on the opening weekend, the institution was filled with feminist performances, lectures, panels, and discussions. Among the performances was . . . *International Dinner Party*, which involved a giant map . . . on which Suzanne pinned up telegrams from people all over the planet who held "dinner parties" in celebration of the opening of my (now iconic) work. Hers was a wonderful, generous work that empowered people from all parts of the world and was a precursor to the marvelous work that Suzanne has been doing since then.

—Judy Chicago, 2018

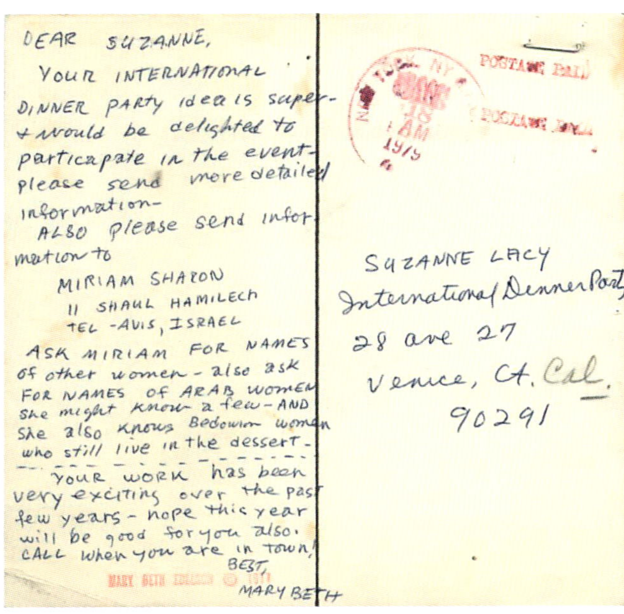

DEAR SUZANNE,

YOUR INTERNATIONAL DINNER PARTY idea is super— + would be delighted to participate in the event— please send more detailed information—

ALSO please send information to

MIRIAM SHARON
11 SHAUL HAMILECH
TEL-AVIS, ISRAEL

ASK MIRIAM FOR NAMES of other women — also ask FOR NAMES OF ARAB WOMEN she might know a few — AND she also knows Bedowin women who still live in the dessert.

— — — — — — — — — — — YOUR WORK has been very exciting over the past few years — nope this year will be good for you also. CALL when you are in town! BEST, MARY BETH

SUZANNE LACY
International Dinner Party
28 ave 27
Venice, Ct. Cal.
90291

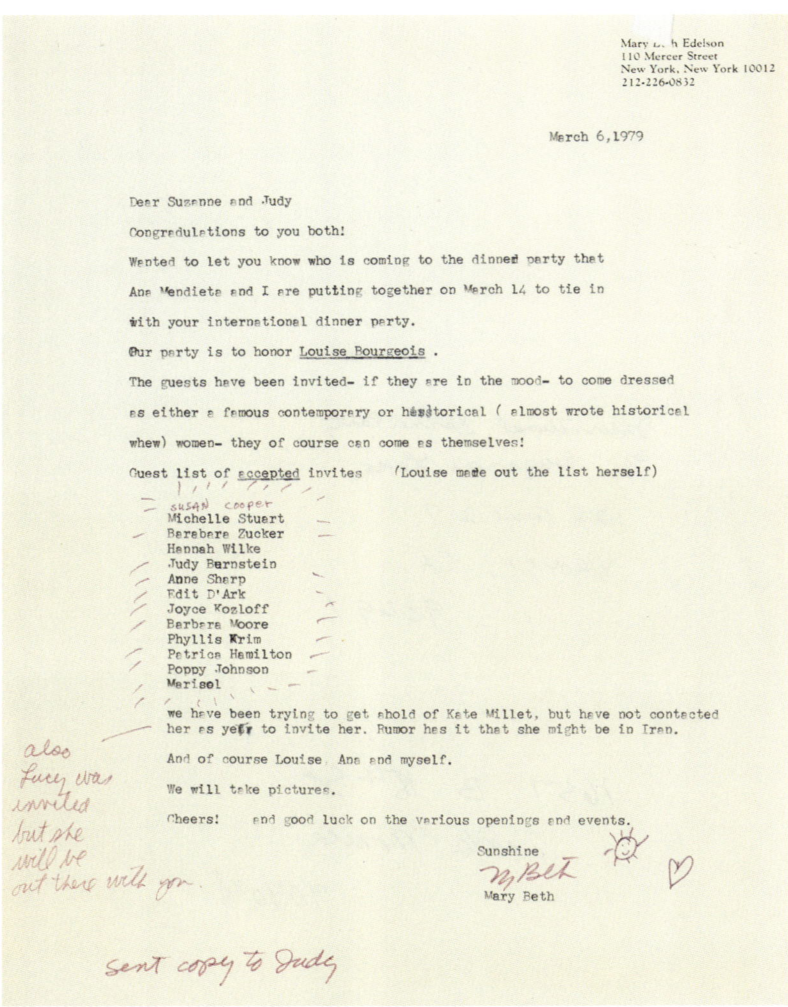

Mary Beth Edelson
110 Mercer Street
New York, New York 10012
212-226-0832

March 6, 1979

Dear Suzanne and Judy

Congradulations to you both!

Wanted to let you know who is coming to the dinner party that Ana Mendieta and I are putting together on March 14 to tie in with your international dinner party.

Our party is to honor Louise Bourgeois .

The guests have been invited- if they are in the mood- to come dressed as either a famous contemporary or herstorical (almost wrote historical whew) women- they of course can come as themselves!

Guest list of accepted invites   (Louise made out the list herself)

Susan Cooper
Michelle Stuart
Barebara Zucker
Hannah Wilke
Judy Bernstein
Anne Sharp
Edit D'Ark
Joyce Kozloff
Barbara Moore
Phyllis Krim
Patrica Hamilton
Poppy Johnson
Marisol

we have been trying to get ahold of Kate Millet, but have not contacted her as yett to invite her. Rumor has it that she might be in Iran.

And of course Louise, Ana and myself.

We will take pictures.

Cheers!   and good luck on the various openings and events.

Sunshine
Mary Beth

also Lucy was invited but she will be out there with you.

sent copy to Judy

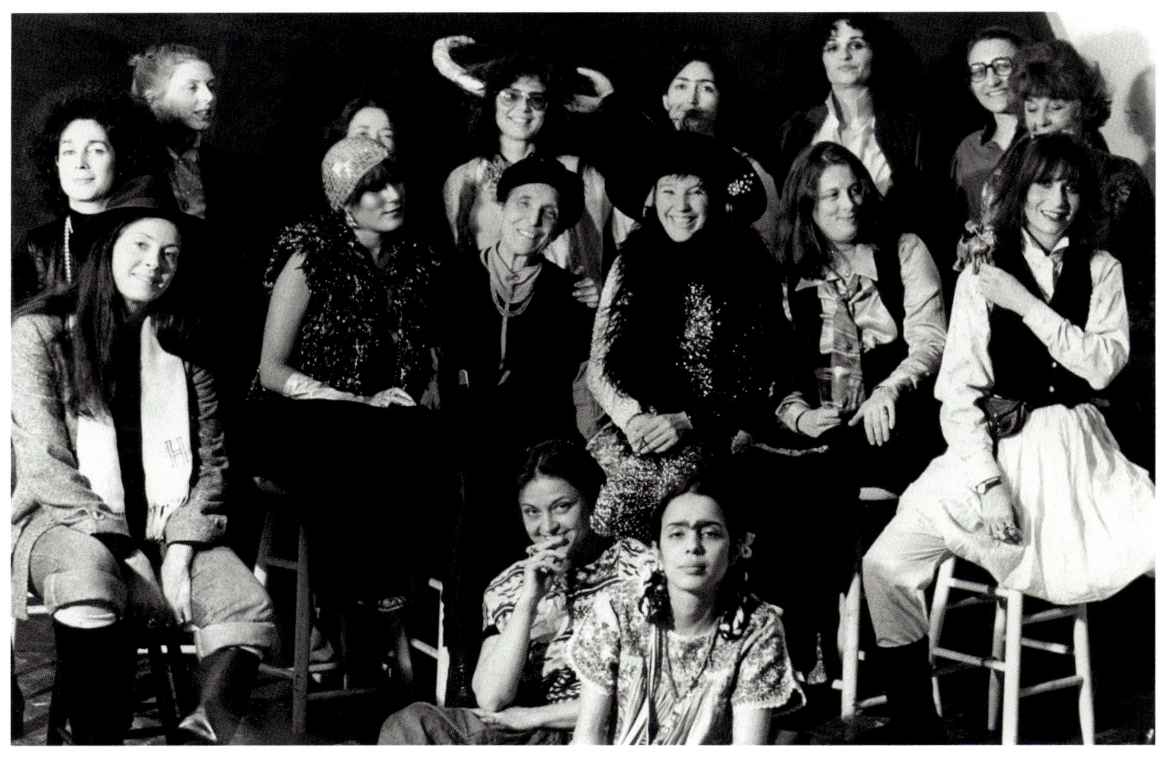

RIGHT: Guests of a dinner hosted by Mary Beth Edelson (back row, center) and Ana Mendieta (front row, right) in honor of Louise Bourgeois (center)

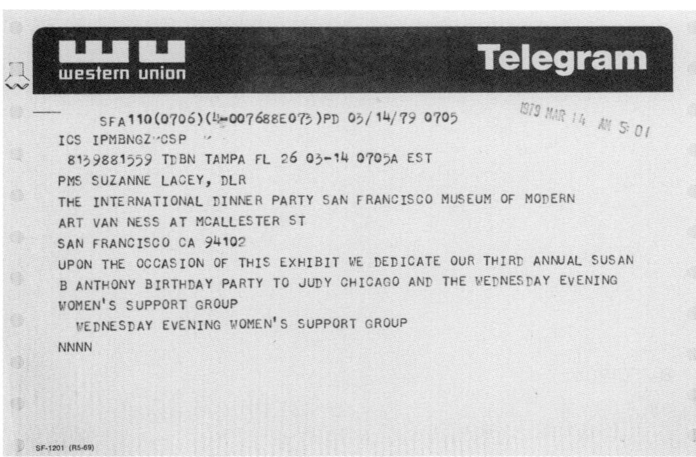

western union   Telegram
1979 MAR 14 AM 5:01
SFA110(0706)(4-007688E073)PD 03/14/79 0705
ICS IPMBNGZ CSP
 8139881559 TDBN TAMPA FL 26 03-14 0705A EST
PMS SUZANNE LACEY, DLR
THE INTERNATIONAL DINNER PARTY SAN FRANCISCO MUSEUM OF MODERN
ART VAN NESS AT MCALLESTER ST
SAN FRANCISCO CA 94102
UPON THE OCCASION OF THIS EXHIBIT WE DEDICATE OUR THIRD ANNUAL SUSAN
B ANTHONY BIRTHDAY PARTY TO JUDY CHICAGO AND THE WEDNESDAY EVENING
WOMEN'S SUPPORT GROUP
    WEDNESDAY EVENING WOMEN'S SUPPORT GROUP
NNNN
SF-1201 (R5-69)

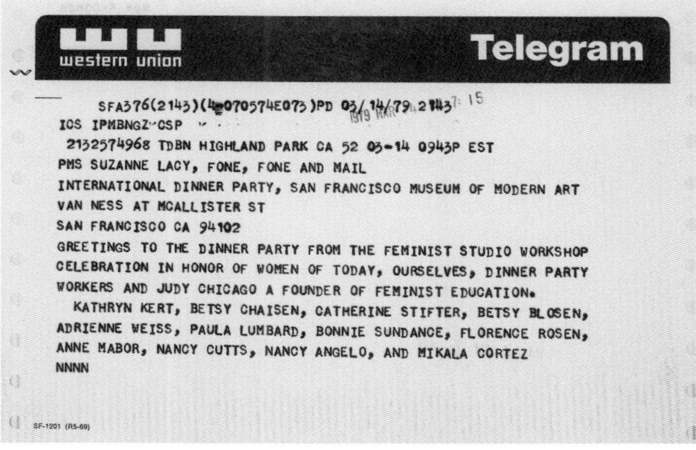

western union   Telegram
SFA376(2143)(4-070574E073)PD 03/14/79 2143
1979 MAR 15
ICS IPMBNGZ CSP
 2132574968 TDBN HIGHLAND PARK CA 52 03-14 0943P EST
PMS SUZANNE LACY, FONE, FONE AND MAIL
INTERNATIONAL DINNER PARTY, SAN FRANCISCO MUSEUM OF MODERN ART
VAN NESS AT MCALLISTER ST
SAN FRANCISCO CA 94102
GREETINGS TO THE DINNER PARTY FROM THE FEMINIST STUDIO WORKSHOP
CELEBRATION IN HONOR OF WOMEN OF TODAY, OURSELVES, DINNER PARTY
WORKERS AND JUDY CHICAGO A FOUNDER OF FEMINIST EDUCATION.
    KATHRYN KERT, BETSY CHAISEN, CATHERINE STIFTER, BETSY BLOSEN,
ADRIENNE WEISS, PAULA LUMBARD, BONNIE SUNDANCE, FLORENCE ROSEN,
ANNE MABOR, NANCY CUTTS, NANCY ANGELO, AND MIKALA CORTEZ
NNNN
SF-1201 (R5-69)

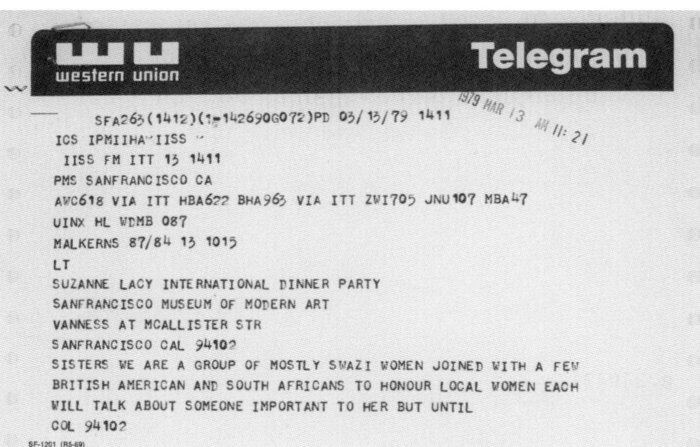

western union   Telegram
1979 MAR 13 AM 11:21
SFA263(1412)(1-142690G072)PD 03/13/79 1411
ICS IPMIIHA IISS
 IISS FM ITT 13 1411
PMS SANFRANCISCO CA
AWC618 VIA ITT HBA622 BHA963 VIA ITT ZWI705 JNU107 MBA47
UINX HL WDMB 087
MALKERNS 87/84 13 1015
LT
SUZANNE LACY INTERNATIONAL DINNER PARTY
SANFRANCISCO MUSEUM OF MODERN ART
VANNESS AT MCALLISTER STR
SANFRANCISCO CAL 94102
SISTERS WE ARE A GROUP OF MOSTLY SWAZI WOMEN JOINED WITH A FEW
BRITISH AMERICAN AND SOUTH AFRICANS TO HONOUR LOCAL WOMEN EACH
WILL TALK ABOUT SOMEONE IMPORTANT TO HER BUT UNTIL
COL 94102
SF-1201 (R5-69)

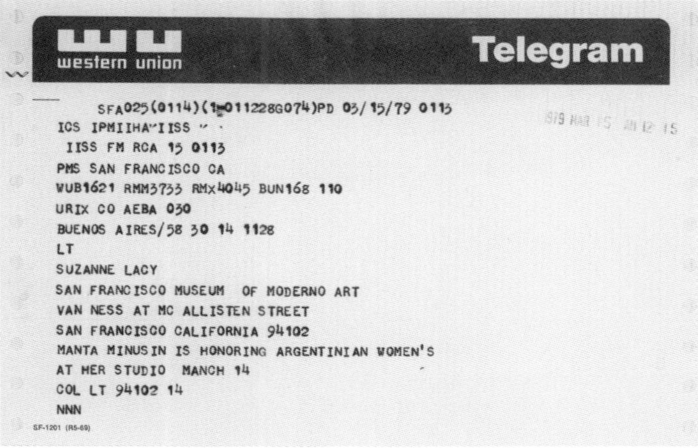

western union   Telegram
SFA025(0114)(1-011228G074)PD 03/15/79 0113
1979 MAR 15 AM 12:15
ICS IPMIIHA IISS
 IISS FM RCA 15 0113
PMS SAN FRANCISCO CA
WUB1621 RMM3733 RMX4045 BUN168 110
URIX CO AEBA 030
BUENOS AIRES/58 30 14 1128
LT
SUZANNE LACY
SAN FRANCISCO MUSEUM OF MODERNO ART
VAN NESS AT MC ALLISTEN STREET
SAN FRANCISCO CALIFORNIA 94102
MANTA MINUSIN IS HONORING ARGENTINIAN WOMEN'S
AT HER STUDIO MANCH 14
COL LT 94102 14
NNN
SF-1201 (R5-69)

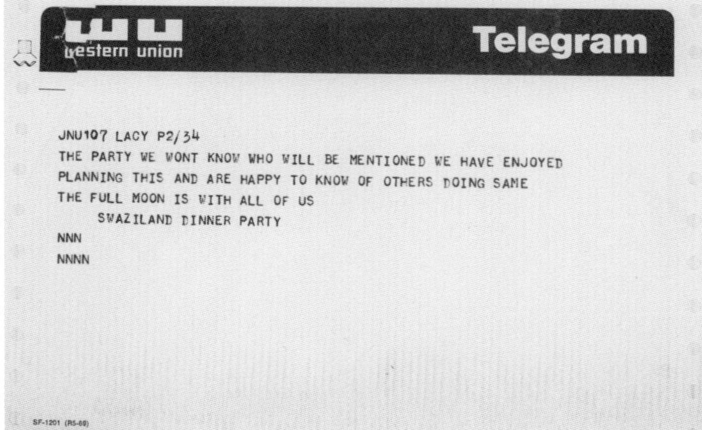

western union   Telegram
JNU107 LACY P2/34
THE PARTY WE WONT KNOW WHO WILL BE MENTIONED WE HAVE ENJOYED
PLANNING THIS AND ARE HAPPY TO KNOW OF OTHERS DOING SAME
THE FULL MOON IS WITH ALL OF US
    SWAZILAND DINNER PARTY
NNN
NNNN
SF-1201 (R5-69)

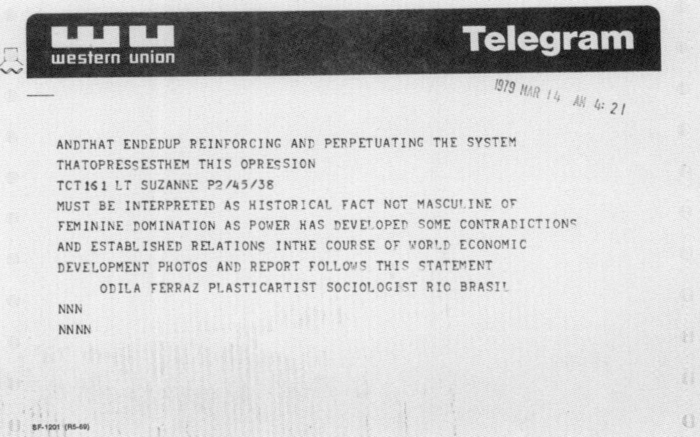

western union   Telegram
1979 MAR 14 AM 4:21
ANDTHAT ENDEDUP REINFORCING AND PERPETUATING THE SYSTEM
THATOPRESSESTHEM THIS OPRESSION
TCT161 LT SUZANNE P2/45/38
MUST BE INTERPRETED AS HISTORICAL FACT NOT MASCULINE OF
FEMININE DOMINATION AS POWER HAS DEVELOPED SOME CONTRADICTIONS
AND ESTABLISHED RELATIONS INTHE COURSE OF WORLD ECONOMIC
DEVELOPMENT PHOTOS AND REPORT FOLLOWS THIS STATEMENT
    ODILA FERRAZ PLASTICARTIST SOCIOLOGIST RIO BRASIL
NNN
NNNN
SF-1201 (R5-69)

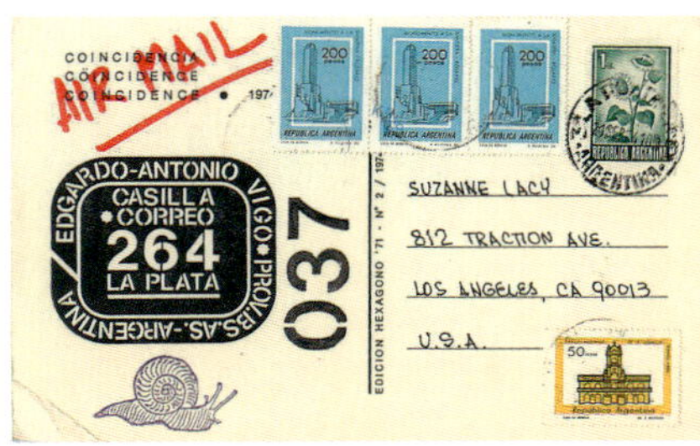
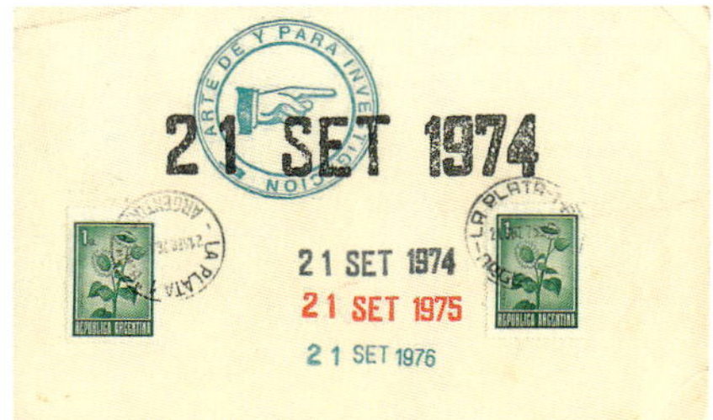

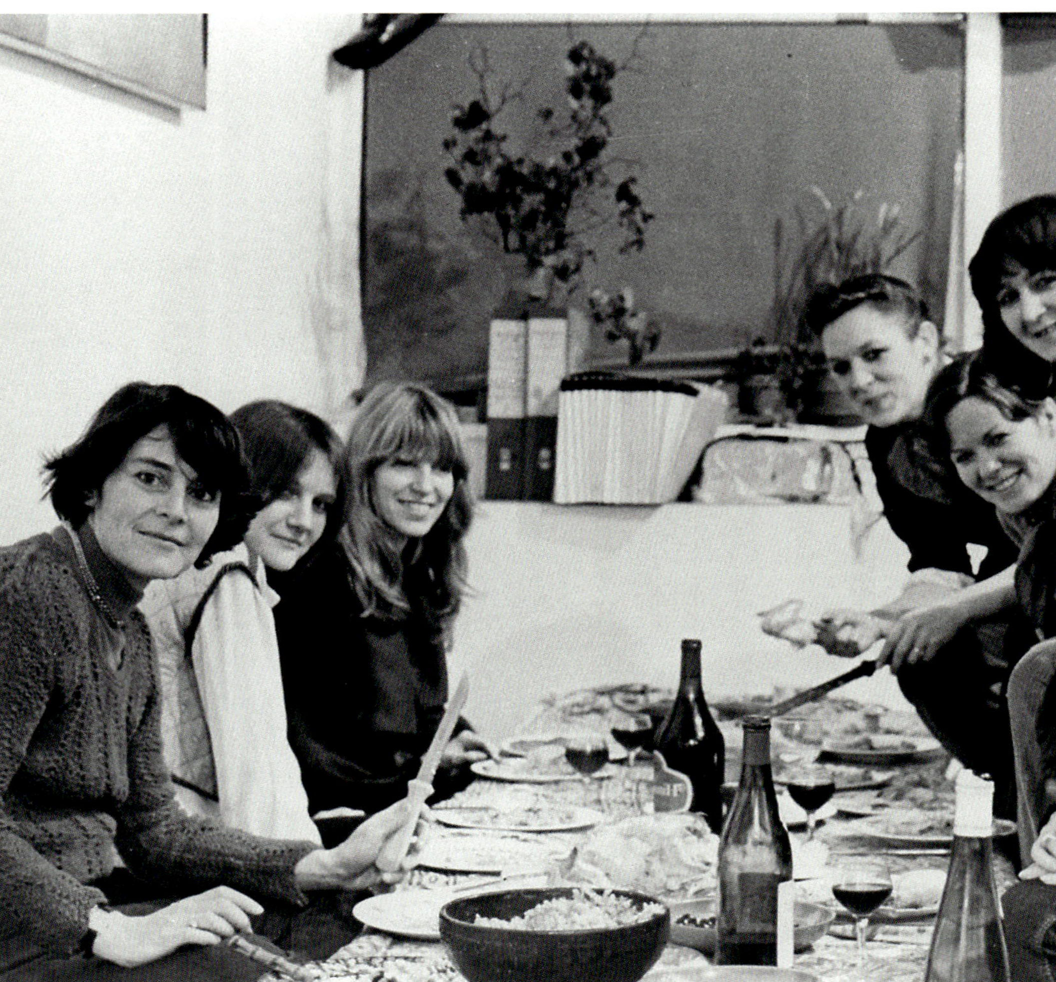
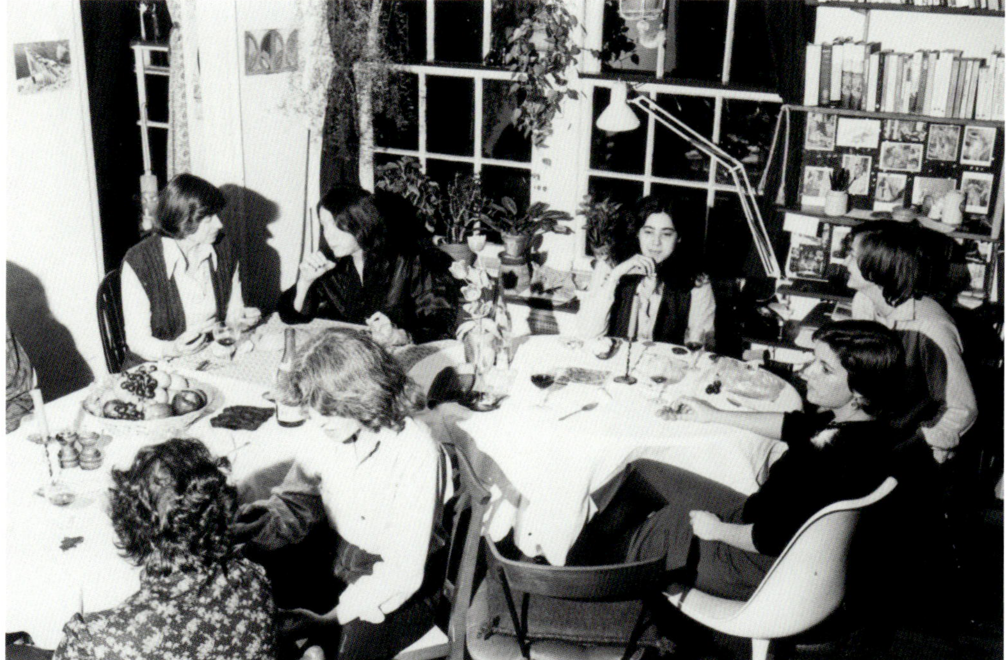

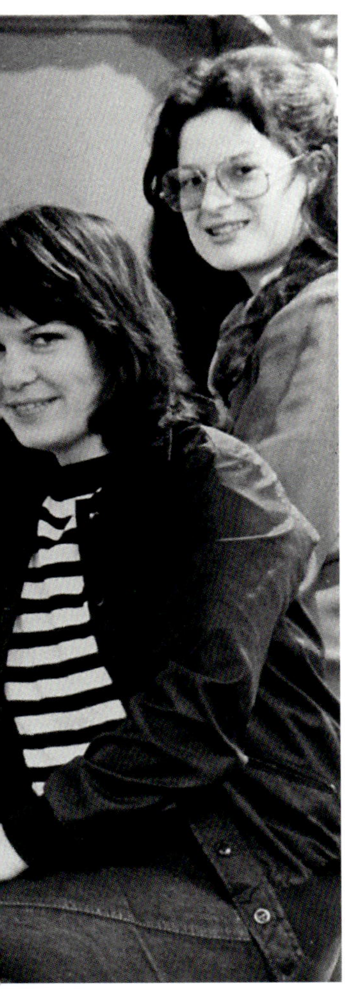
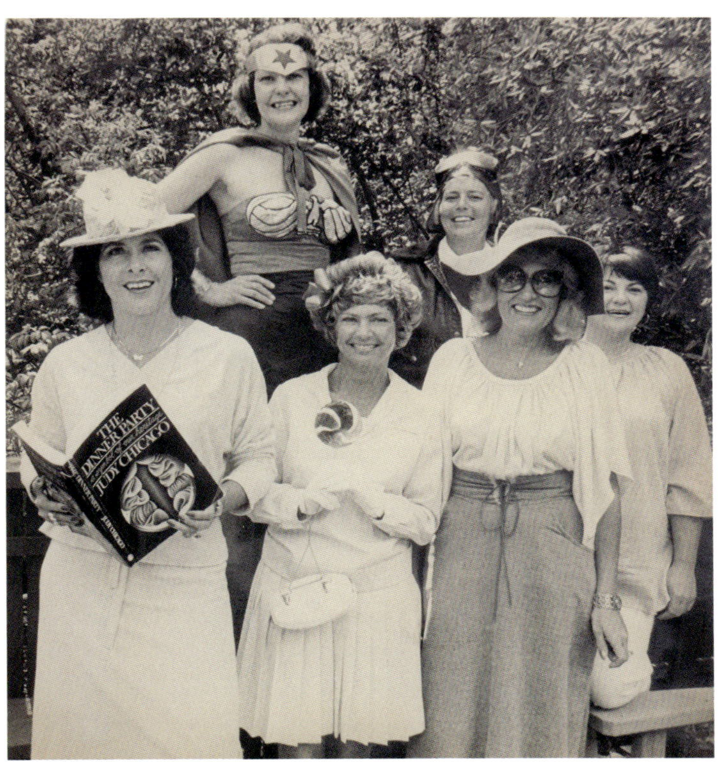
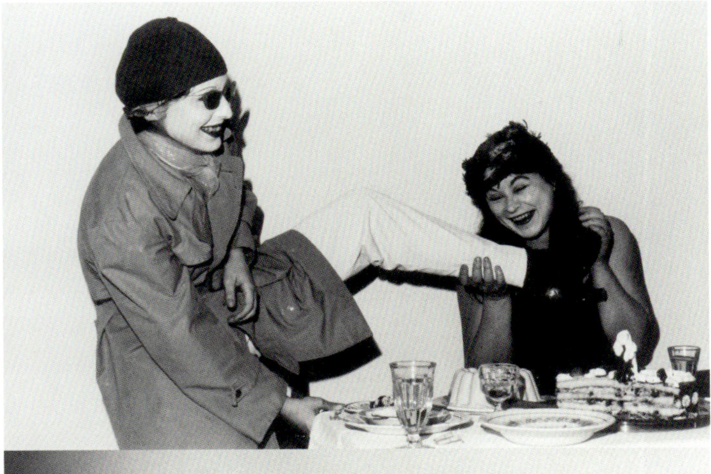
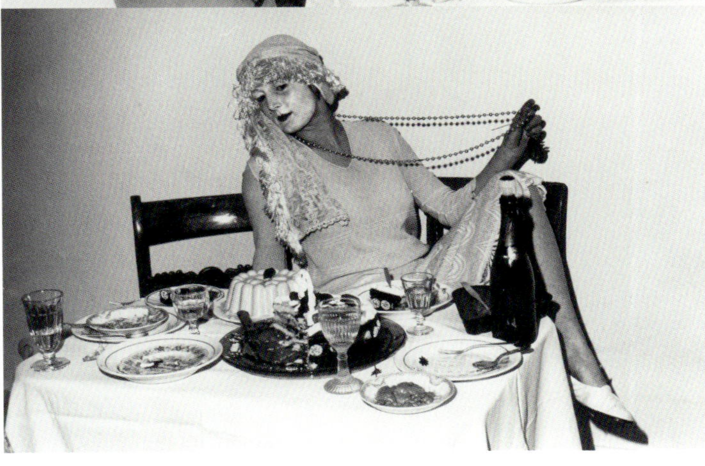
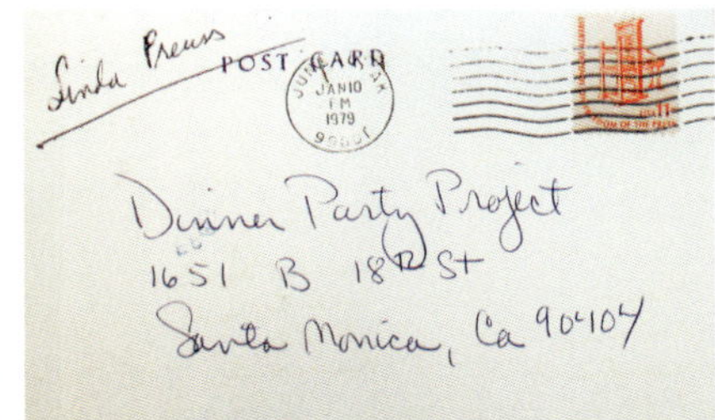

POST CARD
Dinner Party Project
1651 B 18th St
Santa Monica, Ca 90404

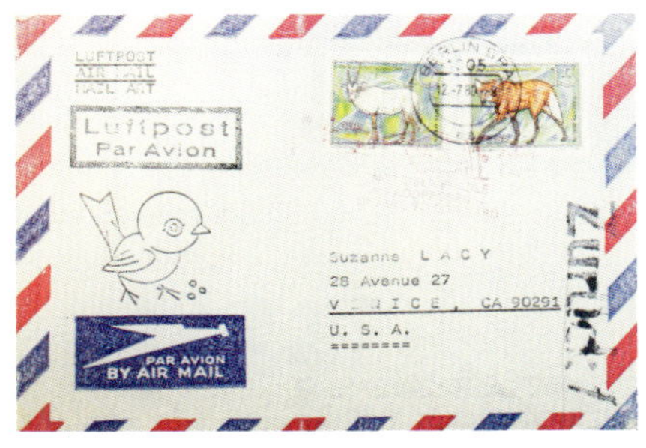

LUFTPOST
AIR MAIL
PAR AVION
Luftpost
Par Avion
PAR AVION
BY AIR MAIL
Suzanne LACY
28 Avenue 27
VENICE, CA 90291
U. S. A.

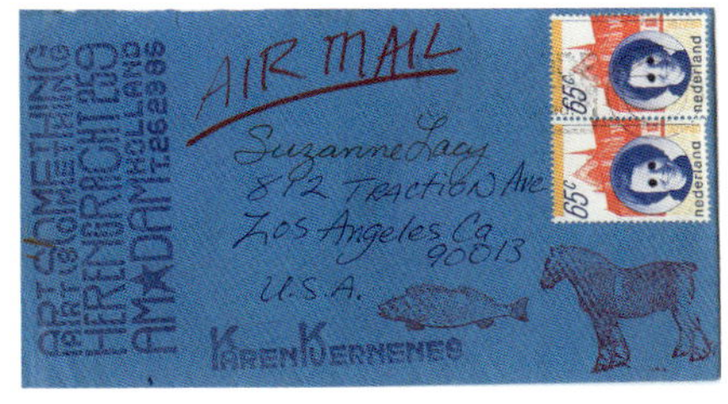

AIR MAIL
ART SOMETHING
PART IS SOMETHING
HERENGRACHT 89
AMSTERDAM HOLLAND
Suzanne Lacy
892 Traction Ave
Los Angeles Ca
90013
U.S.A.
Karen Kvernenes

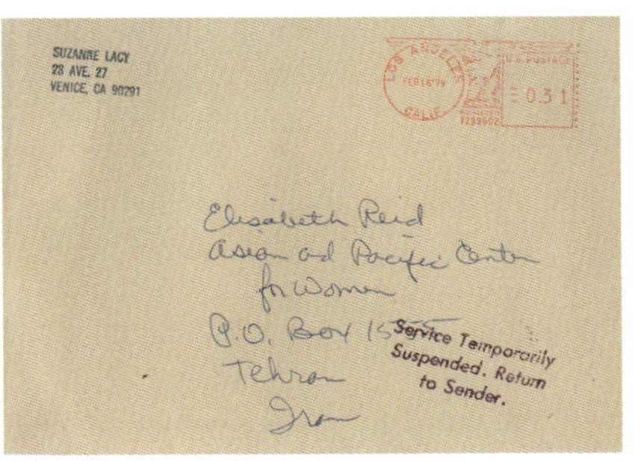

SUZANNE LACY
28 AVE. 27
VENICE, CA 90291
Elizabeth Reid
Asian and Pacific Center
for Women
P.O. Box 14
Tehran
Iran
Service Temporarily
Suspended. Return
to Sender.

River Meetings: Lives of Women in the Delta (1980)

SUZANNE LACY, BETTY CONSTANT, LAVERNE WOODS DUNN, JEANNE NATHAN, AND MARILEE SNEDEKER

In 1980 the College Art Association hosted its annual conference in New Orleans. Despite the feminist boycott on states that had refused to ratify the Equal Rights Amendment—Louisiana among them—the Women's Caucus for Art (WCA) was contractually obligated to attend. Struggling between the desire to boycott and the desire to support Southern women artists, the WCA invited Lacy to produce a performance/political intervention. For the opening of the conference, a potluck-style dinner for five hundred women was organized at the old U.S. Mint building to honor Southern diversity. It featured an array of musical acts, poets, and a performance by twelve actresses representative of the various ethnicities in the region. Throughout the rest of the conference Lacy and her collaborators supported woman-run catering businesses and arranged for WCA members to stay in local women's homes, thereby facilitating dialogue across religious, social, and occupational circles and focusing on the celebration of women rather than on the negative nature of the boycott. Dunn and Lacy posed in conversation in different locations around New Orleans as a way to promote dialogue and increase the visibility of the work. Mary Ann Guerra and Mary Helen Matlick also contributed to the project.

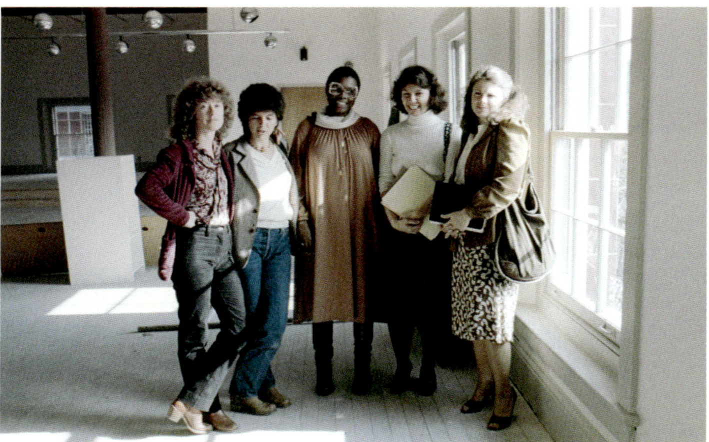

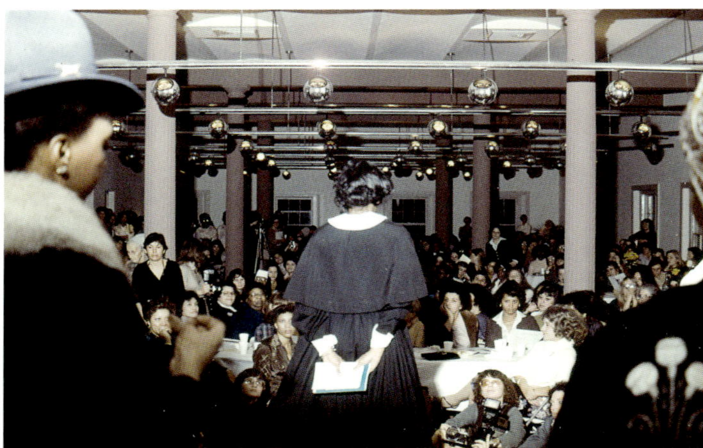

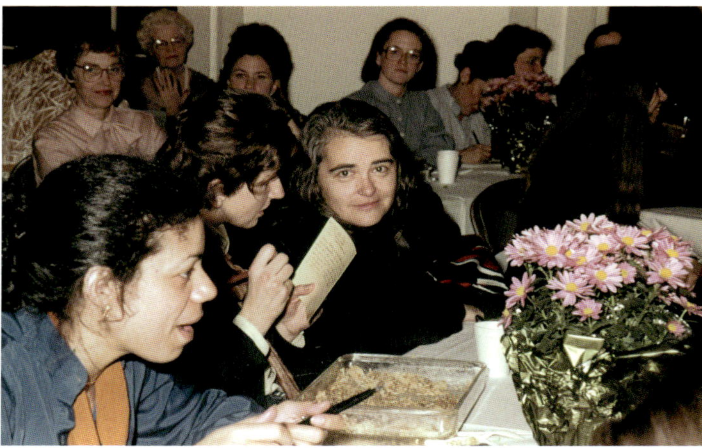

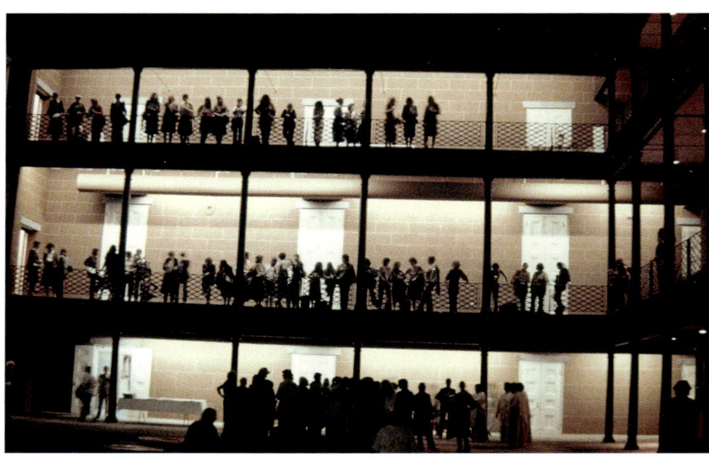

TOP LEFT: Left to right: Lacy, Constant, Dunn, Snedeker, and Nathan
TOP RIGHT AND BOTTOM: Opening event at the old U.S. Mint; guests included feminist writer Kate Millett (bottom left)

It had become a tradition of the WCA for exhibitions of work by women to accompany the panels and other conference activities. . . . At this time, it had not only to reaffirm the quality of women's art today, but also to deal directly with the issue of protest. The idea of women's performance . . . developed concurrently with that of the WCA conference as a whole.

—Mary Jane Jacob, curator, 1983

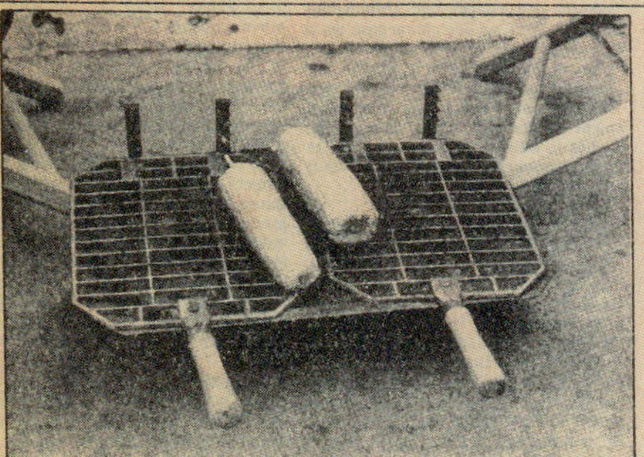

Protestin' ears sizzle for meal at cornstalk fence.

When protest is a picnic

By SHARON LITWIN

Conventioneers come to New Orleans to eat, drink and hold meetings — with the emphasis on the first activity.

But members of the National Women's Caucus for Art are in the unique position of being in a city with one of the world's best cuisines and not being able to dine in its restaurants.

What do you do if your organization, composed of women dedicated to the passage of the Equal Rights Amendment, is committed to attend a conference in a state that has not ratified it?

You come, but you boycott everything in sight.

That's what the members of the caucus are doing, and for the next few days Orleanians will be seeing female artists from all over the nation brown bagging it as they attend workshops and lectures this week.

Several years ago, when the College Art Association, the professional organization of academic artists and art historians, was trying to decide where to hold future meetings, a member of the board mentioned that, while the CAA had met often in the East, West and Midwest, it had never convened in the South. So, New Orleans became the site for the 1980 conference.

The Women's Caucus for Art, which always holds its meetings simultaneously with the CAA, made its plans to come here, never dreaming that in 1980 the ratification of the Equal Rights Amendment would not already be a fact of life in the Crescent City.

As the time for the conference approached, the caucus organizers and members had to decide whether to participate or not.

They decided to come, but to refuse to patronize the established businesses, hotels and restaurants. "We are accommodating the politics of the women who are coming," said Suzanne Lacy, caucus member and conference performance designer. "I don't mean to say that the 150 or 200 women who are not staying in hotels are going to have a great impact on the economy of the city or anything like that. But, we feel it's a gesture — a symbol.

"We're staying in other women's homes during the conference, and we will be providing all the women with box lunches so they won't have to eat in restaurants. We will also be giving out special cards to the people attending."

The cards to be distributed show scenes, photographed in various parts of the city, of "alternate" sources of food and ways to prepare it. They are parodies, says Lacey, of tourist postcards.

"A packet of information, provided to everyone at the conference, will include a list of local legislators and groups like the hotel/motel association, so that women can write to them and express their opinions about ERA."

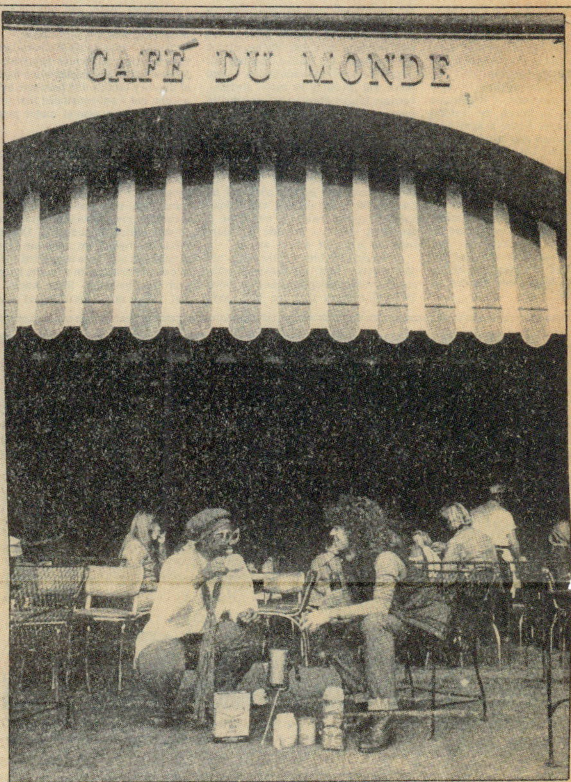

Above, Lavern Dunn and Suzanne Lacey pose for a parody postcard to be distributed to women artists boycotting the city's restaurants and hotels. Below, they demonstrate preparation of a banquette banquet.

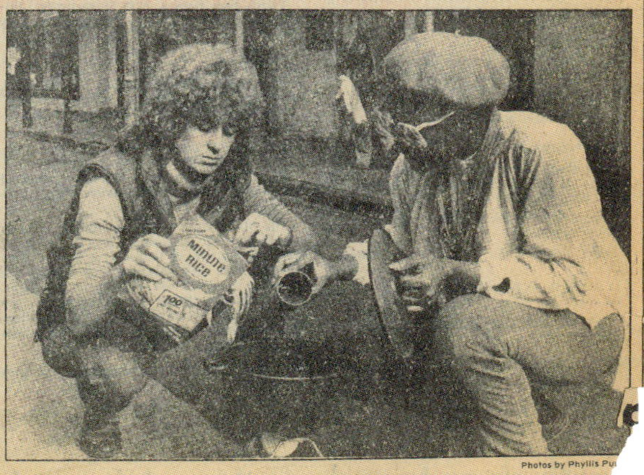

Photos by Phyllis Pu[illegible]

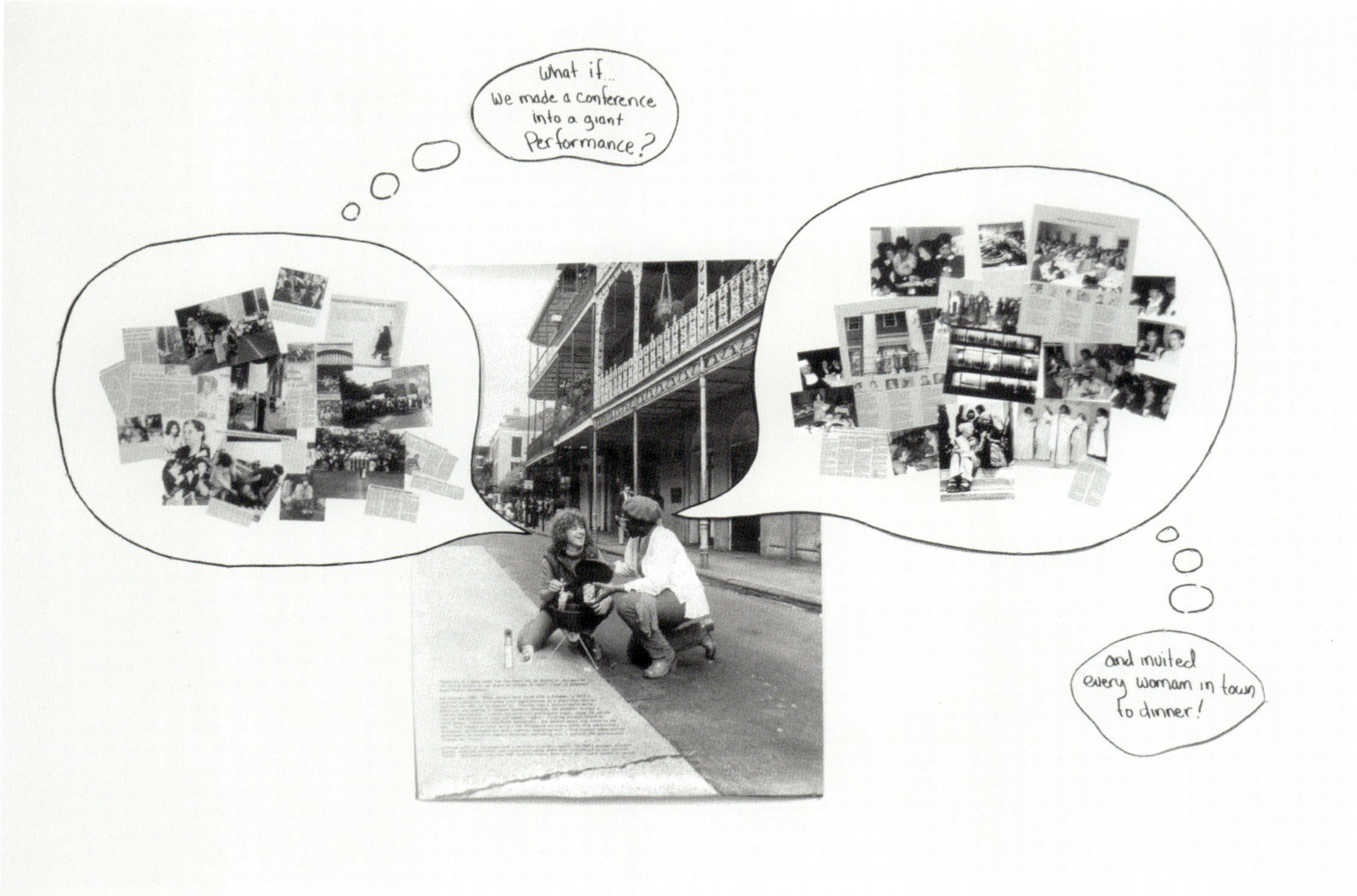

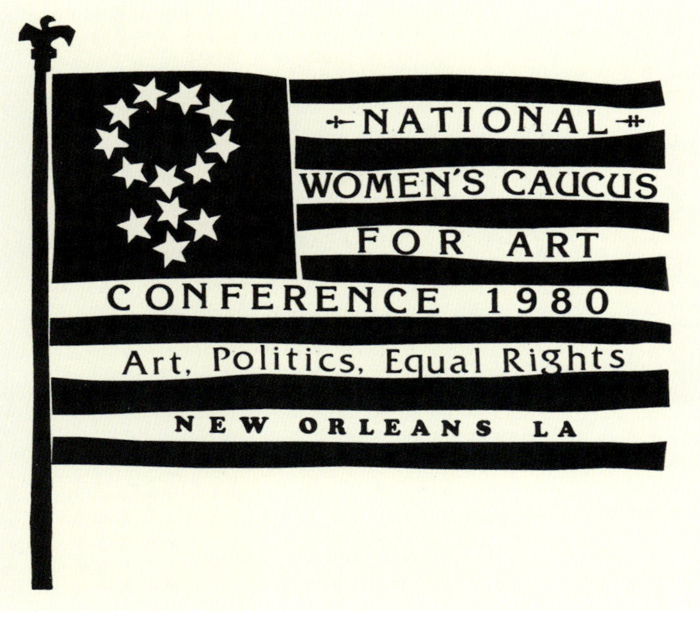

[Suzanne and I] became coconspirators in creating scenes around New Orleans where we pretended to duplicate the food offered by the [nearby] establishment or suggested by the scenery. . . . My pregnancy of five months had been confirmed, yet here I was stooping in the street in front of the famous Café Du Monde pretending to fry beignets. . . . [An] article was published in the *Times-Picayune* for all to read about the adventures of a lifetime for me but [also] a statement about the inequalities faced in our city, state, and nation.

—Laverne Woods Dunn, 2018

River Meeting: Lives of Women in the Delta

RIVER MEETING:
LIVES OF WOMEN OF THE DELTA

In the rich heritage of the South, women of achievement stand out; women who held the land during wars, kept the homes in peace, ran businesses, founded hospitals and charities, work in politics, created art and literature, and entered the professions. In 1980, women of today's achievements pay homage to the rich past of Southern women.

On January 30th, women from all parts of New Orleans will come together in the U.S. Mint for a reception and dinner, sponsored by the Women's Office, City of New Orleans, and the National Women's Caucus for Art. Created by artists from the Caucus and local women, the evening is a large performance in which all are performers creating together a sense of connection, respect and sharing among women in New Orleans.

Long before this evening, however, the art performances began. Beginning in early January women gathered in homes throughout the city for pot luck dinners. The guests at one dinner became the hostesses of yet more dinners. The network has continued to grow, and all will come together at the Mint.

Twelve women from this region's past were chosen to be recalled and honored. These are but few of the many women we could honor, and so each woman attending the dinner in the Mint will describe a woman important to her own life, adding to our lore the names of countless women left out of history.

The profiles of women honored will be collected, published, and kept alive by the Louisiana State Museum.

THE PROGRAM
January 30, 1980
6:30-10:00 p.m.

A Reception

We enter the old U.S. Mint through the majestic Greek Revival entrance on Esplanade Avenue. The elegant stone stairway leads us up to the third floor.

with Actresses

As we wander through the monumental yet graceful halls of the newly renovated Mint, we are greeted by women in costumes of past eras. They share with us the rich heritage of New Orleans women...the writers, teachers, doctors and philanthropists who left their mark on the City and the lives of each of us.

and Music

On the third floor we hear a piano and women's voices performing the music written many years ago by women composers from Louisiana. Walking out on the balcony, we can look over the rooftops of the French Market and view the contemporary towers of the city's business world beyond them. From the courtyard the voices of a women's gospel choir keeps the spiritual connection with the city's past alive. And on other balconies an Acadian racanteur talks and sings of old tales that repeat themselves everyday.

three Flags

Outside our windows, three banners have flown since they were hoisted there Sunday. The banners herald the work of New Orleans and national women artists on themes of River Meetings.

and a Tapestry

Inside we stop at a large canvas on which women are signing names. Each brings a woman to honor, a woman important to her own past, and adds this name to the canvas which will later be beaded by many women.

Dinner is served

Many faces are familiar from the small dinners we have been holding over the past six weeks. New acquaintances formed, old friendships renewed. New faces have joined us tonight.

Collecting our Stories

Together we write down an image, or anecdote, or description of the woman from our past. And together we speak aloud of these women.

Sharing Food

We pass platters and bowls, food prepared by each guest, sharing recipes handed down from generation to generation. Honoring our talent for nurturing, feeding.

Listening

Listening to each other, to women talking about why they created this event. Listening to E. M. Broner, author of **Weave of Women** speak to us of our connections to each other, and listening to Margaret Walker, author of **Jubilee** as she talks from her Southern woman's experience.

and finally, Parting

A ritual of leavetaking, with artist Mary Beth Edelson and Women from New Orleans. Sending us together into the night. Later we will meet again to bead our tapestry, to talk of subsequent gatherings.

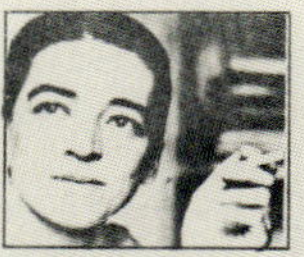 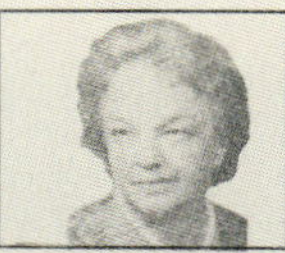

JUANITA GONZALES

Graduated from Newcomb, Juanita Gonzales apprenticed as an artist in New York before returning to New Orleans to become a fulltime instructor for the Newcomb Pottery Department. She was part of an exciting movement of women artists who combined crafts, fine arts, and the radical notion of women earning a living from their art. Her work in clay and sculpture was ahead of its time, influencing art five years after her untimely death at 32.

POKEY McILHENNY

Pokey McIlhenny was a leader in several campaigns to reform Louisiana politics.

She joined New Orleans women in a "Broomstick Brigade" that swept out a corrupt political machine to elect reform Mayor Chep Morrison.

In 1954 she led a women's campaign to elect a non-political school board.

She lobbied unceasingly on behalf of mental health programs, vocational education, and protection of the state's wetlands.

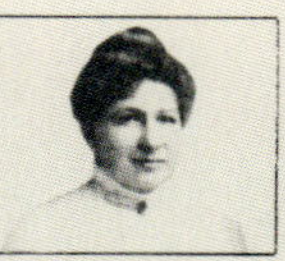 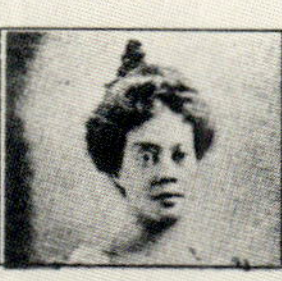

SARAH TEW MAYO

Sarah Tew Mayor graduated from Women's Medical College in Philadelphia in 1898.

In 1905 she joined six other women who had been denied staff hospital positions because of their sex, and opened the New Orleans Hospital and Dispensary for Women and Children. For the first time black women were admitted to a private hospital.

After her death the New Orleand Dispensary was renamed the Sarah Mayo Hospital. Inscribed on her tomb in Metairie Cematery is: "A mother to all mothers".

ALICE DUNBAR NELSON

Born in New Orleans on July 19, 1875, Alice Dunbar became the respected author of **Violets and Other Tales** in 1895; **The Goodness of St. Rochque** in 1890; **Masterpieces of Negro Eloquence** in 1914; and **Romances of the Negro** in 1932.

As editor of the Wilmington Advocate, and associate editor of the African Methodist Review, she was deeply involved in social and political issues. She participated in the NAACP, American Interracial Peace Committee and Delta Sigma Sorority.

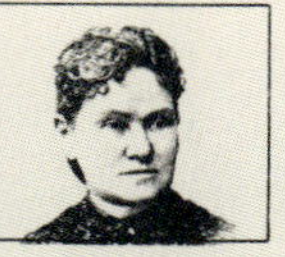 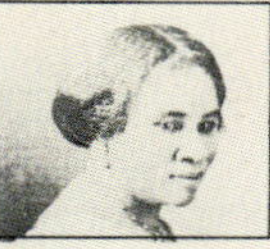

ELIZABETH LYLE SAXON

Elizabeth Lyle Saxon was born in 1832 in Greenville, Tennessee. Motherless at the age of two, her father demanded from her a promise on his deathbed to "never cease working for unfortunate women, so long as your life should last."

Later she devoted herself to the social and legal enfranchisement of her sex. In 1879 she, Caroline Merrick, and Emily Peltier Collins unsuccessfully petitioned the Louisiana State Constitutional Convention for women's suffrage, but gained for women the right to manage school offices and laws.

SARAH McWILLIAMS WALKER

Born in New Orleans December 23, 1867, Sarah McWilliams was orphaned, married and widowed by age twenty. With a child to support she moved to St. Louis, worked as a laundress, and married again.

She invented a hair straightening formula for black women, and peddled it door-to-door. Later, with 500 agents selling the formula and a full line of cosmetics, she became the first black woman millionaire in the United States.

A philanthropist, she sponsored negro artists, writers, the NAACP and black educational institutions.

OPPOSITE, TOP: Collage representing the organizing process, media, and events, created by Lacy for the exhibition *Art socio-critique*, Maison de la Culture, Festival de La Rochelle, France, June 26–September 30, 1982
OPPOSITE, BOTTOM: WCA promotional material distributed in the weeks leading up to the conference
ABOVE: Program brochure for the opening event at the old U.S. Mint

Freeze Frame: Room for Living Room (1982)

SUZANNE LACY AND JULIA LONDON WITH JAN CHATTLER, JOYA CORY,
NATALIA RIVAS, NGOH SPENCER, AND CAROL SZEGO

As part of the International Theater Festival conference and the International Sculpture Conference in San Francisco, Lacy and her collaborators produced a performance that brought women from different demographic groups together to discuss their lives and the topic of survival. In an upscale furniture showroom, 120 women were arranged in nineteen small clusters by age, ethnicity, social position, or occupation, creating a portrait of the diversity of the city. Gathered on couches and chairs to which they had added objects pertinent to their groups, they formed "living paintings" for the audience that wandered among them, listening to their stories. The performance ended with a dialogue between all of the women, directed at the audience. *Freeze Frame* was the first time Lacy organized intentionally structured conversations into aesthetic tableaux and merged theatrical staging with socially engaged topics.

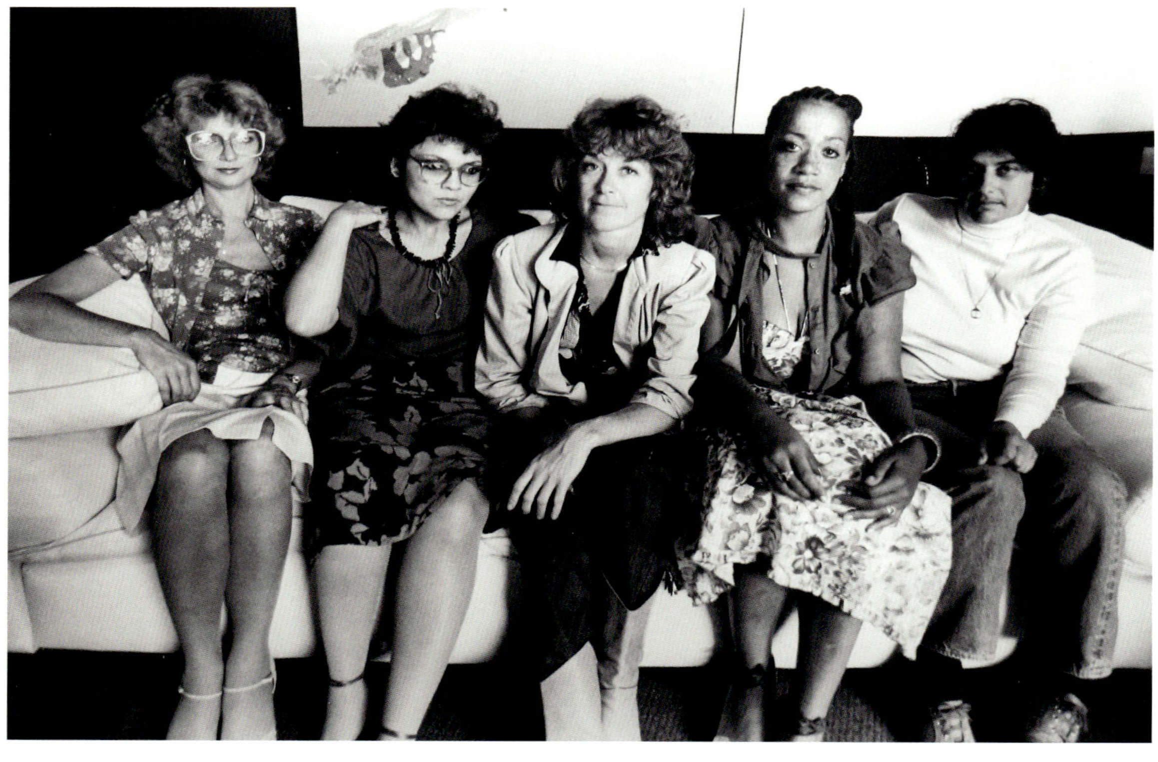

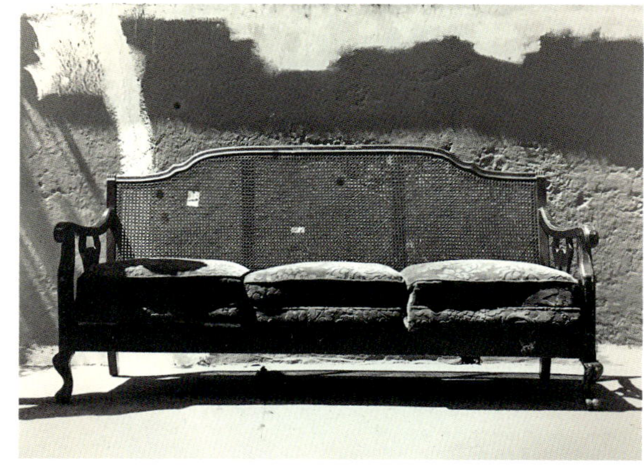

TOP: Left to right: Perney Sampson, Rivas, Lacy, Spencer, and London
BOTTOM AND OPPOSITE: Promotional images of Lacy's own couch on the streets of San Francisco, where women were invited to engage with it
FOLLOWING PAGES: Lacy addressing participants in a rehearsal for the performance

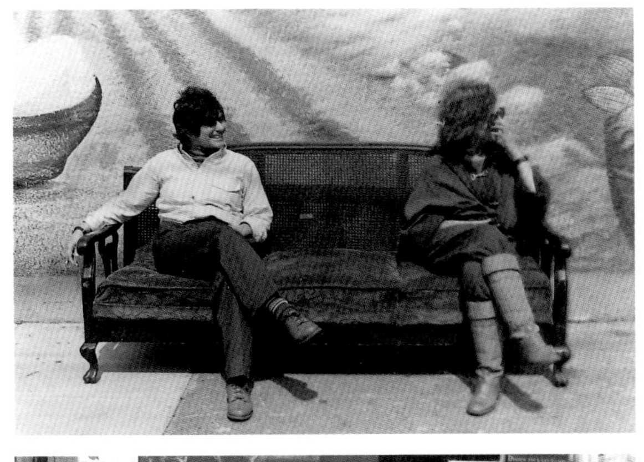
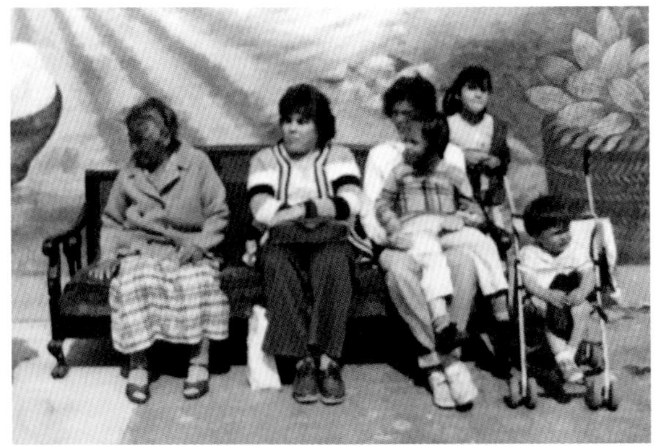
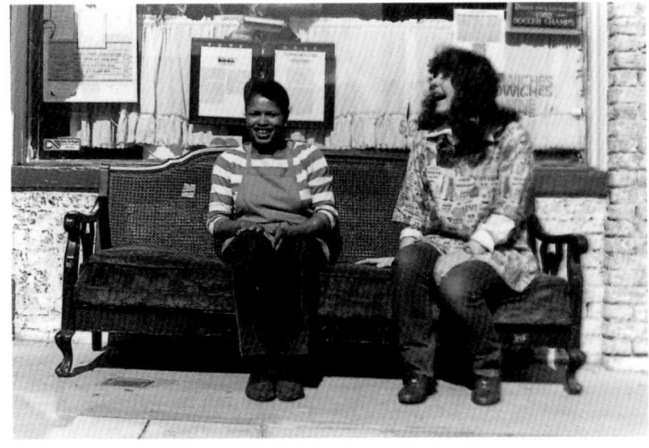
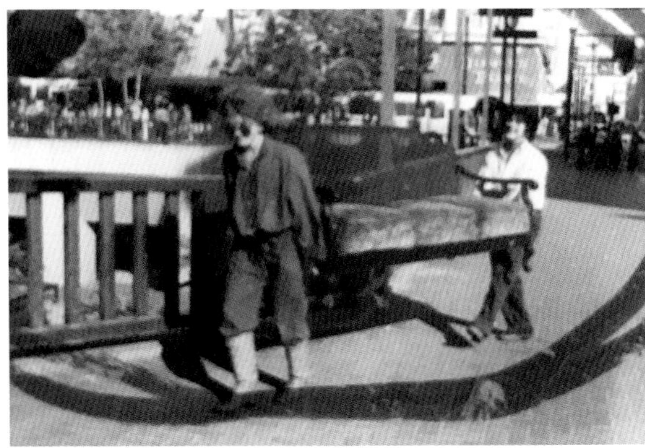
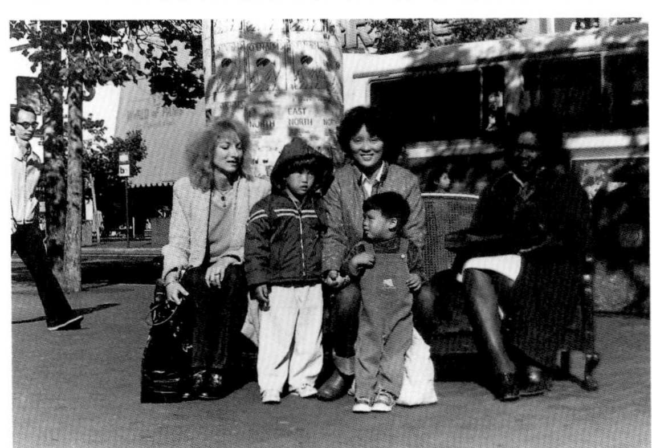
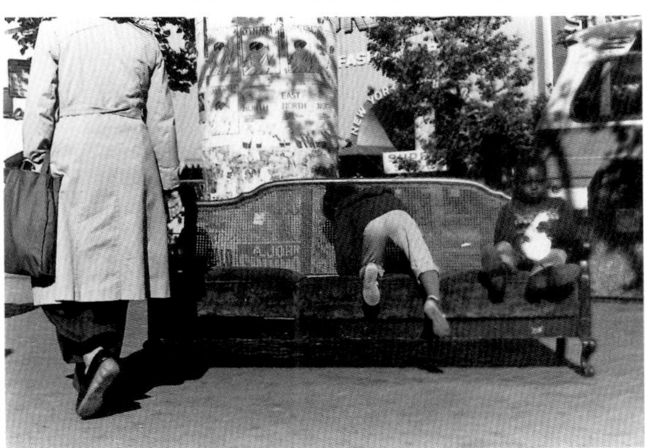
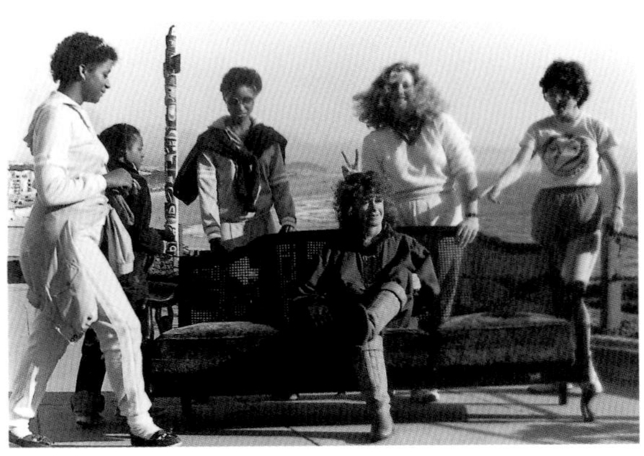
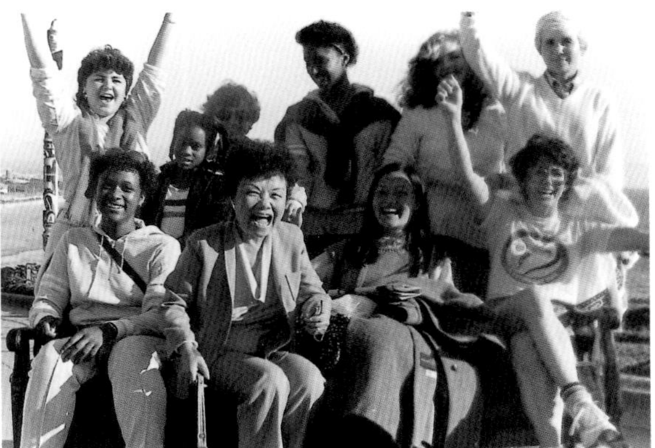

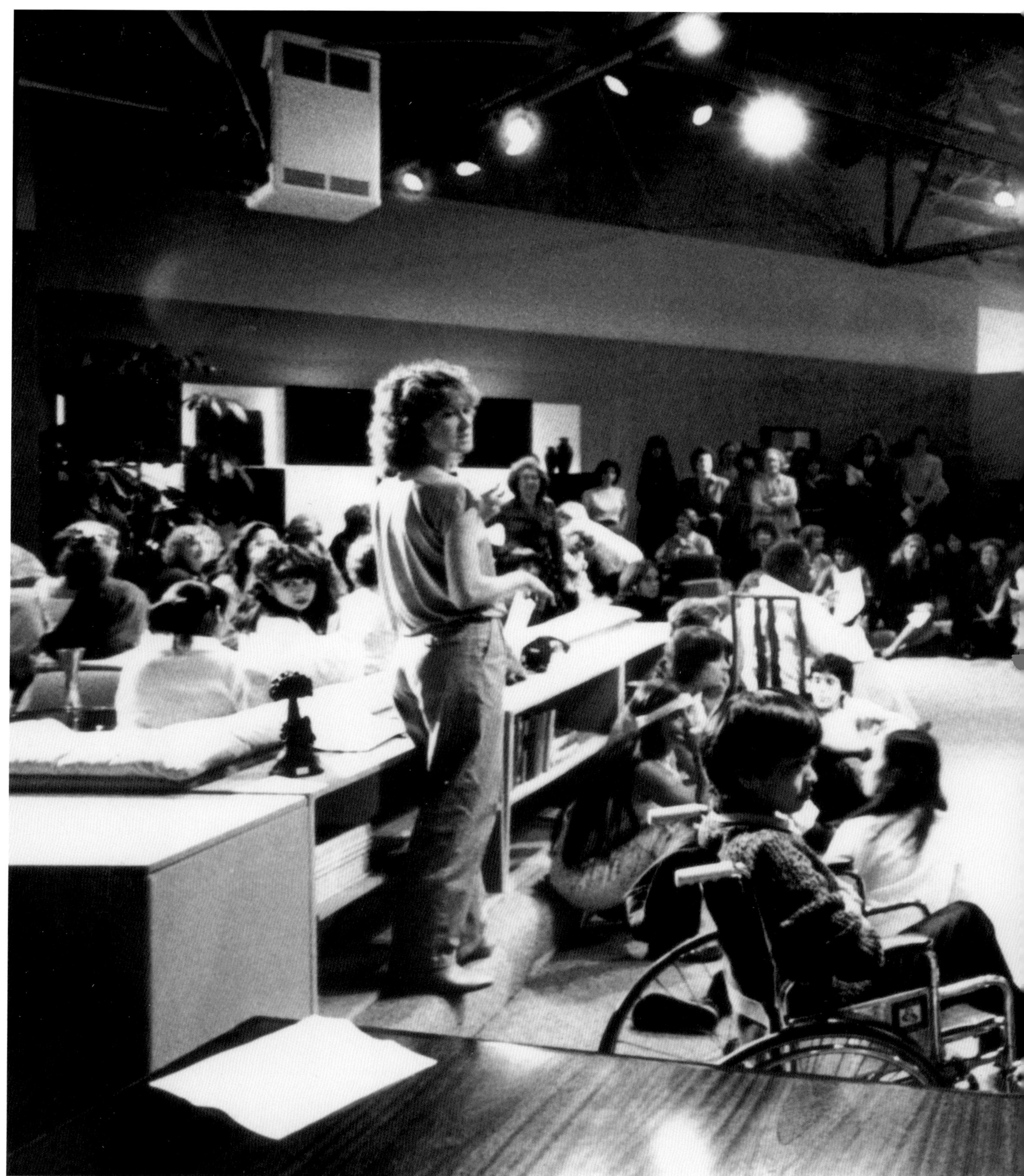

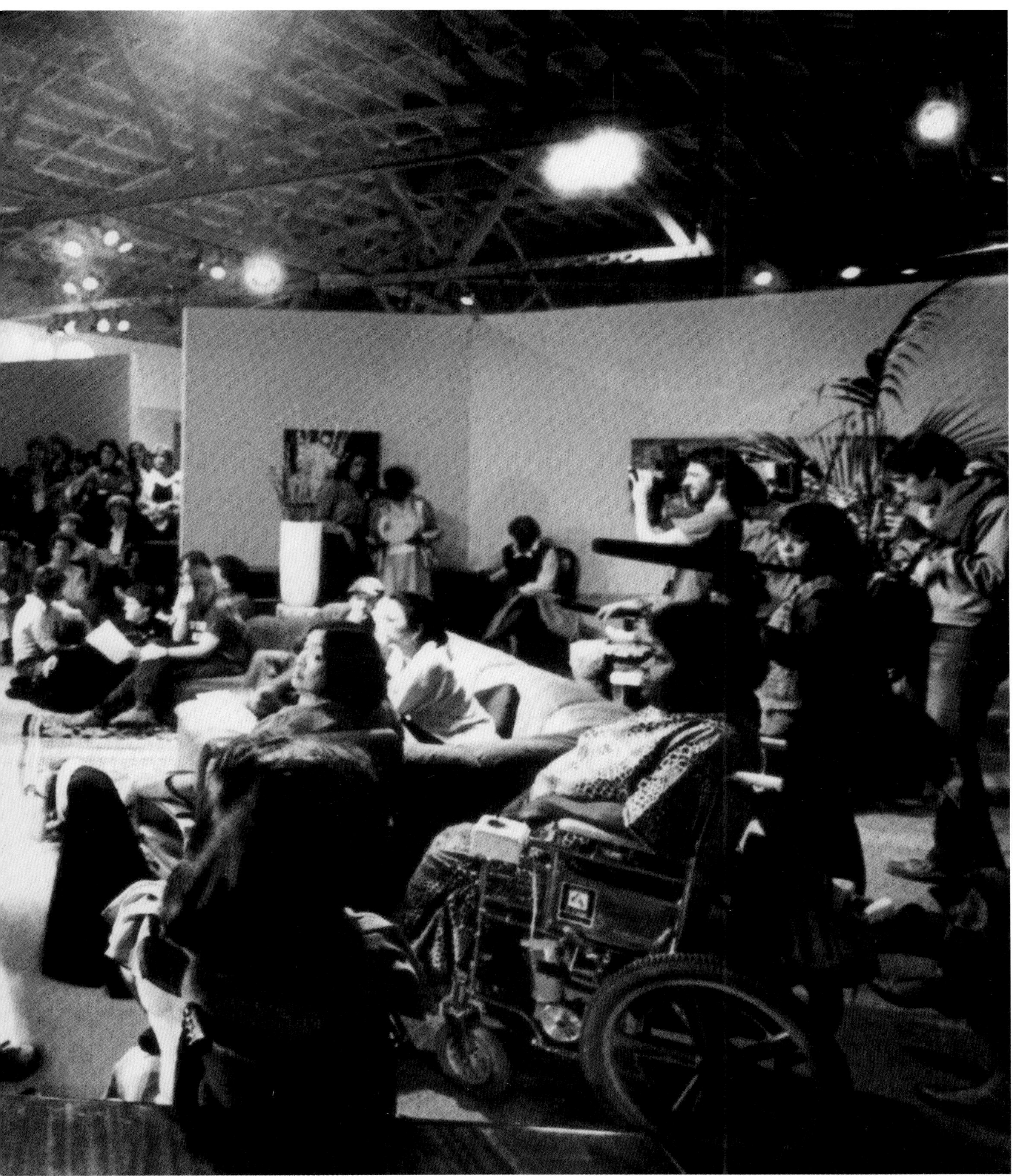

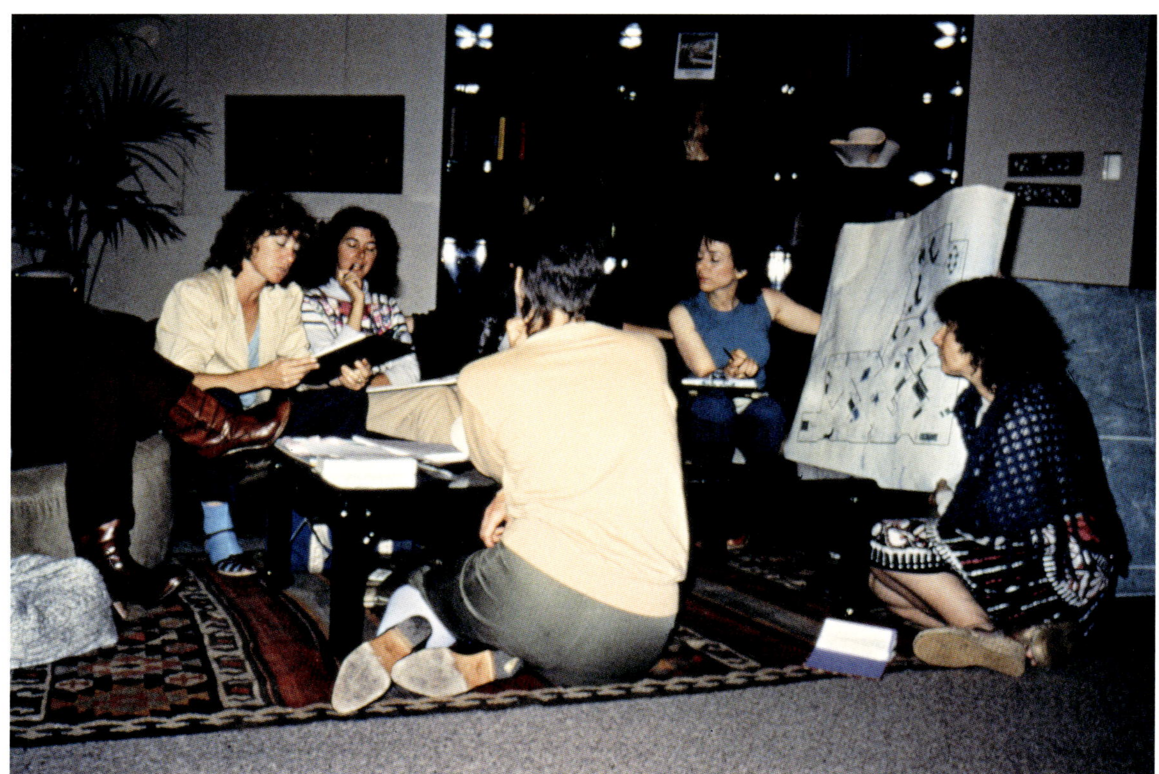

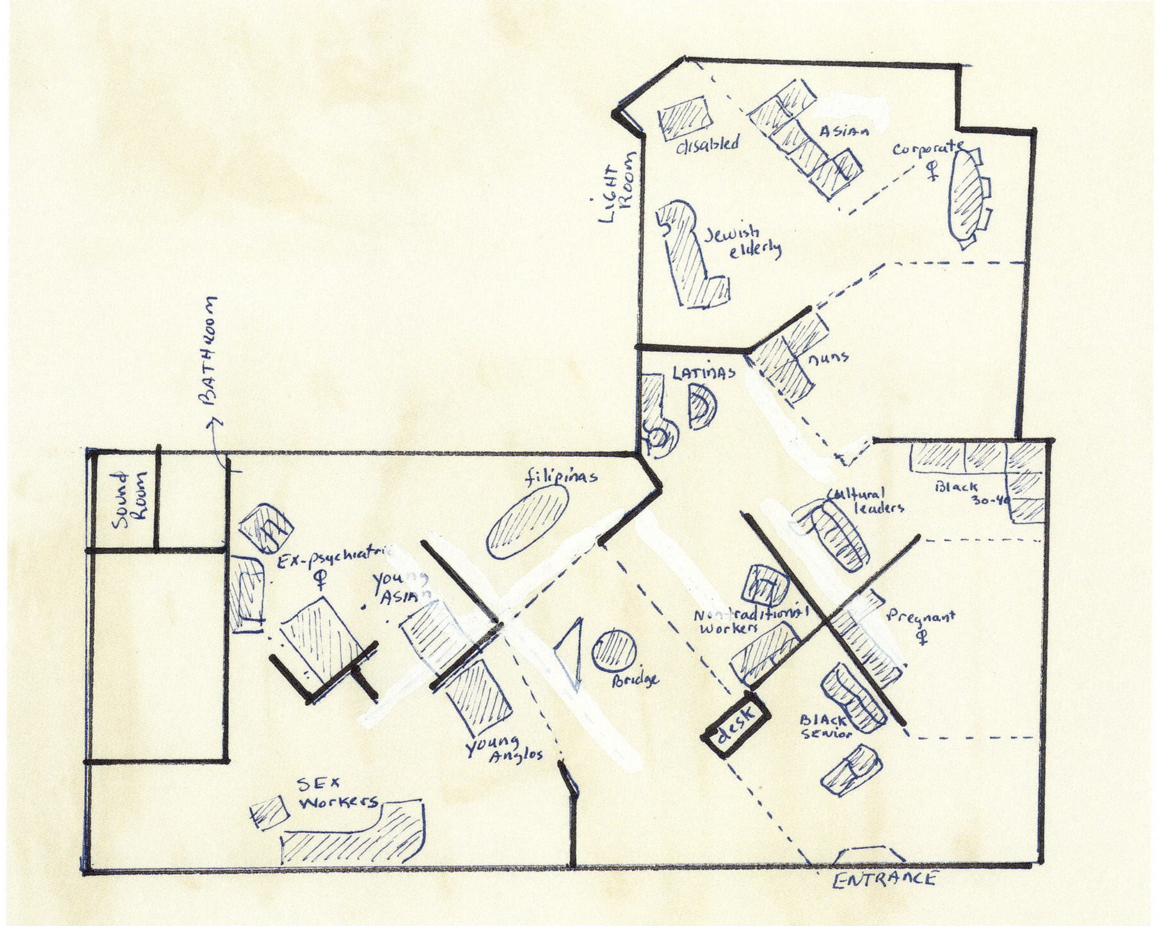

TOP: Lacy and collaborators planning where different groups would be situated
BOTTOM: Diagram of groups and their planned positions in the showroom
OPPOSITE: Stills from *SOFA* (1984), a documentary about *Freeze Frame* edited by Douglas Gayeton Smith, with corresponding excerpts from the transcript

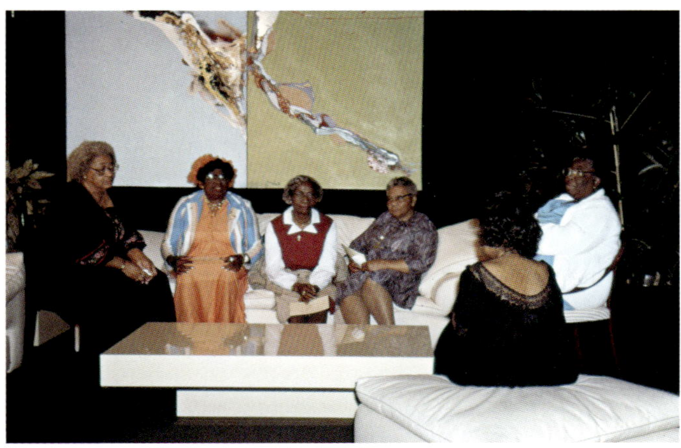

We worked! And if we were turned down on the job because we were black, we searched and found another. Because we knew we had to work. Because we knew, if we didn't work, we [we]re dead. So we worked and it made us strong. We learned to survive by knowing that I've got my children, I've got to work. I've got to have a paycheck. My children are in school. My daughter is going to college. My son is in high school. I've got to work.

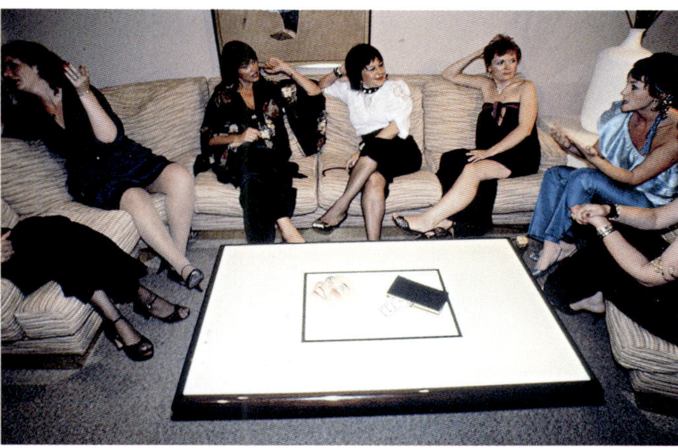

I guess I want to say, I am a prostitute and I put my survival at stake by coming here and saying that. I could get thrown out of my apartment building. I can't get arrested for saying it, but I can conceivably get arrested for being public. I just want to say that I hope everyone understands my position. I know that other women identify with us.

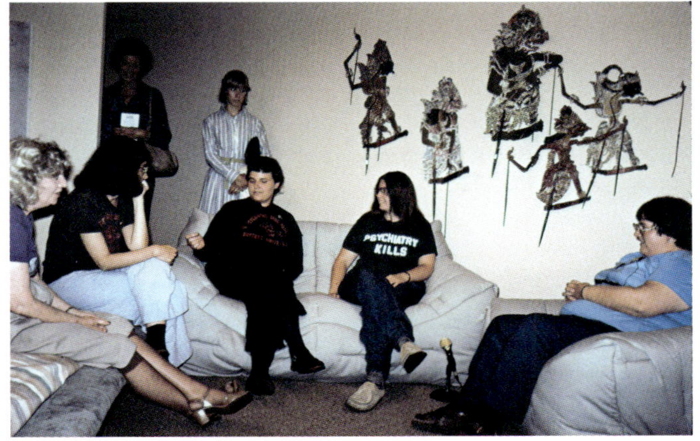

She kind of had a similar experience to me . . . she had been going through a lot of spiritual opening up. And, you know, I guess her family thought it was weird or something. And so they had her committed, and her husband authorized the shock treatments against her will. . . . How could I not get depressed being locked up in this really horrible environment, you know, seeing all these terrible things going on around me? So I did think every day that I could get it next. And then they did this thing, I guess which is real common, to get me to agree to be a voluntary patient. And they said, "If you stay here" — they committed me totally against my will, but then once I was in the hospital they said — "If you agree to be a voluntary patient, then we'll let you out in two weeks. But if you don't agree to be a voluntary patient, then we'll have you court-committed and you'll be in for months and months. And so you better go along with it." And so I agreed to go along with it for two weeks.

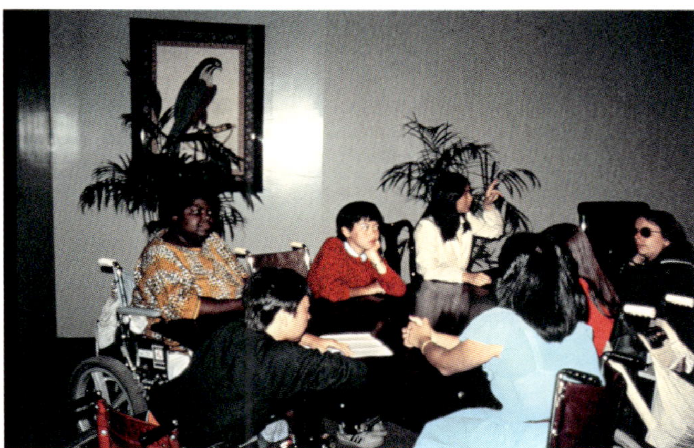

In my personal life, everything that I did, I think, was harder because of my disability. And so just trying to survive socially becomes a whole different technique, not just as a black woman, but as a black disabled woman. And I think some of the things that my mother taught me as a child helped me to become a survivor.

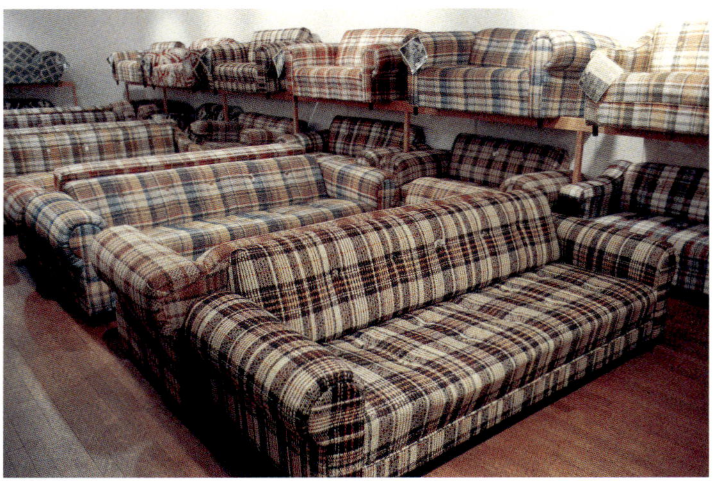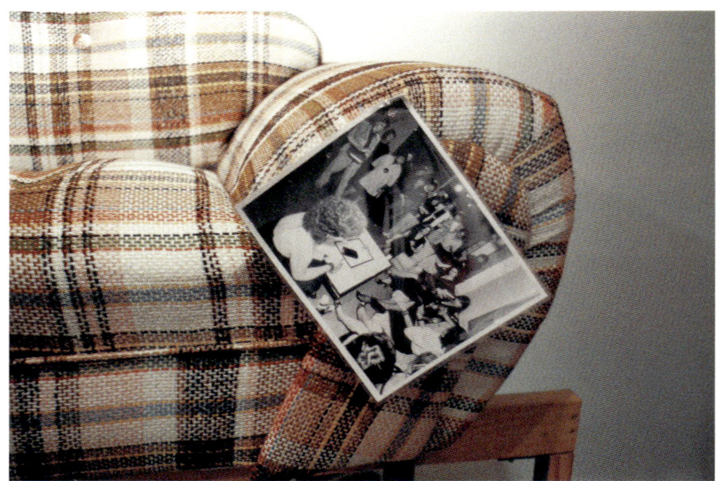

Lacy created an installation based on *Freeze Frame* for the exhibition *At Home*, Long Beach Museum of Art, California, September 4–November 6, 1983. It incorporated sofas with photographs and texts from the original performance and a soundtrack by Jacki Apple.

AT HOME CARDS (SELECTED)

8. The stories of women are beginning and they are filling me up. Talked to Ngoh Spencer—her story of her husband's suicide, how she is raising her daughter, how she found the Lord. Her courage is moving. Talked to Carol Fenton, a manager of a showroom in the Galeria. Wonderful, witty Jewish woman from New York. We talked straight, talked survival. Her third marriage, after ten years and two sons, ending in divorce. She came to San Francisco and began, simply began, with nothing. Now she doesn't have everything, but she's survived. She worries about being booted out of her job when she is no longer young looking.

With Julia later, I began to laugh. It occurred to me finally that I was creating a room full of women talking about what I needed to hear. How did they manage? How did women cope, live through separations, do their work, make independent women of themselves? I need models.

13. And now the last barrier is the creation of the actual evening and clarifying the metaphors we have set in motion. I'm using the visual and aural components of the performance to describe, heighten, and hopefully resolve the basic contradiction in the piece. The tension between the showroom's elegance and overwhelming influence upon our desire and its museum quality that could make objects, beautiful yet rendered useless, out of the women—and between the politics of women's difficulties with survival. The juxtaposition of the furniture of the upper class and the struggles of women who could never buy such luxury is a strong expression here. But maybe the Roche-Bobois ambiance will overwhelm. Maybe people will objectify the women even more.

14. The tableaus are stereotypical, there's no getting around it. And I am arranging the women with the studied elegance of objects on display in a museum. The distance inherent in this arrangement is great, and the audience's potential alienation is reinforced by the role of voyeur I am forcing upon them. Some of our participants are asking, "Aren't we reinforcing social stereotypes by recreating them here?"

It's complicated, and I don't have the answer. I suppose that's part of what makes it art rather than political action. Driven by an image, an intuition or feeling, I try to polish it until its reality becomes one with that of my audience—a reality that hopefully is also a political consciousness raising. But it's almost as if the imagery has its own life, and I'm running along behind trying to clarify and explain and make it reasonably responsible to its constituency. The truth is I'm driven to do this image, with its experience of alienation and otherness. I guess I'm excited by the challenge of turning alienation into responsiveness, caricature into empathy.

17. Interesting thing about performance—when you follow your psyche through the development of a piece, each thing that in the real world might be seen as a diversion from your course, in a performance becomes part of the process of doing it. When a turn of energy comes, it is often with distress in the beginning but later with wonder that one observes how the performance shaped itself.

The audience did not see my own quest for family, for a way to transcend not only the pain from my personal life but the despair out of which art often comes—but perhaps as they watched the performance they felt a resonance with their own similar needs? It was the hardest piece I've ever done, but I think it was also the best. . . .

Stories of Work and Survival (2007)

SUZANNE LACY WITH KELLY AKASHI AND SUSAN BARNET

In conjunction with the exhibition *WACK! Art and the Feminist Revolution* at the Museum of Contemporary Art (MOCA), Los Angeles, Lacy revisited *Freeze Frame: Room for Living Room* (1982, pp. 140–46) and *Immigrants and Survivors* (1983) to unpack how representations of feminism, race, and class in the visual arts had shifted in the intervening years. The project included private conversations in women's homes and workplaces; group conversations behind glass doors at MOCA, seen but not heard by an audience; audio recordings from these conversations, played in an installation; and a dinner for 250 women on the museum's patio. This was the first instance of Lacy's practice of revisiting projects to expand their networks and dialogues and to place them in new political and social contexts.

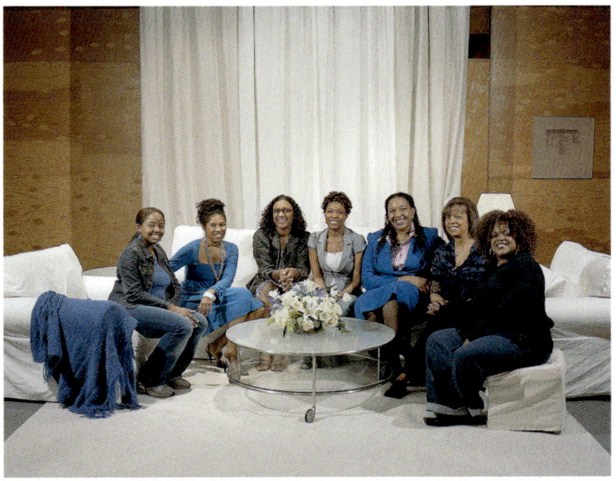
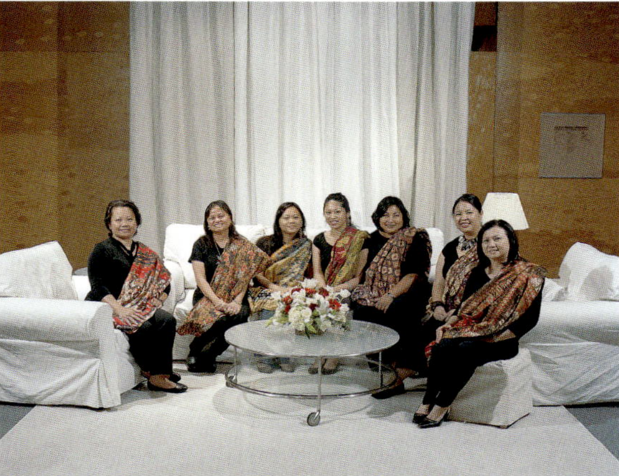
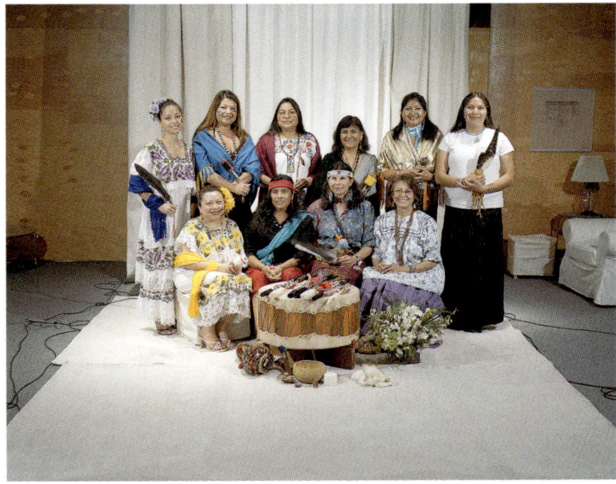
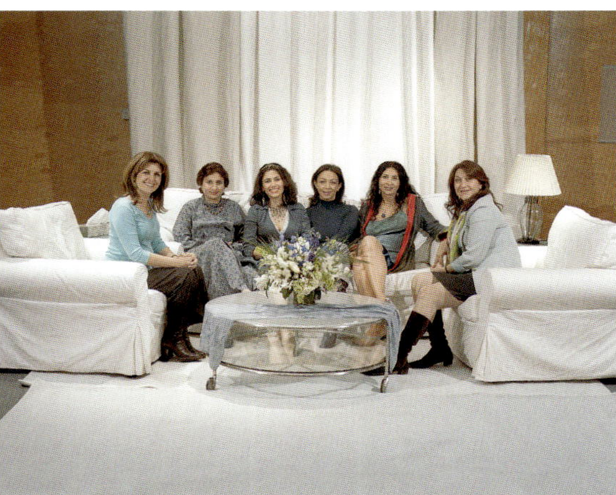

Groups of women from different neighborhoods and occupations that convened behind glass doors at MOCA

Full Circle (1992–93)

SUZANNE LACY WITH A COALITION OF CHICAGO WOMEN

Lacy produced a two-part project for the exhibition *Culture in Action* in Chicago. Bringing attention to the city's lack of monuments to women, the first part, *Full Circle*, comprised one hundred half-ton stones sourced from a female-owned quarry and installed downtown with commemorative plaques honoring the service work of ninety contemporary and ten historical women. Lacy collaborated with residents and a steering committee that solicited public nominations in order to select a diverse, representative range of figures. Displaying names and quotes, the stones drew public and media attention as they appeared almost magically overnight. An awards ceremony was also organized for the honorees, after which small groups dispersed among the stones for simultaneously public and private acts of celebration.

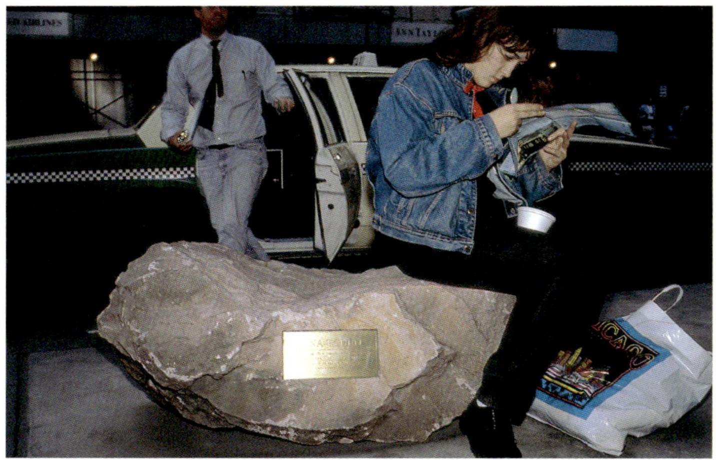

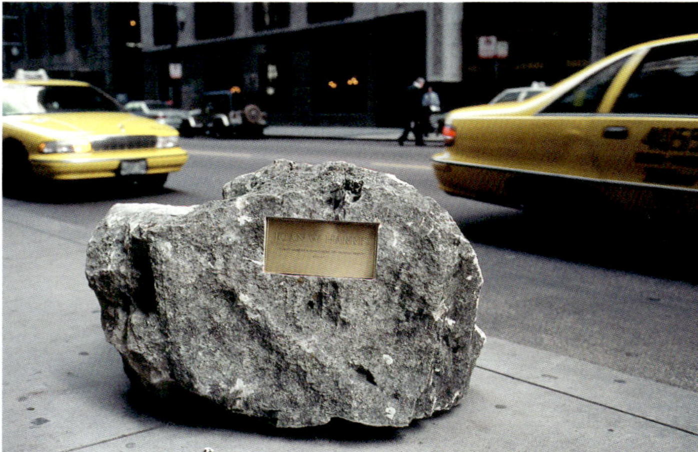

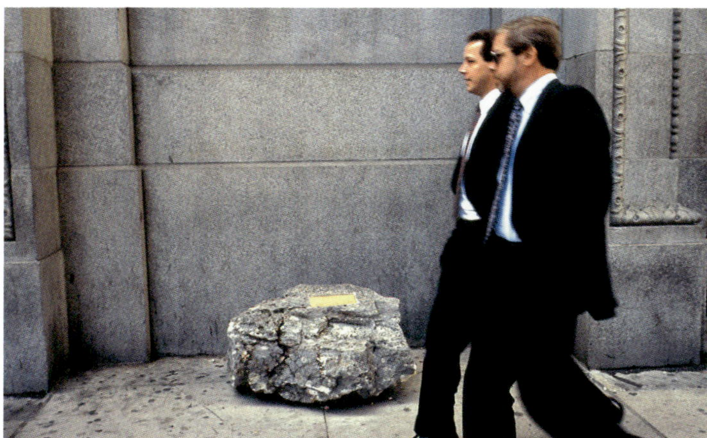

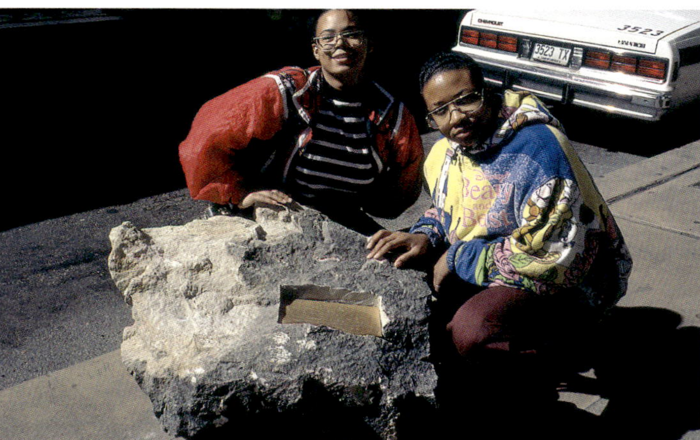

Dinner at Jane's (1993)

The second part of Lacy's project for the exhibition *Culture in Action* was a dinner on September 30, 1993, for fourteen international women activists at Hull-House, Chicago's first and most important settlement house. Founded by Jane Addams in 1889, it provided resources for labor organizing, political reform, other social justice causes, and the arts, and it was the site of scores of dinners where scholars and activists discussed the politics of the time. The act of inviting present-day women to envision the future in a historically significant location effectively combined poetic gesture with public organizing. Participating artists included Phylis Geller, Jane Saks, and Tom Weinberg.

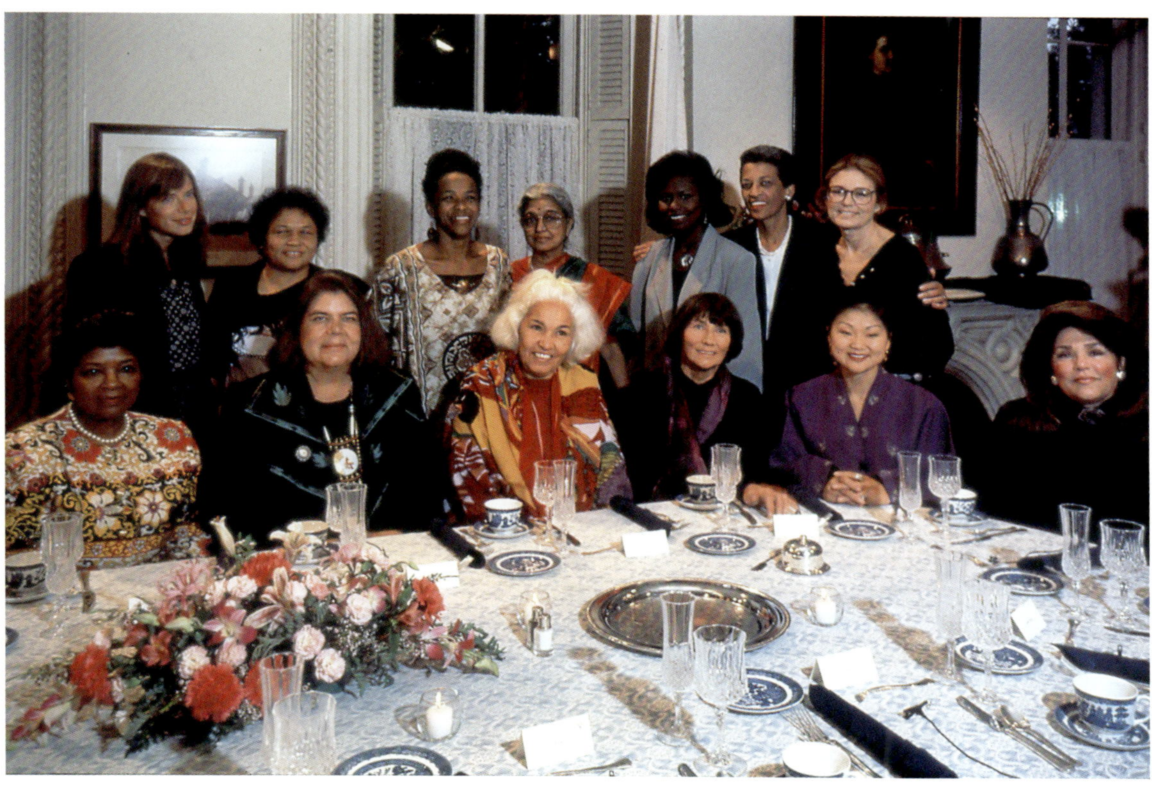

Participants; top row, left to right:
Susan Faludi, Myrna Cunningham,
Cheryl Carolus, Devaki Jain, Anita Hill,
Johnnetta Cole, and Gloria Steinem;
bottom row, left to right: Addie Wyatt,
Wilma Mankiller, Nawal El Saadawi,
Magdalena Abakanowicz, Chung Hyun
Kyung, and Susan Grode (not pictured:
Dolores Huerta)

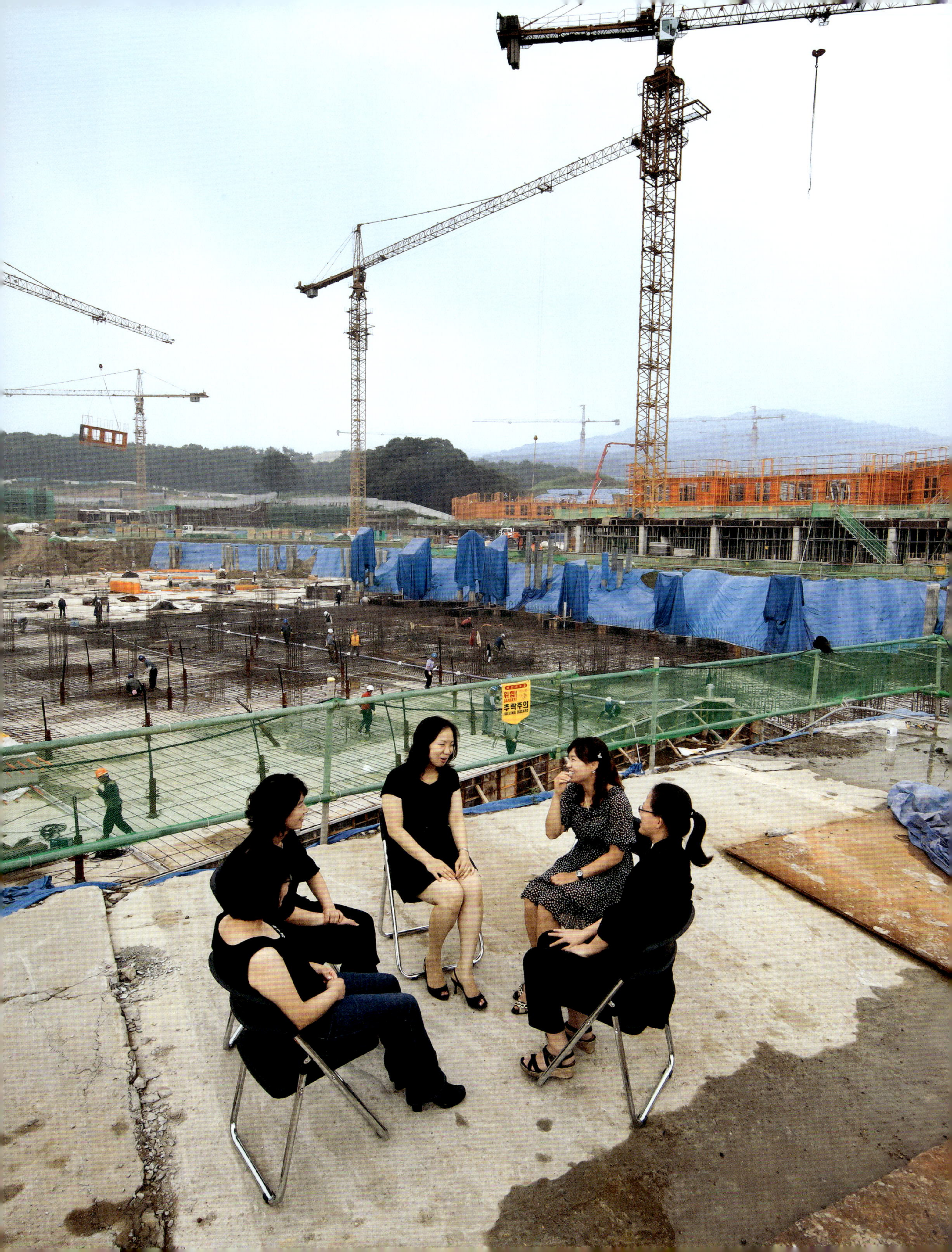
위험!
DANGER
추락주의
FALLING HAZARD

IMAGE AND DIALOGUE

Many of Lacy's performances of the late 1970s and early 1980s aimed to cultivate a sense of common cause among diverse networks of women; this goal would also shape three of her defining projects of the 1980s: *Whisper, the Waves, the Wind* (1983–84, pp. 152–57), *The Dark Madonna* (1985–86, pp. 158–65), and *Whisper Minnesota* (1985–87, pp. 166–73). In these later works, however, Lacy achieved a more fully realized visual resolution, drawing inspiration from the use of pageants and tableaux vivants as forms of feminist resistance in the late nineteenth and early twentieth centuries[1]—frameworks she first deployed in *Freeze Frame: Room for Living Room* (1982, pp. 140–46) and would return to again and again. In *Whisper, the Waves, the Wind*, senior women dressed in white descended stairs to the shoreline of two beaches in La Jolla, California, and sat at tables arranged across the sand, where they discussed the joys, challenges, and questions they faced. Lacy would employ this structure—thoughtfully placed groups engaged in focused conversations in metaphorically rich settings—in many projects to come.

Iconic, almost mythic images like that of the women on the La Jolla beach were born of long periods of planning and discursive engagement with the communities the projects explore. Whereas Lacy's earlier works generally required no more than three months to produce, the development phase alone for many of these projects lasted more than a year and often involved logistical feats such as procuring large, public venues; creating media campaigns; and recruiting and convening vast numbers of participants. In *The Crystal Quilt* (1987, pp. 166–73), a performance within the project *Whisper Minnesota*, Lacy went to great lengths to secure the Crystal Court in the IDS Center, Minneapolis, where she convened around 430 performers. The longer periods of engagement also allowed her to include more symposia, conferences, community groups, and classes in her projects. These discursive elements were designed to build community and create space for the works to unfold in dialogue with the experiences and knowledge of the participants, and to extend the projects' potential to impact public policy.

These multilayered works reveal Lacy's drive to both craft powerful imagery and achieve tangible results. At times these priorities came into competition, causing her to reconsider and revise her methods. In 1982, when she was about to embark on *Whisper, the Waves, the Wind*, she reflected: "If dreams and visions are a source of social transformation, then the realization of metaphors of community, over and over, will have an impact on the cultural zeitgeist if not comparable to a more overt action at least complementary to it. We hope."[2] With *Whisper, the Waves, the Wind*, and in subsequent projects, Lacy played out her dreams and visions, continually questioning and refining her approach as she balanced aesthetic and political motivations.

—TAYLOR SHOOLERY

NOTES
1. "I started reading about the US pageant movement between 1886–1932 or so, and was intrigued with the combination of activism and visuality in tableaux." Suzanne Lacy, conversation with Megan Steinman, January 2018. Education and Public Practice exhibition files, San Francisco Museum of Modern Art.
2. Suzanne Lacy, "Beneath the Seams" (1982), reprinted in *Leaving Art: Writings on Performance, Politics, and Publics, 1974–2007* (Durham, NC: Duke University Press, 2010), 143.

OPPOSITE: Public conversation staged at a construction site as part of *Anyang Women's Agenda* (2010, pp. 176–77)

Whisper, the Waves, the Wind (1983–84)

SUZANNE LACY AND SHARON ALLEN

In 1984, 154 women over the age of sixty-five convened on two contiguous, picturesque beaches in La Jolla, California. Dressed in white, participants sat in groups of three or four around white-cloth-covered tables to discuss their lives, fears, and desires as one thousand people watched from surrounding cliffs. Susan Stone's soundtrack echoed and amplified portions of prerecorded conversations, and the audience was later invited to approach the tables and listen to those occurring in real time. At once a public performance installation staged for film and a consciousness-raising session conceived in the spirit of the populist theater movement, the collective action was organized over the course of a year and a half and monumentalized the commonplace activity of women reflecting on their experiences. The work translated the intimacy of personal disclosure into a public spectacle with greater social and political implications, exploring older women's losses of cultural visibility, dignity, respect, and resources. The setting provided a poignant backdrop as the cyclical washing of waves on the shore resonated with the individual yet universal experiences of womanhood, aging, and mortality that were shared.

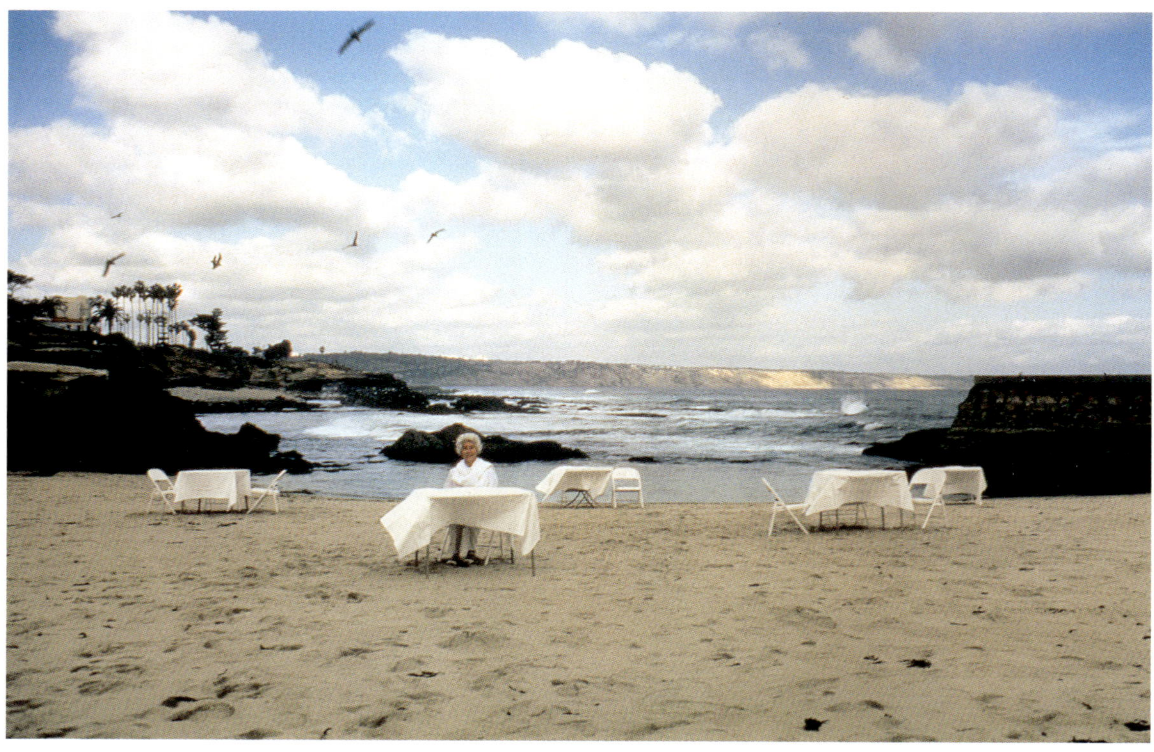

Staged photograph

OPPOSITE, LEFT: Labels for The Whisper Project T-shirts

OPPOSITE, TOP RIGHT: Organizing luncheon at which promotional brochures were distributed

OPPOSITE, BOTTOM RIGHT: Invitation to a fund-raising brunch

Our steering committee, aged sixty-five years and older, were all involved in assisting other aging seniors [to] make the transition from *old* to *older* to *oldest*. At the first of many of our get-togethers Suzanne voiced the hope that all our *actresses* would have white hair. This caused quite a stir, and the women pushed against the idea every time she brought it up. I often think she raised the issue as part of a process to stimulate their thinking and to enjoy the passion of their interactions. It came as no surprise to either of us that "We aren't aging, we're ripening" soon became their mantra. When I asked each of them, *"How old do you feel?"* the majority responded with: "Age is just a number, but how you feel inside is everything!" These words of wisdom have eased me into my own age of ripening.

—Sharon Allen, 2018

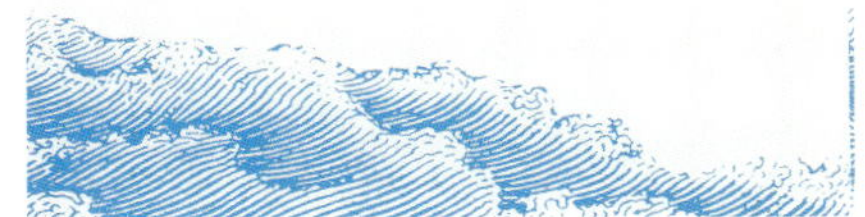

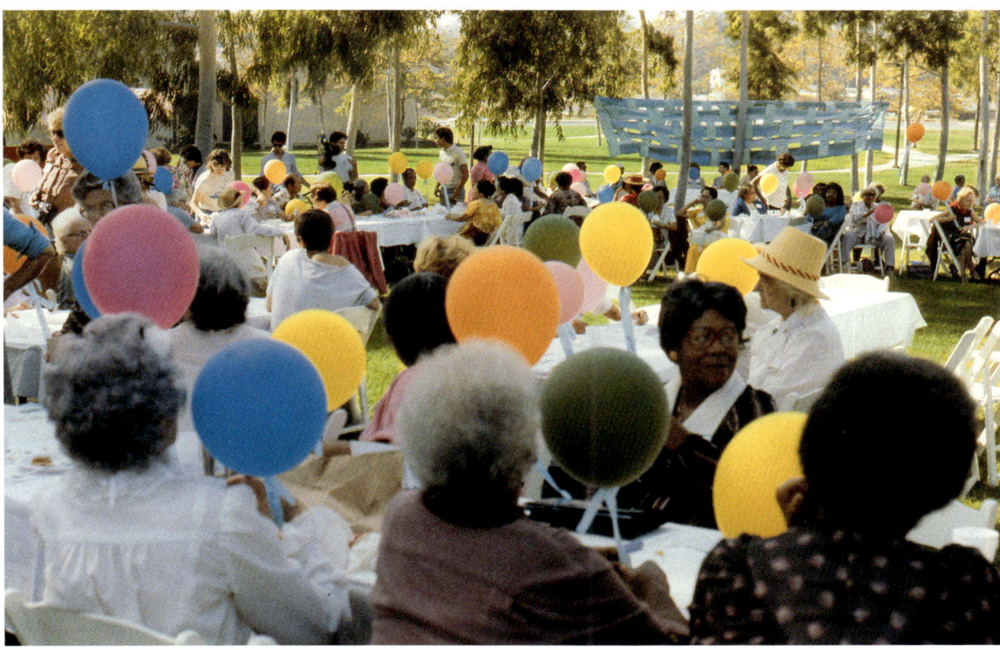

Scheduled for late spring of 1984, *Whisper, the Waves, the Wind* is a performance art event created by artist Suzanne Lacy working with over fifty San Diego residents to illuminate the concerns of older women and to establish, through art, new and positive images of them.

This hand-painted one-of-a-kind t-shirt was created especially for The Whisper Project by Los Angeles artist Julie A. When you buy this, you are making a non-profit contribution that will help make this performance a reality.

The paint on this shirt is made for fabrics and should stand normal care. We recommend dry cleaning or hand washing for best results, and ironing on the wrong side with low heat.

For more information on how you can be involved in The Whisper Project, call 280-2599.

The Whisper Project, P.O. Box 815, La Jolla, CA 92038.

Welcome to "Whispers and Crosscurrents," a unique event celebrating the accomplishments, strengths, and survival abilities of San Diego's older women. In naming our luncheon, we used the name "whispers" to represent information, often hidden from us about older women's contributions to the fabric of our lives. "Crosscurrents" is the place in wind or water where two or more streams come together. Today is such a meeting place, one whose theme, "Women Honoring Women," gives us the opportunity to pay tribute to the individuals who have been important to each of us. We have asked you to bring a special recipe that brings to mind such a woman, and as we share these memories from our past, we will forge stronger bonds between us in the present.

We hope you enjoy today's event, the first in a year-long series called "The Whisper Project."

Program

Music
"Melodiers," Nicholas Fontilla Director
Dr. Ricardo Bielma Director

Welcoming Remarks, Dr. Rose Somerville

Introduction, Special Guests of Honor
  Cindy Hedgecock
  Dr. Lillian Beam
  Dr. Anita Figueredo
  Lucy Killea
  Danah Fayman
  Marguarite Schwarzman
  Judge Madge Bradley
Invitation to Share, Avis Johnson
Lunch
Participating in The Whisper Project, Artist/Director Suzanne Lacy
Closing Ceremony, A Litany of Names, Ellie Stein

Join Us

As a member of The Whisper Project. Your contribution of $25.00 or more will enable this year-long series to bring important information to a wide range of people in San Diego. Tax deductable contributions can be made to: The Whisper Project/San Diego Arts Foundation, P.O. Box 815, La Jolla, CA 92038.

The Whisper Project Continues

Imagine a sunny beach in La Jolla. The waves wash in and out along a single stretch of sand, enclosed on three sides by high rock walls. On the beach a surprizing gathering is taking place: around white cloth-covered tables sit almost 200 older women, dressed in white, talking with each other about their lives — about the special joys, problems and circumstances of aging.

Now in the planning stages, this exciting performance by Los Angeles artist Suzanne Lacy, "Whisper, the Waves, the Wind," eulogizes older women, presenting their experiences in a compelling visual setting. Enhancing communication between older people, sharing their experiences with a broad audience creating positive and beautiful images of women — these are the motivations behind the tremendous community effort going into this production.

This performance is the culminating event in The Whisper Project, a year-long series of events to illuminate the older woman in San Diego. This portrait will be shared with the nation through a Public Broadcast Television special now in the planning stages. If you would like to help make this year-long series, the performance itself and the film a reality.

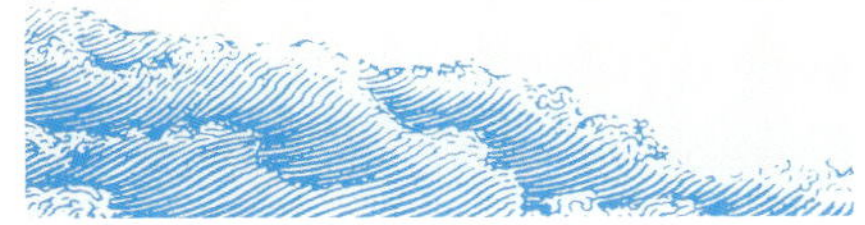

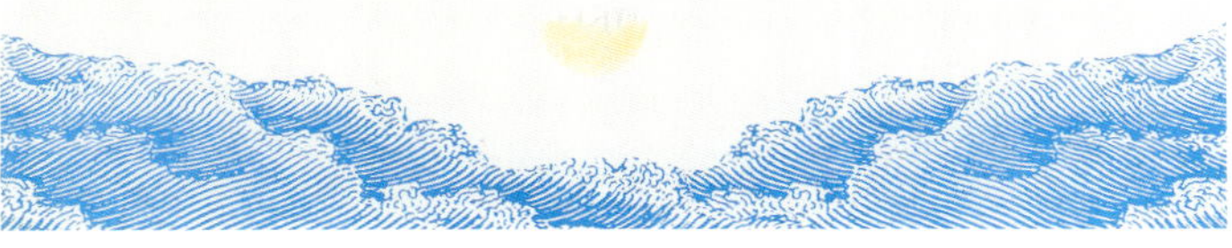

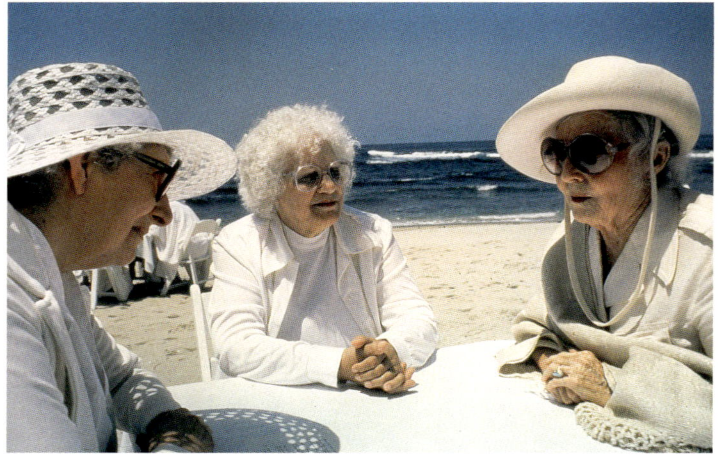

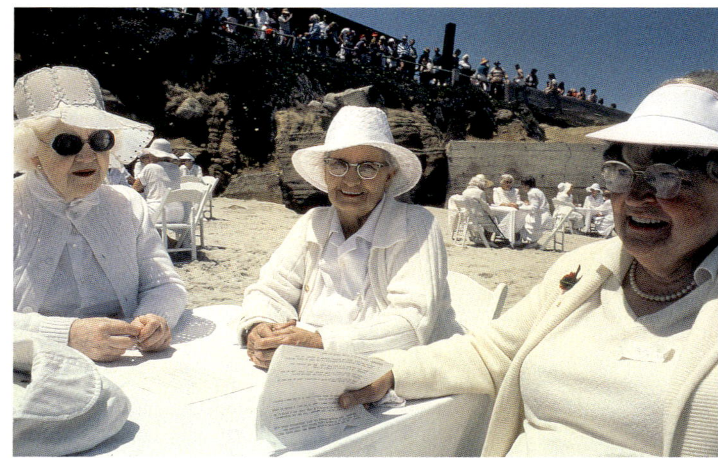

FILM TRANSCRIPT (EXCERPTS)

I still love to dance; I've always loved to dance. So I asked him to go to this dance with me downtown—you know they have this for seniors—and he refused to go, so I said, "You know, I'm going." And he took me and he waited out in the car for two and a half hours while I was in there just having a ball. And I loved it. I loved it.

A perfect stranger was pushing her basket and she stopped and said, "You are beautiful." Of course, I felt very thrilled and very flattered that at my age anybody thought I was beautiful.

I like to think of myself as an elderly woman. To me "elderly" is not a negative term.

What made you attractive to her?

You have that charisma.

- - -

I think that sometimes we are not seen when we're in a public place. There have been times when I've been in a grocery store seeking some help for finding an—an article, and [the] person just looks past, and you feel like you're not there, you know.

Many people look upon the older black woman out of the stereotypes that have been developed through the years. They consider us to have less ability too often; they consider us people who can take what I call "the dregs" and be satisfied. And many times, this permeates not only among the older white women, but the younger white people who come along.

I used to make talks or review books and do things of that sort in front of people, and I find myself still making clippings of ideas that I like that I could base a talk on, but I'm not asked to do those things anymore, and I expect it's because I'm old.

- - -

I think we've made an important statement in that we could amass that number of people, so I think we should do something with that energy other than walk on the beach. Because there are so many problems that face us. That's real to me. World peace. Children going to bed at night hungry is a big issue. You know, my coming to the beach isn't going to change that. It's not going to change the nuclear warfare. But my coming to the beach can make a statement to women that in our strength we together can do something about it. So I think this can be an announcement that we are together—we are standing together, young and old. And just think what we could do if we had this kind of situation in our social problems today. That's my reason for coming, because I needed someplace to see the kind of force that I can dream about coming from women.

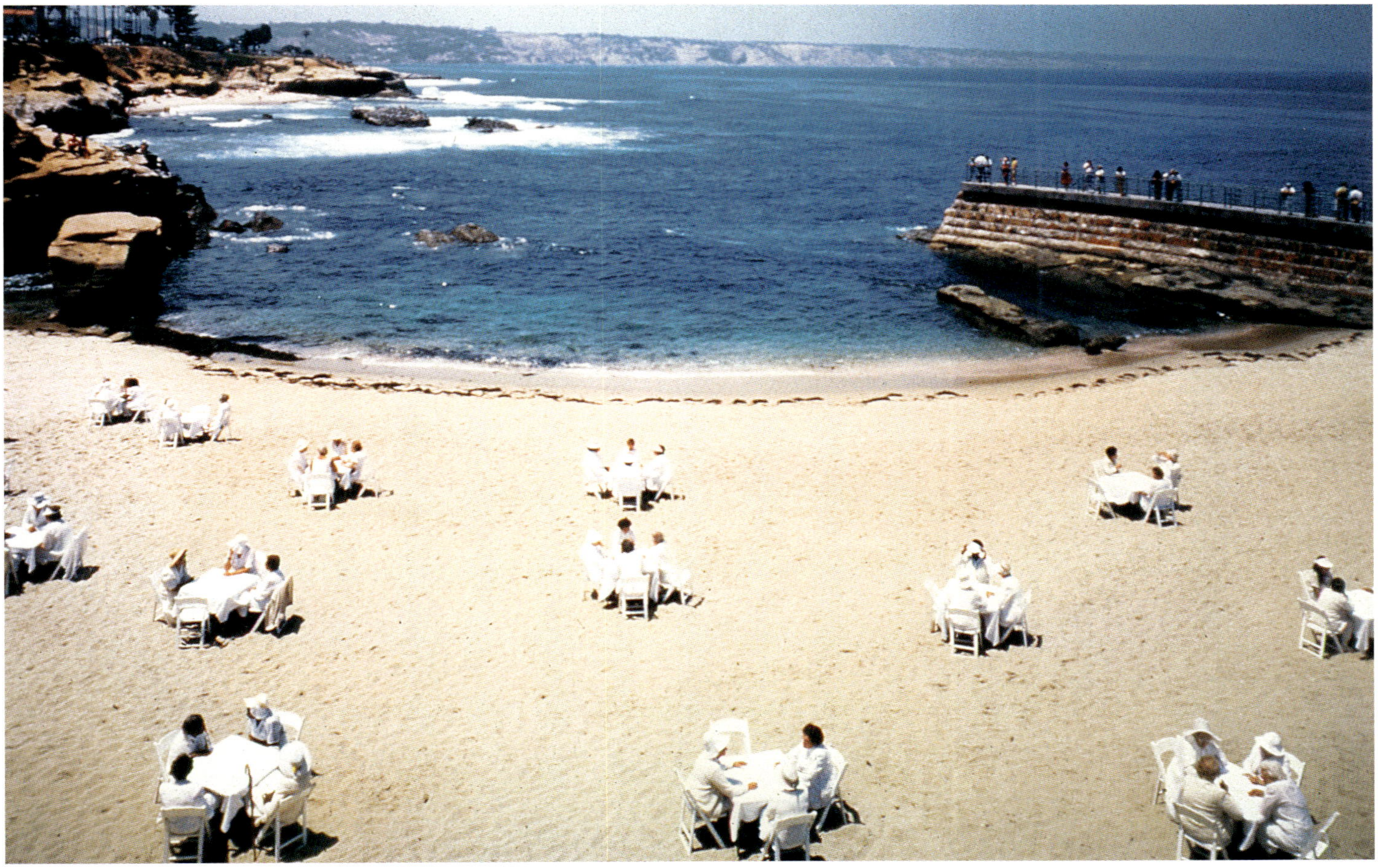

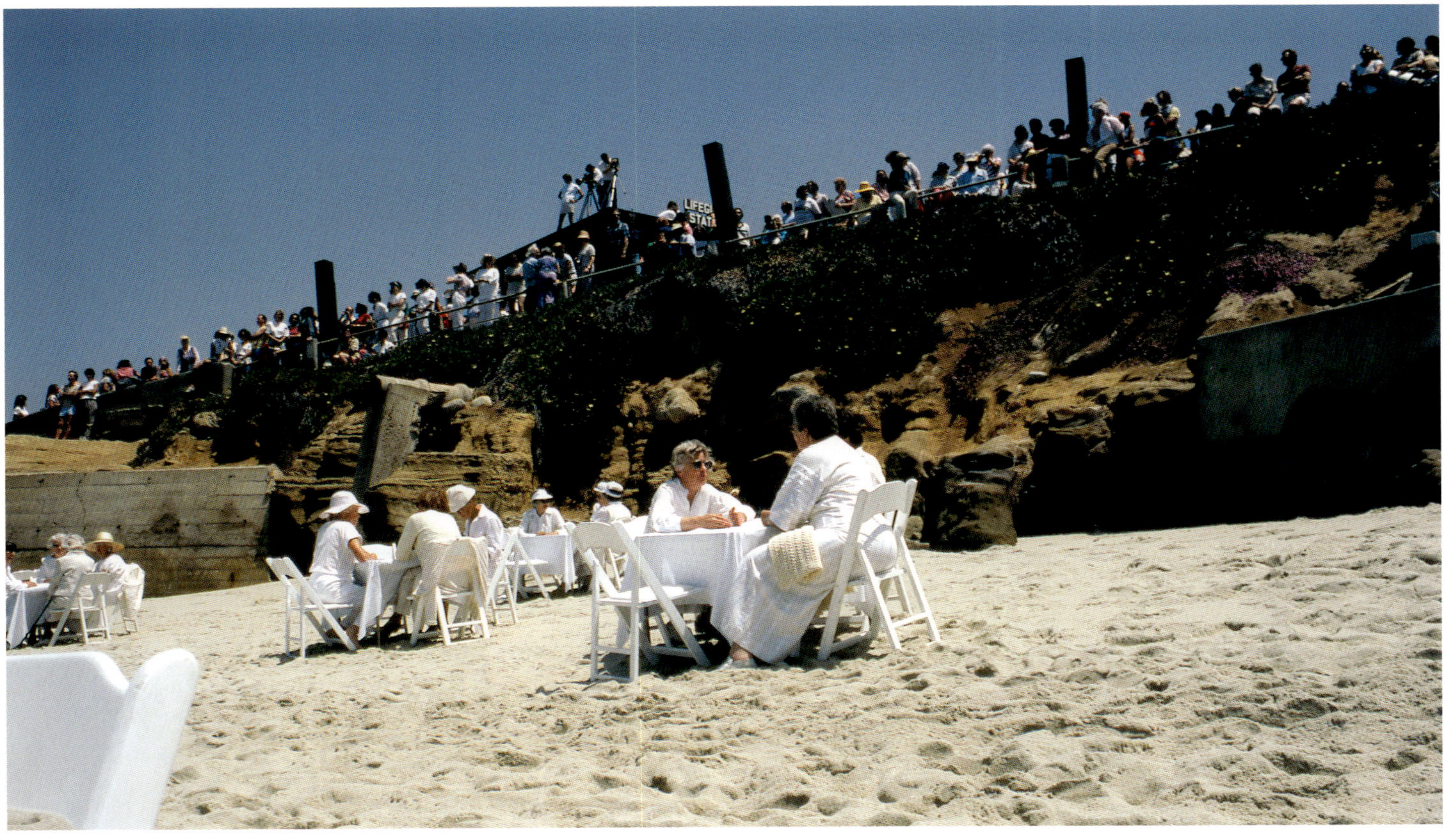

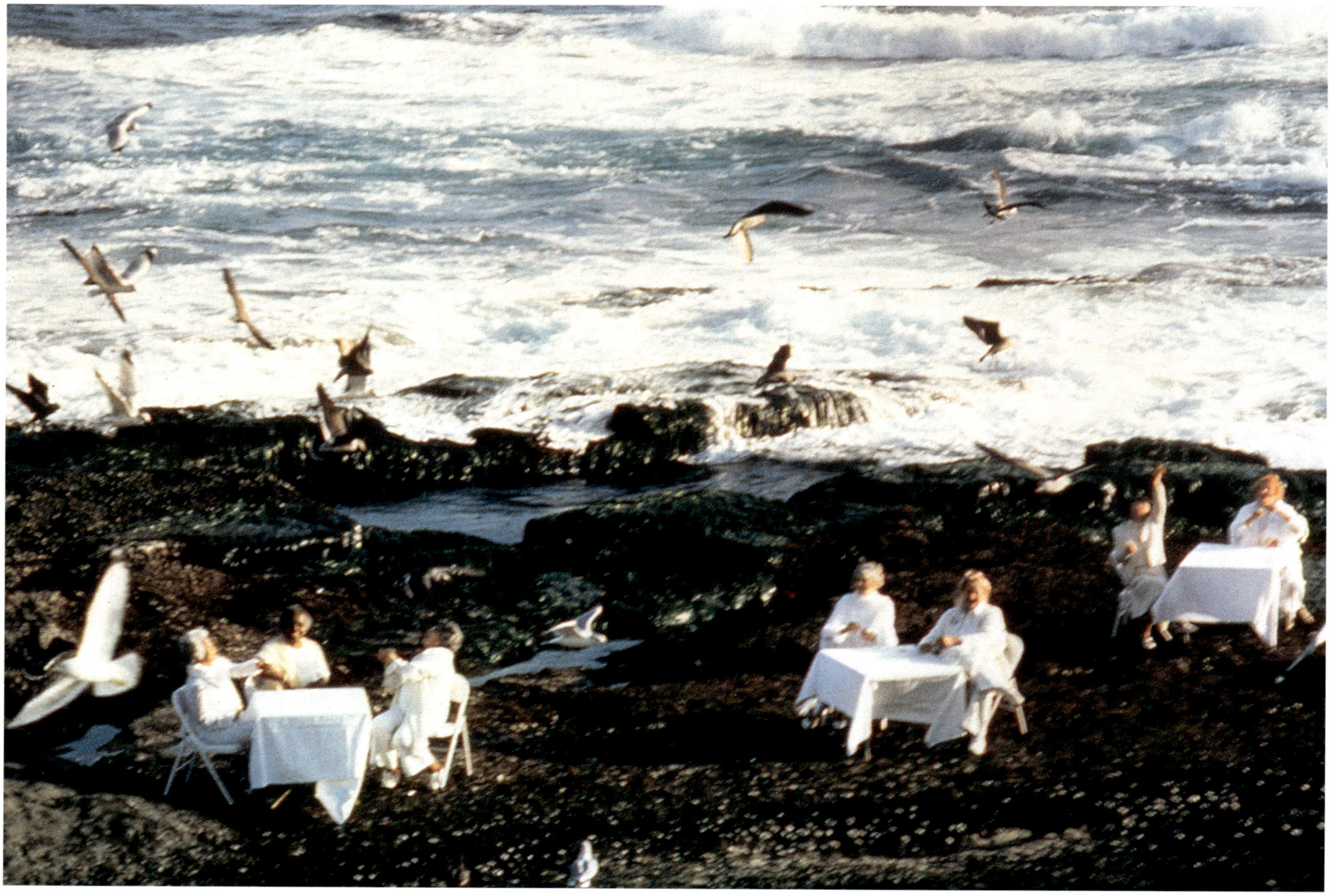

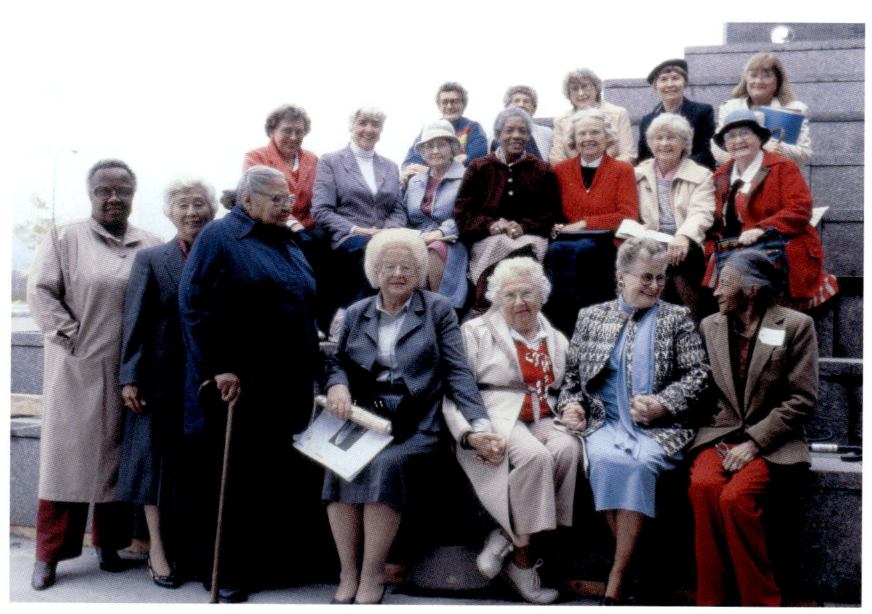

TOP: Staged photograph
BOTTOM: Organizers of *Whisper, the Waves, the Wind* visiting organizers of *Whisper Minnesota* (1985–87, pp. 166–73) in Minneapolis
OPPOSITE: Organizational chart outlining the possible trajectory of The Whisper Project, including *Whisper Minnesota*

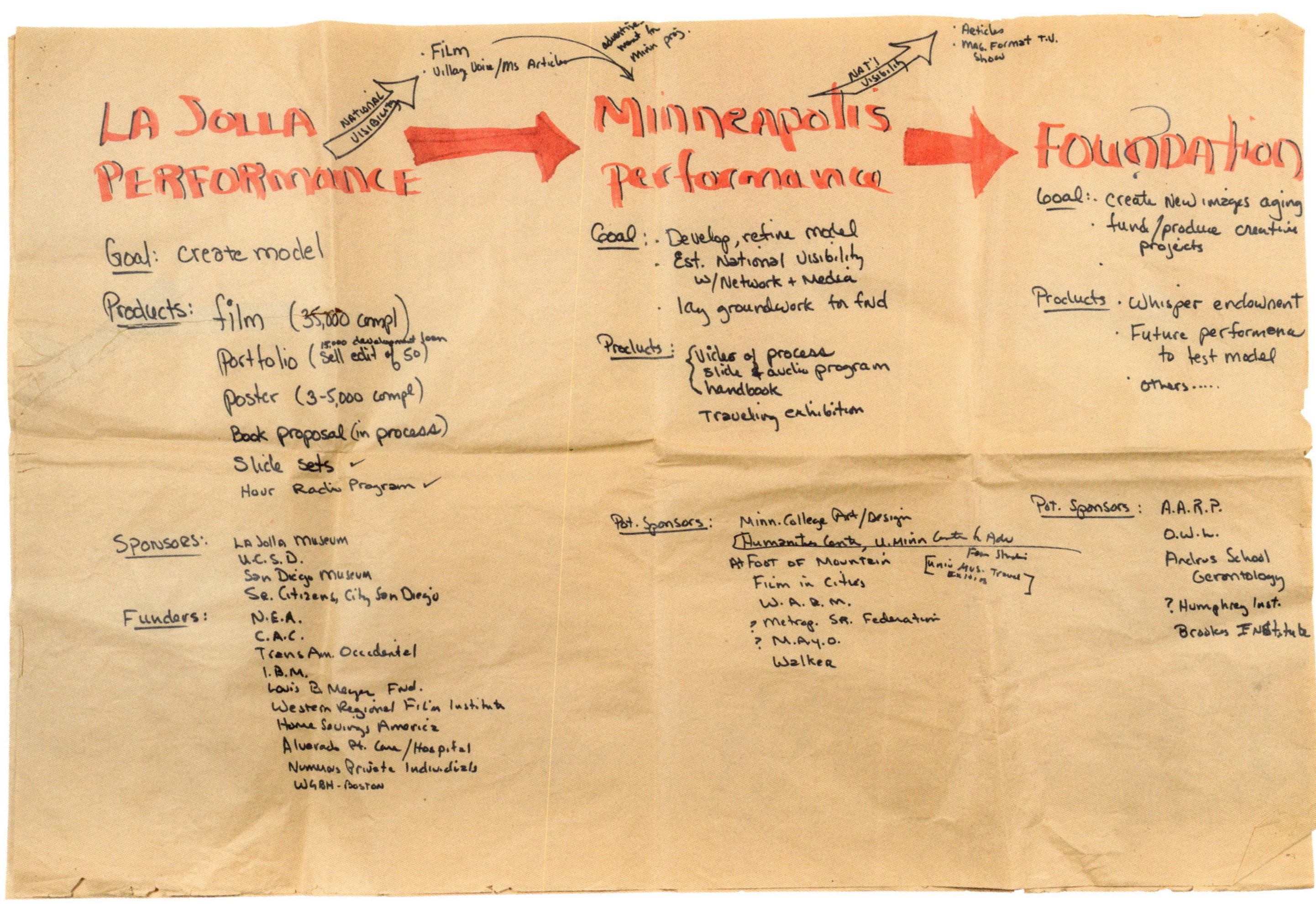

This diagram outlines my thinking about how scale and duration are key elements in mass media's potential for change. After completing *Whisper, the Waves, the Wind* . . . I wondered how I might influence attitudes toward aging women, through art, on a larger scale. All the long-term public change movements tended toward repetition, so when invited to Minneapolis, I wondered what might happen if, rather than changing into a different research area, I should think about broadening the lens on aging. These were the questions we were formulating at the time about art and social change. I decided to work on the same theme but to deepen the exploration by increasing its national influence and visibility, generating larger networks, and focusing on media strategies combined with organizing, consciousness raising, and art performance.

—Suzanne Lacy, 2018

The Dark Madonna (1985–86)

SUZANNE LACY, ANNE BRAY, CAROL HEEPKE, SUSAN STONE, AND WILLOW YOUNG

In 1985 Edith Tonelli, director of the Frederick S. Wight Art Gallery at the University of California, Los Angeles, asked Lacy to create a new work for the Franklin D. Murphy Sculpture Garden, which Lacy noticed was dominated by white European male artists. At dusk on May 31, 1986, an audience of more than one thousand watched fifty women of assorted ages, races, ethnic identities, and body types, all dressed in white, pose on pedestals scattered among the sculptures. An ambient soundtrack by Stone accompanied this "Light Tableau." As night fell, the "Dark Tableau" formed: ten women in black, called "shadows," ran in and cloaked the performers in black as 150 additional women in black entered the garden with flashlights and formed small discussion circles in the dark. The audience was invited to listen or participate.

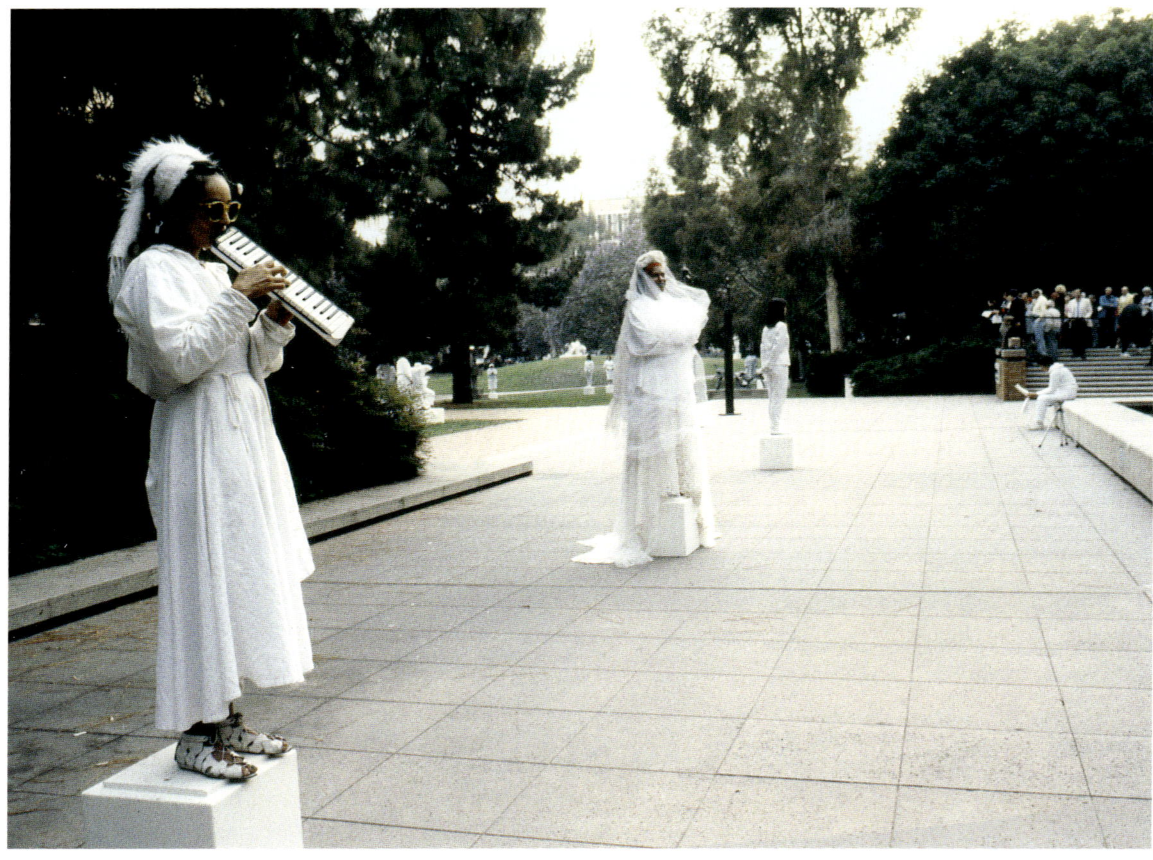

Surely few conferences convened in academe—after a familiar format of scholars delivering papers, moderators fielding questions and comments from the audience—are the emotional workout that the one held by UCLA'S Center for the Study of Women was last weekend.

It set out to be a conference. It wound up a happening.

"The Dark Madonna: Women, Culture and Community Rituals" was the theme of this first public effort of the newly established center, approved in 1984 as an interdisciplinary organized research unit of the university.

Response Called Overwhelming

Partial funding was obtained from the California Council for the Humanities, the flyers went out and, to the organizers' surprise, the response was overwhelming. As people began arriving at Dickson Auditorium Friday evening, Karen Rowe, center director, said more than 600 had pre-registered. More overwhelming, however, was the response of those intrigued, excited people at the opening session. It was a diverse group of all colors, cultures, ages, religions, sexes and sexual persuasions and life styles that had been drawn to the topic.

For a few tense moments at the close of that session, it seemed the whole innovative effort would end prematurely in a shambles, or as one man walking out declared, "a sad blunder."

The brochure had promised the following: "In mythic images of women, we see ourselves reflected. The Dark Madonna symposium will identify goddesses and madonnas from different times and cultures, particularly figures representing women of color. Speakers will consider the origins and transformations of spiritual images of women, the community rituals that celebrate their powers, and the contemporary meanings of female icons in multi-ethnic cultures and in women's lives." Next to the printed message, a logo of a Negroid-featured Madonna and child.

Speakers Tackle Racism

Imagine the audience's surprise then, and discomfort, and consternation as the speakers at the opening session turned out to be six white women whose presentations contained either no reference to the Dark Madonna or tangential ones at best. Considerable reference was made, however, to racism in U.S. society and some of these women's struggles in coming to terms with it.

The evening focused on the political uses of art by women, specifically within the context of the 19th-Century U.S. suffrage movement and the re-emergence of the women's movement in the '60s. Scholars read papers and showed slides of women, mostly upper-middle class, liberal or iconoclastic white women, engaging in rituals, tableaux, pageants and, in later times, performance art.

There was a reason for this: The symposium was conceived as *part* of a project the center is engaged in, which will culminate in the spring with performance art directed by feminist artist Suzanne Lacy in the Franklin D. Murphy Sculpture Garden on campus.

Between the symposium and the performance, the center, and some on-and-off campus co-sponsors, will conduct small group discussions where women will explore women's relationships across racial and ethnic barriers. There was mention of this near the bottom of the brochure, but most arrived unaware of any larger context and it was not fully explained until Saturday when Friday's blow-up required a response.

On Friday night, the first to pose a question from the audience was Esther Broner, a writer from Wayne State University who would speak the following day on modern rituals, especially women's adaptations of Jewish rituals.

Describing herself as a little confused, she asked why there had been no mention of black women. Were there no rituals, or pageants or tableaux they had participated in?

"I hunger for this knowledge," she said.

"Well, God bless you ma'am. God bless you," a black man seated behind her spoke out.

Indeed, a panelist answered, there had been black pageants put on by churches, camps and women's clubs.

Next, a Latina stood and spoke up: "I drove a long ways to get here. I was very excited about learning about the Dark Madonna and the opening session has six white women up there."

Looking somewhat stunned at the direction things seemed to be taking, Karen Rowe answered that there had been no attempt to balance each session, but to balance the conference as a whole. She pleaded, as did the others, that they not be judged by one session. There would be much discussion of women of color, just as there would be panelists of all races.

From a white woman: "Is this really going to be about white women's pain in dealing with racism? I mean, is that why we're here?"

The audience was not through: Charges ranged from one outraged black man who took everyone to task for leaving out reference to the Catholic Church, "the treasurer of the black Madonna," to the incensed response from a goddess worshiper from a local coven who shouted across the room that the church had co-opted that image to oppress women.

In general, there was as much pain as anger in people's voices, both those in the audience and on the stage. No one had come looking to pick a fight. But they had come with high and specific expectations.

"Political Oversight"

Finally, Suzanne Lacy, whose work has often involved interracial explorations, said, "There has been a strategic error and a deep political oversight. One of the problems is the racism evident in the choice of the panel. Also, we're beginning to explore very new material. This kind of confrontation will probably occur again tomorrow. It's important to acknowledge the criticism, react, and act. It's important to stay and stand up."

Her words proved prophetic. Most people did return the next day. As promised there were black, Chicana, Native American and Asian panelists, and much discussion of the history and significance of the Dark Madonna.

The black Madonna of Montserrat in Spain, who continues to be revered by the Catalans, was discussed by historical anthropologist William Christian and historian Mary Elizabeth Perry. The faithful have nicknamed her "La Moreneta," the dark one, having made her one of them. Scholars and churchmen however tend to dismiss her darkness, seeing it as an embarrassment or as insignificant.

Joking somewhat about the tendency of some scholars to attribute the darkness of the black Madonnas found throughout Europe to centuries lof candle smoke rather than design, social anthropologist St. Clair Drake talked about the gradual "attenuation of blackness."

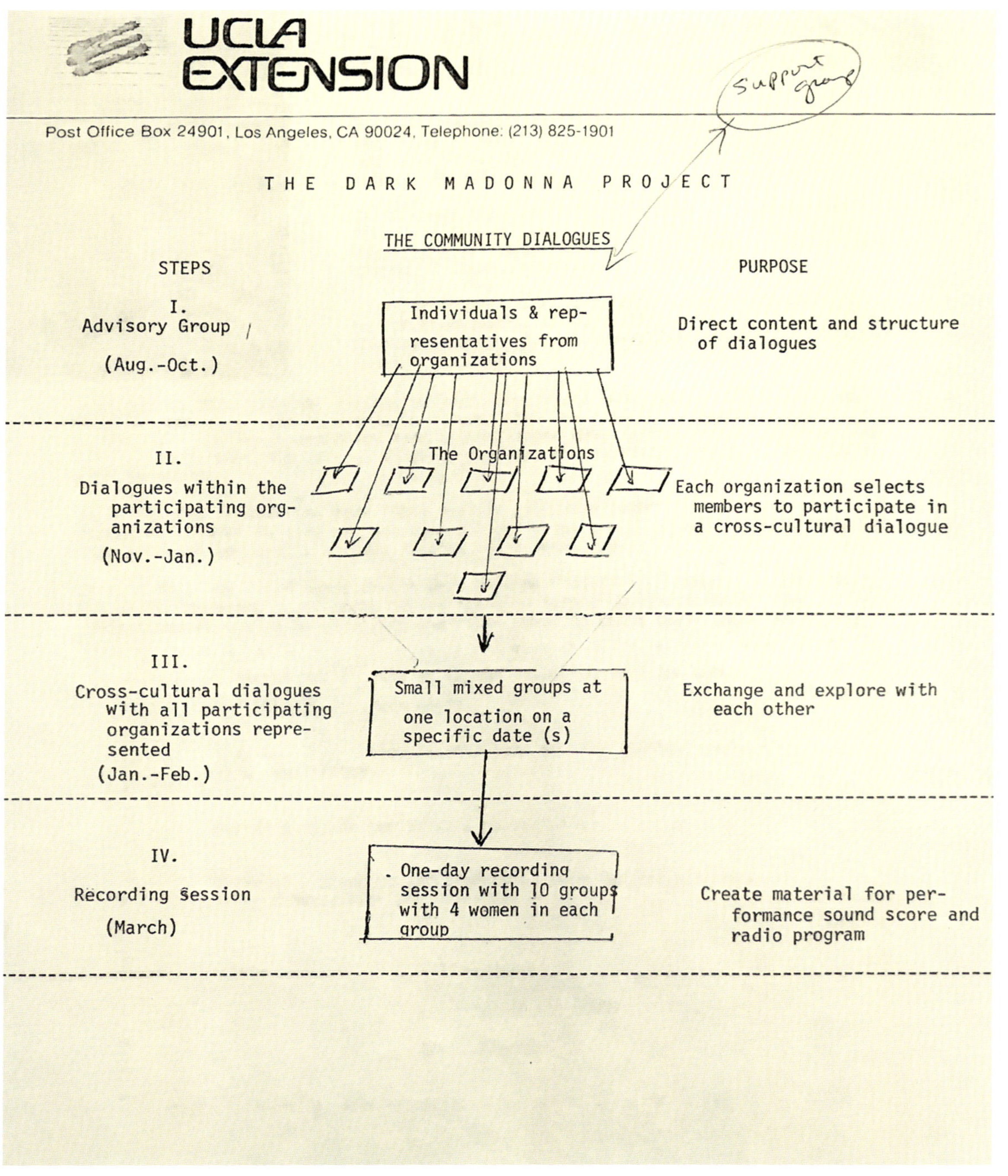

UCLA EXTENSION

Post Office Box 24901, Los Angeles, CA 90024, Telephone: (213) 825-1901

THE DARK MADONNA PROJECT

THE COMMUNITY DIALOGUES

STEPS		PURPOSE
I. Advisory Group (Aug.-Oct.)	Individuals & representatives from organizations	Direct content and structure of dialogues
II. Dialogues within the participating organizations (Nov.-Jan.)	The Organizations	Each organization selects members to participate in a cross-cultural dialogue
III. Cross-cultural dialogues with all participating organizations represented (Jan.-Feb.)	Small mixed groups at one location on a specific date (s)	Exchange and explore with each other
IV. Recording Session (March)	One-day recording session with 10 groups with 4 women in each group	Create material for performance sound score and radio program

I felt strongly about the basis of the project because: I know we live in a mediated culture so I want to personally encounter the viewers sometimes. I know we operate in a commercial world so I want to exchange with them without a price tag. I know we exist in a society which is alienating in both its specialization and its conformity, so I want to encourage interaction among the audience. I want to offer a challenge at low risk in a milieu where change is usually associated with fear. I want to activate people's imaginations and criticality simultaneously. Both artistic and political movements are based on changes of perception.

—Anne Bray, 1986

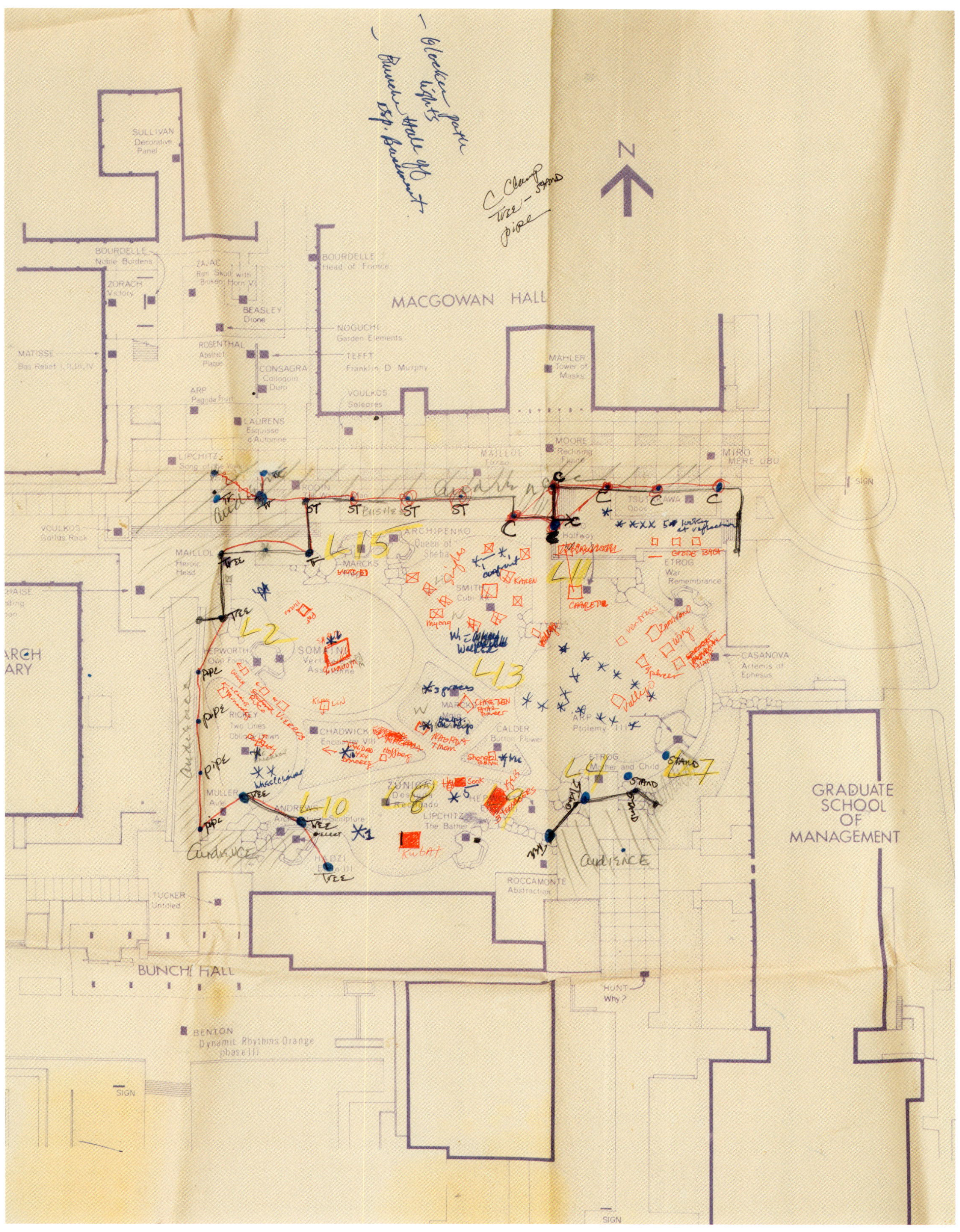

MACGOWAN HALL
SULLIVAN Decorative Panel
BOURDELLE Noble Burdens
ZAJAC Ram Skull with Broken Horn VI
ZORACH Victory
BEASLEY Dione
MATISSE Bas Relief I,II,III,IV
ROSENTHAL Abstract Plaque
CONSAGRA Colloquio Duro
ARP Pagode Fruit
LAURENS Esquisse d'Automne
BOURDELLE Head of France
NOGUCHI Garden Elements
TEFFT Franklin D. Murphy
VOULKOS Soleares
MAHLER Tower of Masks
LIPCHITZ Song of the Vowels
MOORE Reclining Figure
MAILLOL Torso
MIRO MÈRE UBU
VOULKOS Gallas Rock
MAILLOL Heroic Head
RODIN
MARCKS
ARCHIPENKO Queen of Sheba
TSUTAKAWA Obos
SMITH Cubi
CHAISE Standing Woman
HEPWORTH Oval Form
ETROG War Remembrance
RICKEY Two Lines Oblique Down
CHADWICK Encounter VIII
MARCKS
CALDER Button Flower
ARP Ptolemy III
CASANOVA Artemis of Ephesus
MULLER Auto
ANDREWS Architectural Sculpture
ZUNIGA Desnuda Reclinado
LIPCHITZ The Bather
ETROG Mother and Child
HAJDZI Ergo III
ROCCAMONTE Abstraction
TUCKER Untitled
GRADUATE SCHOOL OF MANAGEMENT
BUNCHE HALL
BENTON Dynamic Rhythms Orange phase III
SIGN
HUNT Why?
N

PERFORMERS INSTRUCTIONS
LIGHT TABLEAUX

CURTAIN CALL: <u>Saturday May 31 6:00 pm sharp</u>
                 In front of Wight Art Gallery, UCLA

                 Your Director is: ________________________________

COSTUME:
-    Everything you wear must be completely white — Shoes, Clothes, any props.

-    Be sure to dress warmly

-    Some of you have already been asked to wear something black underneath,
     to be part of the "transforming sculptures". If so, wear white outer
     garment that can be easily removed to reveal the black underneath.

INSTRUCTIONS FOR MAY 31 PERFORMANCE:

5:30   Shuttle bus begins departing from Federal Bldg. ¼ block south of Wilshire on
            Veteran. <u>For campus parking</u>, enter at Hilgard & Wyton — request Lot #3 or
            (Lot #5 as alternative) from Information Kiosk — <u>For passenger drop-off</u>, ask
            at Kiosk for Wight Gallery loading zone.

6:00   Sign-in (please take this opportunity to use the restroom and meet your directors)

6:30—   Orientation
6:45

6:45—   Placement on Pedestals
7:15

7:30—   <u>AUDIENCE WILL BEGIN TO ARRIVE — THEY SHOULD SEE YOU ALL IN PLACE!</u>
8:00

7:45   <u>Intro Soundtrack</u> begins

8:00—   <u>Light Tableaux</u> — The soundtrack will play for audience & for you in the garden
8:30   Please stay very still the entire time. You should have 2 positions so that
                 you can switch from one to the other when you get tired.

            When you switch positions or otherwise move, do so very slowly and subtly.
                 The emphasis is not on the movement but on your apparent stillness.
                 You are representing beautiful "artworks", frozen in time. Practice your 2
                 positions and the movement between them at home in front of a mirror.

8:25—   <u>Transition</u>
8:30

            This is the brief period between day and night. It is also the transition
                 between Light and Dark Tableaux. The soundtrack will change to the sounds
                 of night — insects singing, birds darting and women talking about the dark Madonna.
                 (You will not be able to hear this inside the garden).

On cue, 10 "shadows" (women dressed in black) will dart from their hiding
  spots on the edge of the garden and stop at a pre-arranged white pedestal.
  Very slowly they will step on to the pedestal or drape the white figure with
  a black cloth.

For those of you wearing black clothes underneath, the running figures are
  your cue to very slowly remove the outer layer of white clothes and let them
  drop to the ground.

8:30–
9:00

The Dark Tableau

It is now almost dark. From the edge of the garden, small groups of women in
  black emerge with flashlights. There are approximately 15 to 18 groups.
  They will sit down at designated spots and begin dialogues.

After all the groups of women in black are seated, the White Tableau on
  the top of the hill (5 older women) will leave their pedestal. This is the
  cue for the rest of you to very slowly get down off your pedestals and
  walk [to] join the dialogue group closest to you. The group leader will have a
  slowly [sic] copy of the 3 questions (see below).

9:00–
9:15

Audience enters

At a point determined by the directors, the audience will be handed lit
  flashlights and invited to enter the garden.

When an audience member approaches your group, simply continue your
  conversation, allowing them to listen and illuminate you with their
  flashlights.

Do not ask them to join you, but if they seem eager and initiate the
  participation, graciously include them. At a point determined by the
  directors, the garden lights will go on. One of the directors will approach
  your group to signal [to] you that it is time to leave for the reception. You
  may continue your conversations informally as you leave the garden for
  the reception in front of the Wight Art Gallery.

9:15–
10:00

Reception

This reception is in your honor and enable[s] you to meet with other
  participants, audience, family and friends.

A souvenir program is available for you there. You may also sign up for a
  copy of the audio track by composer Susan Stone. It will be available for
  purchase at cost ($5.00) for performers only. Cost to audience is
  $10.00.

All of us who have worked to produce this performance including the staff and
  directors of the Wight Art Gallery want to thank you for your participation
  in this performance. Your involvement makes it a very special evening!

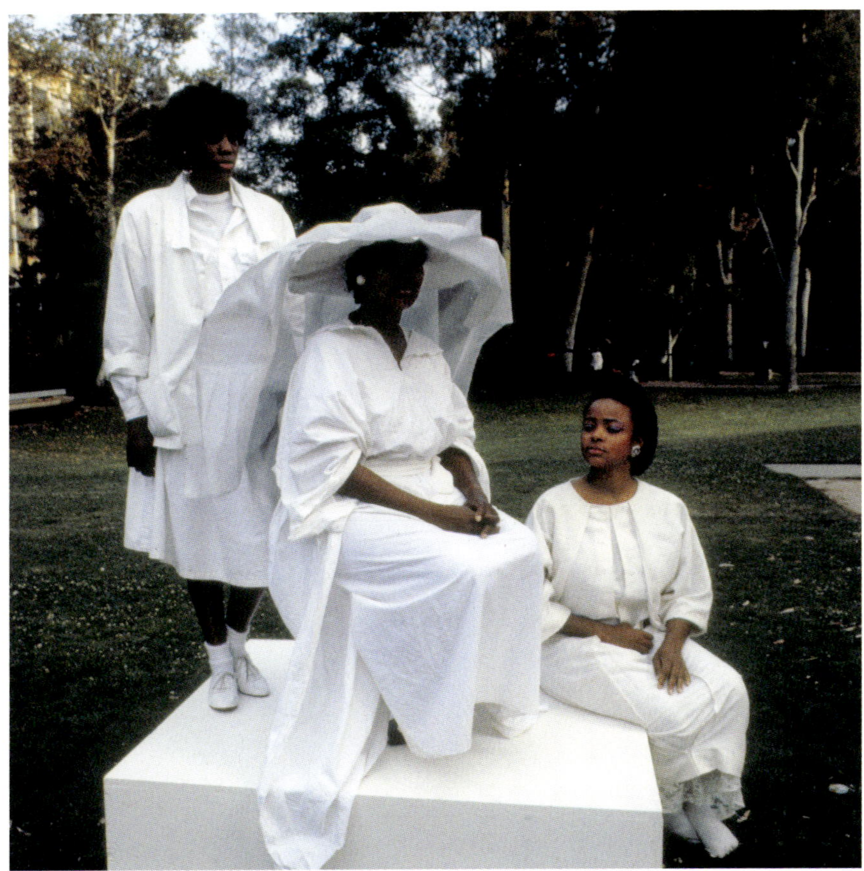
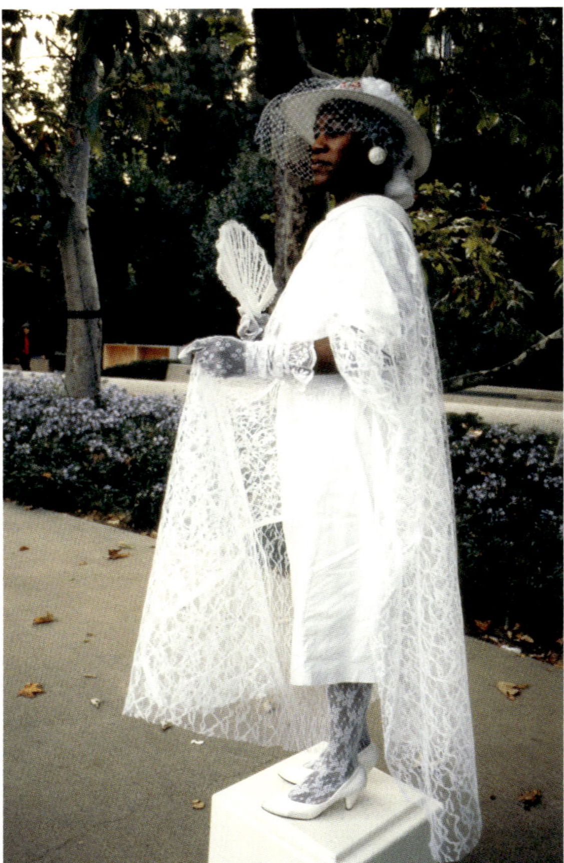
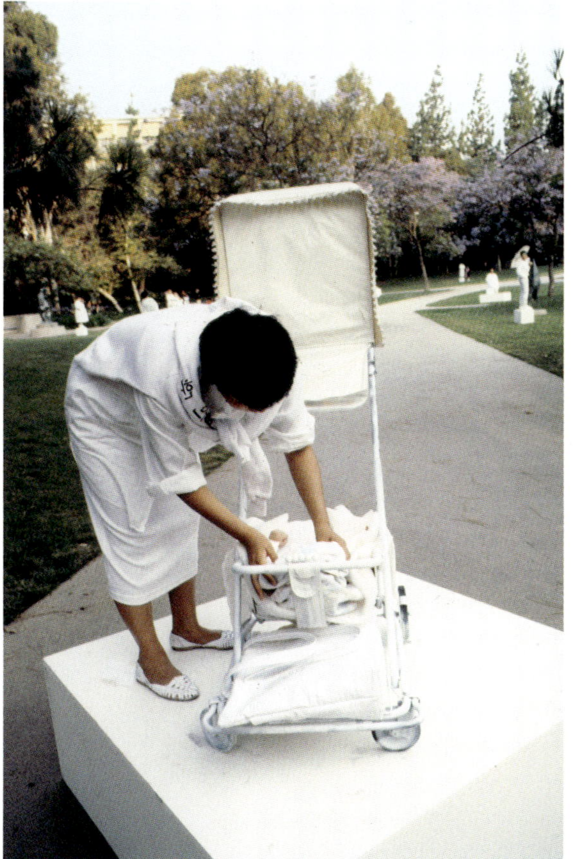
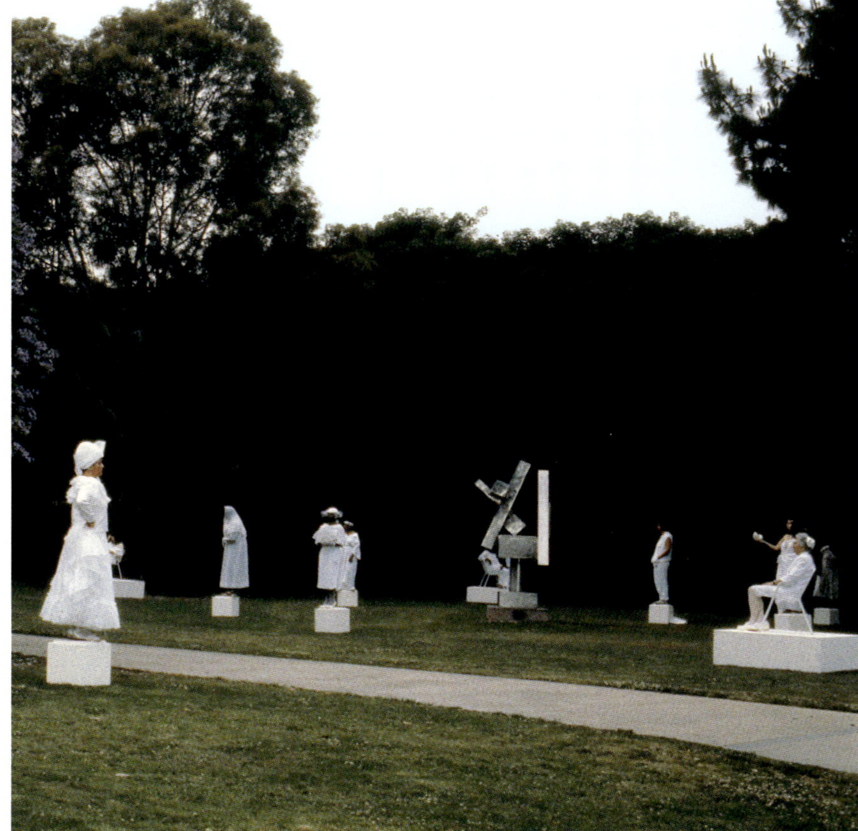

The Dark Madonna, the personification of the dark self, is in actuality the dark earth itself, the nurturing soil that gives life and recovers us after death. I felt connected to this belief as I sat with my baby surrounded by the sculpture garden, wearing traditional clothing and meditating on the impending darkness. I recognized that although the Dark Madonna has a deep, spiritual indigenous meaning for many, she could be appropriated, only superficially grasped, and easily misunderstood by Christian-based white society. . . . One of the discussion questions of the evening was, "What in your heritage gives you strength and resources for endurance?" Indigenous ceremonial rites are often based on endurance and a focus on intention and prayer. Holding my body still felt like home to me as a test of physical endurance [in] the impending crisp, dark night. . . . Women of all colors, races, and orientations, sometimes with their children present, created the prayer on which to focus and contemplate.

—Linda Vallejo, participant, 2018

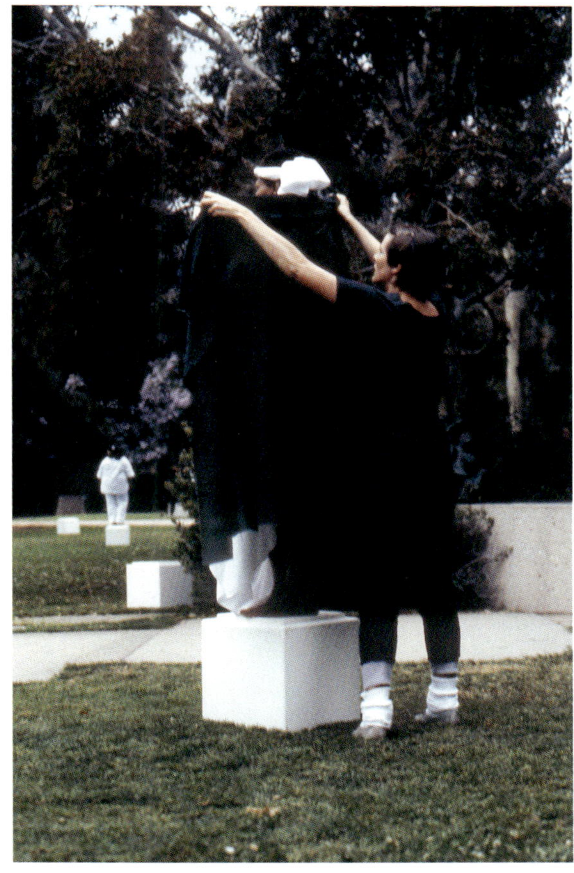

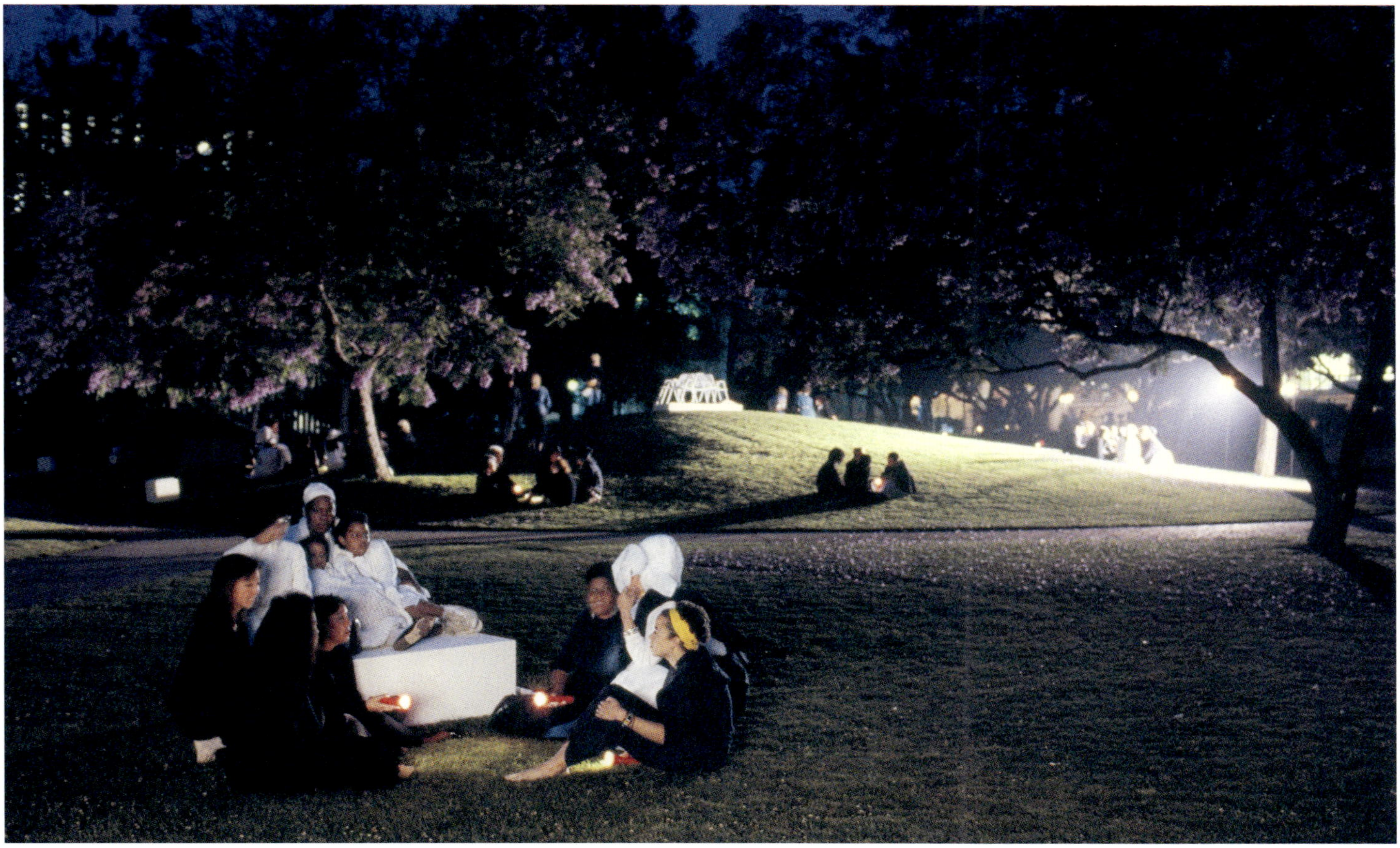

Whisper Minnesota (1985–87)
The Crystal Quilt (1987)

SUZANNE LACY WITH SHARON ROE ANDERSON, SAGE FULLER COWLES,
NANCY DENNIS, JUDY KEPES, PHYLLIS JANE ROSE, AND PHYLLIS SALZBERG

Whisper Minnesota comprised classes, lecture series, film screenings, and a mass-media campaign organized in collaboration with numerous artists and volunteers to continue Lacy's work of highlighting women's experiences of aging.
It included the Older Women's Leadership Series organized by Anderson, a monthly gathering of thirty-five women
leaders from across Minnesota, and *The Crystal Quilt*, a performance installation staged on Mother's Day 1987 in the
IDS Center, a mall in downtown Minneapolis. Dressed in black, participants in *The Crystal Quilt* slowly proceeded into
the atrium, called the Crystal Court, and unfolded black cloths over square tables to reveal yellow and red layers
underneath. The tables and colors were arranged in a pattern designed by Miriam Schapiro, creating a "quilt" visible
from the mezzanine. Sitting four to a table, 430 women over age sixty produced shapes with synchronous hand and
arm movements directed by Lacy and choreographed by Cowles. Susan Stone created the soundtrack that cued the
movements; it included voices of participants singing and telling stories, and sounds gathered in rural Minnesota.
Approximately three thousand people watched the hour-long performance that was live broadcast on PBS. Many
entered the tableau at the end to present participants with scarves painted by Julie Arnoff.

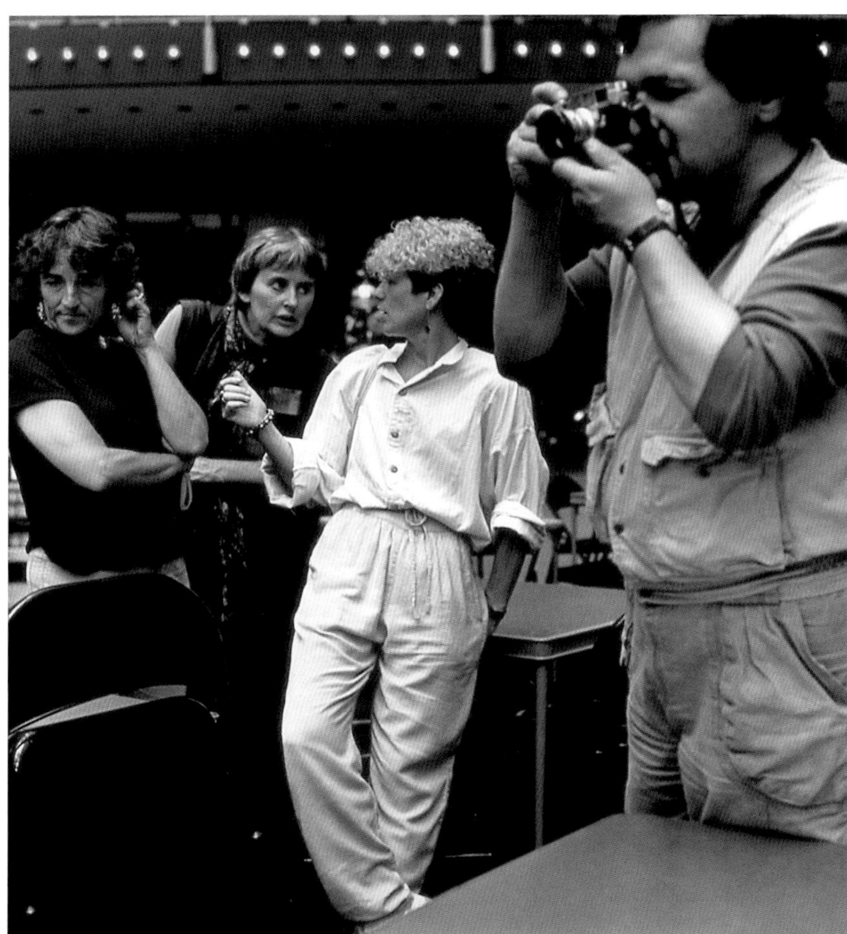

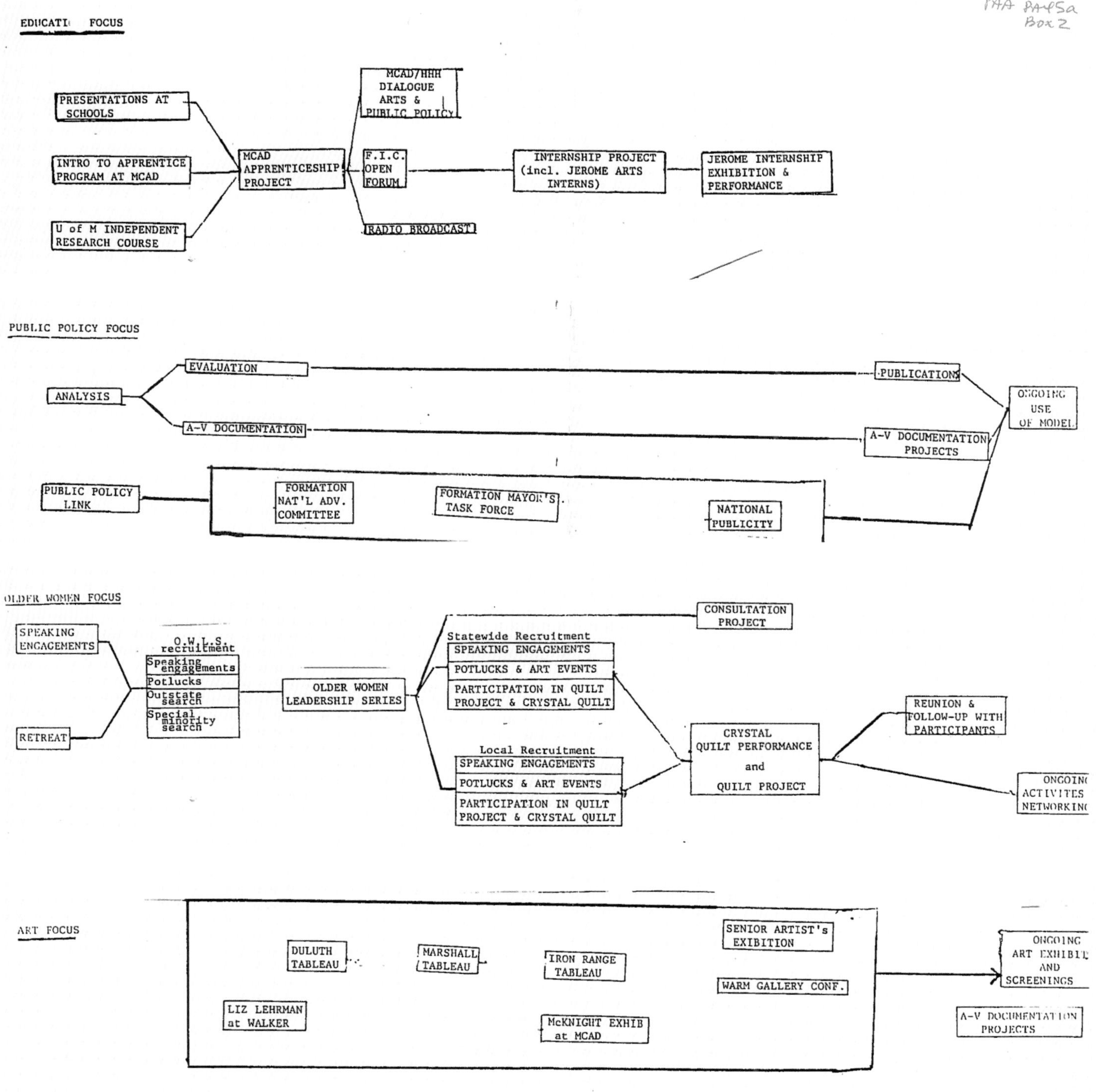

OPPOSITE: Lucy Lippard, Moira Roth, and Lacy on the set of *The Crystal Quilt* as Larry Fink documents the preparations
ABOVE: Organizational chart breaking *Whisper Minnesota* into parallel spheres of activity, including public policy initiatives, community events, *The Crystal Quilt*, and post-performance engagement with the community and participants

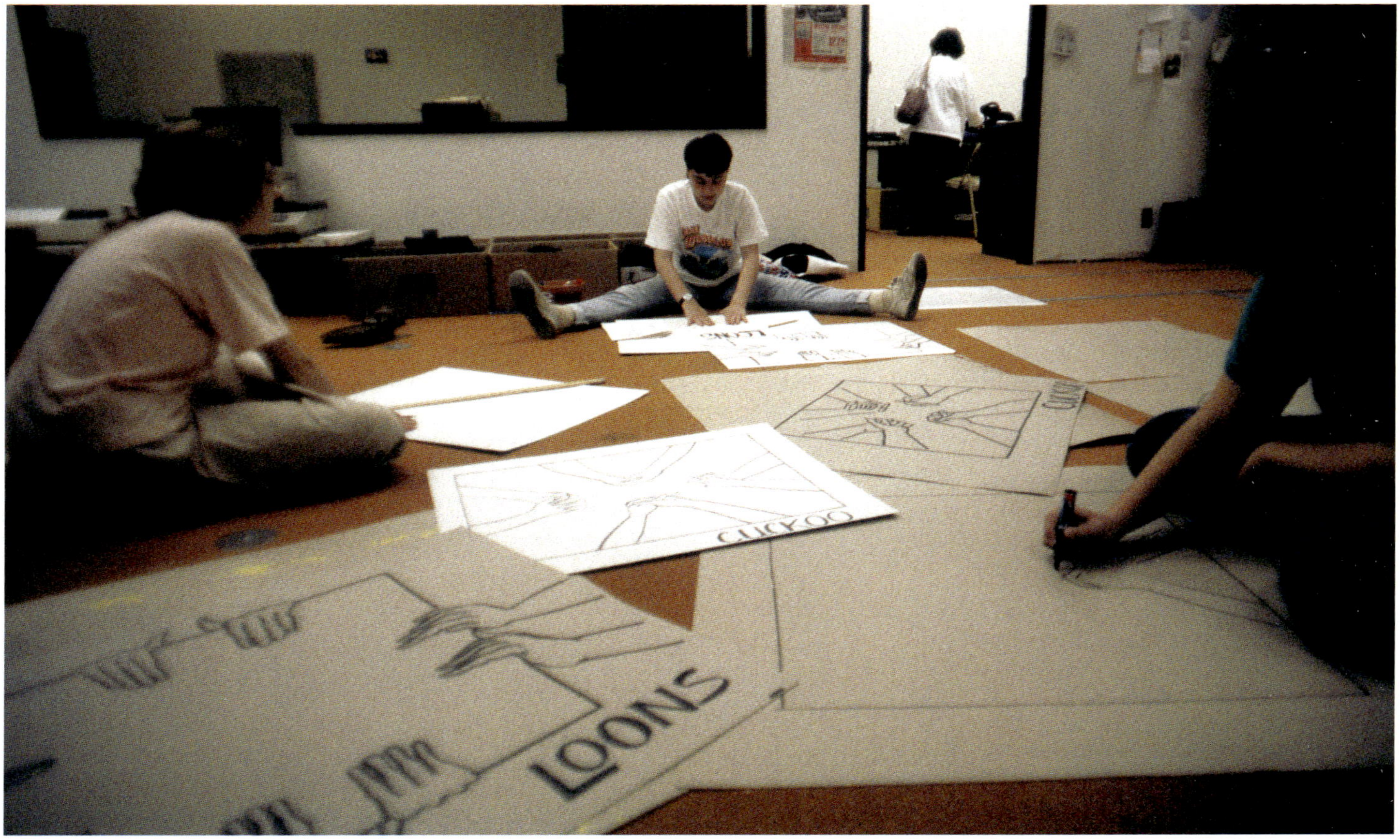

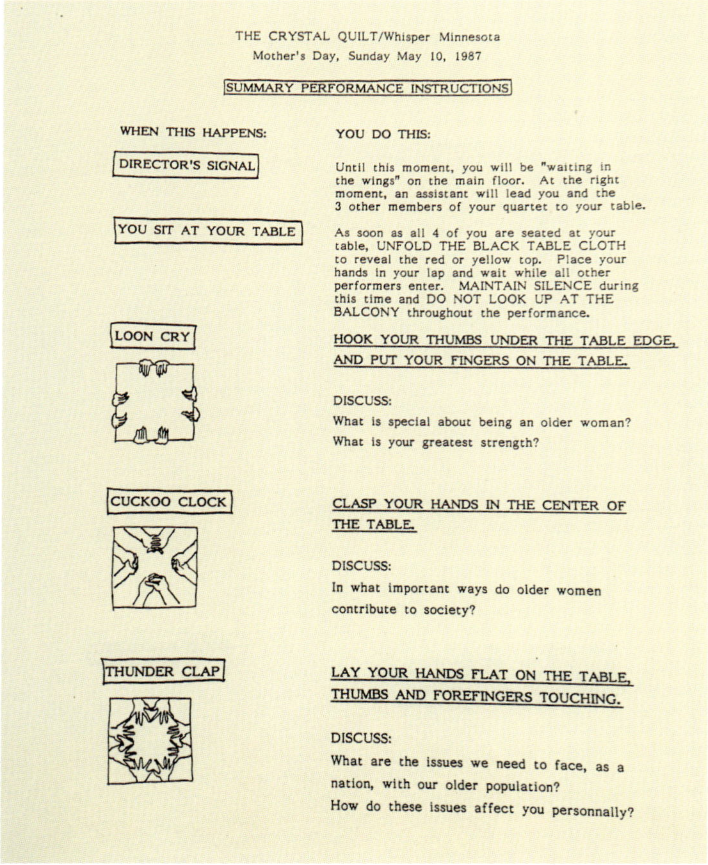

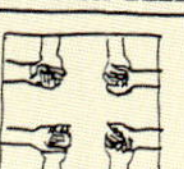

The following is a reproduction of a two-page typed document, "Summary Performance Instructions."

THE CRYSTAL QUILT/Whisper Minnesota
Mother's Day, Sunday May 10, 1987

SUMMARY PERFORMANCE INSTRUCTIONS

WHEN THIS HAPPENS:	YOU DO THIS:
DIRECTOR'S SIGNAL	Until this moment, you will be "waiting in the wings" on the main floor. At the right moment, an assistant will lead you and the 3 other members of your quartet to your table.
YOU SIT AT YOUR TABLE	As soon as all 4 of you are seated at your table, UNFOLD THE BLACK TABLE CLOTH to reveal the red or yellow top. Place your hands in your lap and wait while all other performers enter. MAINTAIN SILENCE during this time and DO NOT LOOK UP AT THE BALCONY throughout the performance.
LOON CRY 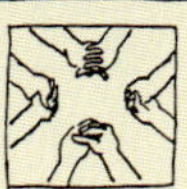	HOOK YOUR THUMBS UNDER THE TABLE EDGE, AND PUT YOUR FINGERS ON THE TABLE. DISCUSS: What is special about being an older woman? What is your greatest strength?
CUCKOO CLOCK 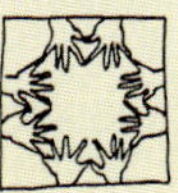	CLASP YOUR HANDS IN THE CENTER OF THE TABLE. DISCUSS: In what important ways do older women contribute to society?
THUNDER CLAP	LAY YOUR HANDS FLAT ON THE TABLE, THUMBS AND FOREFINGERS TOUCHING. DISCUSS: What are the issues we need to face, as a nation, with our older population? How do these issues affect you personnally?

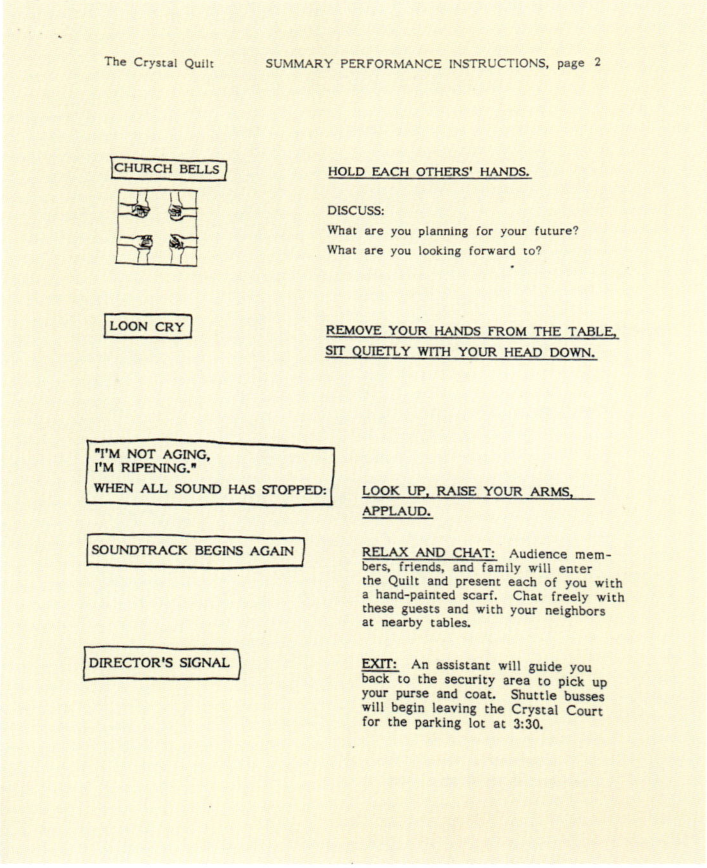

The Crystal Quilt — SUMMARY PERFORMANCE INSTRUCTIONS, page 2

CHURCH BELLS	HOLD EACH OTHERS' HANDS. DISCUSS: What are you planning for your future? What are you looking forward to?
LOON CRY	REMOVE YOUR HANDS FROM THE TABLE, SIT QUIETLY WITH YOUR HEAD DOWN.
"I'M NOT AGING, I'M RIPENING." WHEN ALL SOUND HAS STOPPED:	LOOK UP, RAISE YOUR ARMS, APPLAUD.
SOUNDTRACK BEGINS AGAIN	RELAX AND CHAT: Audience members, friends, and family will enter the Quilt and present each of you with a hand-painted scarf. Chat freely with these guests and with your neighbors at nearby tables.
DIRECTOR'S SIGNAL	EXIT: An assistant will guide you back to the security area to pick up your purse and coat. Shuttle busses will begin leaving the Crystal Court for the parking lot at 3:30.

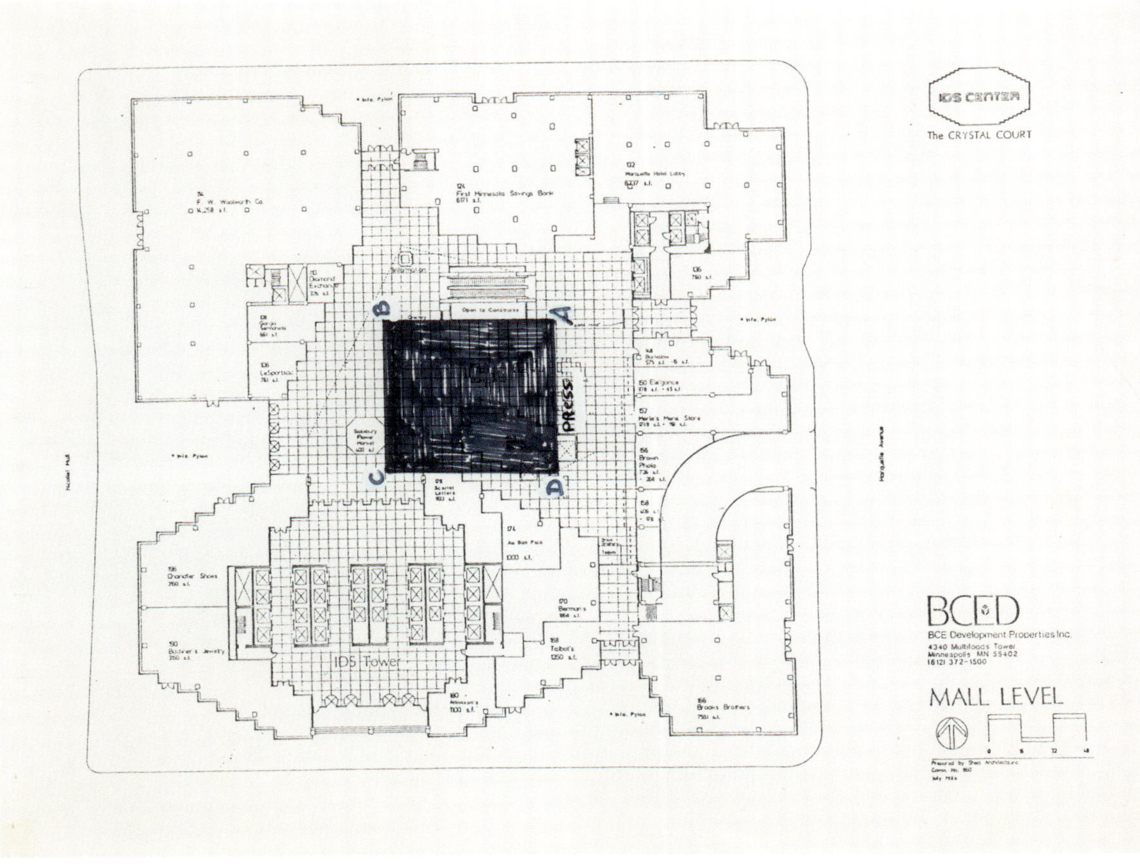

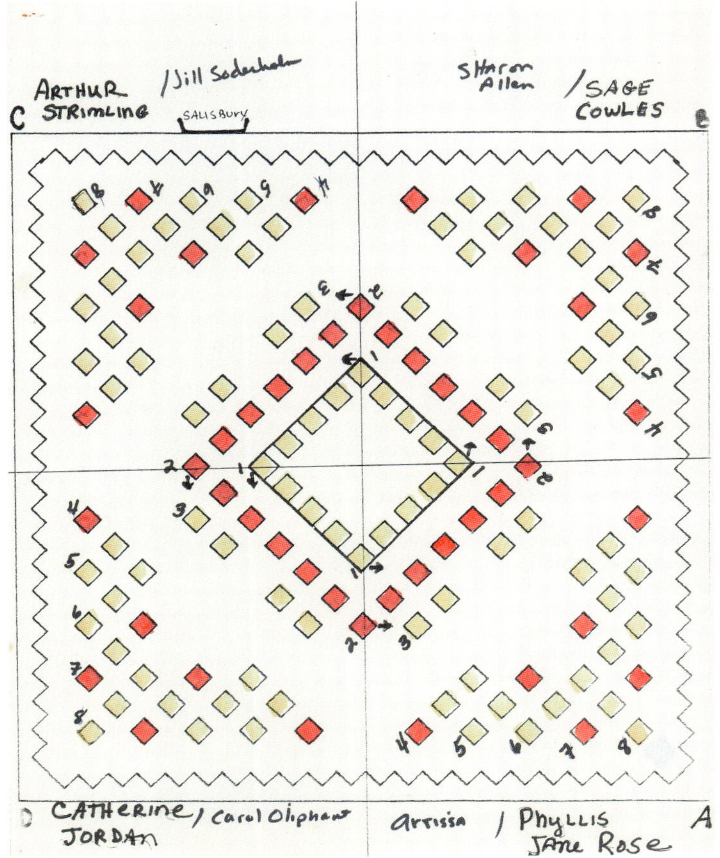

Voices as music; sound as geography: these were my initial audio objectives in composing soundtracks from scores of individual, intimate testimonials designed to accompany Suzanne Lacy's moving, large-scale public performances. Above all, how might the aural weave of personal narratives combined with the natural ambience of the strategically chosen venue put the listener/observer more deeply into the meaning of the place, the message, and the moment? Over a series of months leading up to each of our collaborative projects, I would record, edit, and mix both field and studio recordings, drawing from topic- and location-specific stories of hundreds of multigenerational, multi-cultural women. . . . My goal was to . . . craft a sonic outcome that offered a sense of place, experience, struggle, and triumph: story bits floating up over a larger ebb and flow of voices, much like the evocative procession of women moving singly, then in groups, through the vivid performance locales.

 —Susan Stone, 2018

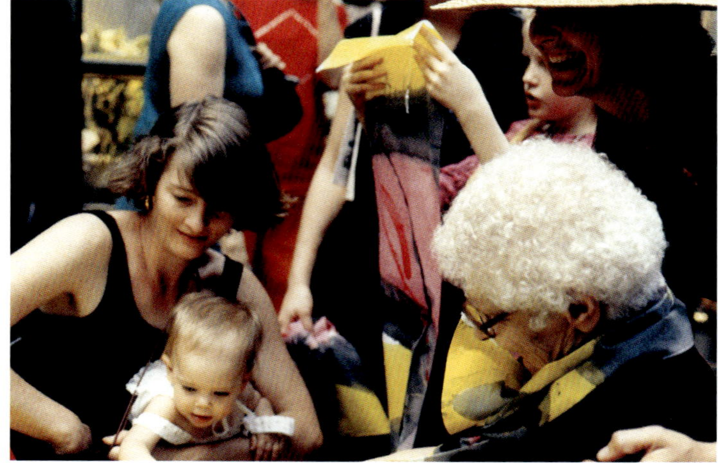

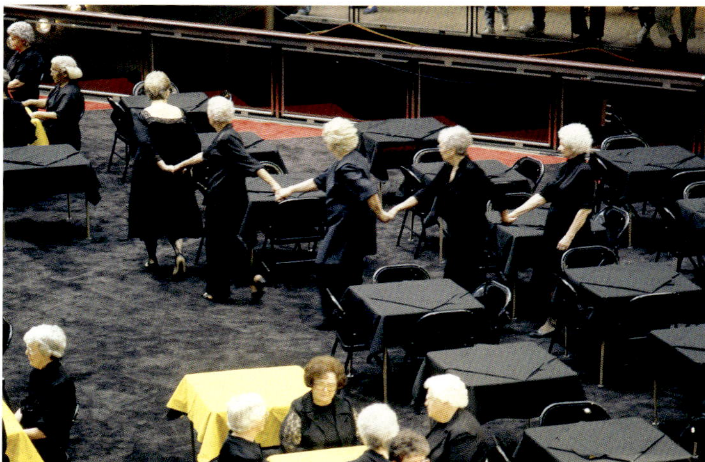

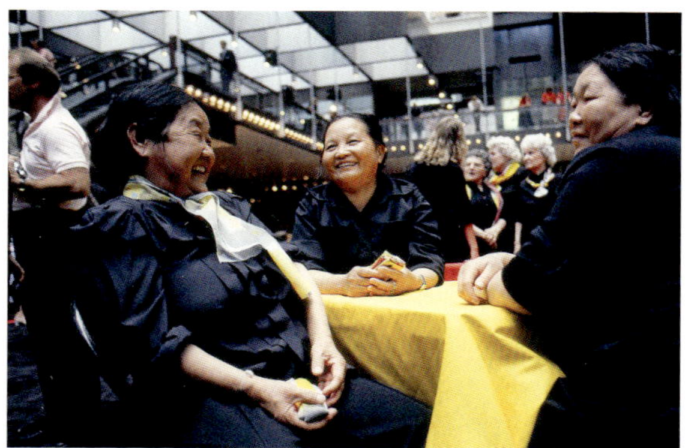

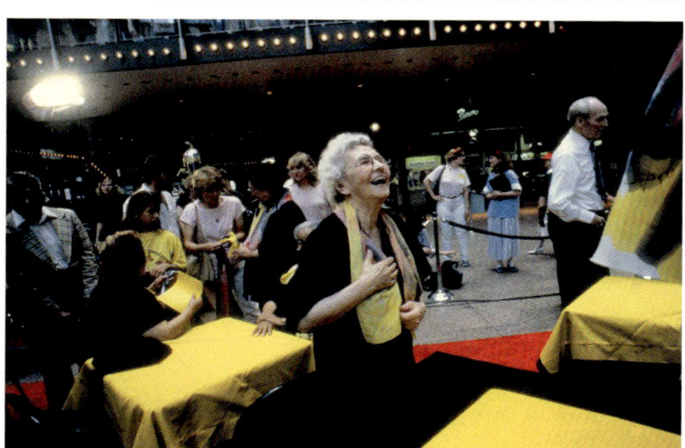

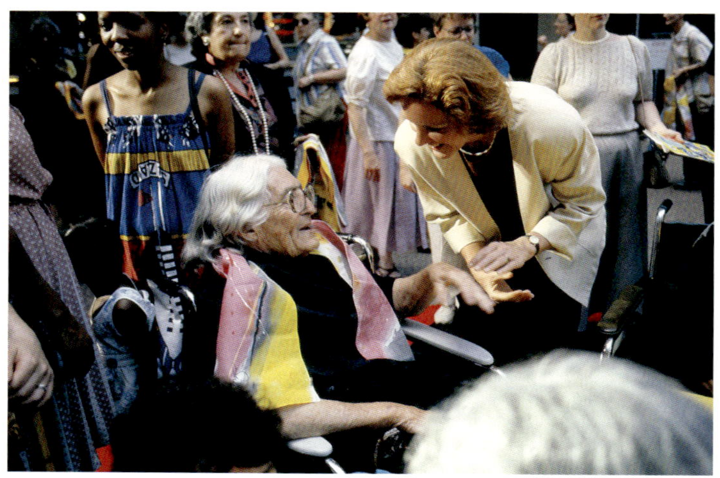

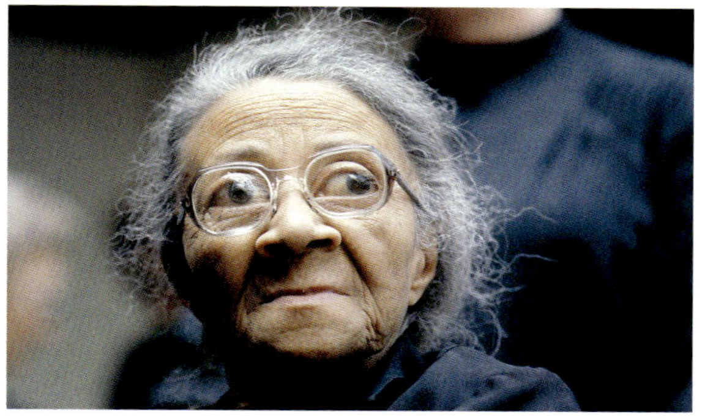

BOTH PAGES: *The Crystal Quilt*
BOTTOM LEFT: Leadership group
member Etta Furlow
ABOVE: Writer Meridel Le Sueur
with Minnesota lieutenant governor
Marlene Johnson

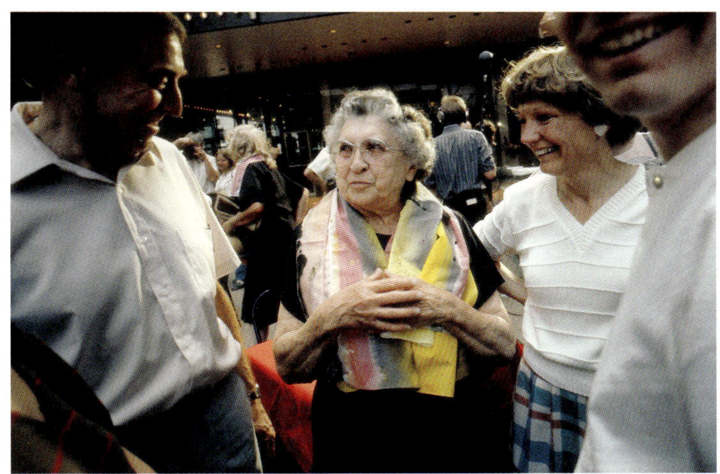

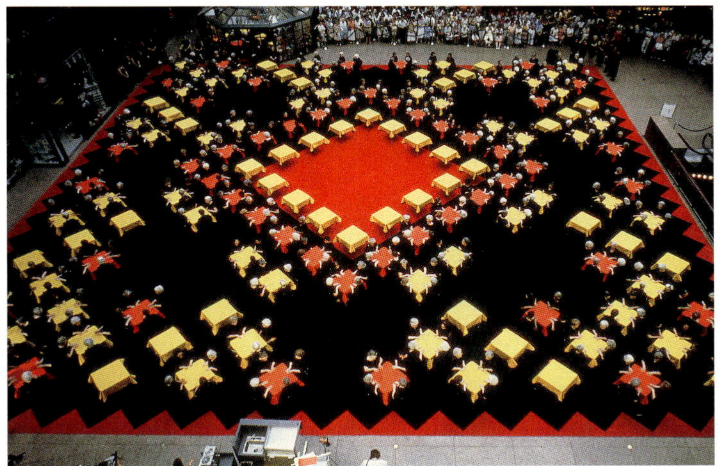

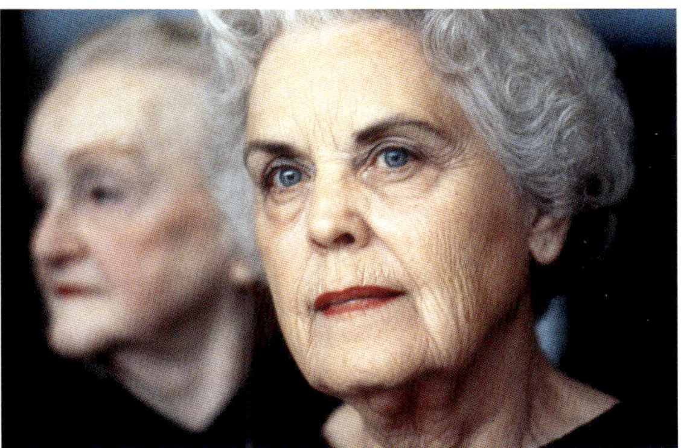

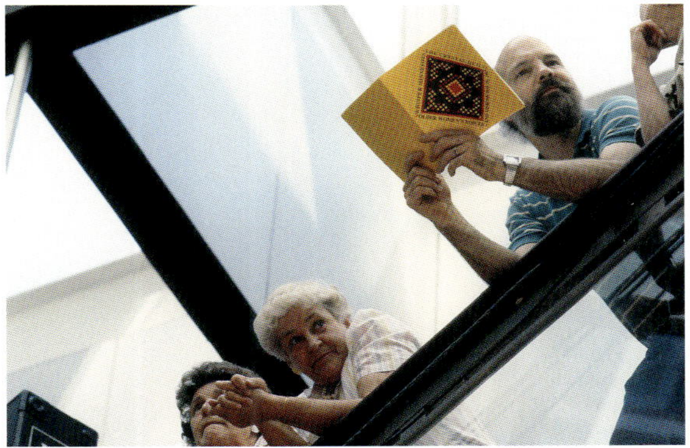

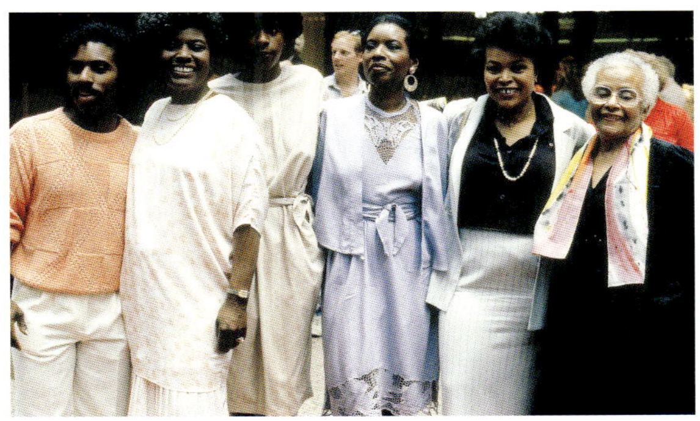

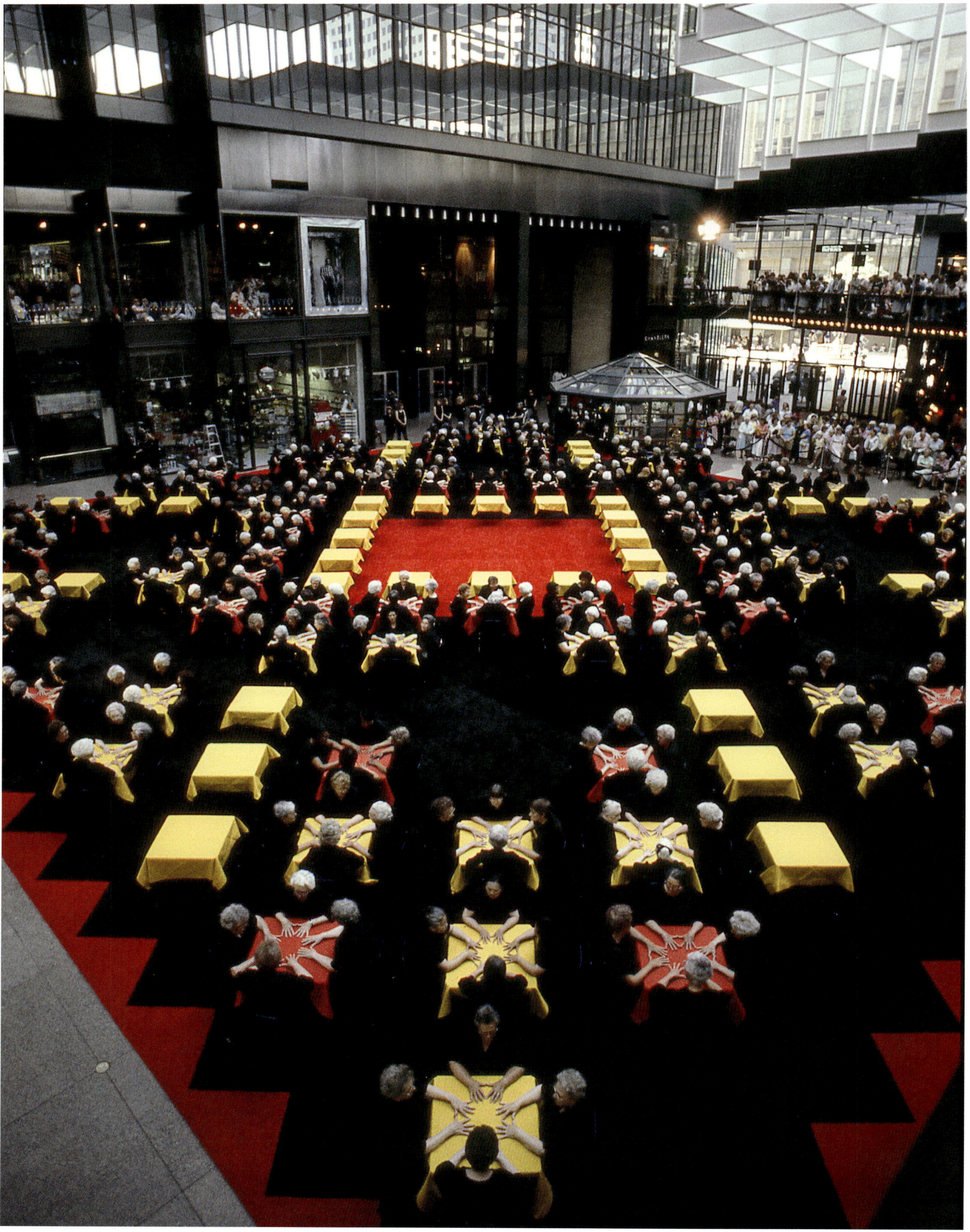

The Crystal Quilt

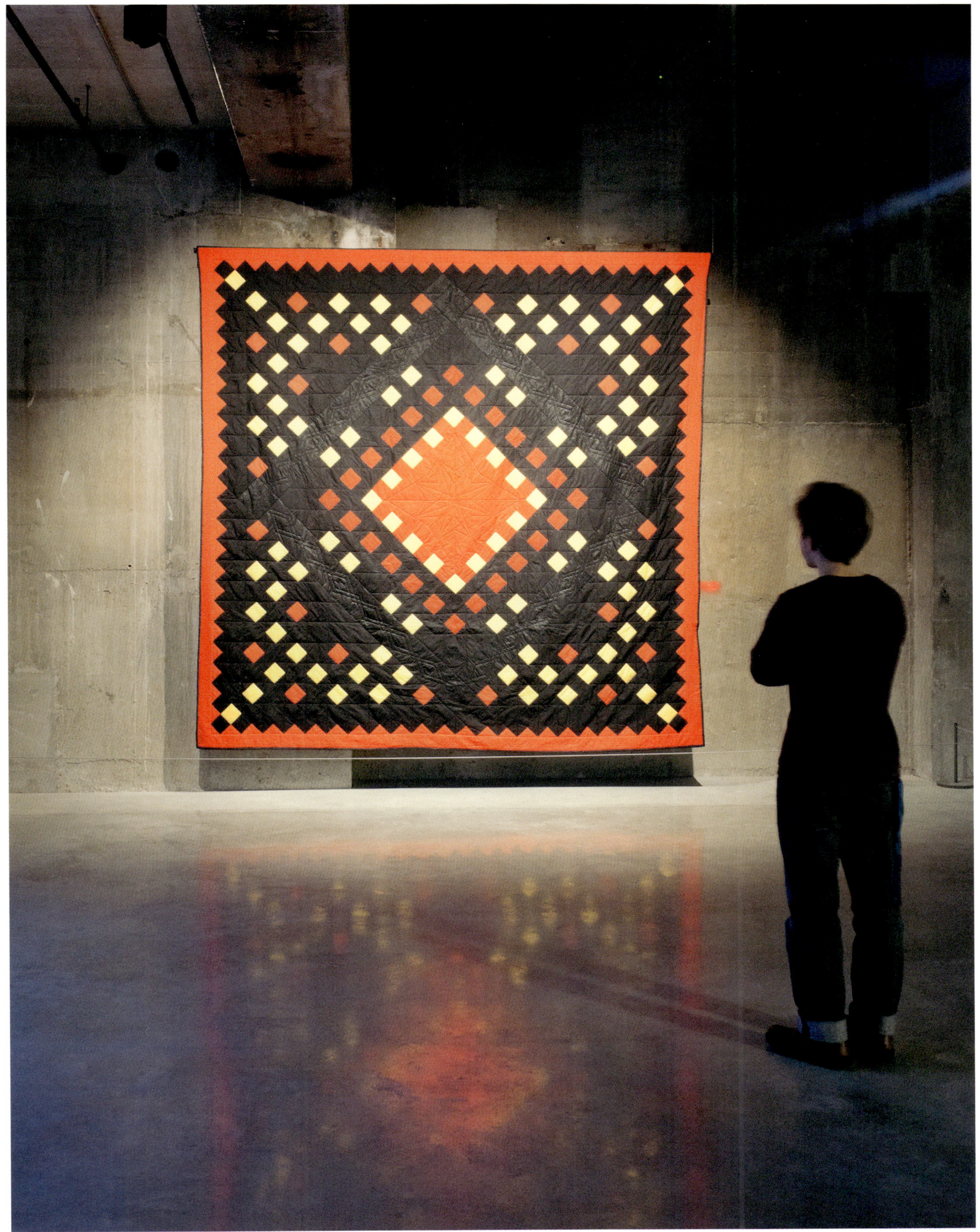

Quilt by the Minnesota Quilters with names of participants stitched on the border, installation view, *The Tanks: Fifteen Weeks of Art in Action*, Tate Modern, London, July 18–October 28, 2012

The Road of Poems and Borders (1989–90)

SUZANNE LACY, ARTHUR STRIMLING, TUULA LINSIÖ, ALLAN KAPROW, AND
PIRKKO KURIKKA WITH IHVA AULA, TUIRE HINDIKKA, PETR REHOR, JUDY BACA,
AND GUILLERMO GÓMEZ-PEÑA

The Road of Poems and Borders explored issues of national identity, international exchange, and border crossing through four theatrical events in Joensuu, Finland. It was part of an international music festival that included concerts, a peace symposium, an art exhibition, and the opening of a nearby border to allow passage into the Soviet Union (now Russia) for a world peace concert. *Talking at the Borders* comprised daily readings of stories, poems, and reflections on border crossings solicited by post from individuals in more than forty countries. *Meeting of the Youth* was a choreographed action at Ilosaari pool. A score composed by Jarmo Kähkönen cued 214 red-clad teenagers to move in synchronicity, waving red flags and creating an amorphous form at the center of the lagoon. *Across Time and Space*, produced by Jouko Blomberg, connected and shared the life stories of three elderly women in Minnesota, Finland, and the Soviet Union by radio broadcast. *Meeting at the Market* was a series of small actions around the Joensuu market in which individuals lay on the ground with their hands touching. Their bodies were outlined in chalk and their meetings photographed. Participants later produced a catalogue about their collaborations and the social and political issues that had inspired them.

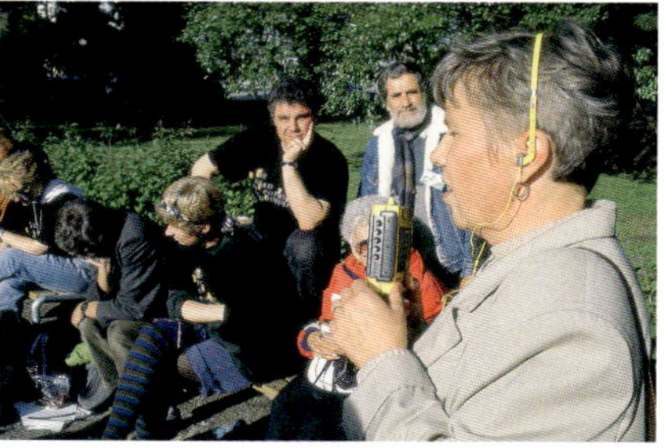

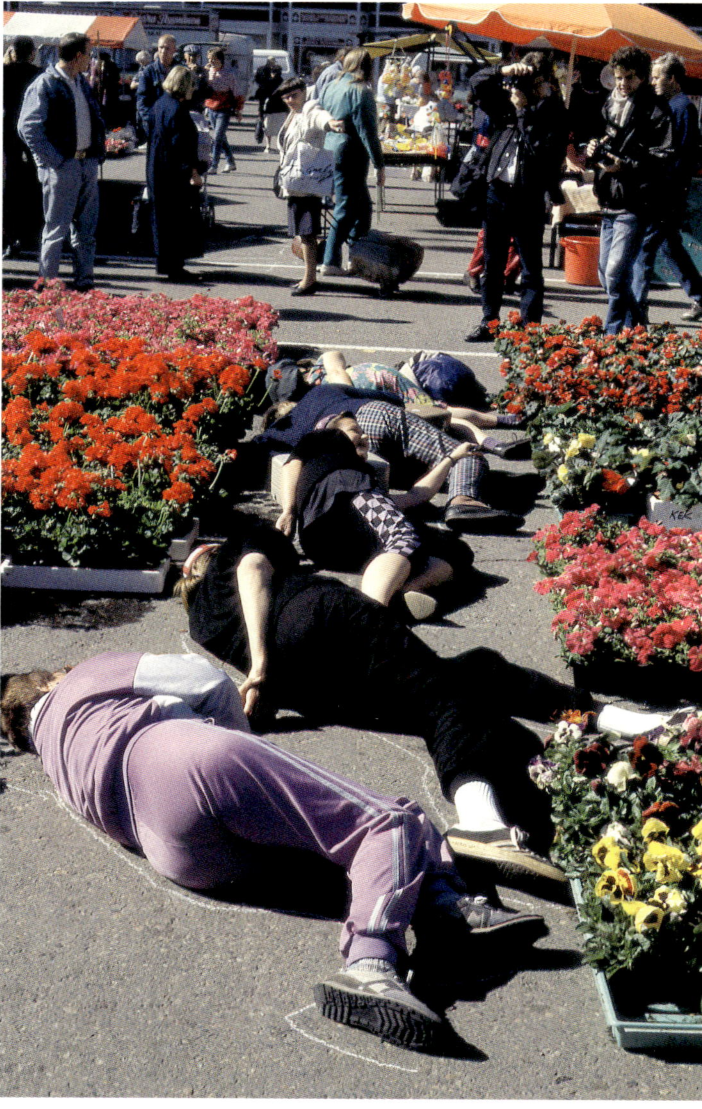

LEFT: *Meeting at the Market*
RIGHT: *Across Time and Space*
OPPOSITE: *Meeting of the Youth*

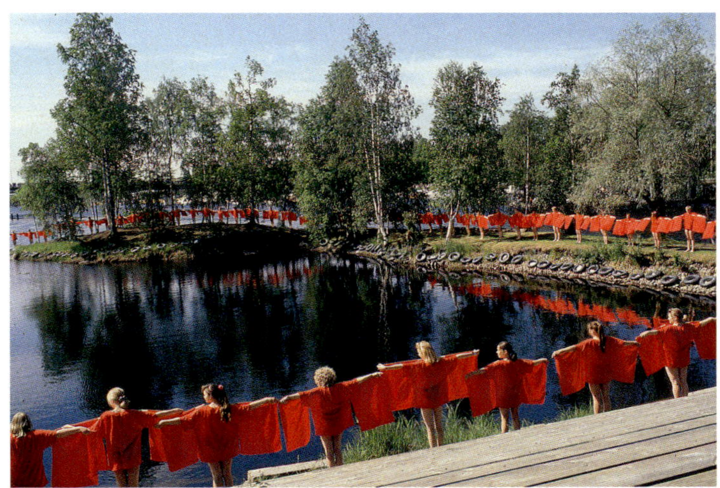 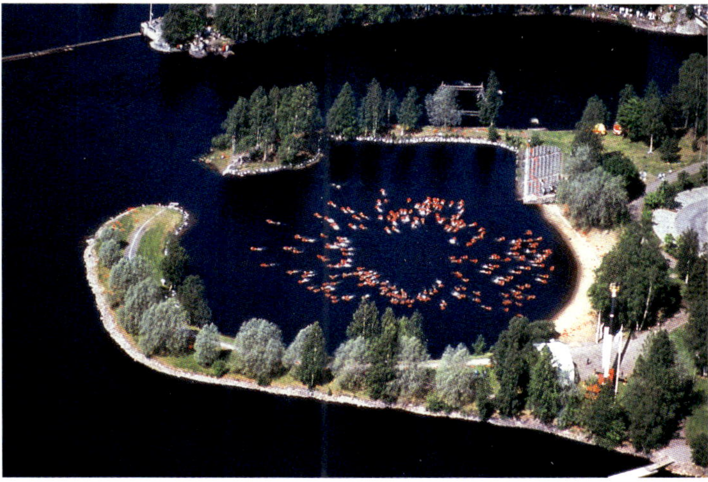

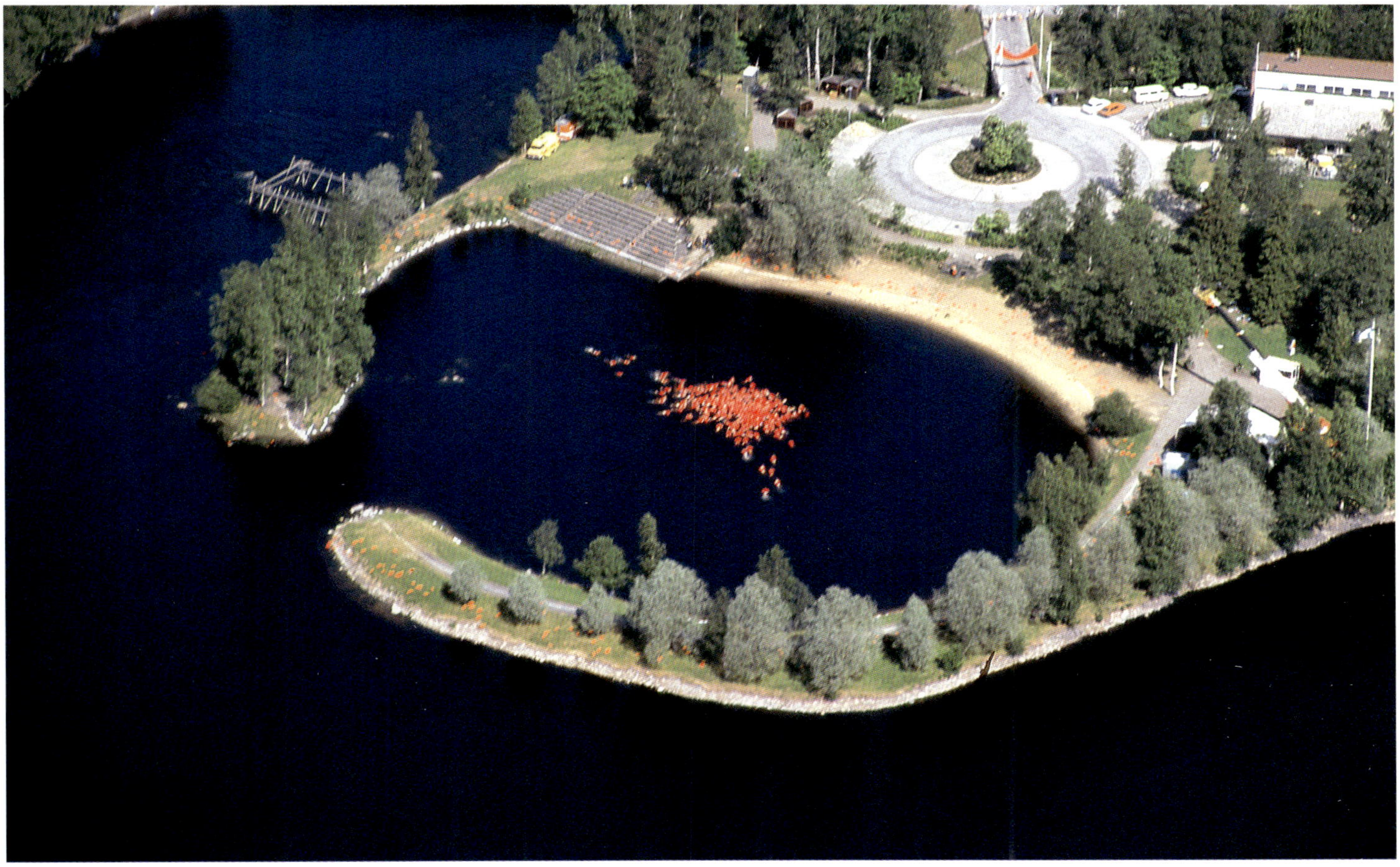

Near the border between a superpower and a small, isolated, always-threatened country, we modeled images and experiences of a peaceful community by organizing large groups of people into beautiful, non-normal, and risky actions, like leaping together into freezing water. . . . We turned satellite technology, until then solely the tool of warriors or entrepreneurs, into a means for elder women to talk across time and space. And we crossed a forbidden physical border to give a concert in a Soviet city that had been closed for generations. To accomplish this, Finns, Americans, and others worked for a month, around the clock, without temporal borders, in a place where, at that time of year, you could barely distinguish day from night. The artists met at cultural, personal, political, and international borders, and sometimes we crossed them and sometimes we stepped back. A border is where fear meets desire.

—Arthur Strimling, 2018

Anyang Women's Agenda (2010)

Organized in collaboration with local politicians and activists, this series of unscripted conversations staged throughout Anyang, South Korea, followed the unprecedented election of six women to the Anyang City Council in 2010. More than one hundred Korean women of different occupations and socioeconomic statuses came together to discuss how their experiences as women intersected with social and political issues they identified as urgent, such as opportunity in employment and education, individual financial stability during economic recession, and human impact on the environment. The conversations were held over the course of ten days in fifteen different locations, including markets, plazas, a swimming pool, a construction site, and a recycling center. The unexpected and unavoidable presence of these women's bodies in public spaces gave visual form to the concerns they voiced about women's representation in the public sphere. Audio recordings of their conversations were used as raw material to create a four-year "women's agenda" for the city, which ninety participants presented to the mayor and city council members in the lobby of City Hall. The project was produced with the assistance of Jun Seung-Boh and Bosuel Kim and was photographed by Raúl Vega.

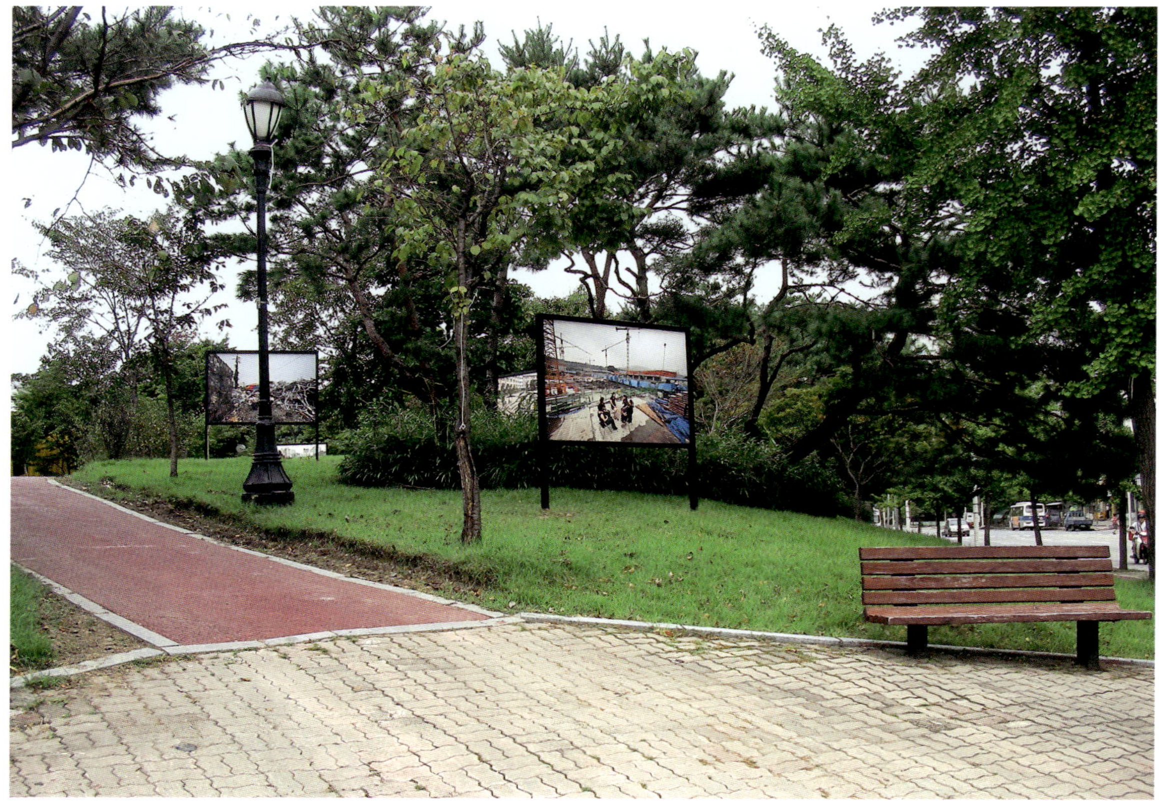

Photographs by Vega, installation view, *Third Anyang Public Art Project*, Hagun Park, Anyang, September 4– October 31, 2010

As the artistic director and chief curator of Anyang Public Art Project 2010 in South Korea, I invited Suzanne Lacy to conceive a project about *ajumma*, a slightly derogatory but embraced term for the middle-aged women in South Korea. This idea came from my childhood memory of seeing *ajummas* carrying heavy loads of cement bags and concrete blocks up to the plentiful construction sites in the 1960s. I wondered how such backbreaking slavery to the developmental economy of South Korea could be contextualized in the contemporary feminist discourses.

—Kyong Park, 2018

#SilverAction Tweets: February 3, 2013 (Selected)

@shanharves: "At a table with women rehearsing, hearing sadness that young women are still having to fight some of the same battles #silveraction"

@themaidsair: "Fundamental changes in society have isolated communities, and left women without networks for help with childcare #silveraction"

@PrincessBelsize: "'Women feel they have more of a voice and domestic violence won't be tolerated' #silveraction"

@gofeminist: "Hearing about women organising as a group of lesbians to have children - so radical then, still challenging now #silveraction"

@ahaworthbooth: "In 1979 one woman started the Incest Survivor Campaign. How did you set it up without the internet, asks another participant? #SilverAction"

@PrincessBelsize: "'Activism is what we do on a day to day basis - what we challenge &how we bring up children.' #silveraction"

@cod_philosophy: "Power of coming together. My table says this gathering of women is v familiar and reminds them of 70s. It's new to me. #silveraction"

@katie_mccrory: "Lots of talk of the active role of daughters, but no mention of sons. Surely we must make equality a shared issue? #silveraction"

@renaldridge: "Emphasis on class struggle. Yes! Feminism is redundant without consideration of class issues. #silveraction"

@shanharves: "Sadness, had to leave the table just as a woman started talking about her work in Women in Black #silveraction"

@TheWomensRoom: "'The austerity regime is stripping older women out of the work force' #silveraction"

@restlessbuddha: "Is it right 4 corporates to have say in the arts? For BP to have a say at the Tate? Never used to happen with arts council #SilverAction"

@themaidsair: "In my experience... I have learnt theres no getting 'rid' of anything. #silveraction"

@amberhsu: "The problem now: youth growing up with lower expectations. Education no longer seen as a route out. Huge debt + no opps #SilverAction"

@jojowelch1: "Lots re domestic violence too then n now.One of1st women's refuges Nottm closed by cuts '10 reopened 2012 by women activists #silveraction"

@ahaworthbooth: "Parliamentary hours and childcare - is that what's restricting women from going into Govt? #SilverAction"

@ahaworthbooth: "'Voluntary sector is mainly women, it's indicative of how society works. Women are flexible, fill gaps & make things happen' #SilverAction"

@ahaworthbooth: "This table knows younger men who've taken on majority of childcare - but I know more grandparents who are primary caregivers. #silveraction"

@themaidsair: "As the stories filter down the tank walls I wonder whether our generation will have stories as great... #silveraction"

@victoriatrinder: "A soft rumbling of voices fill the tanks as women exchange their stories #SilverAction"

@marinewitch: "The silences here are so powerful. #silveraction"

@whatbutlersaw: "'I can't save the world but I can save the local library.. #silveraction wonderful Tate inspiration"

@ProfLizKelly: "There is also something moving and familiar about the intensity with which which women are listening to each other #Silveraction"

@leepster: "'our lives changed at Greenham common' - awesome to hear from Greenham women at #silveraction"

@marinewitch: "Spontaneous post performance singing in Tate Tanks, lights and projectors off and performers home. What a fantastic day. #silveraction"

@anywavewilldo: "do NOT speak to me about #SilverAction"

@broke_grove: "The one thing in was told at #SilverAction on Sunday was that you cannot focus on all things but just one. Got told to choose. made me sad"

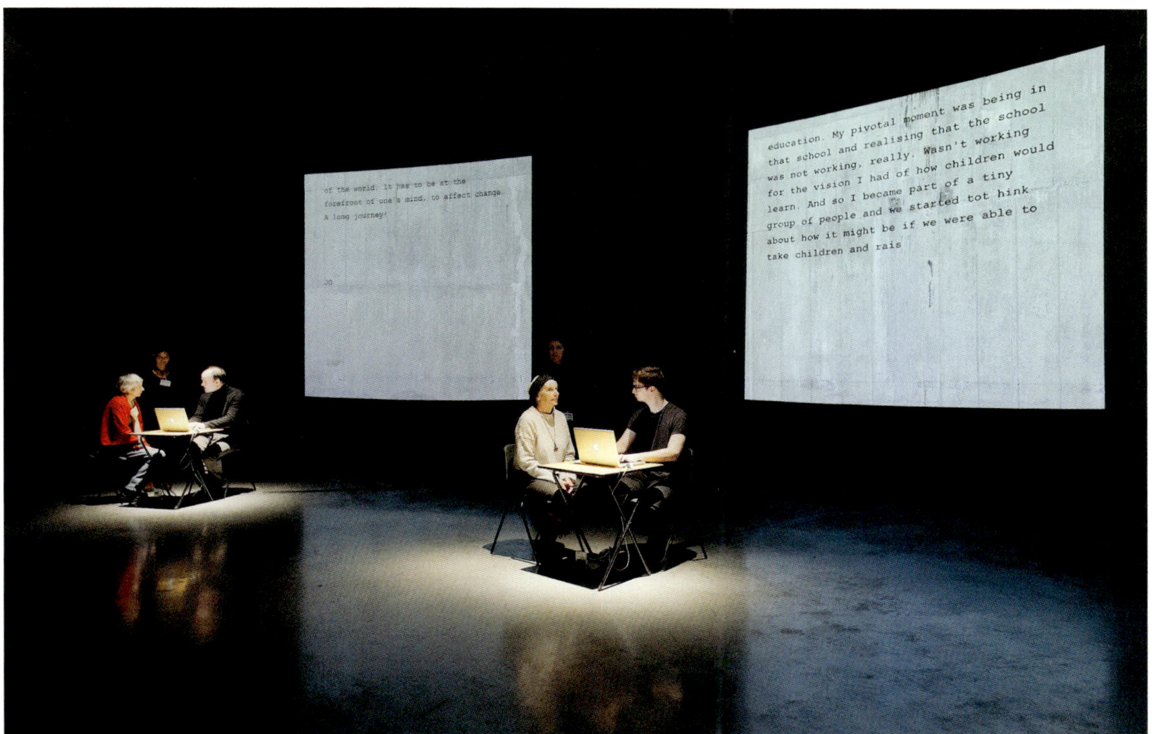

Individuals invited to break away from the conversations in the larger space and relay their stories to typists who generated the transcripts on the walls behind them in real time

Between the Door and the Street (2013)

On October 19, 2013, a residential block in Brooklyn was closed to traffic as nearly four hundred activists gathered to respond to a set of questions about the intersections of race, ethnic identity, class, and feminism in activism. Some twenty-five hundred audience members entered through a sound installation by Bruno Louchouarn, which demarcated the area as an interstitial space for collective conversation and expressions of both personal reflection and public concern. Potted yellow flowers and a yellow line along the curb drew visual attention to the participants—mostly women—who wore yellow pashmina scarves and sat in clusters on sixty different stoops. The event was commissioned and co-presented by Creative Time and the Brooklyn Museum's Elizabeth A. Sackler Center for Feminist Art. Lacy also produced an installation at the Brooklyn Museum, using its grand staircase to pose questions about feminism to the community at large. Anne Pasternak, Nato Thompson, Jennifer Hsu, and Jean Cooney were among those who contributed creatively to the project.

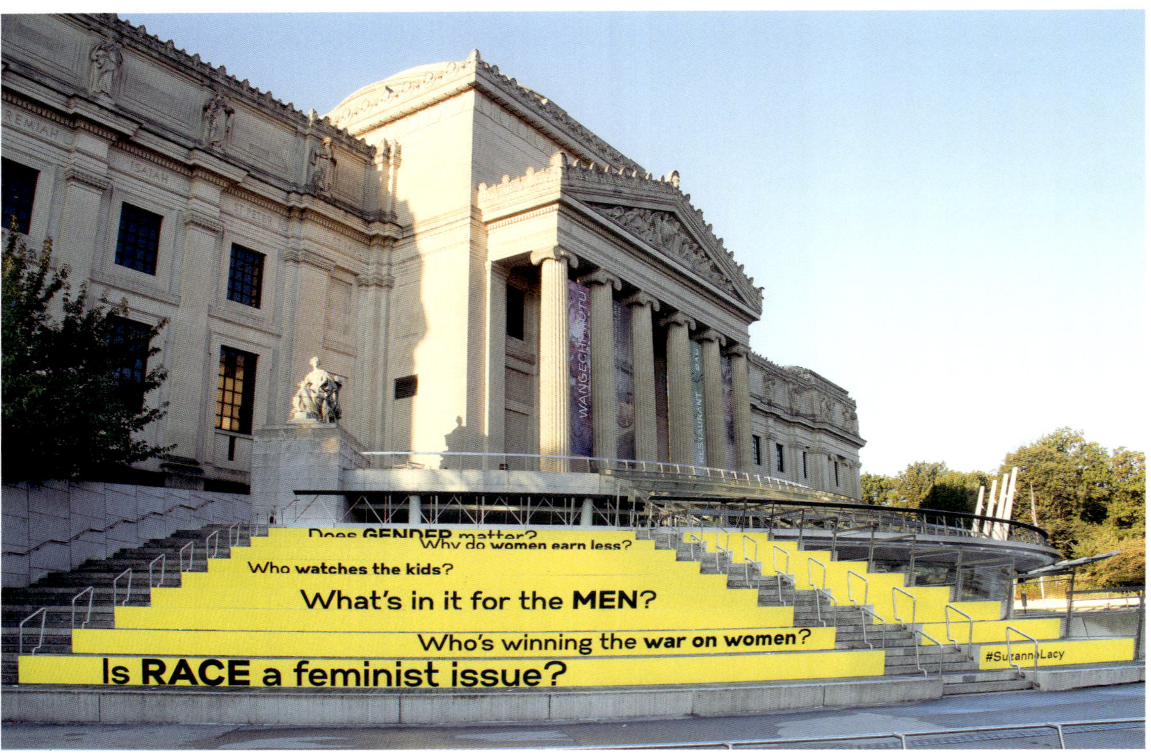

Installation view, Brooklyn Museum,
October 10–20, 2013

Having a real conversation with someone and sharing a part of your story by talking about what's important in your life—your concerns, fears, what brings you joy—requires vulnerability and provides connection. Even if we don't quite catch what's happening at the moment, the connection has a way of staying with us—it stays in the body. We don't have to intellectualize it. This process takes time—it's not something that comes through "discussing the issues" once or twice in a group, but through ongoing, sustained dialogue—through relationship building.

—Unique Holland, 2018

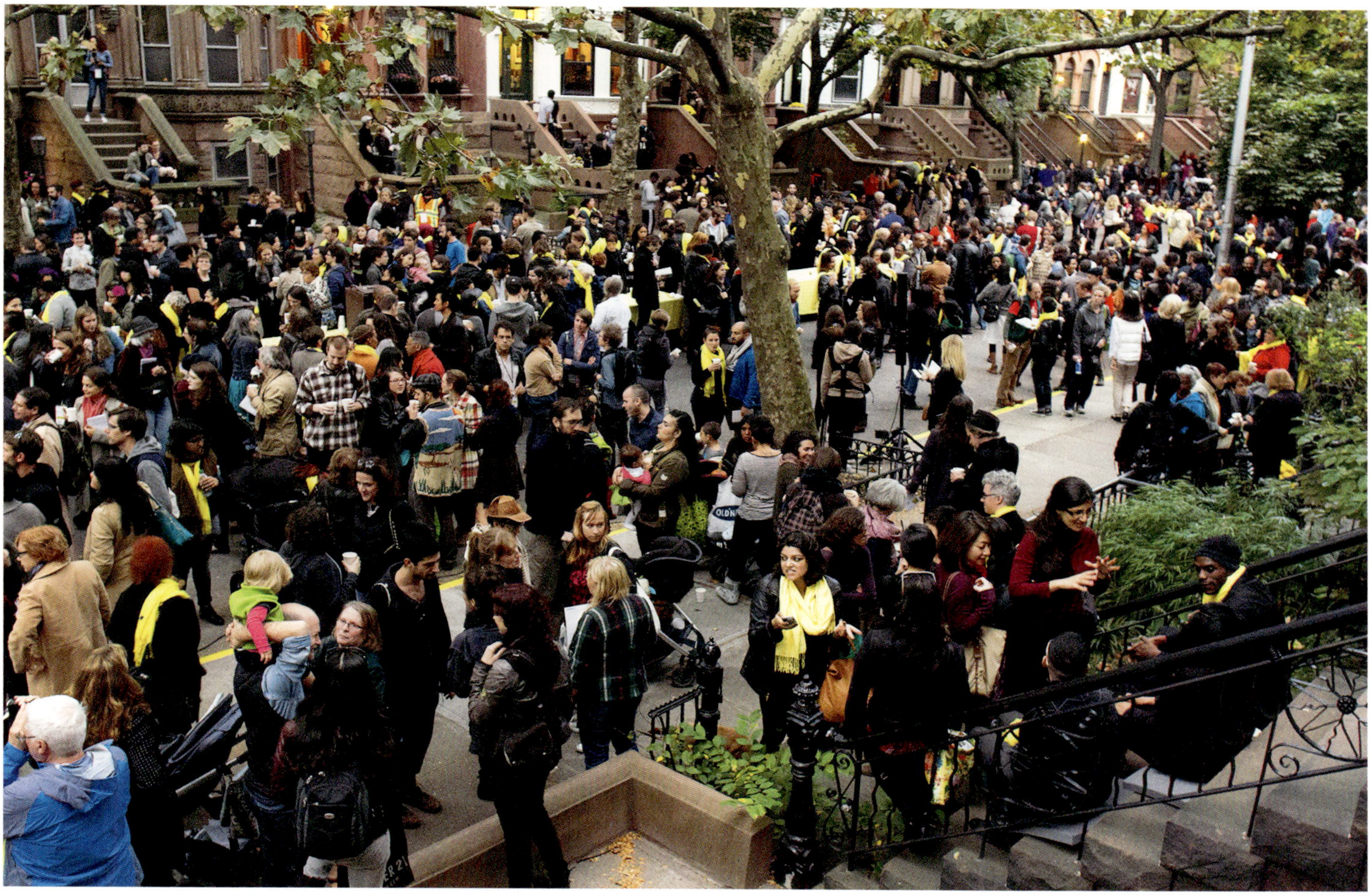

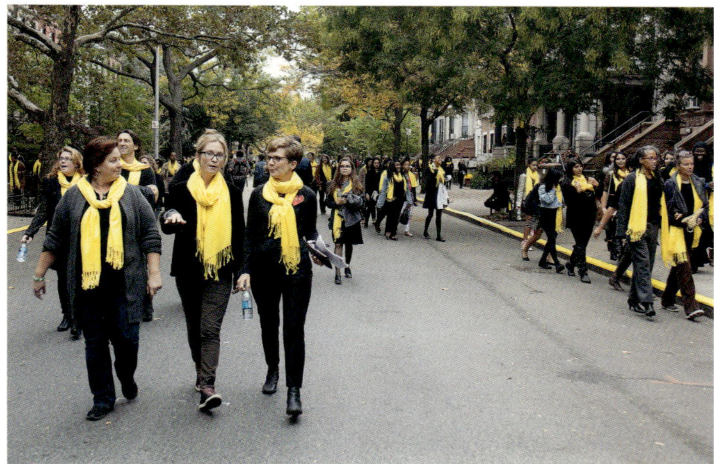
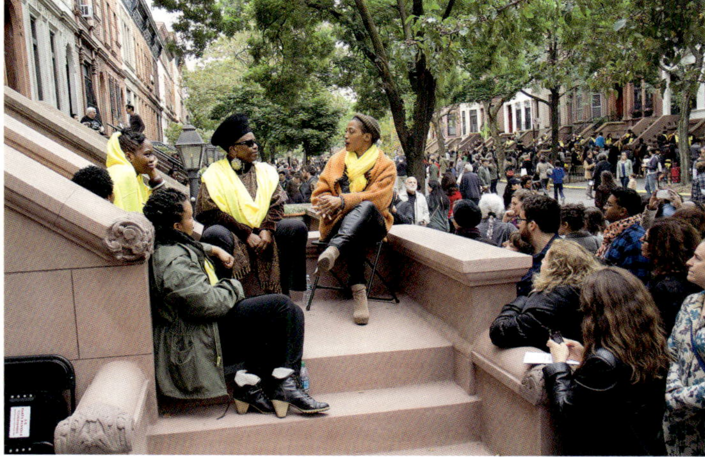

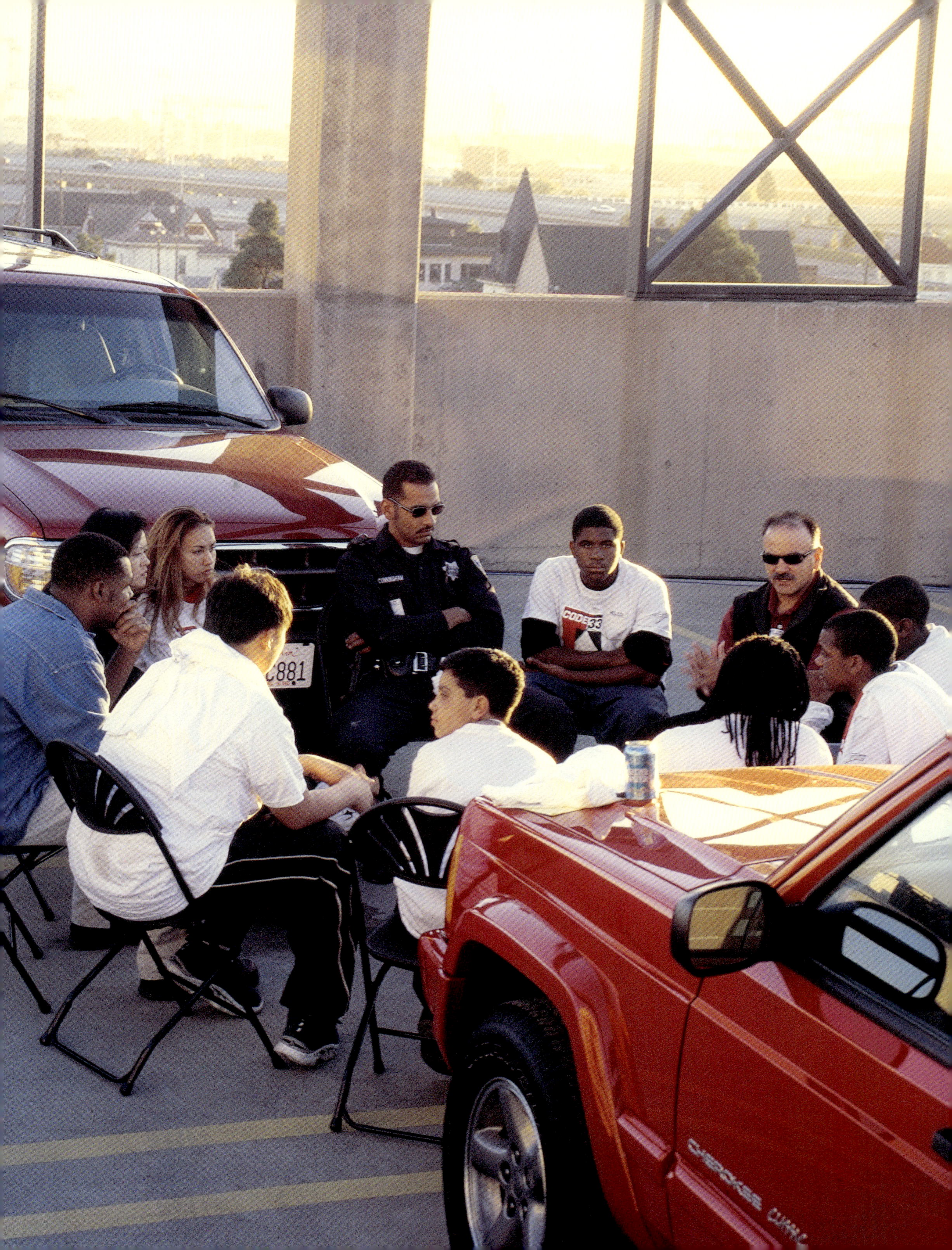

YOUTH

In 1987 Lacy moved to Oakland to become dean of the school of fine arts at the California College of Arts and Crafts (CCAC, now California College of the Arts). This move foreshadowed a shift in her practice away from investigations of old age—present in works such as *The Bag Lady* (1977, pp. 78–79), *Whisper, the Waves, the Wind* (1983–84, pp. 152–57), and *The Crystal Quilt* (1987, pp. 166–73)—and toward explorations of youth, specifically the lives of young people in urban spaces. At CCAC Lacy met Chris Johnson, a fine arts photographer and professor who saw subversive potential in teaching media literacy to high school students in Oakland. Together they aimed to combat the negative stereotypes of youth of color in the media—at a time when their own institution had a fraught relationship with these teenagers, who often waited for the bus in front of the CCAC campus. Lacy and Johnson visited local high schools in search of teachers or principals interested in incorporating media literacy into their curricula. This led to *Teenage Living Room* (1991–92, p. 185), the first work in the ten-year series known as *The Oakland Projects* (1991–2001, pp. 184–211).

Lacy's work with youth in *The Oakland Projects* became widely recognized and inspired her to develop youth-centered projects internationally, including *The Turning Point* (1996–97, p. 212) in Vancouver, Canada; *I.D.Entity* (2004, p. 213) in Taipei; *SWARM* (2007, p. 214) in Los Angeles; and *School for Revolutionary Girls* (2016, p. 215) in Dublin. These works focused on young people's relationships to the forms of institutional authority that had the most bearing on their lives, including education, criminal justice, health care, public policy, and the media. Many of the performance elements of the larger projects— *The Roof Is on Fire* (1993–94, pp. 186–91), *Code 33: Emergency, Clear the Air!* (1997–99, pp. 206–11), and *The Turning Point* among them—demanded the audience's silence, ordering them to "shut up and listen" to a generation whose opinions were so often ignored and whose experiences were so often devalued. Audience members were invited to walk among groups of teenagers discussing topics of their own choosing, ranging from family and sex to power, violence, and their portrayal in the media. While social media was employed in later works such as *I.D.Entity*, *SWARM*, and *School for Revolutionary Girls*, face-to-face conversation remained important to Lacy's process and performances. Her youth-centered projects have also regularly featured pedagogical components, whether through classroom curricula or intensive workshops held outside of school hours. Some works, such as *The Oakland Projects* and *The Turning Point*, incorporated interventions into public policy, in which Lacy partnered with governmental, nongovernmental, and grassroots organizations to take a structural approach to shaping youth policy and ensuring its support and success. These projects pushed back against the ever-present societal alarm about the condition of teenagers through performances in which young people could put their own voices front and center in the "politics of perception."

—CHRISTA CESARIO

OPPOSITE: Teenagers and police gathered for the final performance of *Code 33: Emergency, Clear the Air!* (1997–99, pp. 206–11), Center City West Garage, Oakland, October 7, 1999

THE OAKLAND PROJECTS

(1991–2001)

Teenage Living Room / The Roof Is on Fire / Signs of Violence /
Youth, Cops, and Videotape / Eye 2 Eye at Fremont High / No Blood/No Foul /
Expectations / Code 33: Emergency, Clear the Air!

Oakland in the late 1980s was different from anywhere Lacy had worked before. As the birthplace of the Black Panther movement, it had a rich history of activism and community engagement, and race relations were constantly at the fore. It was also an economically depressed former manufacturing town with high rates of violent crime. Politicians stereotyping young black men as "super predators" and national media representations of Oakland youth as rioters created an urgent need for the city's teens to gain control over the ways they were being portrayed and perceived.

In *The Oakland Projects* Lacy coupled her established strategies of media intervention with programs that explored and expanded young people's power of self-representation. Most often produced in partnership with Annice Jacoby and Chris Johnson, it is her longest-running series of works, with every new project informed by and emerging from the last. Although the large-scale performances, films, and installations have received the most recognition, each work had an extensive preparation period that included combinations of curriculum design, in-school coursework, out-of-school workshops, mentorships, career development programs, video production training, policy interventions, coalition building, and partnerships with government departments and nonprofit organizations. In 1992 Lacy, Jacoby, and Johnson formed T.E.A.M. (Teens + Educators + Artists + Media Makers) as a fund-raising vehicle and to provide a loose administrative structure to the fluid network of artists and activists with whom Lacy would collaborate for a decade—once again demonstrating her long-standing commitment to coalition building as the foundation of her social practice.

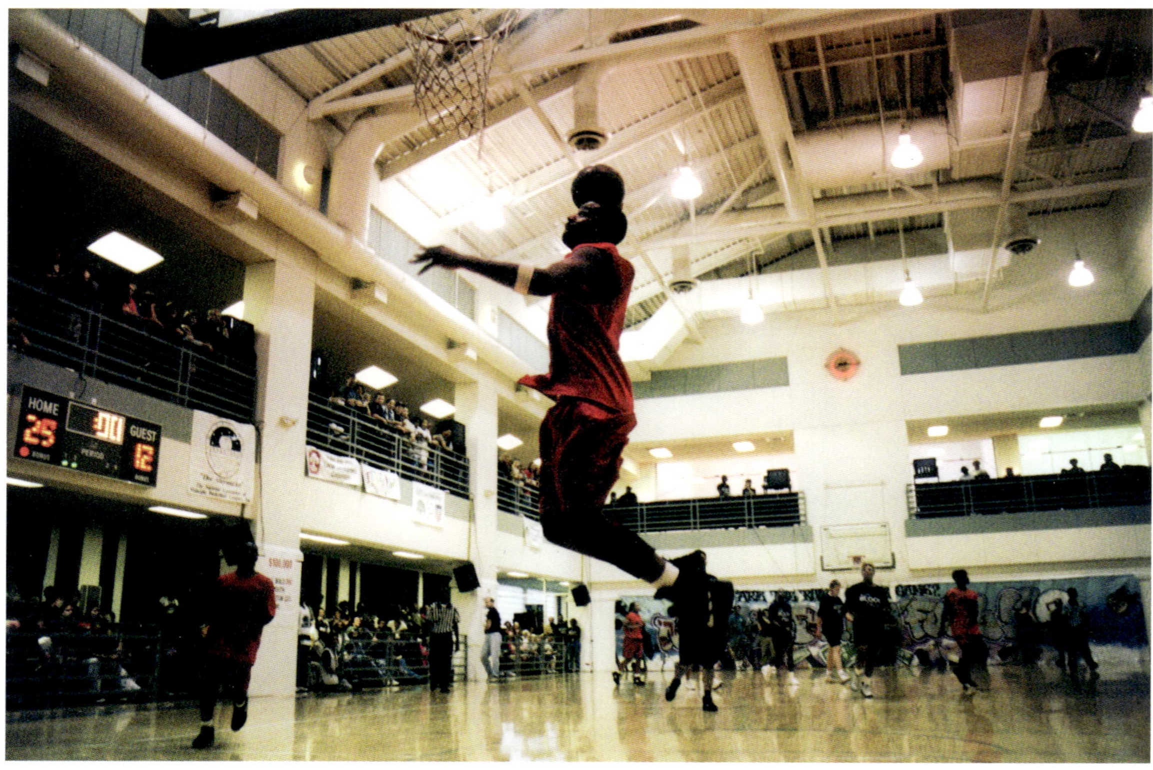

No Blood/No Foul, Club One, Oakland, June 5, 1996

Teenage Living Room (1991–92)

SUZANNE LACY AND CHRIS JOHNSON WITH ANDY HAMNER AND LAUREN MANDUKE

In the fall of 1991 Lacy and Johnson led a media literacy class with Hamner and Manduke, who taught at Oakland Technical High School. The hour-long weekly study block for thirty sophomores explored how mass media portrayed youth, how media is made, what media teaches, and how they could craft their own images. The class continued throughout the school year and culminated in a two-hour public performance in the California College of the Arts parking lot.

During the first hour of the performance students were asked to consider how they wanted to represent their cars and themselves in portraits taken with large-format view cameras. During the second hour an audience entered the lot and the teens hopped into their cars, dropping the self-conscious stances they had adopted in front of the cameras to discuss eight topics they had selected: power, cars, sex, friends, family, violence, money, and media. These improvisational conversations yielded powerfully honest self-portrayals as students revealed their feelings and ideas about the complex world they inhabited, taking the opportunity to "write their own script" for the camera and the audience.

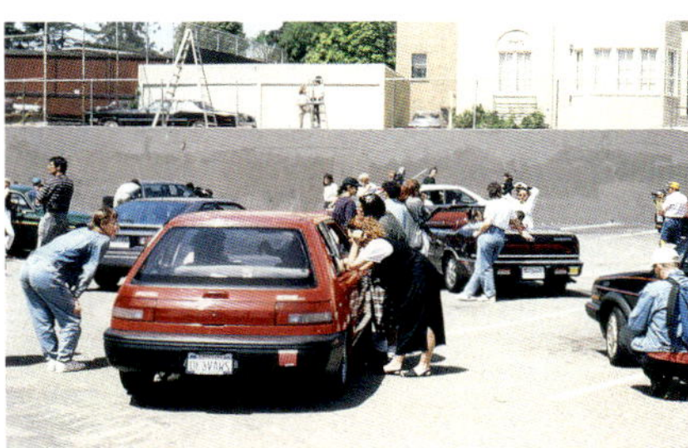

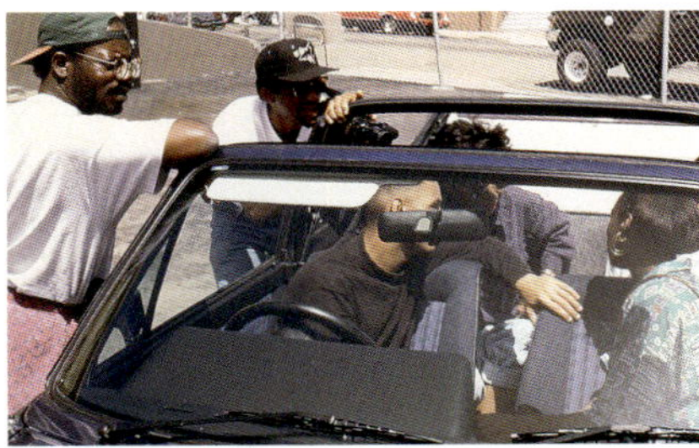

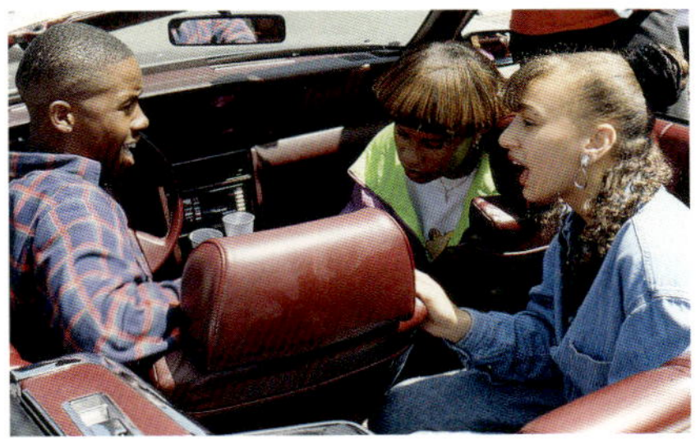

```
                    LESSON PLAN OUTLINE
         Popular Culture and Media Literacy Curriculum

                 Compiled by Lauren Manduke based on
               personal journal notes from Fall 1991 class


The curriculum below is for a one semester course that met once a
week for one hour.  Detailed accounts of each lesson can be found
in the Journal Notes following this section.  It should be noted
that this information was based on the experiences of one class
and could be altered and expanded upon in other settings. (see
Evaluation Section)


WEEK ONE    Objective: To introduce the ideas of image/reality
                       in the context of the media and the self.

            Activities:     --   have all teachers involved sit on a
                                 stage and students define who they
                                 are by what they see.

                            --   write the words popular, media,
                                 culture, image, and you on the
                                 board and introduce curriculum plan
                                 using a discussion of these terms.

                            --   show slides of media pop stars and
                                 ask students to respond to what
                                 they see in terms of media images
                                 and reality.  Examples of slides
                                 might include Madonna, Michael
                                 Jackson, etc.

                            --   assignment: ask students to bring
                                 in something from media that
                                 represents themselves.  Items might
                                 include a magazine clipping or an
                                 object commonly found in media.
                                 Personal  photos of students should
                                 not be included at this point.

WEEK TWO  Objective: Define image and reality in terms of media
                     representations.

          Activities:     --   review last week's class by asking
                               students "What did we do and why?".
                               Include review of words on the
                               board from last week.

                                10
```

The Roof Is on Fire (1993–94)

SUZANNE LACY, ANNICE JACOBY, AND CHRIS JOHNSON

The Roof Is on Fire culminated in the first large-scale performance of *The Oakland Projects*, featuring 220 public high school students in unscripted conversations about family, sexuality, drugs, music, neighborhoods, and the future as they sat in one hundred cars parked on the Center City West Garage rooftop. With cameras rolling and more than one thousand Oakland residents roaming from car to car to listen, the production had the haunting familiarity of images from the evening news—but here, youth represented themselves. The performance was aired as a one-hour documentary by the Bay Area's NBC affiliate and was covered extensively on local news and national CNN.

Over the previous year fifteen teachers from eight Oakland public high schools participated in a certification program designed by Johnson and Lacy. Distinguished faculty including the educator Herb Kohl and the sociologists Todd Gitlin and Troy Duster led workshops helping them develop and deliver media literacy curricula in their classrooms. The teachers then brought forty students to weekly after-school planning sessions for the performance. Fifteen of those students were elected to the Youth Steering Committee, whose members were trained and participated in all aspects of the production and media coverage.

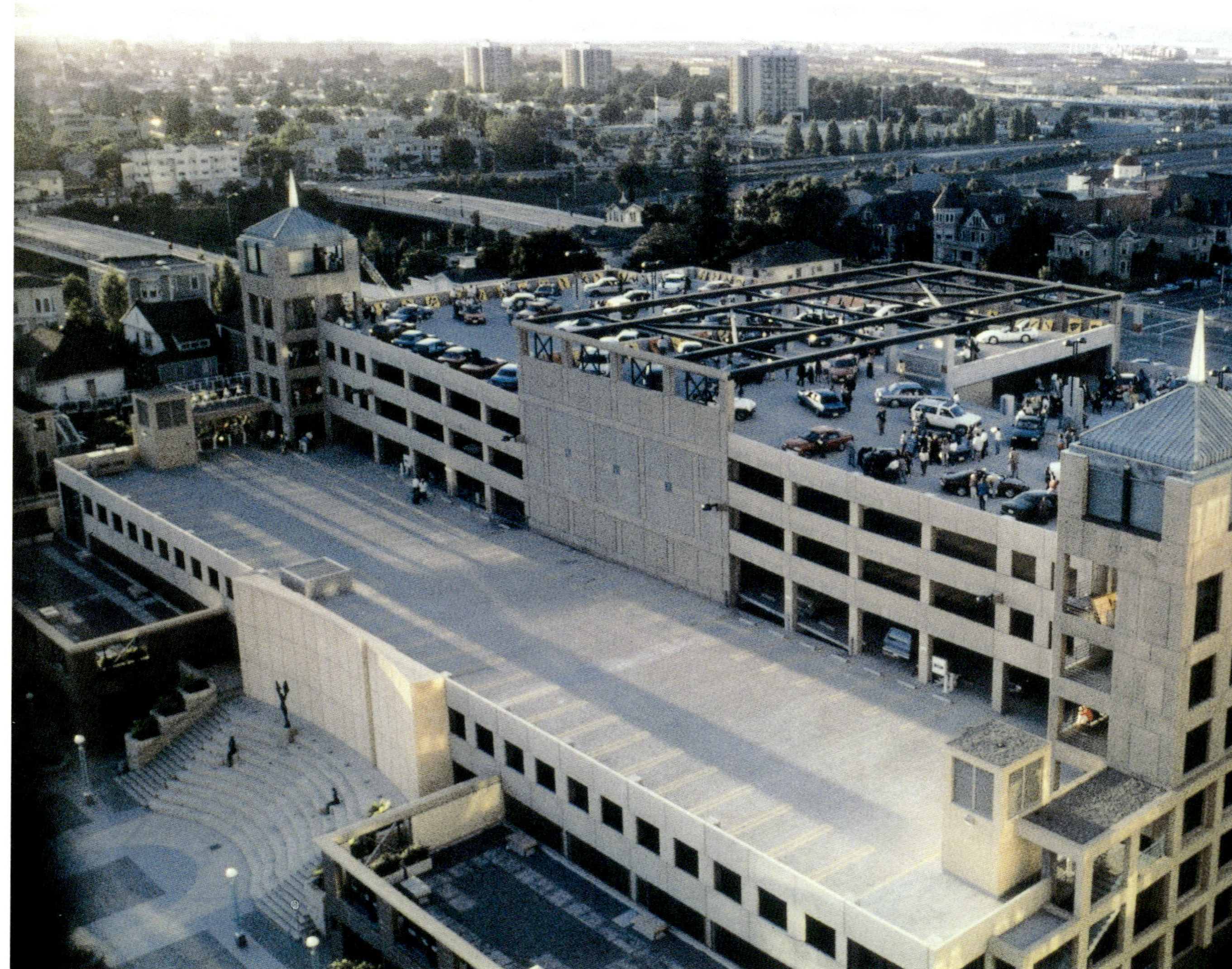

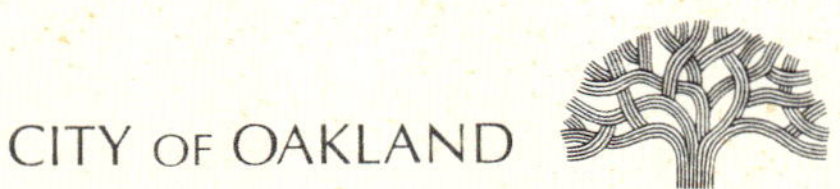

CITY HALL • ONE CITY HALL PLAZA • OAKLAND, CALIFORNIA 94612

Office of the Mayor
Elihu M. Harris
Mayor

510 238-3141
TDD 839-6451

June 21, 1993

Dear Friend,

The City of Oakland endorses and supports the work of T.E.A.M. to develop media literacy awareness for teens in Oakland. T.E.A.M. is an acronym for Teens + Education + Art + Media, an innovative educational alliance designed to fulfill our mission of addressing community issues. T.E.A.M. recognizes the cultural rift between today's teens and the adult world and offers an exciting concept to address these tensions. Building our award as the All American City, the T.E.A.M. approach to problem-solving will put into focus the on-going concerns of Oakland's youth.

Last May, Teenage Living Room, a performance collaboration between California College of Arts and Crafts and Oakland Technical High School, culminated a media study program. The strong response in print and television gave the students a chance to see themselves in the loop of public dialogue. To build on that success, a group of multi-talented people have been working to expand T.E.A. M. to all Oakland high schools.

The economic and cultural diversity of our community makes Oakland a unique and an appropriate national model for educational reform and social transformation. T.E.A.M. is offering an important opportunity to make education a process for the entire community. The benefits to Oakland are extensive; communication, awareness and change. I actively endorse partnerships with T.E.A.M.'s expanded effort to foster community wide action that strengthens education and the arts. As mayor, I encourage all collaboration with T.E.A.M. I believe T.E.A.M. will generate broad public interest in Oakland. I urge your support and cooperation.

Sincerely,

ELIHU M. HARRIS
Mayor

EMH:jd

The fact is that teenagers are a direct reflection of what our society is. I mean, in a sense, teenagers are like the canary in the mine shaft. We can see in the way teenagers behave and react to culture whether or not we are creating a healthy culture, so we need to listen to what they think and what they feel.

—Chris Johnson, 1994

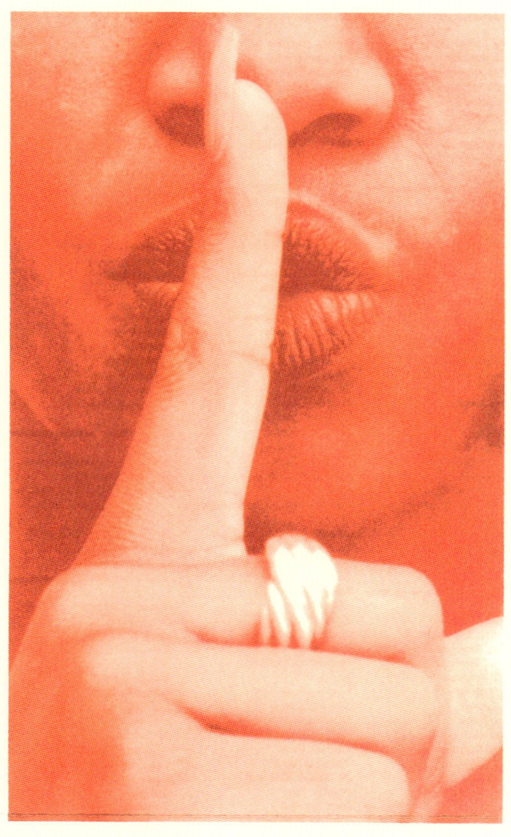

THE ROOF IS ON FIRE

*"At first take the scene in the parking lot has the haunting familiarity of images on the six o'clock news. It is the same tedious tale fueling urban nightmares, complete with a crowd of Oakland teenagers right in the center of the action, surrounded by jostling cameramen, intrusive reporters and curious onlookers. **This time the story has a different twist. The teens are in control of the medium and the message, starring as featured players in an artistically and socially radical performance piece— a lesson in social imagination.**"*

June 9, 1994

A performance event by Suzanne Lacy in collaboration with Annice Jacoby & Chris Johnson. With a Cast of Hundreds of Oakland Youth.

THE ROOF IS ON FIRE is a multi-media public conversation ignited by artists, culminating a three-year collaboration exploring the effects of media on teen lives. One student asks "Who has more power, a man with a gun or a man with an education?" "What makes a woman a woman?" Oakland youth answers.

A chance to eavesdrop.

Presented by T.E.A.M = Teens + Education + Art + Media.

Propaganda
Hype or slander
I won't believe the hype
I understand
Media dictates
The mind and rotates
The way you think
And syncopates slow pace
Brains
Can't maintain
Ascertain...

knowledge is king
by Kool Moe Dee

SPONSORS:
California College of Arts and Crafts
Oakland Unified School District
KRON Channel 4 Kids First
Bramalea U.S. Properties

CORPORATE AND FOUNDATION CONTRIBUTORS:
Rockefeller Foundation
Walter and Elise Haas Foundation
LEF Foundation
Tamarack Foundation
The San Francisco Foundation
McKesson Foundation
The Clorox Foundation
Kaiser Permanente
American President Companies

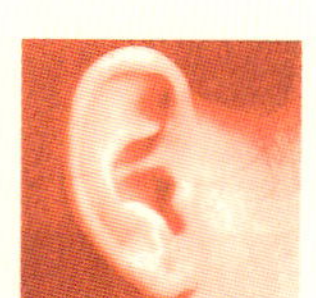

City Center
West Garage,
Oakland

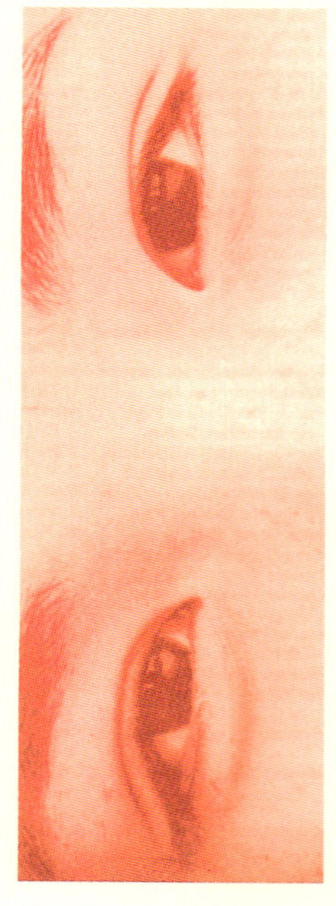

Flyer by Michael Manwaring distributed to the audience
OPPOSITE, TOP: Diagram of the layout of the cars on the rooftop
OPPOSITE, BOTTOM LEFT: Student participant (left foreground) and Oakland mayor Elihu Harris (right foreground) interviewed by the press, Center City West Garage

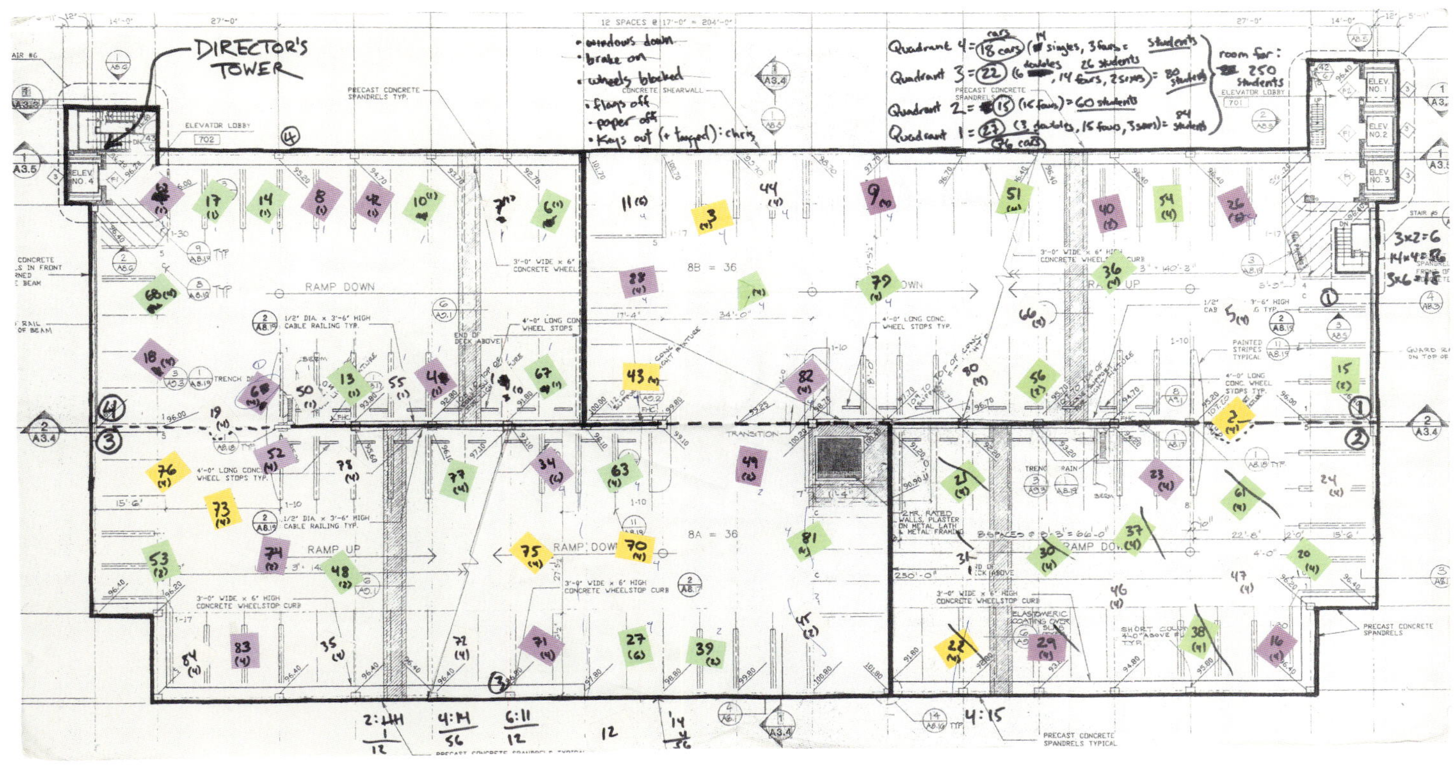

The media *is* powerful. And the fact that the teens were on the six-o'clock news, speaking for themselves, was a tremendous coup d'état. It was in essence showing they could get inside the palace. . . . One event is just like a seed. . . . The agricultural image is [that] we have to keep plowing to keep people using their voices, but we've definitely got lots of seeds out there.

—Annice Jacoby, 1994

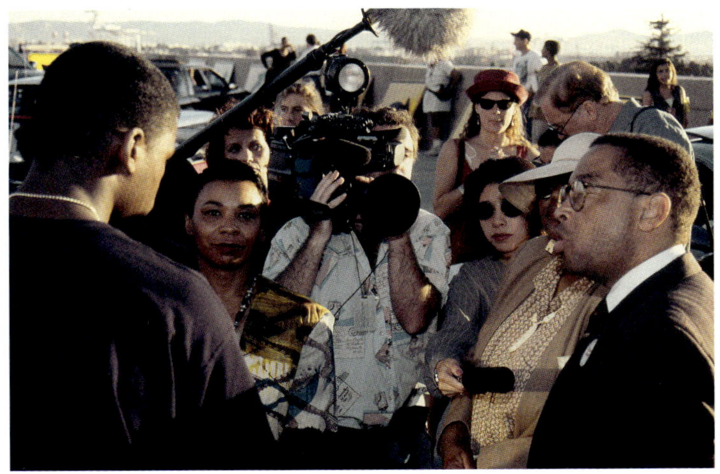

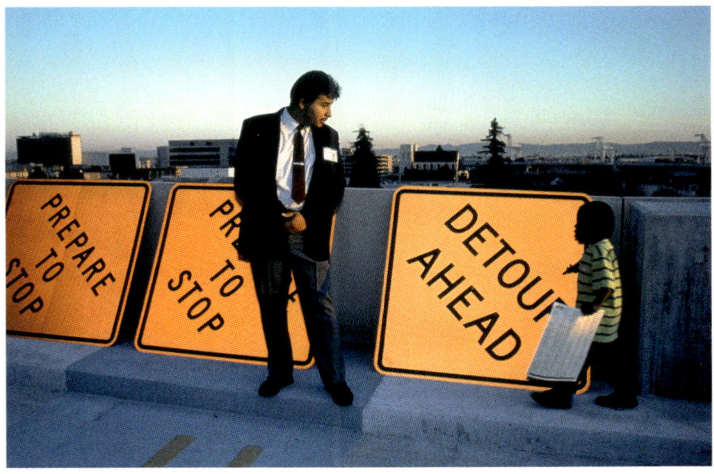

The kids, all the younger people on the thing, all of them started to band together as a group—which was good—but it was out of frustration and resentment and feeling like they weren't being taken seriously, because [they thought], "Oh, if I was taken seriously, you would take my ideas." . . . They wanted to be like student directors. See, this is the thing about ownership, and I guess this gets to the crux of the whole issue of ownership. When you do a project on a group level like that, you give up ownership. You don't take it, you have to give it up. And control. We didn't control any of those kids in the cars. They could say whatever they wanted. They just had to say it in the car. And usually, when [they're] in a situation like that, they're used to being co-opted and are distrustful of being taken advantage of. There was some of that.

—Jacques Bronson, filmmaker, 2007

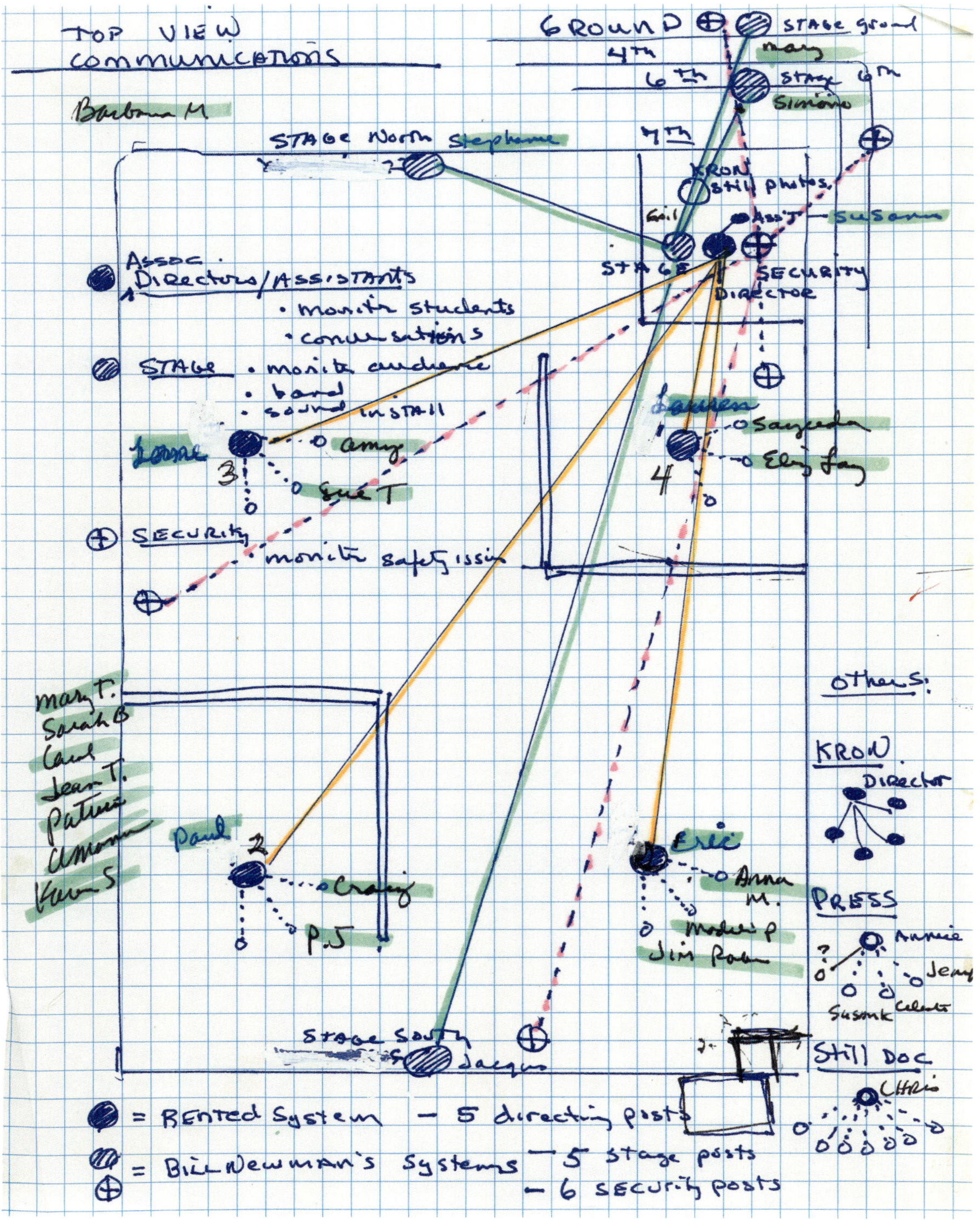

Diagram of production roles and the chain of communication

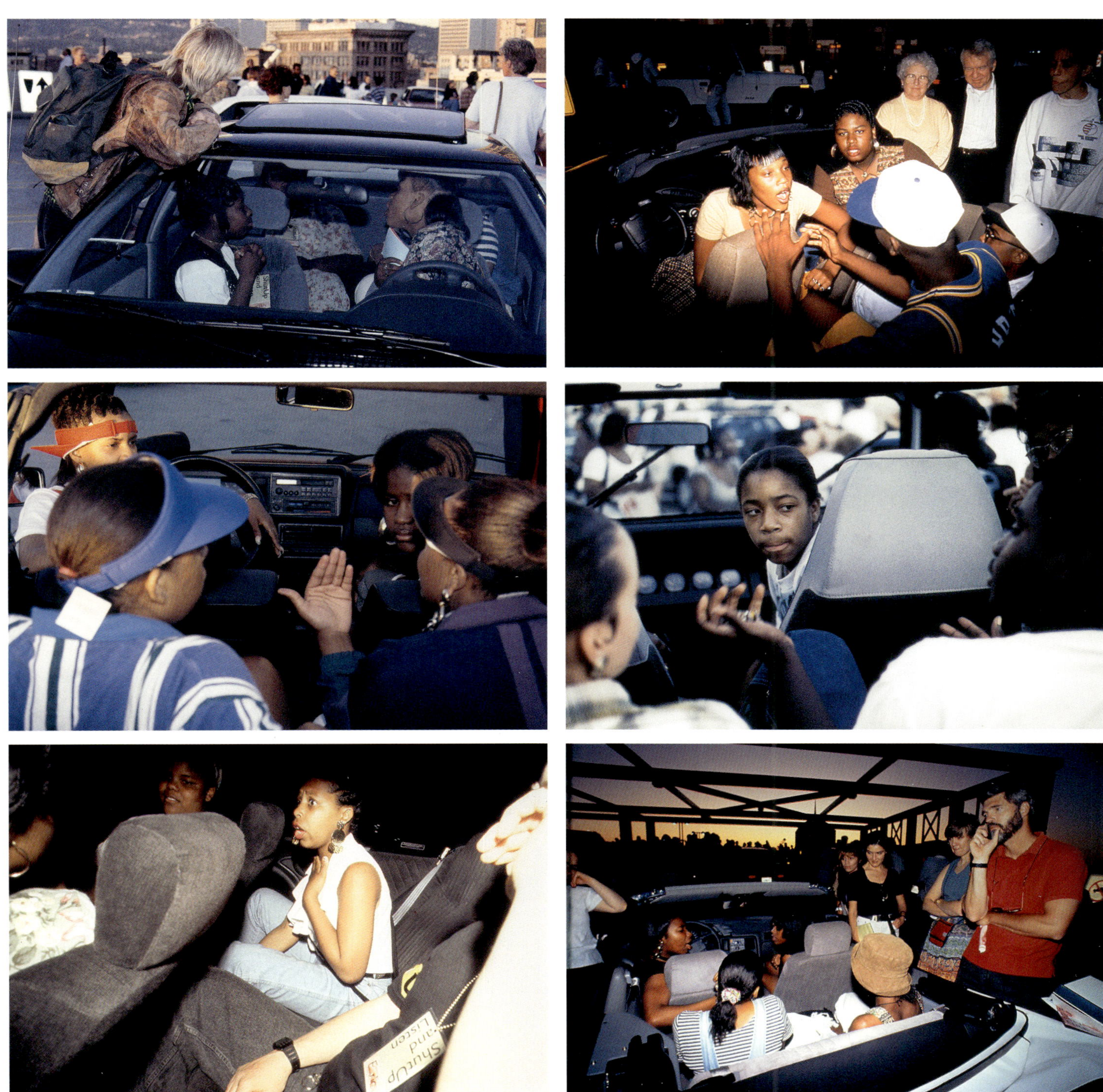

But it was powerful, though, to actually have [the audience] not able to speak. Usually the dynamic between teens and adults is the opposite. Teens are usually the ones that are told to shut up or stay in their place, and adults do a lot of the talking. That within itself was a very powerful statement.
—Leuckessia Hirsh, participant, 2007

Signs of Violence (1994)

SUZANNE LACY, LESLIE BECKER, ANNICE JACOBY,
AND GAIL SMITHWALTER

In *The Roof Is on Fire* (1993–94, pp. 186–91), violence surfaced as a topic of concern for several young women. Channeling their personal experiences, they worked with graphic designers and Becker to create full-scale street signs with text and images reconfigured to address the theme of domestic violence. The signs were fabricated by the California Department of Transportation and exhibited in Lacy's 1994 retrospective at the Snug Harbor Cultural Center and Botanical Garden in Staten Island, New York.

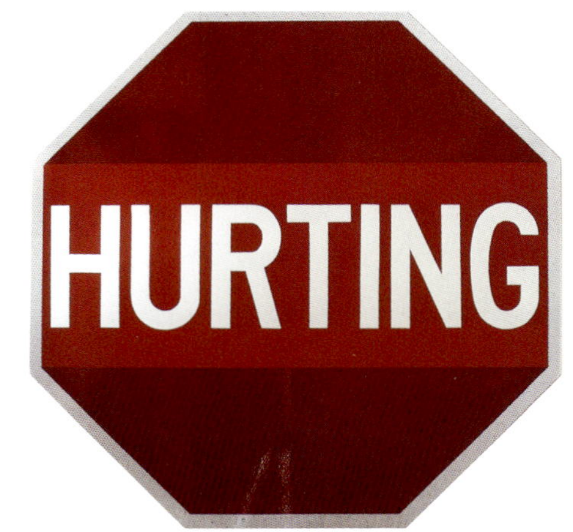

Youth, Cops, and Videotape (1995)

SUZANNE LACY, ANNICE JACOBY, AND CHRIS JOHNSON

After students involved in *The Roof Is on Fire* (1993–94, pp. 186–91) identified conflicts with police as a major concern, Lacy sought to address the mutual distrust between Oakland youth and law enforcement. Police captain Sharon Jones, facilitator from the U.S. Justice Department Booker Neal, and T.E.A.M. organized six weekly dialogues between eighteen teenagers and ten police officers. Jacques Bronson filmed the discussions and created the video *Youth, Cops, and Videotape* for Oakland Police Department community policing trainings.

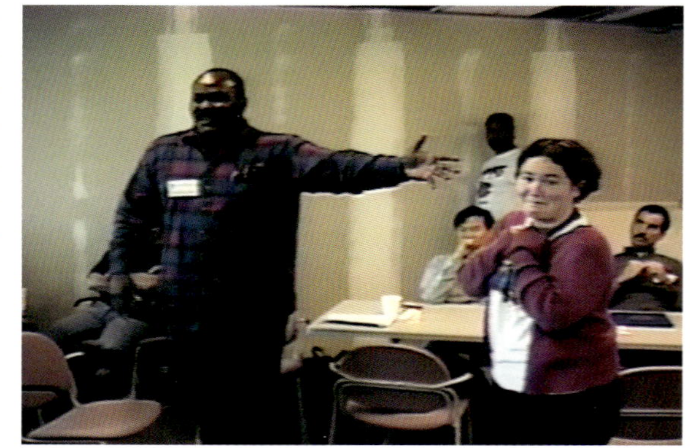

Eye 2 Eye at Fremont High (2000)

SUZANNE LACY AND JULIO CÉSAR MORALES

Eye 2 Eye at Fremont High comprised three facilitated conversations among more than one hundred faculty, students, and staff divided into small groups at Oakland's overpopulated Fremont High School. The final conversation was open to the public as a performance, with colorful T-shirts, banners, video monitors, and a DJ bringing youth to the school's outdoor quad. Problems and recommendations were recorded on blackboards and were later presented to Oakland Unified School District superintendent Dennis Chaconas. Participants included Rosa Chavez, Sara Chavez, Nicole Hickman, Jidan Koon, and Lou Ann Lucke-Aaberg.

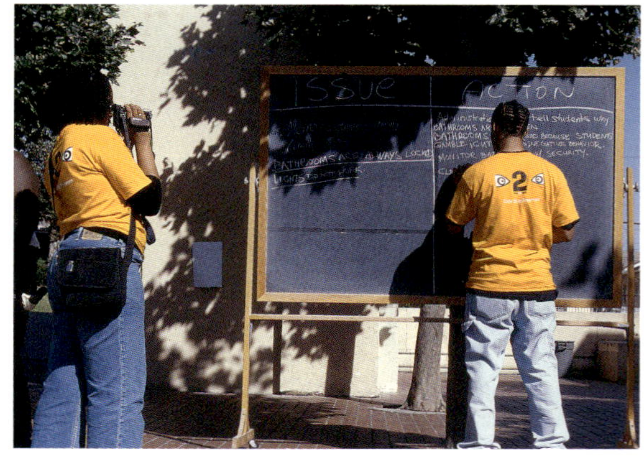

No Blood/No Foul (1995–96)

SUZANNE LACY, ANNICE JACOBY, AND CHRIS JOHNSON

When city councilwoman Sheila Jordan began planning the Oakland Youth Policy Initiative, T.E.A.M. worked with committees to implement focus groups and help draft the proposal. They also designed a performance to announce the policy to the community and urge its passage. *No Blood/No Foul* pitted youth against police officers in a competitive, fast-paced "basketball as performance" artwork staged at a trendy health club. Each quarter introduced a new element: teen referees replaced adult referees in the second quarter; the third quarter followed the rules of street ball, where "if there's no blood, there's no foul"; and in the final quarter, the audience became the referee. The event included live-action video interrupts, prerecorded interviews with players, a halftime dance performance, an original soundtrack, and sports commentators. Murals by local graffiti artists surrounded the court, youth reporters interviewed the crowd, and telephones connected to a hotline were provided for the audience to respond to the policy. *No Blood/No Foul* received extensive local and national television coverage as an example of the policy in action; it was attended by the mayor and several city council members, who subsequently passed the proposal. Lacy also produced a documentary on the project.

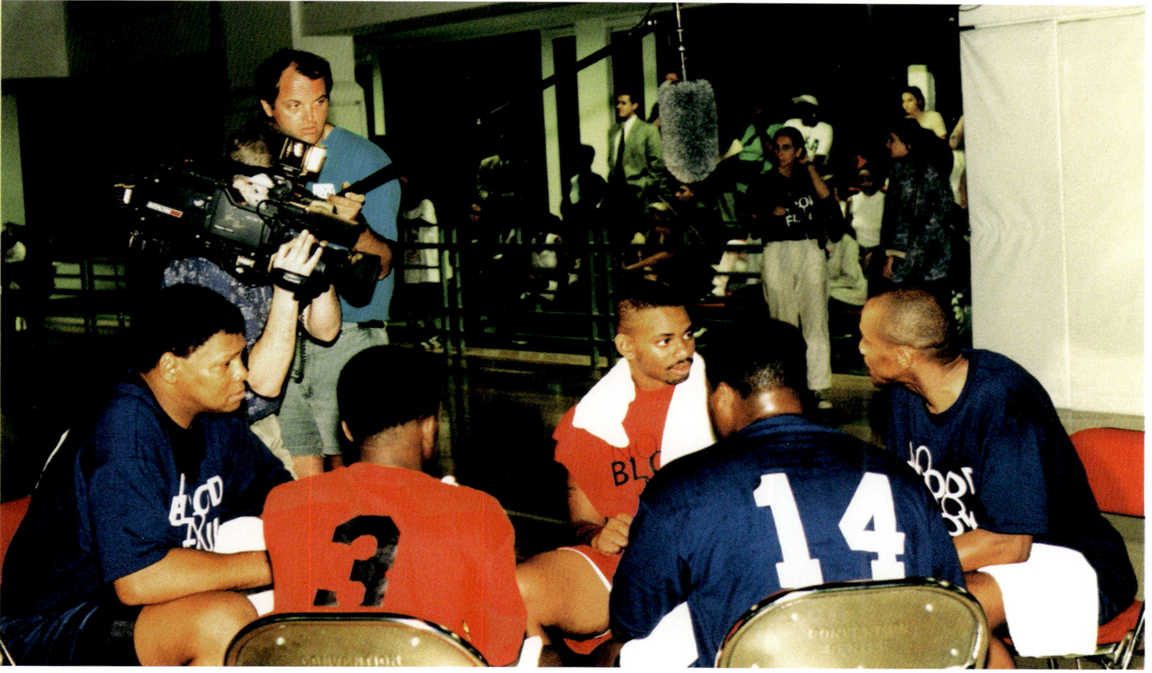

Suzanne Lacy's provocative documentary . . . employs the street basketball metaphor that fouls can't be called unless there's blood. The video begins with statistics (25 percent of Oakland youth live in poverty; homicide is the leading cause of death). . . . The consensus held that teenagers (who then comprised one-fourth of the city's homicides and violent crime arrests) were a "problem to be fixed" via policy initiatives. . . . In hindsight, we now know 1990s approaches (both crackdowns and initiatives) founded in the "problem" view of youth had little effect. . . . However, after Oakland's 2006 murder peak, profound change occurred. Among teens under age twenty, murders fell by 70 percent to below one-tenth of the city's total. . . . A 2018 update of *No Blood/No Foul* is badly needed to illuminate a bold new frame of youth in ways art, language, social science, and politics do not yet imagine: as assets and leaders, not fearsome objects of urban apocalypse.

—Mike Males, senior research fellow, Center on Juvenile and Criminal Justice, 2018

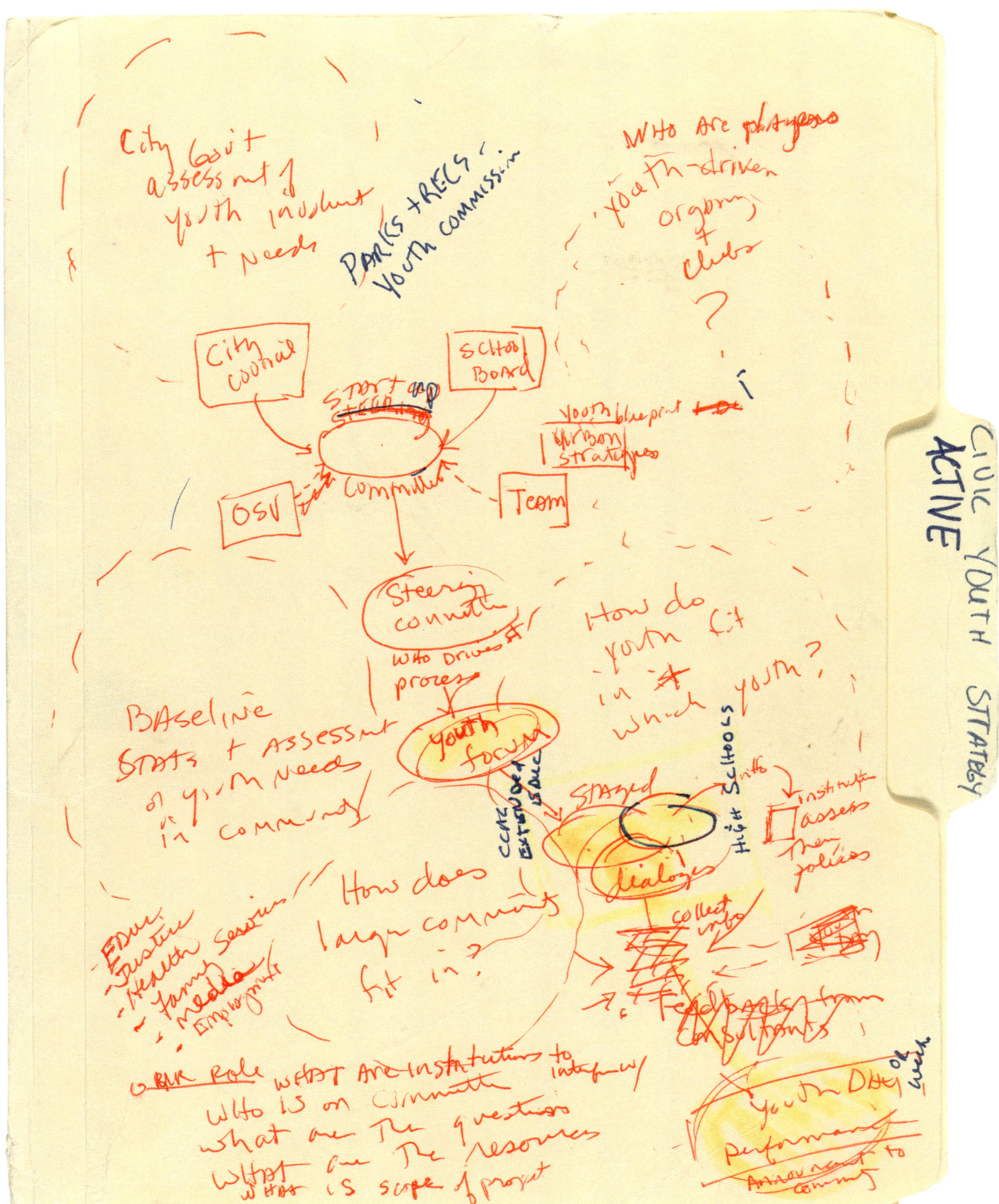
City Gov't assess mt of youth involvmt + Needs
PARKS + RECS / YOUTH COMMISSION
WHo Are players
youth-driven orgns + clubs ?
City Council
School Board
Start up Steering
youth blueprint
Urban Strategies
OSV
Committee
Team
Steering committee
WHo Drives process
BASELINE Stats + Assessmt of youth Needs in community
Youth Forum
How do youth fit in & which youth?
CCNC Extended Issues
Staged
High Schools
institute assess then policies
dialogues
collect info
- Educ
- Justice
- Health Services
- Family
- Media
- Employmt
How does large community fit in?
feedbacks from consultants
OUR ROLE WHAT Are Institutions to interview
WHo is on Committee
what are The questions
what are The resources
What is scope of project
youth Day
performances
Announcemt to community

CIVIC YOUTH STRATEGY ACTIVE

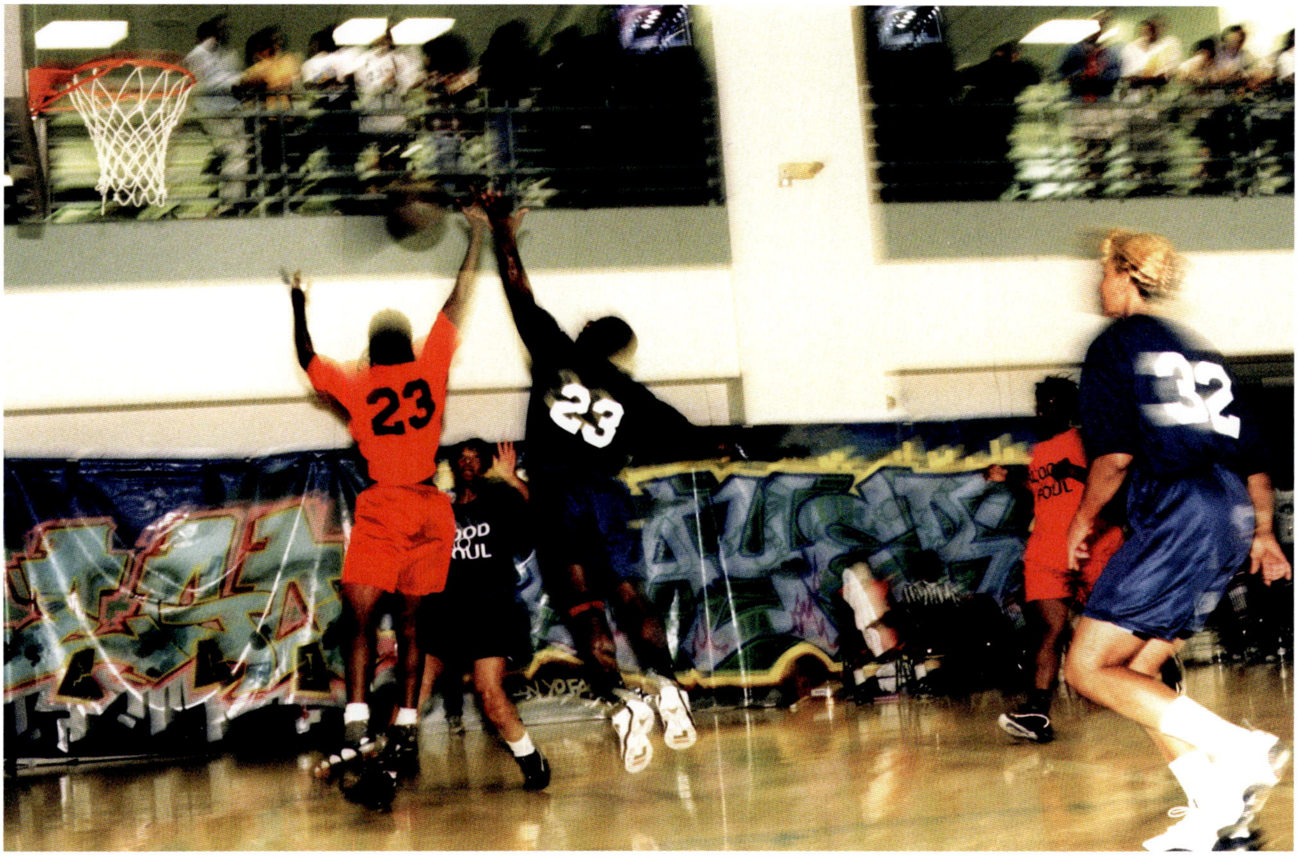

23
23
32

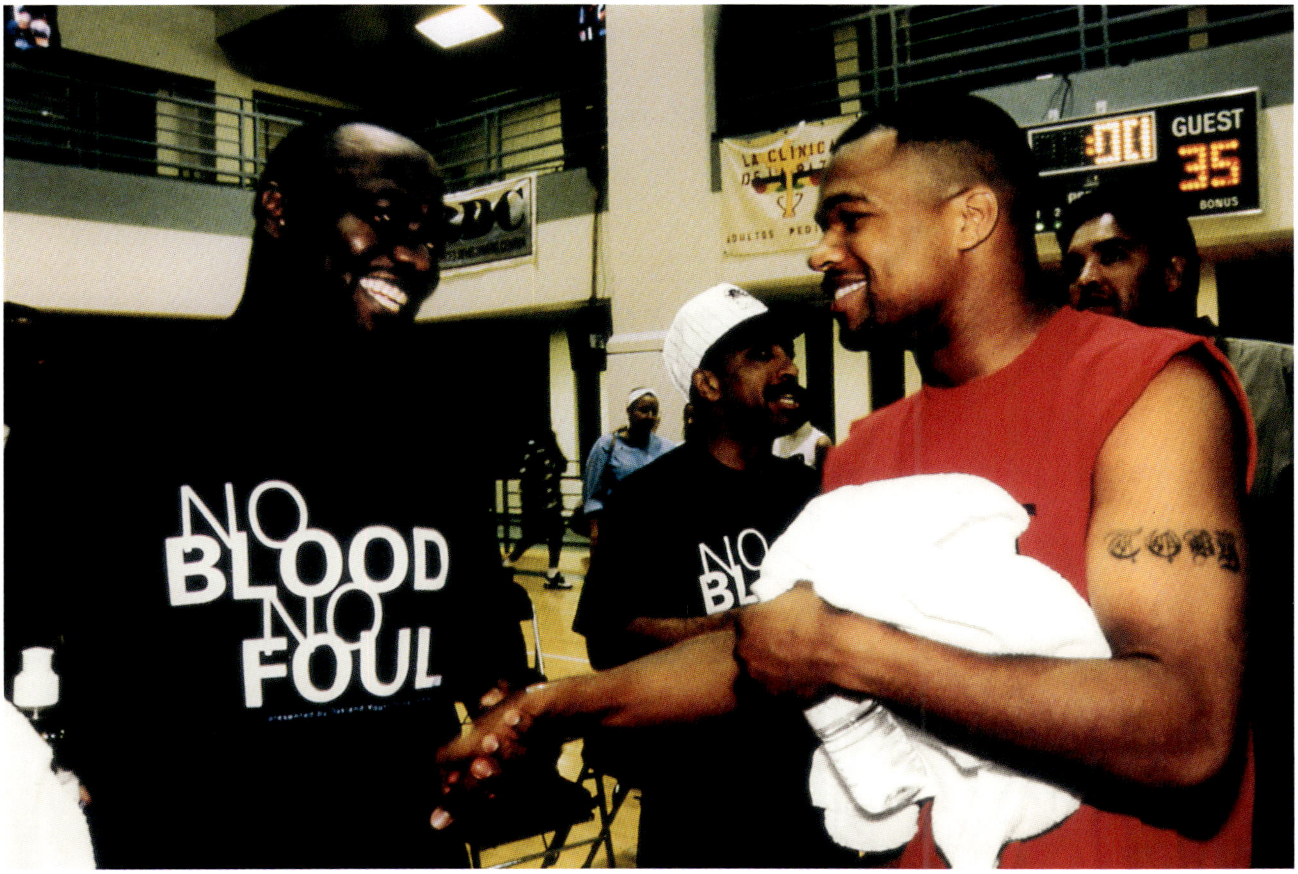

NO
BLOOD
NO
FOUL
GUEST
35
BONUS

Structure

ADVISORY Committee
role: ADVICE + support

AD Hoc planning group
role:
• plan to plan
• set agendas

Planning Council
role:
• identify stakeholders
• guide process
• define issues
• recommend policy

administrative team
media consultant
fundraising committee
tracking coordinator
writing policy

TASK FORCES:

MEDIA, ART, Commun.
role:
• convene youth forum
• plan Media campaign
• involve community
• generate information for task forces
• create staged dialogues

ISSUES:
EDUC
Health
Crimin Just.
Employ ment
Family
Citizen ship + represent ation

role:
• identify issues
• gather background info
• make recommendations
• work w/ media/art/comm task force to identify teen + community leaders for staged dialogues
• work w/ evaluation to create on-going methods to measure success in their areas
• generate series of "good ideas" for later implementation
• develop implementation plan

EVAL- UATION
role:
• create methods to evaluate success, during + after the process

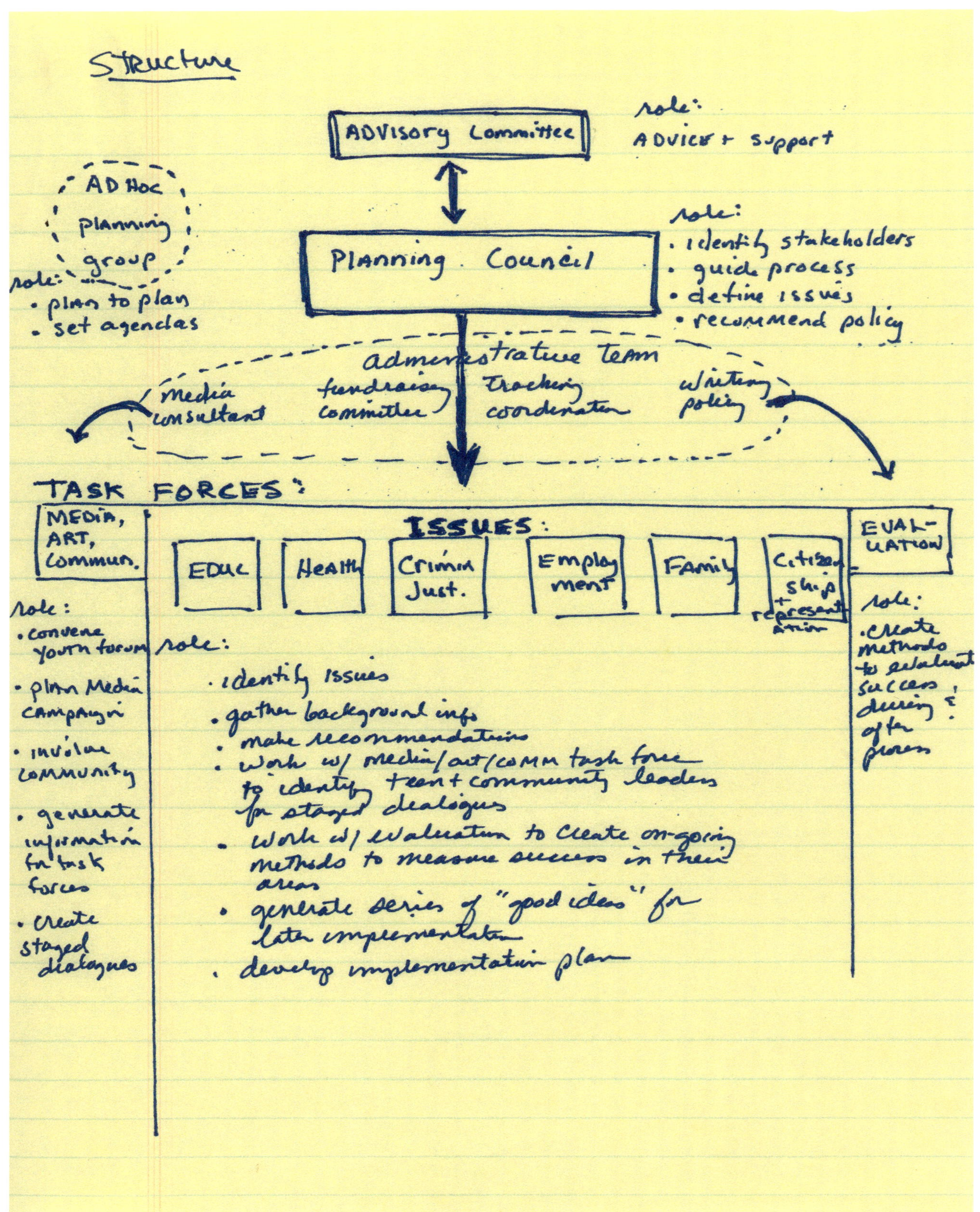

If I had to give an overview of the state of youth in Oakland, what I would say is that we're at a very interesting pcint of sort of chaos and opportunity. A lot of what has happened to young people in this city and around the country is that . . . young people have really been very low on the public agenda, that we tend to only think about young people as problems to be fixed, that we don't think of young people as the assets that they really are.

—Gregory Hodge, executive director, Oakland Urban Strategies Council, 1996

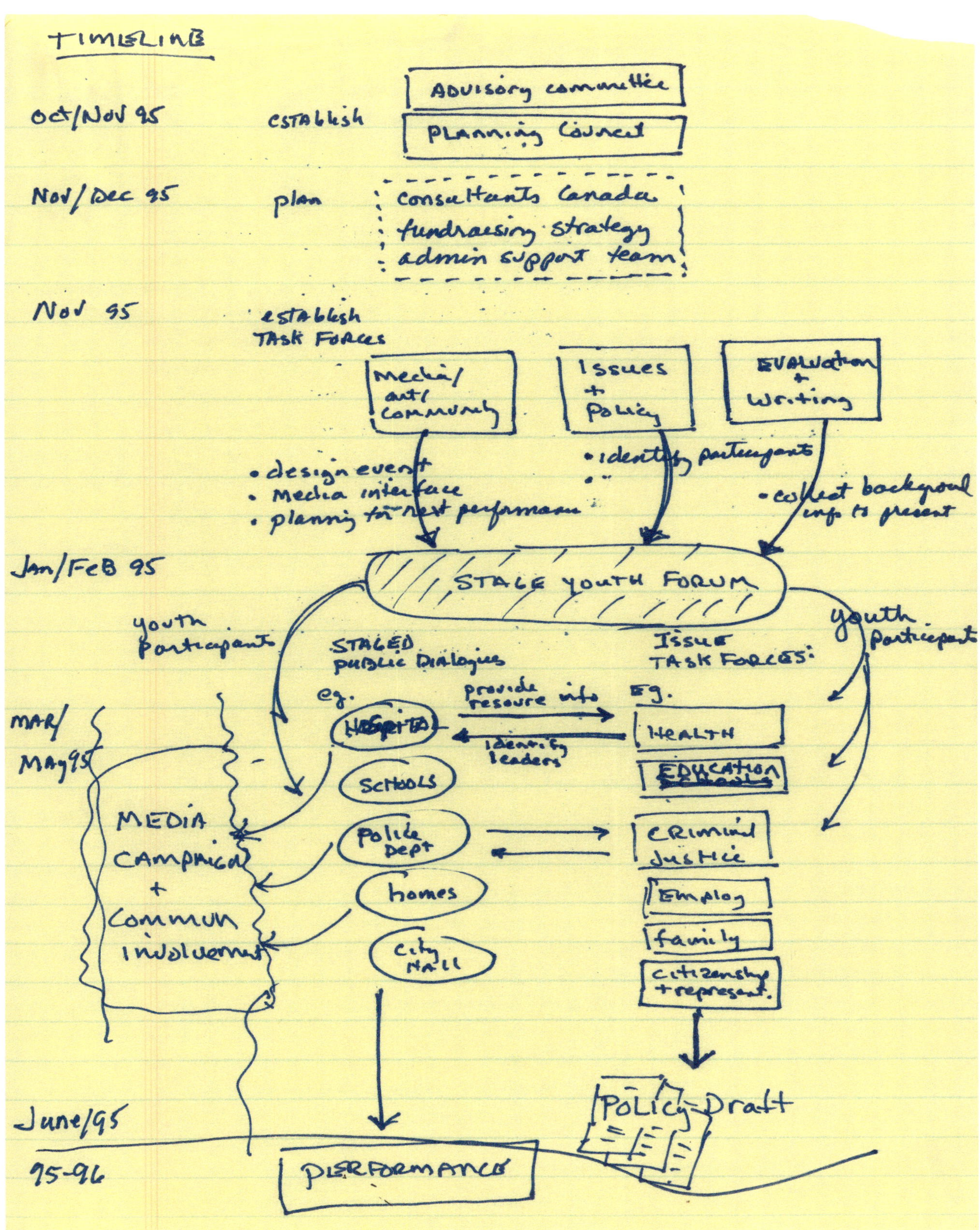

WILLIAM WONG

Cops lose by 30 points — and win

Oakland

HOOPS BEING a city sport, a pickup basketball game in Oakland is no big deal.

But last week, on the hardwood indoor court of a local health club, there was something special about one particular game.

It began with a warm-up shootout between Oakland Mayor Elihu Harris and Oakland City Council member Sheila Jordan. She outgunned the mayor, three baskets to one. And she did it in her dress and heels.

Then there were TV monitors ringing the court, at courtside and along a second-level balcony.

Finally, there were the players themselves. One team, wearing red, was composed of sleek young men and women. The other side wore blue, but some showed considerable paunches and gimpy knees.

The game was no contest. The reds ("Da Rebels") swept past the blues ("Da Rollers") easily, by almost 30 points.

It wasn't really fair, but it was fun. The blues were Oakland police officers, and the reds were young devotees of the city's Midnight Basketball League.

Usually, in Oakland and other cities, it's cops vs. kids on the

William Wong is an independent journalist and Examiner columnist.

streets, in one another's faces, angry, taunting, tense and sometimes violent.

This time, cops and kids were on stage together, playing a real game that was part of an innovative performance art piece. They did so to introduce a new city youth policy and to illustrate the possibility of antagonists finding less confrontational ways of dealing with one another.

The game's rules changed several times. In one quarter, with no referees, the players called fouls on each other. In another, the fans voted on whether a foul took place.

During breaks, the TV monitors rolled videotape of kids and cops expressing honest feelings about each other. They also showed grim statistics about youth afflictions.

The performance art game was designed by Suzanne Lacy, dean of fine arts at the California College of Arts and Crafts in Oakland.

She was also the visionary behind another creative performance art piece, "The Roof Is on Fire," where young people sat in automobiles discussing their problems while adults listened in.

Lacy and her adult and youth collaborators also produced a 20-minute film, "Youth, Cops and Videotape," that brought together teenagers and Oakland police officers.

At first, the two sides were angry and resentful. At the end of the six two-hour sessions, barriers fell.

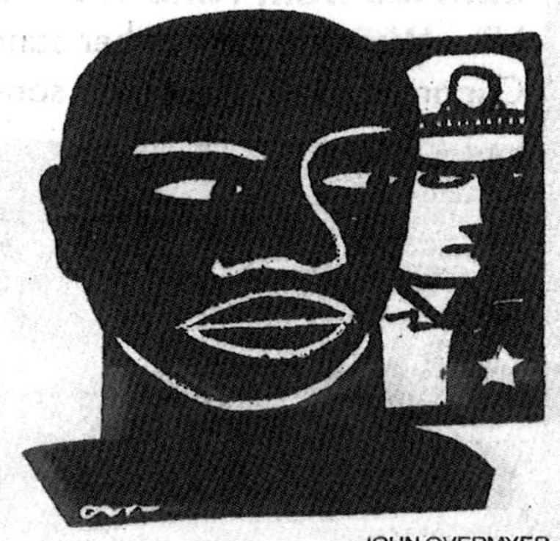

JOHN OVERMYER

Some participants have become friends. The videotape is being used in police training.

The whole idea behind these artistic endeavors is to tackle a seemingly intractable problem using a wildly unconventional approach. The endgame here is to break down stereotypes that cops and kids have of one another.

The hope for the new youth policy, spearheaded by Jordan, is that it will supplement a heavy-handed law-enforcement approach with more official attention and resources on Oakland youngsters.

A pickup basketball game, a videotape and a bunch of words on a new policy won't magically transform hostilities between cops and kids in Oakland. But they can help.

One police officer in the video project, Jeff Israel, was skeptical until he heard the kids' side about sometimes being hassled by men in blue.

After the pickup game last week, opposing players huddled in circles. They agreed they should play each other again because basketball, at least, wasn't the usual kind of interaction they had with one another.

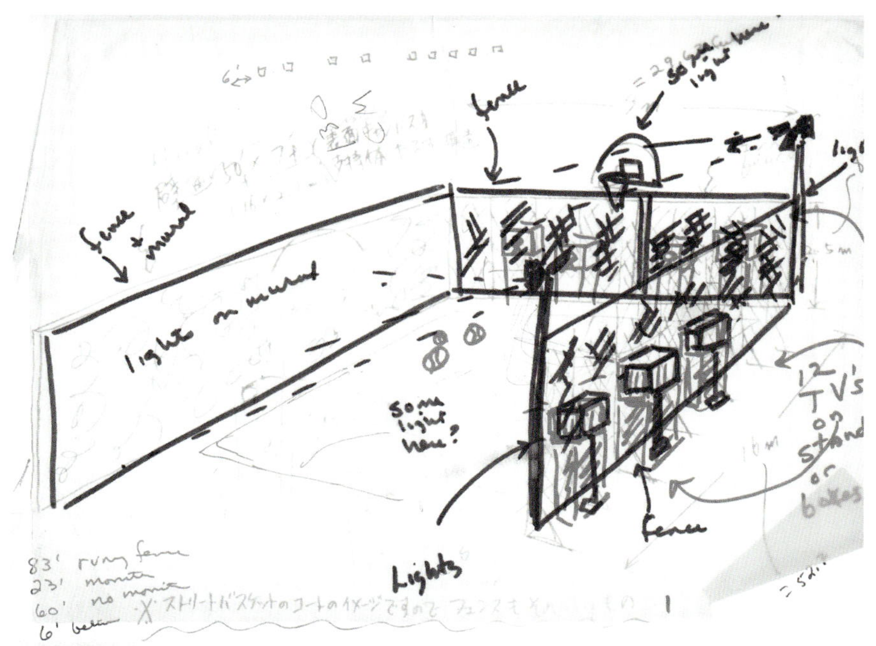

Lacy reimagined *No Blood/No Foul* as an installation for *Atopic Site*, an exhibition of work by international conceptual and installation artists, Tokyo Big Sight, August 1–25, 1996. She created a basketball court surrounded by graffiti murals and video interviews with police and teens, subtitled in Japanese. The installation also included a discussion, led by Unique Holland, with Japanese youth about conflicts between youth and adults. A sketch and the realized installation are seen here.

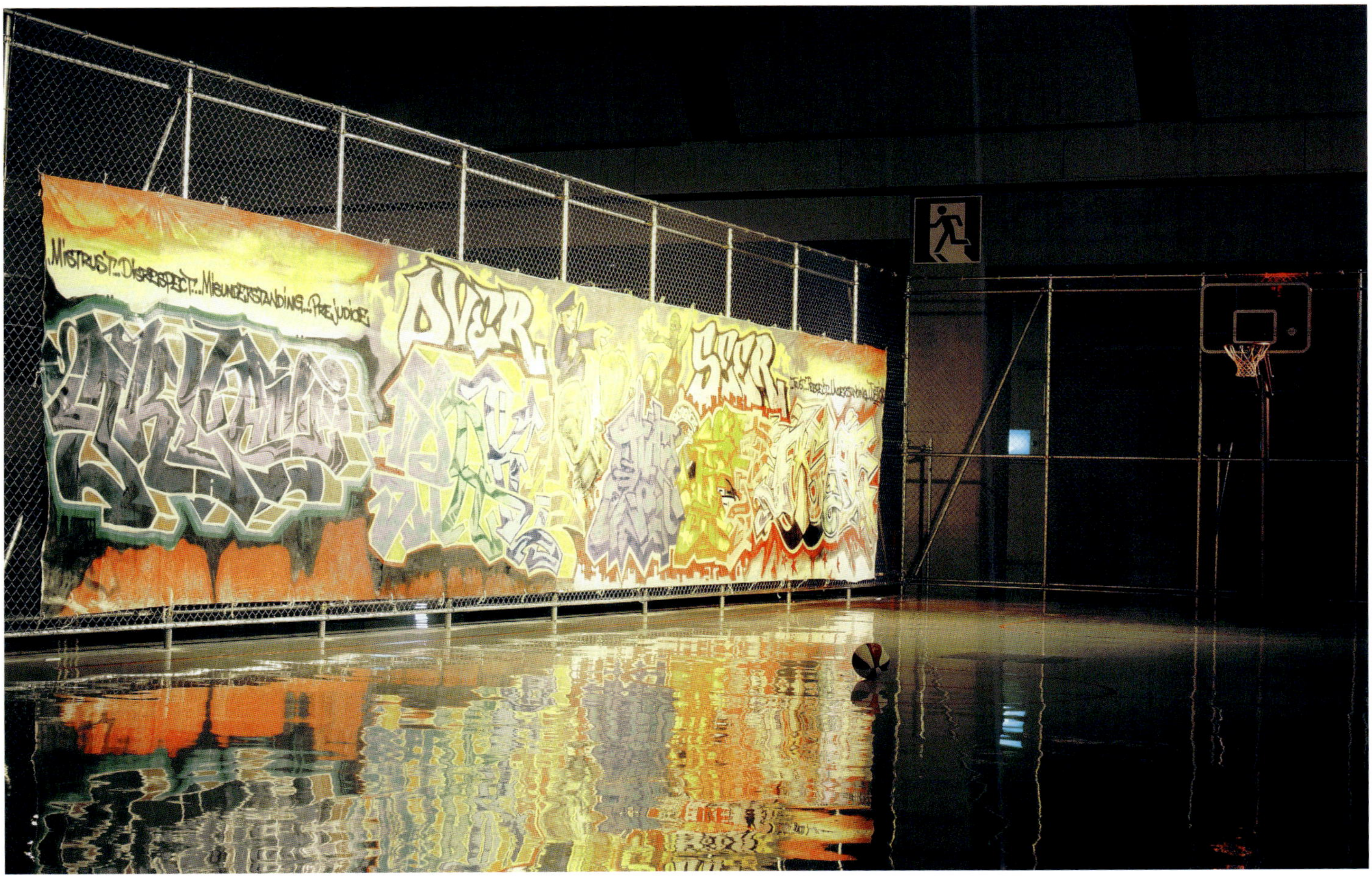

Expectations (1996–97)

SUZANNE LACY WITH LESLIE BECKER, LISA FINDLEY, AMANA HARRIS, LEUCKESSIA HIRSH, UNIQUE HOLLAND, ANNICE JACOBY, SHEILA JORDAN, AND MAXINE WYMAN

Expectations explored a spectrum of issues related to teen pregnancy through a summer art course for thirty-two pregnant and parenting teenagers, an installation, a symposium, and policy work. The class covered a different theme each week—autobiography, health care, relationships, employment and education goals, and public policy—and offered childcare, transportation, lunches, stipends, school credit, and instruction by professional artists. The graduation ceremony included commendations and speeches by local officials.

Fifteen students subsequently enrolled in an internship to create an exhibition at San Francisco's Capp Street Project. The installation comprised drawings of their experiences of pregnancy and a twelve-foot-high crib designed by Findley. Inside the crib, a disordered classroom was piled with desks containing clay sculptures by the teens. A large television featured California governor Pete Wilson's State of the State Address excoriating teen pregnancy, while student Asha Zitani's rebuttal played on a smaller television. A video and sound collages by Holland completed the collective narrative.

Finally, Alameda County Public Health Department director Arnold X. C. Perkins moderated a symposium where the young women spoke with health care providers, educators, and policy makers. Wyman and Becker worked with a team of the teens to create a poster of their writings and drawings to send to leaders throughout the state.

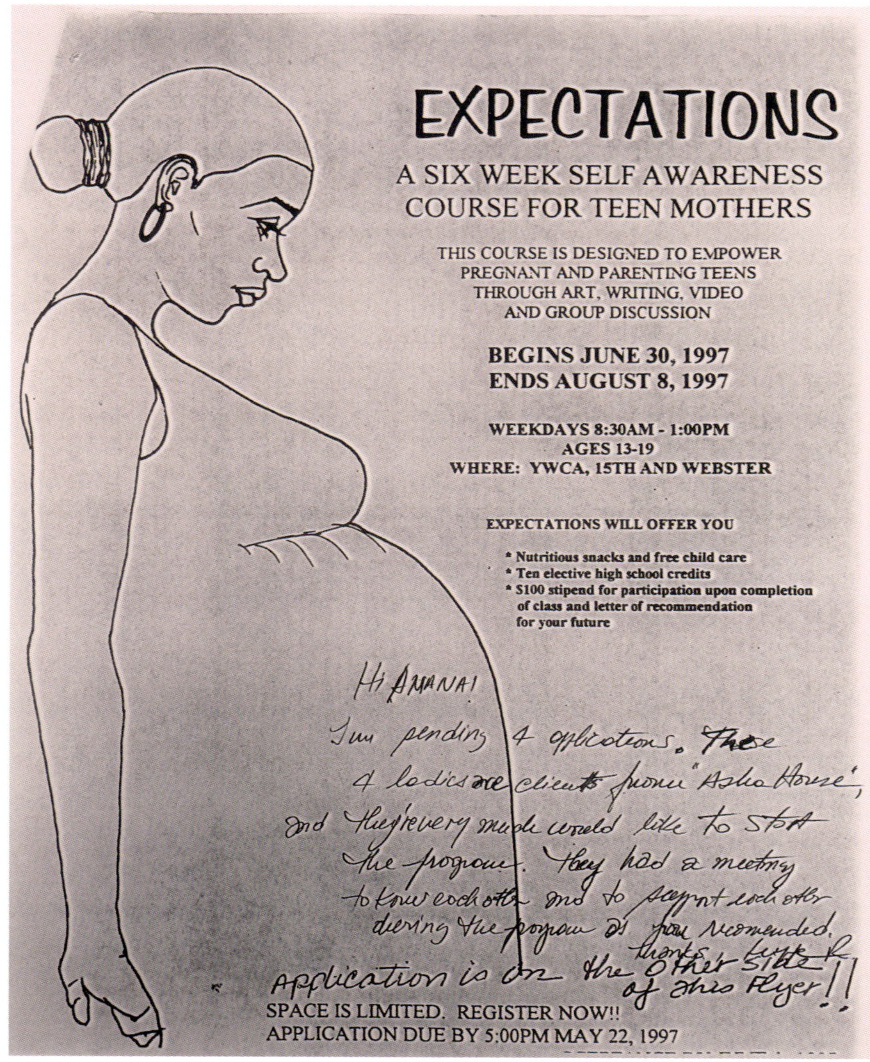

One thing people were really concerned about was that the girls began to share these very personal stories, and they felt like, "Oh my God, they're talking about this, and what's going to happen from now, and are we going to do this and are we going to do that? Yada yada yada." And I think we even had some of these conversations, but I also felt like just the simple fact that these girls were in a space that they felt comfortable to even talk about these issues—people don't really recognize that when you speak about this in a group, that's validating what your experience has been, that that's therapy right there.

—Amana Harris, 2006

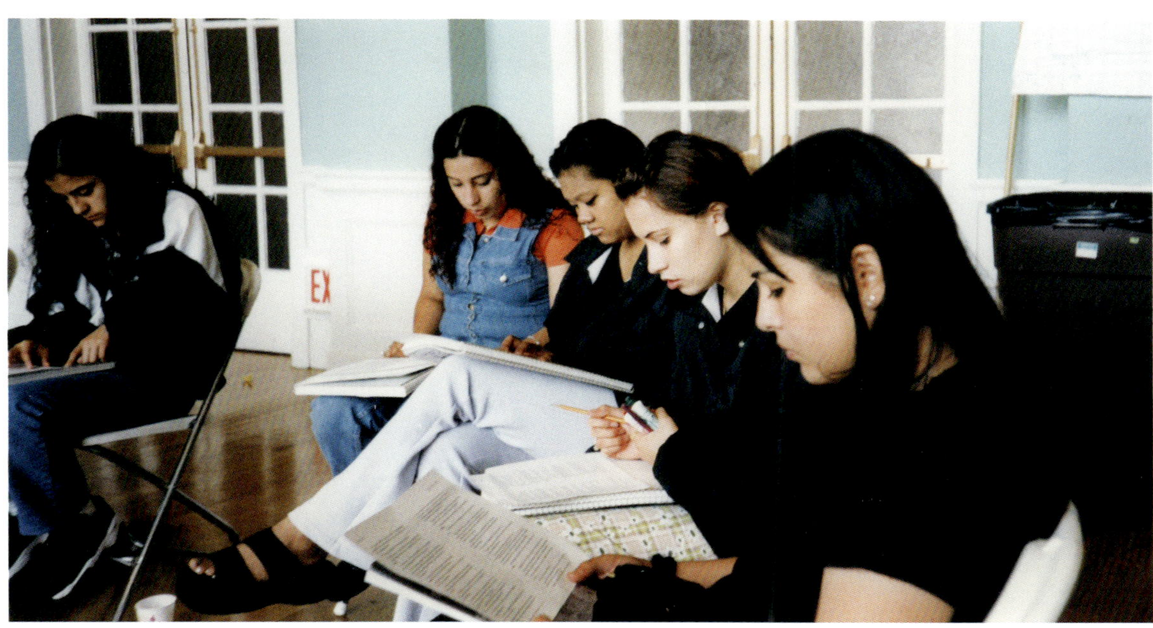

COURSE DESCRIPTION (EXCERPT)

This studio art class will look at your self identity, your relationships with those around you, your relationship with health and medicine, your goals and expectations, and your roles and ideas with respect to social issues. We will talk about these subjects and develop art projects that express your opinions and feelings.

In each study block, you will consider [and] discuss the issues below, and then do class assignments in drawing, writing, sculpture, and videotape. The artworks you create from these assignments will be used for the September art installations in San Francisco and Oakland.

STUDY BLOCK 1: YOURSELF AND YOUR AUTOBIOGRAPHY

SENSE OF SELF — What are social expectations of young women's potential and what opportunities are there for their future? Does having a child constitute a significant barrier to your development? Did/will having a baby [a]ffect your identity?

HOPES AND DREAMS — What do you hope will become of your life? What are your dreams? Who will you be at forty? What do you hope for your children? What are your career goals? How will you support yourself, your children?

PREGNANCY — How did you get pregnant? How do your bodies express your sense of self? What changes (is changing) with pregnancy? How will (or did) childbirth feel? How will mothering [a]ffect your life, and your body?

STUDY BLOCK 2: HEALTH CARE

WHOSE BODY? — Who is making the decisions about your body, the ones that dictate the shape of your lives? How do you make your choices about your body, your health, your future? What [are the] public policies and opinions, for example on abortion, teenagers, and welfare, that [a]ffect your life? Who has the final say on what happens to your body?

SEX EDUCATION IN HIGH SCHOOL — Do young women have accurate information about sexuality and childbirth? What do you remember about sex education classes, and do these play a role in preventing unwanted pregnancy? How informed are you about sexually transmitted diseases, and once informed, has it [a]ffected your behavior?

MEDICAL SYSTEM — What is the quality of support for pregnant teens, from the medical establishment? What is the relationship between teen pregnancy and sex education, contraceptive availability, and abortion availability?

TOP: Students creating family tree mobiles with Wyman (far left) and Julie Caffey (far right)

BOTTOM: Collaborative sculptures by students showing scenes from the worlds they would like to inhabit in five years

RIGHT: Poster by Becker and Wyman displaying student drawings and poems, created for the exhibition *Expectations*, Capp Street Project, San Francisco, September 6–27, 1997

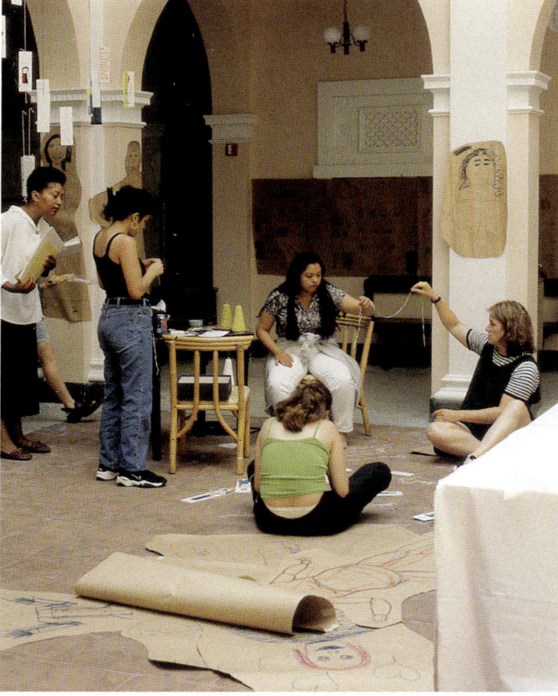

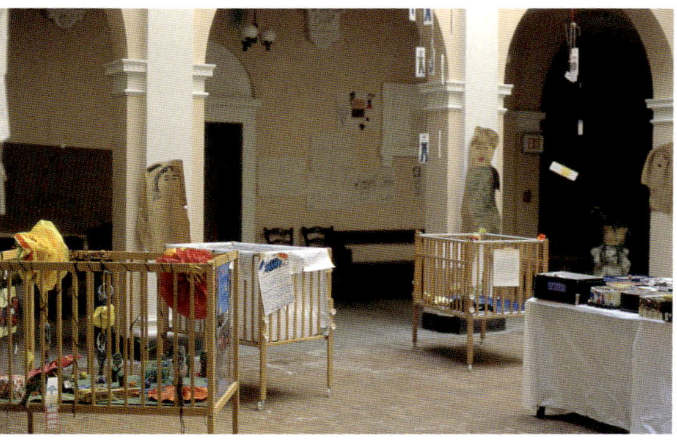

Expectations is a collaborative art proje[ct]

Now, it seems, young parents are being assigned the responsibility for society's failures.
Kristin Luker, "Dubious Conceptions: The Politics of Teenage Pregnancy"

ASIAN FINN   CHRISTINA GADSON   ASHA ZITANI   ALMA MARQUEZ   BLANCA RODRIGU[EZ]

COLLABORATORS/ARTISTS → SUZANNE LACY PROJECT DIRECTOR, UNIQUE HOLLAND SOUND AN[D]

For six weeks in the summer of '97, a group of 36 young women participated in a summer school class at the Oakland YWCA, designed specifically to support self expression and focus on who they are and who they can be.

I love lots of things but one thing I love most is my baby. He's always with me, I'm never alone. He always gives me a smile when I'm sad or mad I get happy when he sees me in the morning he just wakes up with a smile on his face I loved him so much when I didn't know how he looked when he was in my stomach I can just feel the bond between me and him and I love my mom, dad, sister and my boyfriend same way I love my baby.

Welfare doesn't make you comfortable
Doesn't give you love
Doesn't provide for all families needs
You can't make extra money and be legit
You are not idle
Welfare is not easy to get, and many get no help
Not all single mothers are on welfare
Most women on welfare do not stay on welfare it is a start
Not all unmarried mothers need assistance
Not all fatherless homes are the result of unwed mothers
Fatherless children are not always behind bars

I am

I am a tad bit over the limit.
I am a weeping willow blowing in the [wind]
I am a red hot chili pepper that burns t[he]
I am as pretty as a plum that hangs fro[m]

I am a woman with **determination an[d]**

I am a mother.
I am, I am, I am.

I a[m]

STUDENTS: LAURA CUTRER LE CRESHA DUDLEY

I loved and don't know if I still love him. I loved his way of being when he acted normally), I loved his muscles I loved the writings in his body. I loved his hand moving around me. I loved his face when he was asleep I used to kiss without him ever knowing. I love his color, some shades darker than mine, which made him look so manly I loved his lips that ate me with a kiss. I loved his eyes in which really deep down I would see his soul and feelings. I love when he loved me. I loved those instant moments that will last a lifetime. I loved his age. I love the love that was there.

I'm going to see you later, I love you

Bye Daddy

CRYSTAL JEFFERSON   NAI SACCHAO   KENISHA SIMS   JENNIFER SALAZAR

It's the 90's!!! I know when you were young most people got married before they had kids. I'm not saying every one should have kids at an early age or before they are married, but it's a personal thing not a law.

"Fifty years ago, the incidence of out-of-wedlock births was 1 in 15. Today, it's 1 in 3."
Governor Pete Wilson

"And, Governor Pete Wilson

I found your State of the State Address very disrespectful and ignorant. When you implied that "out of wedlock births are the cause of increased public spending for health care for the poor, police protection, drug and alcohol rehabilitation, criminal courts, prisons, probation and parole supervision". This is absurd, just because I am not living in the luxuries of money, does not mean I, or other teen mothers, will ever become delinquents, or abuse drugs or alcohol in any shape or form.

You say "we must insist that individuals on welfare meet the same standards of responsibility, accountability, and decency as do working families". This is very offensive, just because I and others are poor or on welfare definitely does not mean that I don't have responsibilities or that I am not "decent". I work extremely hard as do other poor "welfare families," because I have the biggest responsibility— that of raising the next generation, raising the future. Being a mother takes so much strength and energy. I am on call 24 hours a day, 7 days a week being a teacher 24/7, doctor 24/7, nurturer 24/7, provider 24/7, protector 24/7 and the list goes on.

I would also like to raise the point about you wanting "taxpayers no longer subsiding idleness or promiscuity, and no longer suffer when illegitimacy hatches into social pathology." What does being on welfare have to do with idleness or promiscuity? There are some poor people on welfare who are promiscuous and there are also rich politicians who are promiscuous. You are complaining about more public spending going to criminal courts, prisons and police protection and blaming it all on children living in

I think you need to reevaluate your double standard perceptions.

Governor Pete Wilson's 1997 State

of course, as out-of-wedlock births have increased, so has public spending — massively — for health care for the poor, for police protection, for drug and alcohol rehabilitation, for criminal courts, for prisions, probation and parole supervision."

TAULONA GLASS   JAKKIE STONEWALL   STACY AYUYU   CHRISTINA ANDRADE

TAMSIN DILLON SYMPOSIUM COORDINATION,   JILLIAN PURYEAR PRODUCTION ASSISTANCE

In the recent public focus on tee[n]
obscures their identities, and the[ir]

Fo[r]

it's a personal thing not a law.

he moment that I knew I was pregnant with my first child
didn't feel anything wrong with my body but my boyfriend
as getting sick and he felt everything. I knew because I
issed my menstruation and I was wondering what I was

going to do. I always wanted a baby of my own, because there is nothing like being a mother. A friend will let you baby-sit but they will soon want their child. I don't believe in abortions so that was really out of the question. I was

also thinking about adoption, but on TV everyday I see people struggle, parents trying to find their children and children parents. I couldn't live with knowing my baby was with some family that I didn't know or care about.

RODRIGUEZ SHANIDA SCOTT JAMIA SHUTTLEWORTH   ROSELENE ALPHONSE MIRANDA BOSTON DENA GOSS RISHANI HOWELL MIKA ROBERSON SHANIEA RODGERS

SA FINDLEY INSTALLATION DESIGN, SHEILA JORDAN COURSE DESIGN AND LIAISON WITH ALAMEDA COUNTY OFFICE OF EDUCATION, MAXINE WYMAN BROADSHEET PUBLICATION EDITOR, ANNICE JACOBY

I knew before I took the pregnancy test. I just had a feeling.
hy? Because my period was late. I had morning sickness, and I was
aving unprotected sex with my boyfriend. I think I knew all along
at I was going to get pregnant. It was like my son's spirit was
nging to come to me. It was meant to be. If I didn't want to get
regnant, I would have had protected sex, and so would have his
ther. We didn't talk about having a child, but mentally I think we
oth knew what we were doing.

Once that mission was accomplished, I felt scared happy.
ared to tell my Mom. I didn't want her to feel like I let her down, or
didn't have my priorities straight, even though I didn't. I also felt
cited. Excited for my future excited to tell my baby's dad. Happy
ecause now I am sure I could conceive children.

Dear Colleges, Child Care Providers, Future Employers, and Society,

We are trying to survive this rough life, but it is hard. I am in high school right now, but I would like to go to college. For me to go to college I need scholarships and grants. **I plan to become a psychiatrist.** I feel I can help people with their problems. I want to have a great support system for my daughter, instead of being 35 years-old and on welfare.

I am a pregnant high school graduate. When my baby gets here I will need help with child care on a regular basis in order to continue going to classes at the college of my choice. **I do not want a small thing like child care to hold me back from getting the education I deserve.**

I have worked very hard on my education. One day I hope to get a well paying job in order to save money for my son to go to college. I am not a bad person. I did not commit a crime, but just became a mother. **I know I can succeed.**

We are still human beings. We just need a little help and support.

Sincerely,

Never have [young women and their babies] needed help more, yet never have Americans been less willing to help and more willing to blame.
Kristen Luker, "Dubious Conceptions: The Politics of Teenage Pregnancy"

Americans seem bent on making the lives of teenage parents and their children even harder than they already are.
Kristen Luker, "Dubious Conceptions: The Politics of Teenage Pregnancy"

first 6 months

What I have experienced in the other room is some funny movement. When all of us were closing our eyes, I felt like I was locked inside of a box. It was dark and it seems like even though you open your eyes there will only be darkness.

ze.
he man who eats me.
blossomed plum tree.

ngths.

ird with *blue wings, and pink body that goes out into* the night of my dream place.

When I found out I was Pregnant
Oh toilet seat let me hold you
And turn inside out the rumble in my tummy
The food rising through my throat and into the toilet
For some reason everything
revolved around sandwiches with pickles
I knew I was pregnant.

Bueno yo voy acci madre para mi eso no me perfudica esto me a cambiado mi vida e comprendido que la vide es muy importante. Me siento diferente por que aora soy una persona madura pro que me voy a dedicar a mi bebe esto me separa de muchas cosas pero para mi esta bien por que no en este mundo no encuentra nada bueno.

Mi embarazo no menace sentir mal con las personas, este me cambio much y debo de cuidar mi vida y la de me bebe. Quiero trabaja y estudiar porque quier ser alquien en esta vida.

I am a flower.

Ordinary like a flower, but if one goes to a flower and sees something beautiful like there is in me, that flower becomes special. Reserved because I don't share my thoughts with other people. Aimee is the name should have had, it's perfect for me as a flower.

the night of my dream place.
Everything that I've always longed for.

I am a drop of liquid in a sea of liquid humans.
I am a precious jewel of little value compared
to others. I am ordinary waiting to burst
some day and not be what everybody is. I
am tired of everyday routines.

AKILAH ASKEW LAMEEKA GUARD SHAKEISHA LAVENDER TOMIKA MEANS TINISHA WHISENTON DANIELLE DERDEN TIFFANY SOLIS LAURNECIA FULTON CHASSITY HARRIS ALICIA SINGLETON

CONCEPTUAL AND MEDIA DESIGN, LESLIE BECKER GRAPHIC DESIGN, AMANA HARRIS TEACHER FOR EXPECTATIONS CLASS, LEUCKESSIA HORSE TEACHING ASSISTANT AND COORDINATOR OF THE SPEAKER'S SERIES, LEAH BRODER TEACHING ASSISTANT

I HATE
I hate the way people judge others.
I hate the way people always have something negative to say
about those who doen't have more and those who do
I hate the way my baby's father tries to control me.
I hate the way Mary had a little lamb.
I hate the way my boyfriend talks.
I hate the hate.
I hate it when on Christmas you ask for a pair of Jordans
And you get a pair of socks instead.
I hate the way I curse
I hate that I can't find a good boyfriend that I really like.
I hate that I live in hell on earth.

reconsider your attitude, and open your eyes. Just because our lifestyles are very different does not mean you are better than me.

Yours sincerely,

To all the people that supported me, like I.L.S.P., my group home, my grandmother, my baby's father, my baby's godmother:

I just want to thank all of them for being there with me and the baby.

Much Love,

n I can plan my *future and complete it.*

Getting my NST (Non Stress

UE CAFFEY TEACHING ASSISTANT, CLEO EVANS TEACHING ASSISTANT AND INSTALLATION ASSISTANCE, MORGAN BARNARD SOUND A

BRODER TEACHING ASSISTANT, SARAH HUGHES TEACHING ASSISTANT, BLUE CAFFEY

egnancy, the scapegoating of young people often blems they face.

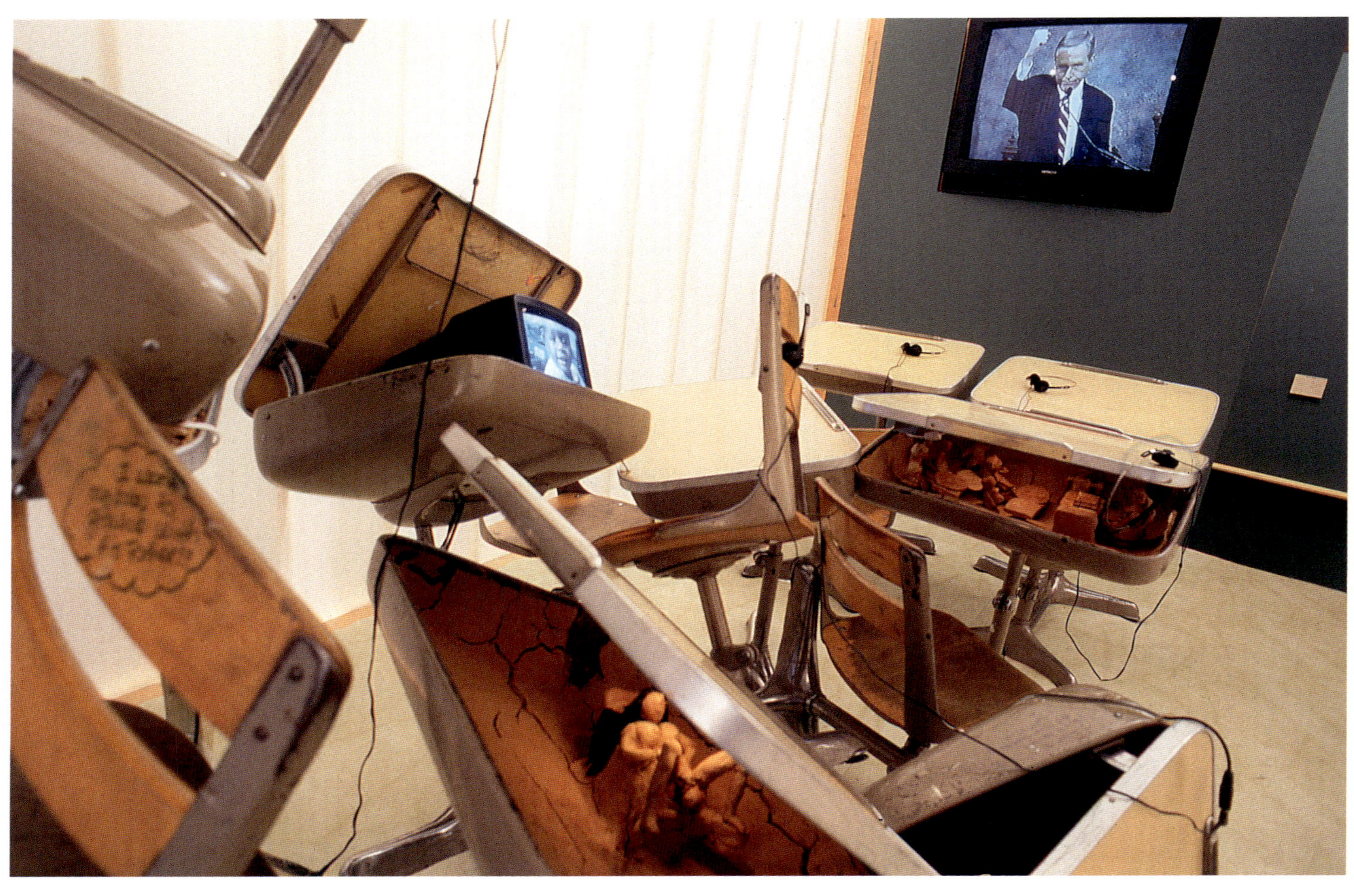

The crib was larger than life, and that blew things up in a way that caused you to see it and caused you to confront some of what's going on in you and what's going on in [your] community. During that period of time, we had a spate of teen pregnancies. A lot of young women [had] the whole notion of "having something of my own." That's a hell of a way to have something of your own, is having a baby. Because it's not a thing that you can just give away. It's something that you have to deal with. So I thought [the crib] brought that to the fore. It also helped members of the community, [through] the art, to understand what some of these women really go through. It's not easy on them.
    —Arnold X. C. Perkins, 2006

Installation view, *Expectations*
OPPOSITE: Drawings by students

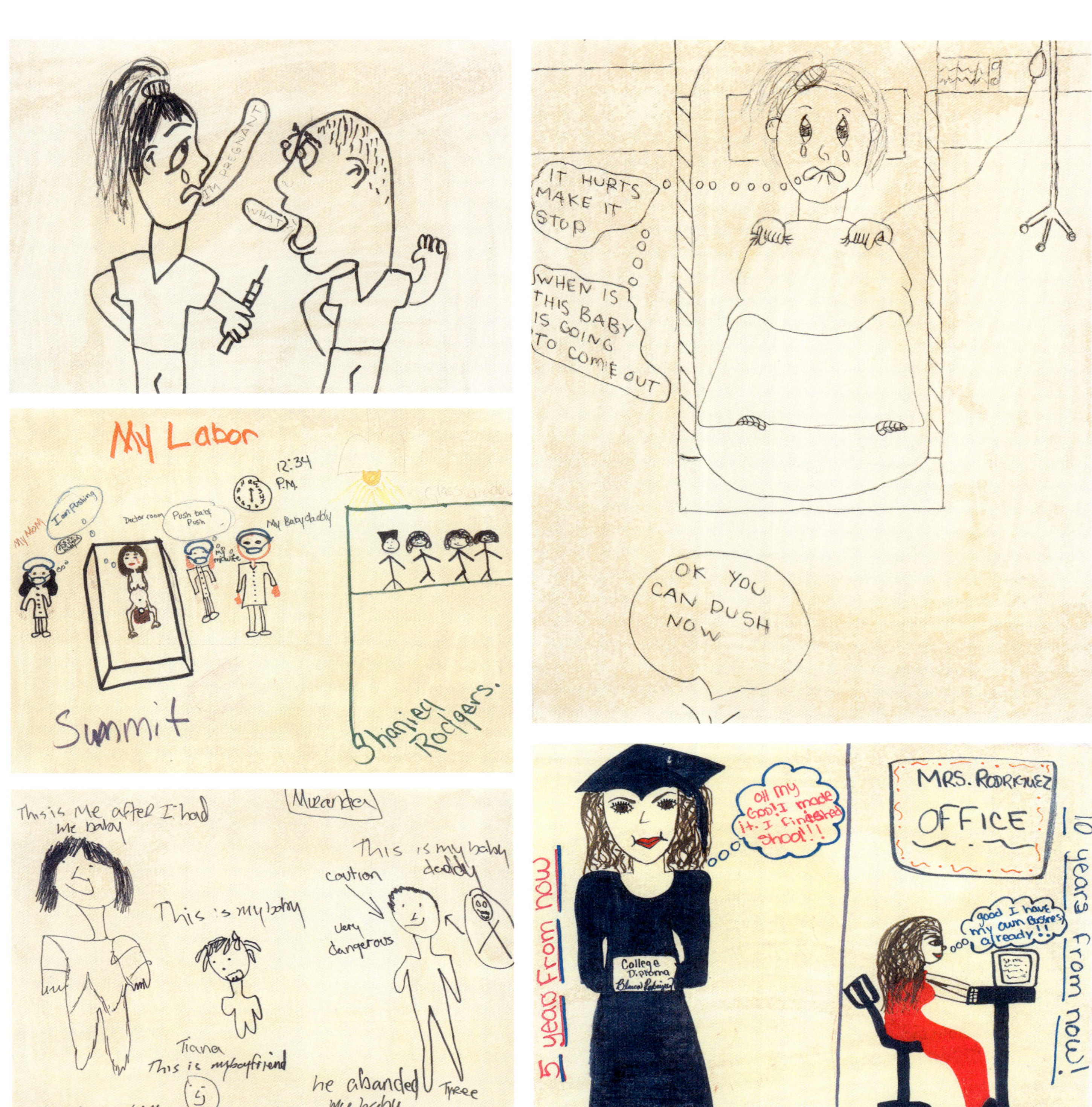

DASHKA SLATER, "NEW PROGRAM TEACHES YOUNG OAKLAND MOMS THE FINE ART OF FIGHTING BACK," *EAST BAY EXPRESS*, 1997 (EXCERPT)

The women looked at their family relationships, creat[ed] mobiles of their family tree, discussed issues like breast feeding, welfare reform, domestic violence, incest, and rape, and began setting educational and employment goals for themselves. . . . They sculpted worlds inside baby cribs that represented their own utopias. . . . [The] class has helped [Tiffany Solis] understand all that has happened to her, Solis says. "Through the self-portraits and the comic strips, I got to see myself, my story, through someone else's eyes. It took me a while to open up. Having to grow up so fast made me build up a wall inside me."

Code 33: Emergency, Clear the Air! (1997–99)

SUZANNE LACY, JULIO CÉSAR MORALES, AND UNIQUE HOLLAND

Named after the police radio code for "emergency, clear the radio waves," *Code 33* explored ways to reduce police hostility toward youth, foster teen participation in their communities, and promote a better understanding of young people's needs. It included a youth leadership team; a speakers bureau and community presentations; art workshops for youth from probation programs, high schools, and organizations; a prototype youth-police training session, aired on local television; and a media campaign, all involving more than one thousand teens. The three-year project drew national attention, engaging fierce opinions about forms of activism around youth, police, and the communities in which they interact.

A performance designed by teens and artists took place on October 7, 1999, with more than one hundred cars arranged in swaths of red, white, and black across the Oakland City Center West Garage rooftop. Videos by teens about Oakland neighborhoods played on thirty monitors as one thousand community members roamed among the cars, where two hundred fifty youth and police officers discussed crime, authority, power, and safety. After an hour of heated conversation—and despite a temporary interruption by Free Mumia protesters on the street below—forty teens replaced their white T-shirts with red and danced through the crowd. Spotlighted by a police helicopter, they led everyone down to a massive balcony where residents of eight neighborhoods sat on grass-covered platforms with picket fences—"front yards"—to discuss police-youth relations. Youth with cameras interviewed audience members, and people signed up for mentorship programs. Kim Batiste, Raúl Cabra, David Goldberg, Anne Maria Hardeman, and Patrick Toebe also contributed to the project.

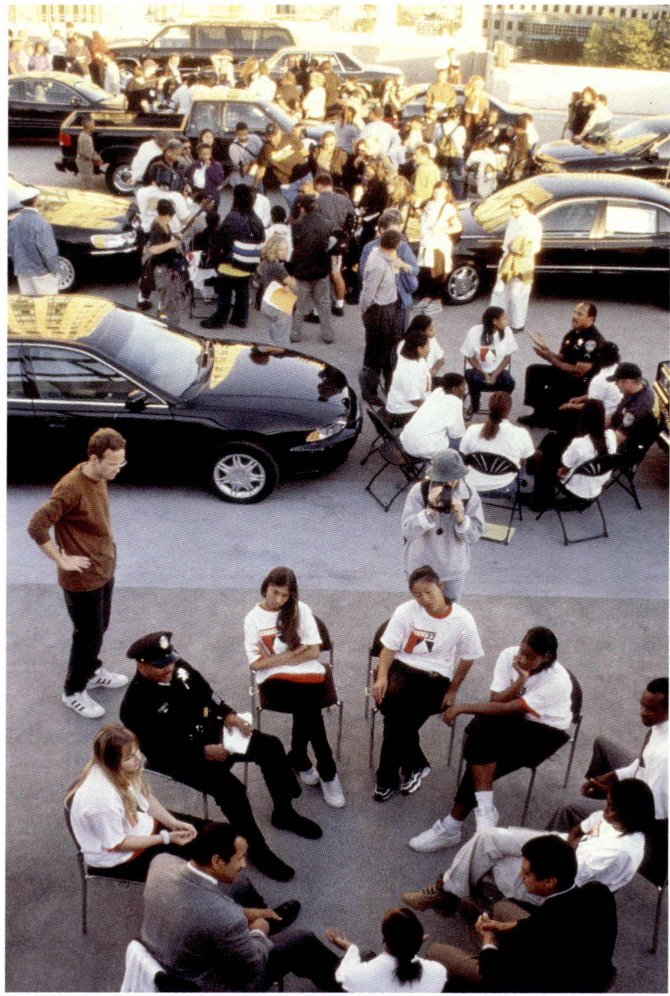

Part of what I think [was] created with *Code 33* and those conversations was a sense of personal power. . . . Young people got a chance to say something straight to a police officer who prior to that would have been seen as somebody they need[ed] to be afraid of, somebody that they couldn't talk to, somebody that was totally inaccessible to them. . . . And they kept pushing up against [the police's attitude], "Well, no, I just don't understand why the kids are whining so much." Because [they've] got all the power! . . . At least in this room, for three hours a night for five or six weeks, we [were] trying to change the power dynamic a little bit.

—Gregory Hodge, executive director, Oakland Urban Strategies Council, 2006

Code 33: Event includes mentor recruitment drive

Continued from NEWS-1

and his mother later died of epilepsy. He was reared by his grandmother.

"I didn't have the things I needed and got influenced by older young men," Newson said. First arrested when he was 13, Newson spent the rest of his youth in and out of juvenile hall.

While serving two years at a California Youth Authority facility in Stockton — a prison that houses some of the state's most violent young men — Newson said he was blessed to have met Martin Jacks, founder of The Mentoring Center.

"At first I didn't want to get involved because other groups that had visited the CYA had made promises they didn't keep. But Mr. Jacks' presentation was different," Newson said. "He gave my life direction and encouraged me to be a productive member of society when I got out."

Code 33 will consist of a series of group dialogues among 100 police officers and 150 teen-agers dealing with the prejudices and misunderstandings of both groups.

It's the fourth such event produced by Teens, Education, Art and Media, an Oakland-based organization of artists, activists and teachers led by artist Suzanne Lacy. This will be the first TEAM event to include a mentor recruitment drive, which takes place during Act IV, or "Act Now" of the performance.

The recruitment drive will occur after the performance, when organizations devoted to servicing teens will be introduced, said Linda Kiehle, administrative director of Code 33.

Sitting behind red tables arranged in a large X will be representatives from The Mentoring Center, Oakland Readers, Police Activities League, court-appointed Special Advocate Program, Big Brothers Big Sisters of the East Bay, Simba, Successful Options for Academic Readiness GEAR-UP and Project Hope.

"X marks the spot," Kiehle said. "The color red is a metaphor for urgency."

African Americans at risk

Statistics from the National Center for Institutional Alternatives in Washington, D.C., project that by 2010, 75 percent of all African-American youths will have had a run-in with the law. Nonprofit groups such as Simba are trying to offer alternatives through mentoring programs and training for organizations that want to work with inner-city residents.

"We help the kids to discover and cultivate their greatness and then give their gifts to the world," said Roland Gilbert, 52, who founded Simba in 1988.

"We're like an interpreter. There are two different languages and we help the groups to communicate."

Simba was originally formed to exclusively pair up African-American men with African-American boys. The group's focus now, Gilbert said, is to train parents to act as mentors to their own children.

"I am listening to my son now. I am more understanding instead of being critical," said Elizabeth Lewis, 42, a March graduate of the weeklong parenting program.

Lewis said she has seen an improvement in the behavior of her son, Ray Wilson, who turns 5 in two weeks, because of the change in her own behavior.

"My parents dictated to me what I was going to do with my life and I dared not disobey," said Lewis, a single mother of three older teen-age children.

Simba also has trained mentors for Big Brothers Big Sisters, a national organization that recruits mentors to help fatherless or motherless children.

Setting an example

Lavell Freeman, 29, an unmarried carpenter who for two years has been a big brother to 12-year-old Stephon Brown, said he joined Big Brothers because he wanted to give back what he received as a boy.

"As an only child growing up in a single-mother household, I wanted a big brother myself," Freeman said.

When Freeman was 15, male church members would take neighborhood children on camping trips twice a year. In his later teens while working as a carpenter's apprentice, Freeman said, his boss would take him skiing with his own family of a half-dozen children.

"We play laser tag, go to the library, water slide, participate in community clean up . . . Lavell's someone I can talk to and he's not like all grouchy and stuff," said Freeman's little brother, Stephon. "He's just cool."

Stephon lives with his mother, Vicki Stocker, and six other siblings.

Freeman said he takes Stephon — and sometimes his 8-year-old brother, Eric, who is on the Big Brothers waiting list — to outdoor events. He tries to set a good example for the boys.

"I tell them constantly that the things you do now will affect your life later on," Freeman said.

Target groups

Martin Jacks, founding director of The Mentoring Center, said the center's two main programs serve "highly at-risk youth" who use group and a combination of group and one-on-one mentoring.

He called Newson a successful product of the transition program.

After Newson was released, he volunteered off and on at The Mentoring Center "to repay my obligation to the community."

YOUTH AND POLICE INSTRUCTIONS
PUBLIC CONVERSATION
OCTOBER 7, 1999

Responsibilities

- To participate you need to have your photo release turned in.
- Please be respectful of each other and observe the ground rules.
- To participate you must follow the event instructions:

Event

- Open to the public at 6:00 p. m.
- Police/youth conversation ends about 7:45 p. m.
- Community response and food from 8:00-9:00. You may leave anytime after your part.

Location and seating

- Walk together to city center west garage, 12th and Jefferson streets.
- Go to 7th floor to be seated with facilitator.
- Your chairs will have your group number.
- Put all back packs and purses into trunk of car to be locked up
- Do not leave your seat during the event.
- If you must go to the restroom, an assistant will escort you through the crowd. Water will be brought to you.

the conversation

- Facilitator and 2 group monitors will direct conversation

- You will be able to discuss about one topic every 20 minutes

- Move on to the next topic when you are ready.

What I did get from it was not so much learning about the cops, but more of an appreciation for my own voice. . . . There [were] things that I wanted to say to the police officers, questions I wanted to ask—but how would a young person do that? How would you do that without risking getting beat up or going to jail? There's no space for that. It helped, for me, being able to express it, because [now] I can see that there are ways that can happen. So, in other arenas of my life—with my teachers at school, I had a couple of things that just didn't work for me in both college and high school—knowing that there's a way to have a dialogue with people who have opposing viewpoints is an important thing. . . . Especially with authority figures.

—Ogubala Atkintunde, participant, 2007

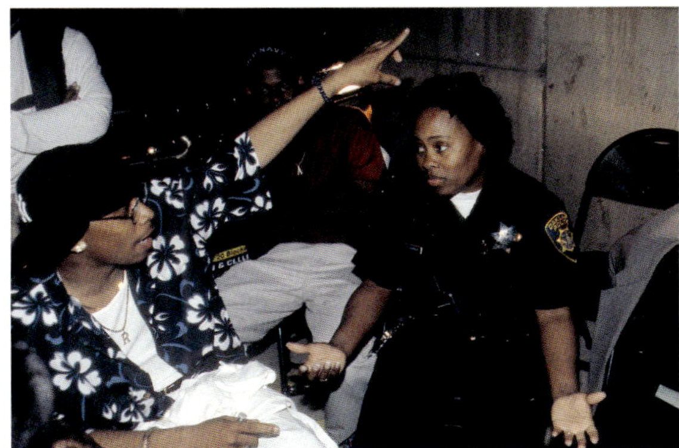

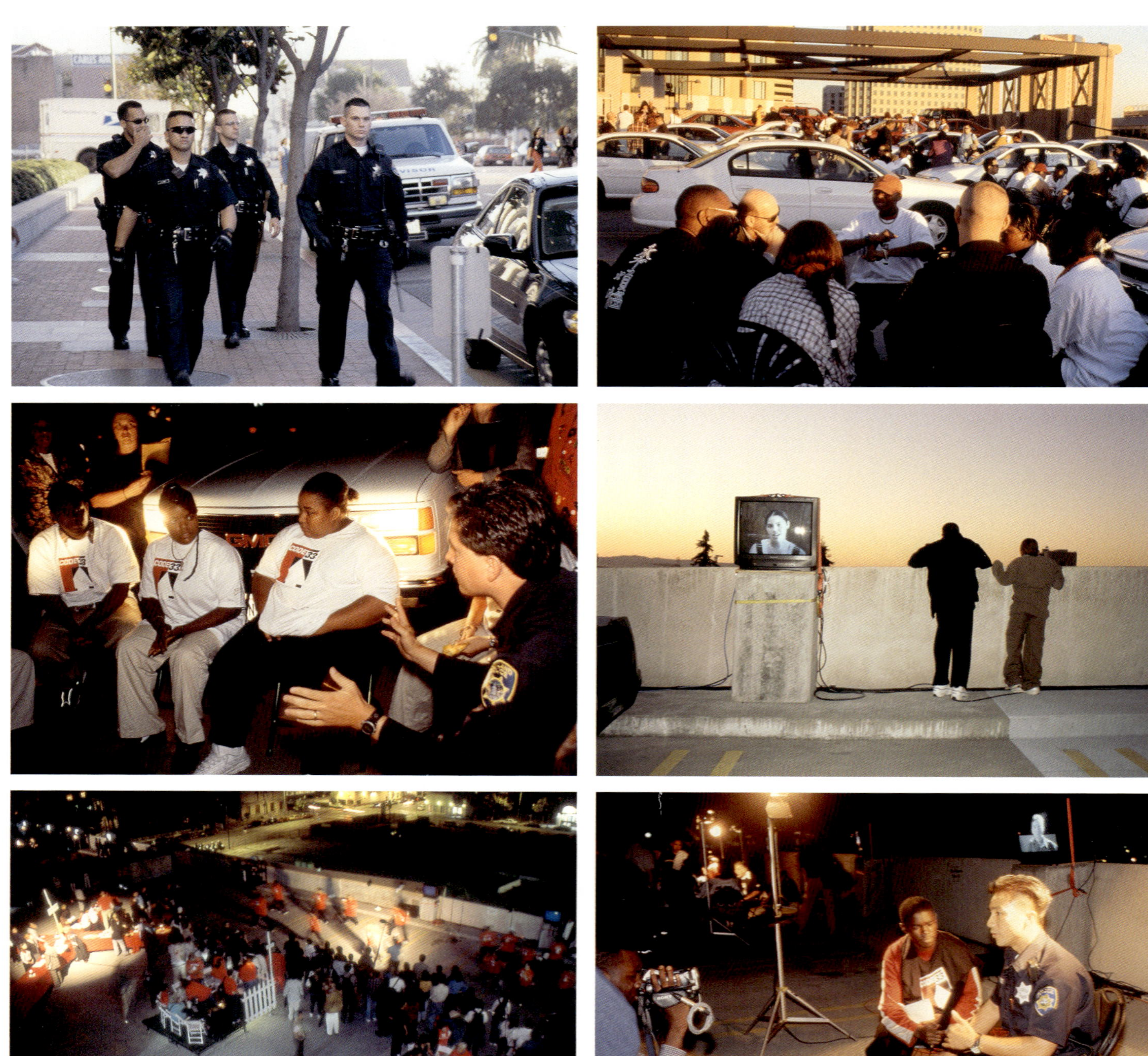

When we look at trying to impact large, prominent institutions and structures within our society, it's important to remember that they are created, operated and sustained by people. . . . Transformation is all about relationships, and it's personal. The project provided the profound experience for police officers to get to know young black and brown people—to look into their eyes, to hear their stories, and to understand more of the context of their lives. It was my hope that the officers could carry those experiences with them when out working on the street and perhaps, perhaps, see something they'd seen "a million times" a little differently and possibly make a different choice. It's the tension of openness and possibility that's intriguing and exciting to me in this type of art form.

—Unique Holland, 2018

Oceana High School

401 Paloma Avenue
Pacifica, Ca 94044
(650) 355-4131   Fax (650) 355-6108

Judith A. Borelli
Principal

Mark W. Loos
Vice Principal

The Honorable Edmund G. Brown, Jr.
1 Franklin H. Ogawa Plaza; Third Floor
Oakland, Calif.   94612

October 8, 1999

Dear Mayor Brown,

I wanted to inform you of a situation that happened with our students last night at the Code 33 event in your fair city. One of our teachers took six students to participate in what he thought would be a wonderful event.

Our students were given stickers by the Mumia protestors at the scene, and as teenagers are apt to do they stuck several stickers on their clothing. Our students did not know who Mumia was nor did they know how offensive this would be to your police officers. Most of our students removed their stickers after our teacher explained the situation. A couple of students however, got separated from the teacher and did not understand the dynamics of the situation. One student in particular, Mario, a 15-year-old Latino boy from Guatemala who earlier had been chanting "Save Mama Mia!", still had stickers on his clothing when the audience was being led into an alternative entrance. This evidently was interpreted by one of your officers as subversive attempt by a Mumia protestor to gain entrance. The officer approached Mario in what we consider to be an aggressive stance and was soon joined by two other officers. This student was then arrested, placed in a patrol car and eventually dragged to a patrol wagon.

Our teacher attempted to intervene with the arresting officers and was rebuffed. He eventually talked with the sergeant and was able to get the officers to agree to release Mario into our teacher's custody.

The unfortunate irony of this situation is that Code 33 was intended to improve police relations with youth and all six of our students came home with an increased cynicism toward police officers. While our student certainly is not blameless (i.e. he acted like an immature, hotheaded 15 year old), the arresting officers did not demonstrate the best side of your force.

Please note that our students refused all requests to be interviewed by the media and, although they have spoken with the ACLU it is not their desire to pursue legal action. What we would like to see is a healing dialogue facilitated by some neutral parties. We feel this would accomplish the intended goal of Code 33.

We are also displeased with the organizers of the Mumia protest and have sent them a separate letter. The Mumia effort is not of concern to us, nor do we wish to involve the Mumia organizers or allow them to use this to their advantage.

The relationship between our youth and the police is of great concern to us, (which is why we were attending Code 33) and we would like to have some follow up to this incident. I would appreciate any ideas your office may have in how to go about setting this up.

Thank you for your time and consideration.

Sincerely,

Elaine E. Collins, MFT
Special Services Counselor

Cc: Code 33

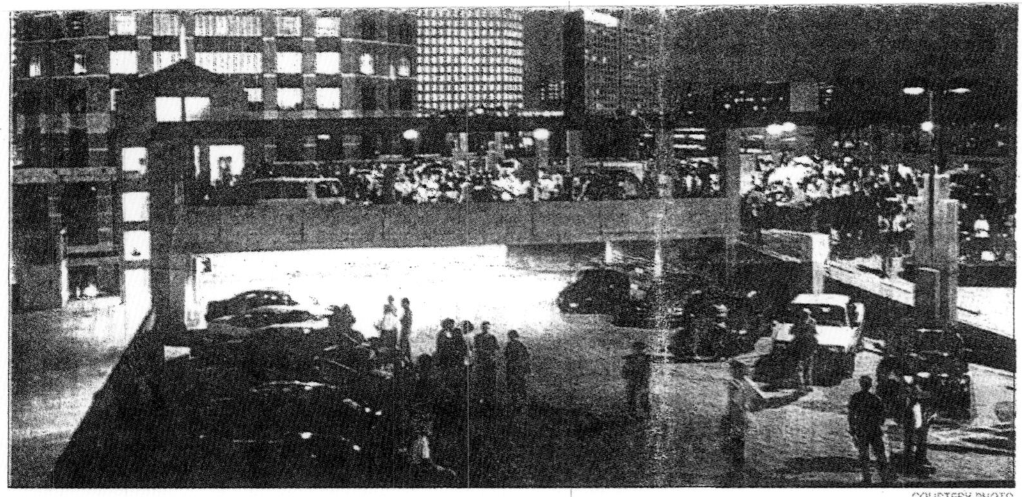

Thousands of Oaklanders gathered in June 1994 for the public performance art event "The Roof Is on Fire," aimed at putting the spotlight on teen-age concerns. In October, Oakland police and young people will come together for a similar event.

Oakland police, teens meet to clear the air

Rooftop performance to be staged at parking lot

By Kathleen Kirkwood
STAFF WRITER

OAKLAND

IT'S AN all-too-common scenario. A teen-ager hanging out is detained by police officers for any number of reasons: a crime nearby, suspicion of gang activity. The list is long. Police might have cause, but the young person has no recourse and no say.

But one night this fall, Oakland police will give local teen-agers more than the right to remain silent. They will call a "Code 33": clear the air and listen.

The cutting-edge public art performance planned for Oct. 7, named for the police code for radio silence, will turn a parking garage rooftop in downtown Oakland into a stage. One hundred police officers and 150 teen-agers will come together to talk candidly.

It is the third, and possibly the edgiest, such performance event to be held in Oakland. It is being staged by the producers behind the 1994 "Roof Is on Fire" and a 1996 basketball game/performance between police and young people called "No Blood, No Foul."

This time, "Code 33: Emergency, Clear the Air" will begin with the police black and whites, lights flashing and sirens going, converging on the City Center West parking garage at 12th and Clay streets.

With that dramatic intro, officers and teen-agers will start talking — sitting in cars on the rooftop — about issues they confront together every day: authority, crime, power and violence. Audience members will be able to wander between conversations, eavesdropping at will.

"Most young people, low-income and people of color don't think the police are there to help you, they are there to get you caught up in something," said Unique Holland, youth coordinator for Code 33.

As a high school student, Holland, now 21, participated in the previous rooftop event in 1994.

Videos produced by local teen-agers of eight Oakland neighborhoods will be broadcast around the rooftop, along with a live video feed giving audience reaction to the conversations they have just witnessed.

Afterward, dancers will take the stage to change the tone and celebrate the event. Then audience members will have an opportunity to sign up as youth mentors with various community organizations.

"The relationship between youth and authority has reached an emergency, and we need to clear the air," said Suzanne Lacy, a public artist and senior faculty member at the California College of Arts and Crafts in Oakland.

And conversely, adults need to listen.

young people through short media sound bytes on the television news. Jacoby said one of the goals of the October event is to sign up youth mentors. "There is no such thing as getting too much attention," Jacoby said.

Police Officer Terence West said police use a "Code 33" to signal there is an emergency, necessitating that radio traffic is cleared.

"The message we are trying to put out there is there's a need for youth and authority to talk," West said. The sense of frustration building in young people is almost tangible, said West, who runs the Police Activities League and deals with local teen-agers on a daily basis.

Outbreaks of violence are symptoms of that frustration, he said.

"It is really a scary time in our history," West said, referring to tragedies such as the shootings at Columbine High School in Colorado in April.

When he was 16, a police officer detained him as a possible robbery suspect in East Oakland.

He was at a gas station with his mother, filling up the car. What he remembers most about it was the officer did not listen to what they had to say. The officer only saw that he fit the general description of a suspect.

An organizing meeting for those who would like to participate in "Code 33" will be held at 7 p.m. Wednesday at We The People, 200 Harrison St. For more information, call 238-6907.

Please see **Teens**, LOCAL-2

Performance art allows teens, Oakland police to talk openly

This is the first in a series of articles about the public art "Code 33" event, to be held at 6 p.m. Thursday in downtown Oakland. It will bring together 100 police and 150 local youth to talk candidly about power, authority and safety. The public is invited to eavesdrop. The topics are scripted but the conversation is not.

By Tracey Compton
STAFF WRITER

OAKLAND — Teen-agers and police officers communicating about misconceptions and stereotypes.

Could it be possible? Eighteen-year-old Neya Doeur questioned whether it could be done when she first joined project "Code 33: Emergency, Clear the Air."

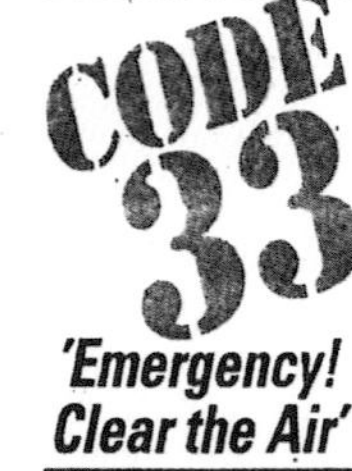

The public art performance links 150 teen-agers with 100 police, all sitting in cars atop a downtown parking garage to talk openly about the tension that divides them. Around them will be listeners and video cameras recording the event, similar to 1994's "The Roof is on Fire."

The title was chosen because it's the police code for radio silence. For one night at least, adults — authority figures in particular — will listen to what young people have to say.

"It's like putting two magnets together, north and north, you know

Please see **Meet**, LOCAL-2

Meet: Th

Continued from LOCAL-1

how they repel," Doeur said.

Doeur, who recently graduated from San Leandro High School, assisted in recruiting young people to participate. The task was difficult at first, she said, but got easier as more understood the event, and brought their friends along.

Workshops were held with the youth participants and police officers to begin choosing topics and raising questions.

Starting a dialogue between the two groups took a lot of hard work and commitment on both sides, they said.

"I found it kind of hard to talk," Doeur said. "It felt like [the police department] was giving me opinions that I want to hear. I'm trying to get them to admit that there are some corrupt cops out there and there always will be, but they never said that."

Doeur said she has been witness to unfair treatment by the police, because her best friend is African American. She says he has been repeatedly stopped by the police for unjust reasons — officers say th

New Police Code In Oakland Lets Teens Speak Out

Protest fails to derail promising forum

By Henry K. Lee
CHRONICLE STAFF WRITER

The teenagers and police officers came by the hundreds last night, converging on top of a downtown Oakland parking garage to speak openly about stereotypes and issues involving crime and authority.

As they spoke in small groups amid the headlights of parked cars at the City Center West Garage, other people mingled, listening in on discussions between two groups that have historically had a tense relationship.

The chats were part of "Code 33: Emergency, Clear the Air" — part catharsis, part performance piece, with the goal of having the police listen to what the youths had to say — instead of the other way around.

Code 33 is the police radio term telling officers to stay off the air unless they have an emergency. Organizers said it was an appropriate title for a forum designed to let teenagers — many of them at-risk youth — vent their opinions.

But the event was marred by a boisterous protest in behalf Mumia Abu-Jamal, convicted of killing a police officer. Plans for a procession of police vehicles and low-rider cars were scrapped after about 150 chanting demonstrators moved from the Oakland Federal Building to Jefferson Street outside the garage.

Police were forced to close the garage gates, limiting access to the event and inconveniencing motorists trying to leave. One protester was arrested for allegedly assaulting a police officer.

Oakland Police Chief Richard Word said Abu-Jamal's supporters had a right to protest. "But they're trying to ruin a very fine event, and they should be ashamed of themselves," said Word, his face grim.

Many of the "Code 33" participants, on an upper floor of the garage, were oblivious to the demonstration. They spoke at length on a variety of topics, from racial profiling to the death penalty.

In response to one teenager's comment that officers can be rude and abrupt in their interactions with youths, Oakland Police Sgt. Rick Andreotti acknowledged that the sheer volume of calls often prevents police from explaining their actions.

"That does a disservice to both of us, and it can leave a sour taste in your mouth," Andreotti said.

Teens hope tonight's 'Code 33' will reduce tension with police

This is the last in a series of articles about "Code 33," which starts at 6 tonight in downtown Oakland. The public art event will bring together 100 police and 150 local youth to talk candidly about power, authority and safety. The public is invited to eavesdrop on the conversations. "Code 33" will be held on the rooftop of Oakland's City Center West Garage, corner of Jefferson and 12th streets.

By Jason Begay
STAFF WRITER

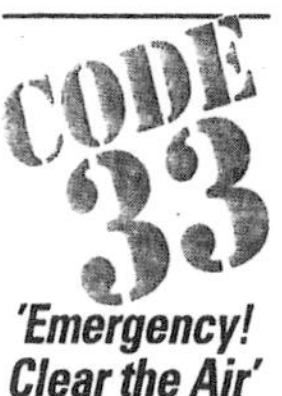

OAKLAND — It can be graffiti, music, poetry, even doodles in the back of a notebook, but art is one of the first mediums of expression recognized by teen-agers.

"Art is really like religion and language, it's available to all of us," said Annice Jacoby, a founding artist of Teens + Education + Art + Media. "It's a way to share and to create beauty and understanding."

TEAM is the producing organization behind "Code 33: Emergency — Clear the Air," a public art event scheduled for tonight. The event is designed to bridge the communication gap between law enforcement and young people. But it's the medium that makes the event a performance rather than a forum.

In an elaborate setup atop the City Center West Garage in downtown Oakland, black and white cars will be strategically placed around a group of red cars. This is the setting where youths will talk candidly with police to "clear the air" and tension be-

Please see **Art**, LOCAL-10

'CODE 33' EVENT

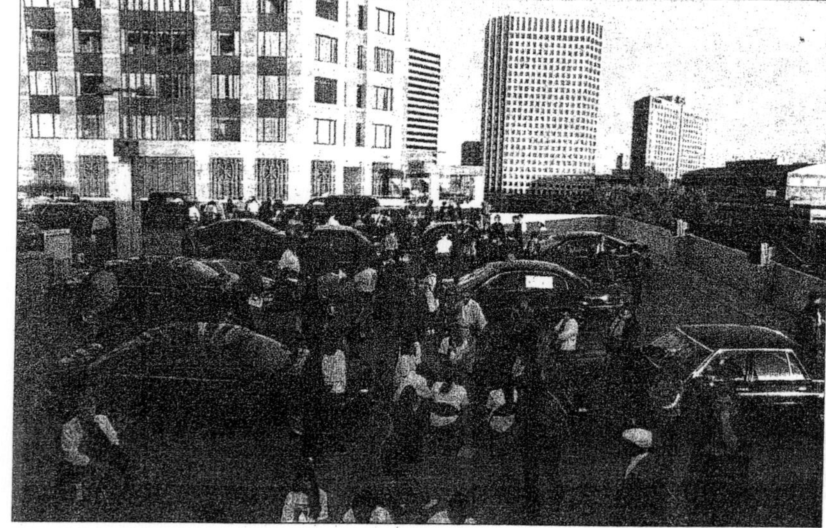

Oakland Police officers and youth talk about power, violence and authority as part of the "Code 33" event held at the City Center Garage rooftop Thursday afternoon.

RAY CHAVEZ — Staff

Police, youth rap on the roof

By Sharon Lerman
STAFF WRITER

OAKLAND — Until the cops chase them away, Lavon Frazier Jr. hangs out with friends outside a liquor store in his East Oakland neighborhood.

Frazier, 18, says the officers are usually familiar, and so is the drill: He is treated like a criminal even though he doesn't deal drugs or harass customers.

Under the glare of an unmarked police car's headlights Thursday night, Frazier told officers he is tired of being Maced, handcuffed and pushed around just for being on the streets. And all around him on a downtown Oakland rooftop, similar scenes were taking place.

About 800 people gathered atop the City Center West Garage as more than 200 police officers and youth tried to

hash out their differences in a program dubbed "Code 33: Emergency! Clear the Air."

Wandering among the small groups, city officials, neighborhood activists and parents listened in on the conversations. Sometimes humorous but often tense, the dialogues focused on such issues as racial profiling, power and harassment.

Officer Troy Jones told Frazier police are often on the defensive, especially in high-crime areas.

"If I'm going to a liquor store where I've seen all this violence, all these drugs . . . In your opinion, how do you suggest I handle it?" Jones asked.

Matthew Williams, 17, suggested police be honest when they stop kids, rather than use their authority to intimidate them.

"Tell us the truth," Williams said. "When they ask, 'Why are you doing this to me?' Let them know."

Officer Leroy Johnson said police are often driven by fear, and that can translate into an explosive situation between an officer and a suspect — sometimes leading to a shooting.

"I'll be the first to admit, when we're out there, we're scared," Johnson said.

Sitting in the same group, Johnson's wife — also an Oakland police officer — said her husband's safety on the streets is her greatest concern.

"My husband puts that uniform on

Please see **Event**, NEWS-15

---

sk was very difficult at first

s license plate, that or the tags have ex-

r night, she says, he d by a patrol car and ter picking her up T station.

u know why he boyfriend? 'Oh be-dn't see the date or on your license said, imitating the

er asked to see his registration and bottle of cologne in nac, Doeur said. Before them proceed, the Doeur's boyfriend to dall and pay $10 to legible.

es and lack of re-ing people, from au-es, are the concerns ants to talk about. ociety is prejudiced g people, and some icularly senior citi-prehensive around

older adults act like k to young people," they act like we don't e language."

Recent workshops, held to facilitate discussion, have given her the opportunity to get police perspectives on various situations as well. The workshop conversations allowed officers to express that they are people too. The police must deal with all types of people — sometimes dangerous ones — and still return home to families when their work is done.

Eighteen-year-old Lavon Frazier also feels that the discussion Code 33 creates is good, but only if it is continued. Frazier, who attends an East Bay charter school, wasn't scared or intimidated during a workshop discussion with police officers because he said he knows most of them from the area.

"I wanted to talk to police about what goes on," Frazier said. That includes harassment, intimidation and abuse of power, he said.

"Police detained me for hanging out in the yard of a friend. Later on the police officer told me he would take me somewhere and beat me up because he said I had a smart mouth."

Frazier said the officers

pulled up to his friend's house in East Oakland, jumped from the car, put the young men in handcuffs and took them to the car for questioning.

Frazier kept asking why he was being searched, but said the officer only whispered in his ear that "he already knew." His mother watched the incident and questioned the officers as well.

Frazier said he had no record, and discovering this, police left without any explanation, he said.

He also spoke about other young people being kicked, stomped and sprayed with mace for no reason.

"Code 33" will be held at 6 p.m. Thursday on the rooftop of Oakland's City Center West Garage, corner of Jefferson and 12th streets. For more information on the event, www.code33.org on the web or call 238-6907.

The Turning Point (1996–97)
Under Construction (1997)

The Turning Point aimed to amplify the public voice of teenage girls in Vancouver, Canada. Thirty young women from diverse backgrounds participated in a two-week introductory workshop about the theory and practice of public art and then collaborated over the next year with Lacy to design their own workshops, public appearances at community events, media reports, *mendhi*-based hand-painting performances, and a zine to recruit additional participants. It culminated in *Under Construction*, a performance at the site of an unfinished luxury residential development. Nearly two hundred teenage girls wearing red T-shirts and construction hats sat on a central concrete slab discussing parental expectations, alienation from school, sexuality, violence, eating disorders, depression, relationships with other girls, and their hopes and dreams. The audience first observed the gathering through holes in the site's enclosure fence while listening to prerecorded conversations and television relays from inside the building. Finally the audience was invited to approach the "stage" and hear the live conversations as performers mixed and poured concrete and painted one another's hands. Attended by five thousand people, the event recognized the ways young women are often positioned for voyeurism instead of activism.

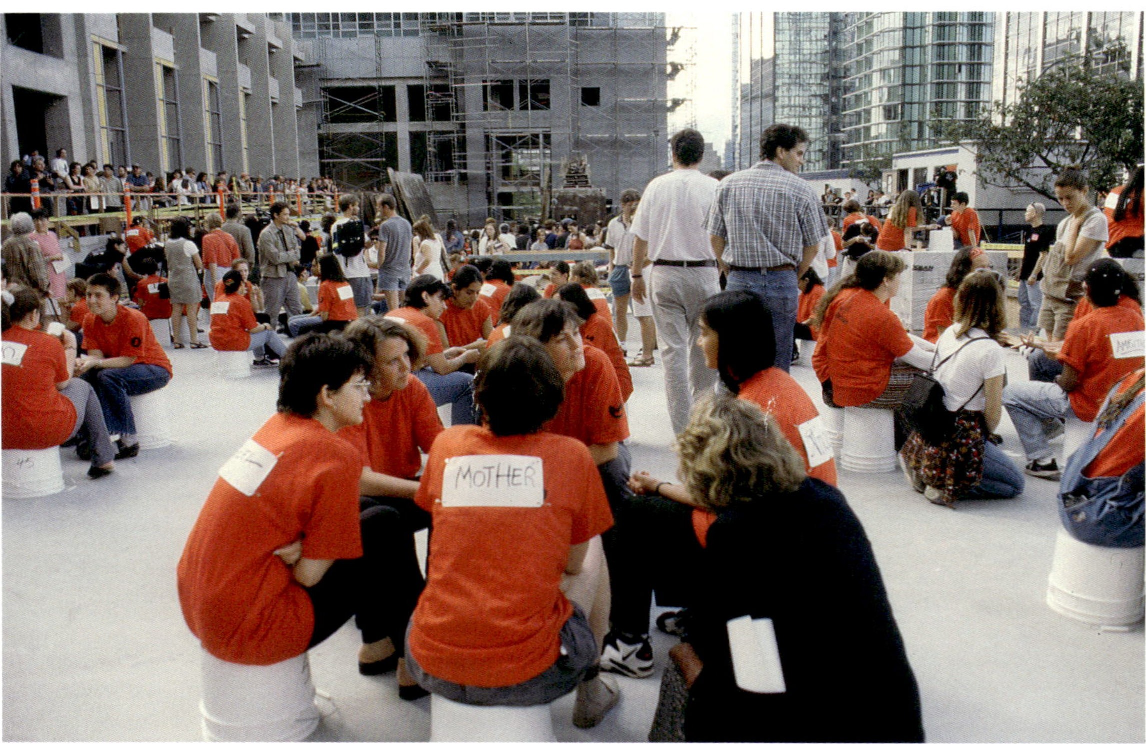

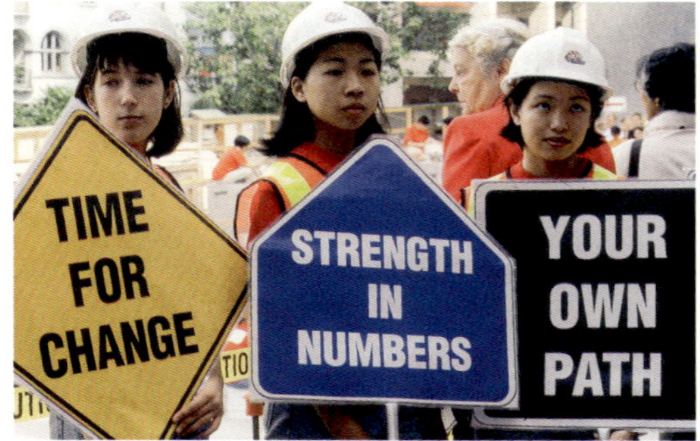

When Suzanne was invited to Vancouver, several institutions within the city were looking at the idea of public art as a key community development strategy for the city, particularly in the context of diversity and multiculturalism. They wanted to bring Suzanne because they thought that of all the artists they knew, her work was the most deeply rooted in community and cultural development. They wanted work that would strengthen relationships in the community from the bottom up.

—Pilar Riaño-Alcalá, collaborator, 2018

I.D.Entity (2004)

SUZANNE LACY WITH ELISHEVA GROSS, UNIQUE HOLLAND, AND ARTHUR OU

On November 13, 2004, in downtown Taipei, 160 Taiwanese youth recruited through text message and email assembled like a flash mob, revealing themselves to one another in an artistic "speak-out." Their conversation explored questions developed with American artists about the impact of technology on life, culture, taboo subjects, and the construction of identity. The performance included an internet-based collaboration between the U.S. and Taiwan, and a subsequent exhibition featured a website that facilitated international youth engagement with issues *I.D.Entity* brought forth.

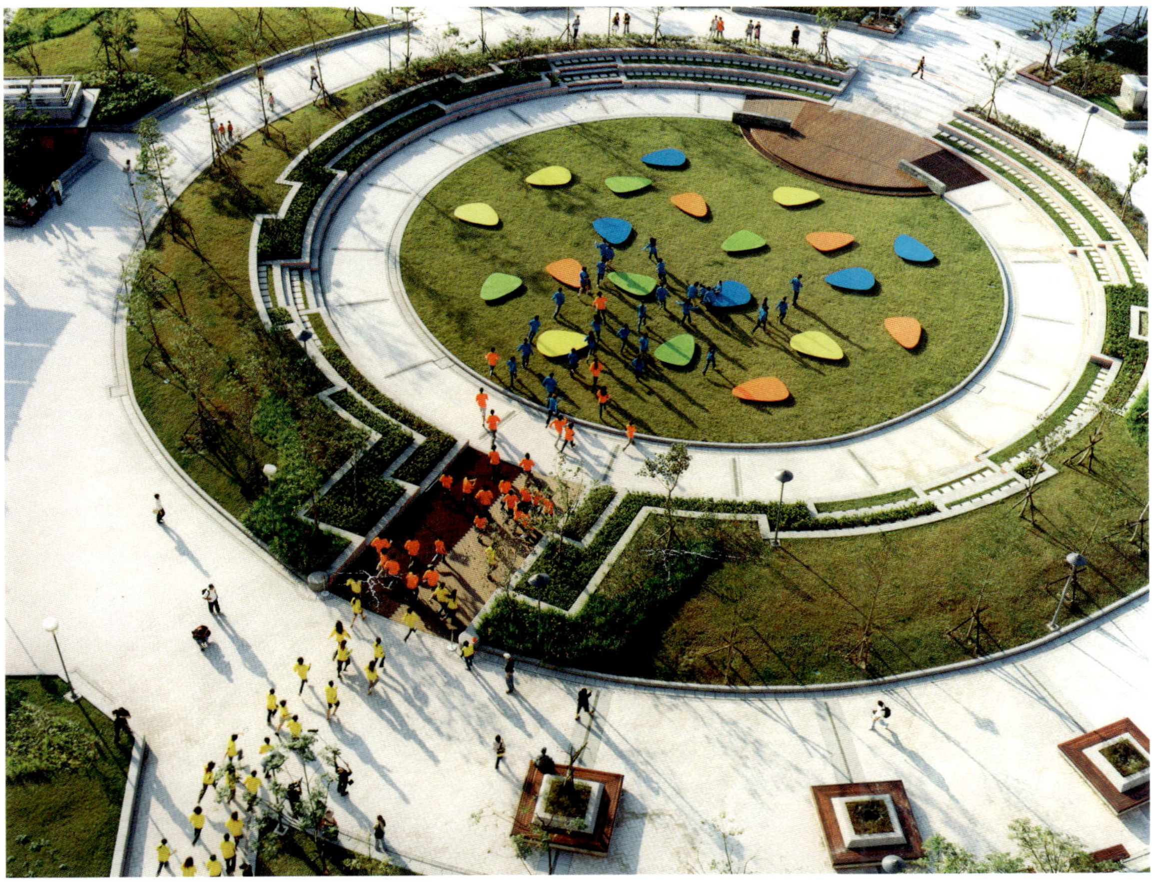

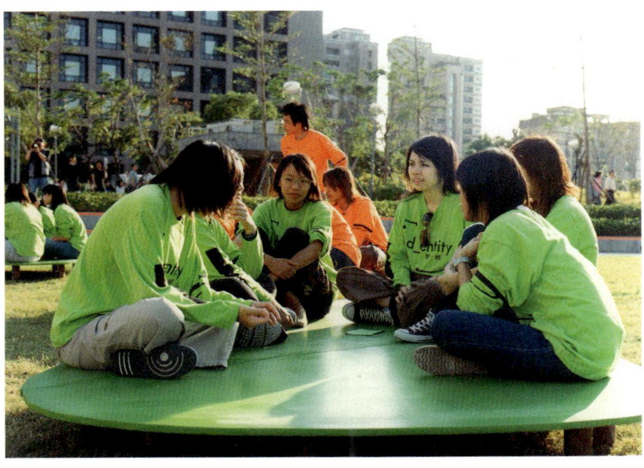

SWARM (2007)

SUZANNE LACY, KIM ABELES, JEFF CAIN, AND ROCHELLE LABOWITZ

SWARM was produced for the twenty-fifth-anniversary celebration of the Los Angeles–based magazine *ArtScene*, held at the Los Angeles County Museum of Art. The performance featured one hundred students from Fairfax and Culver City High Schools enjoying a private party in a café in full view of the dinner guests at the sedate awards ceremony. Dressed in bright yellow T-shirts, they interviewed key figures in local feminist history, including Judy Baca, June Wayne, and Betye Saar, and periodically dashed out to broadcast the interviews to the dinner guests via boom box. A radio tower built by Cain broadcast the interviews throughout the neighborhood over a pirate station, and live video footage from the youth party was projected onto the walls of the museum. In preparation for the performance, the students researched and interviewed twenty-five women artists and created a MySpace page for each to gain a better understanding of the significant role women artists have played in Los Angeles's history.

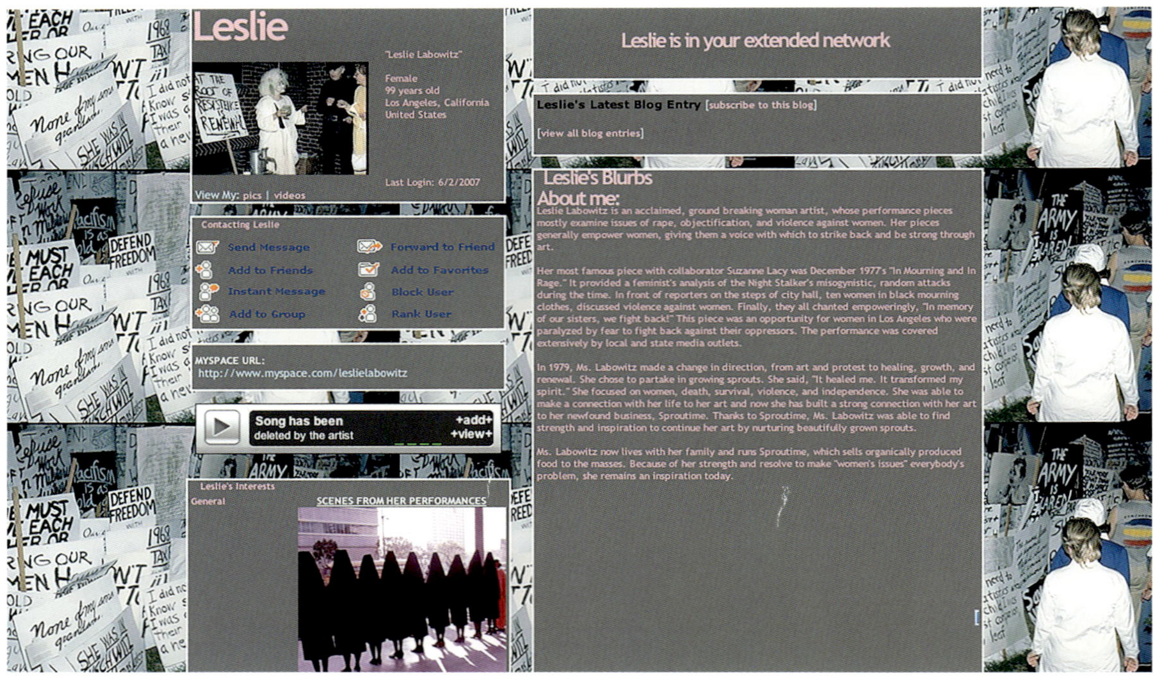

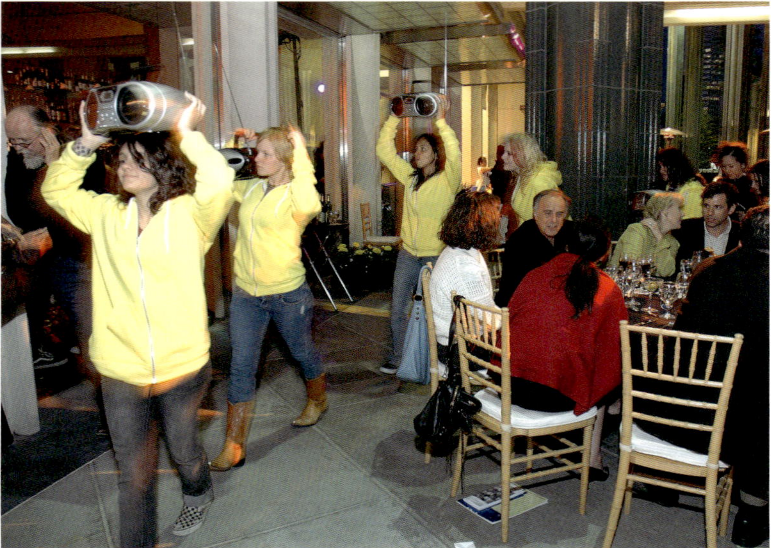

School for Revolutionary Girls (2016)

SUZANNE LACY WITH NICOLA GOODE

School for Revolutionary Girls was a ten-day project with twenty teenage girls exploring their relationship to Ireland's 1916 Easter Rising and to contemporary issues facing young women in Ireland and around the world. This artistic consciousness-raising process combined group discussion, performance, social media, and a reading of manifestos in the courtyard of the Irish Museum of Modern Art, Dublin. Working with the historian Liz Gillis, international students, Irish and American artists, and Create—the national development agency for collaborative arts—the girls imagined the world as it is and as it could be, developing creative expressions of their own unique "public voice."

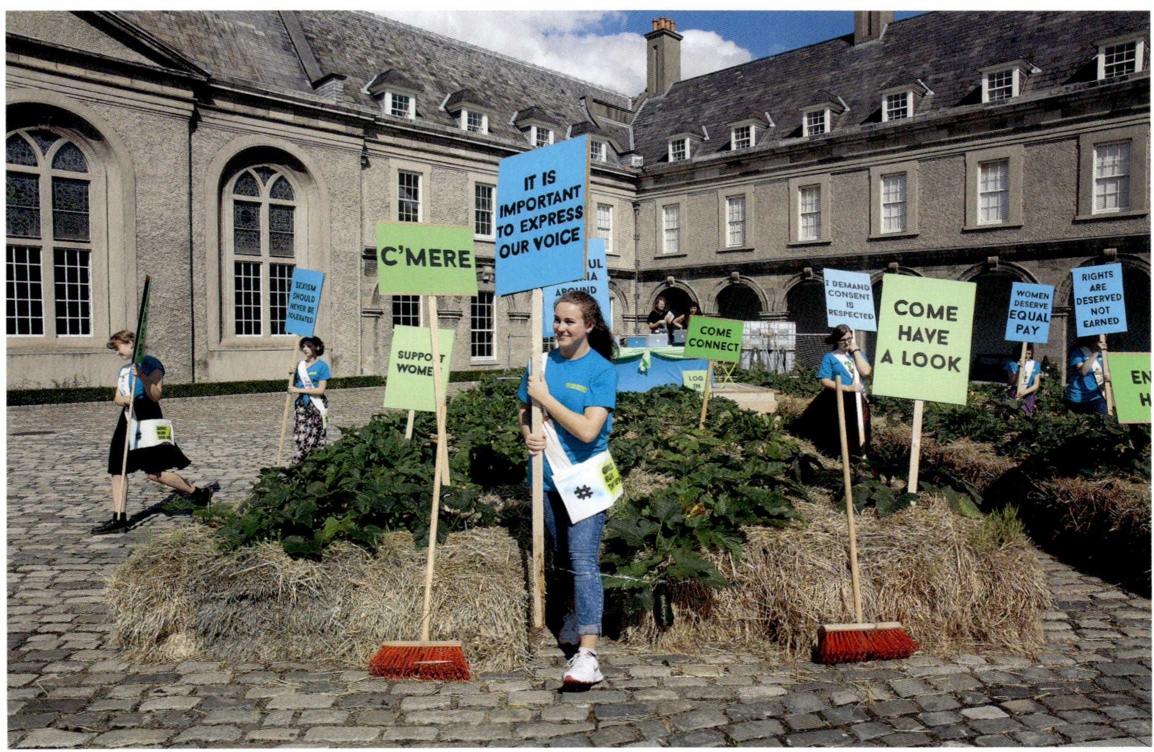

The project blended personal and group experience with care. Young women's personal voices were first shared through consciousness raising and later in the public domain through individual manifestos, placards, and badges. This was complemented by a sense of camaraderie and solidarity achieved through the collective act of working through the week's program in small groups, emerging as one big group in the performance, united as contemporary revolutionary girls. The masters students, in their role as artist/teachers . . . emerg[ed] with many complex questions [that fed] their own practices related to ethics/aesthetics and the challenge in balancing artistic and pedagogical aims.

—Fiona Whelan, artist advisor, 2018

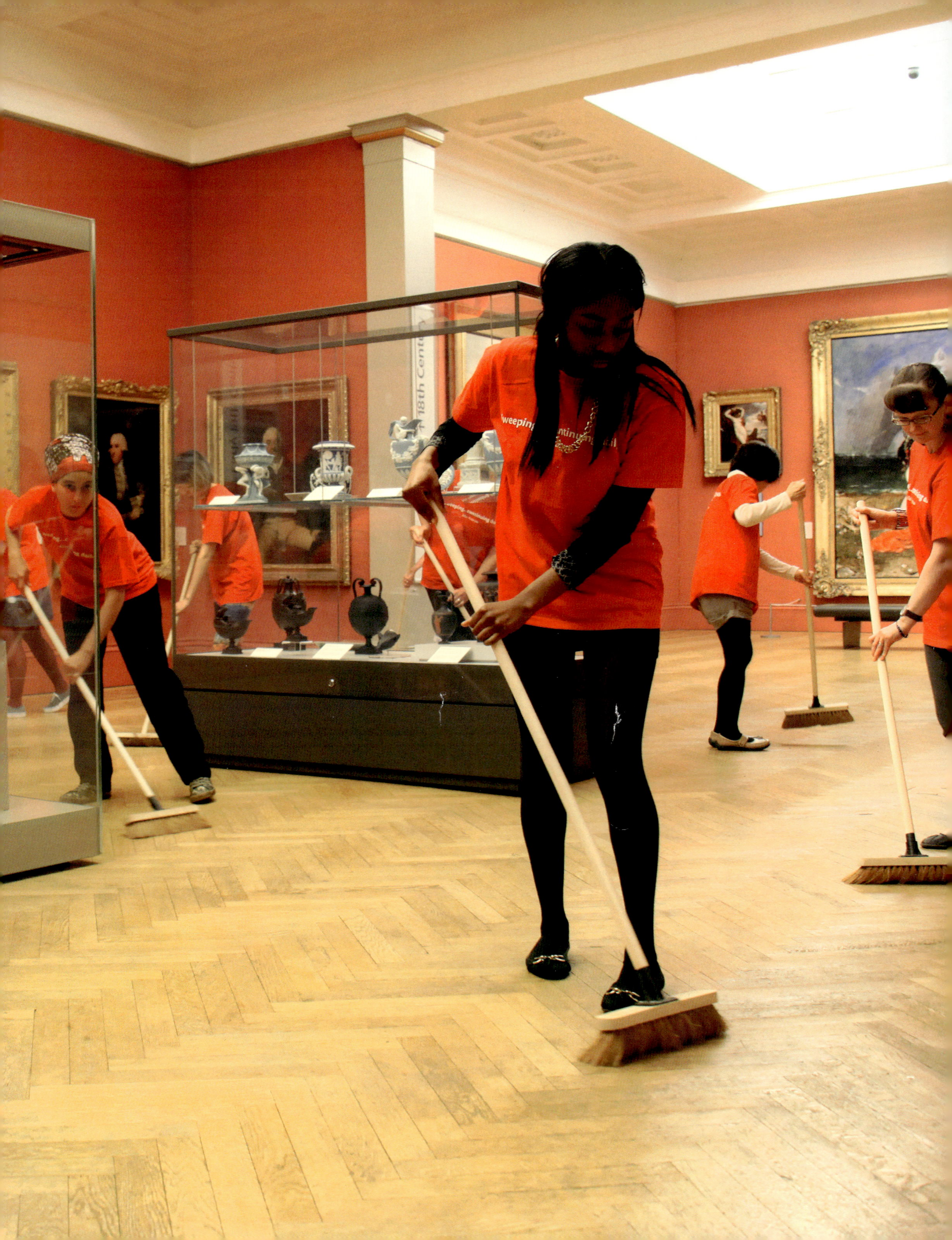

WORK AND CLASS

Lacy continues to ask fundamental questions about what public art can do and what it actually does—interrogations that have animated her entire career. In recent decades many of her works have taken "home" as their primary subject matter, focusing on small-scale communities—regions, towns, neighborhoods, and even individual workplaces and families—as unique and invaluable sources of knowledge and history. Rather than drawing generalized conclusions based on specific experiences, these projects explore the local impacts of large-scale, systemic, and environmental change, especially as skilled labor has become increasingly devalued by global capitalism. Lacy has prioritized her role as a community organizer, identifying appropriate targets for public intervention and proposing and achieving tangible outcomes. The resulting works have comprised temporary events, such as exhibitions, performances, workshops, and dinners, as well as more permanent products, including brochures, websites, videos, photographs, public murals and sculptures, and community gardens.

Lacy has increasingly focused on the intersections between women's labor, the causes and conditions of poverty, and environmental devastation. Works such as *Alterations* (1994–95, p. 218) and *Cleaning Conditions* (2013, pp. 236–37) foreground the visual dissonance of seeing manual labor presented against the backdrop of a gallery or museum exhibition space. *La piel de la memoria / Skin of Memory* (1999–2000, pp. 219–23), *University of Local Knowledge* (2000–ongoing, pp. 224–27), and *The Circle and the Square* (2015–17, pp. 238–45) are all premised on recognizing the inherent value and relevance of autobiography to shared histories. Community initiatives such as *Beneath Land and Water: A Project for Elkhorn City* (2000–2005, pp. 228–31) have responded to the direct effects of environmental devastation, one of global capitalism's most acute consequences, and have sought to harness local resources to create collective visions for the futures of small towns.

Lacy's *Central Valley* series (2008–ongoing, pp. 232–35) engages with the artist's own autobiography, which began in the working-class town of Wasco, California. The series encompasses a collaborative community initiative with her students in the town of Laton, California, with photographic and video works that visualize the local economies of the San Joaquin Valley. Subsequently presented in exhibitions, these projects have tested the efficacy of designated "art spaces" as sites for activism or social reform. Lacy has reflected on the continuous impact of her own family—a community in its smallest form—on the issues of enduring importance to her work as an artist: "Representative of one of many new art audiences, my working-class parents serve as a touch point for me as I consider the conflicts in our values, our profound points of agreement, and the potential role of art in an examination of meaning."[1]

Many of these projects spanned several years, allowing time to conduct the research, connect with the organizations and individuals, and build the relationships needed to identify the most urgent concerns of a given community. These cooperative efforts exemplify Lacy's commitment to initiating conversations and undertakings that have long lives even after she is no longer physically present. Her collaborative projects have become increasingly complex and inclusive, as Lacy has formed networks that incorporate anthropologists, activists, arts organizations, and her own graduate students, pushing her work in public practice further into the realm of pedagogy. Thoughtful communication, skilled organizing, and deference to local expertise are critical to Lacy's recent work.

—JESSICA D. BRIER

NOTES

1. Suzanne Lacy, "Debated Territory: Toward a Critical Language for Public Art" (1995), reprinted in *Leaving Art: Writings on Performance, Politics, and Publics, 1974–2007* (Durham, NC: Duke University Press), 183–84.

OPPOSITE: "Sweepers" in the galleries as part of *Cleaning Conditions* (2013, pp. 236–37), Manchester Art Gallery, England, 2013

Alterations (1994–95)

SUZANNE LACY, SUSANNE COCKRELL, AND BRITTA KATHMEYER

This performance installation was staged for *Old Glory, New Story: Flagging the 21st Century*, an exhibition at Capp Street Project that reimagined the American flag in a variety of media. Lacy, Cockrell, and Kathmeyer placed heaps of used red, white, and blue garments in a gallery and invited women to hand-stitch them together. The women worked quietly, nearly buried in the fabric and tethered by a task that would never be complete, as the piles were replenished daily. Their endeavor called attention to the invisible labor of migrant women working for minimum wage in San Francisco's garment district, where Capp Street Project was located, and of workers abroad whose cheap labor enables excessive American consumerism. The performance sparked a series of conversations, including a high school group discussion about patriotism, race, gender, and disenfranchisement.

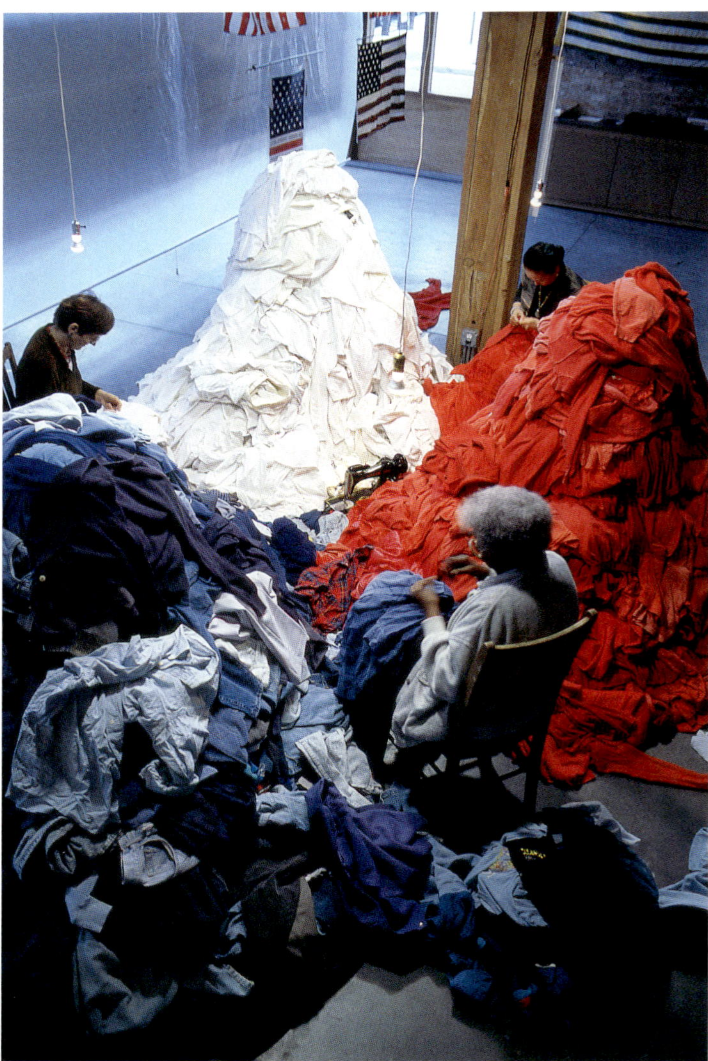

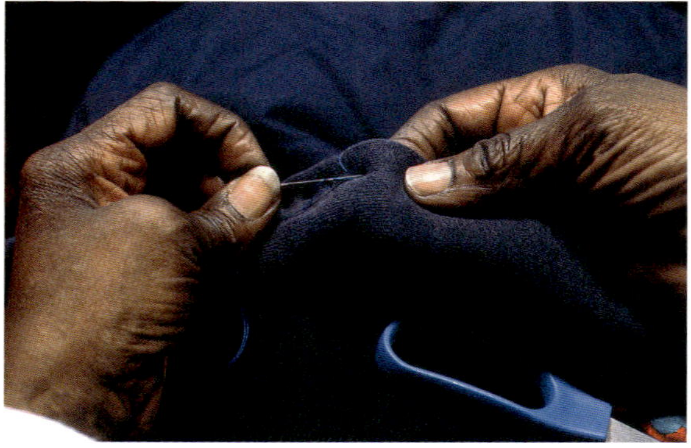

La piel de la memoria/Skin of Memory (1999–2000)
La piel de la memoria revivida/Skin of Memory Revisited (2011)

SUZANNE LACY AND PILAR RIAÑO-ALCALÁ

Instigated by a series of workshops Lacy and Riaño-Alcalá organized in 1998, *La piel de la memoria* was a public project in the Antioquia barrio of Medellín, Colombia, that was both an intimate, collective reflection on the neighborhood's violent and traumatic history and a community initiative to imagine and create a better path forward. Lacy and Riaño-Alcalá worked with a team of youth, women, and community leaders, including members of governmental and non-governmental organizations, to conceive an exhibition and celebration commemorating Antioquia's past and future. They collected approximately five hundred personal objects from residents for display in a roving "memory museum"—a bus that traveled to different sectors of Antioquia for ten days and stopped at the subway station in Medellín, drawing approximately four thousand visitors. Also on view were letters written by Antioquia residents to unknown neighbors, expressing wishes for each other and visions for the future of the barrio. At the conclusion of the exhibition, the letters were distributed ceremoniously to different homes. Local historian Mauricio Hoyos helped collect the objects and strategize an initiative for future community education; other contributors to the project included Raúl Cabra, Vicky Ramirez, Juan Sebastián Vargas, and Rubén Fernández Andrade. The installation culminated in a day of celebration and performances throughout Antioquia by mimes, storytellers, musicians, and stilt-walkers. *La piel de la memoria revivida* revisited the project with an installation, video, and performance in 2011.

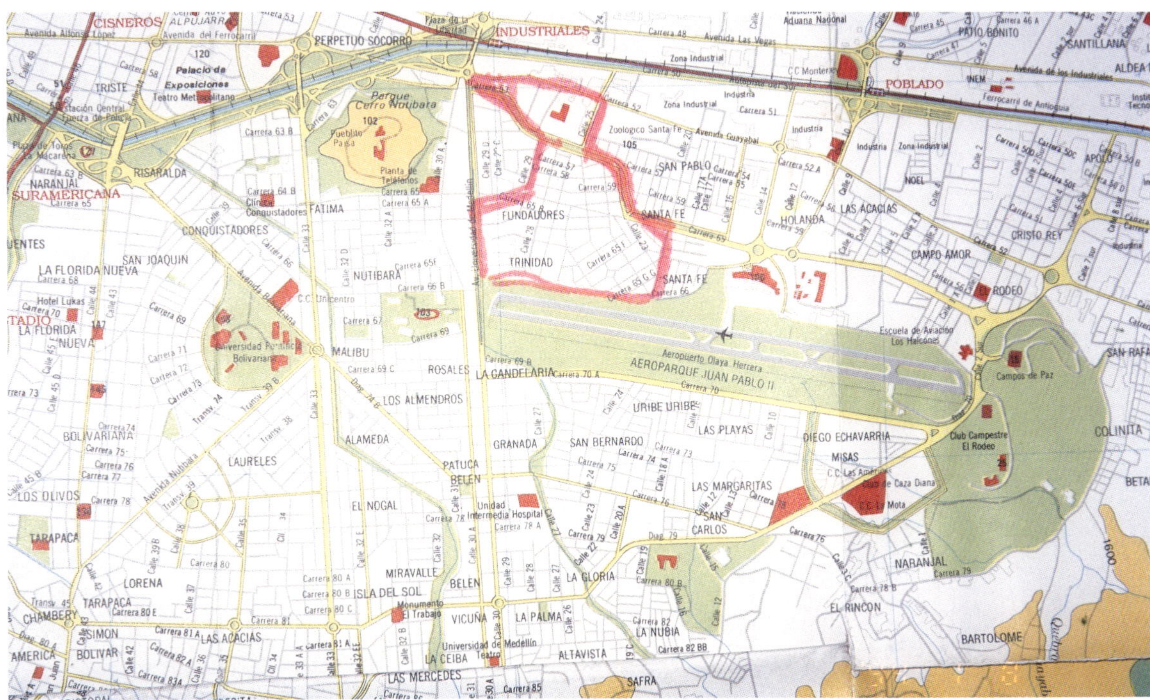

The point of departure for the *Skin of Memory* project was the recognition that the daily experience of violence affects the entire lives of all barrio residents and opens a social wound that lacks expressive and narrative vehicles. In communities such as barrio Antioquia, unarticulated grief obstructs the possibility of establishing emotional connections to face the experience of loss. The excess of violence in daily life, furthermore, deters the possibilities of a collective processing of loss. [We] envisioned a kind of civic pedagogy process to (1) recognize the multiple losses and the fragmentation of the social and moral worlds, (2) acknowledge the ways in which local worlds are altered by larger social forces, (3) create a local context to deal with grief and pain, and (4) develop other *forms of relating to death*.

—Pilar Riaño-Alcalá, 2004

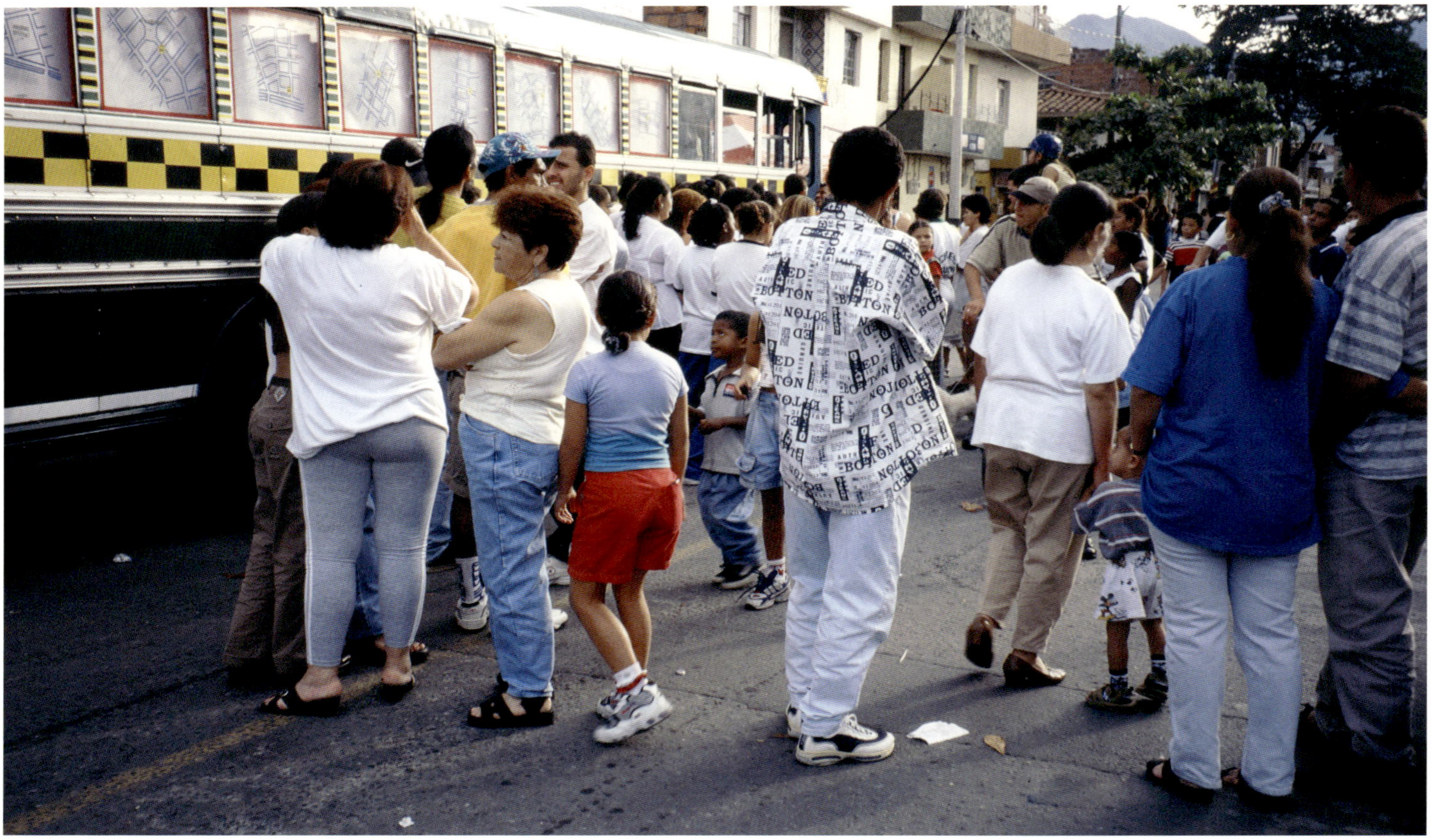

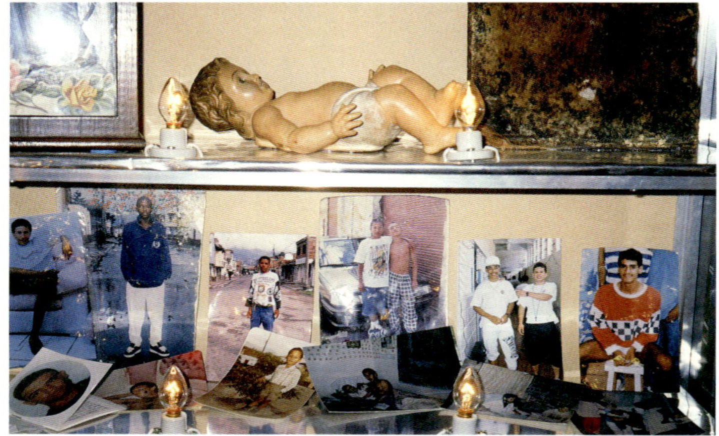

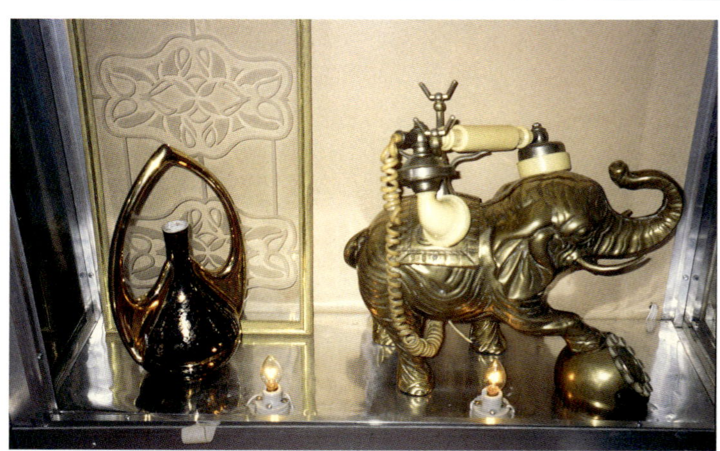

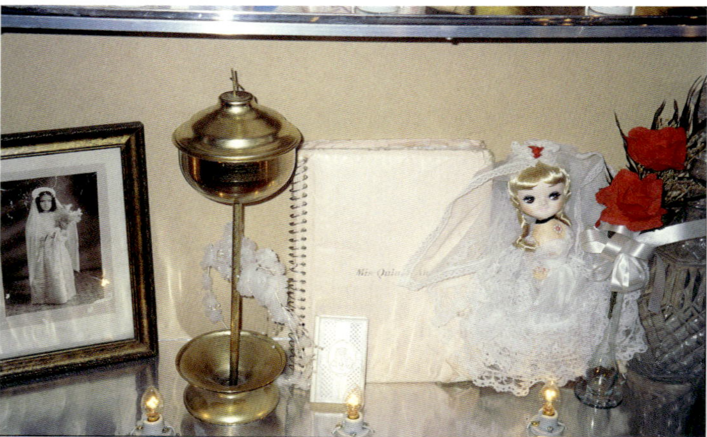

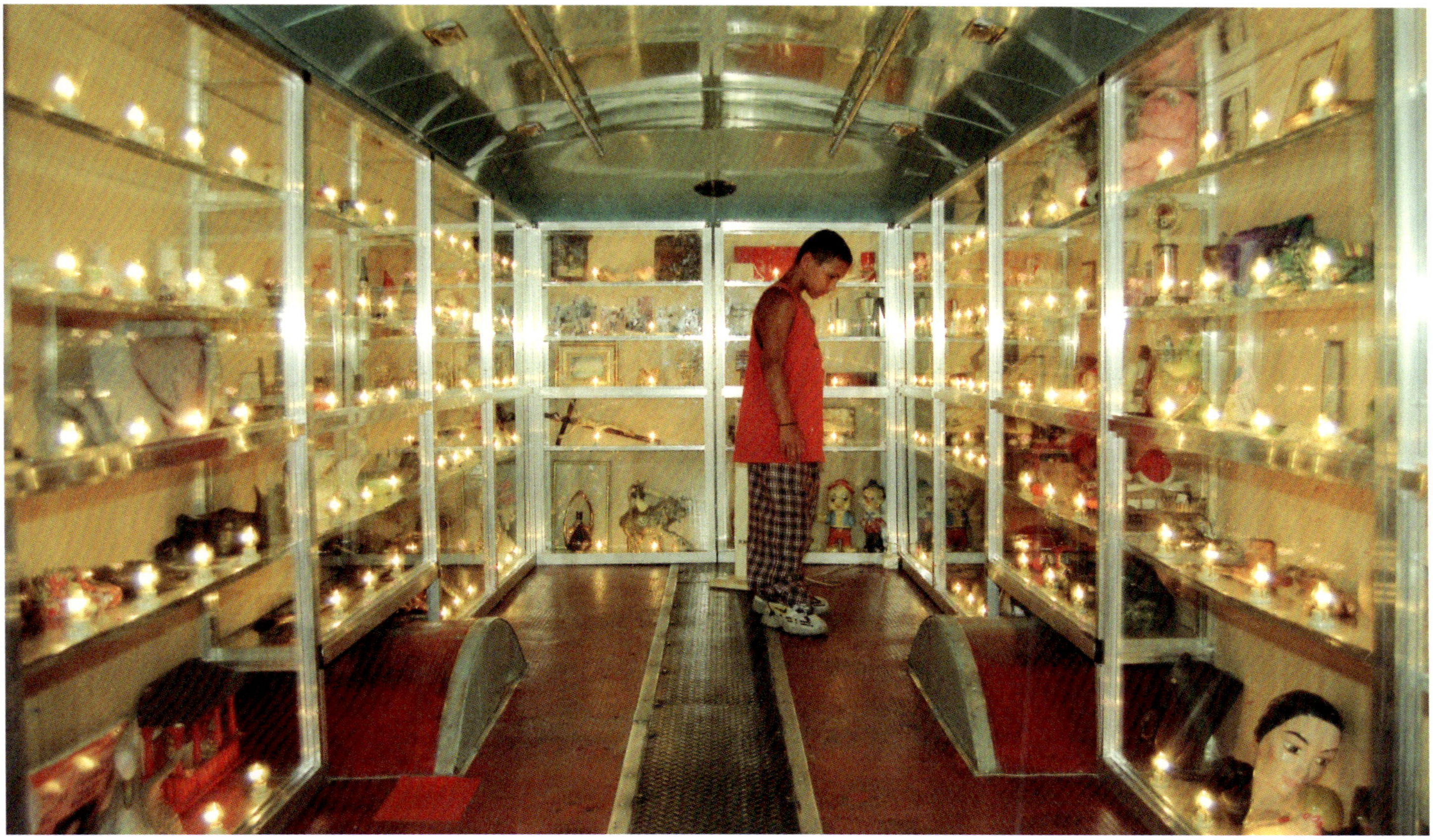

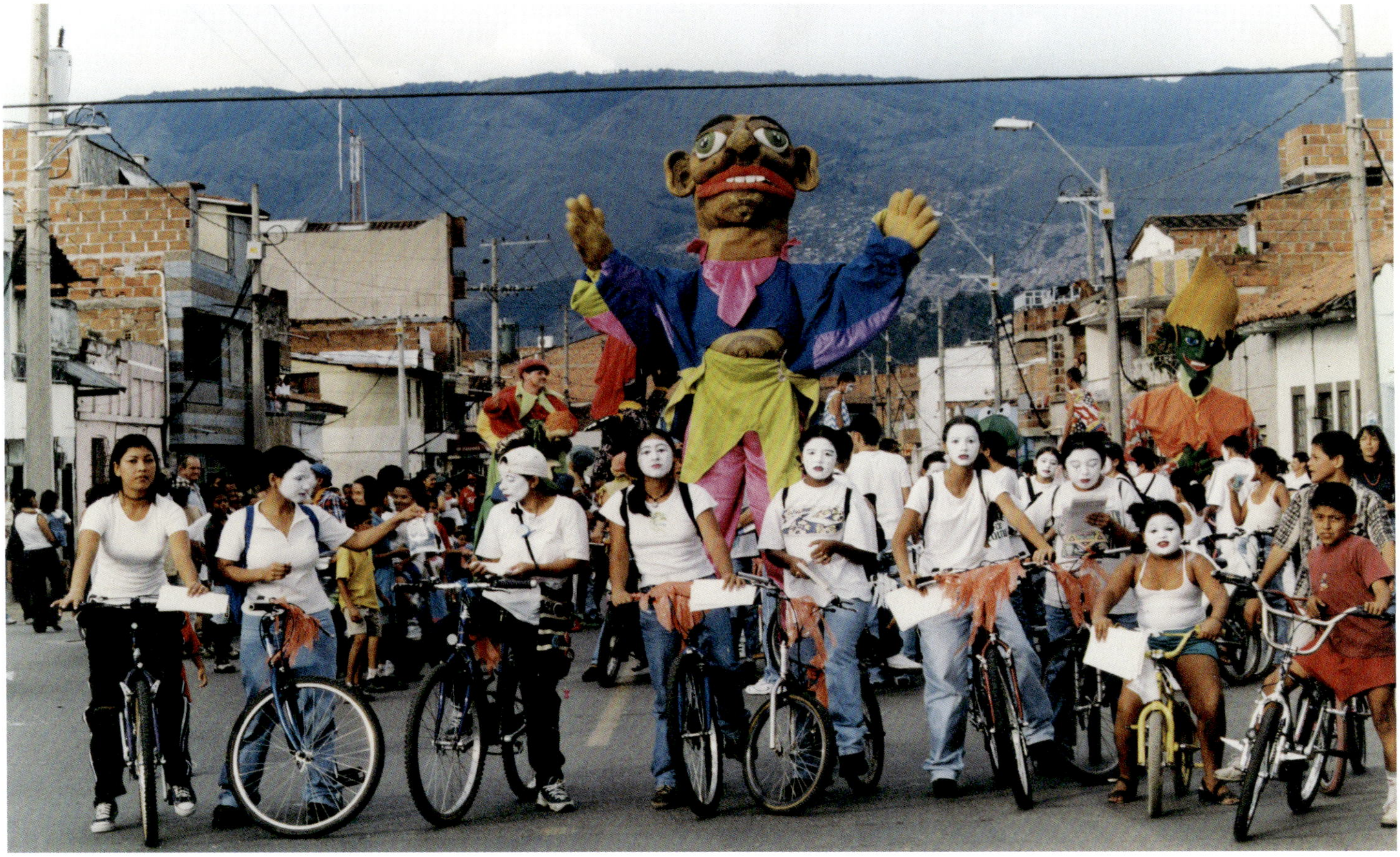

221

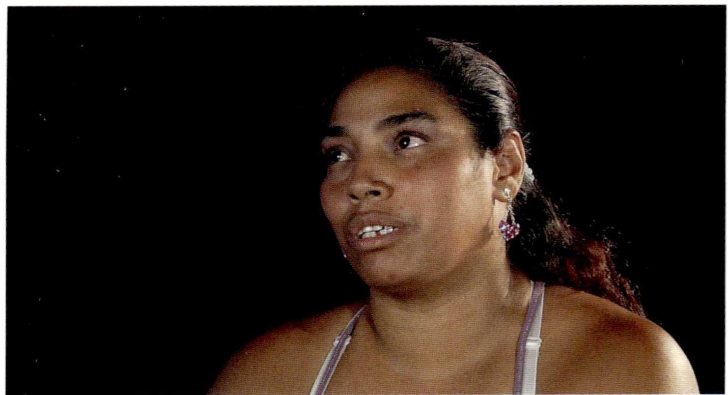

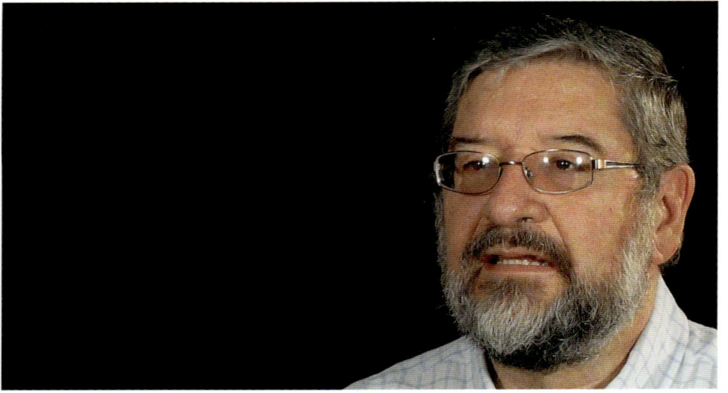

Back then men just couldn't go from one place to another, and we women were also afraid to do so. But we broke through that barrier, and we went into houses that we had never dreamed of going into. And we were made welcome, even if we came from a different sector of the barrio. . . . It [leaves] me so touched that in this moment that I am grieving the personal loss of my son, all those people [are] telling their stories of the killing[s] of their son[s] or the girl that drowned. My participation in *Skin of Memory* really helps me now to come to terms with my own pain.

Skin of Memory registered on two levels: a reflection of the international concern for memory and identity and the particularity of our situation as a society, the great anguish in its configuration. The project, in its artistic expression, had two very evident connotations: In the first place, making visible the scars of memory—and for that reason the name "Skin of Memory" is so accurate, the skin being where these kinds of records and traces are inscribed. I also think it had a very evident ethical/political effect, that of seeing in these scars not just the recognition of a history, of an identity, but of the possibility of building something.

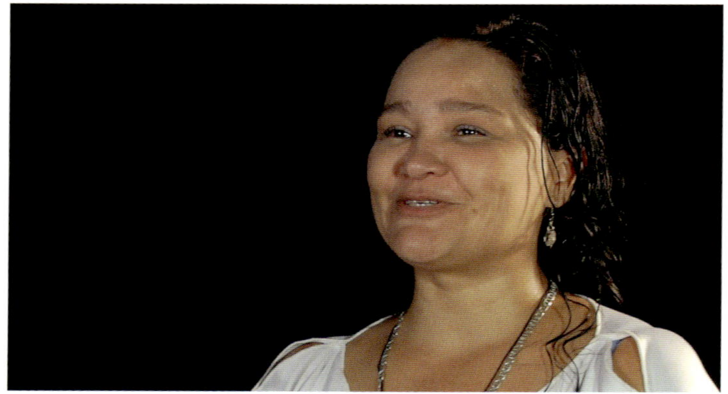

BOTH PAGES: Stills from *La piel de la memoria revivida/ Skin of Memory Revisited* with corresponding excerpts from the transcript

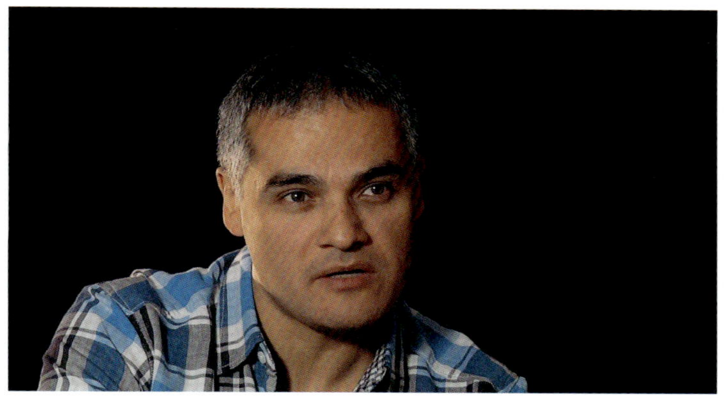

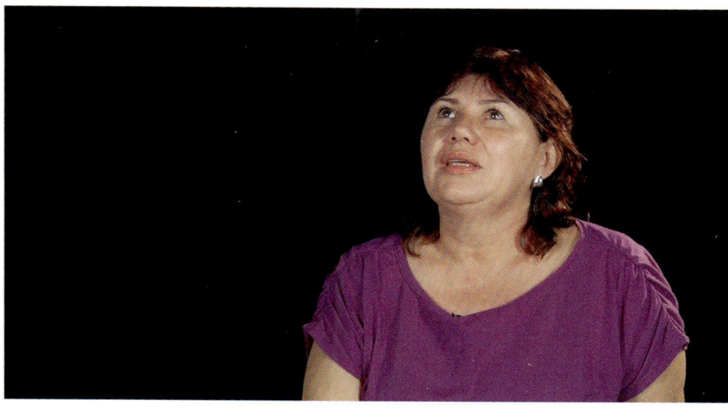

It was a barrio with streets full of life, of relationships, but at the same time it was life surrounded by death. . . . But what are we going to do with everything happening amidst this art? We can't keep thinking that it's only five or ten young men, rappers, murdered in La Comuna 13, or those involved in the project of art being killed today. So I think this project could shine a light on what is happening today, both the marvels of the city and the possibility of negotiating this violence in a different manner that would give us the way once again to touch the skin of these new generations and those who inhabit the city and who walk its streets every day.

A pair of jeans, this was the object of the lover, of a friend, who died and is kept by them. . . . The fundamental thing in a project of memory and history is that it matches art with pedagogy, and this is fundamental in the construction of a city. The public sphere and experiences of community work and pedagogy should be built together permanently.

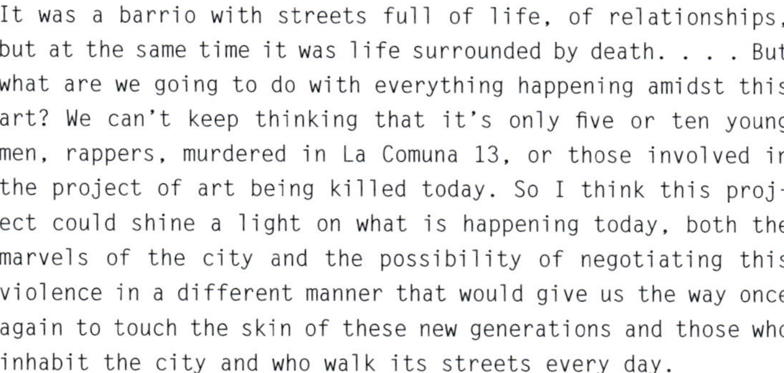

Listen, those letters filled those empty spaces left when the objects were brought to the bus. . . . This was about touching— it was like touching something we have inside. I don't know if we can touch people's hearts again, but I know that it helps, it helps so much to talk about the problems we all have. I had such a good time, and they got me out of the gang, El Combo, you know, that I was in. All those people around me then, they got me out. . . . Where are the mementos of those people? Do they still have them? I have my book. Where is the bus?

University of Local Knowledge (2000–ongoing)

SUZANNE LACY, PENNY EVANS, AND CAROLYN HASSAN

Residents of Bristol's Knowle West housing project, established in the early 1930s for British factory workers and their families, have long struggled with unemployment, crime, stereotyping, and limited access to higher education. Lacy worked with Evans, Hassan, Arnolfini Gallery, and Knowle West Media Centre to create a model for self-generated learning that challenges the hegemony of academic institutions as producers of knowledge. The team recorded one thousand videos, each between thirty seconds and four minutes long, that impart the skills and expertise of residents, cultivated through everything from child-rearing and running family businesses to religious worship and fitness routines. These videos function as "texts" that translate Knowle West into a kind of university, with a website to help find and share the knowledge of community members. Residents and professors also discussed their intersecting knowledge bases in public conversations held at local businesses. Knowle West Media Centre continues this work today, and *University of Local Knowledge* has provided a model for self-organized community education elsewhere.

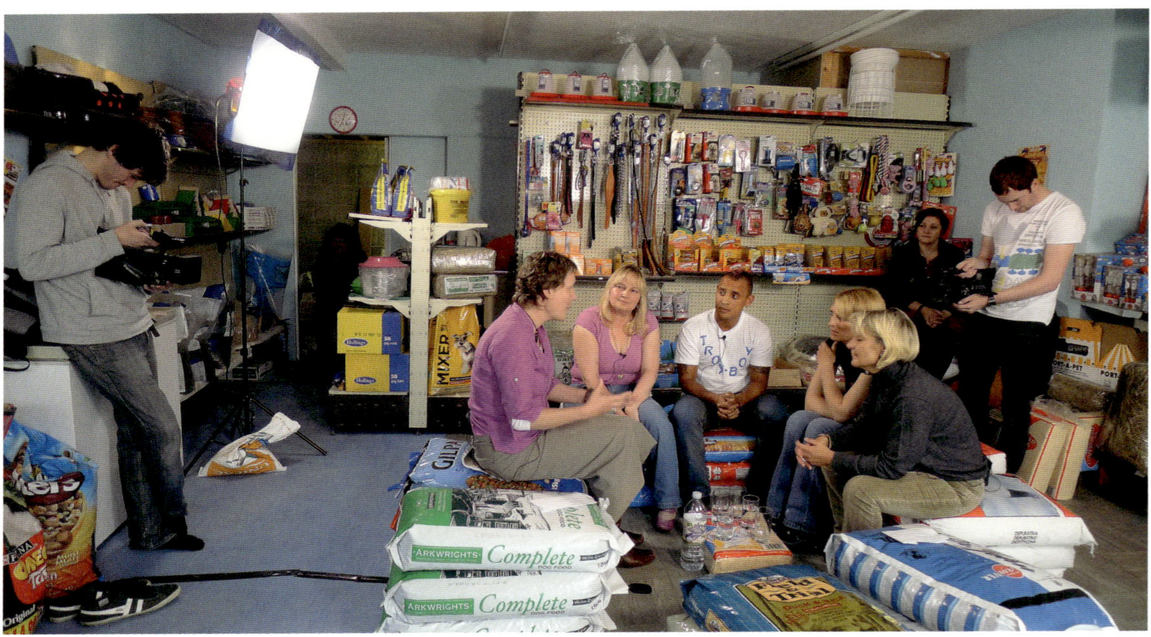

University of Local Knowledge set the groundwork for the organization we [Knowle West Media Centre] are today. It was the means by which we developed our practice, our work with artists; explored our relationship with partners such as the BBC, the universities, local government, the arts world; and, most importantly, committed to a practice that values long-term, deep engagement with our community . . . collaboratively recognizing the assets, experiences, and embodied knowledge in the community, rather than "doing to" or imposing cultural and arts practices on people.
—Carolyn Hassan, 2018

Throughout the project we generated one thousand videos filmed in private homes, garages, dance halls, football pitches, and gardens, always starting with [a] conversation and eliciting and then identifying with the participant the "nugget" of skill expertise, knowledge. Many people started to come forward and tell others. We adopted various strategies to create this momentum and scale, expand networks and a sense of ownership around the project. We hosted workshops around themes and relationships, met existing groups, invited people to discuss ways to share and invite. It launched with a "Lunch on the Green," providing a locally sourced sit-down meal for 250 people and opportunities to create content. The editing process was an understandably significant and highly structured process, both in content and in material. No one video or piece of knowledge resembled another.

—Penny Evans, 2018

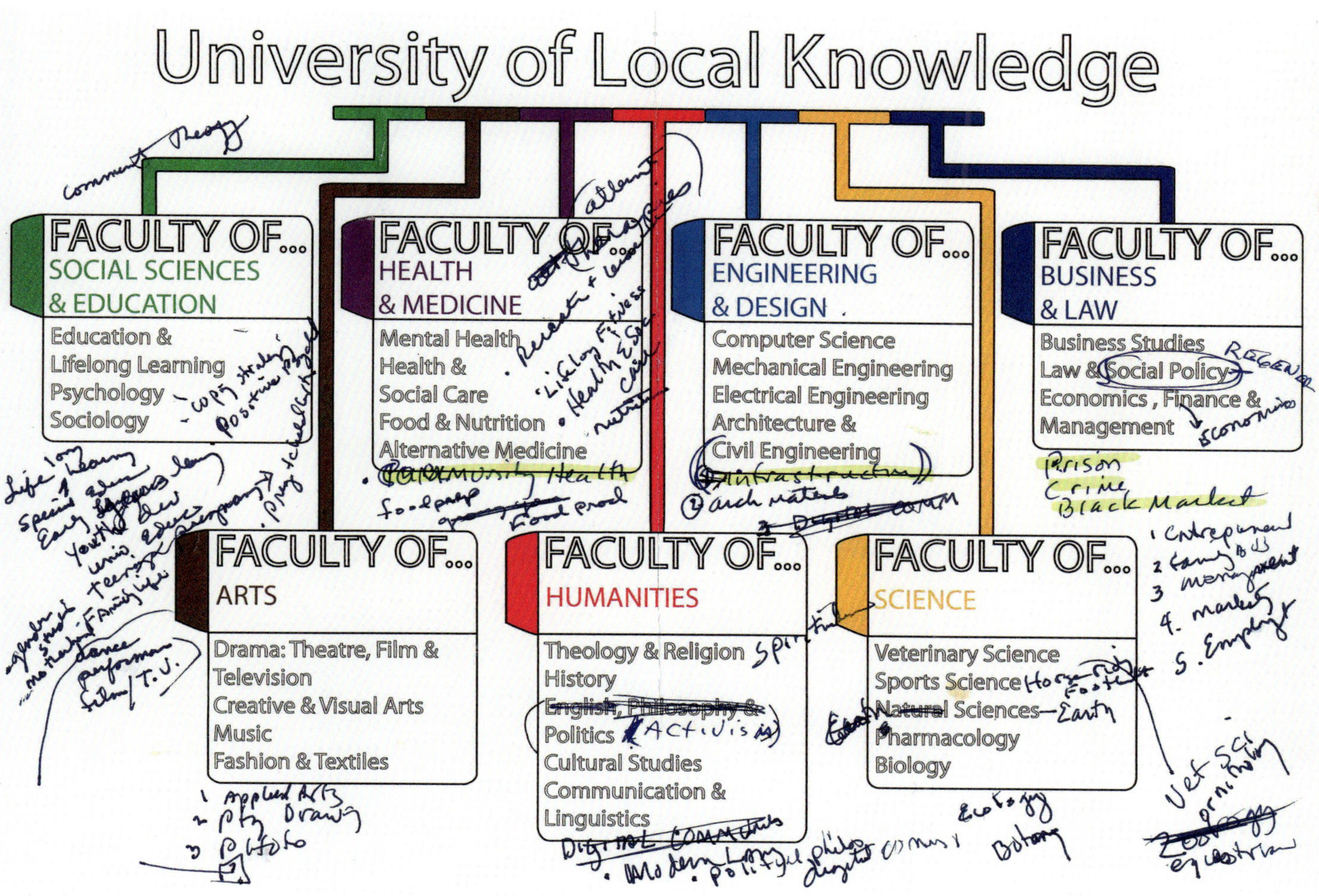

Organizational diagram with notes on the knowledge bases of Knowle West residents, structured according to "schools" and "departments" of the community's metaphorical "university"

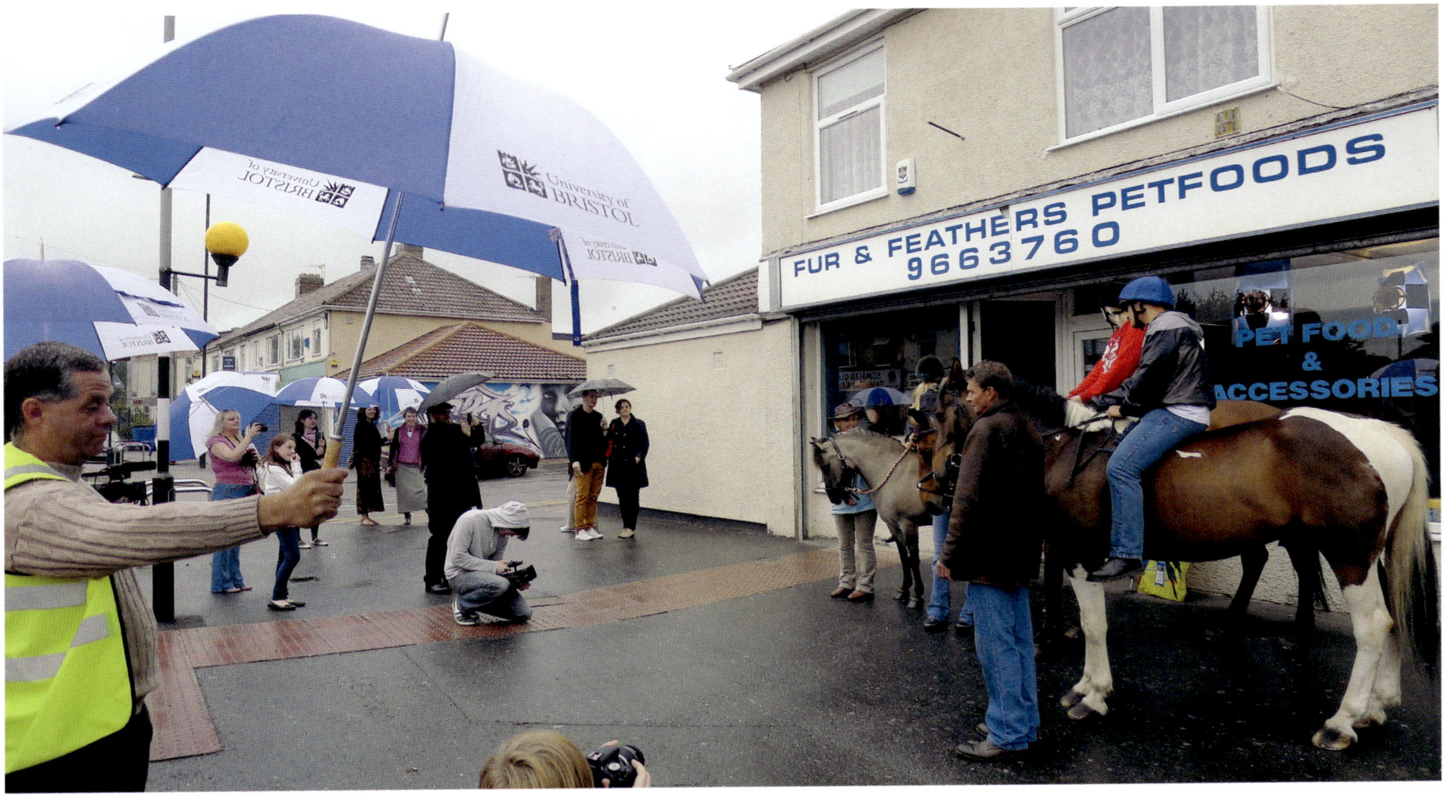

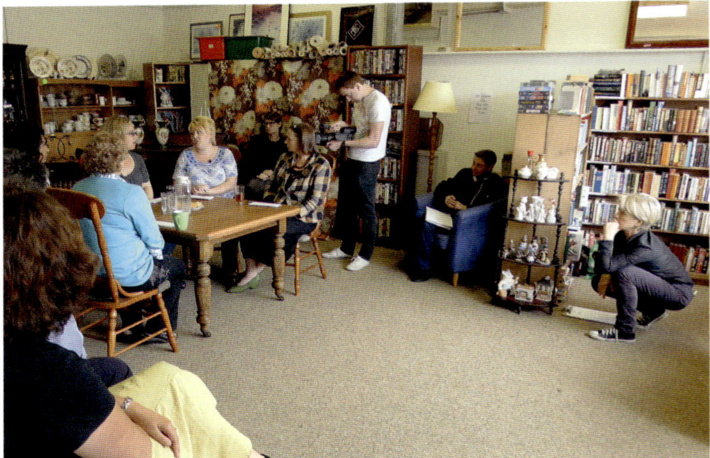

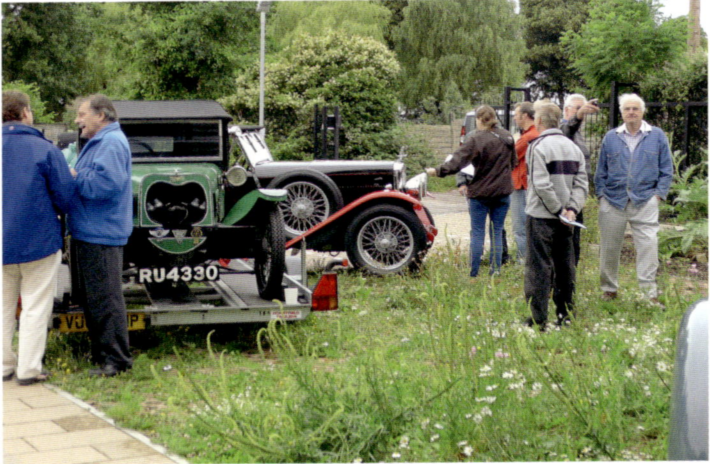

Conversations between community
members and professors
OPPOSITE: Online database of talks
and demonstrations by Knowle
West residents, produced by Knowle
West Media Centre

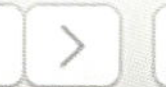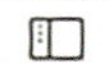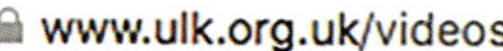 www.ulk.org.uk/videos 

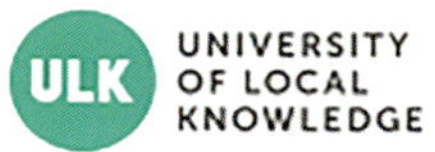

ULK UNIVERSITY OF LOCAL KNOWLEDGE

SEARCH THE SITE

LOGIN | JOIN

COURSES | VIDEOS | RESOURCES

+ ADD YOUR KNOWLEDGE

I want to see [All] videos about [Everything] in the [Global] community

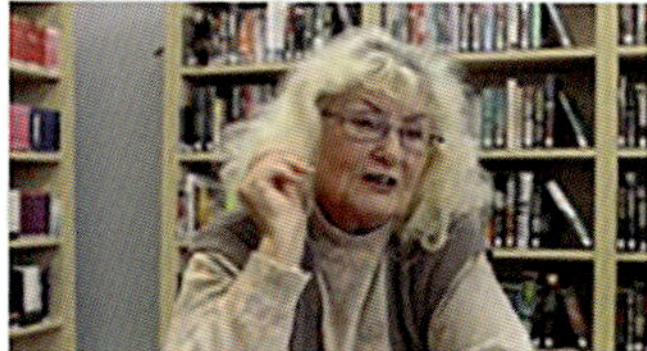

Performing a One Women Show

Added on 18/01/17
by admin
in Performance

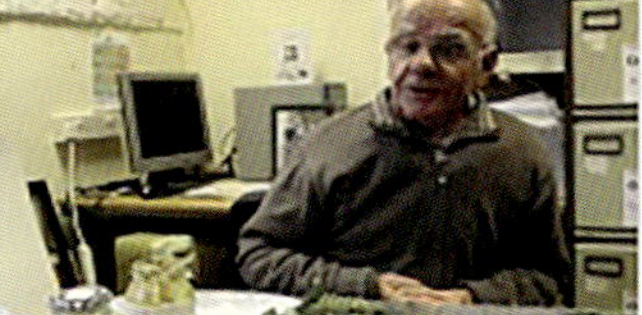

Becoming a Healer

Added on 18/01/17
by admin
in Healing

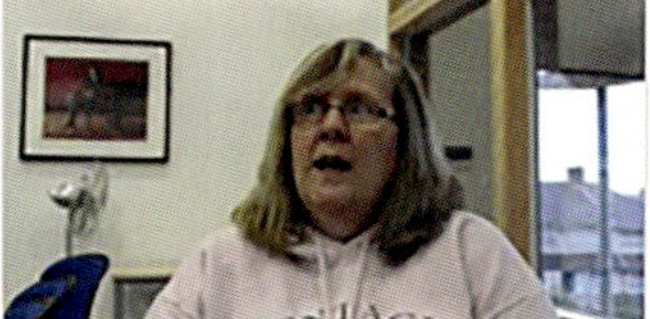

Copying with your Children leaving home

Added on 10/01/17
by admin
in Parenthood

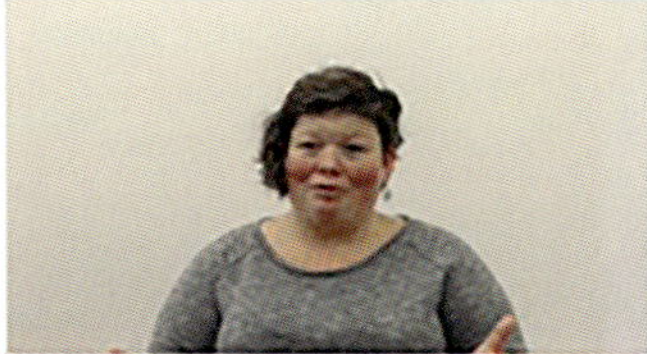

Foraging for Food

Added on 09/01/17
by admin
in Hunting

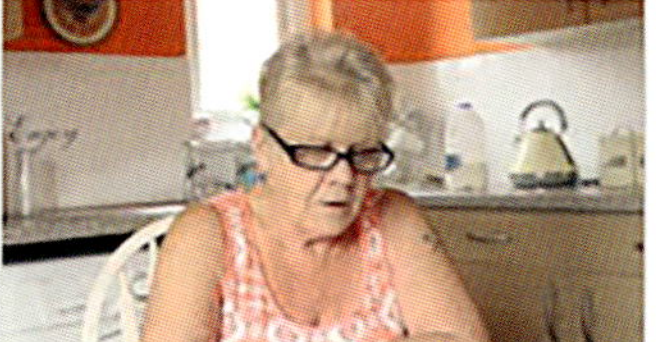

Writing Poems about Knowle West

Added on 30/11/16
by admin
in Learning

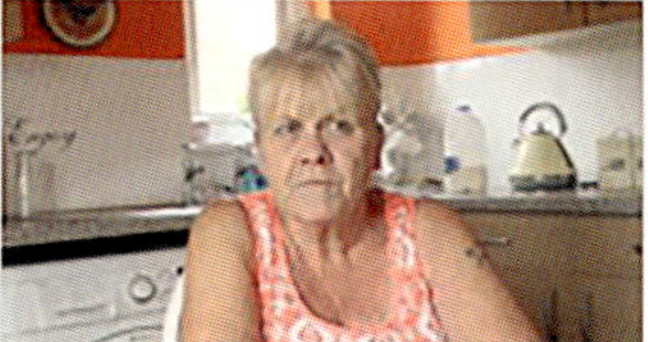

Life in Knowle West

Added on 30/11/16
by admin
in Community & Culture

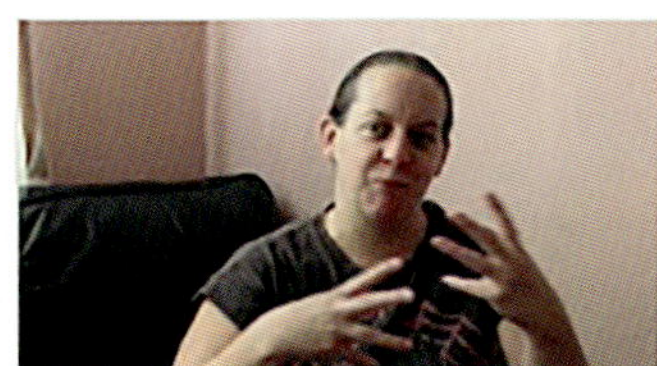

Becoming a Health Champion

Added on 30/11/16
by admin
in Health

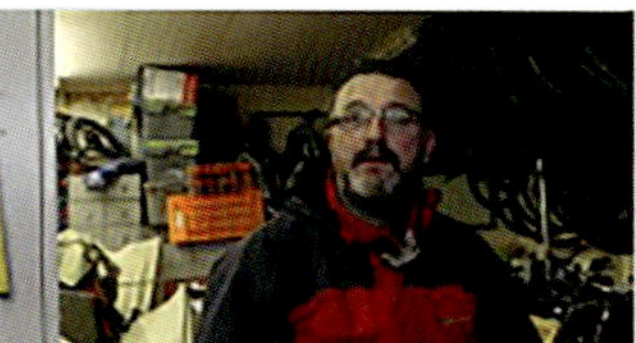

Setting up a Cycle Group

Added on 30/11/16
by admin
in Lifelong Fitness

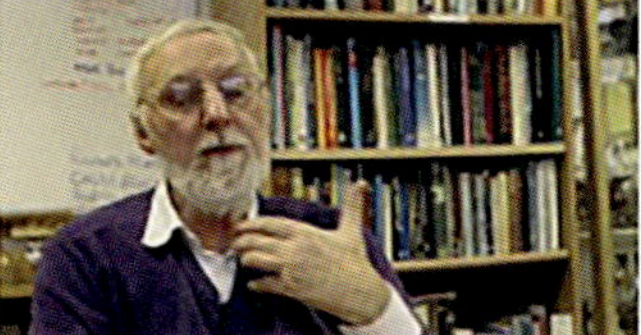

Growing Medicinal Healing Plants

Added on 30/11/16
by admin
in Gardening

‹ Previous   1 of 96   Next ›

Contribute your knowledge and connect with others

Do you have skills, experiences or stories you'd like to share with others? Become a member and add your local knowledge.

Join ULK

Beneath Land and Water:
A Project for Elkhorn City (2000–2005)

SUZANNE LACY, YUTAKA KOBAYASHI, AND SUSAN LEIBOVITZ STEINMAN

For five years Lacy, Kobayashi, and Steinman worked with the local government of Elkhorn City, a mountain town with scarcely one thousand residents in eastern Kentucky, to conceive and execute a community improvement project that would stimulate a sustainable eco-tourist economy. Amid ongoing efforts to clean up the Russell Fork River, which curves through the town center, they initiated a riverfront revitalization plan that drew on both this natural landscape and residents' strong connections to it. The artists collaborated with community members and officials including Nina Aragon, Tim Belcher, Stephanie Richardson, and Peggy Pings on a native plant garden with sculptural benches, a large outdoor mural that was designed by Steinman and painted collectively, and the Blue Line Trail walking path, which visually unifies the center of town with a pale blue line—inspired by the big Kentucky sky—painted along curbs, bridges, and building facades. A website for the project and a new tourism brochure were also produced.

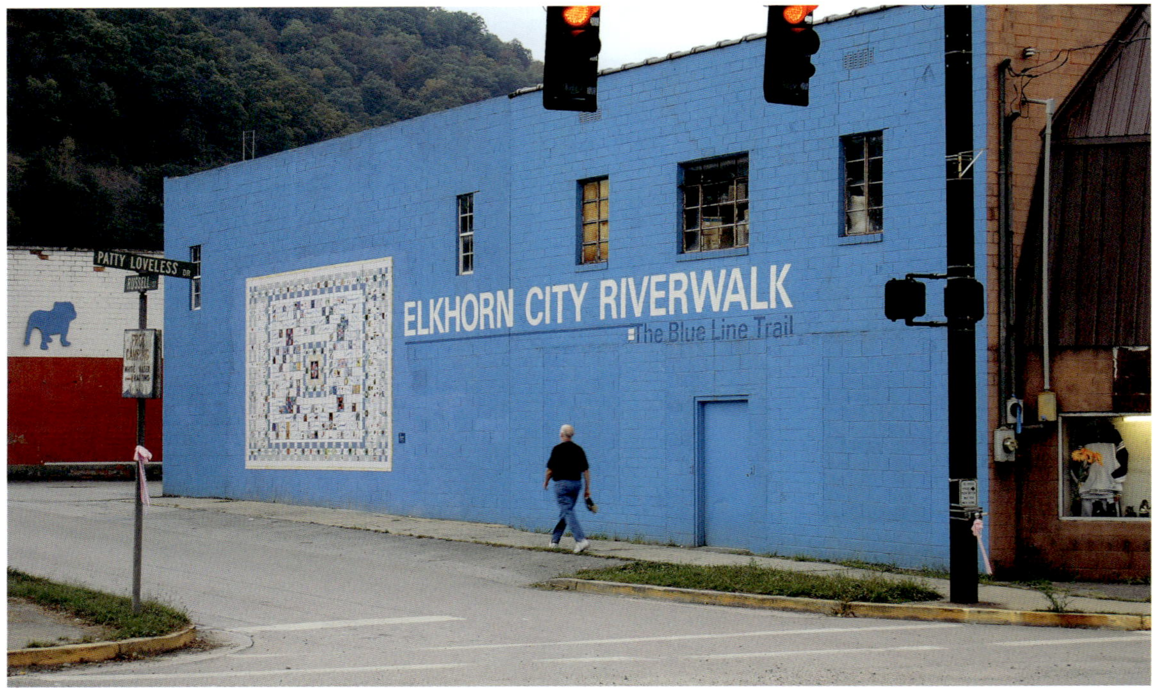

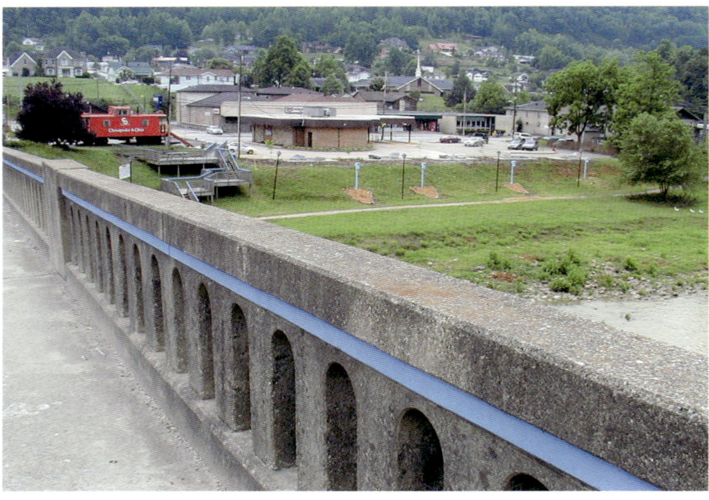

BOTH PAGES: The Blue Line Trail, Elkhorn residents, and community activities, including the planting of a native plant garden and the installation of sculptural benches along the Elkhorn City riverfront

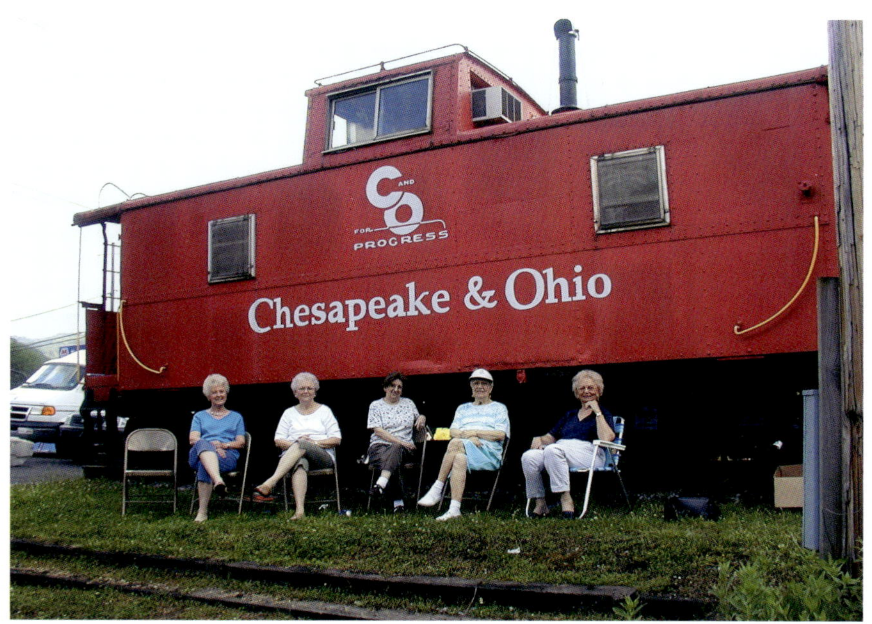

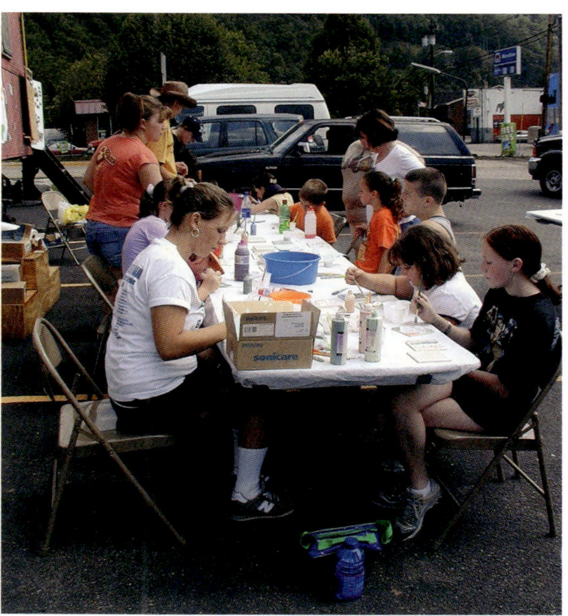

Being here has given me great insight into my totally eccentric working-class father, who called himself a "Tennessee hillbilly." Founded in 1825, Elkhorn City has relied on railroad, logging, and coal industries, fostering a hardy breed of rugged individuals—miners, loggers, Indians, settlers, railroaders, moonshiners, and outlaws. Mountain culture has a history of resistance, from moonshine production during Prohibition to union activism in the twentieth century, when women sat down in front of trucks, rifles were drawn, sheriffs called in, and miners killed.

—Suzanne Lacy, 2006

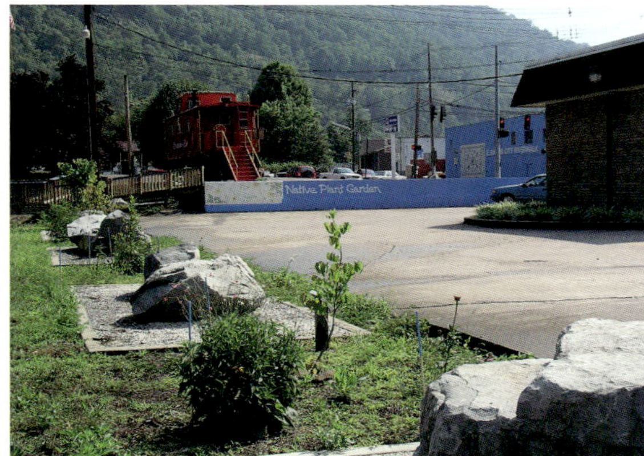

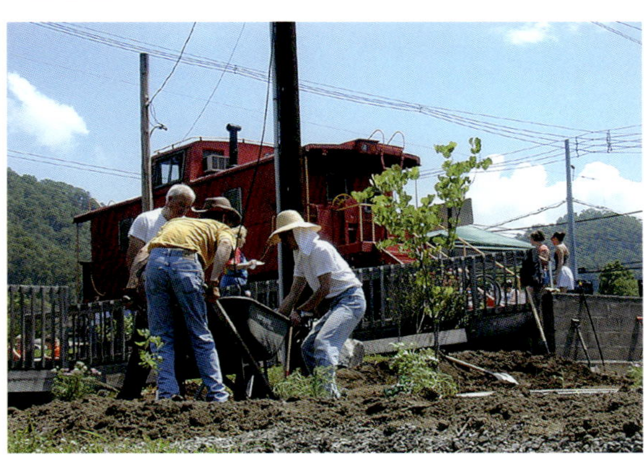

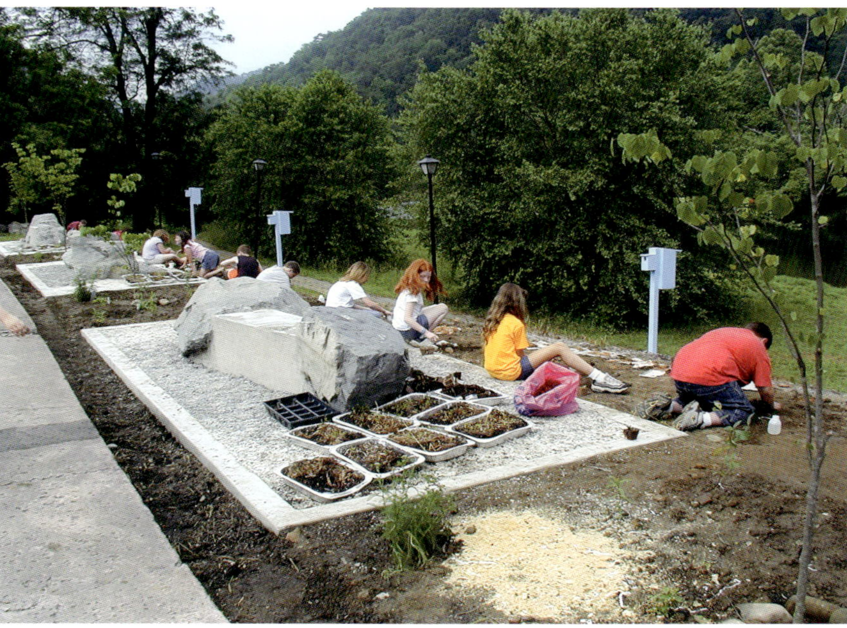

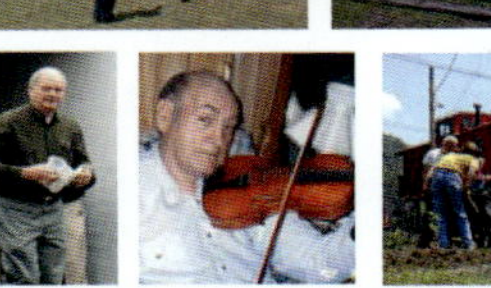
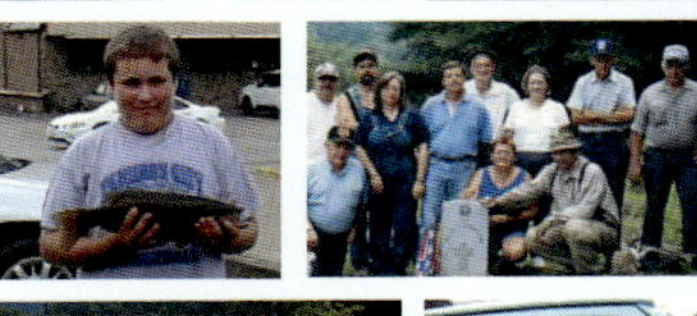
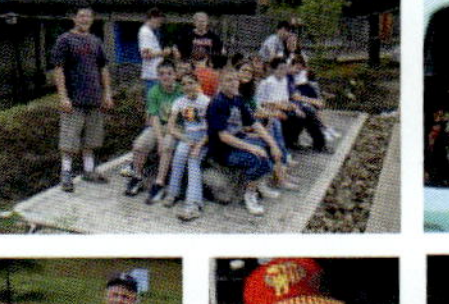
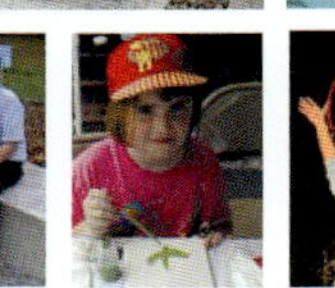
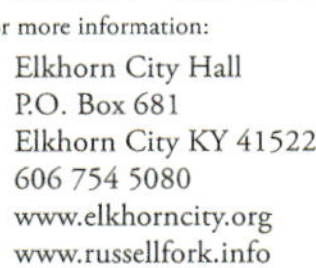

For more information:
Elkhorn City Hall
P.O. Box 681
Elkhorn City KY 41522
606 754 5080
www.elkhorncity.org
www.russellfork.info

ADVENTURE
where nature meets culture

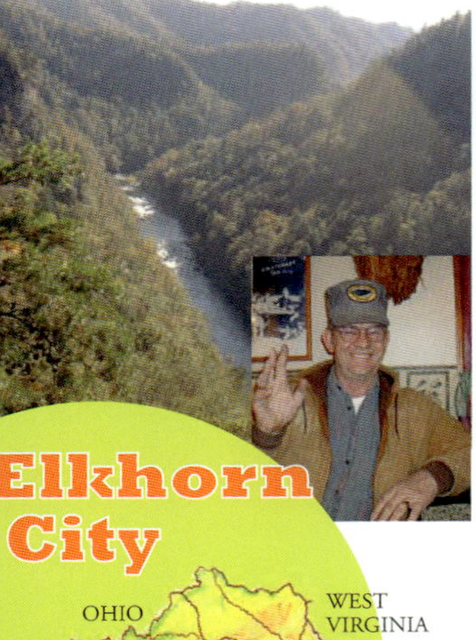

where nature

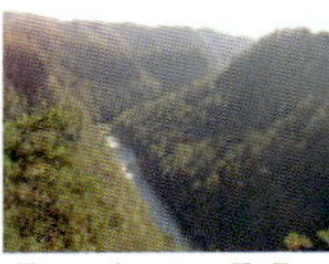
The marvelous view to The Towers from The Breaks.

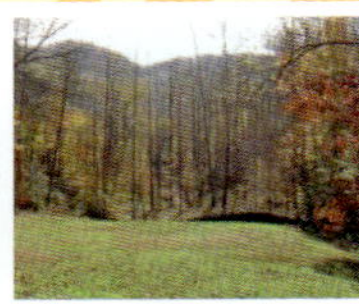
Hiking through Jefferson National Forest.

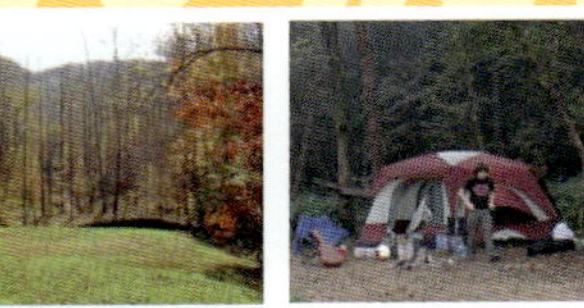
Camping and backpacking in lush Pine Mountain—a back to nature experience.

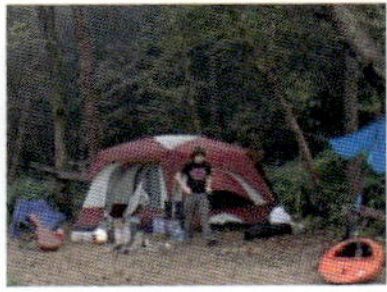
Feeding ducks in the Waterfront Park.

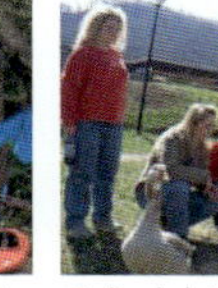

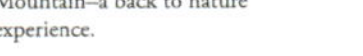

The Grand Canyon of the South

Elkhorn City is the jumping off point for some of the most scenic wilderness in the United States, surrounded by mountains, rivers, forests and meadows.

Travel Route 80, **Patty Loveless Highway** east from Elkhorn City to 4600-acre Breaks Interstate Park and find miles of hiking and horseback trails. Park amenities make it fun & easy for wildlife watching, fishing, camping and other outdoor activities. Campers can enjoy the Park's comfortable lodging and convenient RV hook-ups.

Adventure for All Levels

Imagine a bountiful river where you can fish in pristine wilderness or in the middle of the town in well-stocked **Russell Fork River**. Regional birds and plants, such as the native rhododendron bushes, provide a peaceful distraction on long walks. Avid hunters will find an abundance of wild turkey in the region.

For the more adventuresome, hiking, mountain biking or horseback riding through the historic **Potter's Flats** meadow offers views of archaeological ruins from early pioneer homes. The history of **Potter Flats** is a source of colorful stories about moonshine, stills and revenue agents.

The area surrounding Elkhorn City is a backpacking paradise. The **Jefferson National Forest** extends from Elkhorn City to Raven Rock at Pound Gap. A new trailhead for the **Pine Mountain Trail** establishes Elkhorn City as a starting point for the 210 mile trail to Cumberland Gap National Historic Park in Tennessee.

Adventure in Nature

- Jefferson National Forest
- Potter Flats
- Breaks Interstate Park
- Russell Fork River
- Trailhead of the Pine Mountain Trail
- Ratliff Hole

Fishing, rock climbing and mountain biking for the outdoor enthusiast.

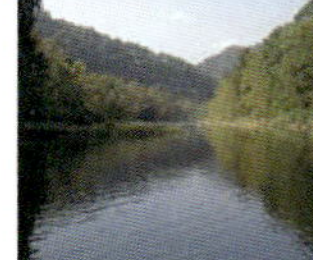

Adventure Variety

- Whitewater boating
- Kayaking, rafting & canoeing
- Trout fishing
- Rock climbing
- Horseback riding
- Hiking
- Hunting
- Long distance biking
- Mountain biking
- Swimming
- Camping

www.elkhorncity.org
www.russellfork.info

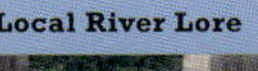

Local River Lore

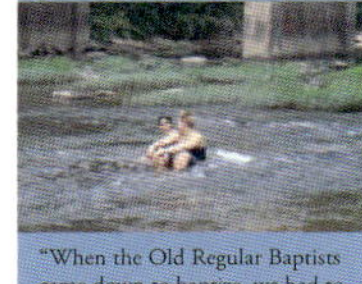
"When the Old Regular Baptists came down to baptize, we had to stay in the water until they finished, because we weren't wearing swimming trunks!"

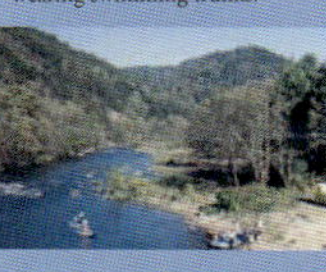
"Before they had kayaks, we used tubes and before that, railroad ties to ride the river into Elkhorn!"

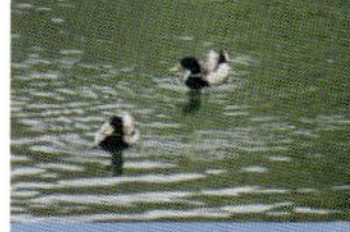
"Every evening I feed the ducks down at the Waterfront Park and, if she's able, my wife comes to watch."

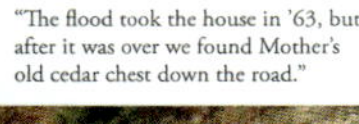
"The flood took the house in '63, but after it was over we found Mother's old cedar chest down the road."

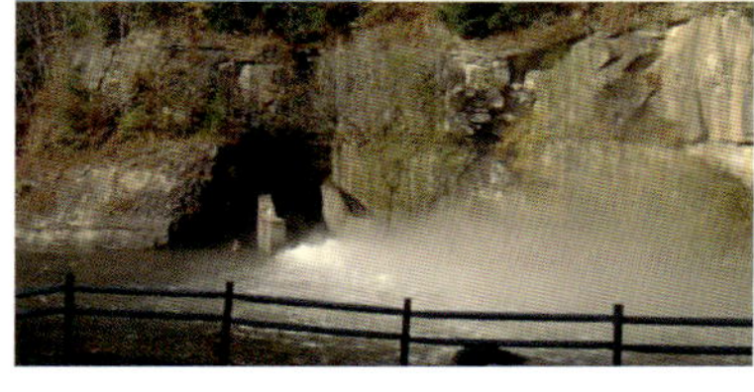

Whitewater Boating

The **Russell Fork River** carved the largest canyon east of the Mississippi, estimated to be as old as 250 million years.

After cutting a 1600 foot gorge through the mountains, the Russell Fork cascades into **Elkhorn City**, a great pull out and place to catch a bite after the day's river trip.

Rafters and kayakers navigate the gorge paddling through some of the best Class IV—V rated whitewater in the United States.

But the greatest thing about the river is that there are sections for beginner and intermediate boaters of all ages and abilities.

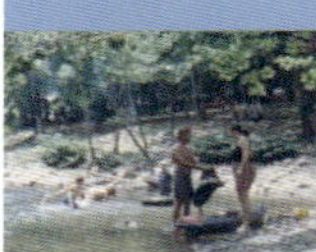
"They threw me overboard and said, 'Sink or swim.' That's how most people around here learned."

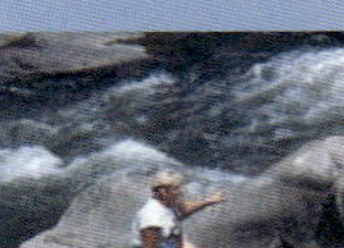
"I lost one of the biggest Smallmouth Bass I ever saw over by that bridge. It was pure heartbreak."

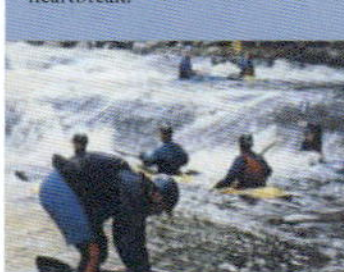
"The loggers rode the logs all the way downriver to Ashland, enjoyed the local saloons, and then took the train back home."

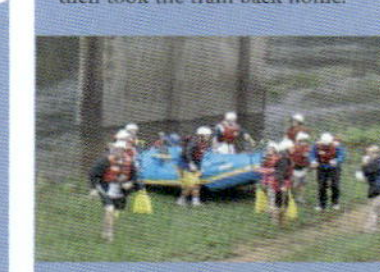
"Before they had kayaks, we used tubes and before that, railroad ties to ride the river into Elkhorn."

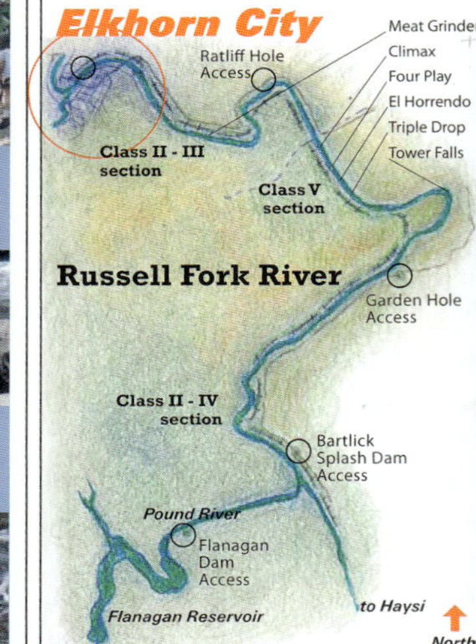

Loggers and kayakers have charted the river on its way from West Virgina to Elkhorn City. Riverside trails allow hikers access to this natural beauty.

For whitewater information, contact www.russellfork.info.

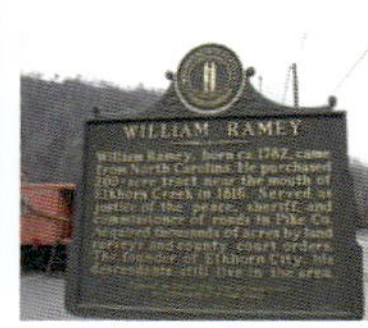

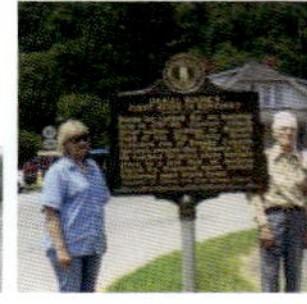

Elkhorn City River Walk

The Elkhorn City River Walk—also called The Blue Line Trail, referring to the City's railroad past—was constructed by local residents and artists from all over the world. The theme of this scenic 15 minute walk is the protection of the natural environment that residents hold dear. The entire community—children, youth, adults, and retirees—worked together to revitalize their town.

The first stop is the (1) Red Caboose & Wm. Ramey Historical Marker and (2) Waterfront Park, a bird habitat with viewing decks above the Russell Fork River. An artist from Japan used stone from a local quarry and concrete to make (3) sculptural seating benches. (4) The Nature Garden and Butterfly Habitat, designed by a California artist, contains native plants from the region. Ducks swim under the bridge and fish break the water surface as they feed. Fishing, swimming, picnicking, sunbathing and inner-tubing area is part of a day's play here at the Waterfront Park.

Don't miss the (5) Children's Mural with a child's eye view of local nature as you head toward the Historic District via the (6) Walking Trestle Bridge across the river. Visit (7) the Railroad Museum on the other side and if you're lucky talk to a retired railroad worker. Continue toward Main Street and the public library, a good source of family genealogy; (8) the Old Bank Building; and (9) the Artists' Collaborative Theatre with its seasonal schedule of plays. Nearby is the Daniel Boone Historical Marker. Turn left and you are on Cantrell Bridge, heading back to the Waterfront Park.

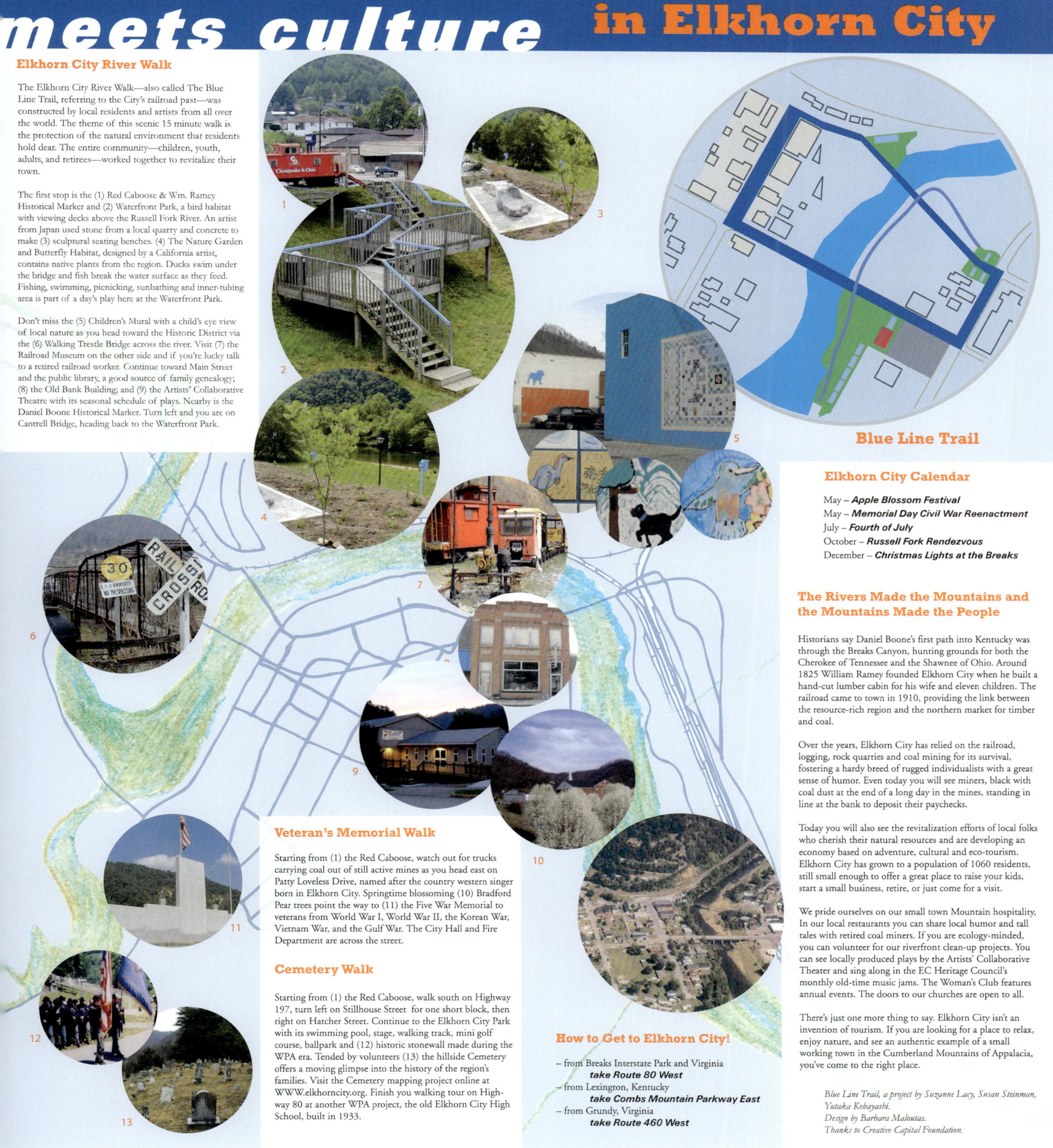

Blue Line Trail

Elkhorn City Calendar

May – **Apple Blossom Festival**
May – **Memorial Day Civil War Reenactment**
July – **Fourth of July**
October – **Russell Fork Rendezvous**
December – **Christmas Lights at the Breaks**

The Rivers Made the Mountains and the Mountains Made the People

Historians say Daniel Boone's first path into Kentucky was through the Breaks Canyon, hunting grounds for both the Cherokee of Tennessee and the Shawnee of Ohio. Around 1825 William Ramey founded Elkhorn City when he built a hand-cut lumber cabin for his wife and eleven children. The railroad came to town in 1910, providing the link between the resource-rich region and the northern market for timber and coal.

Over the years, Elkhorn City has relied on the railroad, logging, rock quarries and coal mining for its survival, fostering a hardy breed of rugged individualists with a great sense of humor. Even today you will see miners, black with coal dust at the end of a long day in the mines, standing in line at the bank to deposit their paychecks.

Today you will also see the revitalization efforts of local folks who cherish their natural resources and are developing an economy based on adventure, cultural and eco-tourism. Elkhorn City has grown to a population of 1060 residents, still small enough to offer a great place to raise your kids, start a small business, retire, or just come for a visit.

We pride ourselves on our small town Mountain hospitality, In our local restaurants you can share local humor and tall tales with retired coal miners. If you are ecology-minded, you can volunteer for our riverfront clean-up projects. You can see locally produced plays by the Artists' Collaborative Theater and sing along in the EC Heritage Council's monthly old-time music jams. The Woman's Club features annual events. The doors to our churches are open to all.

There's just one more thing to say. Elkhorn City isn't an invention of tourism. If you are looking for a place to relax, enjoy nature, and see an authentic example of a small working town in the Cumberland Mountains of Appalacia, you've come to the right place.

Blue Line Trail, a project by Suzanne Lacy, Susan Steinman, Yutaka Kobayashi.
Design by Barbara Maloutas.
Thanks to Creative Capital Foundation.

Veteran's Memorial Walk

Starting from (1) the Red Caboose, watch out for trucks carrying coal out of still active mines as you head east on Patty Loveless Drive, named after the country western singer born in Elkhorn City. Springtime blossoming (10) Bradford Pear trees point the way to (11) the Five War Memorial to veterans from World War I, World War II, the Korean War, Vietnam War, and the Gulf War. The City Hall and Fire Department are across the street.

Cemetery Walk

Starting from (1) the Red Caboose, walk south on Highway 197, turn left on Stillhouse Street for one short block, then right on Hatcher Street. Continue to the Elkhorn City Park with its swimming pool, stage, walking track, mini golf course, ballpark and (12) historic stonewall made during the WPA era. Tended by volunteers (13) the hillside Cemetery offers a moving glimpse into the history of the region's families. Visit the Cemetery mapping project online at WWW.elkhorncity.org. Finish you walking tour on Highway 80 at another WPA project, the old Elkhorn City High School, built in 1933.

How to Get to Elkhorn City!

– from Breaks Interstate Park and Virginia
take Route 80 West
– from Lexington, Kentucky
take Combs Mountain Parkway East
– from Grundy, Virginia
take Route 460 West

CENTRAL VALLEY

(2008–ongoing)

Tulare: Garage Sale / Beer Bucket/Champagne Bucket /
Laton: Free Store / Dad Lessons

Since 2008, Lacy has produced several works in small towns in California's rural San Joaquin Valley. She has likened the region to Appalachia, as its agricultural communities struggle with similar extremes of poverty and pollution; the visual history of the area includes Dorothea Lange's Depression-era photographs of Dust Bowl migrants, one of the populations that was hit hardest by the economic downturn. Lacy's own working-class upbringing in the San Joaquin Valley has informed her interest in foregrounding economic class struggle and disparity in much of her work, and the region has been a touchstone for her thinking about the expressive potential of art. Among these projects are a series of installations and exhibitions in the town of Laton, produced with students from the Graduate Public Practice Program at Los Angeles's Otis College of Art and Design, and photographic and video works that depict daily life in Tulare, produced in collaboration with other artists.

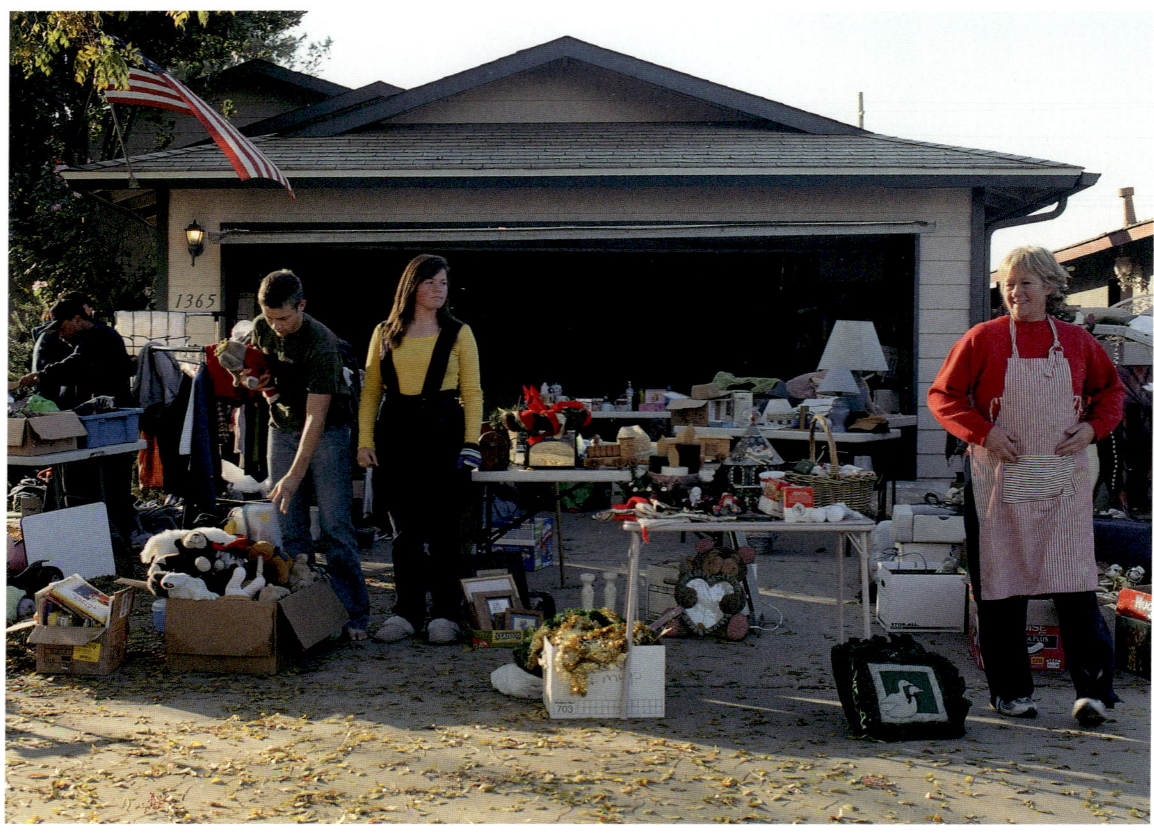

Tulare: Garage Sale, 2008

Tulare: Garage Sale (2008)

SUZANNE LACY WITH KELLY AKASHI

This series of photographic and video installations chronicles the centrality of the yard sale to the economies and social landscapes of small towns in the San Joaquin Valley. The project depicts yard sales as sites where friends and family convene and where neighbors of different ethnic backgrounds come together to create micro-economies on which working-class towns like Tulare depend. Some pictures include members of Lacy's own family. *Tulare: Garage Sale* has been exhibited at the Los Angeles Municipal Art Gallery; Track 16 Gallery, Culver City, California; and Sweeney Art Gallery at the University of California, Riverside. Andy Manoushagian edited the video.

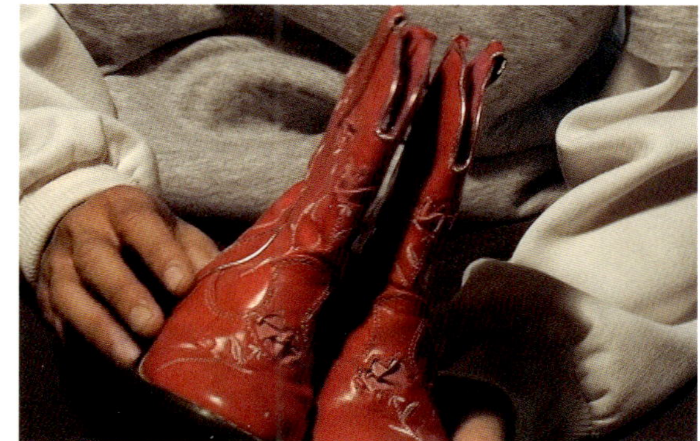

Beer Bucket/Champagne Bucket (2008)

This multimedia installation includes a series of photographs of yard sales in the San Joaquin Valley, lined with stacks of used clothing. Written on the stacks is a narrative on "beer stocks," or stocks that serve low-income households, and "champagne stocks," which serve high-income households, along with advertisements for local yard sales and notes on the movement of California cotton agriculture to foreign countries.

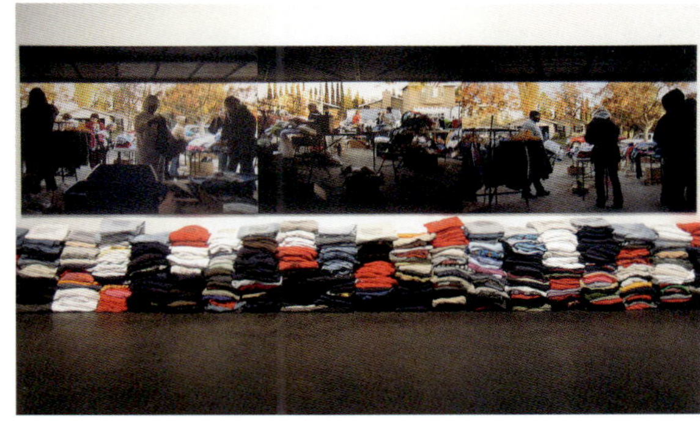

Laton: Free Store (2009)

SUZANNE LACY AND ANDREA BOWERS

Lacy organized a number of events and community revitalization projects for the small town of Laton with invited artists and her students in the Graduate Public Practice Program at Otis College of Art and Design, Los Angeles. Among the projects was *Laton: Free Store*, a hub for residents to donate and trade used clothing and household items. It was created at Laton's United Methodist Church, where the collaborators met with community members to learn about what was needed and how their partnership could have a lasting impact on the lives of residents. The donated clothing was solicited by Lacy and Bowers for the 2009 exhibition *Your Donations Do Our Work*, organized at the Sweeney Art Gallery at the University of California, Riverside.

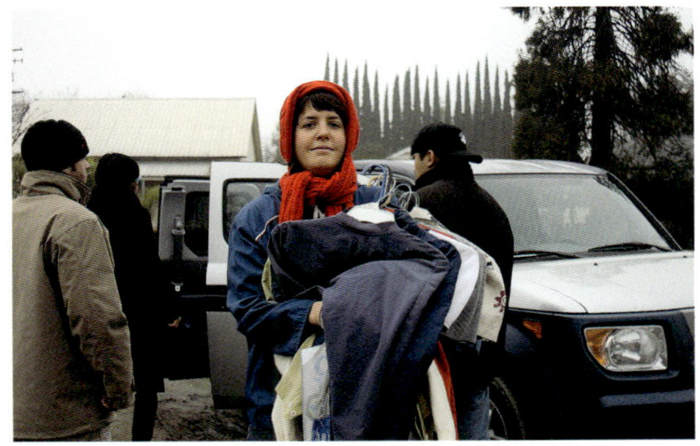

Dad Lessons (2019)

Lacy made two video works featuring her elderly father, Larry Lacy. Alone in the camera's frame, he recalls his service in the United States Air Force. Lacy captures his moments of struggle against the deterioration of memory, as well as his sense of humor. Shot against sweeping backdrops of Tulare, California, in the San Joaquin Valley, these works evoke the simple act of a daughter listening to her father reflect on his life and observe the changing surroundings in which he finds himself.

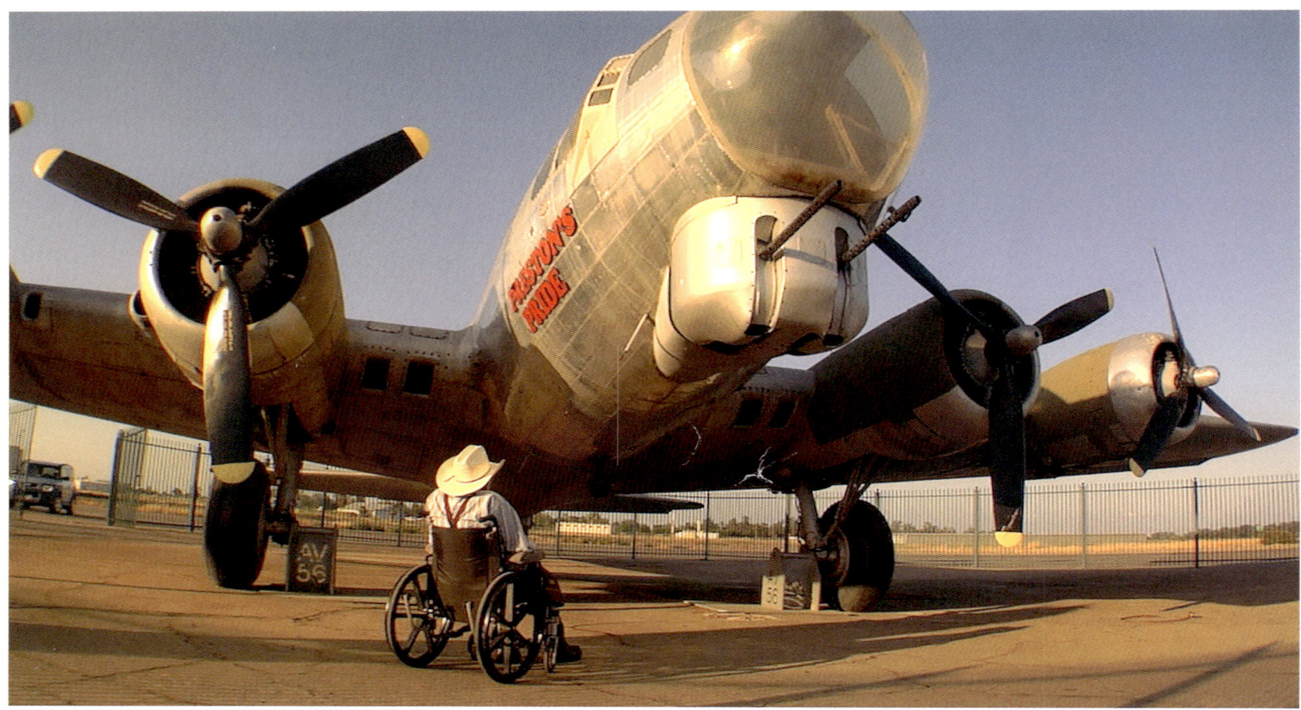

TRANSCRIPT (EXCERPTS)

Well, I felt a lot better about fitting in the cockpit of a B-17. I flew the B-24 for two years trying not to get killed every year, and I just thanked God when they transferred me out of B-24s and sent me to the war in B-17s. Because a B-24, if you damage the body a little bit, or the tail a little bit, the plane, it would fall apart, but the B-17, you could have the tail half shot off and the guys could make it back to safe times and safe places, usually.

It's just a stronger geometric structure. It's round, instead of a square box, and it had one real strong vertical tail instead of two of them. . . .

There's just so much that I've forgotten, ah, it seems like a hundred years ago, but there's so much I've forgotten about these planes. . . .

Yeah, I was a pilot. I flew for three and a half years in the air force. And I enjoyed it. I had a lot of good friends, ah, but one of the problems of living [to] almost ninety, is you outlive all your friends. I don't know where a single one of my friends is now. They are probably all gone from this earth because most people don't live [to be] as old as I am.

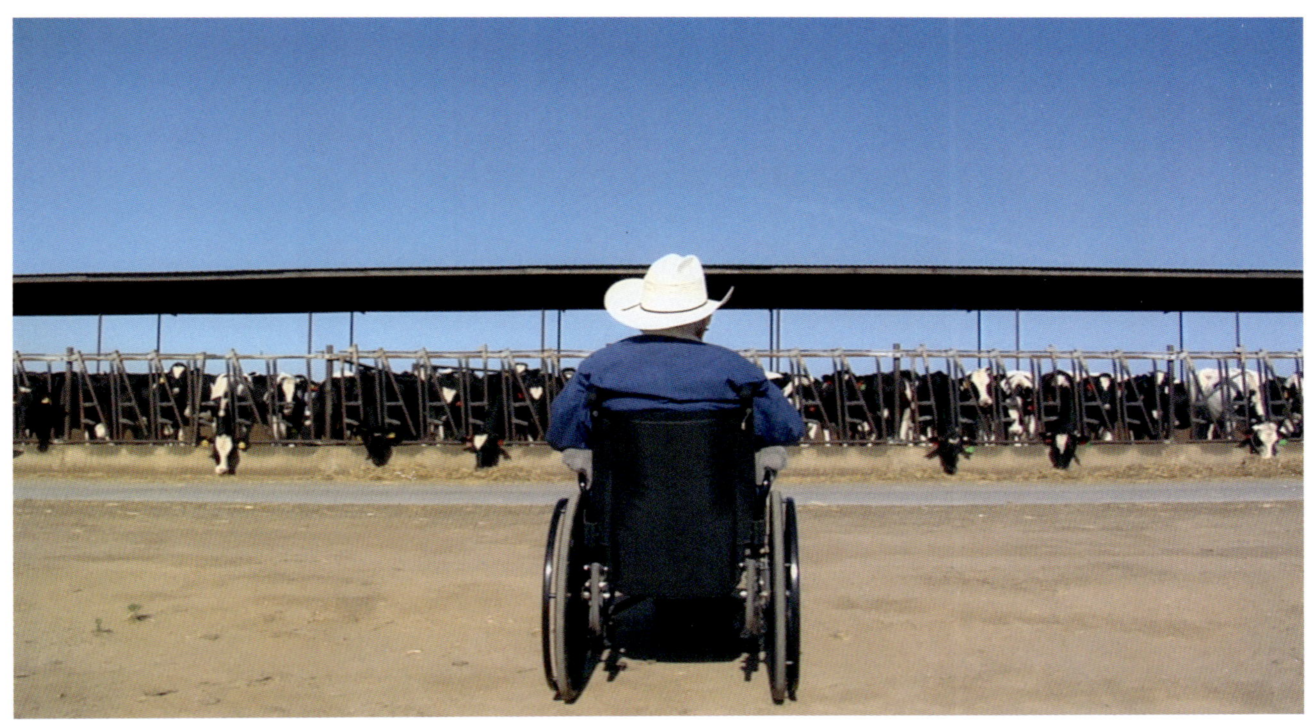

When we were growing up in the South, most of the milk cows we had were Jerseys. And, my God, my feeble brain, Holsteins, I'd forgotten the name of Holsteins. I don't think these are Holsteins. I don't know what kind of cows they are. But they're the most common cow here in our dairy, and in all of California.

A lot of my dairy information is dated, though. I, I get confused, now at my age, about what kind of cows they are and how much money they're making. . . . A cow's milk production will dwindle off after she delivers a calf. And sometimes the calves around here, the conditions we are under today, the feed and everything costs more than they can get out of the milk. So, at best, they're just breaking even or treading water. They're not going very far with their product, because they're not making a profit on it like they once did. . . .

Might mention too, this wind is picking up, and it's blowing some of the haze away. And we can just barely see the snow-capped Sierra Mountains, over there to the east. So on a clear day, it's just beautiful to watch the snow. And that snow probably won't come off till June or July.

Cleaning Conditions (2013)

SUZANNE LACY WITH MEG PARNELL

Cleaning Conditions paid homage to Lacy's mentor Allan Kaprow, who was a faculty member at the California Institute of the Arts, Valencia, when she was a student, by interpreting his text *Chores* (1995) as a two-week performance installation at the Manchester Art Gallery, England. Lacy recruited a team of "sweepers" from local labor and immigration organizations, clad in matching red T-shirts, to sweep the galleries daily, beginning in front of Ford Madox Brown's large oil painting *Work* (1852–65). The sweepers followed Kaprow's instructions by redistributing not "dust" on the gallery floors, but political ephemera printed on brightly colored paper, and like Kaprow's practice of holding post-performance discussions, the daily sweepings were followed by public conversations among activists, politicians, students, and museum visitors on the subject of labor in service industries and its intersections with questions of immigration, gender, and living wages. Private conversations with museum staff also formed around these issues. The performance was realized as part of the Manchester International Festival 2013.

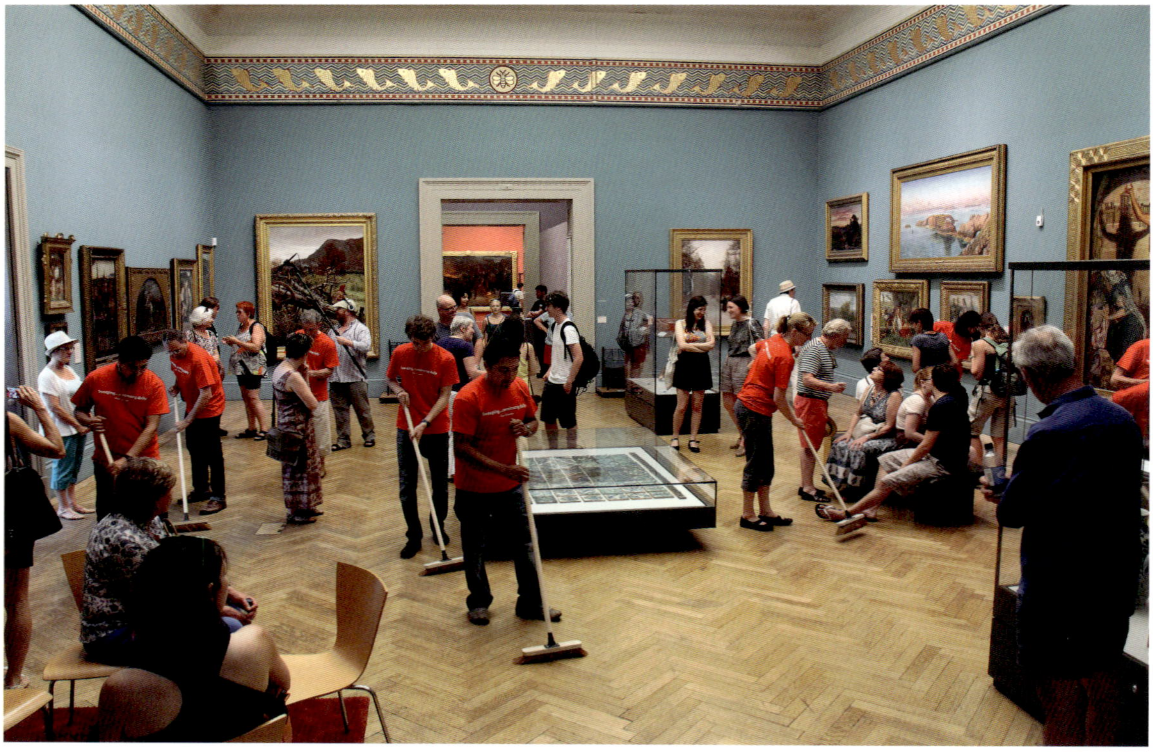

OPPOSITE: Parnell's diagram of the organizational structure of *Cleaning Conditions*, including notes on institutions, groups, and individuals identified to participate as performers and discussants, as well as topics for post-performance conversation

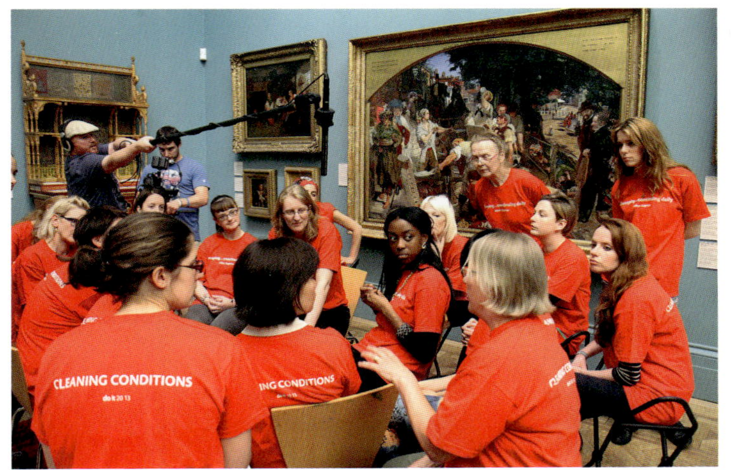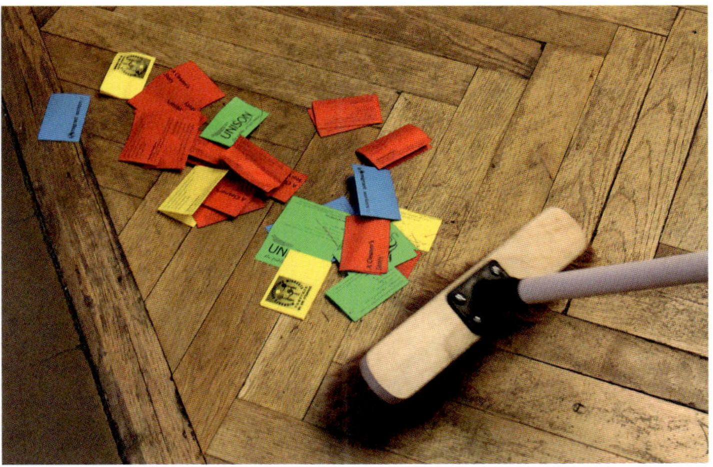

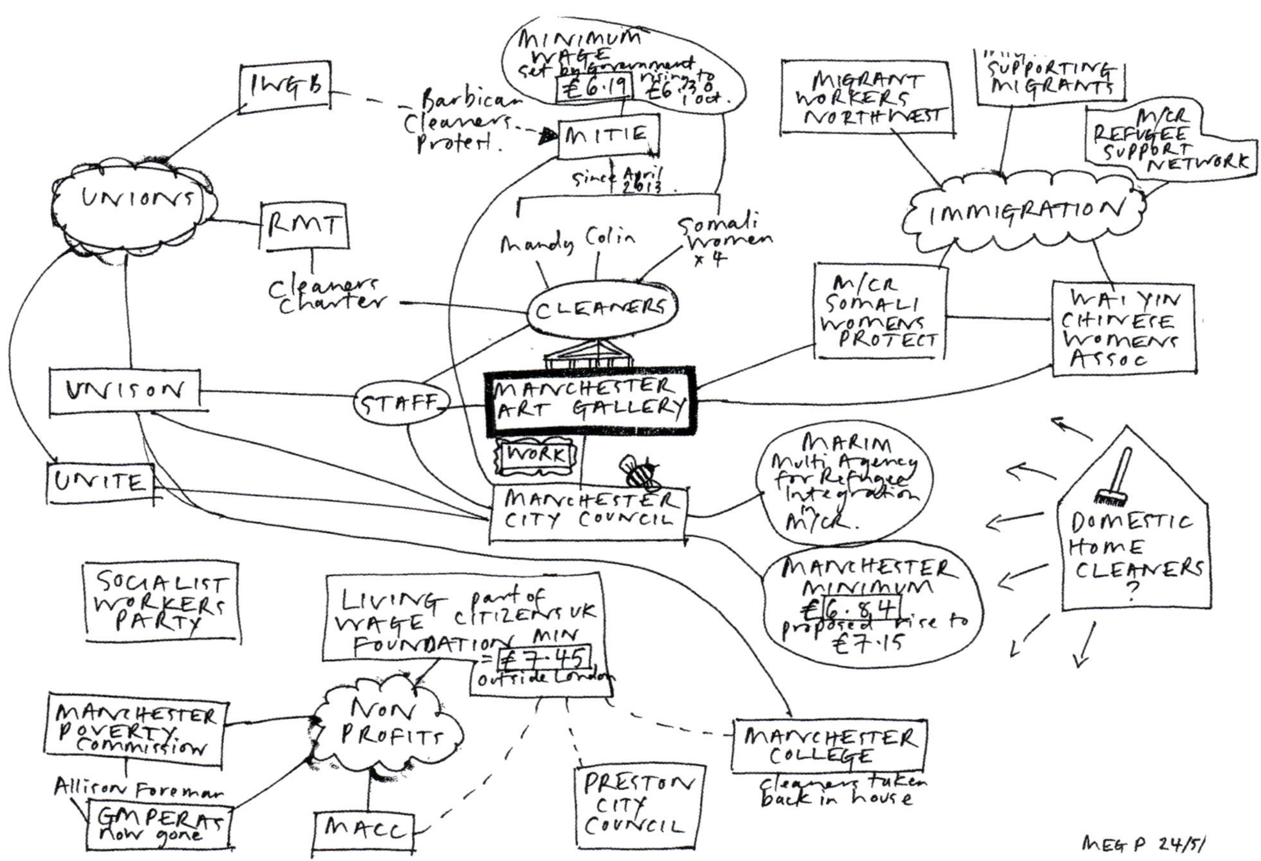

Suzanne created a space for people to talk and to exist *outside* of their everyday lives whilst at the same time talking about and creating something *with* their lives and jobs. The art gallery provided this space. I have often thought of the gallery as a neutral space. I know that it is not, and like everything it has a politics of its own, but it is a noncommercial, free space, and as such I've always felt it to be a great place to facilitate debate. It can put a frame around it. Even though we were dealing with and exposing difficult issues for the council, at no point was there any contention from council leaders. . . . This is probably due to the fact that they were unaware that it was happening . . . or is it because it happened in an art gallery and came under the guise of "art"?

I think the visitors found it difficult at times to work out if it was a public or private conversation. The conversation was taking place in a public gallery space; however, the group of people were huddled together (mainly to hear each other in a [space with] difficult acoustic[s]), but as such and wearing red T-shirts [they] looked to the outside as if [they were having] a closed conversation. Did this matter? No, the conversation was about bringing together the people in that group, and the collective action was important.

—Meg Parnell, 2013

The Circle and the Square (2015–17)

The Circle and the Square was commissioned by the arts program Super Slow Way and took place in Pendle, England. The project was a two-year collaboration between Lacy, the local arts nonprofit In-Situ, and the interfaith educational initiative Building Bridges Pendle. Lacy also worked with Ron Pen, Paul Hartley, Rauf Bashir, Massimiliano Mollona, and many Pendle residents to organize community meetings and singing sessions, which culminated in a three-day performance event and installation. Its site was also its subject: Brierfield Mill, previously one of Britain's largest textile mills, had closed a decade prior and was emblematic of the local consequences of globalized capitalism, including the segregation of once-integrated, ethnically diverse populations. The context of the dying textile industry became a catalyst for a celebration of local history and culture. Lacy and her collaborators reopened the mill, which had sat empty and was slated for redevelopment, as a space for residents to share food, music, and conversation about their experience of the ramifications of globalization. The event also included volunteer-led tours of the mill, a reunion of former textile mill workers, a daylong performance of Sufi chanting and shape note singing, and a final dinner for five hundred Pendle residents. The resulting video installation, with films by Mark Thomas of Soup Collective, Graham Kay, and Elena Adorni, features interviews with individuals reflecting on the region's past and future.

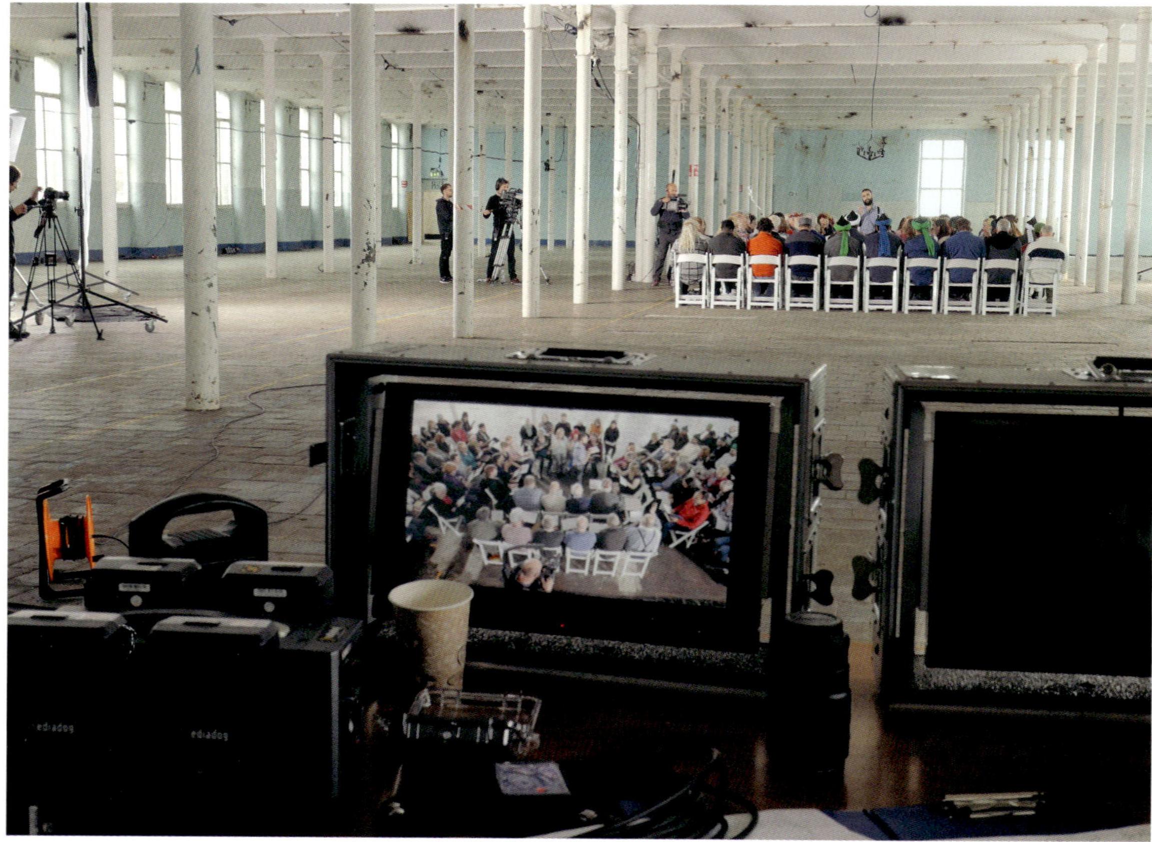

It's been enriching to see that we found something new and fresh, when you think about community cohesion work. [As a] community worker I'm quite interested to see what happens after [the performance], in terms of how people continue to engage with each other and engage with the issues that we have within Pendle. Because it's all about making Pendle a strong place, and this project is sowing the seeds for that.

—Rauf Bashir, 2017

Suzanne's projects are about having conversations with people about what is important in their community, what are the challenges that they face in those communities. . . . The idea of the community dinner—[for] exploring these forms of vocalization, the commonalities between people, you know—using that point as a safe space to kind of come and talk together became really important. . . . Over time we've been collecting questions from people in the community . . . [asking] what is that key question that you've always wanted to ask about either another culture or something around an issue that we're facing with our communities? What is that question?

—Paul Hartley, 2017

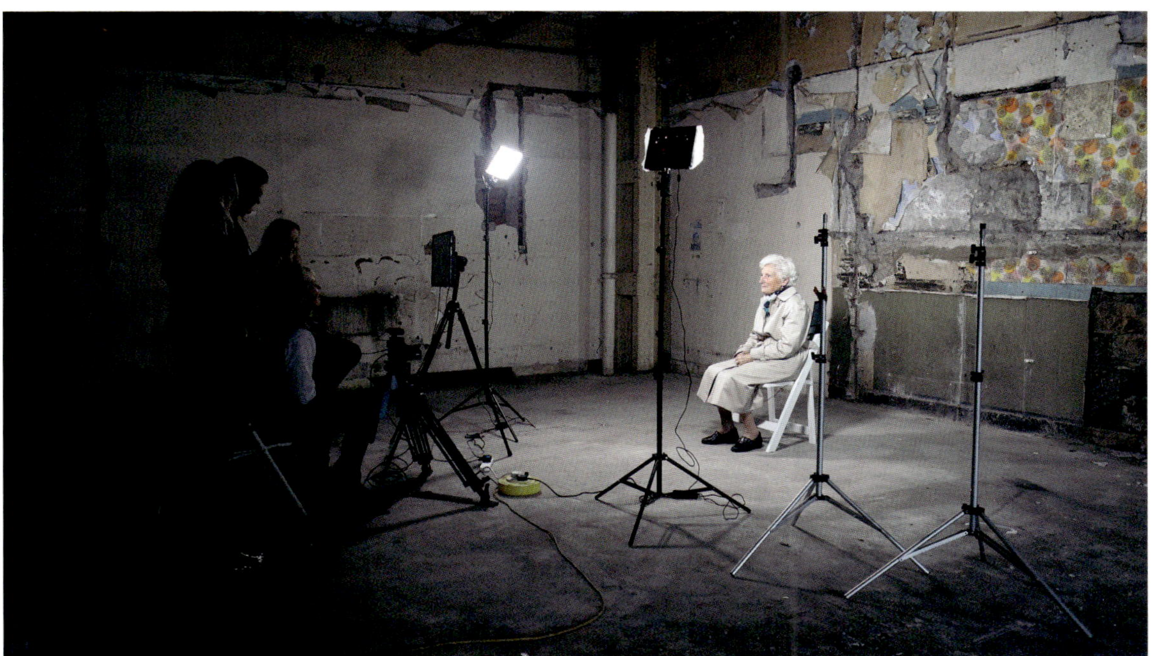

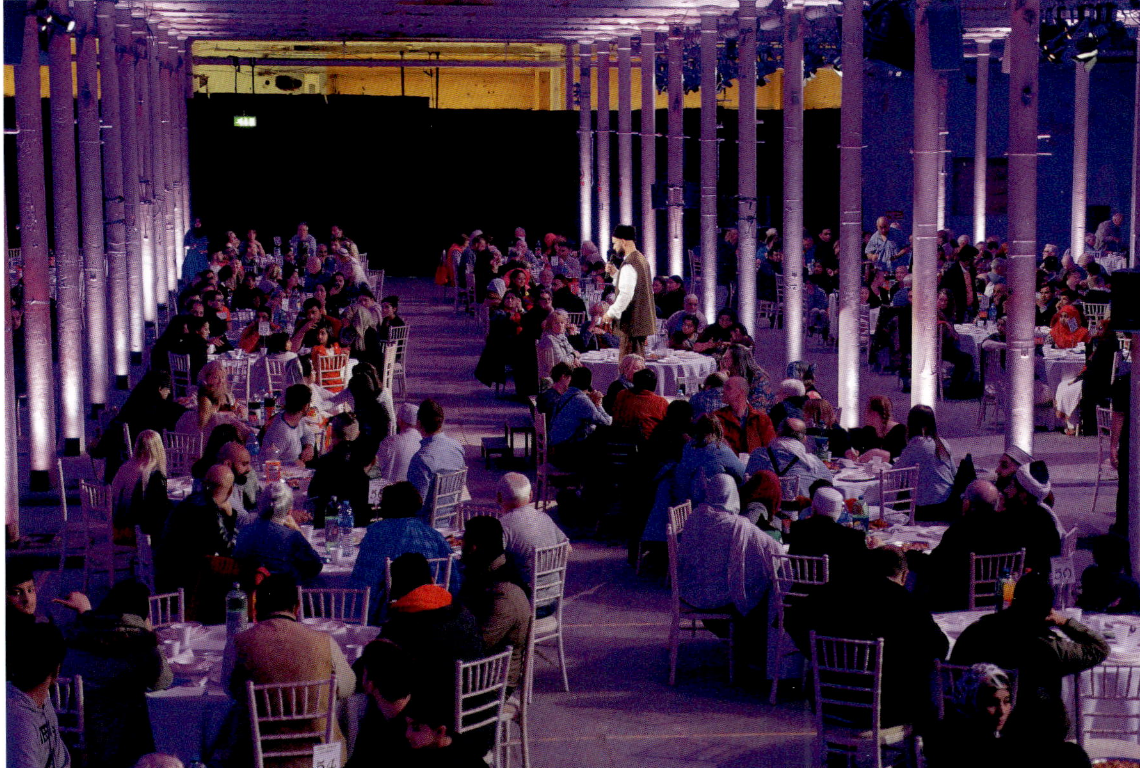

TOP: Filming of interviews with Pendle residents, Brierfield Mill, 2016
BOTTOM: Participants thinking about the future of Brierfield during a community dinner, Brierfield Mill, 2016
FOLLOWING PAGES: Time line of relevant histories produced for the project and film stills with corresponding excerpts from the transcript

LOCAL AND GLOBAL HISTORIES

1742 — Lancashire Sol-fa (known as shape note in America) singing sessions start in Dean, Rossendale, with Wesleyan preacher John Nuttall

1750 — Baptist Chapel built in Lumb, Rossendale, with Nuttall, where the group "Larks of Dean" sing

1760 — New Baptist Chapel built in Goodshaw Booth, Rossendale, to accommodate growing congregation/singers

1790 — Coal mining begins in Little Marsden, later known as Brierfield

1796 — Construction of Leeds & Liverpool canal in progress through Pendle

1821 — Population in Little Marsden is 2,052

1833 — Factory Act passed, minimum employment age 9 years, with maximum 48-hour working week for children

1834 — Henry Tunstill opens Brierfield Mill to spin and weave cotton with 106 power looms

1845 — Sarah Ann Glover publishes "A Manual of the Norwich Sol-fa System" to teach sol-fa singing, widely used in Mechanics Institutes

1858 — The British Crown takes over the East India Company's Indian possessions, commencing the British Raj

1861 — Depression in the North West England textile industry, brought about by overproduction and compounded by the loss of raw cotton during the American Civil War, is called the Cotton Famine

1862 — *Manchester Examiner and Times* reports on strength of singing culture of Rossendale in "Home Life of the Lancashire Factory Folk during the Cotton Famine"

1868 — Brierfield becomes a legal township

1878 — Factory & Workshops Act passed, minimum worker age 10 years, maximum 60-hour working week for women

1879 — Brierfield Mill has 92,000 spinning mule spindles, 2,235 weaving looms, and employs 1,500 people

1879 — John Greenwood publishes the *Lancashire Sol-fa Primer*, noting that sol-fa "has been handed down from generation to generation orally in that county"

1884 — Northern Counties Amalgamation Association of Weavers established

1885 — National Confederate Association of Power Loom Overlookers established

1887 — William Henry Quilliam founds the first mosque in Britain, the Liverpool Muslim Institute

1893 — Nelson branch of Independent Labour Party founded, first in country

1901 — Tunstill House becomes Brierfield Town Hall, with a market on the grounds

1904 — Tunstill Mill is renamed Brierfield Mills Ltd.

1911 — Brierfield population is 8,200

1936 — First recorded Sufi lodge in the UK, for devotional chanting in South Shields

1938 — The Holidays With Pay Act gives UK workers the right to one week's paid holiday per year

1946 — Britain ends British rule in India

1947 — Leaders in India partition the country along religious lines. Twelve million people flee across the new borders to escape sectarian violence

1956 — The closure of Brierfield Mill is announced; 360 people lose their jobs

1956 — Pakistan becomes an Islamic republic

1957 — Smith & Nephew buys Brierfield Mill, with a workforce of 800, and replaces steam power with electric

1961 — Construction of the Mangla Dam in Mirpur, Pakistan, displaces 100,000 people; some come to North West England, including Pendle

1962 — Commonwealth Immigrants Act introduces first entry restrictions with the work voucher system

1964 — First Asian grocery shop in Brierfield opens

1968 — Commonwealth Immigrants Act requires migrants to supply proof that their parents or grandparents are born in Britain

1970 — The first mosque in Pendle is founded in Nelson

1972 — Smith & Nephew has 1,600 employees working on a three-shift system

1974 — Town hall closes and Brierfield ceases to be an urban district

1974 — First mosque in Brierfield opens

1981 — The first section of the highway M65, connecting Burnley to Colne, opens

1991 — Building Bridges, charity to improve understanding of cultural diversity, established in Nelson

1996 — First UK Shape Note Convention held

1999 — Sufi chanting programme begins at Ghausia Mosque, Nelson

2001 — Free Spiritual Centre established

2002 — Brierfield Action in the Community established

2007 — Brierfield Mill closes, moving production to Germany and Mexico

2011 — Population of Brierfield is 8,193

2012 — In-Situ art collective established in Pendle

2012 — Pendle Council buys empty Brierfield Mill to be developed in a joint venture with Barnfield Construction

2013 — Jamia mosque opens in Brierfield with private money raised locally and nationally

When my father arrived in this country, he told me that he worked his socks off. Their [my parents'] original intention was to come here for a few months and go back home, just to earn a bit of money and go back home, because they were farmers.

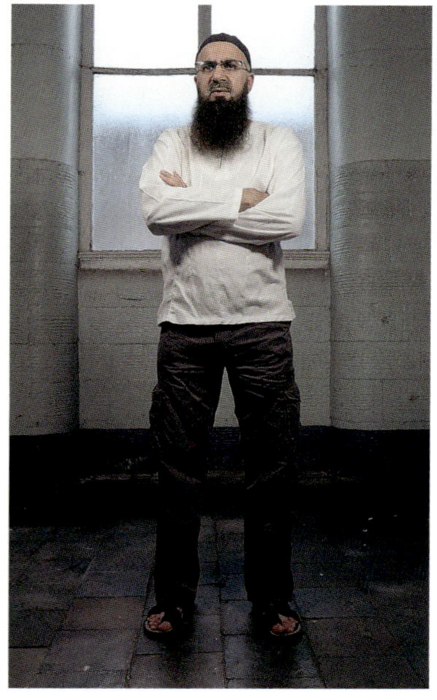

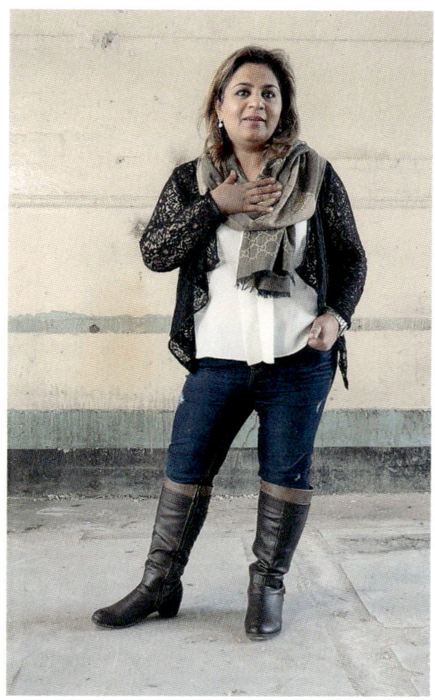

If I look back down, I think my parents . . . they were a lot more tolerant and believed [more] in interfaith dialogue than what I see today. And I question that as well today, when I come back—because I live away—and I come back and I question why there isn't that integration, especially that I grew up with. Because I see a huge gap. And that for me is very scary, because I wasn't raised like that.

I socialize with both sides of the community. Growing up, you know—[I] had a lot of Asian friends, a lot of English friends, so I've never had any issues at all, where generally some people out of our area usually do.

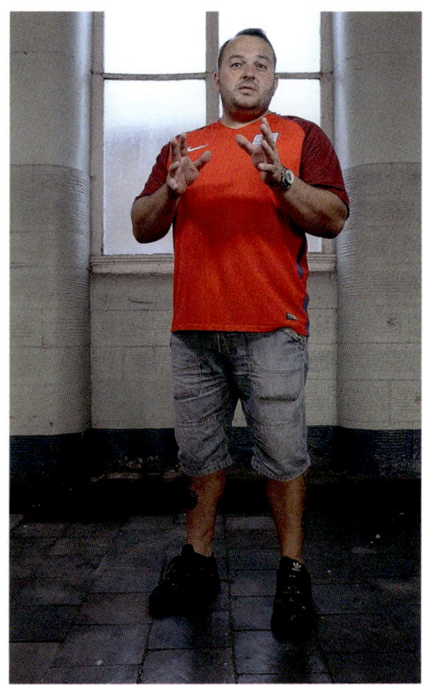

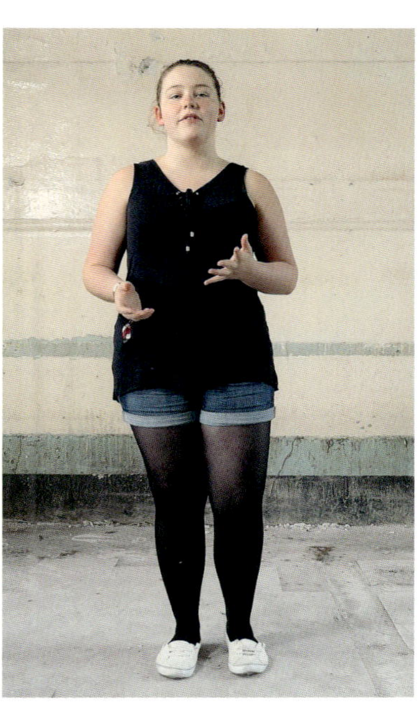

I feel like I'm a lot more open-minded and just more open in general—to other people, and wanting to speak to them and know about their own cultures and their own interests and things like that—than possibly some people I know are, because they haven't grown up with the same kind of cultural diversity I have.

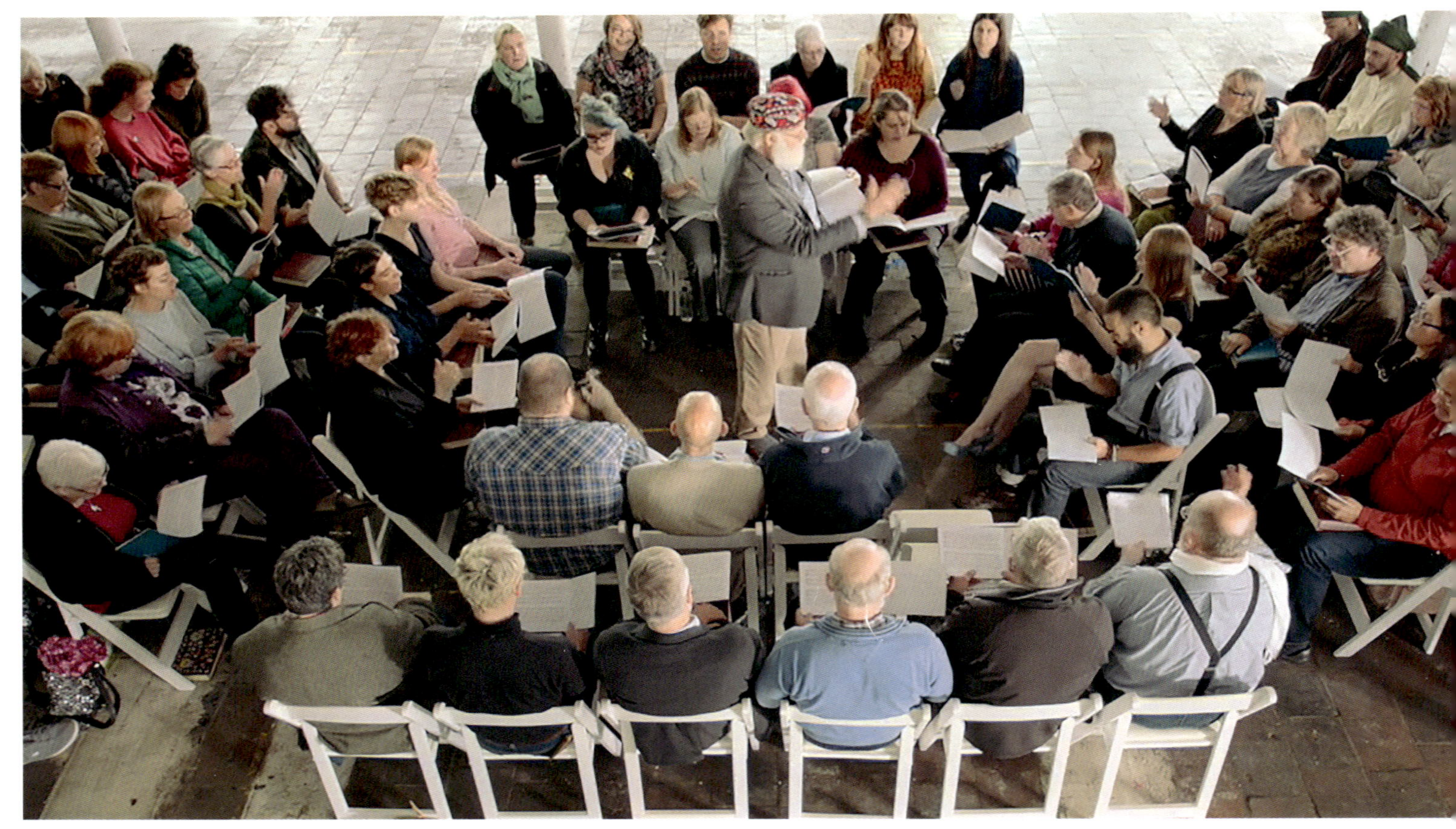

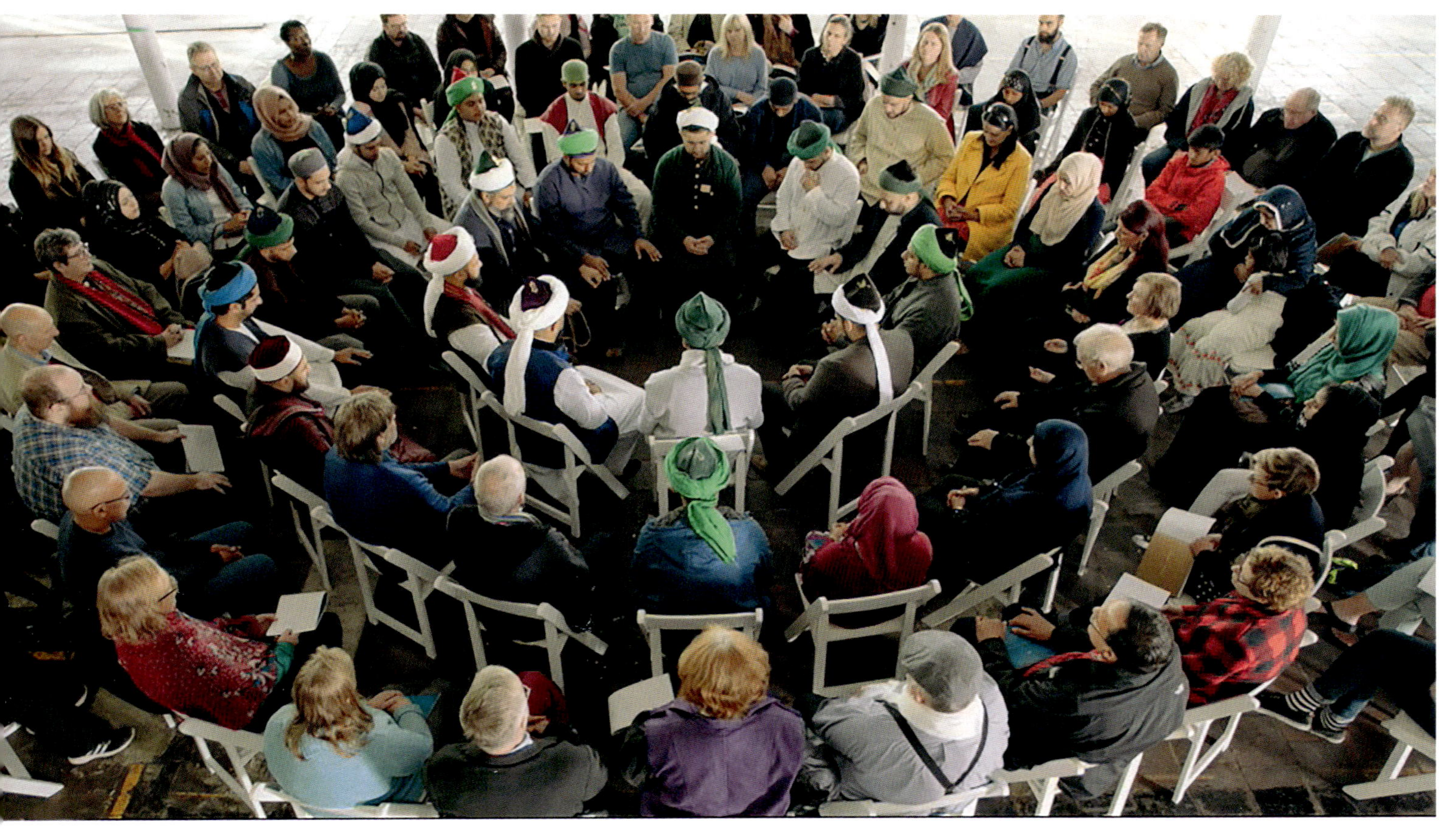

Musical harmony forges social harmony. Active engaged participation in communal vocal expression in both Sufi chant and shape note singing complements diversity with unity. Our distinct individual personalities are sustained, yet our commonalities are reinforced through the act of shared music. Participants in shape note singing are seated in a hollow square in which the four vocal parts—treble, counter, lead, and bass—sing with one another and to one another rather than facing outwards to an audience. Similarly, Sufi chant is sung in concentric circles in which our human diversity is subsumed in unity and concord.

—Ron Pen, 2016

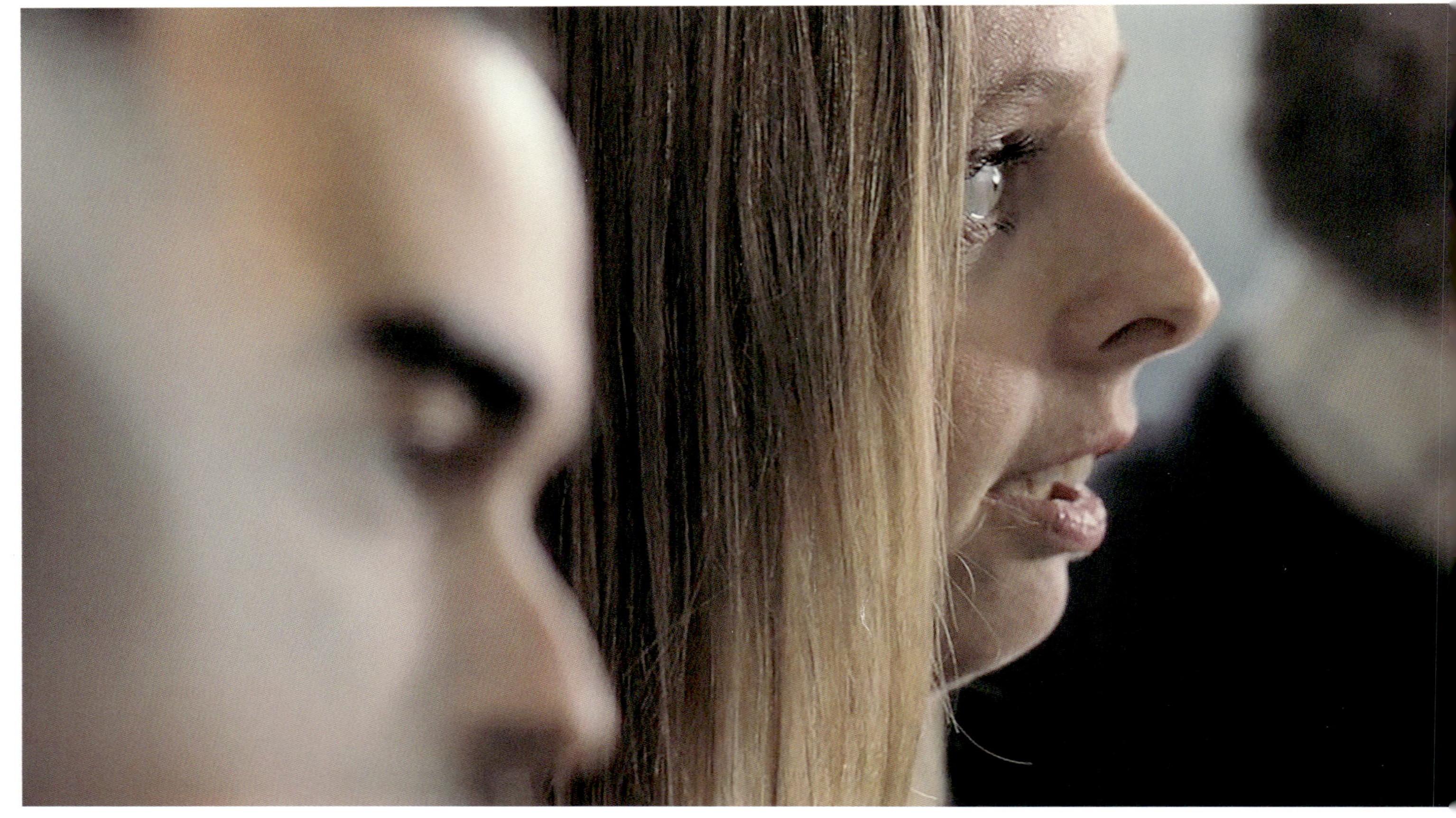

BOTH PAGES: Film still

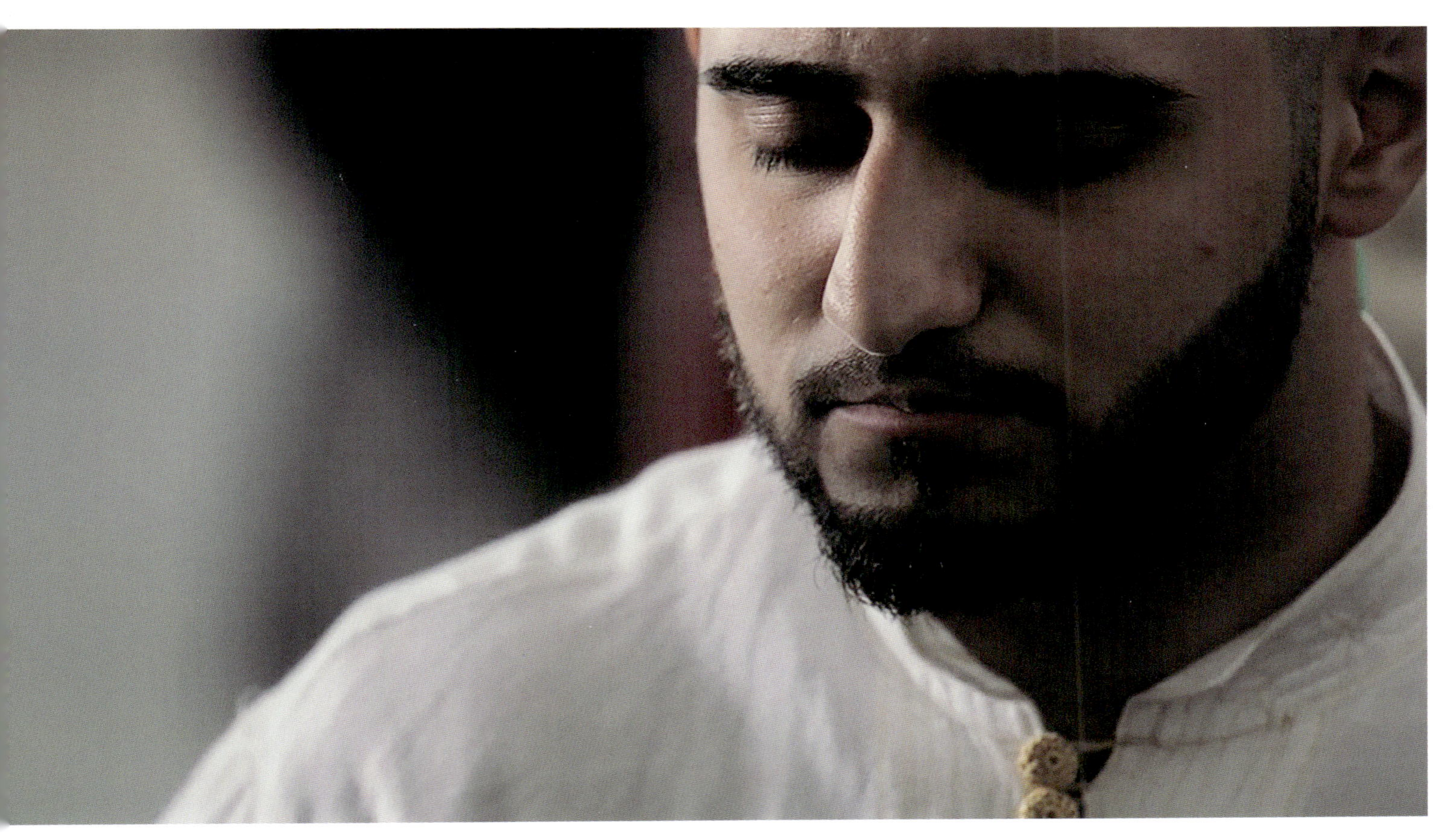

ACKNOWLEDGMENTS

In their curatorial introduction to this book, Rudolf Frieling, Lucía Sanromán, and Dominic Willsdon acknowledge their challenge: "to present two contexts at once, to enable visitors and readers to hold in their minds the reality that the work was of its time and yet persists." My challenge as an artist is quite different but also exists on a continuum of mindfulness: to navigate that tenuous line connecting "my" and "our" and to remember and acknowledge how and with whom the works were constructed.

My work is based on a complex web of relationships, and its very subject is relationality. Underneath everything is an unusual sort of family made up of teachers, collaborators, writers, curators, sponsors, and many, many, volunteers—a group too numerous to name. This extended family, born through practicing art together, has made this work a shared effort, a gesture of their friendship, a common cause.

I don't use the word "family" casually, perhaps because my birth family was so exceptional. I was fortunate to have a mother, father, brother, and sister—Jean Marie Graff—who were consistently loyal and supportive, and from this base my "family" has grown to include more sisters, brothers, cousins, aunts, uncles, daughters, and sons. Because naming in this limited space those intimates and others co-responsible for work made over almost five decades profoundly risks overlooking too many, I won't list names here. Acknowledgments are found throughout the catalogue and exhibition and, most fulsomely, they are recorded in my archives.

However, I will make these exceptions: Included in family is the idea of honoring those upon whose shoulders, and work, each of us stands. The idea of independent and isolated originality has never been attractive to me, and my work emerges from legacies left by others, including the intellectual contributions of early feminist writers such as Simone de Beauvoir and activists like Saul Alinsky and Martin Luther King Jr. I have been fortunate to learn directly from great teachers, among them Sensei Joko Beck; psychologist Dick Farson; writers Moira Roth, Arlene Raven, and Lucy Lippard; and artists Judy Chicago, Sheila Levrant de Bretteville, and Allan Kaprow. Thus feminism, antiracism, activism, social psychology, and visual art are always present in some way.

Finally, I have been fortunate to have had not one but three excellent curators to guide me through the process of this major retrospective. I thank Rudolf, Lucía, and Dominic, and I acknowledge the hard work of all those others at the San Francisco Museum of Modern Art and Yerba Buena Center for the Arts who put so much care and creativity into this exhibition.

—SUZANNE LACY

Suzanne Lacy: We Are Here was developed in a spirit of collaboration on multiple levels. First and foremost we extend deepest thanks to Suzanne Lacy, our close collaborator throughout this process, for her generosity, her commitment, and the invaluable perspective she offered on her works and their larger contexts. It has been intensely rewarding and a great pleasure to have had the opportunity for such an extended dialogue over the three and a half years spent planning this exhibition. We are equally grateful for the early and full support of this endeavor by Neal Benezra, Helen and Charles Schwab Director, San Francisco Museum of Modern Art (SFMOMA); Deborah Cullinan, Chief Executive Officer, Yerba Buena Center for the Arts (YBCA); Ruth Berson, Deputy Museum Director for Curatorial Affairs, SFMOMA; and Scott Rowitz, Chief Operating Officer, YBCA. Their commitment to civic engagement allowed us to take on the complexities and curatorial challenges of executing such a project across two institutions.

We used this retrospective as an occasion for sustained inquiry and an opportunity to engage in dialogues with wider circles of colleagues, as well as with the artist's former collaborators. A generous curatorial fellowship grant from The Andy Warhol Foundation for the Visual Arts allowed us to undertake critical research and stage two professional convenings: *Curatorial Research Convening: Exhibiting Social Practice in Museums* (February 27–March 1, 2017), co-organized with Independent Curators International, and *The Oakland Projects Intensive* (March–June 2017), coordinated with the assistance of educator and activist Unique Holland and historian and archivist Moriah Ulinskas, in which we sought oral histories of *The Oakland Projects* (1991–2001) from participants. SFMOMA and YBCA also co-hosted the roundtable discussion *What Role Should Art Have in Civic Life?* as part of *Does Art Have Users?* (September 28–30, 2017), a symposium exploring the politics, ethics, and value of working artistically in the public sphere. Directed by Deena Chalabi and Alessandra Saviotti with assistance from Stella Lochman, the symposium was presented in partnership with the Asociación de Arte Útil, YBCA, and the exhibition *Tania Bruguera: Talking to Power / Hablándole al Poder*. We thank all the participants and contributors involved in these gatherings.

Early on we decided to think of this catalogue as a research tool that would provide broader access to source materials and documents than the exhibition could offer. Purtill Family Business brought uncommon ingenuity and elegance to the book's design. The publication was overseen by SFMOMA senior editor Amanda Glesmann and editor Lucy Medrich, who managed all aspects of its complex production gracefully. We are indebted to them for their thoughtful feedback and rigorous attention to detail. Polly Watson and Lindsey Westbrook also brought their editorial acumen to bear on the project. Dominic Willsdon led the research and publication effort in close dialogue with the artist, and former SFMOMA colleague Taylor Shoolery was instrumental in preparing the selection of archival materials. In addition to authoring texts for the Illustrated Survey, Taylor, Jessica D. Brier, Christa Cesario, Lucia Fabio, and Tanya Zimbardo contributed vital research on Lacy's multifaceted projects. SFMOMA publications associate Jessica DeCamp and media arts curatorial intern Priscilla Chung helped with bibliographic research, as did Sharon Irish, author of *Suzanne Lacy: Spaces Between* (2010). SFMOMA's Don Ross and Los Angeles–based photographer Jeff McLane provided invaluable imaging assistance. We are also grateful to Tony Manzella and his team at Echelon Color for the exceptional care they brought to preparing the images throughout this volume for publication. Mary DelMonico, Katie Hands, and their colleagues at DelMonico Books•Prestel were supportive copublishing partners, and we thank them for championing this unprecedented monograph.

At SFMOMA, Jessica Woznak and Jillian Aubrey shepherded all phases of this co-organized retrospective. Steve Dye and Joshua Churchill lent their technical expertise to the presentation of a range of time-based media works. Sarah Choi developed creative solutions for the overall exhibition design and display of archival materials. Brandon Larson, Kimberly Walton, Greg Wilson, Joshua Pieper, and the entire installation crew deftly managed the ambitious installation. Olga Charyshyn and Molly Fishman facilitated multiple shipments of loans. Michelle Barger, Amanda Hunter Johnson, Roberta Piantavigna, and Martina Haidvogl provided assessment and care for several historical works. Bosco Hernández and Jody Hanson, supported by Laura Santizo, developed the graphic identity and assisted with the production of select works for this presentation, notably *Between the Door and the Street* (2013), which was adapted for the stairs in SFMOMA's Haas Atrium. We also extend our gratitude to Chad Coerver, Ana Fox-Hodess, and Vincent Sulit, Content Strategy and Digital Engagement; Jennifer Northrop, Jill Lynch, Clara Hatcher Baruth, Janet Ozzard, and Antonio Campos, Marketing and Communications; Sriba Kwadjovie, Collections Information and Access; Leigh Brawer and Julie Knight, Membership and Community Enterprise; Ginger Davis, Visitor Experience; and Elizabeth Waller, Caroline Stevens, Sara Pinto, Caroline Armstrong, Lanlian Szeto, Misty Youmans, and Maggie Azary, Development. Karen Cheung, Media Arts, managed the performers who activated *Alterations* (1994–95), and Stella

Lochman, Education and Public Practice, executed a version of *Cleaning Conditions* (2013) with staff and local organizers. In Education and Public Practice we are grateful as well to Megan Brian, Tomoko Kanamitsu, Julia Askenase, Claire Bradley, and Michelle Kim. We would also like to thank David Senior, Peggy Tran-Le, Andrew Pierce, Abby Bridge, and Brian Lucas, Library and Archives, for facilitating our catalogue research and for supporting the presentation of artist publications in the exhibition.

At YBCA we are thankful for the enthusiasm and rigor with which Dorothy Dávila, Director of Visual Arts, managed all aspects of this show and guided staff toward its successful implementation. Her team—John Foster Cartwright, Tesar Freeman, Susie Kantor, Elena Morrison Lyman, and Rebecca Silberman—contributed exceptional energy and effort to this undertaking. Christa Cesario, Community Organizing Manager and a Mellon/American Council of Learned Societies (ACLS) Public Fellow hired specifically for this project, worked tirelessly on the exhibition in a range of roles, including performing archival research, writing, co-writing a grant with YBCA's Development team and Lucía Sanromán, and leading and managing relationships with partner organizations. We are deeply grateful for her attention to detail, critical insight, and patience. Valerie Brown developed a robust communications and public relations strategy with the assistance of Voleine Amilcar, James Im, Lin Kung, Caitlin Lee, John Mavroudis, Sam Mende-Wong, and Harley Wong. Sarah Cathers and Martin Strickland dove headfirst into programming this nontraditional exhibition. We are grateful to Angela Carrier and Rebeka Rodriguez, Civic and Community Engagement, for their many contributions, and especially for their engagement with external youth and education participants. In Development, Sandie Arnold led grant-writing efforts, securing a key Mellon/ACLS Public Fellowship, and Maggie Pico, Emily Lakin, Angela Mathews, Flynn O'Brien, Janet Oh, and Charles Ward worked hard to engage donors and raise funds. Marc Bamuthi Joseph and Jonathan Moscone were important sounding boards for content and engagement strategies. Lisa Elliott, Jason Zimmerman, and their teams negotiated with partners in our shared spaces; Emily Quist, Jeffrey Mason, and Ben Cooper, Visitor Experience, led a vibrant team key to visitors' understanding of and participation in the exhibition; and Daniela Lencioni was an invaluable liaison between leadership and staff.

Suzanne Lacy: We Are Here features several of Lacy's earliest collaborations with fellow feminist artists. In particular, we thank her coauthors Leslie Labowitz and Nancy Youdelman, who made available original work and materials. It was important for us to include major examples of Lacy's work from other institutions; we extend our thanks to Ann Philbin, Hammer Museum, Los Angeles; Philippe Vergne and Klaus Biesenbach, Museum of Contemporary Art, Los Angeles; and Maria Balshaw and Catherine Wood, Tate, London. We are deeply grateful for the tireless work of Anna Ayeroff, Lacy's studio assistant, and her former assistant Lucia Fabio, who facilitated our access to the artist's papers, photographic and negative materials, and collection storage. Megan Steinman, director of the Underground Museum, Los Angeles, and producer of Lacy's survey exhibition organized by the Centro per l'Arte Contemporanea Luigi Pecci at Museo Pecci, Milan, also assisted us onsite. Peter Kirby, Lacy's longtime video editor, was invaluable in helping us gather and remaster media materials and also helped develop new video works with Lacy along with Bruno Louchouarn, Daniel Andrade, and Oderay Game. Unique Holland, Chris Johnson, and Annice Jacoby worked closely with Lacy to develop a new installation of *The Oakland Projects*, for which Moriah Ulinskas's re-cataloging of *The Oakland Projects* archives was fundamental.

Over these three years we were privileged to work with a number of organizations and individuals. We are profoundly grateful to Anyka Barber, Roberto Bedoya, Randolph Belle, Miguel Buenrostro, Ellen Sebastian Chang, Unique Holland, Chris Johnson, Pilar Riaño-Alcalá, and Ted Russell; Cristy Johnston Limón, Cassie Newman, Isa Nakazawa, and Gabriel Cortez at Youth Speaks; Maeven McGovern, Oliver Rodriguez, Aria Bendy, Cole Anderson, Symone Woodruff-Hardy, Noel Anaya, Jacob Armenta, and David Lawrence at YR Media (formerly Youth Radio); Malkia Cyril, Eteng Ettah, and Imran Siddiquee at the Center for Media Justice; Shaghayegh Cyrous, Michael Essien, Michelle Hemminger, Leslie Hu, Katy Hugo, Jackson Whittington, Vanessa "DJ AGANA" Espinoza, Leticia Hernandez, Ajuan Mance, and the sixth- and eighth-grade students at Dr. Martin Luther King Jr. Academic Middle School, San Francisco Unified School District; Caleb Duarte at Fremont High School, Oakland; and EDELO En Donde Era La Onu (Where the United Nations Used to Be). At the time of this publication, not all participants had joined the process; while they may not be named here, we are indebted to their contributions.

Last but not least, we wouldn't have been able to pursue these extended phases of research and dialogue without the support of our respective partners, Giacomo Castagnola, Moriah Ulinskas, and Sybille Weber-Frieling.

—RUDOLF FRIELING, LUCÍA SANROMÁN, AND DOMINIC WILLSDON

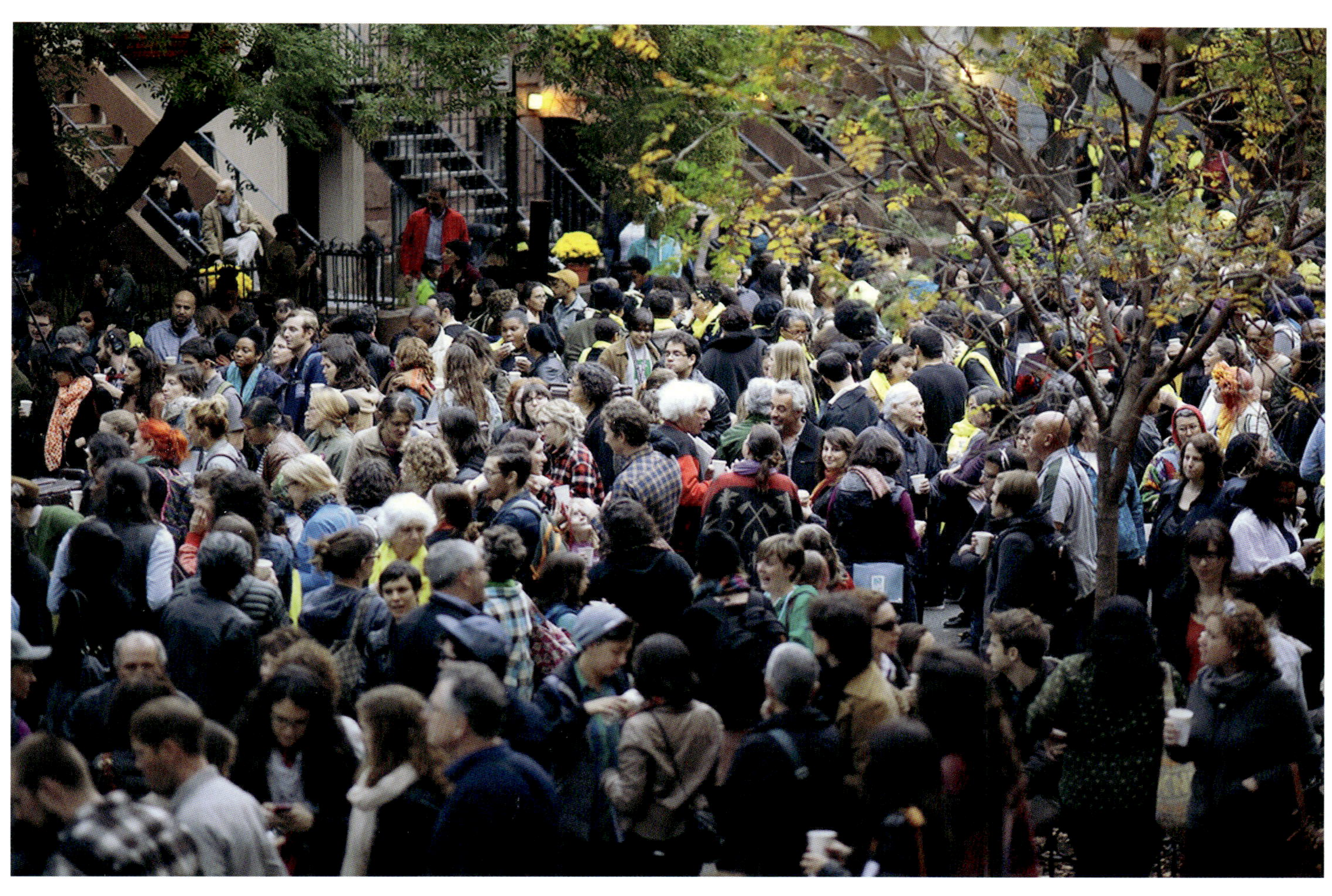

Suzanne Lacy, *Between the Door and the Street*, 2013. Production photo

CHRONOLOGY OF SELECTED WORKS

Suzanne Lacy's projects often encompass a range of media and forms of social engagement; involve the collaboration, participation, and support of numerous individuals and organizations; and may be re-envisioned in later iterations or documentation formats. What follows is an overview of her key works since graduate school. Primary coauthors and collaborators are noted; full production credits are not included. Within each year, works without known dates are listed first, alphabetically by title, followed by a chronological listing of performances and installations with known dates. Reinstallations and associated exhibitions and events other than the first are not indicated. Unique objects in public collections are noted. Projects represented in Suzanne Lacy: We Are Here, *San Francisco Museum of Modern Art and Yerba Buena Center for the Arts, are indicated with an asterisk. This listing reflects the complete information available at the time of publication.*

1972

Car Renovation. Installation, Route 126, Fillmore, California. Created for Judy Chicago's class at California Institute of the Arts, Valencia

**Rape Is.* Artist's book, edition of 1,000. Second edition published 1976

The Menopause Tapes, Lacy, Sheila Levrant de Bretteville, Jill Soderholm, and the Women's Design Program, California Institute of the Arts, Valencia. Video, black and white, with sound

**Ablutions,* Lacy, Judy Chicago, Sandra Orgel, and Aviva Rahmani. Performance, studio of Guy Dill, Venice, California

East-West Coast Eating Event, Lacy and Susan Mogul. Performance, Saugus Café, Saugus, California

**I Tried Everything,* Lacy, Dori Atlantis, Jan Lester Martin, and Nancy Youdelman. Installation/mail art and black-and-white photographs, California Institute of the Arts Library, Valencia

1973

Bound Penis. Black-and-white and color photographs

**Lamb Construction.* Performance, Womanspace Gallery, Los Angeles, and the Woman's Building, Los Angeles

**Maps.* Performance, California Institute of the Arts, Valencia; to Pomona, California; to Vernon, California. Created for Allan Kaprow's class at California Institute of the Arts

Mother Venus, Lacy, Vanalyne Green, Laurel Klick, and Susan Mogul. Performance, Womanspace Gallery, Los Angeles. Related documentary: *Mother Venus* (2019)

**Net Construction.* Performance, University of California, Santa Barbara

1974

**Body Contract.* Fourteen-page document, prepared with California Lawyers for the Arts

Mice and Penis. Video, color, with sound, and black-and-white photographs

The Teeth Series. Video, black and white, with sound

Exchange. Performance, University of California, Irvine

Wall Construction. Performance, private home, Pacific Palisades, Los Angeles

ca. 1974–1975

**Autobiography of a Young Vampire.* Photocollages

1974–1975

**Prostitution Notes.* Performative research project, San Francisco and Los Angeles, and ten ink and collage works on paper, Museum of Contemporary Art, Los Angeles. See also: *Prostitution Notes* (2010)

1974/1975

**Monster Series: Construction of a Novel Frankenstein,* Lacy with Sarah Macy. Performance with film, black and white, silent, and slide show, the Woman's Building, Los Angeles (1974), and Western Washington State College (now Western Washington University), Bellingham (1975)

ca. 1975

Basic Urine. Hand-tinted black-and-white photographs

Cold Hands, Warm Heart. Black-and-white photographs

Mice, Kidney, and Dinner Plate. Color photographs

1975

One Woman Shows. Installation/performance, Grandview Galleries, Los Angeles
Running to San Francisco. Performance, Los Angeles to San Francisco Art Institute

1975–1976

**Three Love Stories*. Three sets of six captioned black-and-white photographs: *A Gothic Love Story* (1975), *A True Romance Story, or She's Got Quite a Set of Lungs* (1976), and *Under My Skin: A Pornographic Novel* (1976). Related artist's book, edition of 500, published 1978

1975/1977

**Under My Skin: A True-Life Story*. Performance, San Francisco Art Institute (1975) and Museum of Contemporary Art, Chicago (1977), and film, two versions (black and white and color), silent

1975–1980

**Evalina and I: Crimes, Quilts, and Art*, Lacy and Evalina Newman. Research project, Watts, Los Angeles; performances and installations with Newman, including *Bus Ride from Watts* (1978), Guy Miller Homes, Watts, to downtown Los Angeles, and *Living Here* (1978), Guy Miller Homes Resident's Gallery; and exhibition, *Evalina and I: Crimes, Quilts, and Art* (1980), the Woman's Building, Los Angeles
WOW (Women of Watts). Residency with performances and social events with women of Watts Arms Housing Project, Watts, Los Angeles

1976

**Anatomy Lesson: After Baldessari*. Photocollage of color photographs on board
**Anatomy Lesson: Untitled*. Two-part photocollage of color photographs on board
**Anatomy Lesson #1: Chickens Coming Home to Roost (for Rose Mountain and Pauline)*. Set of four captioned black-and-white photographs and set of four black-and-white postcards, edition of 200
**Anatomy Lesson #2: Learn Where the Meat Comes From*. Set of twelve color photographs
**Anatomy Lesson #3: Falling Apart*. Photocollages (two versions)
**Falling Apart*. Artist's book, edition of 20. Part of *Anatomy Lessons* (1976–77)
**Learn Where the Meat Comes From*. Video, color, with sound, directed by Hildegarde Duane. Part of *Anatomy Lessons* (1976–77)
Vaginal Valentine. Black-and-white photograph. Later versions: *Vaginal Valentine #1* (1976/1995), black-and-white photograph, frame, paint, and mirror, Berkeley Art Museum and Pacific Film Archive, California, and *Vaginal Valentine #2* (1976/1995), black-and-white photograph, frame, paint, and mirror
**Cinderella in a Dragster*. Performance, California State College, Dominguez Hills (now California State University, Dominguez Hills), Carson, and University of California, San Diego
**Inevitable Associations*. Two-day performance, Biltmore Hotel, Los Angeles

1977

**Anatomy Lesson #4*. Color photographs and photocollages: *After Mantegna, Swimming, Dreaming, Floating, Flying, Still Life*, and *Untitled*
An Old Wives' Tale about How to Tell the Size of a Man's Penis . . . without Really Looking. Two-part photocollage of black-and-white photographs on board
**How to Deliver a Crippling Blow to Your Gynecologist If He Gets Fresh with You*. Photocollage of black-and-white photographs on board
Edna, May Victor, Mary, and Me: An All-Night Benediction. Performance, Hilton Hotel, Los Angeles. Part of the College Art Association conference
Lamb Chop at the Meat Market, Lacy with Susan Mogul. Performance intervention in David A. Ross's California Art Association Talk Show, Hilton Hotel, Los Angeles. Part of the College Art Association conference
**Three Weeks in May*. Expanded performance/curation of events by other artists and activists, Los Angeles. Lacy's installation/performance: *She Who Would Fly*, Garage Gallery, Los Angeles. Related artist's book, edition of 20, published 1982. Related documentary: *Three Weeks in May* (2011), by Christina Sanchez. Part of *Ariadne: A Social Art Network* (1977–82)
**Three Weeks in May*. Six-panel map, Hammer Museum, Los Angeles. Part of *Ariadne: A Social Art Network* (1977–82)
**The Life and Times of Donaldina Cameron*, Lacy and Kathleen Chang. Performance, Angel Island State Park, California. Part of the performance series *(H)errata*, organized by The Floating Museum
**The Bag Lady*. Performance, Fine Arts Museums of San Francisco Downtown Center. Part of the exhibition *Cityscapes: San Francisco and Los Angeles*
**In Mourning and in Rage*, Lacy and Leslie Labowitz. Performance, Los Angeles City Hall. Related documentary: *In Mourning and in Rage* (1978), by the Woman's Video Center at the Woman's Building, Los Angeles. Part of *Ariadne: A Social Art Network* (1977–82)

1977–1978

**Travels with Mona*, Lacy with Arlene Raven. Performance, Europe and Latin America, and accordion-fold postcards of twelve color photographs and text, edition of 2,000

1978

The Lady and the Lamb, or The Goat and the Hag. Performance, Mills College, Oakland

The Vigil/Incorporate, Lacy and Barbara T. Smith. Two-part performance: *The Vigil*, University Art Gallery, University of California, Irvine, and *Incorporate*, Los Angeles Contemporary Exhibitions

From Reverence to Rape to Respect, Lacy, Leslie Labowitz, and Claudia King. Expanded performance with events, performances, and installations, Las Vegas. Lacy's installation: *There Are Voices in the Desert.* Part of Ariadne: A Social Art Network (1977–82)

Here We Are There, Lacy with Nancy Buchanan and Norma Jean Deak. Telephone performance, University of Nevada, Las Vegas, and Center of Music Experiment, San Diego. Part of Ariadne: A Social Art Network (1977–82)

Mona by Number. Installation/performance, San Francisco Museum of Modern Art. Part of the exhibition *The Floating Museum: Global Space Invasion Phase II*

Take Back the Night, Lacy and Leslie Labowitz. Performance/curation of work by other feminist artists, San Francisco. Part of the Feminist Perspectives on Pornography conference, organized by Women against Violence in Pornography and the Media. Part of Ariadne: A Social Art Network (1977–82)

Hardcore Screening, Lacy and Leslie Labowitz. Screening and critique of the movie *Hardcore*, Columbia Pictures Studio, Los Angeles. Part of Ariadne: A Social Art Network (1977–82)

1979

**International Dinner Party*, Lacy and Linda Preuss. Performance, San Francisco Museum of Modern Art

Making It Safe. Performance and exhibition, Main Street, Ocean Park, Santa Monica. Part of Ariadne: A Social Art Network (1977–82)

1980

Boycott Performance, Lacy and Laverne Woods Dunn. Performance, New Orleans; black-and-white photographs; and black-and-white postcards

River Meetings: Lives of Women in the Delta, Lacy, Betty Constant, Laverne Woods Dunn, Jeanne Nathan, and Marilee Snedeker. Performance/intervention in the College Art Association conference, New Orleans

**In the Last Throes of Artistic Vision.* Installation/performance, Los Angeles. Part of the festival Public Spirit: Live Art LA

1981

Tree: A Performance for Women of Ithaca, Lacy with Marilyn Rivchin, Nancy Bereano, and Carolyn Whitlow. Performance, Cornell University, Ithaca, New York

1982

**Freeze Frame: Room for Living Room*, Lacy and Julia London with Jan Chattler, Joya Cory, Natalia Rivas, Ngoh Spencer, and Carol Szego. Performance, Roche Bobois furniture showroom, San Francisco. Part of the International Theater Festival conference and the International Sculpture Conference. Related documentary: *SOFA* (1984), executive produced by Lacy, edited by Douglas Gayeton Smith, photography directed by Steve Hirsch

1983

**Immigrants and Survivors.* Performance, Immaculate Heart High School cafeteria, Los Angeles

1983–1984

**Whisper, the Waves, the Wind*, Lacy and Sharon Allen. Performance, La Jolla, California. Related documentary: *Whisper, the Waves, the Wind* (1985), produced by Lacy, edited by Kathleen Laughlin. Related portfolio of eight color photographs printed 1984

1985–1986

**The Dark Madonna*, Lacy, Anne Bray, Carol Heepke, Susan Stone, and Willow Young. Symposium, Center for the Study of Women, University of California, Los Angeles (1985), and performance, Franklin D. Murphy Sculpture Garden, University of California, Los Angeles (1986)

1985–1987

**Whisper Minnesota*, Lacy with Sharon Roe Anderson, Sage Fuller Cowles, Nancy Dennis, Judy Kepes, Phyllis Jane Rose, and Phyllis Salzberg. Project, Minnesota. Culminating performance: *The Crystal Quilt* (1987), IDS Center, Minneapolis. PBS live broadcast: *The Minnesota Whisper Project* (1987), directed by Emily Goldberg. Related documentary: *The Crystal Quilt* (1997), produced by Lacy, edited by Michelle Baughan. Related installation: *The Crystal Quilt* (2012), cotton quilt designed by Miriam Schapiro; set of thirty-six color and black-and-white photographs; signed poster; performance soundtrack by Sharon Stone; and 16mm time-lapse film, color, with sound, Tate Modern, London. See also: *The Crystal Quilt* (1992/2015)

1989–1990

The Road of Poems and Borders, Lacy, Arthur Strimling, Tuula Linsiö, Allan Kaprow, and Pirkko Kurikka with Ihva Aula, Tuire Hindikka, Petr Rehor, Judy Baca, and Guillermo Gómez-Peña. Performances, Joensuu, Finland

1991

Cancer Notes: Seven-Day Genesis. Performance, Roswell Park Memorial Institute (now Roswell Park Comprehensive Cancer Center), Buffalo, New York

1991–1992

*Teenage Living Room, Lacy and Chris Johnson with Andy Hamner and Lauren Manduke. Project, Oakland Technical High School. Culminating performance, California College of Arts and Crafts (now California College of the Arts) parking lot, Oakland, 1992. Related documentary: *Teenage Living Room* (1992), by Craig Franklin, KRON 4. Part of *The Oakland Projects* (1991–2001)

1992–1993

Full Circle, Lacy with a coalition of Chicago women. Performance and installation, the Loop, Chicago. Related documentary: *Full Circle* (2014). Part one of two-part piece for the exhibition *Culture in Action*

*1992/2015

The Crystal Quilt. Two ink works on paper (1992) and two videos, color, with sound (2015). See also: *Whisper Minnesota* (1985–87)

1993

Dinner at Jane's. Performance, Jane Addams Hull-House Museum, Chicago. Part two of two-part piece for the exhibition *Culture in Action*. Related documentary: *Dinner at Jane's* (2000), produced by Lacy, edited by Michelle Baughan

1993–1994

Auto on the Edge of Time. Five projects: *Underground* (1993), Lacy with Carol Kumata, installation, Three Rivers Park, Pittsburgh; *Doing Time* (1993), Lacy with Charlotte Watson, Virginia Cotts, David Katzive, and Sharon Smolick, installation, Bedford Hills Correctional Facility, New York; *Auto on the Edge of Time* (1993), installation, Niagara Falls, New York; *The Children's Car* (1994), Lacy with Carol Kumata and Susanne Cockrell, installation, Museum of Contemporary Art Cleveland; *Children Speak* (1994), Lacy with Virginia Cotts and David Katzive, televised public service announcement. Related documentaries: *Underground* (1994), by Mia Houlberg, produced by Lacy; *Auto: Body* (1998), produced by Lacy with Virginia Cotts and Michelle Baughan

*The Roof Is on Fire, Lacy, Annice Jacoby, and Chris Johnson. Project, Oakland. Culminating performance, City Center West Garage, Oakland, 1994. Related documentary: *The Roof Is on Fire* (1994), by Craig Franklin, KRON 4. Part of *The Oakland Projects* (1991–2001)

1994

*Signs of Violence, Lacy, Leslie Becker, Annice Jacoby, and Gail Smithwalter. Installation, multiple locations. Part of *The Oakland Projects* (1991–2001)

1994–1995

*Alterations, Lacy, Susanne Cockrell, and Britta Kathmeyer. Installation/performance, Capp Street Project, San Francisco. Part of the exhibition *Old Glory, New Story: Flagging the 21st Century*. Related documentary: *Alterations* (2009), by Jacques Bronson

1995

*Youth, Cops, and Videotape, Lacy, Annice Jacoby, and Chris Johnson. Videotaped workshops, Oakland. Related documentary: *Youth, Cops, and Videotape* (1995), produced by Lacy, edited by Jacques Bronson. Part of *The Oakland Projects* (1991–2001)

1995–1996

*No Blood/No Foul, Lacy, Annice Jacoby, and Chris Johnson. Project, Oakland. Culminating performance, Club One, Oakland, 1996, and installation for the exhibition *Atopic Site* (1996), Tokyo Big Sight. Related documentary: *No Blood/No Foul* (1996), produced by Lacy, edited by Michelle Baughan. Related installation: *No Blood/No Foul and the Oakland Youth Policy* (2014), multichannel video installation. Part of *The Oakland Projects* (1991–2001)

1996–1997

The Turning Point. Project, Vancouver, Canada. Culminating performance: *Under Construction* (1997), Residences on Georgia construction site, Vancouver. Related documentary: *Under Construction: A Public Art Project* (1998), art directed by Lacy, produced and directed by Darlene Haber

*Expectations, Lacy with Leslie Becker, Lisa Findley, Amana Harris, Leuckessia Hirsh, Unique Holland, Annice Jacoby, Sheila Jordan, and Maxine Wyman. Project, YWCA, Oakland; poster; and installation, Capp Street Project, San Francisco. Part of *The Oakland Projects* (1991–2001)

1997–1999
*Code 33: Emergency, Clear the Air!, Lacy, Julio César Morales, and Unique Holland. Project, Oakland. Culminating performance, City
    Center West Garage, Oakland, 1999. Related documentary: Code 33: Emergency Clear the Air (2002), produced by Lacy, edited
    by Michelle Baughan. Part of The Oakland Projects (1991–2001)

1999–2000
La piel de la memoria/Skin of Memory, Lacy and Pilar Riaño-Alcalá. Performances and installation, Medellín, Colombia. Related documen-
    tary: Skin of Memory (2006), art and consultation by Lacy, produced by Dorothy Kidd. See also: La piel de la memoria revivida/
    Skin of Memory Revisited (2011)

2000
*Eye 2 Eye at Fremont High, Lacy and Julio César Morales. Performance, Fremont High School, Oakland. Related documentary: Eye2Eye:
    Code 33 at Fremont High School (2000), by Oakland youth, directed by Nicole Fleetwood. Part of The Oakland Projects (1991–2001)

2000–2005
Beneath Land and Water: A Project for Elkhorn City, Lacy, Yutaka Kobayashi, and Susan Leibovitz Steinman. Project, Elkhorn City, Kentucky

2000–ongoing
University of Local Knowledge, Lacy, Penny Evans, and Carolyn Hassan. Project with Knowle West Media Centre, Arnolfini Gallery, and
    the University of Bristol, England

2002
The Borough Project, Lacy and Tumelo Mosaka. Performance, Charleston, South Carolina. Part of Spoleto Festival USA. Related docu-
    mentary: The Borough Project (2002), by Tumelo Mosaka

2003
Latitude 32 Degrees: Navigating Home, Lacy, Rick Lowe, and Rob Miller. Installation/performance, Ansonborough Field, Charleston,
    South Carolina. Part of Spoleto Festival USA

2004
I.D.Entity, Lacy with Elisheva Gross, Unique Holland, and Arthur Ou. Performance, Taipei. Part of the exhibition Cities on the Move

2006
Mapping Allan Kaprow: A Memorial. Performance, University of California, San Diego

2007
*Stories of Work and Survival, Lacy with Kelly Akashi and Susan Barnet. Installation/performance, The Geffen Contemporary at the
    Museum of Contemporary Art, Los Angeles. In conjunction with the exhibition WACK! Art and the Feminist Revolution
The Performing Archive: Restricted Access, Lacy and Leslie Labowitz. Videos and installation, 18th Street Art Center, Santa Monica,
    California. Part of Ariadne: A Social Art Network (1977–82)
SWARM, Lacy, Kim Abeles, Jeff Cain, and Rochelle Labowitz. Performance, Los Angeles County Museum of Art

2008
Trade Talk, Lacy, Peter Kirby, and Michael Rotondi. Installation/performance, Museum of Contemporary Art, Los Angeles. Part of the
    exhibition Allan Kaprow—Art as Life. Related documentary: Trade Talk (2008), by Lacy and Kirby
*Beer Bucket/Champagne Bucket. Color photographs and installation. Part of Central Valley (2008–ongoing)
Tulare: Garage Sale, Lacy with Kelly Akashi. Color photographs and video installation, including Yardsale, color, with sound. Part of
    Central Valley (2008–ongoing)

2009
Laton: Free Store, Lacy and Andrea Bowers. Project, Laton, California. Related exhibition: Your Donations Do Our Work: Andrea Bowers
    and Suzanne Lacy (2009), Sweeney Art Gallery, University of California, Riverside. Part of Central Valley (2008–ongoing)

2010
Anyang Women's Agenda. Performances and installation, Anyang, South Korea
Prostitution Notes. Performance with video, color, with sound, Serpentine Galleries, London. See also: Prostitution Notes (1974–75)
*Esqueleto tatuado (Tattooed Skeleton). Project and performances, Museo Nacional Centro de Arte Reina Sofía, Madrid. Related
    documentary: Esqueleto tatuado (Tattooed Skeleton) (2010), by Cecilia Barriga, art directed by Lacy

2011

La piel de la memoria revivida/Skin of Memory Revisited, Lacy and Pilar Riaño-Alcalá. Installation, videos, and performance, Museo de Antioquia, Medellín, Colombia. Part of the biennial Encuentro Internacional de Medellín 2011 (MDE11). Related documentary: *La piel de la memoria revivida/Skin of Memory Revisited* (2011), by Lacy, Riaño-Alcalá, and Peter Kirby. See also: *La piel de la memoria/ Skin of Memory* (1999–2000)

2012

Three Weeks in January. Project and installation, Los Angeles Contemporary Exhibitions. Culminating performances by Lacy: *Storying Rape*, Los Angeles City Hall, and *Call to Action/Candlelight Vigil*, Los Angeles Police Department Parker Center. Part of Pacific Standard Time Performance and Public Art Festival. Related documentary: *Storying Rape* (2012), produced by Lacy, edited by Peter Kirby. Related project: *Storying Rape* (2012), part of the Liverpool Biennial

Re/Locating Learning: Public Practices as Art, Lacy, Sara Daleiden, Sally Tallant, and Pablo Helguera. Performance, Los Angeles Convention Center. Part of the College Art Association 100th Annual Conference

2013

Silver Action. Performance, The Tanks, Tate Modern, London

Cleaning Conditions, Lacy with Meg Parnell. Performance and installation, Manchester Art Gallery, England. Part of the exhibition *do it 2013* and the Manchester International Festival. Related artwork: *Cleaning Conditions (An Homage to Allan Kaprow)* (2017), broadsheet

Between the Door and the Street. Performance, Brooklyn, and text-based installation, Brooklyn Art Museum steps. Sponsored by Creative Time and the Elizabeth A. Sackler Center for Feminist Art, Brooklyn Museum. Related video installation: *Between the Door and the Street* (2019), San Francisco Museum of Modern Art

2014

Artists Read Baldessari. Performance, The Geffen Contemporary at the Museum of Contemporary Art, Los Angeles. Part of the Printed Matter LA Art Book Fair

Andrea Bowers and Suzanne Lacy: Drawing Lessons, Lacy and Andrea Bowers. Installation/performance, The Drawing Center, New York

Three Weeks in May Re-creation, Lacy and Megan Steinman with Franziska Rauh. Performance, Museo Pecci, Milan

2014–2015/2019

De tu puño y letra (By Your Own Hand). Performance, Plaza Belmonte bullring, Quito, Ecuador (2014–15), and multichannel video installation (2019)

2015–2017

The Circle and the Square. Project, Pendle, England, and multichannel video installation. Related documentary: *The Circle and the Square* (2017), by Huckleberry Films

2016

School for Revolutionary Girls, Lacy with Nicola Goode. Project and performance, Irish Museum of Modern Art, Dublin. Part of the Irish Museum of Modern Art and Grizedale Arts project A Fair Land

Performance Lessons: Suzanne Lacy Teaches Andrea Bowers Performance Art. Performance and installation, Beta Main, Los Angeles

2018

ONE/US, Lacy and Anna Ayeroff. Billboard, Crosstown Connection and Albany Street, Albany, New York. Designed for For Freedoms as part of the #50stateinitiative

Across and In-Between, Lacy with Cian Smyth, Garrett Carr, Eva Grosman, Helen Sharp, Helen Sloan, Pedro Rebelo, and Mark Thomas. Performance/project and multichannel video installation, Ulster Museum, Belfast, Ireland, and Stormont Parliament Buildings, Belfast. Part of 14-18 NOW and the Belfast International Arts Festival. Related documentary: *Across and In-Between* (2018), by Conan McIvor

2019

Dad Lessons. Videos and installation. Part of *Central Valley* (2008–ongoing)

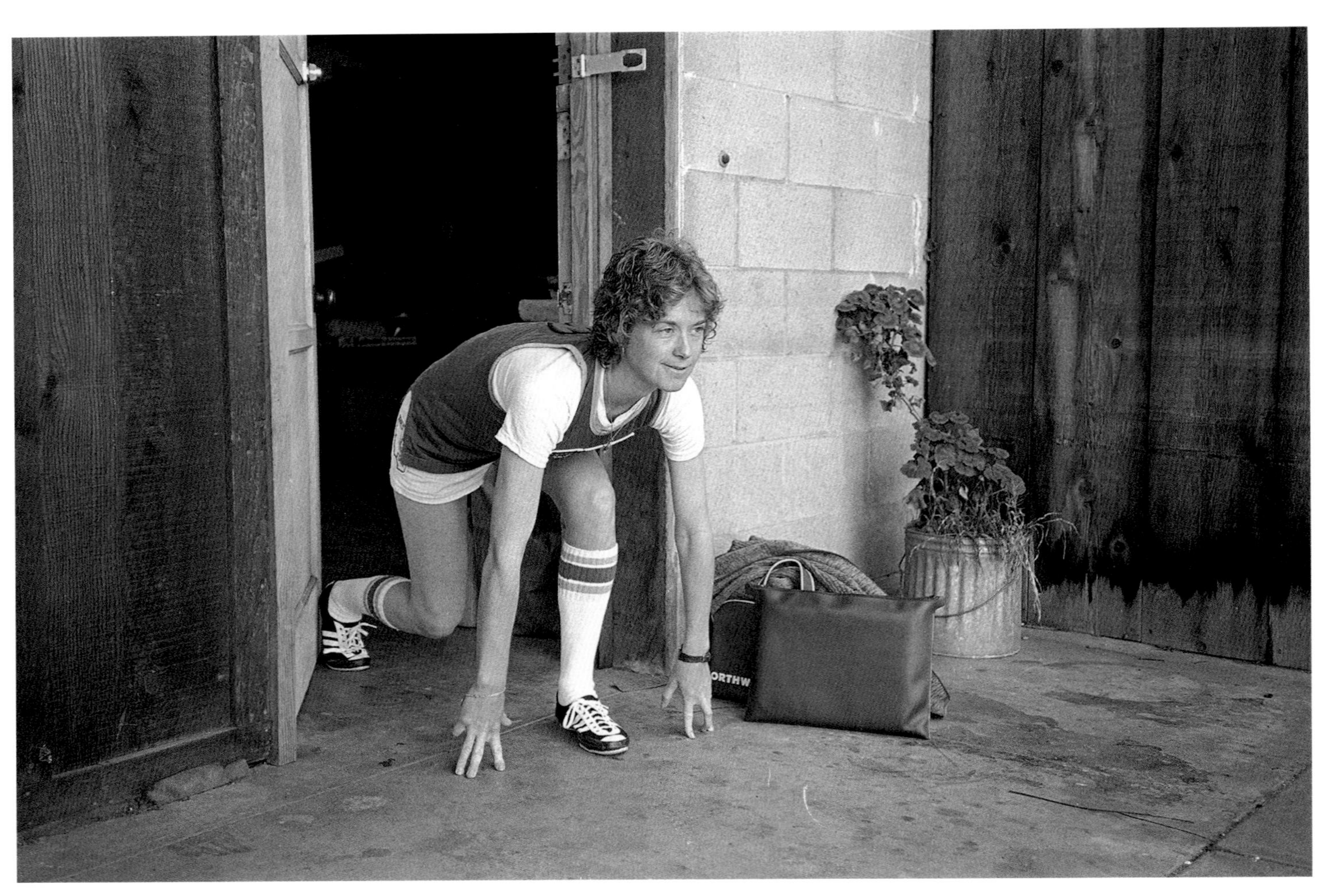

Suzanne Lacy, *Running to San Francisco*, 1975. Production photo

Suzanne Lacy (b. 1945, Wasco, California) is based in Los Angeles.

EDUCATION

2013
PhD, Gray's School of Art, Robert Gordon University, Aberdeen, Scotland

1973
MFA, social design, California Institute of the Arts, Valencia

1969–71
Graduate work in psychology, Fresno State College (now California State University, Fresno)

1968
BA, zoological sciences, with honors, University of California, Santa Barbara

1965
AA, premedical sciences, with honors, Bakersfield College, CA

PROFESSIONAL EXPERIENCE

Professor, Roski School of Art and Design, University of Southern California, Los Angeles, 2016–present
Founding Chair, MFA in Public Practice, Otis College of Art and Design, Los Angeles, 2007–16
Visiting Faculty, Gray's School of Art, Robert Gordon University, Aberdeen, Scotland, 2007–8
Chair of Fine Arts, Otis College of Art and Design, Los Angeles, 2001–6
Founding Director, Center for Art and Public Life, California College of Arts and Crafts,* Oakland, 1999–2002
Special Assistant to the President on Service Learning, California College of Arts and Crafts,* Oakland, 1997–99
Artist in Residence, Oakland Sharing the Vision, 1996–2000
Founding Faculty, California State University, Monterey Bay, 1995–96 (full professorship, highest step level)
Dean of Fine Arts, California College of Arts and Crafts,* Oakland, 1987–97
Dayton Hudson Distinguished Visiting Artist, Carleton College, Northfield, MN, 1987
Faculty, School of the Art Institute of Chicago, 1986, 1992
Faculty, Minneapolis College of Art and Design, 1985–86
Faculty, University of California, Irvine, 1982
Faculty, University of California, San Diego, 1976, 1977, 1979
Faculty, San Francisco Art Institute, 1975–77
Founding Faculty, Feminist Studio Workshop, the Woman's Building, Los Angeles, 1974–79
Faculty, University of California, Los Angeles, Extension, 1974

*California College of Arts and Crafts (CCAC) changed its name to California College of the Arts (CCA) in 2003.

SELECTED BIBLIOGRAPHY

This listing of texts authored or coauthored by Suzanne Lacy includes selected reprints and translations and reflects the complete information available at the time of publication. Many texts were also reprinted in Lacy's Leaving Art: Writings on Performance, Politics, and Publics, 1974–2007 *(Durham, NC: Duke University Press, 2010).*

Lacy, Suzanne. "After Consciousness Raising—What?" *Everywoman* 2, no. 7, issue 18 (May 7, 1971): 10–11.

Herbert, Martha Reed, and Suzanne Lacy. "Women's Design Program." *Networks* 1, no. 2 (June 1972): 20–23.

Lacy, Suzanne. "Gothic Love Story." *La Mamelle* 1, no. 2 (Fall 1975): 18–19.

———. "Cinderella in a Dragster." *Criss Cross Double Cross* 1 (Fall 1976): 15–17.

———. "'Three Weeks in May': Speaking Out on Rape, a Political Art Piece." *Frontiers: A Journal of Women Studies* 2, no. 1 (Spring 1977): 64–70.

Lacy, Suzanne, and Leslie Labowitz. "Evolution of a Feminist Art: Public Forms and Social Issues." *Heresies: A Feminist Publication on Art and Politics* 2, no. 2, issue 6 (1978): 76, 78–85.

Labowitz-Starus, Leslie, and Suzanne Lacy. "In Mourning and in Rage . . ." *Frontiers: A Journal of Women Studies* 3, no. 1 (Spring 1978): 52–55.

Labowitz, Leslie, and Suzanne Lacy. "Mass Media, Popular Culture, and Fine Art: Images of Violence against Women." In *Social Works*, exh. cat., edited by Nancy Buchanan, 26–31. Los Angeles: Los Angeles Institute of Contemporary Art, 1979. Reprinted in *Obscura: The Journal of the Los Angeles Center for Photographic Studies* 1, no. 5 (May/June 1981): 7–9.

Lacy, Suzanne, and Linda Palumbo. "The Life and Times of Donaldina Cameron." *Chrysalis: A Magazine of Women's Culture*, no. 7 (1979): 29–35.

Labowitz, Leslie, and Suzanne Lacy. "Two Approaches to Feminist Media Usage." In *Proceedings of the Caucus for Marxism and Art* (January 1979), 2–5.

Lacy, Suzanne. "Take Back the Night." *High Performance* 2, no. 4 (Winter 1979–80): 32–34.

———. "Broomsticks and Banners: The Winds of Change." *Artweek* 11, no. 17 (May 3, 1980): 3–4.

———. "Battle of New Orleans." *High Performance* 3, no. 2 (Summer 1980): 2–9.

———. "Falling Apart." *Dreamworks: An Interdisciplinary Quarterly* 1, no. 3 (Fall 1980): 234–41.

———. "Great Masterpieces Series #2: The Last Throes of Artistic Vision." *High Performance* 3, nos. 3/4 (Fall/Winter 1980): 68–69.

Labowitz, Leslie, and Suzanne Lacy. "Feminist Artists: Developing a Media Strategy for the Movement." In *Fight Back! Feminist Resistance to Male Violence*, edited by Frédérique Delacoste and Felice Newman, 266–72. Minneapolis: Cleis Press, 1981.

Lacy, Suzanne. "A Gothic Love Story." *Scree*, nos. 19–21 (1981): 41–47.

———. "Learning to Look: The Relationship between Art and Popular Culture Images." *Exposure* 19, no. 3 (September 1981): 8–15. Excerpted and reprinted in *Media Report to Women* 10, no. 3 (March 1, 1982): 2, 8.

———. "Made for TV: California Performance in Mass Media." *Performing Arts Journal* 6, no. 2 (1982): 52–61.

———. "The Bag Lady." *Block*, no. 7 (1982): 32–35.

———. "The Forest and the Trees." *Heresies: A Feminist Publication on Art and Politics* 4, no. 3, issue 15 (1982): 62–63.

———. "The Greening of California Performance: Art for Social Change—A Case Study." *Images and Issues* 2, no. 4 (Spring 1982): 64–67.

———. "In Mourning and in Rage: An Analysis Aforethought." *Ikon* 2, no. 1 (Fall/Winter 1982): 60–67. Reprinted in *Femicide: The Politics of Woman Killing*, edited by Jill Radford and Diana E. H. Russell, 317–24. New York: Twayne Publishers, 1992.

———. "Art of Protest." *MS. Magazine* 11, no. 4 (October 1982): 64–67.

———. "Speak Easy." *New Art Examiner* 10, no. 1 (October 1982): 7, 9.

Lacy, Suzanne, and Lucy R. Lippard. "Political Performance Art: A Discussion by Suzanne Lacy and Lucy R. Lippard." *Heresies: A Feminist Publication on Art and Politics* 5, no. 1, issue 17 (1984): 22–25.

Lacy, Suzanne, and Leslie Labowitz. "Feminist Media Strategies for Political Performance." In *Cultures in Contention*, edited by Douglas Kahn and Diane Neumaier, 122–33. Seattle: The Real Comet Press, 1985. Reprinted in *The Feminism and Visual Culture Reader*, edited by Amelia Jones, 302–13. New York: Routledge, 2003.

Lacy, Suzanne. "Fragments in a Rose Garden." *WARM Journal* 6, no. 2 (Summer 1985): 4–6.

———. "Statement." *High Performance* 11, nos. 41/42 (Spring/Summer 1988): 51–52.

———. "Fractured Space." In *Art in the Public Interest*, edited by Arlene Raven, 287–301. Ann Arbor: UMI Research Press, 1989.

———. "Skeptical of the Spectacle." *The Act* 2, no. 1, issue 4 (1990): 36–42.

———. "In the Shadows: An Analysis of the Dark Madonna." *Whitewalls: A Journal of Language and Art*, no. 25 (Spring 1990): 61–70.

———. "Footnotes: A Conversation Continued." *Gallerie Magazine* 9 (June 1990): 25–29.

———. "Finland: The Road of Poems and Borders." *Journal of Dramatic Theory and Criticism* (The University of Kansas) 5, no. 1 (Fall 1990): 211–19.

———. "Wrestling the Beast." *Public Art Review* 2, no. 2, issue 4 (Fall/Winter 1990): 14–15.

———. "Practicing Pluralistic Discourse: Blurring the Boundaries." In *Sunbird: Final Report on the Proceedings of the Sunbird Seminar on Preservice Art Education, Long Beach, May 1989, and Summaries of the Preservice Art Education Projects at Sixteen of the California State University Campuses*, 75–81. Long Beach: The California State University; Los Angeles: The Getty Center for Education in the Arts, 1991.

———. "The Name of the Game." *Art Journal* 50, no. 2 (Summer 1991): 64–68. Reprinted in *Theories and Documents of Contemporary Art: A Sourcebook of Artists' Writings*, edited by Kristine Stiles and Peter Selz, 783–86. Berkeley: University of California Press, 1996.

Lacy, Suzanne, and Rachel Rosenthal. "Saving the World: A Dialogue between Suzanne Lacy and Rachel Rosenthal." *Artweek* 22, no. 29 (September 12, 1991): 1, 14–16.

Lacy, Suzanne. "Debated Territory: Artists' Roles in a Culture of Visibility." *NACA Journal* (Napa Contemporary Arts Foundation), no. 1 (1992): 65–79.

———. "Mapping the Terrain: The New Public Art." Pts. 1 and 2. *Public Art Review* 4, no. 2, issue 8 (Spring/Summer 1993): 14–17; 5, no. 1, issue 9 (Fall/Winter 1993): 26–33. Reprinted in Theory and Practice (Russian), 2015, http://special.theoryandpractice.ru/suzanne-lacy.

———. "Montages from the Series, *The Anatomy Lesson*." *Creative Camera*, no. 324 (October/November 1993): 39.

———. "Affinities: Thoughts on an Incomplete History." In *The Power of Feminist Art: The American Movement of the 1970s, History and Impact*, edited by Norma Broude and Mary D. Garrard, 264–75. New York: Harry N. Abrams, 1994.

———. "Toward a Culturally Inclusive Art Education." In *Worlds in Collision: Dialogue on Multicultural Art Issues*, edited by Carlos Villa, 283–84. San Francisco: International Scholars Publications, 1994.

———, ed. *Mapping the Terrain: New Genre Public Art*. Seattle: Bay Press, 1995. Chinese edition, translated by Wu Mali et al., Taipei, Taiwan: Yuan-Liou Publishing, 2004. Korean edition, translated by Yoengwuk Lee and Ingyu Kim, Seoul: Munhwagwahak-sa, 2010.

———. "Bird's Nests, Boxes and Spinning Tops: A Meditation for Bella, on Her Work." In *Bella*, edited by Bella Feldman, 78. Self-published, 1996.

———. "Pink Blouse and False Teeth: On 'The Relationship of Artist to Writer—Real to Ideal.'" In *Sniper's Nest: Art That Has Lived with Lucy R. Lippard*, edited by David Frankel, 56–60. New York: Bard College, 1996.

———. "Some Notes on 'The Crystal Quilt.'" In *Expanding Circles: Women, Art, and Community*, edited by Betty Ann Brown, 175–80. New York: Midmarch Arts Press, 1996.

———. "Love, Cancer and Memory." *Public Art Review* 7, no. 2, issue 14 (Spring/Summer 1996): 5–13.

Lacy, Suzanne, and Susanne Cockrell. "Alterations: A Series of Conversations." *Fiber Arts: The Magazine of Textiles* 23, no. 2 (September/October 1996): 36–40.

Lacy, Suzanne. "Lisbon in Motion." In *Junction '96: Lisbon Worldwide Conference on Art and Public Transport*. Metropolitano de Lisboa, 1997.

———. "Prostitution Notes." In *Veiled Histories: The Body, Place and Public Art*, edited by Anna Novakov, 147–69. New York: Critical Press; San Francisco: San Francisco Art Institute, 1997.

Steinman, Susan Leibovitz, and Suzanne Lacy. "Jo Hanson." In *Women's Caucus for Art Honor Awards*, 8–9. Women's Caucus for Art, 1997.

Lacy, Suzanne. "Seeing Mud Houses." In *Accidental Audience: Urban Interventions by Artists*, edited by Kym Pruesse, 68–75. Toronto: off\site Collective, 1999.

Lacy, Suzanne, Julio Morales, and Unique Holland. "Code 33: Emergency—Clear the Air." *New Observations*, no. 127 (Fall/Winter 2000): 48–49.

Lacy, Suzanne. "'Comments on *Code 33: Emergency Clear the Air*,' Letter to Author, May 23, 2000." In *Modern Art in the USA: Issues and Controversies of the 20th Century*, edited by Patricia Hills, 452–54. Upper Saddle River, NJ: Prentice Hall, 2001.

Lacy, Suzanne, and Ann Wettrich. "What It Takes." In *CO-LAB: New Generations, Creative Partnerships in Art and Learning*, exh. cat., edited by Julia Marshall, 12–22. San Francisco: San Francisco Arts Commission Gallery and Fine Arts Gallery, San Francisco State University, 2002.

Roth, Moira, and Suzanne Lacy. "Exchanges." In *Art/Women/California 1950–2000: Parallels and Intersections*, exh. cat., edited by Diana Burgess Fuller and Daniela Salvioni, 295–309. San Jose: San Jose Museum of Art, 2002.

Riaño Alcalá, Pilar, Suzanne Lacy, and Olga Cristina Agudelo Hernández. *Arte, memoria y violencia: Reflexiones sobre la ciudad*. Medellín, Colombia: Corporación Región, 2003.

Lacy, Suzanne. "Finding Our Way to the Flag: Is Civic Discourse Art?" *Public Art Review* 14, no. 2, issue 28 (Spring/Summer 2003): 26–32.

———. "Having It Good: Reflections on Engaged Art and Engaged Buddhism." In *Buddha Mind in Contemporary Art*, edited by Jacquelynn Baas and Mary Jane Jacob, 97–111. Berkeley: University of California Press, 2004.

———. "Seeking an American Identity (Working inward from the Margins)." In *Civic Dialogue, Arts and Culture: Findings from Animating Democracy*, edited by Pam Korza, Barbara Schaffer Bacon, and Andrea Assaf, 191–209. Washington, D.C.: Americans for the Arts, 2005.

———. "Engagement in Buddhism and Art." *Urthona*, no. 22 (Fall 2005): 19–23.

———. "Activism in Feminist Performance Art." In *A Boal Companion: Dialogues on Theatre and Cultural Politics*, edited by Jan Cohen-Cruz and Mady Schutzman, 91–102. New York: Routledge, 2006.

———. "Tracing Allan Kaprow." *Artforum* 44, no. 10 (Summer 2006): 323.

———. "Allan Kaprow: Art as Life." *Artforum* 45, no. 4 (December 2006): 115.

———. "Small Observations on Leaving Art and Other Issues." *EXIT* (Winter 2006).

Lacy, Suzanne, and Pilar Riaño-Alcalá. "Medellín, Colombia: Reinhabiting Memory." *Art Journal* 65, no. 4 (Winter 2006): 96–112.

Lacy, Suzanne. "Mirando alrededor. Sobre las prácticas públicas." *EXIT Book, Arte público*, no. 7 (2007): 74.

———. "time between is the spine of this book . . ." *interReview*, issue 7 (2007): 47–54.

Lacy, Suzanne, and Leslie Labowitz. "The Performing Archive." *interReview*, issue 7 (2007): 36–46.

Lacy, Suzanne. "Suzanne Lacy," part of "WACK! Art and the Feminist Revolution." *MOCA The Contemporary* (June–August 2007): 6.

———. "Time in Place: New Genre Public Art a Decade Later." In *The Practice of Public Art*, edited by Cameron Cartiere and Shelly Willis, 18–32. New York: Routledge, 2008.

———. "The Artist Arlene Raven." *Critical Matrix: The Princeton Journal of Women, Gender and Culture* 17 (Spring 2008): 80–86.

Lacy, Suzanne, and Arlene Raven. "Travels with Mona." *Critical Matrix: The Princeton Journal of Women, Gender and Culture* 17 (Spring 2008): 32–41.

Lacy, Suzanne, Susan Leibovitz Steinman, and Yutaka Kobayashi. "Beneath Land and Water: A Project for Elkhorn City." *Public Art Magazine* (Japan) 1 (October 2008): 7–9.

Lacy, Suzanne. "The Public Body." *Public Art Review* 20, no. 2, issue 40 (Spring/Summer 2009): 39.

———. "Reintroductions: Feminist Performance Art, Meet Public Practice; Activist Art Meet Live Art." *Public Art Review* 21, no. 1, issue 41 (Fall/Winter 2009).

———. "Beyond Necessity: The Street as Studio." In *The Studio Reader: On the Space of Artists*, edited by Mary Jane Jacob and Michelle Grabner, 317–20. Chicago: The University of Chicago Press, 2010.

———. "Dislocated Conversations: Why Public Art Is Essential." In *New Community in the Open City: Anyang Public Art Project 2010*, exh. cat. Anyang, South Korea: Anyang Public Art Project Foundation, 2010.

———. "In Mourning and in Rage." In *Donna: Avanguardia femminista negli anni '70 dalla Sammlung Verbund di Vienna*, exh. cat., edited by Gabriele Schor, 82–89. Vienna: Sammlung Verbund, 2010.

———. *Leaving Art: Writings on Performance, Politics, and Publics, 1974–2007.* Durham, NC: Duke University Press, 2010.

———. "Killing Women and Other Issues in Art." *The Museum of Non Participation*, edited by Karen Mirza and Brad Butler, a supplement of *The Daily Jang*, September 20, 2010, 6.

———. "Activism in Feminist Performance Art." In *Education, Documents of Contemporary Art*, edited by Felicity Allen, 87–91. London: Whitechapel Gallery, 2011.

———. "Serious Work." In *Pearls of Wisdom: End the Violence*, exh. cat., edited by Suvan Greer and Sandra Mueller, 80–83. Los Angeles: A Window Between Worlds, 2011.

———. "Service and Art: Artists and Buddhists Engage." *Public Art Review* 22, no. 2, issue 44 (Spring/Summer 2011): 27.

———. "It Speaks to Me: Suzanne Lacy on Andrea Bowers." *Los Angeles Times Blog*, September 21, 2011. http://latimesblogs.latimes.com/culturemonster/2011/09/it-speaks-to-me-suzanne-lacy-on-andrea-bowers.html.

———. "The Uncertainty of Land and the Mutability of Art." Nowhereisland, August 26, 2012. http://nowhereisland.org/resident-thinkers/51/.

———. "Distracting Vaginas and the Body Politic." *Creative Time Reports*, October 7, 2012. http://creativetimereports.org/2012/10/07/distracting-vaginas-and-the-body-politic/.

———. "Suzanne Lacy," part of "Sensibility of the Times, Revisited," by Cathy Lebowitz. *Art in America* 100, no. 11 (December 2012): 165.

———. "Suzanne Lacy *do it* Instruction." In *Do It: The Compendium*, edited by Hans Ulrich Obrist, 234. New York: Independent Curators International, 2013.

———. "Suzanne Lacy: Silver Action: Performance Recreation." *Tate Modern Blog*, February 20, 2013. http://www.tate.org.uk/context-comment/blogs/suzanne-lacy-silver-action-performance-recreation.

———. "Between the Door and the Street." *Creative Time Reports*, October 10, 2013. http://creativetimereports.org/reports-360/between-the-door-and-the-street-a-performance-initiated-by-suzanne-lacy/.

———. "Suzanne Lacy," part of "Social Practice in Questions," by Bill Kelley Jr. In *18th Street Arts Center: 2012–2013*, edited by Pilar Tompkins Rivas, 55. Santa Monica, CA: 18th Street Arts Center, 2014.

Lacy, Suzanne, and Christopher G. Robbins. "Reclaiming the Public in Public Pedagogy: A Conversation between Christopher G. Robbins and Suzanne Lacy." In *Problematizing Public Pedagogy*, edited by Jake Burdick, Jennifer A. Sandlin, and Michael P. O'Malley, 149–60. New York: Routledge, 2014.

Lacy, Suzanne, and Andrea Bowers. "After the Slumber Party . . ." *The Brooklyn Rail*, September 4, 2014, 78.

Lacy, Suzanne. "Pedagogies in the Oakland Projects." In *The Routledge Companion to Art and Politics*, edited by Randy Martin, 309–20. London: Routledge, 2015.

Lacy, Suzanne, and Megan Steinman. "Not New: Reclaiming the Radical in Feminism." *WEAD: Women Eco Artists Dialog*, no. 8 (December 31, 2015). http://weadartists.org/not-new-reclaiming-the-radical-in-feminism.

Lacy, Suzanne. "Continuing Silver Actions . . . A Proposal." In *Perform/Experience/Re-live: BMW Tate Live*, edited by Cecilia Wee, 94–107. London: Tate, 2016.

———. "Practical Strategies: Framing Narratives for Public Pedagogies." In *A Companion to Public Art*, edited by Cher Krause Knight and Harriet F. Senie, 239–44. Chichester, UK: Wiley-Blackwell, 2016.

Riaño-Alcalá, Pilar, and Suzanne Lacy. "Skins of Memory: Art, Civic Pedagogy, and Social Reconstruction." In *Collective Situations: Readings in Contemporary Latin American Art, 1995–2010*, edited by Bill Kelley Jr. and Grant H. Kester, 203–19. Durham, NC: Duke University Press, 2017.

Thompson, Nato, and Suzanne Lacy. "Perceptions of Care." In *Curating Context: Beyond the Gallery and into Other Fields*, edited by Magdalena Malm, 95–109. Stockholm: Art and Theory and Statens konstråd, 2017.

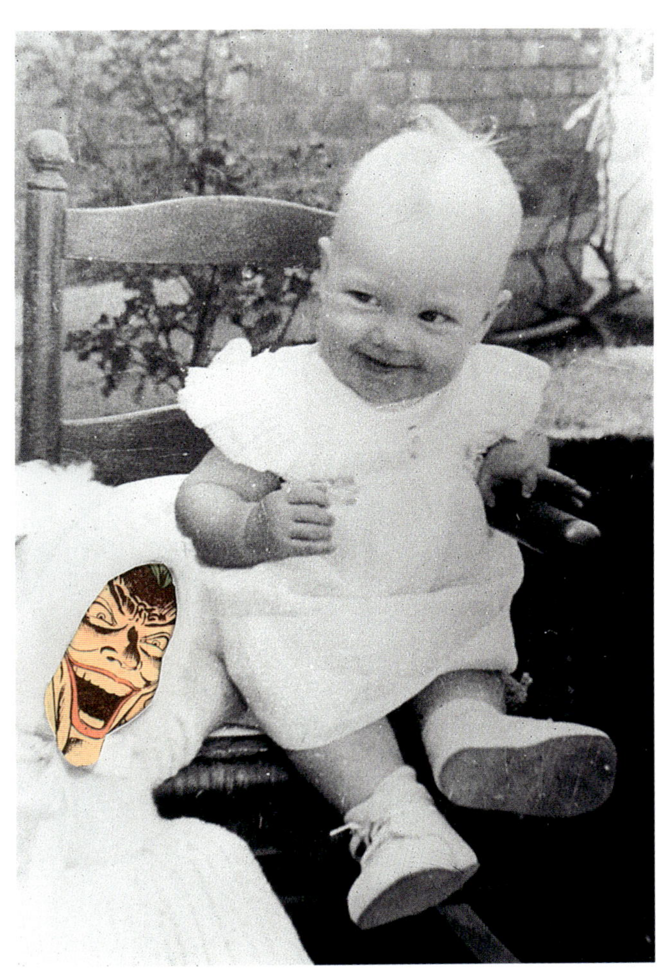

Suzanne Lacy, photograph from *Autobiography of a Young Vampire*, ca. 1974–75

Projects featured in the Illustrated Survey (pp. 42–245) are listed below.

Ablutions (1972), 44–45

Alterations (1994–95), 218

Anatomy Lesson #1: Chickens Coming Home to Roost (for Rose Mountain and Pauline) (1976), 59

Anatomy Lesson #2: Learn Where the Meat Comes From (1976), 60–62

Anatomy Lesson #3: Falling Apart (1976), 63

Anatomy Lesson #4 (1977), 65–67

Anatomy Lessons (1976–77), 58–67

Anyang Women's Agenda (2010), 176–77

Ariadne: A Social Art Network (1977–82), 94–109

Autobiography of a Young Vampire (ca. 1974–75), 70

Auto on the Edge of Time (1993–94), 110–11

Bag Lady, The (1977), 78–79

Beer Bucket/Champagne Bucket (2008), 233

Beneath Land and Water: A Project for Elkhorn City (2000–2005), 228–31

Between the Door and the Street (2013), 180–81

Body Contract (1974), 56–57

Central Valley (2008–ongoing), 232–35

Cinderella in a Dragster (1976), 72

Circle and the Square, The (2015–17), 238–45

Cleaning Conditions (2013), 236–37

Code 33: Emergency, Clear the Air! (1997–99), 206–11

Crystal Quilt, The (1987), 166–73

Dad Lessons (2019), 234–35

Dark Madonna, The (1985–86), 158–65

De tu puño y letra (By Your Own Hand) (2014–15/2019), 118–23

Dinner at Jane's (1993), 149

Edna, May Victor, Mary, and Me: An All-Night Benediction (1977), 73

Esqueleto tatuado (Tattooed Skeleton) (2010), 112–15

Evalina and I: Crimes, Quilts, and Art (1975–80), 126–29

Expectations (1996–97), 200–205

Eye 2 Eye at Fremont High (2000), 192

Falling Apart (1976), 64

From Reverence to Rape to Respect (1978), 106

Freeze Frame: Room for Living Room (1982), 140–46

Full Circle (1992–93), 148

Hardcore Screening (1978), 107

I.D.Entity (2004), 213

Incest Awareness Project (1979–80), 107

Inevitable Associations (1976), 74–77

In Mourning and in Rage (1977), 100–102

International Dinner Party (1979), 130–35

In the Last Throes of Artistic Vision (1980), 86–87

I Tried Everything (1972), 47

Lamb Construction (1973), 49

La piel de la memoria/Skin of Memory (1999–2000), 219–23

La piel de la memoria revivida/Skin of Memory Revisited (2011), 219–23

Laton: Free Store (2009), 233

Life and Times of Donaldina Cameron, The (1977), 82–83

Making It Safe (1979), 106

Maps (1973), 50–51

Mona by Number (1978), 85

Monster Series: Construction of a Novel Frankenstein (1974/1975), 52–53

Net Construction (1973), 48

No Blood/No Foul (1995–96), 193–99

Oakland Projects, The (1991–2001), 184–211

Performing Archive: Restricted Access, The (2007), 108–9

Prostitution Notes (1974–75), 90–93

Rape Is (1972), 46

Record Companies Drag Their Feet (1977), 103

River Meetings: Lives of Women in the Delta (1980), 136–39

Road of Poems and Borders, The (1989–90), 174–75

Roof Is on Fire, The (1993–94), 186–91

Running to San Francisco (1975), 71

School for Revolutionary Girls (2016), 215

Signs of Violence (1994), 192

Silver Action (2013), 178–79

Stories of Work and Survival (2007), 147

SWARM (2007), 214

Take Back the Night (1978), 106

Teenage Living Room (1991–92), 185

Three Love Stories (1975–76), 54

Three Weeks in January (2012), 116–17

Three Weeks in May (1977), 95–99

Travels with Mona (1977–78), 84

Tulare: Garage Sale (2008), 233

Turning Point, The (1996–97), 212

Under Construction (1997), 212

Under My Skin: A True-Life Story (1975/1977), 55

University of Local Knowledge (2000–ongoing), 224–27

Vigil/Incorporate, The (1978), 80–81

Whisper Minnesota (1985–87), 166–73

Whisper, the Waves, the Wind (1983–84), 152–57

Woman's Image of Mass Media, A (1979), 104–5

Youth, Cops, and Videotape (1995), 192

COLLABORATORS, PARTICIPANTS, AND ASSOCIATES

Suzanne Lacy has engaged a wide array of organizations, institutions, artists, and other individuals in her practice. The following listing reflects those noted in the Illustrated Survey (pp. 42–245). Numbers in italics point to quotations.

Abakanowicz, Magdalena, 149

Abeles, Kim, 214

Adams, Britni, *113*

Adorni, Elena, 238

Akashi, Kelly, 147, 233

Allen, Sharon, 152, *152*

Anderson, Sharon Roe, 166

Andrade, Rubén Fernández, 219

Angelo, Nancy, 73, 80, 107

Antin, David, 74

Apple, Jacki, 146

Aragon, Nina, 228

Ariadne: A Social Art Network, 89, 94–109

Arnoff, Julie, 166

Arnolfini Gallery, 224

Atkintunde, Ogubala, *207*

Atlantis, Dori, 47

Aula, Ihva, 174

Baca, Judy, 174, 214

Barnet, Susan, 147

Barriga, Cecilia, 112, 113

Bashir, Rauf, 238, *238*

Batiste, Kim, 206

Becker, Leslie, 192, 200, 202

Belcher, Tim, 228

Belt, Leslie, 107

Blomberg, Jouko, 174

Bourgeois, Louise, 132

Bowers, Andrea, 233

Bray, Anne, 158, *160*

Bronson, Jacques, *190*, 192

Brooks, Betty, 102

Building Bridges Pendle, 238

Burnham, Linda, 80

Cabra, Raúl, 206, 219

Caffey, Julie, 202

Cain, Jeff, 214

California Advocates for Trollops, 107

California National Organization for Women, 103

Carolus, Cheryl, 149

Cartagena, María Fernanda, 118

Chang, Kathleen, 69, 82, *83*

Chattler, Jan, 140

Chavez, Rosa, 192

Chavez, Sara, 192

Chicago, Judy, 43, 44, *44*, 130, *131*

Cockrell, Susanne, 110, 218

Cole, Johnnetta, 149

Communitas, 106

Constant, Betty, 136

Cooney, Jean, 180

Cory, Joya, 140

Cotts, Virginia, 110

Cowles, Sage Fuller, 166

COYOTE (Call Off Your Old Tired Ethics), 94

Create, 215

Creative Time, 180

Cunningham, Myrna, 149

Deak, Frantisek, 74

Deak, Norma Jean, 74

de Bretteville, Sheila Levrant, 46

Dennis, Nancy, 166

Dill, Guy, 44

Dowse, Signe, 99

Duane, Hildegarde, 60, *61*

Dunn, Laverne Woods, 124–25, 136, *138*

Duster, Troy, 186

Ebner, Amanda, *113*

Edelson, Mary Beth, 132

Elizabeth A. Sackler Center for Feminist Art, Brooklyn Museum, 180

El Saadawi, Nawal, 149

Evans, Penny, 224, *225*

Faludi, Susan, 149

Feldman, Deborah, 106

Feminist Art Workers, 106

Findley, Lisa, 200

Fink, Larry, 166–67

Furlow, Etta, 170

Game, Oderay, 118

Gaulke, Cheri, 74–75, *75*

Geller, Phylis, 149

Gillis, Liz, 215

Gitlin, Todd, 186

Goldberg, David, 206

Gómez-Peña, Guillermo, 174

Goode, Nicola, 215

Grode, Susan, 149

Gross, Elisheva, 213

Guerra, Mary Ann, 136

Hamner, Andy, 185

Hardeman, Anne Maria, 206

Harris, Amana, 200, *201*

Hartley, Paul, 238, *239*

Hassan, Carolyn, 224, *224*

Heepke, Carol, 158

Hershman Leeson, Lynn, 69, 85, *85*

Hickman, Nicole, 192

Hill, Anita, 149

Hindikka, Tuire, 174

Hirsh, Leuckessia, *191*, 200

Hodge, Gregory, *197*, *207*

Holland, Unique, *180*, 199, 200, 206, *208*, 213

Hoyos, Mauricio, 219

Hsu, Jennifer, 180

Huerta, Dolores, 149

In-Situ, 238

Irons, Betsy, 106

Jacob, Mary Jane, *136*

Jacoby, Annice, 184, 186, *189*, 192, 193, 200

Jain, Devaki, 149

Johnson, Chris, 183, 184, 185, 186, *187*, 192, 193

Jolly, Margaretta, 178

Jones, Sharon, 192

Jordan, Sheila, 193, 200

Kähkönen, Jarmo, 174

Kaprow, Allan, 50, 51, *51*, 74, 174, 236

Kathmeyer, Britta, 218

Katzive, David, 110

Kauffman, Kathy, 106

Kay, Graham, 238

Kepes, Judy, 166

Kim, Bosuel, 176

King, Claudia, 106

Klix, Ann, 106

Knowle West Media Centre, 224, 226

Kobayashi, Yutaka, 228

Kohl, Herb, 186

Koon, Jidan, 192

Kroeger, Timm, 118

Kumata, Carol, 110

Kurikka, Pirkko, 174

Kyung, Chung Hyun, 149

Labowitz, Leslie, 89, 94, 99, 100, 102, *102*, 103, 104, *104–5*, 106, 107, 108, *109*

Labowitz, Rochelle, 214

Lacy, Larry, 234
Lee, Lois, 107
León, Paulina, 118
Lesbian and Gay Community Services Center (now
    the Lesbian, Gay, Bisexual, and Transgender
    Community Center), 94
Le Sueur, Meridel, 170
Linsiö, Tuula, 174
Lippard, Lucy R., 166–67
London, Julia, 140
Los Angeles Commission on Assaults against
    Women (now Peace over Violence),
    94, 100–101
Louchouarn, Bruno, 116, 118, 180
Lowe, Bia, 51, 100, 107
Lucke-Aaberg, Lou Ann, 192
Lumbard, Paula, 107
Macy, Sarah, 52
Males, Mike, *193*
Manduke, Lauren, 185
Mankiller, Wilma, 149
Manley, Beatrice, 80
Manoushagian, Andy, 233
Manwaring, Michael, 188
Martin, Jan Lester, 44, 47
Matlick, Mary Helen, 136
Mayer, Mónica, 106
Mendieta, Ana, 132
Metzger, Deena, 46, 99
Minnesota Quilters, The, 173
Mogul, Susan, 59, 63
Mollona, Massimiliano, 238
Montano, Linda (Rose Mountain), 59, 73
Morales, Julio César, 192, 206
Moreira, Mónica, 118
Nathan, Jeanne, 136
Neal, Booker, 192
Near, Holly, 100, 101, 106
Newman, Evalina, 125, 126, 128
Oliveros, Pauline, 59
Orgel, Sandra, 44
Ou, Arthur, 213
Oxenberg, Jan, 44–45
Park, Kyong, *176*
Parnell, Meg, 236, *237*
Pasternak, Anne, 180
Pen, Ron, 238, *243*
Perkins, Arnold X. C., 200, *204*
Phillips, Lynn, 80
Phranc, 80
Pings, Peggy, 228
Polletta, Francesca, *113*
Ponce, Gabriela, 118
Preuss, Linda, 130
Prins, Rose Marie, 106
Rahmani, Aviva, 44, *44*

Ramirez, Vicky, 219
Rape Hotline Alliance, 100–101
Raven, Arlene, 84
Rehor, Petr, 174
Riaño-Alcalá, Pilar, *212*, 219, *219*
Richardson, Stephanie, 228
Rivas, Natalia, 140
Rose, Phyllis Jane, 166
Ross, David A., 60, *62*
Roth, Moira, *51*, 166–67
Saar, Betye, 214
Saks, Jane, 149
Salzberg, Phyllis, 166
Sampson, Perney, 140
Schapiro, Miriam, 166, 169
Seung-Boh, Jun, 176
Smith, Barbara T., 80, 81
Smith, Douglas Gayeton, 144
Smithwalter, Gail, 192
Smolick, Sharon, 110
Snedeker, Marilee, 136
Spencer, Ngoh, 140
Steinem, Gloria, 149
Steinman, Susan Leibovitz, 228
St. James, Margot, *91*, 106
Stone, Susan, 152, 158, 166, *169*
Strimling, Arthur, 174, *175*
Super Slow Way, 238
Szego, Carol, 140
T.E.A.M. (Teens + Educators + Artists + Media
    Makers), 184, 192, 193
Thomas, Mark, 238
Thompson, Nato, 180
Toebe, Patrick, 206
Tonelli, Edith, 158
Toxic Lesbian, *114*
Trigoso, Monica, *113*
Vallejo, Linda, *165*
Vargas, Juan Sebastián, 219
Vega, Raúl, 60, 176
Watson, Charlotte, 110
Wayne, June, 214
Weinberg, Tom, 149
Whelan, Fiona, *215*
Wollenman, Shawnee, 44–45
Wolverton, Terry, 107
Women against Violence against Women, 94, 103
Women's Caucus for Art, 136, 137, 139
Wood, Catherine, *178*
Wyatt, Addie, 149
Wyman, Maxine, 200, 202
Youdelman, Nancy, 47
Young, Willow, 158
Zitani, Asha, 200

CREDITS

PHOTOGRAPHY

Photography credits are listed below by page number.

8, 88, 115: Juan Cruz Ibáñez Gangutia

12–13, 42, 48, 51, 58–59, 63, 72 (left), 75 (bottom left), 100 (bottom), 101 (left), 102 (bottom): Susan Mogul

15, 147, 202–3, 232, 233 (middle): Kelly Akashi

17 (top): Christina Sánchez Juárez

17 (bottom): Courtesy of the Museo de Antioquia

18 (top): Hammer Museum, Los Angeles

18 (bottom): Zeno Zotti

21 (top): Carmen Uriarte

21 (bottom): Courtesy of the Santa Monica Museum of Art. Photo by Jeff McLane

25, 119 (top): Patricio Estévez

26, 39–40, 50, 52 (left), 54, 64, 72 (right), 85 (bottom left), 90, 91, 92, 93, 95, 96 (bottom left; bottom right), 97 (bottom left; bottom right), 99, 102 (top left; top right), 103 (top), 106 (top; bottom), 110 (bottom), 111 (bottom left; bottom right), 126, 128 (bottom left; bottom right), 129, 131 (top), 132 (top left), 134 (left, top to bottom), 135 (right, top to bottom), 138 (bottom), 139, 146, 201, 202 (left top; left bottom), 204, 220, 224, 226, 233 (bottom): Suzanne Lacy

27: The Getty Research Institute (980063). Photographed by Robert R. McElroy, © J. Paul Getty Trust

31: Ben Blackwell

32, 37, 83 (left), 190, 194, 196, 197, 200, 207 (top left), 209: Don Ross

38: © Museum of Fine Arts Boston. © 2018 Artists Rights Society (ARS), New York

44, 45: Lloyd Hamrol

46, 56, 57, 60 (top), 74 (top), 75 (top; bottom right), 76 (bottom), 85 (bottom right), 94, 127, 128 (top), 132 (top right), 133, 137, 144 (bottom), 153 (left top; left bottom; right bottom), 157, 161, 169, 205: Jeff McLane

49: Jed Wilcox

52 (right), 70, 73, 130–31, 131 (right bottom), 136 (left top; left bottom), 168 (top): Courtesy Suzanne Lacy

60 (bottom left; bottom right), 61, 74 (bottom), 76 (top), 77 (bottom), 86, 87, 98, 150, 176, 177: Raúl Vega

65, 66–67, 77 (top), 82, 84 (top left; top right; bottom left), 106 (middle): Rob Blalack

68: Susan Mogul, courtesy Linda Frye Burnham, Suzanne Lacy, and Susan Mogul

78, 79: Terry Schutte

80, 81: Courtesy Suzanne Lacy and Barbara Smith

84 (middle left): Iole de Freitas

84 (middle right): D. E. Steward

85 (top): Cheri Gaulke

96–97: Grant Mudford

100 (top), 101 (right): Maria Karras

103 (bottom): Courtesy Women against Violence against Women

104–5: Leslie Labowitz

107 (top): HARDCORE/Courtesy of Columbia Pictures

107 (bottom): Courtesy Leslie Labowitz

108: 6th Street Studio, San Francisco

110 (top): Richard Hurst

111 (top; middle right): Sue Heinrich

113: Tracy Johnson

114 (bottom): © REUTERS/Eloy Alonso

116 (top): Neda Moridpour

116 (bottom): Ceara Conway

118: Raúl Peñafiel

119 (bottom), 120–21, 123: Christoph Hirtz

124, 138 (top): Phyllis Parun

132 (bottom): Mary Beth Edelson

136 (right top; right bottom): J. Grezaffi

140 (top), 142–43, 144 (top): f-stop Fitzgerald

140 (bottom), 141: Candace Compton

148: Melissa Ann Pinney

149: John McWilliams

152, 154, 155, 156 (top), 158, 164 (top left; top right; bottom left), 170 (right top), 171 (left bottom; right middle): Edith Kodmur

153 (top right): John Warner

156 (bottom): Terry Gydesen

164 (bottom right): Basia Kenton

166, 171 (right bottom): Linda Brooks

170 (left, top to bottom; right middle; right bottom), 171 (left top; right top), 172: Ann Marsden

171 (left middle): Gus Gustafson

173, 178, 179: © Courtesy Tate Modern

174 (left): Chris Crickmay

174 (right): Timo Jerkku

175 (top left): Tone Arstila

175 (top right; bottom): Matti Mäkijärvi

180, 181 (bottom right): Jonathan Dorado

181 (bottom left), 215, 249: Nicola Goode

182, 206, 208 (top right): Kelli Yon

184, 189 (bottom right): Chris Johnson

185 (left): Courtesy Lauren Manduke

185 (right top; right middle; right bottom), 193, 195: Courtesy Chris Johnson and students

186–87, 218: Gary Nakamoto

189 (bottom left), 191 (top left; top right; middle left; bottom right): Nathan Bennett

191 (middle right): Alfredo Sosa

191 (bottom left): Rubén Guzmán

192 (top): Gail Smithwalter

192 (bottom): D. Gorell

207 (bottom), 208 (top left; bottom left): Lily Rodríguez

208 (middle left; bottom right): Paul Carter

208 (middle right): Romy Suskin

212 (top): Skai Fowler

212 (bottom): Daniel Collins

213: Arthur Ou

214 (bottom): Niku Kashef

216, 236, 237 (top left; top right): Alan Seabright
221 (top): Carlos Sánchez/Pregón Ltda
221 (bottom): Pilar Riaño-Alcalá
226: Penny Evans
228, 229: Susan Leibovitz Steinman
238, 239 (bottom): Graham Kay
239 (top): Matthew Savage

QUOTATIONS

All script and transcript excerpts in the Illustrated Survey (pp. 42–245) are from the Suzanne Lacy papers unless otherwise noted below. Quotations dated 2018 are from email and telephone conversations with the authors conducted in the summer and fall of that year. Credits for other quotations in the Illustrated Survey are listed below by page number.

46: Susan Griffin, "Rape: The All-American Crime," *Ramparts* 10, no. 3 (September 1971): 35.

51: Suzanne Lacy, Allan Kaprow, and Moira Roth in conversation, 1981, 4–5. Unpublished transcript, Suzanne Lacy papers.

72: Suzanne Lacy, "Cinderella in a Dragster" (1977), reprinted in *Leaving Art: Writings on Performance, Politics, and Publics, 1974–2007* (Durham, NC: Duke University Press, 2010), 50–51.

78: Suzanne Lacy, "The Bag Lady," *Block*, no. 7 (1982): 35.

83: Kathleen Chang in Suzanne Lacy, Kathleen Chang, and Linda Palumbo, "The Life and Times of Donaldina Cameron" (1978), reprinted in Suzanne Lacy, *Leaving Art: Writings on Performance, Politics, and Publics, 1974–2007* (Durham, NC: Duke University Press, 2010), 61–62.

90–91: Suzanne Lacy, "Prostitution Notes" (1974), in *Leaving Art: Writings on Performance, Politics, and Publics, 1974–2007* (Durham, NC: Duke University Press, 2010), 5.

91: Margot St. James in Anne Gray Fischer, "Forty Years in the Hustle: A Q&A with Margot St. James," *Bitch* magazine, no. 58 (Spring 2013).

99: Untitled poem from Deena Metzger, *Skin: Shadows/Silence, A Love Letter in the Form of a Novel* (Reno: West Coast Poetry Review, 1976), 56–57.

101: "I Am Here . . .," in *In Mourning and in Rage*, 1977, https://vimeo.com/100465745, 3:01–6:43 min.
"Fight Back," written and composed by Holly Near, published by Hereford Music.

102: Leslie Labowitz in *Leslie Labowitz Discusses Activist Performance and the Media*, by Teresa Flores, 2011, https://www.youtube.com/watch?t=15s&v=362L2ff7Flc, 2:04–3:49.

109: Leslie Labowitz, Suzanne Lacy, and Dominic Willsdon in conversation, 218. Unpublished transcript, Education and Public Practice exhibition files, San Francisco Museum of Modern Art. Lightly edited.

113: Francesca Polletta, Monica Trigoso, Britni Adams, and Amanda Ebner, "The Limits of Plot: Accounting for How Women Interpret Stories of Sexual Assault," *American Journal of Cultural Sociology* 1, no. 3 (October 2013): 289–320.

116: Charlie Beck in *Three Weeks in January*, by Getty Pacific Standard Time, 2012, https://vimeo.com/99378013, 0:04–0:39 min.

136: Mary Jane Jacob, "Introduction," in Moira Roth, *The Amazing Decade: Women and Performance Art in America, 1970–1980* (Los Angeles: Astro Artz, 1983), 11.

145: *SOFA*, edited by Douglas Gayeton Smith, executive produced by Suzanne Lacy, 1984, 8:11–54 min., 18:19–39 min., 5:12–6:06 min., 11:11–43 min.

159: Kathleen Hendrix, "An Emotional Conference on Women, Myth," *Los Angeles Times*, November 13, 1985. Copyright © 1985. Los Angeles Times. Used with Permission.

160: Anne Bray, artist's statement on *The Dark Madonna*, 1986.

187: Chris Johnson in *The Roof Is on Fire*, written and produced by Craig Franklin (San Francisco: Chronicle Broadcasting, 1994), https://vimeo.com/39865636, 3:27–45 min.

189: Annice Jacoby in *The Roof Is on Fire*, written and produced by Craig Franklin (San Francisco: Chronicle Broadcasting, 1994), https://vimeo.com/39865636, 21:19–33 min., 21:49–22:06 min.

190: Jacques Bronson interview with Suzanne Lacy, 2007. Suzanne Lacy papers.

191: Leuckessia Hirsh interview with Suzanne Lacy, 2007. Suzanne Lacy papers.

197: Gregory Hodge in *No Blood/No Foul*, executive produced by Suzanne Lacy, 1996, https://vimeo.com/39865098, 0:33–0:54 min.

201: Amana Harris interview with Suzanne Lacy, 2006. Suzanne Lacy papers.

204: Arnold X. C. Perkins interview with Suzanne Lacy, 2006. Suzanne Lacy papers.

205: Dashka Slater, "New Program Teaches Young Oakland Moms the Fine Art of Fighting Back," *East Bay Express*, August 15, 1997, 3, 23.

207: Gregory Hodge interview with Suzanne Lacy, 2006. Suzanne Lacy papers. Ogubala Akintunde interview with Suzanne Lacy, 2007. Suzanne Lacy papers.

219: Pilar Riaño-Alcalá, "Encounters with Memory and Mourning: Public Art as Collective Pedagogy of Reconciliation," in Francisco Ibáñez-Carrasco and Erica R. Meiners, *Public Acts: Disruptive Readings on Making Curriculum Public* (New York and London: RoutledgeFalmer, 2004), 219.

222–23: *Projection Skin of Memory 2011 Subtitled*, 2011, 0:27–42 min., 5:25–53 min.; 3:43–4:46 min.; 1:43–51 min., 9:07–52 min.; 1:09–19 min., 1:55–2:16 min.; 1:01–8 min., 4:52–5:23 min., 6:51–7:04 min.

229: Suzanne Lacy, "Hard Work in a Working-Class Town" (2006), in *Leaving Art: Writings on Performance, Politics, and Publics, 1974–2007* (Durham, NC: Duke University Press, 2010), 308.

237: Meg Parnell, *Cleaning Conditions* work journal, 2013. Suzanne Lacy papers.

238: Rauf Bashir in *Shapes of Water*, by Huckleberry Films, 2017, https://vimeo.com/228592195, 20:24–47 min.

239: Paul Hartley in *Shapes of Water*, by Huckleberry Films, 2017, https://vimeo.com/228592195, 2:11–18 min., 3:03–15 min., 16:02–16 min.

241: *Shapes of Water, Sounds of Hope: Interview Promo*, by Fully Formed Films, 2016, https://vimeo.com/183619230, 1:16–34 min., 1:35–2:01 min., 2:14–35 min., 2:02–14 min.

243: Ron Pen, "Shapes of Water/Sounds of Hope, The Circle and the Square, The Shape Note Perspective," 2016.

This catalogue is published on the occasion of the exhibition *Suzanne Lacy: We Are Here*, held at the San Francisco Museum of Modern Art and Yerba Buena Center for the Arts, San Francisco, April 20–August 4, 2019.

Suzanne Lacy: We Are Here is co-organized by the San Francisco Museum of Modern Art and Yerba Buena Center for the Arts, San Francisco.

At the San Francisco Museum of Modern Art, this exhibition is made possible by the following:

Major support is provided by The Andy Warhol Foundation for the Visual Arts.

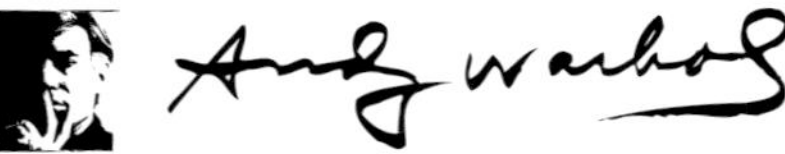

The Andy Warhol Foundation for the Visual Arts

Generous support is provided by Lionel F. Conacher and Joan T. Dea.

The Yerba Buena Center for the Arts (YBCA) presentation is made possible in part by the Circle of Advisors for Changing the Ratio: Female Artists at YBCA. Additional support is provided by Amanda Weil.

YBCA Exhibitions are made possible in part by The Andy Warhol Foundation for the Visual Arts, Panta Rhea Foundation, Mellon/American Council of Learned Societies Public Fellows Program, and Kevin King and Meridee Moore.

YBCA Programs are made possible in part by Bloomberg Philanthropies and The James Irvine Foundation, with additional funding by the National Endowment for the Arts, Grosvenor, and YBCA Members.

Yerba Buena Center for the Arts is grateful to the City of San Francisco for its ongoing support.

San Francisco Museum of Modern Art
151 Third Street
San Francisco, CA 94103
sfmoma.org

Published in association with DelMonico Books • Prestel
DelMonico Books, an imprint of Prestel Publishing, a member
of Verlagsgruppe Random House GmbH

Prestel Verlag
Neumarkter Strasse 28
81673 Munich

Prestel Publishing Ltd.
14-17 Wells Street
London W1T 3PD

Prestel Publishing
900 Broadway, Suite 603
New York, NY 10003

www.prestel.com

This catalogue was produced by the publications department at the San Francisco Museum of Modern Art: Kari Dahlgren, director of publications; Amanda Glesmann, senior editor; Lucy Medrich, editor; Jessica DeCamp and Brianna Nelson, publications associates.

PROJECT EDITOR: Amanda Glesmann
EDITOR: Lucy Medrich
EDITORIAL ASSISTANCE: Jessica DeCamp and Lindsey Westbrook
RESEARCH LEAD: Taylor Shoolery
RESEARCHERS: Jessica D. Brier, Christa Cesario, and Tanya Zimbardo
PROOFREADER: Polly Watson
DESIGNER: Purtill Family Business
COLOR SEPARATIONS: Echelon, Santa Monica, California
PRINTING: Cantz, Esslingen, Germany
PAPER: GardaMatt 150# and F Color 120#
FONTS: Gill Sans, Dutch 766, Letter Gothic, and **Beton**

FRONT COVER: Suzanne Lacy, *The Circle and the Square* (2015–17). Production photo, Brierfield Mill, Pendle, England, 2016. © Suzanne Lacy. Photo: Graham Kay. See pages 238–45.

LIBRARY OF CONGRESS CONTROL NUMBER: 2018962501

A CIP catalogue record for this book is available from the British Library.

ISBN: 978-3-7913-5838-3